Children's
Literature
Review

Guide to Gale Literary Criticism Series

For criticism on	Consult these Gale series
Authors now living or who died after December 31, 1959	*CONTEMPORARY LITERARY CRITICISM (CLC)*
Authors who died between 1900 and 1959	*TWENTIETH-CENTURY LITERARY CRITICISM (TCLC)*
Authors who died between 1800 and 1899	*NINETEENTH-CENTURY LITERATURE CRITICISM (NCLC)*
Authors who died between 1400 and 1799	*LITERATURE CRITICISM FROM 1400 TO 1800 (LC)* *SHAKESPEAREAN CRITICISM (SC)*
Authors who died before 1400	*CLASSICAL AND MEDIEVAL LITERATURE CRITICISM (CMLC)*
Authors of books for children and young adults	*CHILDREN'S LITERATURE REVIEW (CLR)*
Dramatists	*DRAMA CRITICISM (DC)*
Poets	*POETRY CRITICISM (PC)*
Short story writers	*SHORT STORY CRITICISM (SSC)*
Black writers of the past two hundred years	*BLACK LITERATURE CRITICISM (BLC)*
Hispanic writers of the late nineteenth and twentieth centuries	*HISPANIC LITERATURE CRITICISM (HLC)*
Native North American writers and orators of the eighteenth, nineteenth, and twentieth centuries	*NATIVE NORTH AMERICAN LITERATURE (NNAL)*
Major authors from the Renaissance to the present	*WORLD LITERATURE CRITICISM, 1500 TO THE PRESENT (WLC)*

ISSN 0362-4145

volume 53

Children's Literature Review

Excerpts from Reviews,
Criticism, and Commentary
on Books for Children
and Young People

Deborah J. Morad
Editor

The Gale Group

DETROIT • SAN FRANCISCO • LONDON • BOSTON • WOODBRIDGE, CT

STAFF

Deborah J. Morad, *Editor*

Sara Constantakis, Catherine Goldstein, Alan Hedblad, Motoko Fujishiro Huthwaite, Arlene Johnson, Paul Loeber,
Karina Kerr, Thomas McMahon, Malinda Mayer, Gerard J. Senick, Diane Telgen, Timothy Wrublewski,
Renee Wrublewski *Contributing Editors*

Karen Uchic, *Technical Training Specialist*

Joyce Nakamura, *Managing Editor*

Maria Franklin, *Permissions Manager*
Sarah Chesney, Edna Hedblad, Michele Lonoconus, *Permissions Associates*

Victoria B. Cariappa, *Research Manager*
Corrine A. Stocker, *Project Coordinator*
Tracie A. Richardson, Cheryl D. Warnock, *Research Associates*
Patricia Tsune Ballard, Phyllis P. Blackman, Wendy K. Festerling *Research Assistants*

Mary Beth Trimper, *Production Director*
Cindy Range, *Production Assistant*

Gary Leach, *Graphic Artist*
Randy Bassett, *Image Database Supervisor*
Robert Duncan, Michael Logusz, *Imaging Specialists*
Pamela A. Reed, *Imaging Coordinator*

Library of Congress Catalog Card Number 76-643301
ISBN 0-7876-2081-5
ISSN 0362-4145
Printed in the United States of America

10 9 8 7 6 5 4 3 2 1

Contents

Preface vii
Acknowledgements xi

Preface

Literature for children and young adults has evolved into both a respected branch of creative writing and a successful industry. Currently, books for young readers are considered among the most popular segments of publishing. Criticism of juvenile literature is instrumental in recording the literary or artistic development of the creators of children's books as well as the trends and controversies that result from changing values or attitudes about young people and their literature. Designed to provide a permanent, accessible record of this ongoing scholarship, *Children's Literature Review (CLR)* presents parents, teachers, and librarians—those responsible for bringing children and books together—with the opportunity to make informed choices when selecting reading materials for the young. In addition, *CLR* provides researchers of children's literature with easy access to a wide variety of critical information from English-language sources in the field. Users will find balanced overviews of the careers of the authors and illustrators of the books that children and young adults are reading; these entries, which contain excerpts from published criticism in books and periodicals, assist users by sparking ideas for papers and assignments and suggesting supplementary and classroom reading. Ann L. Kalkhoff, president and editor of *Children's Book Review Service Inc.,* writes that "*CLR* has filled a gap in the field of children's books, and it is one series that will never lose its validity or importance."

Scope of the Series

Each volume of *CLR* profiles the careers of a selection of authors and illustrators of books for children and young adults from preschool through high school. Author lists in each volume reflect:

- an international scope.

- representation of authors of all eras.

- the variety of genres covered by children's and/or YA literature: picture books, fiction, nonfiction, poetry, folklore, and drama.

Although the focus of the series is on authors new to *CLR*, entries will be updated as the need arises.

Organization of This Book

An entry consists of the following elements: author heading, author portrait, author introduction, excerpts of criticism (each preceded by a bibliographical citation), and illustrations, when available.

- The **Author Heading** consists of the author's name followed by birth and death dates. The portion of the name outside the parentheses denotes the form under which the author is most frequently published. If the majority of the author's works for children were written under a pseudonym, the pseudonym will be listed in the author heading and the real name given on the first line of the author introduction. Also located at the beginning of the introduction are any other pseudonyms used by the author in writing for children and any name variations, including transliterated forms for authors whose languages use nonroman alphabets. Uncertainty as to a birth or death date is indicated by question marks.

- An **Author Portrait** is included when available.

- The **Author Introduction** contains information designed to introduce an author to *CLR* users by presenting an overview of the author's themes and styles, biographical facts that relate to the author's literary career or critical responses to the author's works, and information about major awards and prizes the author has received. The introduction begins by identifying the nationality of the author and by listing the genres in which s/he has written for children and young adults. Introductions also list a group of representative titles for which the author or illustrator being profiled is best known; this section, which begins with the words "major works include," follows the genre line of the introduction. For seminal figures, a listing of major works about the author follows when appropriate, highlighting important biographies about the author or illustrator that are not excerpted in the entry. The centered heading "Introduction" announces the body of the text.

- **Criticism** is located in three sections: **Author's Commentary** (when available), **General Commentary** (when available), and **Title Commentary** (commentary on specific titles).

  - The **Author's Commentary** presents background material written by the author or by an interviewer. This commentary may cover a specific work or several works. Author's commentary on more than one work appears after the author introduction, while commentary on an individual book follows the title entry heading.

  - The **General Commentary** consists of critical excerpts that consider more than one work by the author or illustrator being profiled. General commentary is preceded by the critic's name in boldface type or, in the case of unsigned criticism, by the title of the journal. *CLR* also features entries that emphasize general criticism on the oeuvre of an author or illustrator. When appropriate, a selection of reviews is included to supplement the general commentary.

  - The **Title Commentary** begins with the title entry headings, which precede the criticism on a title and cite publication information on the work being reviewed. Title headings list the title of the work as it appeared in its first English-language edition. The first English-language publication date of each work (unless otherwise noted) is listed in parentheses following the title. Differing U.S. and British titles follow the publication date within the parentheses. When a work is written by an individual other than the one being profiled, as is the case when illustrators are featured, the parenthetical material following the title cites the author of the work before listing its publication date.

    Entries in each title commentary section consist of critical excerpts on the author's individual works, arranged chronologically by publication date. The entries generally contain two to seven reviews per title, depending on the stature of the book and the amount of criticism it has generated. The editors select titles that reflect the entire scope of the author's literary contribution, covering each genre and subject. An effort is made to reprint criticism that represents the full range of each title's reception, from the year of its initial publication to current assessments. Thus, the reader is provided with a record of the author's critical history. Publication information (such as publisher names and book prices) and parenthetical numerical references (such as footnotes or page and line references to specific editions of works) have been deleted at the discretion of the editors to provide smoother reading of the text.

- Centered headings introduce each section, in which criticism is arranged chronologically; beginning with Volume 35, each excerpt is preceded by a boldface source heading for easier access by readers. Within the text, titles by authors being profiled are also highlighted in boldface type.

- Selected excerpts are preceded by **Explanatory Annotations**, which provide information on the critic or work of criticism to enhance the reader's understanding of the excerpt.

- A complete **Bibliographical Citation** designed to facilitate the location of the original book or article precedes each piece of criticism.

- Numerous **Illustrations** are featured in *CLR*. For entries on illustrators, an effort has been made to include illustrations that reflect the characteristics discussed in the criticism. Entries on authors who do not illustrate their own works may also include photographs and other illustrative material pertinent to their careers.

Special Features: Entries on Illustrators

Entries on authors who are also illustrators will occasionally feature commentary on selected works illustrated but not written by the author being profiled. These works are strongly associated with the illustrator and have received critical acclaim for their art. By including critical comment on works of this type, the editors wish to provide a more complete representation of the artist's career. Criticism on these works has been chosen to stress artistic, rather than literary, contributions. Title entry headings for works illustrated by the author being profiled are arranged chronologically within the entry by date of publication and include notes identifying the author of the illustrated work. In order to provide easier access for users, all titles illustrated by the subject of the entry are boldfaced.

CLR also includes entries on prominent illustrators who have contributed to the field of children's literature. These entries are designed to represent the development of the illustrator as an artist rather than as a literary stylist. The illustrator's section is organized like that of an author, with two exceptions: the introduction presents an overview of the illustrator's styles and techniques rather than outlining his or her literary background, and the commentary written by the illustrator on his or her works is called "illustrator's commentary" rather than "author's commentary." All titles of books containing illustrations by the artist being profiled are highlighted in boldface type.

Other Features: Acknowledgments, Indexes

- The **Acknowledgments** section, which immediately follows the preface, lists the sources from which material has been reprinted in the volume. It does not, however, list every book or periodical consulted for the volume.

- The **Cumulative Index to Authors** lists all of the authors who have appeared in *CLR* with cross-references to the biographical, autobiographical, and literary criticism series published by The Gale Group. A full listing of the series titles appears before the first page of the indexes of this volume.

- The **Cumulative Index to Nationalities** lists authors alphabetically under their respective nationalities. Author names are followed by the volume number(s) in which they appear.

- The **Cumulative Index to Titles** lists titles covered in *CLR* followed by the volume and page number where criticism begins.

A Note to the Reader

CLR is one of several critical references sources in the Literature Criticism Series published by The Gale Group. When writing papers, students who quote directly from any volume in the Literature Criticism Series may use the following general forms to footnote reprinted criticism. The first example pertains to material drawn from periodicals, the second to material reprinted from books.

[1]T. S. Eliot, "John Donne," *The Nation and the Athenaeum,* 33 (9 June 1923), 321-32; excerpted and reprinted in *Literature Criticism from 1400 to 1800,* Vol. 10, ed. James E. Person, Jr. (Detroit: Gale Research, 1989), pp. 28-9.

[1]Henry Brooke, *Leslie Brooke and Johnny Crow* (Frederick Warne, 1982); excerpted and reprinted in *Children's Literature Review,* Vol. 20, ed. Gerard J. Senick (Detroit: Gale Research, 1990), p. 47.

Suggestions Are Welcome

In response to various suggestions, several features have been added to *CLR* since the beginning of the series, including author entries on retellers of traditional literature as well as those who have been the first to record oral tales and other folklore; entries on prominent illustrators featuring commentary on their styles and techniques; entries on authors whose works are considered controversial; occasional entries devoted to criticism on a single work or a series of works; sections in author introductions that list major works by and about the author or illustrator being profiled; explanatory notes that provide information on the critic or work of criticism to enhance the usefulness of the excerpt; more extensive illustrative material, such as holographs of manuscript pages and photographs of people and places pertinent to the careers of the authors and artists; a cumulative nationality index for easy access to authors by nationality; and occasional guest essays written specifically for *CLR* by prominent critics on subjects of their choice.

Readers who wish to suggest authors to appear in future volumes, or who have other suggestions, are cordially invited to contact the editor. By mail: Editor, *Children's Literature Review,* The Gale Group, 27500 Drake Road, Farmington Hills, MI 48331-3535; by telephone: (800) 347-GALE; by fax: (248) 699-8065.

Acknowledgments

The editors wish to thank the copyright holders of the excerpted criticism included in this volume and the permissions managers of many book and magazine publishing companies for assisting us in securing reproduction rights. We are also grateful to the staffs of the Detroit Public Library, the Library of Congress, the University of Detroit Mercy Library, Wayne State University Purdy/Kresge Library Complex, and the University of Michigan Libraries for making their resources available to us. Following is a list of the copyright holders who have granted us permission to reproduce material in this volume of *CLR*. Every effort has been made to trace copyright, but if omissions have been made, please let us know.

COPYRIGHTED EXCERPTS IN *CLR*, VOLUME 53, WERE REPRODUCED FROM THE FOLLOWING PERIODICALS:

The ALAN Review, v. 10, Fall, 1982. Reproduced by permission.—*Appraisal: Science Books for Young People,* v. 18, Winter, 1985; v. 20, Winter, 1987. Copyright © 1985, 1987 by the Children's Science Book Review Committee. Both reproduced by permission.—*Booklist,* v. 73, April 1, 1977; v. 74, June 15, 1978; v. 75, September 1, 1978; v. 76, March 15, 1980; v. 78, March 15, 1982; v. 78, May 1, 1982; v. 78, June 15, 1982; v. 79, December 1, 1982; v. 79, February 1, 1983; v. 80, January 15, 1984; v. 80, July, 1984; v. 81, September 1, 1984; v. 81, June 1, 1985; v. 81, August, 1985; v. 82, March 15, 1986; v. 82, April 1, 1986; v. 83, November 1, 1986; v. 83, March 15, 1987; v. 83, June 15, 1987; v. 83, July, 1987; v. 83, August, 1987; v. 84, May 1, 1988; v. 85, September 1, 1988; v. 86, October 15, 1989; v. 86, December 15, 1989; v. 86, January 1, 1990; v. 86, May 15, 1990; v. 87, July, 1991; v. 88, September 15, 1991; v. 88, March 1, 1992; v. 88, May 15, 1992; v. 88, July, 1992; v. 89, October 15, 1992; v. 89, November 15, 1992; v. 89, January 15, 1993; v. 89, February 1, 1993; v. 89, April 1, 1993; v. 89, August, 1993; v. 90, September 1, 1993; v. 90, October 1, 1993; v. 90, January 1, 1994; v. 90, February 15, 1994; v. 90, April 1, 1994; v. 90, May 1, 1994; v. 91, September 1, 1994; v. 91, November 1, 1994; v. 91, December 15, 1994; v. 91, March 15, 1995; v. 91, April 15, 1995; v. 91, June 1, 1995; v. 91, July, 1995; v. 92, February 1, 1996; v. 92, May 1, 1996; v. 92, June 1, 1996; v. 93, September 15, 1996; v. 93, November 1, 1996; v. 93, November 15, 1996; v. 93, March 1, 1997; v. 93, May 1, 1997; v. 93, June 1 & 15, 1997; v. 94, September 15, 1997; v. 94, March 15, 1998; v. 94, April 1, 1998. Copyright © 1977, 1978, 1980, 1982, 1983, 1984, 1985, 1986, 1987, 1988, 1989, 1990, 1991, 1992, 1993, 1994, 1995, 1996, 1997, 1998 by the American Library Association. All reproduced by permission.—*The Booklist,* v. 66, June 1, 1970; v. 66, June 15, 1970; v. 67, May 15, 1971; v. 70, December 1, 1973. Copyright © 1970, 1971, 1973 by the American Library Association. All reproduced by permission.—*Books for Keeps,* n. 97, March, 1996. © School Bookshop Association 1996. Reproduced by permission.—*The Booktalker,* v. 65, September, 1990 for a review of "The Call of the Wolves" by Susan Wolfe. © 1990 by the H. W. Wilson Company. All rights reserved. Reproduced by permission of the author.—*Bulletin of the Center for Children's Books,* v. 27, January, 1974; v. 29, July-August, 1976; v. 31, March, 1978; v. 32, December, 1979; v. 33, May, 1980; v. 35, June, 1982; v. 36, January, 1983; v. 37, September, 1983; v. 37, April, 1984; v. 37, May, 1984; v. 37, July-August, 1984; v. 38, May, 1985; v. 39, April, 1986; v. 40, June, 1987; v. 40, July-August, 1987; v. 41, January, 1988; v. 41, June, 1988; v. 42, September, 1988; v. 42, April, 1989; v. 43, September, 1989; v. 43, November, 1989; v. 43, February, 1990; v. 44, January, 1991; v. 44, July-August, 1991; v. 45, October, 1991; v. 45, January, 1992. Copyright © 1974, 1976, 1978, 1979, 1980, 1982, 1983, 1984, 1985, 1986, 1987, 1988, 1989, 1990, 1991, 1992 by The University of Chicago. All reproduced by permission. / v. 46, March, 1993; v. 46, June, 1993; v. 47, September, 1993; v. 47, January, 1994; v. 47, March, 1994; v. 47, June, 1994; v. 47, July-August, 1994; v. 48, November, 1994; v. 48, December, 1994; v. 48, January, 1995; v. 48, March, 1995; v. 48, May, 1995; v. 49, May, 1996; v. 49, June, 1996; v. 50, October, 1996; v. 50, December, 1996; v. 50, January, 1997; v. 50, May, 1997; v. 50, July-August, 1997; v. 51, March, 1998; v. 51, June, 1998. Copyright © 1993, 1994, 1995, 1996, 1997, 1998 by The Board of Trustees of the University of Illinois. All reproduced by permission.—*Chicago Tribune—Books,* January 18, 1987 for "Young Dr. Seuss: Early Wit and Whimsy from a National Treasure" by George Garrett. © copyrighted 1987, Chicago Tribune Company. All rights reserved. Reproduced by permission of the author.—*Children's Literature Association Quarterly,* v. 16, Winter, 1991-92. © 1992 Children's Literature Association. Reproduced by permission.—*Children's literature in education,* v. 20, September, 1989 for "Seuss as a Creator of Folklore" by Francelia Butler. © 1989, Agathon Press, Inc. Reproduced by permission of the publisher and the Literary Estate of Francelia Butler. / v. 21, June, 1990. © 1990, Agathon Press, Inc. Reproduced by permission of the publisher.—*The Christian ScienceMonitor,* April 3, 1987 for "Tales of Courage and Love: Here's Quality for Children" by Diane Manuel. © 1987 by Diane Manuel. All rights reserved. Reproduced by permission of the author.—*English Journal,* v. 82, December, 1993 for a review of "The Long Road to Gettysburg" by Aileen Pace Nilsen. Copyright © 1993 by the National Council of Teachers of English. Reproduced by permission of the publisher and the author.—*Growing Point,* v. 14, September, 1975 for a review of "The Search for Delicious" by Margery Fisher; v. 27, January, 1989 for a review

Children's
Literature
Review

Maya Angelou

1928-

(Born Marguerite Annie Johnson) African-American author of fiction, nonfiction, autobiography, poetry, picture books, plays, and screenplays.

Major works include *I Know Why the Caged Bird Sings* (1970), *Gather Together in My Name* (1974), *I Shall Not Be Moved* (1990), *My Painted House, My Friendly Chicken, and Me* (1994), *Kofi and His Magic* (1996).

Major works about the author include *Maya Angelou: Greeting the Morning* (by Sara E. King, 1994), *Heart of a Woman, Mind of a Writer, and Soul of a Poet: A Critical Analysis of the Writings of Maya Angelou* (1996), *Maya Angelou: More Than a Poet* (by Elaine Slivinski Lisandrelli, 1996).

INTRODUCTION

Although her work as a poet and performer has brought her acclaim, Angelou is best known for her innovative examinations of her life as an African-American woman. Her first two volumes of autobiography, *I Know Why the Caged Bird Sings* and *Gather Together in My Name,* can be appreciated by adolescents as well as adults. While Angelou once noted that she told the story of her childhood because "there were so few books for a black girl to read that said 'This is how it is to grow up,'" her works are enjoyed by a broad audience. According to critics, the widespread appeal of Angelou's work lies in her ability to not just examine, but re-create the events of her life, involving her readers in the emotion and atmosphere of her experiences and thus highlighting their universality. The significant themes of her autobiographies—the struggle to establish one's identity, the value of reading and learning, the persistence to overcome obstacles such as racism and sexism, taking pride in one's heritage—appear throughout all of Angelou's work, including her more recent picture book set in Africa and enjoyed not only by elementary graders, but also by readers of all ages. Her writings are both affirmations of the black experience and testimonials to the human condition. As Doris Grumbach commented, "A truly remarkable person, [Angelou] is able to re-create events of her own life and make them seem part of the reader's imaginative experience."

Biographical Information

Angelou was born Marguerite Annie Johnson on April 4, 1928, in St. Louis, Missouri. Her parents divorced when she was three, and she and her older brother were sent to live with their paternal grandmother in Stamps, Arkansas. At eight, she was sent to rejoin her mother in

St. Louis, but soon returned to Stamps after being raped by her mother's boyfriend. By age seventeen, Angelou had moved to San Francisco, become the city's first black female streetcar conductor, and had a son. These events and others of her childhood, both traumatic and triumphant, are vividly recalled in her first volume of autobiography, *I Know Why the Caged Bird Sings.*

Although she found inspiration in literature throughout her childhood, as a young mother on her own, Angelou had little inkling that a stellar literary career lay ahead of her. She was briefly involved in drugs and prostitution before starting a career as an actress, singer, and dancer. She married and divorced a white ex-sailor, and joined an international touring company of the musical *Porgy and Bess.* Angelou eventually began writing her own performance pieces and joined the Harlem Writers Group, where she met renowned author James Baldwin. Inspired by Dr. Martin Luther King, Jr., she created, produced, and starred in a musical benefit for Dr. King's Southern Christian Leadership Conference. During the 1960s, the author travelled to Africa and Europe and worked as a journalist, actress, activist, and film director before returning to California. Challenged by Baldwin and his publisher, she wrote *I Know Why the Caged Bird Sings,* which was published in 1970 and received immediate critical and popular acclaim. Angelou has since published four additional volumes of autobiography, and has continued her work as a poet, playwright, screenwriter, director, and actress. While her diverse talents have earned her recognition as a performer and poet—she was named Inaugural Poet for President Bill Clinton's 1993 inauguration—Angelou remains best known for her skillful portrayals of her own life that also examine the nature of the era. As she explained to Cheryl Wall: "A good autobiographer seems to write about herself and is in fact writing about the temper of the times. A good [autobiography] is writing history from one person's viewpoint."

Major Works

In *I Know Why the Caged Bird Sings* Angelou recounts the experiences of her childhood, from her arrival at her grandmother's home in rural Arkansas, to her return to her mother's home in St. Louis, to her family's move to wartime San Francisco. The key event during this time, however, is Maya's rape at age eight by her mother's boyfriend; she testifies against the man at his trial, after which he is murdered. She associates her words with his death, and remains mute for the next five years. The work continues by recounting the people and experiences that shaped Maya's transformation into a independent, self-confident, and proud young woman. Maya's story resumes in *Gather Together in My Name,* a somewhat darker volume than the first, in which Maya remembers her struggle as a teenage mother trying to raise her son alone. Her missteps include relationships with men who take advantage of her naiveté, a stint as a madam and then as a prostitute, and a brief flirtation with drug use. Her misadventures are related with confidence and humor, however, and Annie Gottlieb noted that "Angelou accomplishes the rare feat of laying her own life open to a reader's scrutiny without the reflex-covering gesture of melodrama or shame." Both volumes were hailed for their use of language, their honesty, and the author's ability to depict another place and time.

Angelou's writing style, at turns both lyrical and full of down-to-earth metaphors, also serves her well in her poetic endeavors. In *Now Sheba Sings the Song* (1987), a picture book intended for all ages, Angelou created a poem celebrating the strength and beauty of black women, to accompany the original drawings of noted artist Tom Feelings. While Feelings's drawings received more attention, critics also praised Angelou's poem for its rich imagery and moving themes. Angelou's collection *I Shall Not Be Moved* addresses many of the same topics found in her autobiographies, including her pride in the resilience of African Americans and the strength humanity exhibits in diversity. Reviewers praised the poet's ability to address such issues personally and without sentimentality, in poems that are "funny, reflective, illuminating, and honest," according to Jacqueline Gropman. Another illustrated individual poem is *Life Doesn't*

Frighten Me (1993), which combines Angelou's song of defiant bravery with the startling urban images of the late painter Jean-Michel Basquiat. Critics enjoyed the read-aloud, chant-like quality of the text, and felt that children would both identify with and respond to the lively banishing of fears found in the words and pictures.

In the 1990s, Angelou began writing books specifically intended for a young audience. With her literary skill and experience living in Africa, she was the ideal choice to collaborate with photographer Margaret Courtney-Clarke to produce picture books exploring the everyday life of African children. The first, *My Painted House, My Friendly Chicken, and Me,* is told in the voice of eight-year-old Thandi, a member of the South African Ndebele culture. While reviewers disagreed as to the effectiveness of the book's unusual design, they generally found Angelou's text engaging, humorous, and informative. A similar approach was used in *Kofi and His Magic,* which is related from the point of view of a young West African boy. Kofi's "magic" is his ability to use his imagination, and he uses it throughout the book to transport his readers to nearby towns and places. While one reviewer was disappointed by a lack of specific information in the text, others enjoyed the lyricism and creativity which would encourage readers to learn more about other cultures. As Mary Harris Veeder noted, there is "no whiff of the anthropology museum about this book." Angelou's intent, after all, is to show her readers the strength and beauty that can be found in the diversity of the world's peoples, despite the obstacles put in front of them. As the author told George Plimpton in the *Paris Review:* "There is, I hope, a thesis in my work: we may encounter many defeats, but we must not be defeated. . . . We are much stronger than we appear to be, and maybe much better than we allow ourselves to be."

Awards

Angelou received a National Book Award nomination in 1970 for *I Know Why the Caged Bird Sings,* and was also nominated for the Pulitzer Prize in 1972 for her poetry collection *Just Give Me a Cool Drink of Water 'fore I Diiie.* Her performing has earned her Tony and Emmy Award nominations. Angelou was selected as Inaugural Poet by President Bill Clinton in 1993, and her recording of her inaugural poem, "On the Pulse of Morning," earned her a Grammy Award in 1994. In addition, Angelou has received fifty honorary degrees from institutions including Smith College and Laurence University.

AUTHOR'S COMMENTARY

Maya Angelou with Cheryl Wall

SOURCE: An interview in *Women Writers Talking,* Holmes & Meier Publishers, 1983, pp. 59-68.

Cheryl Wall: You have just published *The Heart of a Woman,* the fourth volume of an autobiography that began with *I Know Why the Caged Bird Sings* in 1969. Yet from passages in all four books, a reader may infer that Maya Angelou is a private person. If this inference is correct, how difficult has it been to relinquish that privacy in order to share your experiences with readers?

Maya Angelou: The difficulty is met early on by making a choice. I made a choice to become an autobiographer. You know the saying, "You make your bed and do whatever you want in it." I find autobiography as a form little used. I know no serious writer in the United States who has chosen to use autobiography as the vehicle for his or her most serious work. So as a form, it has few precedents. But I decided to use it. Now, I made that choice, I ain't got no choice. Unless I found it totally untenable—if it was running me totally mad or if I lost the magic—then that would be a different matter. I would start to look at fiction or go back to plays. But having said I'm going to write autobiography as literature and to write history as literature, then I have made that agreement with myself and my work and I can't be less than honest about it. So I have to tell private things, first to remember them and then to so enchant myself that I'm back there in that time. . . .

C.W.: Autobiographies by black women have been exceedingly rare, and to my knowledge, none of the few before yours has probed personal experience very deeply. Why and how did you select the form?

M.A.: The form is intriguing. Maybe third, certainly half into *Caged Bird,* I realized that a good autobiographer (whatever that means and I don't know what that means *yet*—I'm learning the form. I am molding the form and the form is molding me. That's the truth of it.), a good autobiographer seems to write about herself and is in fact writing about the temper of the times. A good one is writing history from one person's viewpoint. So that a good one brings the reader into a historical event as if the reader was standing there, bridled the horse for Paul Revere, joined Dred Scott, actually was there. What I'm trying to do is very ambitious, because I am trying, I hope, to lay a foundation for a form. And I know it's ambitious, it's egomaniacal. I know all that, I don't mind. There it is. I mean, I do mind; I'd love to be nice and sweet and loved by everyone, but there it is.

There are writers now and coming who will develop that form. It is important to remember how new the novel as a form is. So somebody in the next twenty, thirty, five years, or next year will write autobiography going through the door I have opened, or cracked anyway, and really show us what that form can be. One has to see it as stemming from the slave narrative and developing into a new American literary form. It's ambitious, I told you, it's ambitious.

Oh, yes. Not just for my art, but for the pantheon of

moral values: how to act, how to behave, how to interact. By the time I left Momma, I knew what was right and what wasn't. I have a painting now by Phoebe Beasley called *Sister Fannie's Funeral.* It depicts women sitting on fold-up chairs, and it reminds me of all the women in my grandmother's prayer-meeting group. There's one empty chair that for me is Momma's. Whenever I have a debate within myself about right action, I just sit down and look at that and think now, what would Momma say? So, morals and generosity, good things, I believe I got at Momma's lap.

C.W.: Your grandmother and her teachings seem always to have been an anchor. Many black children coming of age today don't have that link to their past; is there anything that can replace it?

M.A.: Nothing. I see nothing. It's tragic. There is no substitute for parental and/or family love. And by love, I do not in any way mean indulgence. I mean love . . . that quality so strong it holds the earth on its axis. The child needs that carrying over of wisdom from the family to the child directly, and there is no substitute. Society cannot do it, despite the 1984 concepts of Big Brother and a larger society caring for a child and imbuing the child with values. One needs it from someone to whom one is physically attached.

C.W.: That whole theme of the maternal figure is apparent in the work of many black women writers and white women as well. That leads me to wonder, is there a community of writers of which you feel a part—Afro-American writers, women writers, particular individual writers?

M.A.: That's a question . . . I'm a member of the community of writers, serious writers; I suppose much like a drug addict is a member of a community. I know what it costs to write . . . as soon as that is so, one is part of that community.

I'm part of the Afro-American writing community, because that is so. I'm writing out of my own background, but it is also the background of Toni Morrison, Toni Cade Bambara, Nikki Giovanni, Carolyn Rodgers, Jayne Cortez. All the black women who are writing today and who have written in the past: we write out of the same pot.

C.W.: I know that the title of *Caged Bird* is taken from a poem by Paul Laurence Dunbar. Does the new book's title allude to the poem by Georgia Douglas Johnson, the poet of the Harlem Renaissance?

M.A.: It certainly does. "The heart of a woman goes forth with the dawn . . . " I love that woman. I have *Bronze* [Johnson's second book, published in 1922]. It's in my nightstand. I will not put it even in my own private bookcases, let alone in the library. It's in my nightstand and there it will stay.

C.W.: How long have you known of her work?

M.A.: Since I was a very young person. I love Anne Spencer too. So different . . . born a year apart . . . but so different.

C.W.: Many Afro-American writers cite music as a primary influence on their work. References to music recur in your prose and poetry. In fact, you begin *Singin', Swingin', and Gettin' Merry Like Christmas* with the statement: "Music was my refuge." Do you believe Afro-American music in particular has shaped your work as well as your life?

M.A.: So much. I listen for the rhythm in everything I write, in prose or poetry. And the rhythms I use are very much like the blues and the spirituals. So that more often than not they are in 3/4 or 4/4 time. For example: [she reads from *The Heart of a Woman*] "The drive to the airport was an adventure in motoring and a lesson in conversational dissembling." "His clear tenor floated up over the heads of the already-irate passengers. The haunting beauty of the melody must have quelled some of the irritation, because no one asked Liam to shut up." "It seemed to me that I washed, scrubbed, mopped, dusted and waxed thoroughly every other day. Vus was particular. He checked on my progress. Sometimes he would pull the sofa away from the wall to see if possibly . . . " It is *always* there, wherever; it seems to me that there is the rhythm. And the melody of the piece, I work very hard for that melody.

A young woman told me that I had it easy because I have the art which Graham Greene has of making writing, a complex thing, seem so simple. So I said yes, it's hard work, and she replied, yes, but you have the art. But [to paraphrase Hemingway] "easy reading is damned hard writing."

C.W.: Until I read *The Heart of a Woman,* I had not realized how very much involved you had been with the civil rights movement. In this book you really capture the incredible sense of momentum, the vitality, and the hope. How important were those experiences as catalysts for your art?

M.A.: I suppose it's so important for me in my life that it must come through in the work. Despite living in the middle of murk, I am an optimist. It is *contrived* optimism; it is not pollyanna. I have to really work very hard to find that flare of a kitchen match in a hurricane and claim it, shelter it, praise it. Very important. The challenge to hope in a hopeless time is a part of our history. And I take it for myself personally, for me, Maya. I believe somewhere just beyond my knowing now, there is knowing and I shall know. *This* I shall overcome. There is a light, no larger than a pinhead, but I shall know. When I say I take it personally, I take that tradition of hoping against hope, which is the tradition of black Americans, for myself.

C.W.: That may perhaps be defined as a spiritual quality. Do you see your writing as political as well as spiritual?

M.A.: Well, yes. In the large sense, in that everything is political. If something I write encourages one person to save her life, then that is a political act. I wrote *Gather Together in My Name*—the most painful book until *The Heart of a Woman.* In the book I had to admit, confess; I had to talk about prostitution, and it was painful. I talked to my son, my mother, my brother, and my husband, and they said, "Tell it." I called the book *Gather Together in My Name,* because so many people lie to young people. They say, "I have no skeletons in my closet. Why, when I was young I always obeyed." And they lie like everything. So I thought all those people could gather together in my name. I would tell it.

I had a lot of really ugly things happen as a result right after the book's publication. Then I arrived in Cleveland, Ohio, and I was doing a signing in a large department store. Maybe one hundred fifty people were in line. Suddenly I looked and there were black fingers and long fingernails that had curved over in the mandarin style. And I looked to follow those up and the woman had a wig down to here, a miniskirt, a fake-fur minicoat, which had been dirtied—it might have been white once—false eyelashes out to there. She was about eighteen, maybe twenty. She leaned over and said, "Lady, I wanna tell you something, you even give me goddamn hope." If she was the only person . . . The encouragement is: you may encounter defeats, but you must not be defeated.

C.W.: Apart from your grandmother, can you identify what gave you that belief?

M.A.: My mom, my mom is outrageous. And I'm a Christian or trying to be. I'm very religious. I try to live what I understand a Christian life to be. It's my nature to try to be larger than what I appear to be, and that's a religious yearning.

C.W.: Although all your books give insight into a quintessentially female experience, *The Heart of a Woman* seems to explore the most explicitly feminist themes. For example, your treatment of single motherhood and the portrayal of your marriage to a South African freedom fighter. Has the feminist movement influenced your reflections on your past?

M.A.: No. I am a feminist, I am black, I am a human being. Now those three things are circumstances, as you look at the forces behind them, over which I have no control. I was born as a human being, born as a black, and born as a female. Other things I may deal with, my Americanness for example, or I may shift political loyalties. But, these three things I *am.* It is embarrassing, in fact insulting, for a woman to be asked if she's a feminist, or a human, if he's a humanist, or a black if he's black inside. It goes with the territory. It is embarrassing for a woman to hear another woman say, "I am not a feminist." What do you mean?! Who do you side with?

The book is about a woman's heart, about surviving and

being done down, surviving and being done down. If I were a man, I hope I would have the presence of mind to write "The Heart of a Man" and the courage to do so. But I have to talk about what I see, what I see as a black woman. I have to speak with my own voice.

C.W.: One of the most moving passages in **The Heart of a Woman** involves a conversation among women married to African freedom fighters. You and the other women—most of whom are African, one of whom is West Indian—forge a powerful common bond. Is there a broader lesson in that scene; are there bonds linking black women on several continents?

M.A.: If you have the luck to encounter women who will tell. That experience had to do in particular with African women. In Egypt, through the poet Hanifa Fahty, I met a group of Egyptian women involved with the Arab Women's League. They were at once struggling against the larger oppressor, colonialism, and against a history of masculine oppression from their own men. I understood it. Unfortunately. I would like to say it's such a rare occurrence that it was exotic; unfortunately, I understood it clearly. It would be the same if I were in Vietnam and talked to the Vietnamese women. It is one of the internationally pervasive problems, and women today are choosing to take courage as their banner. Courage is the most important virtue because without it you can't practice any of the other virtues with consistency.

C.W.: Do you see alliances being formed among women in various societies who are facing like problems?

M.A.: I haven't seen them yet. It must happen. But you have to consider that certain movements are very new. One of the many American problems built into the fabric of the country, beyond the woven-in lie of "we hold these truths to be self-evident that all men are created equal," beyond the inherent lie that the people who were writing those statements owned other human beings, one of the serious problems has been looking at the idea of freedom as every human being's inherent right. Just by being born, you've got it. It is ridiculous as a concept. It is wishful, wistful, and foolish. Freedom and justice for a group of animals is a dream to work toward. It is not on every corner waiting to be picked up with the Sunday paper.

As a species we have not evolved much beyond the conceiving of the idea. Now that's fabulous, and for that we need to salute ourselves. But to say that we have conceived the idea and the next moment it is in our laps is ridiculous. We have to work diligently, courageously, without ceasing, to bring this thing into being. It is still in the mind. It will take us hundreds of years, if not thousands, to actually bring it so that we can see it. We need to tell our children that this quality which has been conceived of most recently by human beings is something wonderful to work for. And your children's children and your children's children's children and everybody will be working to pull this order out of disorder.

C.W.: The joy then is in the struggle.

M.A.: Yes, yes, then you begin to understand that you love the process. The process has as its final end the realization, but you fall in love with the process.

We are new as a species. We just got here yesterday. The reptiles were on this little ball of spit and sand 300 million years. We just grew an opposing thumb—I think it was last week—and grew it by trying to pick up something to beat somebody down.

The terrifying irony is that we live such a short time. And it takes so long for an idea to be realized. Can you imagine the first person who had these fingers and saw this little nub growing and said, "Got the nub, pretty soon we're going to be able to hold on to the whole hatchet?" Not to know that it was to be another three million years. You see?

Thomas Wolfe calls us "dupes of time and moths of gravity." We're like fireflies—lighted by an idea and hardly any time to work at it. Certainly no time if we don't realize it has to be worked for. At least in this brief span, we can try to come to grips with how large an idea it is and how much work it demands, and try to pass it on to one other person. That's more than some people can achieve in a lifetime.

Maya Angelou with Carol E. Neubauer

SOURCE: An interview in *The Massachusetts Review*, Vol. XXVIII, No. 2, Summer 1987, pp. 286-92.

NEUBAUER: I see autobiography in general as a way for a writer to go back to her past and try to present what is left in memory but also to recover what has been lost through imagination and invention.

ANGELOU: Autobiography is for me a beloved which, like all beloveds, one is not given by family. One happens upon. You know, you turn the corner to the left instead of to the right. Stop in the parking lot and meet a beloved, or someone who becomes a beloved. And by the time I was half finished with *Caged Bird* I knew I loved the form—that I wanted to try to see what I could do with the form. Strangely enough, not as a cathartic force, not really; at any rate I never thought that really I was interested or am interested in autobiography for its recuperative power. I liked the form—the literary form—and by the time I started *Gather Together* I had gone back and reread Frederick Douglass' slave narrative. Anyway, I love the idea of the slave narrative, using the first person singular, really meaning always the third person plural. I love that. And I see it all the time in the black literature, in the blues and spirituals and the poetry, in essays James Baldwin uses it. But I've tried in each book to let the new voice come through and that's what makes it very difficult for me not to impose the voice of 1980 onto the voice I'm writing from 1950, possibly.

NEUBAUER: And so when you say you look for a new voice you don't mean the voice of the present or the time of writing the autobiographical account, but rather of that period of your past. That must be difficult.

ANGELOU: Very. Very difficult, but I think that in writing autobiography that that's what is necessary to really move it from almost an "as told to" to an "as remembered" state. And really for it to be a creative and artistic literary art form. I believe I came close to recreating the voice in *Gather Together* of that young girl—erratic, sporadic, fractured. I think in each case I've come close. Rather a sassy person in *Singin' and Swingin'*.

NEUBAUER: It seemed that in *The Heart of a Woman*, either the voice was more complex or else there was more than one voice at work. There seemed to be the voice of that time in your life and yet another voice commenting on that time.

ANGELOU: It seems so, but I looked at that quite carefully and at the period I think it is the voice because I was really coming into a security about who I was and what I was about, but the security lasted sometimes for three or four days or maybe through a love affair or into a love affair or into a job. I think it would be like smoke in a room. It would just dissipate and I would suddenly be edgewalking again. I would be one of those children in the rye, playing very perilously close to the precipice and aware of it. I tried very hard for the voice. I remember the woman very well.

NEUBAUER: What I saw in *Heart of a Woman* was not so much that there were two voices talking against one another, but rather that a voice from a more recent time commented ironically on the predominant voice of that time in the past. The irony of you as the writer and the autobiographical presence coming through.

ANGELOU: It is really one of the most difficult. First, well, I don't know what comes first in that case. Whether it is the insistence to write well while trying to speak in a voice thirty years ago. I'm now writing a new book and trying to speak in that voice—the voice of 1963 and what I know about writing in 1984. It really is difficult.

NEUBAUER: Does it become more difficult the closer you get to the present?

ANGELOU: Yes, absolutely. Because by '63 my command of English was *almost* what it is today and I had been very much influenced by Vus Make. He had really influenced my thinking, and his English was exquisite. My reading in other languages also by that time had very much influenced my speaking and I was concerned about eloquence by 1960. So this book is really the most difficult and I've been ducking and dodging it too. I know this morning I should call my editor and tell him I have not forgotten him. He's very much on my mind and the work is very much on my mind. I don't know what I'm going to do when I finish this book. I *may* try

to go back and pick up some of the incidents that I left out of maybe *Caged Bird* or *Gather Together* or any of the books. I don't know how to do that.

NEUBAUER: Are you thinking of autobiography?

ANGELOU: Yes.

NEUBAUER: That's fascinating. One of the things I'm interested in particularly is how the present influences the autobiographical past. I think what you're engaged in doing now and have been since *Caged Bird* is something that's never been done before in this scope. Each volume of yours is a whole and has a unity that works for that volume alone. If you were to go back to the period of *Caged Bird* that would add another wrinkle in this question of time and different voices.

ANGELOU: I don't know how I will do it, and I don't know if I'll be able to do it. But I think there are facets. When I look at a stained glass window, it's very much like this book. I have an idea that the books are very much like the Everyman stories so that there is greed and kindness and generosity and cruelty, oppression, and sloth. And I think of the period I'm going to write about and I try to see which of the incidents in which greed, say it's green, which of these that happened to me during that period will most demonstrate that particular condition. Now some are more rich, but I refuse them. I do not select them because it's very hard to write drama without falling into melodrama. So the incidents I reject, I find myself unable to write about without becoming melodramatic. I just can't see how to write it. In *Gather Together* there is an incident in which a man almost killed me—tried to, in fact—and kept me for three days and he was a mad man, literally. My escape was so incredible, literally incredible, that there was no way to write it, absolutely, to make it credible and not melodramatic.

NEUBAUER: Have you ever chosen to take another incident in that case, perhaps one that might not have even happened, and use that as a substitute?

ANGELOU: No, because there are others which worked, which did happen, and which showed either cruelty or the irony of escape. So I was able to write that rather than the other.

NEUBAUER: I see. So you didn't have to sacrifice the core of the experience.

ANGELOU: No, I never sacrificed. It's just choosing which of those greens or which of those reds to make that kind of feeling.

NEUBAUER: It's a beautiful metaphor, the greens, the reds and the light coming through the window. Because in a sense, memory works that way; it filters out past work. And yet an autobiographer has a double task—at least double, probably triple or quadruple—in some ways the filtering has been done beyond your control on an unconscious level. But as a writer working in the present you, too, are making selections or choices, which complicate the experience.

ANGELOU: There is so much to talk to you about on this subject. I have, I think, due to all those years of not talking, which again, I chose to minimize in *Caged Bird* because it's hard to write that without, again, the melodramas leaking in. But because of those years of muteness, I think my memory was developed in queer ways, because I remember—I have total recall—or I have none at all. None. And there is no pattern to the memory, so that I would forget all the good and the bad of a certain time, or I will remember *only* the bad of a certain time, or I will remember *only* the good. But when I remember it, I will remember *everything* about it. *Everything.* The outside noises, the odors in the room, the way my clothes were feeling—everything. I just have it, or I remember nothing. I am sure that is a part of the sort of psychological problems I was having and how the memory went about its business knitting itself.

NEUBAUER: Almost as a treasure chest or a defense.

ANGELOU: Yes, both, I guess. But in a sense, not really a defense, because some of the marvelous things I've not remembered. For instance, one of the promises I've exacted from every lover or husband who promised to be a permanent fixture was that *if* I die in the house, if something happened, get me outside. Please don't let me die in the room, or open the window and let me see some rolling hills. Let me see, please. Now, my memory of Stamps, Arkansas, is flat, dirt, the trees around the pond. But everything just flat and mean. When I agreed to go to join Bill Moyers for his creativity program, I flew to Dallas and decided to drive to Stamps because I wanted to sneak up on Stamps. It's, I guess, 200 miles or more. When I drove out of Texas into Arkansas, Stamps is 30 miles from Texas. I began to see the undulating hill. I couldn't believe it! I couldn't believe it! It's beautiful! It's what I love. But the memory had completely gone.

NEUBAUER: When you're working, for example, on your present book, are there things that help you remember that period or any period in the past better?

ANGELOU: Well, a curious thing has happened to me with every book. When I start to work—start to plan it—I encounter people whom I have known in that time, which is really queer. I've wondered if I would encounter them anyway, or if it's a case of "when the student is ready the teacher appears." If I simply wouldn't see their value if I would encounter them and wouldn't see their value for what I'm working on, because I wouldn't be working on that. That is one of the very interesting things. I'm working on Ghana now and this summer I went to London to write a play. I saw a sister friend there from Ghana and suddenly about fifteen Ghanaians; soon I was speaking Fanti again and they were reminding me, "Do you remember that time when?" and suddenly it all came right up my nostrils. But what I do is

just pull myself away from everything and everybody and then begin the most frightening of the work. And that is going back. I'm always afraid I'll never come out. Every morning I wake up, usually about 5:30 and try to get to my work room. I keep a little room in a hotel. Nothing on the walls, nothing belonging to me, nothing. I go in and I try to be in by 6:30 and try to get back, get back. Always, for the first half hour is spent wondering if anybody cares for me enough to come and pull me out. Suppose I can't get out?

NEUBAUER: That's a difficult road to retrace—to find.

ANGELOU: Like an enchanted . . . I know that sounds romantic, but you know how I mean. But I do get back and I remember one thing and I think, "Yes, and what are the other things like that that happened?" And maybe a second one will come. It's all there. *All of it* is there.

NEUBAUER: Even down to the finest details and the dialogues, what you said to the people you were with.

ANGELOU: The sound of the voices. And I write wurrrrrrrrrrrrrrrr.

NEUBAUER: How long do you write if you go in at 6:30?

ANGELOU: Well, I'm out by 12:30, unless it's really happening. If it's really happening I'll stay till 2:00, but no longer. No longer. And then get out and go home and shower and make a lovely lunch and drink a lot of wine and try to come down. Get back. Stop in a shop, "Hi, how are you? Fine. . . . " So I can ascertain that I do live and people remember me.

NEUBAUER: Do you leave it in the middle of an incident so that you have a way back, or do you write to the end of each one?

ANGELOU: No, I can't write to the end of the incident. I will write to a place that's safe. Nothing will leak away now; I've got it. Then at night I'll read it and try to edit it.

NEUBAUER: The same night?

ANGELOU: The same night. Try to edit it for writing, a little of it. And then begin again the next day. Lordy.

NEUBAUER: Is it a frightening journey because of the deep roots from that time to the present? Do you feel a kind of vulnerability?

ANGELOU: I am not afraid of the ties. I cherish them, rather. It's the vulnerability. It's like using drugs or something. It's allowing oneself to be hypnotized. That's frightening, because then we have no defenses, nothing. We've slipped down the well and every side is slippery. And how on earth are you going to come out? That's scary. But I've chosen it, and I've chosen this mode as my mode.

NEUBAUER: How far will the fifth volume go?

ANGELOU: Actually, it's a new kind. It's really quite a new voice. I'm looking at the black American resident, me and the other black American residents in Ghana, and trying to see all the magic of the eternal quest of human beings to go home again. That is maybe what life is anyway. To return to the Creator. All of that naivete, the innocence of trying to. That awful rowing towards God, whatever it is. Whether it's to return to your village or the lover you lost or the youth that some people want to return to or the beauty that some want to return to.

NEUBAUER: Writing autobiography frequently involves this quest to return to the past, to the home. Sometimes, if the home can't be found, if it can't be located again, then that home or that love or that family, whatever has been lost, is recreated or invented.

ANGELOU: Yes, of course. That's it! That's what I'm seeing in this trek back to Africa. That in so many cases that idealized home of course is non-existent. In so many cases some black Americans created it on the spot. On the spot. And I did too. Created something, looked, seemed like what we have idealized very far from reality. It's going to be a painful, hard book to write, in that not only all the stuff that it cost me to write it, but there will be a number of people who will be disappointed. So I have to deal with that once the book is out. The main thing is getting it out.

NEUBAUER: Are their opinions becoming more and more of a consideration as you move closer to the present in your autobiographies?

ANGELOU: Yes, indeed, because in some cases I can't use names. When I use names I have to get permission from people who are alive. I called Vus Make just when I was about half way through *Heart of a Woman* and I told him. He lives in Darsalan now. And I said I'm writing a book in the time which you featured. So he said, "I will sign any permission. I will give any rights to you, for I know you will not lie. However, I am sure I shall disagree with your interpretation of the truth."

NEUBAUER: I know I speak for many in saying how much I am looking forward to your next book or your next "interpretation of the truth."

Maya Angelou

SOURCE: "The Writer and Her Craft," in *Readings on Maya Angelou*, Greenhaven Press, 1997, pp. 31-4.

[The following excerpt is from Angelou's essay "Shades and Slashes of Light," originally published in Black Women Writers (1950-1980), *in 1983.]*

Why and how frequently does a writer write? What shimmering goals dance before the writer's eyes, desirable, seductive, but maddeningly out of reach? What happens to the ego when one dreams of training Russian bears to dance the Watusi and is barely able to teach a friendly dog to shake hands?

Those are questions, frightful questions, too intimate and obscenely probing. I could say I write because I like words and the way they lie passively on a page, or that I write because I have profound truths to reveal. I could say that I love the discipline which writers must employ to translate their nebulous thoughts into practical phrases. If I claimed any of the above as my reasons for writing I would not be telling the whole truth. I have too often hated words, despised their elusive nature. Loathed them for skittering around evading their responsibility to convey my meaning. Conversely, they have frequently infuriated me by being inert, heavy, ponderous. Lying like stones on a page, unwilling to skip, impervious to my prodding.

As for truth, I'm quiveringly uncertain of it. Reality has changed chameleonlike before my eyes so many times, that I have learned, or am learning, to trust almost anything except what appears to be so. If morning brings me a stated truth before I can find my pen and yellow pad, the principle flees and leaves in its place either ashes of itself or a dictate of opposite meaning. No, I know no absolute truths which I am capable of revealing.

And I certainly do not adore the writer's discipline. I have lost lovers, endangered friendships, and blundered into eccentricity, impelled by a concentration which usually is to be found only in the minds of people about to be executed in the next half hour.

I write for the Black voice and any ear which can hear it. As a composer writes for musical instruments and a choreographer creates for the body, I search for sound, tempos, and rhythms to ride through the vocal cord over the tongue, and out of the lips of Black people. I love the shades and slashes of light. Its rumblings and passages of magical lyricism. I accept the glory of stridencies and purrings, trumpetings and sombre sonorities.

Having said that, I must now talk about content. I have noted most carefully for the past twenty years our speech patterns, the ambiguities, contradictions, the moans and laughter, and am even more enchanted at this time than I was when I began eavesdropping.

After, and during pestilential assaults of frustration, hate, demeanings, and murders, our language continues to expand and mature. Our lives, made inadequate and estranged by the experience of malice, loathing, and hostility, are enriched by the words we use to, and with, each other. By our intonations, our modulations, our shouts and hollers.

I write because I am a Black woman, listening attentively to her talking people.

When I turn my conscious mind to writing (my unconscious or subconscious is always busy recording images, phrases, sound, colors, and scents) I follow a fairly rigid habit. I rise early, around 5:30 or 6 A.M., wash, pray, put on coffee, and arrange my mind in writing order. That is, I tell myself how lucky I am that this morning is new, a day never seen before, that ideas will come to me which I have never consciously known. I have coffee and allow the work of the day before to flood my mind. The characters and situations take over the chambers of my existence until they are all I see and hear. Then I go to my writing room, most times a little cubicle I have rented in a cheap but clean hotel; rarely but sometimes it is a room in my own home.

I keep in my writing room a Bible, a dictionary, Roget's Thesaurus, a bottle of sherry, cigarettes, an ashtray, and three or four decks of playing cards. During the five hours I spend there I use every object, but I play solitaire more than I actually write. It seems to me that when my hands and small mind (a Southern Black phrase) are engaged in placing the reds on the blacks and blacks on the reds, my working mind arranges and rearranges the characters and the plot. Finally when they are in a plausible order, I simply have to write down where they are and what they say.

Later, after I have resumed home or if I have worked at home, when I have left my writing room, I bathe and change clothes. This seems to signal my total mind that it may now stop working for the writer and begin to think for the woman, the wife, the friend, and the cook.

I begin thinking about dinner midafternoon. I love to cook and find it both creative and relaxing. After I have planned dinner and possibly begun a dish which demands long stewing, I take the morning's work to my dining room table and polish it, straighten out the grammar, clear up the syntax, and try to eliminate repetitions and contradictions. By dinnertime, I am ready to join my family or friends (although truthfully, when I'm working on a book I am never totally away from it). I know that they are aware that they and their concerns are not of great importance to me during the creative period (as long as a year, sometimes less), but we all pretend. The discipline I use to be in company stands me in good stead on the following morning when I must go alone into my small writing room and face a host of new ideas and headstrong characters, yet keep myself open so that they can interact, grow, and become real.

I also wear a hat or a very tightly pulled head tie when I write. I suppose I hope by doing that I will keep my brains from seeping out of my scalp and running in great gray blobs down my neck, into my ears, and over my face.

TITLE COMMENTARY

I KNOW WHY THE CAGED BIRD SINGS (1970)

Kirkus Reviews

SOURCE: A review of *I Know Why the Caged Bird Sings,* in *Kirkus Reviews,* Vol. XXXVII, No. 23, December 1, 1969, pp. 1292-93.

Maya Angelou is a natural writer with an inordinate sense of life and she has written an exceptional autobiographical narrative which retrieves her first sixteen years from "the general darkness just beyond the great blinkers of childhood." Her story is told in scenes, ineluctably moving scenes, from the time when she and her brother were sent by her fancy living parents to Stamps, Arkansas, and a grandmother who had the local Store. Displaced they were and "If growing up is painful for the Southern Black girl, being aware of her displacement is the rust on the razor that threatens the throat." But alternating with all the pain and terror (her rape at the age of eight when in St. Louis with her mother) and humiliation (a brief spell in the kitchen of a white woman who refused to remember her name) and fear (of a lynching—and the time they buried afflicted Uncle Willie under a blanket of vegetables) as well as all the unanswered and unanswerable questions, there *are* affirmative memories and moments: her charming brother Bailey—her own "unshakable God"; a revival meeting in a tent; her 8th grade graduation; and at the end, when she's sixteen, the birth of a baby. Times when as she says "It seemed that the peace of a day's ending was an assurance that the covenant God made with children, Negroes and the crippled was still in effect." However charily one should apply the word, a beautiful book—an unconditionally involving memoir for our time or any time.

James Baldwin

SOURCE: "Maya Angelou," in *Writers for Young Adults, Vol. 1,* Charles Scribner's Sons, 1993, p. 44.

[The following review was originally published in the New York Times, *March 20, 1970.]*

This testimony from a black sister marks the beginning of a new era in the minds and hearts and lives of all black men and women . . . *I Know Why the Caged Bird Sings* liberates the reader into life simply because Angelou confronts her own life with such a moving wonder, such a luminous dignity. I have no words for this achievement, but I know that not since the days of my childhood, when people in books were more real than the people one saw every day, have I found myself so moved. . . . Her portrait is a biblical study of life in the midst of death.

Ruth P. Bull

SOURCE: A review of *I Know Why the Caged Bird Sings,* in *The Booklist,* Vol. 66, No. 20, June 15, 1970, p. 1256.

A well-written, honest, and moving episodic autobiographical account of the growing-up years of a Southern black girl. The author describes her early years living with her indomitable grandmother, who owned the only Negro general merchandise store in Stamps, Arkansas; a stay with her mother in St. Louis that ended when the then eight-year-old Maya was raped; the resumption of life in Stamps; and her eventual return to her mother in California, ending the narrative when at sixteen, and unmarried, she gives birth to a son. She elicits the reader's empathy by effectively evoking the harshness of black Southern life and yet recalling good times as well as bad and bringing to life the people who played a part in her life.

Regina Minudri

SOURCE: A review of *I Know Why the Caged Bird Sings,* in *School Library Journal,* Vol. 17, No. 1, September, 1970, p. 184.

Miss Angelou writes with conviction, some anger, much humor and a good deal of frankness about her girlhood in a small Arkansas town, St. Louis and San Francisco. The characters of Maya and her brother Bailey are lovingly shaped by Momma, their grandmother, a truly remarkable woman of strength, virtue and black dignity. The whites of Stamps, Arkansas live in another world and are creatures to be feared because of their power. Even Momma bows to them, and Maya deeply resents this because she knows Momma is, at the least, the equal of any person and better than most. Then, the children live for a time with their mother in St. Louis, where Maya, at age eight, is raped by her mother's boyfriend (a realistically handled scene). The children return to Stamps and their grandmother, finish grammar school, and move to San Francisco when Maya is 14. She goes through the usual adolescent changes, worries and doubts, and the book ends with her graduation from high school and the birth of her illegitimate son. Miss Angelou is a poet, and this is apparent in the flow and style of her writing. Hers is a moving, very real, most evocative story, which will be enlightening to whites who know little or nothing of the world Miss Angelou describes.

Ernece B. Kelly

SOURCE: A review of *I Know Why the Caged Bird Sings,* in *Harvard Educational Review,* Vol. 40, No. 4, November, 1970, p. 32.

[I Know Why the Caged Bird Sings] is a poetic counterpart for the more scholarly *[Growing Up in the Black Belt: Negro Youth in the Rural South* by Charles S. Johnson]. For it is an autobiographical novel about a "too big Negro girl, with nappy black hair, broad feet and a space between her teeth that would hold a number-two pencil" . . . scratching out the early outlines of self in a small Arkansas town.

Miss Angelou confidently reaches back in memory to pull out the painful childhood times: when children fail to break the adult code, disastrously breaching faith and laws they know nothing of; when the very young swing easy from hysterical laughter to awful loneliness; from a hunger for heroes to the voluntary Pleasure-Pain game of wondering who their *real* parents are and how long before they take them to their authentic home.

Introducing herself as Marguerite, a "tender-hearted" child, the author allows her story to range in an extraordinary fashion along the field of human emotion. With a child's fatalism, a deep cut ushers in visions of an ignoble death. With a child's addiction to romance and melodrama, she imagines ending her life in the dirt-yard of a Mexican family—among strangers! It is as if Miss Angelou has a Time Machine, so unerringly does she record the private world of the young where sin is the Original Sin and embarrassment, penultimate.

While she expertly reminds us of the pain of children trapped by time in the unsympathetic world of adults, she stretches out to the human environment too. Although the elements that go to make up the Black southern and rural experience—customs, values, superstitions—most interest Miss Angelou, she carries us "across the tracks" occasionally to the white world in experiences which corroborate the observation Marguerite's uncle makes: "They don't know us. They mostly scared." . . .

[Marguerite's] view of the truth about interracial encounters in this land is often expressed in phrasing that seems dated in its naturalistic grounding. Speaking of a white receptionist who gives her the run-around about a job, for instance, she says, "I accepted her as a fellow victim of the same puppeteer." . . . Such a fatalistic point-of-view would be quickly smothered in the current climate of social/political activism. Activists see the possibility and necessity for change—moderate to revolutionary—in the racial roles this society assigns us. Interestingly, the author moves out from under her fatalism by the end of the novel when she successfully demands a job as a streetcar conductor in San Francisco, a position traditionally denied women who are Black.

Miss Angelou accommodates her literary style to the various settings her story moves through. She describes a rural vignette which is "sweet-milk fresh in her memory." . . . Her metaphors are strong and right; her similes less often so. But these lapses in poetic style are undeniably balanced by the insight she offers into the effects of social conditioning on the life-style and self-concept of a Black child growing up in the rural South of the 1930's.

This is a novel about Blackness, youth, and white American society, usually in conflict. The miracle is that out of the War emerges a whole person capable of believing in her worth and capabilities. On balance, it is a gentle indictment of white American womanhood. It is a timely book.

Opal Moore

SOURCE: "Learning to Live: When the Bird Breaks from the Cage," in *Censored Books: Critical Viewpoints,* The Scarecrow Press, Inc., 1993, pp. 306-16.

I Know Why the Caged Bird Sings, the autobiography of Maya Angelou, is the story of one girl's growing up. But, like any literary masterpiece, the story of this one black girl declaring "I can" to a color-coded society that in innumerable ways had told her "you can't, you won't" transcends its author. It is an affirmation; it promises that life, if we have the courage to live it, will be worth the struggle. A book of this description might seem good reading for junior high and high school students. According to People for the American Way, however, *Caged Bird* was the ninth "most frequently challenged book" in American schools. *Caged Bird* elicits criticism for its honest depiction of rape, its exploration of the ugly spectre of racism in America, its recounting of the circumstances of Angelou's own out-of-wedlock teen pregnancy, and its humorous poking at the foibles of the institutional church. Arguments advocating that *Caged Bird* be banned from school reading lists reveal that the complainants, often parents, tend to regard any treatment of these kinds of subject matter in school as inappropriate—despite the fact that the realities and issues of sexuality and violence, in particular, are commonplace in contemporary teenage intercourse and discourse. The children, they imply, are too innocent for such depictions; they might be harmed by the truth.

This is a curious notion—that seriousness should be banned from the classroom while beyond the classroom, the irresponsible and sensational exploitation of sexual, violent, and profane materials is as routine as the daily dose of soap opera. . . .

In truth, what young readers seem most innocent of these days is not sex, murder, or profanity, but concepts of self empowerment, faith, struggle as quest, the nobility of intellectual inquiry, survival, and the nature and complexity of moral choice. *Caged Bird* offers these seemingly abstract (adult) concepts to a younger audience that needs to know that their lives are not inherited or predestined, that they can be participants in an exuberant struggle to subjugate traditions of ignorance and fear. Critics of this book might tend to overlook or devalue the necessity of such insights for the young.

Caged Bird's critics imply an immorality in the work based on the book's images. However, it is through Angelou's vivid depictions of human spiritual triumph *set against a backdrop* of human weakness and failing that the autobiography speaks dramatically about moral choice. Angelou paints a picture of some of the negative choices: white America choosing to oppress groups of people; choosing lynch law over justice; choosing intimidation over honor. She offers, however, "deep talk" on the possibility of positive choices: choosing life over death (despite the difficulty of that life); choosing courage over safety; choosing discipline over chaos; choosing voice over silence; choosing compassion over pity, over hatred, over habit; choosing work and planning and hope over useless recrimination and slovenly despair. The book's detractors seem unwilling to admit that morality is not edict (or an innate property of innocence), but the learned capacity for judgment, and that the necessity of moral choice arises only in the presence of the soul's imperfection.

Self empowerment, faith, struggle as quest, survival, intellectual curiosity, complexity of choice—these ideas are the underpinning of Maya Angelou's story. To explore these themes, the autobiography poses its own set of oppositions: Traditional society and values vs. contemporary society and its values; silence vs. self expression; literacy vs. the forces of oppression; the nature of generosity vs. the nature of cruelty; spirituality vs. ritual. Every episode of *Caged Bird* engages these and other ideas in Maya Angelou's portrait of a young girl's struggle against adversity—a struggle against rape: rape of the body, the soul, the mind, the future, of expectation, of tenderness—towards identity and self affirmation. If we cannot delete rape from our lives, should we delete it from a book about life?

Caged Bird opens with the poignant, halting voice of Marguerite Johnson, the young Maya Angelou, struggling for her own voice beneath the vapid doggerel of the yearly Easter pageant:

"What you lookin at me for?"

"I didn't come to stay. . . . "

These two lines prefigure the entire work. "What you lookin at me for . . . " is the painful question of every black girl made self-conscious and self-doubting by a white world critical of her very existence. The claim that she "didn't come to stay" increases in irony as the entire work ultimately affirms the determination of Marguerite Johnson and, symbolically, all of the unsung survivors of the Middle Passage, to do that very thing—to stay. To stay is to affirm life and the possibility of redemption. To stay—despite the circumstance of our coming (slavery), despite the efforts to remove us (lynching) or make us invisible (segregation).

Angelou, in disarmingly picturesque and humorous scenes like this opening glimpse of her girl-self forgetting her lines and wetting her pants in her earliest effort at public speech, continually reminds us that we survive the painfulness of life by the tender stabilities of family and community. As she hurries from the church trying to beat the wetness coursing down her thighs, she hears the benedictory murmurs of the old church ladies saying, "Lord bless the child," and "Praise God."

This opening recitation lays a metaphorical foundation for the autobiography, and for our understanding of the trauma of rape that causes Marguerite to stifle her voice for seven years. In some ways, the rape of Marguerite provides the center and the bottom of this autobiographical statement.

Critics of the work charge that the scenes of seduction and rape are too graphically rendered:

> He [Mr. Freeman] took my hand and said, "Feel it." It was mushy and squirmy like the inside of a freshly killed chicken. Then he dragged me on top of his chest with his left arm, and his right hand was moving so fast and his heart was beating so hard that I was afraid that he would die. . . . Finally he was quiet, and then came the nice part. He held me so softly that I wished he wouldn't ever let me go.

The seeming ambivalence of this portrait of the dynamics of interfamilial rape elicits distaste among those who prefer, if rape must be portrayed at all, for it to be painted with the hard edges of guilt and innocence. Yet, this portrait reflects the sensibilities of eight year old Marguerite Johnson—full of her barely understood longings and the vulnerability of ignorance:

> Mama had drilled into my head: "Keep your legs closed, and don't let nobody see your pocketbook."

Mrs. Baxter has given her daughter that oblique homespun wisdom designed to delay the inevitable. Such advice may forewarn, but does not forearm and, characteristic of the period, does not even entertain the unthinkable improbability of the rape of a child. Aside from this vague caution, and the knowledge that "lots of people did 'it' and they used their 'things' to accomplish the deed . . . ," Marguerite does not know how to understand or respond to the gentle, seemingly harmless Mr. Freeman because he is "family," he is an adult (not to be questioned), and he offers her what appears to be the tenderness she craves that had not been characteristic of her strict southern upbringing.

When asked why she included the rape in her autobiography, Angelou has said, "I wanted people to see that the man was not totally an ogre. And it is this fact that poses one of the difficulties of rape and the inability of children, intellectually unprepared, to protect themselves. If the rapists were all terrible ogres and strangers in dark alleys, it would be easier to know when to run, when to scream, when to "say no." But the devastation of rape is subtle in its horror and betrayal which creates in Marguerite feelings of complicity in her own assault. When queried by Mr. Freeman's defense attorney about whether Mr. Freeman had ever touched her on occasions before the rape, Marguerite, recalling that first encounter, realizes immediately something about the nature of language, its inflexibility, its inability to render the whole truth, and the palpable danger of being misunderstood:

I couldn't . . . tell them how he had loved me once for a few minutes and how he had held me close before he thought I had peed in my bed. My uncles would kill me and Grandmother Baxter would stop speaking, as she often did when she was angry. And all those people in the court would stone me as they had stoned the harlot in the Bible. And Mother, who thought I was such a good girl, would be so disappointed. . . .

Some schools that have chosen not to ban *Caged Bird* completely have compromised by deleting "those rape chapters." It should be clear, however, that this portrayal of rape is hardly titillating or "pornographic." It raises issues of trust, truth and lie, love, the naturalness of a child's craving for human contact, language and understanding, and the confusion engendered by the power disparities that necessarily exist between children and adults. High school students should be given the opportunity to gain insight into these subtleties of human relationships and entertain the "moral" questions raised by the work: should Mr. Freeman have been forgiven for his crime? (After all, he appears to be very sorry. When Marguerite awakens from the daze of trauma, Mr. Freeman is tenderly bathing her: "His hands shook.") Which is the greater crime, Mr. Freeman's rape of Marguerite, or Marguerite's lying about the nature of their relationship (which might be seen as having resulted in Mr. Freeman's death)? What should be the penalty for rape? Is the community's murderous action against Mr. Freeman's unthinkable crime merely a more expedient form of the state's statutes on capital punishment? Might we say he was "judged by a jury of his peers"? Which is the greater crime—if Marguerite had told the truth and Mr. Freeman had been acquitted, or Marguerite's lie, and Mr. Freeman's judgement by an outraged community? What *is* the truth? Didn't Marguerite actually tell the basic truth, based on her innocence, based on her inability to understand Mr. Freeman's motives? As Maya Angelou might say, "Those are questions, frightful questions, too intimate and obscenely probing." Yet, how can we deny young readers, expected to soon embark upon their own life-altering decision-making, the opportunity to engage in questions so relevant as these . . .

Caged Bird, in this scene so often deleted from classroom study, opens the door for discussion about the prevalent confusion between a young person's desire for affection and sexual invitation. Certainly, this is a valuable distinction to make, and one that young men and women are often unable to perceive or articulate. Angelou also reveals the manner by which an adult manipulates a child's desire for love as a thin camouflage for his own crude motives. A further complication to the neat assignment of blame is that Marguerite's lie is not prompted by a desire to harm Mr. Freeman, but out of her feelings of helplessness and dread. Yet, she perceives that the effect of that lie is profound—so profound that she decides to stop her own voice, both as penance for the death of Mr. Freeman and out of fear of the power of her words: " . . . a man was dead because I had lied."

This dramatization of the ambiguity of truth and the fearfulness of an Old Testament justice raises questions of justice and the desirability of truth in a world strapped in fear, misunderstanding, and the inadequacy of language. The story reveals how violence can emerge out of the innocent routines of life; how betrayal can be camouflaged with blame; that adults are individual and multi-dimensional and flawed; but readers also see how Marguerite overcomes this difficult and alienating episode of her life.

However, the work's complexity is a gradual revelation. The rape must be read within the context of the entire work from the stammer of the opening scene, to the elegant Mrs. Flowers who restores Marguerite's confidence in her own voice to the book's closing affirmation of the forgiving power of love and faith. Conversely, all of these moments should be understood against the ravaging of rape.

Marguerite's story is emblematic of the historic struggle of an entire people and, by extension, any person or group of people. The autobiography moves from survival to celebration of life and students who are permitted to witness Marguerite's suffering and ascendancy might gain in the nurturing of their own potential for compassion, optimism and courage.

This extended look at the scene most often censored by high school administrators and most often criticized by parents should reveal that Angelou's *Caged Bird,* though easily read, is no "easy" read. This is, perhaps, part of the reason for the objections of parents who may feel that the materials are "too sophisticated" for their children. We should be careful, as teachers, designers of curriculum, and concerned parents, not to fall into the false opposition of good vs. easy. What is easier for a student (or for a teacher) is not necessarily good. In this vein, those parents who are satisfied to have this work removed from required lists but offered on "suggested" lists should ask themselves whether they are giving their kids the kind of advice that was so useless to Maya Angelou: "keep your legs closed and don't let nobody see your pocketbook." Without the engagement of discussion, *Caged Bird* might do what parents fear most—raise important issues while leaving the young reader no avenue to discover his or her relationship to these ideas. Perhaps the parents are satisfied to have controversial works removed to the "suggested" list because they are convinced that their children will never read anything that is not required. If that is their hope, we have more to worry about than booklists.

If parents are concerned about anything, it should be the paucity of assigned readings in the junior high and high school classrooms, and the quality of the classroom teaching approach for this (and any other) worthwhile book. Educators have begun to address the importance of the preparation of teachers for the presentation of literature of the caliber of *Caged Bird* which is a challenge to students, but also to teachers who choose to bring this work into the classroom. *Caged Bird* establishes oppo-

sitions of place and time: Stamps, Arkansas vs. St. Louis and San Francisco; the 1930s of the book's opening vs. the slave origins of Jim Crow, which complicate images related to certain cultural aspects of African-American life including oral story traditions, traditional religious beliefs and practices, ideas regarding discipline and displays of affection, and other materials which bring richness and complexity to the book, but that, without clarification, can invite misapprehension. For example, when Marguerite smashes Mrs. Cullinan's best pieces of "china from Virginia" by "accident," the scene is informative when supported by its parallels in traditional African-American folklore, by information regarding the significance of naming in traditional society, and the cultural significance of the slave state practice of depriving Africans of their true names and cultural past. The scene, though funny, should not be treated as mere comic relief, or as a meaningless act of revenge. Mrs. Cullinan, in insisting upon "re-naming" Marguerite Mary, is carrying forward that enslaving technique designed to subvert identity; she is testing what she believes is her prerogative as a white person—to establish *who* a black person will be, to call a black person by any name she chooses. She is "shock[ed] into recognition of [Marguerite's] personhood." She learns that her name game is a very dangerous power play that carries with it a serious risk.

With sufficient grounding, *I Know Why the Caged Bird Sings* can provide the kinds of insights into American history and culture, its values, practices, beliefs, lifestyles, and its seeming contradictions that inspired James Baldwin to describe the work, on its cover, as one that "liberates the reader into life simply because Maya Angelou confronts her own life with such a moving wonder, such a luminous dignity," and as " . . . a Biblical study of life in the midst of death." A book that has the potential to liberate the reader into life is one that deserves our intelligent consideration, not rash judgements made from narrow fearfulness. Such a work will not "teach students a lesson." It will demand an energetic, participatory reading. It will demand their seriousness. With the appropriate effort, this literary experience can assist readers of any racial or economic group in meeting their own, often unarticulated doubts, questions, fears, and perhaps assist in their own search for dignity.

GATHER TOGETHER IN MY NAME (1974)

Annie Gottlieb

SOURCE: "Gather Together in My Name," in *The New York Times Book Review,* June 16, 1974, pp. 16, 20.

Maya Angelou writes like a song, and like the truth. The wisdom, rue and humor of her storytelling are borne on a lilting rhythm completely her own, the product of a born writer's senses nourished on black church singing and preaching, soft mother talk and salty street talk, and on literature: James Weldon Johnson, Langston Hughes,

Richard Wright, Shakespeare and Gorki. Her honesty is also very much her own, even when she faces bitter facts or her own youthful foolishness. In this second installment of her autobiography, as in her much praised first book, *I Know Why the Caged Bird Sings,* Maya Angelou accomplishes the rare feat of laying her own life open to a reader's scrutiny without the reflex-covering gesture of melodrama or shame. And as she reveals herself so does she reveal the black community, with a quiet pride, a painful candor and a clean anger.

Gather Together in My Name is a little shorter and thinner than its predecessor; telling of an episodic, searching and wandering period in Maya Angelou's life, it lacks the density of childhood. In full compensation, her style has both ripened and simplified. It is more telegraphic and more condensed, transmitting a world of sensation or emotion or understanding in one image—in short, it is more like poetry. . . .

"The South I returned to . . . was flesh-real and swollen-belly poor." "I clenched my reason and forced their faces into focus." Even in these short bits snipped out of context, you can sense the palpability, the precision and the rhythm of this writing. The reader is rocked into pleasure, stung into awareness. And the migrant, irresolute quality of the story—a faithful reflection of her late adolescence in the forties—resolves into a revelation. The restless, frustrated trying-on of roles turns out to have been an instinctive self-education, and the book ends with Maya Angelou finally gaining her adulthood by regaining her innocence.

In *Gather Together in My Name,* the ridiculous and touching posturing of a young girl in the throes of growing up are superimposed on the serious business of survival and responsibility for a child. Maya Angelou's insistence on taking full responsibility for her own life, her frank and humorous examination of her self, will challenge many a reader to be as honest under easier circumstances. Reading her book, you may learn, too, the embrace and ritual, the dignity and solace and humor of the black community. You will meet strong, distinctive people, drawn with deftness and compassion; their blackness is not used to hide their familiar but vulnerable humanity any more than their accessible humanity can for a moment be used to obscure their blackness—or their oppression. Maya Angelou's second book about her life as a young black woman in America is engrossing and vital, rich and funny and wise.

Doris Grumbach

SOURCE: "Fine Print: Summer Miscellany," in *The New Republic,* Vol. 171, Nos. 1 and 2, July 6 & 13, 1974, pp. 30-32.

[Gather Together in My Name] is the second volume in the story of [Maya Angelou's] life, a series that she intended to continue "every three years until she is recognized as the contemporary Black Proust." It may be

that she will fall short of that avowed ambition but, if one recalls her first successful book *I Know Why The Caged Bird Sings* . . . , and reads this second one, it is apparent that Angelou is keen, sharp, earthy, imaginative, lyrical, spiritually bold, and seems destined for distinction.

The book concerns her travails in California between the ages of 17 and 19 at the end of World War II. . . . Rita [the name Maya calls herself in this book] scrapes, in these two frantic years, from the bottom to the level at the end of the book when, like Voltaire's Candide, she asserts: "I had given a promise and found my innocence. I swore I'd never lose it again."

Angelou has kept that promise. . . . A truly remarkable person, she is able to re-create events of her own life and make them seem part of the reader's imaginative experience.

Lynn Sukenick

SOURCE: A review of *Gather Together in My Name,* in *The Village Voice,* July 17, 1974, p. 31.

Maya Angelou's rendering of three years of her innocent, awkward, and admirably nervy late adolescence in *[Gather Together in My Name],* the second volume of her autobiography, resembles the performance of a professional dancer trying to imitate someone who can't dance. The grace and competence show through and it's hard to believe in the high incidence of failure she describes in her youth. Thus we are entertained but kept safe from the roughness and painful uncertainty of real ineptitudes.

Angelou's prose is sculpted, concise, rich with flavor and surprise, exuding a natural confidence and command. The fault—since I have found one—lies more in the tone of the book. It is healthy, warm, and tough, winning our affection partly through its refusal to gloss over stupidities, mistakes, and cruelties. Yet this refusal to let her earlier self get off easy, and the self-mockery which is her means to honesty, finally becomes in itself a glossing over; although her laughter at herself is witty, intelligent, and a good preventative against maudlin confession (she shrugs off deprivations of family feeling that would make our ordinary psychoanalyzed citizen curl up in self-pity), it eventually becomes a tic and a substitute for a deeper look.

The book is a comedy of self-deception. I don't mean to say that it should be something sober and earnest—indeed, Angelou's style and flair come from her ability to move rather than brood. Yet a revelation of youthful foolishness usually implies that something will take its place, build slowly to edge it out, and the book does not build; it is a chain of anecdotes, and Maya's innocence must re-establish itself at the start of each in order for her mistakes to function as the punch lines they tend to be. Comedy is liberating precisely because there is in it an absence of long-range consequences, and it is not consequences but transitions that I miss—whether of motivation, or musing, or adjustments of emotion. Transitions are a graph of how people cope, and wanting to know how people cope is one of our most urgent reasons for reading autobiography. That Angelou is within the space of three years a mother, a Creole cook, a madam, a tap dancer, a prostitute, a chauffeurette, and so on, is amazing, but I'm not content to be amazed, and I'm annoyed when flippancy runs interference; she gets me to like her and I want to know what it is inside her that makes those choices, however little they may have seemed like choices at the time. . . .

The realest thing about autobiography is the teller, not the tale. Temperament tends to linger and infuse us long after the anecdotes are forgotten. On the strength of *I Know Why the Caged Bird Sings* I will continue to read whatever autobiographical prose Maya Angelou produces, but I hope that next time she will let simmer a little longer and make it a little less Entertaining, however much a publisher, or even her readers, urge her on.

📖 *NOW SHEBA SINGS THE SONG* (1987)

Penny M. Spokes

SOURCE: A review of *Now Sheba Sings the Song,* in *Booklist,* Vol. 83, No. 14, March 15, 1987, pp. 1089-90.

Popular poet Angelou, author of *I Know Why the Caged Bird Sings* and *All God's Children Need Traveling Shoes,* among other works, gets top billing, but the black-and-sepia tones of Tom Feelings' 84 drawings—primarily portraits—are the main attraction in this tribute to black women. The award-winning artist describes his subjects as ordinary but beautiful females whom he observed and sketched over a 25-year period in the Caribbean Islands, North and South America, and Africa. Feelings' essentially realistic depiction of faces and bodies, sometimes enhanced by tonal gradations and elsewhere modified by soft or blurred lines, illustrates physical and spiritual qualities that are concatenated by the poet's sparse, often strong, images: "peanut butter colored cheeks . . . impertinent buttocks . . . A moan for our burned visions . . . We have played together on the floor of the world." A combination of accessible art and poetry that's likely to be requested in public libraries.

Juana D. Kennedy

SOURCE: A review of *Now Sheba Sings the Song,* in *Los Angeles Times Book Review,* August 9, 1987, p. 6.

Tom Feelings, the award-winning children's book illustrator and Maya Angelou, an accomplished writer, performer and activist, have combined their talents to create a paean to black women though drawings and poetry

in a book intended for readers of all ages. In its evocative, celebratory style, this short book is in many ways reminiscent of similar efforts done in the 1960s, works that glorified the beauty, wisdom and resilience of black women. And therein lies both its weakness and its strength.

The simplistic tone of the book may have been part of the publishers' effort to "cross adult and juvenile frontiers." But its historic references and sensual allusions may be a bit obscure for younger audiences. While its insistent focus on the "beauty" and "spirit" of black women, without real attention to their more cerebral attributes, may seem stereotypical to more sophisticated readers—regardless of hue. This is a limited view black parents probably would not want to encourage.

Despite the considerable talent behind the project, its very nature makes it seem somewhat dated. One would like to *think* that in 1987 we would have progressed beyond the need for revelations about qualities that at long last simply should be accepted as obvious.

The 84 sepia and black-and-white illustrations were born out of Feeling's own discovery of the "power" and "balance" of these women over the course of 25 years of travels throughout the world. He chose his long-time friend Angelou to write the accompanying verse because of her shared perspective as a black woman.

Angelou was not a bad choice. She has published five volumes of autobiography, including the acclaimed *I Know Why the Caged Bird Sings,* as well as four collections of poetry.

Although her poetry in this book lapses into I-am-woman, hear-me-roar kinds of cliches in spots, it nevertheless is the stronger portion of the effort. She opens with:

> Mother told her secrets to me
> When I rode
> Low in the pocket
> Between her hips.
>
> History does not dissolve
> In the blood.

Later, she writes:

> I must stiffen my back
> Quieten my face and teach a lesson
> in Grace.

As for Feelings, his skill as an artist certainly is apparent in the drawings—a few are so striking that they should be framed. But too many of them have an undistinctive, student-sketchbook quality that fails to capture the complexity and endless physical diversity of his subjects.

Ironically, Feelings' written introduction to the book is richer than his illustrations. . . .

Sheba began long before Feelings was aware of it. During trips to Africa, the United States, South America and the Caribbean, he took to making "random" drawings of what he calls "the extraordinary ordinary women" he observed along the way.

"I tried to capture a sense of the primal importance of black women, fueled by my growing awareness of their strength and beauty, so undervalued in the world."

One hot day as he was standing by the side of the road waiting for a bus in Ghana, he saw "a middle-aged Ghanaian woman . . . with all her kitchenwares piled . . . gracefully high on her head. She flashed a sunlit smile at me. . . ."

"I knew at that moment that all I had . . . been taught about black being ugly was a lie. For based on those values, this woman was supposed to be ugly, yet I was looking at the most beautiful sight my eyes had ever seen.

"For me . . . as an artist and as a *man* that's what I had come to Africa to see, feel and have affirmed."

It is tragic that history has made this sort of affirmation still necessary for so many.

Joseph Harper

SOURCE: A review of *Now Sheba Sings the Song,* in *School Library Journal,* Vol. 34, No. 2, October, 1987, pp. 146-47.

An excellent choice for poetry lovers and lovers of poignant portraiture, this book combines a sensual poem by Angelou with Feelings' exquisite portraits of black women. The poetry is rich in imagery, rhythm, and beauty, while the art transcends the boundaries of most works which merely capture a person on paper, going on to portray the essence of a people. The sketches have a universal quality to them, and they should remind readers of people they know. The poetry and the art blend to celebrate the life and the beauty of black women everywhere, a beauty of the soul.

Mary K. Chelton

SOURCE: A review of *Now Sheba Sings the Song,* in *Voice of Youth Advocates,* Vol. 10, No. 4, October, 1987, pp. 182-83.

Drawings of black women of all ages from all over the world are unified and "illustrated" by Maya Angelou's poem, which is the title of this oversized, exquisitely beautiful book. A sort of "Song of Songs" in the black female voice, Angelou's poem is proud, wistful, earthy, and sensual, but Feelings' drawings are simply breathtaking. Nearly all are done with black lines on sepia, a very successful attempt to convey the beauty of women

who are of these colors. Feelings creates an aesthetic of black women similar to that of Japanese printmakers which emphasize the head and neck of women, although Feelings' aesthetic is unique to his skill and subjects, perhaps typified by the cover profile drawings. He is as extremely adept at capturing the planes and shadings of black women's faces, as he is at capturing their various and vibrant lives. This is more Feelings' book than Angelou's; moving though her poem is, his drawings do not need it, although good booktalkers will use it to attract attention to the drawings. Senior high art teachers will also be able to use the book to inspire young artists.

I SHALL NOT BE MOVED (1990)

Publishers Weekly

SOURCE: A review of *I Shall Not Be Moved,* in *Publishers Weekly,* Vol. 237, No. 12, March 23, 1990, p. 69.

Angelou's poems embrace opposite poles: the laughter of old folks who "generously forgive life for happening to them," and the "helpless hope" on the faces of starving children. Though she can be directly political, as in a stinging letter to **"These Yet to Be United States,"** more often, a political dimension emerges naturally from ordinary lives observed with keen irony ("Even minimal people can't survive on minimal wage"). Angelou's themes include loss of love and youth, human oneness in diversity, the strength of blacks in the face of racism and adversity. The book's title is also the refrain of **"Our Grandmothers,"** a moving history poem about the struggles of black women. Some of these lyrics are freeform, while others use conventional rhyme and meter to good effect. Angelou *(I Know Why the Caged Bird Sings)* writes with poise and grace.

Hazel Rochman

SOURCE: A review of *I Shall Not Be Moved,* in *Booklist,* Vol. 86, No. 18, May 15, 1990, p. 1773.

"Big ships shudder / down to the sea / because of me / Railroads run / on a twinness track / 'cause of my back." In Angelou's exquisitely simple worksong, both wit and longing seem to be rooted in physical action. Like Paul Robeson's singing, like Langston Hughes' "Florida Road Workers," rhythm and sense are one. The other poems in this collection don't come up to **"Worker's Song"**—some are too polemical—but in the best of them, the sensuous detail livens the abstraction ("Old folks / allow their bellies to jiggle like slow / tambourines . . . / When old folks laugh, they free the world"). There's no false sentiment ("Preacher, don't send me / when I die / to some big ghetto in the sky"); Angelou's paradise has no "grits and tripe"; but "the music is jazz / and the season is fall." The dying fall of many lines combined with the strong beat reinforces the feeling of struggle and uncertainty: "Why do we journey, muttering / like rumors among the stars?"

Jacqueline Gropman

SOURCE: A review of *I Shall Not Be Moved,* in *School Library Journal,* Vol. 36, No. 9, September, 1990, p. 268.

Angelou's fifth book of poetry conveys the complexity, richness, exuberance, and tragedy of the black experience in language that is personal, pithy, and immediate. "I shall not be moved" is the haunting refrain from the poem **"Our Grandmothers,"** a pledge of moral courage referring to the most heartfelt stand from which one will not budge. It is a majestic poem about the immense pain of history and the moral stamina needed to remain true to oneself. In other poems, Angelou's style varies from the lighthearted fun of **"Seven Women's Blessed Assurance,"** to the clever wordplay of **"Man Bigot,"** to the inspiring pathos of **"Ailey, Baldwin, Floyd, and Killens."** Funny, reflective, illuminating, and honest, the poems in this slim volume possess the drama of the storyteller and the imagery and soul of the poet.

LIFE DOESN'T FRIGHTEN ME (1993)

Publishers Weekly

SOURCE: A review of *Life Doesn't Frighten Me,* in *Publishers Weekly,* Vol. 240, No. 38, September 20, 1993, p. 71.

[Editor Sara Jane] Boyers, a TV producer and art collector, deserves a standing ovation for her performance in pairing Angelou's poem with abstract paintings by the late [Jean Michel] Basquiat. "Dragons breathing flame / On my counterpane / That doesn't frighten me at all. / I go boo / Make them shoo / I make fun / Way they run / I won't cry / So they fly"—had it been teamed with representational or whimsical illustrations, the verse might well have lost its dignity; instead, the proximity of Basquiat's edgy, streetwise pictures adds even greater power and authenticity to Angelou's refrain, "Life doesn't frighten me at all." Conversely, the affirming quality of the poem mediates Basquiat's disquieting urban images. Basquiat's first works were drawn onto the walls of Manhattan buildings, and the frenzied, sometimes angry compositions here have the rawness of graffiti. The reproductions invite close scrutiny, implicitly teaching the viewer a way of approaching contemporary art and reinforcing the tough beauty of the poem.

Roger Sutton

SOURCE: A review of *Life Doesn't Frighten Me,* in *The Bulletin of the Center for Children's Books,* Vol. 47, No. 5, January, 1994, p. 146.

The presence of an editorial credit on the title page seems to indicate that Boyers is responsible for this melding of Angelou's poem, originally published in 1978, and Basquiat's paintings, created throughout the early 1980s. It's an apt if arresting synthesis, far more effective than most of the artsy picture books that have been regularly coming down the pike. "Panthers in the park / Strangers in the dark"—Angelou's poem, really a chant, catalogs a host of spooky possibilities and banishes them with the iterated affirmation, "Life doesn't frighten me at all." It does, though, and that's why we need the poem. Basquiat's images capture this same contradiction: they're both scary and intensely vulnerable, with childlike scratches and scrawls and totemic stick-figures facing a dangerous world. The poem is firmly rooted in childhood; the art is New York street-sophisticated and sometimes sadly crazy, but kids will recognize their own drawings and imaginings in these pictures and should be able to see the bravery that drives the images.

Hazel Rochman

SOURCE: A review of *Life Doesn't Frighten Me,* in *Booklist,* Vol. 90, No. 9, January 1, 1994, p. 829.

Both a handsome art book and a rhythmic read-aloud, this is great for sharing with audiences of many ages. Angelou's direct, lovely poem is the text of a dramatic large-size picture book with paintings in glowing color by young New York City artist Basquiat. Words and pictures work together because the editor has made no attempt to match literal images. Both poet and artist confront our archetypal fears, out there and in our nightmares ("Panthers in the park / Strangers in the dark / No, they don't frighten me at all"). Fear is answered with dancing energy and daring imagination and laughter ("Mean old Mother Goose / Lions on the loose / They don't frighten me at all"). Basquiat's work has the directness of street art, with a bold combination of magic realism and abstract geometric shapes—sometimes Picasso, sometimes African mask, sometimes child's scribble.

Jane Marino

SOURCE: A review of *Life Doesn't Frighten Me,* in *School Library Journal,* Vol. 40, No. 3, March, 1994, p. 224.

A unique book that combines the words of a renowned African-American poet laureate and the primitive, modern paintings of a young Haitian-American artist. With lines of verse that shout exuberantly from each page, a young voice rails against any and all things that mean to do her harm. Whether they are "Shadows on the wall/ Noises down the hall" or even "Mean old Mother Goose/ Lions on the loose"—to one and all she responds—"they don't frighten me at all." In the middle, the pace and intensity quicken as "I go boo/ Make them shoo/ I make fun/ Way they run." Despite the scary things around her, the poet's determined courage remains. The art provides a jolting counterpoint to the optimistic words, reflecting a dark, intense vision. Violent splashes of color bleed and drip one into another, and white letters are scratched into black backgrounds. Stark figures with grotesque features face off against one another. Symbols such as arrows, birds, crowns, and letters emphasize the artist's anger and sense of irony. The choice of the paintings, taken as they were from an extant body of work, give levels of meanings to a poem already strong with images of its own. A powerful exploration of emotion and its expression through the careful blend of words and art.

📖 *MY PAINTED HOUSE, MY FRIENDLY CHICKEN, AND ME* (1994)

Publishers Weekly

SOURCE: A review of *My Painted House, My Friendly Chicken, and Me,* in *Publishers Weekly,* Vol. 241, No. 37, September 12, 1994, p. 91.

The poet laureate here adopts the voice of an eight-year-old Ndebele girl of South Africa, who addresses the reader as her "stranger-friend." Thandi, whose name means Hope, describes some of her favorite things: the chicken to whom she confides her secrets, the intricately painted houses in her village, the beads her mother strings. Thandi's narration is strong and direct, and provides a lively introduction to a long-neglected people and culture. Its attempts to embrace the reader, however, seem somewhat strained ("You may call me friend, and I would like to call you friend"), and the use of many sizes and arrangements of type creates some choppiness. The accompanying photographs [by Margaret Courtney-Clarke], on the other hand, do full justice to the brilliant colors of the beadwork, blankets and decorated houses of Thandi's village, and to the various attitudes of the carefully adorned people in it. Regrettably, they offer no more than a glimpse of the landscape nor any larger view of the village as a whole, thus inadvertently narrowing the book's scope.

Kirkus Reviews

SOURCE: A review of *My Painted House, My Friendly Chicken, and Me,* in *Kirkus Reviews,* Vol. LXII, No. 18, September 15, 1994, p. 1264.

A beguiling collaboration between the renowned poet and a Namibian-born photojournalist. Thandi, an eight-year-old Ndebele girl from a South African village, is first glimpsed in European school clothes but talks mostly about her traditional culture, in which "people do not call anything beautiful. They will say that the best thing is good." She tells how their intricately patterned houses are painted and describes her mother's beadwork, focusing on the contrast between these arts and the sober modern world of town and school. Thandi's sunny, childlike voice is gracefully honed and has delightful

touches of humor, especially about her "best friend," a chicken: "When I tell my friend secrets, she can talk all she wants . . . but no one can understand her . . . except another chicken, of course" (ellipses in original). In the expertly composed color photos, Thandi and the other children glow with mischief, laugh out loud, or "just sit back deep inside themselves"; the crafts are also handsomely displayed. The design here (by Alexander Isley Design) is inspired, setting off words and photos to perfection. Vibrant color blocks and pages echo hues in the photos and contrast with white pages. Spacing and different sizes of sans-serif type enhance the cadence and emphasis of the first-person narrative.

A fine introduction to these young South Africans.

Deborah Stevenson

SOURCE: A review of *My Painted House, My Friendly Chicken, and Me,* in *The Bulletin of the Center for Children's Books,* Vol. 48, No. 4, December, 1994, pp. 118-19.

"I am Thandi, a Ndebele girl in South Africa," says the eight-year-old narrator, and she shows us her best friend the chicken, her village of painted houses, and her family and pastimes. Angelou's text has a friendly, singing quality, helped by the repetition of "of course" ("The women wear their best blankets and best neck rings and very good leg rings, of course"); Courtney-Clarke's photographs of the villagers and the intricately beautiful paintings on their houses are sharp and immediate, although they are sometimes reduced to a size that makes details hard to distinguish. The format of the book, however, occasionally clouds the issue of audience: the text is too simple for a readalone audience, but the games with print going across pages and appearing in different sizes and colors (and not always with sufficient contrast with the background) will be lost on the lap crowd and difficult for readers-aloud to convey. The text also leaves questions unanswered. Where did the occasional marginal drawings come from—did Thandi draw them? Where do the mules that take Thandi to the city live? Which of the pictures are taken in the city? This is ultimately a glossy entry, with some composition problems, in the old "children of many lands" genre, but the direct address and sly humor of the text will woo some young viewers.

Kevin Steinberger

SOURCE: A review of *My Painted House, My Friendly Chicken, and Me,* in *Magpies,* Vol. 10, No. 1, March, 1995, p. 35.

A curious title, and words and pictures to excite the senses and invigorate the spirit. Angelou and Courtney-Clarkes' photo-documentary is a most unusual book that gives novel insight into the world of eight-years-old Thandi, an Ndebele girl in South Africa.

Since the pioneering work of Axel Poignant *(Piccaninny Walkabout),* Astrid Bergman Sucksdorff *(Chendru: The Boy and the Tiger)* and Sonia and Tim Gidal *(My Village Series)* the daily life of children in particular cultures has been the subject of many excellent photo-documentaries. What makes this title so different and outstanding is Thandi's whimsical first-person narration and the very colourful, eccentric book design that perfectly suits the energy and joy of the delightful child.

Thandi takes the reader on a little tour of her village focusing on her pet chicken, the remarkable mud dwellings decorated in vibrantly coloured geometric designs, the womens' handicrafts, her family, and her friends and their play. There is no obvious artifice in matching text with pictures; the narration is too capricious and animated for that. Instead, the words, delivered in a fragmented text of playful typographical variety, blend naturally with Courtney-Clarke's excellent variegated photography. The mix of candid and studied shots set off against coloured pages capture the joie de vivre that so apparently abounds in Thandi's village.

KOFI AND HIS MAGIC (1996)

Patricia Manning

SOURCE: A review of *Kofi and His Magic,* in *School Library Journal,* Vol. 43, No. 3, March, 1997, p. 170.

A young Ashanti boy invites readers to visit his West African village, famous for fine kente cloth, and to share his "magic"—a masterful imagination. Artistic typesetting composition is accompanied by appealing color photos that bring the lyrical text into sharp focus. Kofi is an engaging scamp whose vivid "daydreams" that transport him to other places will speak to children everywhere and present them with a clear vision of his beloved West African world. Kofi's joy in his life is reflected in both text and pictorial content and will be an eye-opener to more materialistic children in technically developed environments. A winner.

Julie Corsaro

SOURCE: A review of *Kofi and His Magic,* in *Booklist,* Vol. 93, No. 13, March 1, 1997, p. 1168.

As in the poet and photographer's ***My Painted House, My Friendly Chicken, and Me*** (1995), this second picture-book collaboration about Africa has great photographs but a disappointing text. The narrator is Kofi, a seven-year-old West African boy who uses "magic" to move from his home-town to a jitney, then to a place "up north." Kofi, whose magic comes from closing his eyes and opening his mind, is an engaging tour guide, but the lack of specifics about the setting is perplexing. What country does Kofi live in? What language does he speak? And the story line about magic is a flop. However, if you want to know what West Africa looks like, take a look at the vibrantly striking photographs. You'll see a bustling marketplace, powerful men and women decorated in their richest gold, and people of all ages wearing colorful *kente* cloth. Although there isn't much of a story here, this is a positive and realistic visual portrait.

Additional coverage of Angelou's life and career is contained in the following sources published by Gale Research: *Authors and Artists for Young Adults,* **Vol. 20;** *Black Writers,* **Vol. 2;** *Contemporary Authors,* **Vols. 65-68;** *Contemporary Authors New Revision Series,* **Vol. 42;** *Contemporary Literary Criticism,* **Vol. 77;** *Dictionary of Literary Biography,* **Vol. 38; and** *Something about the Author,* **Vol. 49.**

Natalie (Zane Moore) Babbitt
1932-

American author and author/illustrator of fiction.

Major works include *The Search for Delicious* (1969), *Kneeknock Rise* (1970), *Tuck Everlasting* (1975), *The Eyes of the Amaryllis* (1977), *The Devil's Other Storybook* (1987).

For more information on Babbitt's career prior to 1975, see *CLR*, Vol. 2.

INTRODUCTION

Although starting out as an illustrator, Babbitt thinks of herself primarily as a writer and has a firm belief that, somewhere within, everyone has a story to tell. While she once professed a dislike for awards, believing they often limit the focus of good literature to a select few and cause readers to pass over many other good writers and stories, certainly Babbitt has not been passed over. She has proven to be a diverse and talented writer, with works that span various genres and styles. Writing for a wide audience of children, from preschoolers to adolescents, Babbitt once commented, however, that her favorite age group is fifth graders. Convinced that this is the best age to be, she shapes many of her stories for this audience. She is best known for her fantasy stories that have folktale attributes, including unusual characters, magical settings, the importance of nature, and a touch of the mythical. In entertaining narratives, her characters confront many basic human needs, including the need to be loved, the need for growth, change and independence, the need to overcome fear, and the need to believe in something unexplainable.

Babbitt's works have been consistently praised for their poetic style and their carefully wrought structures. Her originality and courage when facing challenging and complex themes have also established her reputation as a notable children's book author. Yet, with all her seriousness of theme, Babbitt's stories still evoke humor and playfulness while expressing an amused tolerance for human folly and an affirmation of enduring hope in the human spirit. Her writing is often described as eloquent and full of imagery, with prose that is descriptive, evocative, and colorful. She pays attention to the way her sentences sound. For example, in *Tuck Everlasting* she writes about "the man in the yellow suit," choosing yellow, as she once commented, because a two-syllable color has better cadence than a one syllable color (and purple was out of the question!). On the subject of writing, Babbitt once explained, "You have to give writing your full attention, you have to like the revision process, and you have to like to be alone." She further added, "I write for children because I am inter-

ested in fantasy and the possibilities for experience of all kinds before the time of compromise. I believe that children are far more perceptive and wise than American books give them credit for being." Not limited in her talents, Babbitt's artwork is as engaging as her writing. Most of the artwork in her books is pen and ink drawings, but her picture books contain colorful, evocative paintings in soft hues that leap off the page. Through poetic, stimulating texts and charming pictures, Babbitt displays a remarkable versatility of style and artistry. A reviewer for *The Horn Book Magazine* concluded, "Babbitt's infectious sense of humor, her wisdom and perspective on life, and her ability not to take herself too seriously—but to take what she writes and her audience very seriously—have shaped a magnificent body of work."

Biographical Information

Born in Dayton, Ohio, Babbitt grew up during the Great Depression. It was during this difficult time that she learned from her parents what things were of meaning and value in life. Her father saw humor in almost everything and instilled in her the importance of merriment and a sense of humor. From her mother, who read children's books to her daughters, Babbitt learned to love books and art. Growing up, she was a quiet, withdrawn girl who read often. Impressed with Spanish artist Luis de Vargas's airbrushed figures of glamorous women popular during the Second World War, the young artist imitated them using colored pencils. Discouraged by the difference between Vargas's finished drawings and her own, she was inspired by Sir John Tenniel's illustrations in *The Adventure's of Alice in Wonderland* to work with pen and ink, which became her specialty. Later she attended the Laurel School in Cleveland and then Smith College, where she earned a bachelor's degree in art. While at Smith, she met Samuel Babbitt, whom she married in 1954. After taking time to raise her three children, she illustrated her first book—*The Forty-Ninth Magician*, published in 1966 and written by her husband, an aspiring writer. At this time, she was planning on being an illustrator. However, when her husband went back to work as a college administrator and became too busy to write the stories, she started writing and illustrating books on her own, eventually producing over thirteen titles.

Major Works

Borrowing from the folktale tradition, *The Search for Delicious* takes the reader on an enchanting journey through the countryside. During the compilation of a dictionary, a controversy breaks out among the royal court on the definition of delicious. Young Gaylen is, therefore, sent out to scour the countryside in search of a definition. Along the way he meets with a villain, the queen's evil brother, and must save the kingdom. Throughout Gaylen's adventures, he encounters the woldwellers, the mermaids, the dwarfs, and the winds, all of which are far removed from the foolish disputes of human beings. Continuing with the folktale style, *Kneeknock Rise* focuses on a small community's legend of the "Mammoth Mountain" and of its resident monster, the Megrimum. It is a provocative tale about the function of myth and imagination, about the pride and pretensions of ordinary human beings. The hero of the story, Egan, a visitor to the community, sets off one day to climb the mountain and slay the monster. Instead, he discovers his long lost uncle Ott and learns that the Megrimum is nothing more than the whistlings of a hot spring on cool, rainy nights. Yet when Egan tries to explain the truth of this village's favorite superstition, he is chagrined to find that the villagers refuse to believe him and remain faithful to their monster, half convincing him that the Megrimum is up there after all.

Although *Kneeknock Rise* is a Newbery Honor book, it is perhaps *Tuck Ever-lasting* that is Babbitt's most acclaimed work. Critics have praised its style and structure, as well as its perceptive handling of a significant theme. The story revolves around the Tuck family who has discovered a secret spring that makes the drinkers immortal. However, they find out that living forever without ever growing or changing is not very pleasant;

this is explained to Winnie, a ten-year-old girl who discovers the family by accident. The Tucks' explanation of the role of mortality in the cycle of nature "is one of the most vivid and deeply felt passages in American children's literature," *Ms.* reviewer Michele Landsberg declared.

The Eyes of the Amaryllis is the haunting and mysterious story of Geneva Reade, a sea captain's widow who for thirty years waits and watches for a sign of her husband from the sea. When Geneva hurts her ankle, her young granddaughter, Jenny, comes to visit and help. Jenny finds herself torn between her grandmother's obsessive madness at the edge of a mysterious other world and the mundane inland world of her father's store. The story comes to a climax during a horrific sea storm. When it is over, each character has undergone a transformation and growth. The potentially tragic story ends on a note of conciliation and hope. The novel marks the first time Babbitt has departed from the framing devices that usually surround her narratives. *The Devil's Other Storybook*, the sequel to *The Devil's Storybook* (1974), once again pits the devil against animals and humans who leave the trickster in the dust. Humorous rather than frightening, this collection of stories portrays the devil at his best. The punishments given out are appropriate and comical, as the devil gets his just rewards. There is a moral lesson even in the stories where the devil gives "hell, literally, to those who deserve it," noted Laurel Graeber in the *New York Times Book Review*, adding that "Ms. Babbitt's ethical lessons . . . rarely undermine her narrative gifts."

A departure from Babbitt's usual audience, style, and theme, *Herbert Rowbarge* (1982) is a novel for young adults. Darker and bleaker than her other books, this is the story of a man separated from his twin brother at birth. The book takes readers through the dismal life of Herbert Rowbarge, an uncaring man who has always felt that something was missing from his life. Rejecting the affections of his twin daughters, Babe and Louisa, and even of his old and devoted friend Dick, he is haunted by his failure to love and a sense of hollow incompleteness. The prevailing tone of the novel is comically ironic. Herbert's existence is at once pathetic, absurd, and ordinary. Yet Babbitt manages to suggest enormous emotional waste. Even more important perhaps is a subdued feminist theme. In this wry and toughminded novel, Babbitt asks her readers to take a close look at traditional American values, to examine them without sentimentality and false emotion.

Awards

Babbitt was awarded the Best Book of 1969 for Children Ages Nine to Twelve citation from the *New York Times* for *The Search for Delicious*. She was also awarded the American Library Association (ALA) Notable Book citation in 1970, the 1971 John Newbery Honor Book Award, and the *Horn Book* Honor citation all for *Kneeknock Rise*. For *Tuck Everlasting* she received the ALA

Notable Book citation, the *Horn Book* Honor List citation, and the Christopher Award for juvenile fiction, all in 1976, and The International Reading Association choices list citation, the U.S. Honor Book citation, and the Congress of the International Board on Books for Young People citation, all in 1978. In 1977 she received the ALA Notable Book citation for *The Eyes of Amaryllis*. She has also received awards for her body of work as a whole, including the George C. Stone Center for Children's Books award in 1979, the Hans Christian Andersen Medal nomination in 1981, and the Keene State College Award in 1993.

AUTHOR'S COMMENTARY

Natalie Babbitt

SOURCE: "Drawing on the Child Within: Writing Entertaining Children's Books with Honest Characters," in *The Horn Book Magazine,* Vol. LXIX, No. 3, May-June, 1993, pp. 284-90.

Over the years I have noticed that an awful lot of people don't seem to remember what it felt like to be a child. This is hard for me to understand. My childhood is very vivid to me, and I don't feel very different now from the way I felt then. It would appear I am the very same person, only with wrinkles. We keep getting told by psychologists that our characters are pretty much formed by the time we're four years old. I would place the time even earlier, myself, after observing my own children. Based on their personalities as infants, I think it would have been possible to predict with amazing accuracy what they'd be like as adults. You can go back and read what I wrote in their baby books and recognize the people they are today.

So maybe those adults who say they don't remember what it was like to be a child are only saying it because they imagine it must have been somehow different from the way it is now. I don't know. I do know that it's helpful to remember, if you want to write children's books. That's why, whenever I've had writing students, I've always tried to get them to look back, to think about what they were really like. It's the best way to figure out what kind of book you could be writing.

All of us are different, of course. Different kinds of people, I mean. We were different kinds of people when we were children, too. That's a very important thing to keep in mind because once you recognize the fact that there's no such singular, amalgamated thing as "the child," it frees you to write the kind of story that is special to you. Otherwise, you're asking yourself questions like "But would a child like this?" or "Would a child understand this?" You can answer those kinds of questions with another question—"What child?" And the answer to that question is, simply, "Me, as I was then and still am, to a very large extent, today."

As for myself, I was a fairly average child. Very skinny, but fond of toasted-cheese sandwiches and anything chocolate. By turns confident and scared to death. A loner who spent a lot of time drawing and reading, but who liked birthday parties and going to a friend's house after school. A good child who did plenty of bad things. In other words, like everyone else, a person full of contradictions. I did some weird things sometimes, like stringing up a noose from the catalpa tree in our backyard and hanging my dolls. Or only putting five of my weekly allotment of ten pennies into the collection plate at Sunday school because Sunday school, in my opinion, wasn't worth ten pennies. I never got away with anything, though. No matter how clandestine I tried to be, my mother always found me out. Always. She's been dead for thirty-five years, but I have this feeling that even now she's watching.

Everyone has memories like these, and they are indispensable for people who write children's books. Some of us write about the actual experiences we had, and that's fine as long as we remember that though they may seem funny now, they weren't all that funny at the time. I tend, myself, to write not about specific incidents but rather about the feelings I had. Not that I think my feelings were unique. In no way were they unique. I know that now. But I didn't at the time, and that's important to remember, too. None of us is unique in the way we used to think we were. The moment when you realize you're not unique is one of the most important moments in life. At first there's terrible disappointment. But close on the heels of that comes a sense of profound relief: "I'm not unique; I'm just like everyone else, and don't have to feel like an odd person out any more."

But when we're children, we are the odd man out. Some of the reason for this is that we don't know how to communicate our feelings very well, except through actions, but our actions are very often misinterpreted, and we are not very often treated like people. We are treated mostly like lumps of clay to be molded, blank pages to be written on, unformed and in continual need of being taught.

Ah, there's the rub. In continual need of being taught. If there is one thing wrong with books written for children—most from the nineteenth century and too many written since—it is exactly that: too many adults saying to themselves that a children's book is a tool for teaching.

When I was a child, I hated stories that tried to teach me things. Mostly those things were moral things: "You'd better be good or else." This is one reason why I loved *Alice in Wonderland* so much. It didn't—and doesn't—have anything to teach except, maybe, that adults are extremely silly. There is one particular passage that is worth remembering for writers of children's books. It comes in the beginning when Alice finds a little bottle with a label that says "DRINK ME":

It was all very well to say "Drink me," but the wise little Alice was not going to do that in a hurry. "No, I'll look first," she said, "and see whether it's marked 'poison' or not;" for she had read several nice little stories about children who had got burnt, and eaten up by wild beasts and other unpleasant things, all because they would not remember the simple rules their friends had taught them.

Ah, yes, those nice little stories. We remember them well. Let us hope we will never write any.

But the sad thing is that even if you aren't writing teaching books, the children, poor things, accustomed as they are to being taught, will very often assume that you are trying to teach them. I get letters from readers explaining to me, in a tired way, what they have learned from my books, especially *Tuck Everlasting.* This is one of the downsides to this business of using stories instead of textbooks to teach reading. The stories are turning, themselves, into textbooks. I worry about that. Reading stories ought to be for pleasure, not schoolwork. So I say, when I answer letters like those I've just described, that I wasn't trying to teach anything.

Stories that don't try to teach, stories that share remembered feelings—those are the stories that strike to the hearts of children and are never forgotten. A few years ago, Maurice Sendak came up to Providence, where I'm living now, and gave a talk at Brown University. The hall was jammed with Brown students. There wasn't an inch of unfilled space. Sendak talked about *Where the Wild Things Are,* about where it came from, and the letters he's had from children about it. Some of those letters may well have been written by some of the students listening. When he was finished, the applause was thunderous, and the waves of love that flowed from the audience up and over him as he stood there were enough to bring tears to your eyes. For *Where the Wild Things Are* was one of the very first books that was really for children. It came out of Sendak's vivid memories of his own feelings as a child trying to make a place for himself in a world of adults. Its honesty is instantly recognized by children everywhere. It tells the truth, and tells it in a symbolic language that is wholly accessible. It was, when it was first published, a phenomenon. We have learned from it since, we who needed to learn from it. The children haven't needed to learn from it—they already knew.

So I say to writing students, "Try to remember." Because we all knew things when we were children. Those things we knew are still there inside our heads, layered over, maybe, but ready to show themselves if we're willing to dig for them. Some of those things are painful and not necessarily fun to remember, but bringing them out and using them, in however veiled or symbolic a way, will bring to a story the honesty it needs to make it worth the reading.

Those things will also give our young characters three dimensions; keep them from being mere paper dolls. I've been reading a biography of Anthony Trollope by the British novelist and critic C. P. Snow. Because he was a novelist himself, Snow saw and admired things in Trollope's work that the average biographer might not see. Here is what he says about Trollope's uncanny ability to create three-dimensional characters:

> He could see each human being he was attending to from the outside as well as the inside, which is an essential part of the total gift. That is, he could see a person as others saw him: he could also see him as he saw himself.

I like that. It's a nice description of what we all ought to try to do: see our child characters not only from the outside, but also from the inside as they see themselves. And the only way to do that is to try as hard as we can to remember what it was like, what we were like, inside a ten-year-old skin. Or whatever skin we're trying to re-create.

Another thing I've brought out of my childhood into this strange little island called Children's Book Land is an impatience with a story that presents an all-pink world. My life, and the lives of all the children I knew, was never all pink. Mine was free of genuine grief in that no one I loved died until I was well into my teens. But I knew about grief from observing it in less lucky friends, and I knew about poverty and disabilities, too, in the same way. I had, if not grief, certainly sorrows of my own, and plenty of unsolvable problems. And more than anything else, I had all the frustrations of being powerless. So did we all. And then, since World War II began for the United States when I was in the fourth grade, I also knew about nationally sanctioned hatred of other countries and fear of enemy bombers. Our grammar school was a testing place for air-raid sirens, and so we all knew about that particular fear. We dealt with it, one way or another, but we knew the world wasn't all pink. I resented books that tried to tell me it was, and if I came across one, I wouldn't finish it.

But as adults we seem to be afraid, some of us, of telling the truth. We seem to feel we need to protect children from anything that will show that their all-pink world has a lumpy underbelly with discolored spots on it. We'd rather tell them that everything's perfect and keep the truth for later, when they're teenagers, maybe, at which point we seem to think it's time to throw despair at them as a kind of rite of passage. I like to call it the "last chance for gas before the thruway" syndrome.

And yet, if we can look back at our child selves, honestly and openly, we find every time that we knew the hard stuff, the bad stuff, was there. There wasn't any way to protect us from it. So perky little stories with cute little pictures were very often anathema. At least they were to me. I insisted on happy endings, but they had to be happy endings that followed logically from the action of the story. Anything else was irritating.

One final thing that I brought along out of childhood is a distaste for earnestness. It is perfectly true that the children we write for are the future of the world, and it is perfectly true that the world is a mess. In addition to the usual messes, which the world has always had, now we've got a lacerated ozone layer and nuclear waste to worry about. But we won't solve these problems, assuming they can be solved, by writing earnest stories for children. I don't mean serious stories; I mean earnest stories. Earnestness to me means solemn, humorless sincerity; whereas seriousness means honesty—and honesty, in this case, means showing as many sides of life as you can. There is always a humorous side, even if the humor is rueful.

My father thought almost everything was funny except the Republican Party. He was passionately fond of the Republican Party and never laughed at it, ruefully or otherwise. But for everything else he had a clear and sympathetic eye that always seemed to see things in all three dimensions. One of the most valuable things I learned from him was that humor does not trivialize problems. What it does do is relax us and make it easier for us to solve those problems. It puts things in their proper perspective.

My sister had a very tough time in seventh grade. Adolescence, while you're going through it, can be dreadful. But my father told stories at the dinner table—wonderful, made-up, funny stories that always began, "When I was in the seventh grade." They made my sister laugh. They made things a little easier. And when I was having trouble with arithmetic—which was all the time—my father, with mock earnestness, would make up what we used to call thought problems. You know, those terrible things that begin, "If it takes three men two hours to dig a ditch." Here is one my father made up that I've always remembered: "If cross-eyed potatoes are ten cents a jugful, how long will it take a bowlegged cinch bug to crawl through a bag of moldy flour?"

Earnestness doesn't get us very far. At its worst it only increases a feeling of being pressed, stressed, and driven. But humor can take us a long way. It doesn't have to be a pie-in-the-face kind of humor, though there's certainly a place for that. What it does have to be, for me, anyway, is an acknowledgment, rueful or otherwise, of the craziness of humanity. Lewis Carroll understood it perfectly, and expressed it in ways that made me laugh out loud when I was nine years old. Nine-year-olds don't have a lot of rue in their natures. That comes later. I wouldn't have been especially moved and amused by a quote from Mark Twain which I now keep nearby at all times: "When we remember we are all mad, the mysteries disappear and life stands explained."

If that is a kind of philosophy for me now, it was certainly implied in the books I loved when I was in the fifth grade, whether there was up-front ruefulness in my sense of humor or not. So when I write stories for myself and my fifth-grade classmates, I keep at the front of my mind at all times the importance of not being earnest.

Here are three things, then, that my own inner child keeps reminding me to be careful about: don't preach, don't be dishonest, and don't be earnest. Maybe that sounds as if there isn't a lot that you can do in a story for children. But yes, there is one thing that is the single most important thing of all: you can tell an entertaining story. I don't seem to have any more ideas for entertaining stories, I'm sorry to say. Not stories, anyway, for those very special people who are in what is clearly the last, best, greatest year of childhood—the fifth grade. After the age of ten or eleven, if you ask me, things don't get really good again until you're thirty. So I'm concentrating on picture books now. I always liked picture-making better than story-making, anyway. When I was picture-book age, I never thought about growing up to be a book illustrator, the way I did in fifth grade. No, as I recall, when I was four years old I wanted to be a pirate. But I was just as demanding then, where books were concerned, as I was six or seven years later. I disliked *The Little Engine That Could* and loved *Millions of Cats*. Which is to say that I loved books that didn't preach, weren't dishonest, and never sounded earnest.

As I said before, I know now that I was not unique. So when I remember myself as the kind of child I really was, I know I am describing, to a very large extent, all children. I will conclude with a quote about the child within, from *The Rebel Angels* by Canadian writer Robertson Davies, which says it better than anyone else ever said it.

> What really shapes and conditions and makes us is somebody only a few of us ever have the courage to face: and that is the child you once were, long before formal education ever got its claws into you—that impatient, all-demanding child who wants love and power and can't get enough of either and who goes on raging and weeping in your spirit till at last your eyes are closed and all the fools say, "Doesn't he look peaceful?" It is those pent-up, craving children who make all the wars and all the horrors and all the art and all the beauty and discovery in life, because they are trying to achieve what lay beyond their grasp before they were five years old.

If we can just remember that, how can we go wrong?

TITLE COMMENTARY

📖 *THE SEARCH FOR DELICIOUS* (1969)

Anne Carter

SOURCE: "War over Words," in *Times Literary Supplement,* No. 3813, April 4, 1975, p. 365.

Delicious is fried fish. No, apples, says the King. Wrong again, it's Christmas pudding, claims the Queen. And so *The Search for Delicious* is on, and civil war nearly breaks out, all because of the Prime Minister's Dictionary. Which goes to show that even in that happy state where Prime Ministers are lexicographers communication is not all it might be.

Natalie Babbitt's gentle and endearing fantasy describes how the boy Gaylen goes out as poll-taker, looking forward to a holiday, and ends with a desperate race to stop Hemlock, the malcontent, from holding the country to ransom by depriving it of the one thing nobody can do without. In spite of what might seem, at first sight, its somewhat whimsical title, this is in no way a soft or sentimental book. It has its share of sadness as well as fun, but the invention is fresh and unflagging and the author has a care for language which matches the subtlety of her line drawings. Here is a writer in the direct line of Andrew Lang and with something of the same clear-eyed humanity. The book is nicely produced and full marks to Chatto and Windus for printing an explanation for the American spelling. The result was that I didn't notice it at all.

Margaret Hobbs

SOURCE: A review of *The Search for Delicious*, in *The Junior Bookshelf*, Vol. 39, No. 3, June, 1975, pp. 191-92.

This is a fairytale in modern style; the Prologue, however, belongs to ancient myth. There are many traditional features of the Quest, but the subject of the search is disappointingly trivial, amid all the authentic trappings, and the author's delightful delicate decorations. A disagreement over the definition of "delicious" in the Prime Minister's dictionary, his spare time hobby, causes the King to send Gaylen (the Minister's assistant and adopted son) to record a national vote on the subject. The little country is divided and brought to war by its personal preferences, a situation actively inflamed by the Queen's wicked brother Hemlock. Alongside this plot runs the Prologue story of how the little mermaid Ardis lost her dwarf-made doll when she lost the key to the springhouse beneath the lake. Gaylen is able to restore it to her, and, in gratitude, she thwarts Hemlock's plans to take over the country's vital water supplies. Everyone at last agrees on the meaning of "delicious", and life reverts to normal. Gaylen, however, keeps in touch with those beings of an earlier world he has met in his search. The combination of plot-level and styles succeeds on the whole, because of the crisp humorous writing and the beauty of vivid poetic phrases and descriptions.

Margery Fisher

SOURCE: A review of *The Search for Delicious*, in *Growing Point*, Vol. 14, No. 3, September, 1975, pp. 2686-87.

The Search for Delicious is a neo-fairy-tale, with a touch of Thurber in the way wit and irony persuade one to take a fresh look at chivalry and magic. In a kingdom that has long forgotten its fairy origins, the King and Queen are at odds regarding a definition for the Dictionary which the Prime Minister is preparing. The King insists that an apple would be the best illustration for "delicious", the Queen counters with Christmas pudding, and so varied and so hotly defended are the suggestions from members of the court that the monarch decides to conduct a referendum throughout the country. His decision brings opportunity to two individuals in particular. For Gaylen, the Prime Minister's Special Assistant, the ride through the kingdom collecting opinions looks like being a holiday and proves an exciting and rewarding adventure: for Hemlock, the Queen's disaffected and ambitious brother, it provides the chance to foment rebellion. The intellectually-conceived mixture of politics and magic, the juxtaposition of gossiping peasants, mysterious woldweller, friendly minstrel and unhappy mermaid, make a captivating story told in a style that is wittily apt and attractively lilting in tone. The book is elegantly produced and each chapter is signalled by a decorative initial letter incorporated in a tiny, delicate and expressive drawing.

📖 *TUCK EVERLASTING* (1975)

Lance Salway

SOURCE: A letter to Nancy Chambers on November 3, 1977, in *Signal*, Vol. 23, May, 1977, pp. 97-8.

Yes, I was put off by the opening sentence of Natalie Babbitt's *Everlasting Tuck*—sorry, *Tuck Everlasting.* I think you're probably too sensitive about the rampant *faux naiveté* in American children's books and I had hoped to prove you wrong by quoting similar examples of winsome prose from British authors. But a random check on my shelves produced only one example. . . .

But far worse than *Tuck's* Prologue is the first chapter with its whimsical description of the road winding round the wood; both the Prologue and Chapter One will deter most children from reading further into the book and this will be a pity. Had I been Ms. Babbitt's editor, I would have suggested that she cut the Prologue and the first two chapters and begin the story at Chapter Three, which is where the *story* begins anyway.

And it's not just the opening pages which do the book a disservice; the title, too, is misleading for British readers. *Tuck Everlasting* suggests a schoolboy's dream come true (as an American you may not appreciate the English meaning of "tuck" but try the title on any handy Britishers you have around and see how they react) but any child picking up this book expecting an English public school fantasy will be disappointed. Once one has disposed of these obstacles to enjoyment, *Tuck Everlasting* proves to be a fascinating book—[the] adjectives "tasteful" and "flavourful" (like tuck?) seem wholly apt.

I missed, though, the elemental terror that should have been part of this story: the terror that a small girl would feel when she is kidnapped; the terror of the Tucks' predicament: doomed to remain ageless while the world around them withers; the horror which must arise from the fact that the Tucks will—and do—commit murder to prevent the rest of the world from suffering their own fate. The people in this book, especially the amiable Tuck family, are far too *nice*. Still, I admire the book and I hope that children will fight through the opening chapters to find the story beyond. And, for all its occasional whimsy and for all its reluctance to meet the implications of the plot head-on, I was moved by this book and I find it difficult, even now, to dispel its enticing flavour from my memory.

Betsy Hearne

SOURCE: "The American Connection," in *Signal,* Vol. 33, September, 1980, pp. 151-59.

Babbitt's style is skillful, original, and pared down to graphic details. She also keeps symbols on a concrete level rather than letting them become abstract. *Tuck Everlasting* is about the cycle of life and death, focused on one family who has drunk from a stream of eternal waters and on a child who becomes involved with them. She finally chooses not to join them in their everlasting life. In spite of her love for their son she pours her vial from the secret spring onto a toad.

The book is full of cycles and circles, but subtly. Babbitt's own wisdom is contained within hints, suggestions, metaphors, all framed in the familiar. The epilogue telescopes time by the Tucks' return to Treegap more than a half century after the story is over. Not knowing her choice, they read the actual ending on a gravestone inscribed with the dates of their once-young friend's long life and recent death. Nearby, they almost run over a toad that arrogantly refuses to budge from the road. 'Durn fool thing must think it's going to live forever,' says one. The complex issues of living and dying have been personified in everyday flesh, blood, and language.

Kim Aippersbach

SOURCE: "*Tuck Everlasting* and the Tree at the Center of the World," in *Children's literature in education,* Vol. 21, No. 2, June, 1990, pp. 83-97.

Tuck Everlasting, by Natalie Babbitt, is a meaningful and moving account of a girl reaching an important stage in her spiritual and moral development. It is a simple story that deals effectively with its complex theme because of its tight interweaving of structure and symbolism, both of which are borrowed from fairy tale and mythology and displaced only slightly in this folkloristic novel. The fairy tale journey, seen through female eyes, is an apt metaphor for Winnie Foster's discovery of her responsibility to herself and to others, and her growing understanding of the forces of life and death is rendered more powerfully because the mythic symbols used to illuminate her journey summon these forces into the novel. Babbitt uses the forms and devices of folk-tale to depict Winnie Foster's struggle to understand her place in the world, and at the same time Winnie's journey to self-fulfillment becomes a metaphor for the understanding of mortality that Tuck, and Natalie Babbitt, are trying to teach.

According to Max Lüthi, the cardinal characteristic of fairy tale style is the "absence of all desire to describe unessential details." Removing the unessential details from Natalie Babbitt's story makes clear the fairy tale nature of its plot. A young girl lives in a cottage by the edge of a wood, where she is treated with great strictness by her mother and grandmother. One day she decides to run away. Following an animal guide—in this case a toad, who had "bounced itself clumsily off towards the wood" the day before—she enters the magical forest. Reassured by the toad's presence she explores the wood and soon encounters one of the guardians of a magic spring.

She challenges him by asking for a drink from the spring. In response to the challenge, the guardians, called Tucks, kidnap her and carry her off, first to the side of a river, where she is entrusted with the secret of the spring of immortality, and then to their cottage in the hills. Here she is offered food, compassion, and wisdom, in return for which she agrees to keep their secret. The villain then arrives and reveals that he, too, knows the secret and wants to exploit it. When the Tucks refuse to cooperate, he attempts to kidnap the heroine, but the mother Tuck saves her by killing the villain. Mae Tuck thus places herself in the power of the town law, and the constable takes her to jail. The heroine must now save her savior. She enters the underworld of the jail and takes Mae's place, allowing her to return to the world of the Tucks. When the heroine gets out of jail, it is to return to her world, to be accepted back into her family with a new status.

This plot closely follows Joseph Campbell's summary of the mythological hero's journey:

> A hero ventures forth from the world of common day into a region of supernatural wonder: fabulous forces are there encountered and a decisive victory is won: the hero comes back from this mysterious adventure with the power to bestow boons on his fellow man.

Babbitt's only "supernatural wonder" is the immortality of the Tucks, the "decisive victory" is won not over "fabulous forces" but over a greedy man, and the boon is bestowed on the supernatural characters rather than on the heroine's "fellow man," but the basic "separation-initiation-return" pattern can be seen. The nature of the journey can change from hero to hero, and from hero to heroine, but the journey itself remains a practicable metaphor. As Lüthi describes it for fairy tales, the [young girl] sets out to see the world, but at once demands are made on [her] and, later, [she] steps forward to solve the difficult tasks. This course, or one similar to it, is followed in most fairy tales. It corresponds to the course followed by the maturing or matured human being throughout life. Fairy tales are unreal but they are not untrue; they reflect essential developments and conditions of man's existence.

With a few minor emendations regarding gender, this description applies accurately to *Tuck Everlasting,* which is about the essential development of one particular girl.

But, to quote Lüthi again, the "characters of the fairy tale are not personally delineated; the fairy tale is not concerned with individual destinies." If *Tuck Everlasting* is about one particular girl, then it must be a novel and not a fairy tale. Although, as in fairy tales, every character in the novel has a specific role in the plot (in paring down all unessential details we did not leave out a single one), and although each character can be seen as a type (the yellowman trickster, the lawman, the fairy godmother with her magic music box, the green-world lover, the wise old man), each is also given unique characterization. Winnie and the Tuck family are not just variations on a theme; they are individual characters, with recognizable personalities. Tuck is a wise old man, but he is also sad and confused sometimes, often dreams of unattainable happiness, and sometimes gets frightened. Mae is matronly and practical, but she panics on occasion, is sometimes hesitant and unsure, wears a shawl when she does not need one, and owns "one pretty thing" which she never goes anywhere without. Jesse and Miles have equally unique habits and feelings that raise them from types to individuals. As for the heroine, Winnie lives in a cottage by a wood, but hers is "a square and solid cottage with a touch-me-not appearance, surrounded by grass cut painfully to the quick and enclosed by a capable iron fence some four feet high," and Winnie talks to toads.

Babbitt combines fairy tale with psychological realism in a way many children's authors do, using the motif of the hero's journey as a metaphor for a character's changing perceptions of himself or herself and the world. Just as Winnie the heroine makes a circular journey from home to a magic land through an underworld and back home, so Winnie the protagonist must leave home, be exposed to new circumstances and ideas, come face to face with her greatest fears, and return home better equipped to deal with her life there. She follows the pattern of most circular journeys, in which the main character begins with a certain problem, generally one that alienates her from her home in some way. Her attempts to deal with it lead her into another world, where she meets the same problem in a different form and learns to overcome it, returning to her own world with an increased ability to integrate with it.

Winnie's problem is given clear visual representation when we first see her:

Winnie Foster sat on the bristly grass just inside the fence. . . . "Look here, toad," she said, thrusting her arms through the bars of the fence and plucking at the weeds on the other side. "I don't think I can stand it much longer."

She is trapped inside the "touch-me-not" cottage, within the indomitable fortress of duty, and she wants to escape. It is not so much the physical restraint that bothers her, but the frustration of her soul, which longs to be free of touch-me-not impositions. "'I'm tired of being looked at all the time. I want to be by myself for a change,'" she complains to the toad. "'It'd be better if I could be like you, out in the open and making up my own mind.'" She needs the freedom of self-definition, and she looks for it beyond the iron bars of the fence: "'I'll never be able to do anything important if I stay in here like this. I expect I'd better run away.'" . . .

For Winnie, already trapped within a role she did not choose, defined by her parents and grandmother, the forest is a potential escape, a place to be by herself, making up her own mind. Babbitt offers a positive alternative to [Annis] Pratt's vision of feminine heroes when she gives Winnie the chance to run away to the forest.

When Winnie does run away, she meets a family all of whom have essentially the same problem as she. The Tucks are trapped in their immortality: trapped physically, because they cannot die, and also trapped mentally, unable to grow or change or adapt. As Tuck explains to Winnie,

> "this rowboat now, it's stuck. If we didn't move it out ourself, it would stay here forever, trying to get loose, but stuck. That's what us Tucks are, Winnie. Stuck so's we can't move on. We ain't part of the wheel no more. Dropped off, Winnie. Left behind."

Jesse will always be seventeen, will always have a seventeen-year-old's attitudes, ambitions, desires, problems. Miles wants to "find a way to do something important," and Winnie understands. "That was what *she* wanted." But what can Miles do? It has been eighty-seven years and he has yet to find anything "useful." He will go on wanting and hoping and not succeeding forever.

Winnie, who wants change and freedom to choose, meets the Tucks, who cannot change, and who have no choice in the matter. It cannot but be a fruitful encounter. She is embarking on "the first work of the hero," which is, according to Campbell, "to retreat from the world scene of secondary effects to those causal zones of the psyche where the difficulties really reside." Winnie's separation from her former connections allows her to make new "essential contacts"—with the Tucks and with herself. Meeting her problem in a different form in this new world she has entered will enable her [according to Campbell] to "clarify the difficulties" and "eradicate them in [her] own case." Removed from her everyday life, she can see everyday things in a new light . . .

The Tucks help her to open her mind and discover her own potential: they make her feel "special. Important . . . a warm, spreading feeling, entirely new," and they introduce her to a different set of priorities and values, the "whole new idea . . . that people could live in such disarray." But this very difference, the challenge their existence offers her, forces her to recognize her limitations. Her encounter with their bizarre story and "revolutionary" way of life makes her feel real fear, and she responds with anger to what she perceives as their threat to her.

> They had kidnapped her, right out of the middle of her very own wood, and now she would be expected to sleep—*all night*—in this dirty, peculiar house. She had never slept in any bed but her own in her life. All these thoughts flowed at once from the dark part of her mind.

In the first thrill of running away, she believed she was escaping from "[h]er mother's voice, the feel of home," but now without "her own nightgown . . . and the regular bedtime routine . . . she [is] painfully lonely for home." Winnie is getting closer to discovering "where [her] difficulties really reside" [according to Campbell]. The iron bars that hold her in are not in the fence at all. She finds that she has carried her entrapment with her, for she is as "helpless" in this new situation as she was at home.

Problems in fairy tales are generally made easier to overcome by being made concrete: that is what villains are for. Winnie's problem is a psychological one—she cannot free herself from dependency on her family—but Babbitt externalizes it in the yellow man. When Winnie remembers that the man in the yellow suit saw her riding off with the Tucks, she feels "a surge of relief. 'He'll tell my father he saw me,'" she hopes. He is someone to pass responsibility onto, "a kind of savior," someone who will get her out of the situation without her having to do anything. The thought of other people taking care of her is a source of strength: "remembering the man in the yellow suit was the only thing that kept her from weeping. . . . 'Papa will find me. They're out looking for me right now.'" When the yellow man actually arrives, however, she senses "something unpleasant" in his face and is made "instantly suspicious." It turns out that he poses a far greater threat to the Tucks than they ever did to her. His arrival confuses Winnie, for he is not the comforting link to home she thought he was, and his quiet assault on the Tucks frightens her. Up to now, she has been "helpless" in the hands of the Tucks because she believed herself to be, because she accepted her parents' association of freedom with unnamed terrors. When she sees the Tucks threatened by the man she once thought of as "a kind of savior," she is forced to change radically her understanding of her own situation.

Winnie has gradually been accepting the Tucks' good intentions toward her, realizing that "[p]erhaps they *were* crazy, but they weren't criminals" and even wishing "that she could stay with them forever in that sunny, untidy little house by the pond," but until now she has seen herself in a passive role. She thought they were imposing on her, then she thought they were being nice to her, when in truth they have all along needed *her* to help *them*. This finally dawns on her after Mae rescues her from the yellow man and the constable accuses Mae of kidnapping. Winnie could do nothing against the yellow man's attack, but now she can defend her beloved Tucks. "'They didn't kidnap me,' she said, 'I came because I wanted to.'" For the first time in the story she takes responsibility for herself. When Mae is being taken away, possibly to be hanged, she recognizes Tuck's helpless fear and responds almost instinctively:

> And then Winnie said something she had never said before, but the words were words she had sometimes heard, and often longed to hear. They sounded strange on her own lips and made her sit up straighter. "Mr. Tuck," she said, "don't worry. Everything's going to be all right."

Winnie, in her concern for Tuck, has stopped being afraid. Change cannot frighten her now because she feels that she can be responsible for it, and she has earned the freedom to choose it:

> Winnie saw again the wide world spread before her, shimmering with light and possibility. But the possibilities were different now. They did not point to what might happen to her but to what she herself might keep from happening.

Having eaten of the fruit of self-knowledge, she is ready to leave her paradise of innocent dependence and go out to "make a difference in the world." . . .

The turning point in Winnie's development of "[s]ensitivity to the needs of others and [her] assumption of responsibility for taking care" began when she was still very confused and frightened, lying on the couch in the Tuck's cottage:

> Winnie lay with her eyes wide. She felt cared for and—confused. And all at once she wondered what would happen to the Tucks when her father came. What would he do to them? . . .

"All at once" Winnie thinks of someone besides herself, sees the world from someone else's perspective. . . .

Winnie's jail scene is the moment of self-definition she was looking for when she first reached beyond her fence to the toad. It is an ultimate assertion of her independence, the final breaking of the bonds of trust and fear that had restricted her behind the fence in the beginning. In entering prison she finally escapes the yard. The decision to betray her family's trust is painful to her:

> she was struck by the realization that, if she chose, she could slip out night after night without their knowing. The thought made her feel more guilty than ever that she should once more take advantage of their trust.

But she must challenge the ties that hold her to her family in order to be truly bound to them. She recognizes that those ties are "too ancient and precious to be broken. But there [are] new threads now, tugging and insistent, which [tie] her just as firmly to the Tucks." When she returns to her family she must be accepted on her own terms, as someone with the right to choose her affections.

She gains the courage and resolve to perform her heroic act from the ties of love and belonging she has created with the Tucks. She finds "that she love[s] them, this most peculiar family. They [are] her friends, after all. And hers alone." "They [belong] to her." This sense of belonging is far different from the possessiveness queried by Babbitt in the first chapter: "[t]he ownership of land is an odd thing when you come to think of it. How deep, after all, can it go?" Winnie's parents are possessive, owning the wood, the touch-me-not cottage, and owning Winnie just as surely. She does not want to belong to them in that way, "cooped up in a cage" as if she were a pet toad. It is only when she has broken free of that possession and proved that she is an individual with an equivalent capacity to own that she can return and belong to them the way she belongs to the Tucks. . . .

When she betrays them in order to save her new friends, it is the final proof that she is able to love with a free, adult love, able to bind and be bound to others by choice, not compulsion, and her family accepts this new love and welcomes her back. . . .

Winnie thus completes her journey and gains the hero's reward. . . .

At the end of the novel she has entered a new relationship with the people around her and also a new relationship with her world. Babbitt weaves this latter spiritual development through the moral development of Winnie's journey using a network of mythical symbols, motifs, and allusions to underlie and support her text: as the fairy tale structure makes clear the stages that Winnie goes through on her way to maturity, so the symbolism makes concrete the concepts of life and living that she begins to understand.

The yellow man, whom we have already seen as a representation of Winnie's immature desire to be dependent and protected, works at the same time as an externalization of her desire to live forever. Tuck's discussion helps Winnie see why death is necessary: "If all the mosquitoes lived forever—and if they kept on having babies—it would be terrible." But she still does not want to die, does not see what would be so terrible about *her* living forever. Then the yellow man threatens her with changeless, deathless immortality, and suddenly this becomes more frightening than death. "'I won't go with you! I won't!'" she screams. Mae saves her from eternal life by killing the yellow man, and as Winnie later realizes, "[i]f it's true about the spring, then he has to die. He must." This is only the beginning of her under-

standing, and we do not learn until the Epilogue that she does finally choose death, but she has been changed by this encounter. Her family "sense[s] that she [is] different now from what she [was] before. As if some part of her [has] slipped away," and in truth a great part of her childhood innocence is gone. She knows what death is; she has seen it.

The yellow man, as the villain, is the central symbol for the two kinds of immaturity Winnie must overcome, but Babbitt uses other image patterns that link Winnie's two journeys together as they make each one concrete and visual. By comparing possession and belonging with fence bars and ribbons, for example, she shows us the difference between them and helps us to see how the jail is Winnie's transition from one to the other. Ribbons, threads, and ties are useful representations of Winnie's relationships with her two families, suggesting flexibility yet permanence, as opposed to the permanent yet inflexible fence. They join with the road and the music box as images of connection, linking Winnie to the Tucks, the yellow man to Winnie, and the constable to the yellow man. But they are also part of a larger motif, introduced in the first image of the Ferris wheel with its hub and radiating spokes. For ribbons, roads, and spokes to connect things together there must be a center point, a point of departure, a hub: the world is a circle, life is a circle, and Winnie must find the center if she is to make her connections to the wheel. . . .

The center is vital but it is the turning that is life. The Ferris wheel is a vivid and appropriate image with which to begin the novel because it so clearly indicates the relationship between fixity and motion, between permanence and cycle. Babbitt's narrative world is a circle of timeless cycles, the seasons swinging round the "live-long year" to pause "at the very top of summer" for the story to take place, the events swinging around the day from "dawn" to "noontime" to "sunset." *Tuck Everlasting* takes place in a moment of rest, "like the highest seat of a Ferris wheel when it pauses in its turning." All the action takes place in this one week "at the very top of summer," when time seems to stand still. But the premise of the book is that the motion will continue: the weeks will "drop to the chill of autumn" and the year's cycle will repeat itself. It is important that we feel the tension inherent in such a pause and the subsequent relief when it comes to an end, because Babbitt uses the same image to describe the immortality of the Tucks. "We ain't part of the wheel no more," explains Tuck to Winnie. They are stuck within the pause, stuck at the center, and while everything around them, from the turning music box Mae carries to the wheels of the "rusty Hudson automobile," indicates the need to keep moving, they cannot.

The agonizing sterility of this pause is illustrated by the anxious waiting for rain that characterizes the story's atmosphere. That "the first week in August is motionless, and hot" is emphasized over and over again: "There is no thunder, no relieving rain." We meet Winnie "very near the boiling point on a day that was itself near to boiling," and the next day is "another heavy morning, already hot and breathless." The day before Mae's escape is "the hottest day yet"; the earth is "cracked, and hard as a rock, a lifeless tan color," and the toad looks "dried out today, parched." Winnie's attempt to relieve it with a dish of water foreshadows her gift to it of the spring water, and her pouring the water onto the dirt is a miniature of the rainfall that will relieve "the tension in the parched earth" once Mae's escape is effected. That tension is built up all through that day, "the longest day: mindlessly hot, unspeakably hot, too hot to move or even think." As the haze thickens in preparation for rain the air "presse[s] on Winnie's chest and [makes] her breathing difficult." She tells "the prostrate group in the parlor" that she thinks it is going to rain, and her grandmother responds, "'What a week *this* has been! . . . Well, thank the Lord, it's almost over.' And Winnie thought to herself: Yes, it's almost over." Her anticipation of Mae's momentous escape is paralleled in the weather: "Outside, the night seemed poised on tiptoe, waiting, waiting, holding its breath for the storm." Finally, as they arrive at the jail, "a low mumble, still far away, announce[s] at last the coming storm. A fresh breeze [lifts] Winnie's hair, and from somewhere in the village behind them a dog bark[s]." The first drop of rain falls as soon as Mae is freed, and, as the Tucks escape into the darkness, "[t]he tension in the parched earth eased and vanished. Winnie felt it go. The muscles of her stomach loosened, and all at once she was exhausted." The pause has ended, the wheel has started to turn, and Winnie has rejoined the cycle.

Tuck uses the image of water in a different way when he describes this continual cycle to Winnie in terms of the pond they are rowing on.

> "This water, you look out at it every morning, and it *looks* the same, but it ain't. All night long it's been moving, coming in through the stream back there to the west, slipping out through the stream down east here, always quiet, always new, moving on. . . . and someday, after a long while, it comes to the ocean. . . . Know what happens then?" said Tuck. "To the water? The sun sucks some of it up right out of the ocean and carries it back in clouds, and then it rains, and the rain falls into the stream, and the stream keeps moving on, taking it all back again. It's a wheel, Winnie. Everything's a wheel, turning and turning, never stopping."

Water has always been an image of life, and its powerful symbolic value gives conviction and clarity to Tuck's explanation. The strange paradox that in a wheel that never stops turning each life must come to an end is made clear by Tuck's analogy.

> "The frogs is part of it, and the bugs, and the fish, and the wood thrush, too. And people. But never the same ones. Always coming in new, always growing and changing, and always moving on. . . . You for instance. A child now, but someday a woman. And after that, moving on to make room for the new children."

Winnie is frightened and confused by the understanding that she will someday die, but she comes to understand that to choose life is also to choose death, and she makes that choice. We as readers are prepared for Tuck's explanation and for Winnie's choice by the water imagery that ties the book together as a whole: what Tuck's analogy is to Winnie the whole book is to the reader— a representation of the cycle and a demonstration of its necessity.

Babbitt ties her imagery together in the little details as well as the larger structures, teaching always by example as well as by precept. In little incidents like throwing the fish back into the pond, killing mosquitoes, and killing a wasp, Winnie comes to understand the larger implications of Tuck's message. Through Winnie's actions the reader is invited to view death from different angles and to grasp in individual events the astonishing truth that life cannot be without death. The complicated themes of the book are thus illustrated in simple things, and the whole becomes apparent through the parts . . .

Tuck Everlasting is a remarkably down-to-earth story. Toads and music boxes seem almost pathetically simple symbols for the great questions of life and death that the novel deals with, but they work. After all, none of us can really understand philosophy except as it impinges upon what we have for breakfast in the morning; being alive, we are hopelessly concrete creatures. That is why we need fairy tales: to show us the whys and wherefores that words cannot make clear to us; to give us a feeling for the mysteries we cannot conceive. The tree at the center of the world figures in so many mythologies because it is a potent visualization of the way the world fits together—we are so sure it does fit together somehow—and it is thus an apt borrowing for this story, which is all about patterns and links and centers. This is a children's book. A ten-year-old may not be able to formulate hypotheses concerning the nature of life and death and the importance of interrelationships within the human community, but she can sense the joy that is the other side of sadness that illuminates this story. And, in the end, that is all any of us can do.

Louis Rauch Gibson and Laura M. Zaidman

SOURCE: "Death in Children's Literature: Taboo or Not Taboo?" in *Children's Literature Association Quarterly*, Vol. 16, No. 4, Winter, 1991-92, pp. 232-33.

Natalie Babbitt's *Tuck Everlasting* (1975) is one book that challenges the reader's perceptions about life and death. Having found the fountain of eternal life, Pa Tuck shares his family's secret with young Winnie Foster but discourages her from choosing life without death:

> [D]ying's part of the wheel, right there next to being born. You can't pick out the pieces you like and leave the rest. Being part of the whole thing, that's the blessing . . . You can't have living without dying.

Winnie follows Pa Tuck's advice, ultimately agreeing with him that the Tucks, who live eternally, "just *are* . . . just *be,* like rocks beside the road." Her choice to live and not just be is also a choice to grow and change—and die.

📖 THE EYES OF THE AMARYLLIS (1977)

Selma G. Lanes

SOURCE: "Love Story, Sea Story," in *The New York Times Book Review,* November 13, 1977, p. 37.

Indisputably one of our most gifted and ambitious writers for children, Natalie Babbitt has taken an almost dangerously outmoded theme for her fifth and latest novel: the constancy of love. To today's young readers, as familiar with separation and divorce as they are with the institution of marriage, the emotional terrain of this eerie romance may well seem as alien as the landscape of the moon.

Mrs. Babbitt's tale concerns the obsessive 30-year-long vigil by Geneva Reade, widow of Capt. Morgan Reade, as she awaits some seaborne sign from her lost love. ("It will come, it *will,* on the high tide some day.")

The Amaryllis was Captain Reade's two-masted brig, sunk without a trace during a hurricane in the 1850's—just off shore—as his wife and 14-year-old son George watched helplessly. The amaryllis is also an exotic flowering plant, which the Captain had tried in vain to bring back alive from his voyages to the West Indies. Its color reminded him of his wife's red hair.

Out of these elements, Mrs. Babbitt spins a ghost story as involuted as a chambered nautilus. Gone is the playful banter with words and sunlit ideas that was the hallmark of the author's earlier works, *The Search for Delicious* and *Goody Hall.* Absent, too, is the robust framework of fantasy that held the reader firm—and all believing—within the fabricated reality of her . . . best book to date, *Tuck Everlasting.* But here her admirers have the rare pleasure of witnessing a versatile author extend her literary reach in a stark and chilling novel.

When the elder Geneva Reade breaks an ankle, she sends for her 11-year-old granddaughter and namesake, Jenny, to take up the daily search for a "sign." At first, the child suspects the old woman may be mad. But slowly Jenny is drawn into her grandmother's tide-ruled world. She encounters the mysterious Seward, "guardian of the sea," who is invisible to all but grandmother and granddaughter. She also comes to see how Geneva's single-minded devotion to a long-dead husband has robbed her only child, Jenny's father, of any maternal affection or understanding.

At last, the figurehead from the Amaryllis's prow—a carved likeness of Geneva herself—floats in on the morning tide. The old woman is exultant. But not for long. In a climactic hurricane scene as electrifyingly spooky as the best of H. H. Munro, grandmother sits cradling the wooden head while the roof blows off her seaside cottage and the ocean laps at her doorsill.

Only when Geneva reluctantly gives up the head (a symbol of the narcissism of her own love?), in response to Jenny's frightened pleas, does she receive a truly miraculous living sign from the briny deep.

Though there are occasional awkward scenes and some wooden dialogue, Mrs. Babbitt's prose, like Sarah Orne Jewett's, is as admirably clean and spare as the wind-swept New England landscape she describes. Yet there are strong and sensuous images, too: "tender cowrie shells as pearly as a baby's toes"; "The sea can swallow ships, and it can spit out whales upon the beach like watermelon seeds."

The Eyes of the Amaryllis is a ghost story, yet its concerns are not with grand guignol effects but with real-life "things you can't explain" and with the painful truth that "people do strange things for love sometimes." The confidences exchanged between proud grandmother, still basking in the warmth of her lost love's regard, and diffident grandchild, convinced she is plain and without the gift ever to attract any other being, provides the tale's most touchingly human moments. In the end, mother and son are at last reconciled, and a wiser, more self-assured Jenny returns home open to the possibility of a love of her own.

Like the sea, this work of Mrs. Babbitt's does not yield its treasures lightly. But they are well worth the finding.

Kirkus Reviews

SOURCE: A review of *The Eyes of the Amaryllis,* in *Kirkus Reviews,* Vol. XLV, No. 22, November 15, 1977, pp. 1195-96.

An atmospheric, romantic tale: of the sea, which "will take what it wants and keep what it has taken," of a captain's widow who (truly forsaking all others) has been waiting 30 years for a sign from her drowned husband; of the old woman's son who fled in his youth from the treacherous sea—and perhaps from his mother's indifference; and of the granddaughter, also named Geneva, who goes to help when Gram breaks her ankle and who thus becomes involved in her desperate nightly search along the shore. There's another character too, named Seward, but only the two Genevas can see him or his footprints as he prowls the shore in the sea's employ, hoping to find the "sign" before Gram does so that he can return it according to the bargain he made with the sea when he was drowning years before. It was Seward who told Gram that the swallowed ships, with "all the poor drowned sailors," are kept at the bottom of the sea to guard its treasures, and that her husband was down there struggling to send her some sort of token. And when young Geneva retrieves from the waves the wooden figurehead carved in Gram's image long ago, it is Seward who warns that the sea will have it back because "the ship can't see without its eyes." But Gram is stubborn and it takes a hurricane to wrest it from her—and her son's arrival at the crucial moment to save her from drowning. This fortuitous last undercuts the seriousness of the tale, and there is more to come. Also, unlike *Tuck Everlasting* (which also had more life and incident), the plot of . . . *the Amaryllis* is somewhat precariously based—on a notion (the drowned treasure patrol) that is just not compelling enough for the elemental magnitude of the struggle. Still, as Babbitt projects it, Gram's devotion—whether steadfast or obsessive—has its fascination.

Mary M. Burns

SOURCE: A review of *The Eyes of Amaryllis,* in *The Horn Book Magazine,* Vol. LIV, No. 1, February, 1978, pp. 42-3.

Set in a late nineteenth-century Atlantic coastal village, the story of the two Geneva Reades—one a woman in her seventies, the other her eleven-year-old granddaughter—has as its central theme the idea that love can be mistaken or misunderstood but that it can never be fully satisfied or completely destroyed. For thirty years the elder Geneva had daily searched the beach for a sign from her husband who, with his crew and ship *Amaryllis,* had vanished in a hurricane, while she and her fourteen-year-old son watched—helpless—from the shore. Haunted by the mysterious Seward, who guarded the sea's treasures, she confided in no one. Many thought her obsessions foolish and felt that she had ignored the son who later moved inland and avoided bringing his daughter to the house which "stood at the edge of another world." Now young Jenny was to stay with her grandmother who was temporarily incapacitated by a broken ankle. Aware of her father's unspoken fears yet impressed by the conversation in which woman to woman—rather than grandmother to child—Jenny learned that she was needed to continue the search, and she began to feel a subtle transformation in her own sensibilities. Like her grandmother, she was infused with a feeling of invincibility and freedom drawn from her proximity to the sea. Yet when an equinoctial hurricane threatened to destroy them, she recognized that invincibility and freedom have limitations. And with the recognition came the knowledge and wisdom to appreciate love in its many forms. An intricate combination of patterns, like a jacquard weave, the book succeeds as a well-wrought narrative in which a complex philosophic theme is developed through the balanced, subtle use of symbol and imagery. It is a rare story, accessible to the discriminating preadolescent; because of its perfect scale and transcendent style, it neither diminishes the subject nor the audience.

Zena Sutherland

SOURCE: A review of *The Eyes of the Amaryllis,* in *Bulletin of the Center for Children's Books,* Vol. 31, No. 7, March, 1978, p. 106.

Set in the late 19th century, this is a story in which the sea sets the mood, not an ocean of sparkling waves but an ocean of fog and storm, an enemy. It has taken the ship *Amaryllis,* and for three decades Geneva Reade, the captain's widow, has waited for some sign, some message. When her grandchild Jenny comes to visit, she too is drawn into Gran's obsessive searching for the sign, is asked to prowl the beach at high tide whatever the hour. Only Jenny and her grandmother recognize the existence of a third watcher, the wraithlike Mr. Seward. The sign, the figurehead of the *Amaryllis,* is washed up but Gran returns it during a hurricane that she interprets as a wrathful demand for a return of the "eyes," the eyes of the figurehead that can see and guard the wrecked ship. Babbitt does a superb job of establishing mood and sustaining tension, but there's a pat note to the ending that weakens the impact of the story, as Jenny's father (who hates the sea and hasn't wanted ever to be near it) shows up to rescue his mother and daughter, as Gran—who had steadfastly refused to be away from the sea—capitulates and agrees to live with her son's family, and as Jenny (homeward bound in the buggy) preens herself at a boy's obvious admiration.

D. A. Young

SOURCE: A review of *The Eye of the Amaryllis,* in *The Junior Bookshelf,* Vol. 43, No. 1, February, 1979, p. 46.

It is a ghost story, set beside the sea in which Jenny's grandfather lost his ship and his life. Jenny's stay with her grandmother brought her within the ambit of the strange link which still existed between the living and the dead. It is an eerie moving story with a touch of lyricism in the telling. The interplay of light and dark, of the living and the dead and the sea and its victims rises to a splendid climax as the storm breaks over the cottage and the heaving sea breaks through to claim back what it has made its own. A sensitive reader may well be pleased to look up from the pages of this powerful little tale and rejoice in the re-discovery of homely and familiar surroundings.

HERBERT ROWBARGE (1982)

Anne Tyler

SOURCE: "Good Things Come in Twos," in *The New York Times Book Review,* November 14, 1982, p. 44.

Someone ought to start spreading the word that Natalie Babbitt is not only a children's writer. Granted, her books have the firmly defined story line that children love—as anyone knows who's watched a youngster sit mesmerized by *Knee-Knock Rise* or *The Eyes of the Amaryllis.* They're certainly plotted in a way that will lure the phlegmatic young reader. But the style is so fine and subtle that grownups too will take real pleasure. *Tuck Everlasting,* for instance, is one of the best books ever written—for any age. You can picture a child re-reading it every year or so, on into adulthood, and appreciating it at a deeper level each time.

Her 10th novel, *Herbert Rowbarge,* has in common with many of her others an almost folktale-like tone and plot. Never mind that it contains its share of Buicks and bridge parties; it still possesses the hushed, concentrated, stripped quality of a legend. And like a legend, it draws us in. It's spellbinding.

Herbert, who was separated from his twin in infancy, has always felt something missing. His mirror image fascinates him; his talisman is a malicious lion from a toy Noah's Ark; he is obsessed by merry-go-rounds where the animals spin two by two. His identical twin daughters, who are devoted to each other, arouse in him less love than envy.

Alternating with Herbert's story are chapters describing the cozy, rather sad routine of the daughters. They are forced to spend their adult lives apart—one tending Herbert, one tending an aunt. Yet they're so much a unit that they speak of their matching clothes in the singular: "'Our blue linen sailor,' 'our little green print'—as if they were both always zipped together into a single costume." They say things like "We're not even a mother," and when a legacy is divided between them and a cousin it's divided only two ways. Even the author, succumbing to the general view of them, mentions that their father was loved "three times in his life by his only friend, Dick Festeen; by his wife, Ruby; and by his twin daughters, Babe and Louisa."

What gives the story its pull is its constant sense of barely missed connections, always with the hope of re-connecting. Herbert, though heartless, can't be blamed: He's only half a man, and what's worse, he doesn't even know it. He has no conscious notion that he ever had a twin. His daughters, meanwhile, pine for each other's company and meet for brief, wistful outings, wearing "our denim wrap skirt." There is an aching feeling of loss here that reminds us how important it is to be linked to another human being.

Each character, no matter how minor, is fully formed—from the family minister ("a heavy man with a barrel chest and large red hands who is playing in life the role of a pale, narrow man with small white hands") to the aunt who, all alone in her empty nest, rejoices that her house is finally "dust-free, scratch-free, flawless as a scalpel."

Herbert Rowbarge is slightly more difficult reading than Natalie Babbitt's other books. There's a foreword—and young readers tend to skip forewords. There's a dryer,

more formal, more tongue-in-cheek tone, though it's balanced nicely by the interjection of those charmingly dotty twin sisters. And there's not the satisfying click of an ending that occurred in *Tuck Everlasting.* But for anyone willing to expend some time and care, this book is richly rewarding.

Hazel Rochman

SOURCE: A review of *Herbert Rowbarge,* in *School Library Journal,* Vol. 29, No. 4, December, 1982, pp. 69-70.

Separated soon after birth from his identical twin, Herbert Rowbarge has never felt whole. From his childhood in the orphanage to his success as a rich and powerful "self-made" man, he has sensed a "long-lost other," although he has never known that he has a twin. All his life the sight of his own reflection has brought him terror and delight. Angry, clever, cold, unable to love even his wife and twin daughters, he has hidden his loneliness; and he has created "his soul's own country," a huge amusement park, where he has found his only deep satisfaction in the merry-go-round with its twin animals. Now he is 72 and his careful control is slipping. We see his life in a series of flashbacks, alternating with scenes of the present that focus mainly on the dull complacent drift of his twin daughters, Babe and Louisa—middle-aged, unmarried, dressing and thinking alike—whose togetherness has always tormented him. Some of the flashbacks are dramatic, as when Herbert confronts the distorted fragments of himself in the mirrored maze of his park's fun house; or when he is trapped in a confined space with "something terrible," a menacing tramp, who asks him who he is and then recognizes him as his twin and calls him by his twin's name, which Herbert does not know. But in spite of some sharp and funny characterization, many of the present scenes with the chatter of the bland twin daughters are static and repetitive. This difficult book is not easily accessible, even to a young adult reader. The power is in the language—the subtle punning, as in "self-made" man; the rebirth imagery of the death scene when Herbert finally achieves union with the twin he has unknowingly killed—and in the complex figure of a man struggling to maintain his fragile sense of self.

Zena Sutherland

SOURCE: A review of *Herbert Rowbarge,* in *Bulletin of the Center for Children's Books,* Vol. 36, No. 5, January, 1983, p. 82.

Separated in infancy from his twin, Herbert Rowbarge (named by staff at the orphanage where a woman had left the two boys deserted by their mother, a dance-hall girl) never knew he *had* a twin. All of his life, however, he had strange yearnings when he saw himself in a mirror; all his life there was an emotional void that kept him from loving anyone. The story follows two patterns, one set in 1952, when Rowbarge dies, little-mourned by the middle-aged twin daughters he had tolerated and resented, and the other in a series of flashbacks that cover the years from his birth to his death. Babbitt has created some interesting characters, and the writing style is deft and polished, but the lack of child characters (except in flashback glimpses) and the slow start and pace of the story, as well as its lack of action, may limit the interest of adolescent readers.

Sally Estes

SOURCE: A review of *Herbert Rowbarge*, in *Booklist*, Vol. 79, No. 11, February 1, 1983, p. 719.

More adult in tone and subject matter than the usual junior novel, Babbitt's latest story is a complex study of twinship that depends more on characterization and symbolism than on action. One of the two alternating narratives (couched in the past tense) follows the life span of Herbert Rowbarge, abandoned at birth in 1880 and separated from the twin brother he never knew he had—though, without knowing why, Herbert constantly experiences a sense of loss, especially when he looks into a mirror. As an adult Herbert methodically manipulates his only friend and coldheartedly marries a banker's daughter, whom he doesn't even like, to achieve his dream of owning an amusement park, complete with its own merry-go-round with paired animals poised forever side by side. The other carefully juxtaposed (present-tense) narrative focuses on the day-to-day routine of Babe and Louisa Rowbarge, Herbert's indiscernible, identical-twin daughters, during the critical period from May 20 through June 5, 1952, when their father's life comes full circle. None of the characters is really likable, but readers come to know and understand all of them very well. The climactic O. Henry twist involving Herbert's unwitting, ill-fated encounter with his twin surprises despite its reliance on what could be either fate or heavy-handed coincidence—depending on one's outlook. Polished in style and cadence and strongly flavored by a midwestern small-town ambience, this will reward the special teenage reader as well as the discerning high school literature student.

Neville Shack

SOURCE: "Double Trouble," in *Times Literary Supplement*, No. 4248, August 31, 1984, p. 977.

Herbert Rowbarge contains a secret within a secret which is coated in the cheerless floss of small-town America. The twins, Babe and Louisa, are two ageing spinsters who stir their tea in the same lack-lustre way as they do most other things. They are simply, and very effectively, one personification of domestic tedium split into two. The fact that they are stuck in this chintzy realm means that they can be turned back on the scenario like defenses which ensure the stagnation of a backwater in northwestern Ohio.

Eponymous Herbert, their father, is the self-made owner of the Rowbarge Pleasure Dome, an oasis of fun. Despite his business, he is obviously lacking in personable qualities and an appetite for fun, and insists on deceiving even his family about his own origins. These were in an orphanage until he came of age and could find an identity and a fortune for himself. Forever afterwards, only Dick Festeen, his life-long confidant, knows the truth.

Intriguingly, Herbert's shabby, unaffluent beginnings are not the ultimate secret of the book. He doesn't know that, in fact, he was born one of twins and that his brother was adopted and removed from him soon after they were both abandoned as babies. This unknown detail becomes fatefully important towards the end. Babe and Louisa conspire harmlessly and tiresomely. Herbert, not knowingly a twin because a "vital piece of him was wrenched away" so young, becomes a victim of a mutually destructive conspiracy of a far more extraordinary kind.

Herbert is mercenary in his dealings. Ruby, his rich and plain wife, deceives herself about him before he works his own trickery, and then she dies when the twins are still very young. Ruby is truly hapless and innocent; never quite a conscious human being, she can't get to grips with womanhood. One of the strengths in the telling of this story is the clear resonance of mood: commonplaceness occupies every corner. But the modulated narrative gives its study of environment and characters a lasting significance. Natalie Babbitt, an established children's writer, can build interest up out of apparently insipid, extremely provincial matter; she relishes the privilege of being straightforward and gently ironical.

Dorothy Atkinson

SOURCE: A review of *Herbert Rowbarge*, in *The School Librarian*, Vol. 33, No. 1, March, 1985, pp. 77-8.

The cover illustration—of a man's face dissolving into second and third versions—is alarming, and with good reason. The main character in this book is a twin, separated in infancy from his brother. They meet again, in the final pages, when Herbert drives crazily through a town and kills his brother without knowing it. He is, and always has been, questing for that other part of himself, for which he found compensation in a business venture, a Pleasure Dome with a Hall of Mirrors and a Merry-Go-Round. The latter is an adult substitute for the Noah's ark animals, two-by-two, obsessively loved by the infant Herbert. In pursuing his dream, the grown man uses and discards the friend who put him in business, makes a marriage of business convenience, cannot distinguish between his twin daughters, whom he despises, and dies in the Tunnel of Love, floating deep into the mirror.

It is a story not written with young readers particularly in view, but for anyone who can find an interest in the pieces which, together, make up the complete account of the motivation of a seemingly cold and unattractive man.

There is no reason why many should not find such an interest. The serious intention is never solemn; the writing is vivid—nowhere more so than in the inspired description of the steam calliope; and the social irony informing the description of the twin daughters and their world is both amusing and gentle. Their father, victim of the separation of twins, had separated them. Their humble ambition is realised when he dies: they can be together now, go to the cinema and row on their father's Ornamental Lake.

THE DEVIL'S OTHER STORYBOOK (1987)

Betsy Hearne

SOURCE: A review of *The Devil's Other Storybook,* in *Bulletin of the Center for Children's Books,* Vol. 40, No. 11, July-August, 1987, pp. 202-03.

Ten more stories about the disarming creature featured in *The Devil's Storybook* further characterize him as playing off the foibles of ridiculous human beings and sometimes demonstrating a few human-like failures himself. Plotwise, these are not quite as strong as the first batch, but they're craftily written and mischievous. One pokes fun at a soldier who can hardly wait to go to the next campaign, another recounts the fate of a hunter followed down to Hell by a rhinoceros who pursues him eternally, a third derides the incomprehensible speech of both a pickpocket and his educated victim, and a fourth leaves three snooty sisters boating on the Styx forever because they won't associate with the rabble entering Hell. Babbitt's style is as clean and elegant as ever, the unexpected homey expression contrasting with the classical flow for calculated effect. Her pen-and-ink hatch drawings are equally meticulous. A choice morsel to be savored with tongue in cheek.

Ilene Cooper

SOURCE: A review of *The Devil's Other Storybook,* in *Booklist,* Vol. 83, No. 22, August, 1987, p. 1740.

In this companion piece to Babbitt's popular *Devil's Storybook,* the wily Devil makes a return appearance, fouling up lives, meting out justice, and performing an unintentional good deed every once in a while. Among those who have encounters with Lucifer this time around are a sweet little man who fancies himself a famous opera singer and escapes the Devil's clutches; a fast-talking pickpocket and a highfalutin writer, who are doomed to spend eternity talking to each other in one very small room; and three snobby old women who don't want to mingle with the hoi polloi in Hell. Some of the humor in these tales is rather obscure, and children may need discussion to understand what the crafty old Devil has up his sleeve. Others, however, are delights that youngsters will relish. Babbitt provides her own line drawings to illustrate these 10 imaginative reports of hellish happenings. The cover (similar in design to the first volume but in teal blue rather than red) features the Devil reading his very own *Other Storybook.*

Ruth S. Vose

SOURCE: A review of *The Devil's Other Storybook,* in *School Library Journal,* Vol. 33, No. 11, August, 1987, p. 78.

Babbitt's Devil is sly, vain, and as her black-and-white drawings show, slightly paunchy, with a very long pointed tail. Readers first met him in *The Devil's Storybook,* and in these ten new stories he runs true to form. When not making his guests uncomfortable in Hell, he likes to journey through the world causing trouble and misfortune for its inhabitants. Sometimes the tables are turned, however, notably by the very ornery or the very innocent, and the Devil gets a surprise. All of these stories are humorous, but many have a wry sadness hiding close to the surface. Readers will encounter a talented parrot and a bumbling fortuneteller, an opera singer named Doremi Faso, a pair of mixed-up lovers, and other unique characters. The unhurried jaunty rhythm of the text seems an echo of the Devil's own personality, and reads well aloud. Characterization is enhanced by an illustration in each story, and the visual appeal is supported by the book's thick, creamy pages with wide margins and well-spaced print. This book is a pleasure to look at, to hear, and to read.

Ethel R. Twichell

SOURCE: A review of *The Devil's Other Storybook,* in *The Horn Book Magazine,* Vol. LXIII, No. 5, September-October, 1987, pp. 607-08.

As in *The Devil's Storybook,* many of the ten stories find Old Scratch getting his well-deserved comeuppance. Depicted more as a scamp or scalawag, the Devil is a source of mischief rather than the dark alter ego of good, and he provides more opportunities to laugh than to weep. For those who do suffer at the Devil's hand, the treatment seems amply deserved. Who could blame the Evil One for setting permanently adrift the three impossible women whom neither Heaven nor Hell wish to keep? A couple of ill-matched lovers are forever separated when a playful Old Nick switches around a signpost but immediately find and marry more suitable partners. But best of all are the stories in which the Devil is outwitted. In one his camel dumps him in the sand in order to follow the curious star that hovers over a certain baby that "had been born up there who was going to be nothing but trouble for a long, long time," while in another a parrot says the magic words, "'Parson, pastor, priest, and preacher. And *Pope*'" and dispatches the Old Fiend off in a cloud of smoke. An opera singer named Doremi Faso provides an irresistible joke, as does a big game hunter in his endless pursuit of a rhinoceros, who bursts through the bushes like a "bus downhill with no brakes." Told in a pleasing, conversational style, the stories have an originality and a humor that will appeal to all ages. The author's black-and-white illustrations nicely match the whimsical and eminently readable collection.

Laura Graeber

SOURCE: A review of *The Devil's Other Storybook,* in *The New York Times Book Review,* November 1, 1987, p. 36.

It's tempting to say that Natalie Babbitt has more than given the Devil his due. In 1974, the talented author and artist published **The Devil's Storybook,** a collection that portrayed Satan as a character more given to prodding human souls with a well-tuned verbal barb than a pitchfork. Now she has given us **The Devil's Other Storybook,** 10 more tales to entertain—and edify—young readers. But far from being a surfeit of Satan's tricks, this book is likely to give hell a better reputation than it has enjoyed for some time.

The appeal is partly due to Ms. Babbitt's not-unlikable fiend. Her Devil is a cultured fellow who drinks cider, reads novels and gives concerts for the damned. He also has a sense of humor, frequently employed at human expense. What he lacks, however, is real malevolence. Parents who are concerned about their children's reading matter will be relieved to see that this book has virtually no violence, making it a tame match for the average cartoon—or, for that matter, Grimm's fairy tales. And if the Devil seems to be getting his comeuppance somewhat less often here than in the previous collection, it's because he's giving hell, literally, to those who deserve it.

In **"Justice,"** for example, a brutal and boastful hunter arrives in the nether world shortly after it has received one of its few unexpected visitors: a rhinoceros. The Devil instructs the hunter, somewhat eponymously called Bangs, to capture the creature. Bangs gleefully sets off, only to find the task a bit hellish: the rhino is hotter on his trail than he is on the beast's. After a few weeks, he's reduced to an existence of constant vigilance and flight—just like a wild animal.

A similar reversal takes place in **"Boating."** Three snobbish sisters arrive in hell, where they are amazed that "anyone at all can get in." After promising to investigate this strange mingling of classes, the Devil leaves them circling on a raft in the Styx. (Ms. Babbitt may be forgiven here for mixing her mythologies.) Ultimately, the trio is forgotten, even by the Devil, much as they forgot the poor and unfortunate in life.

Too much moralizing? Although Ms. Babbitt's ethical lessons are seldom subtle, they rarely undermine her narrative gifts. Like old-fashioned fables, these stories take place in an ancient world whose characters symbolize universal concerns. Unlike those in fables, however,

Ms. Babbitt's peasants and demons have refreshingly comical quirks and contemporary preoccupations. When the Devil expresses annoyance that a victim of drowning is dripping all over his carpet, or says that he wants to pen up hell's errant rhinoceros and charge admission to see it, it doesn't much matter that his story also delivers a message. The sole exception is **"How Akbar Went to Bethlehem,"** a tale of the Devil's pet camel, who sacrilegiously decides to follow the Three Wise Men on their journey. While spirited in the telling, the story sounds a regrettably sectarian note; Ms. Babbitt is better at battling evil when she doesn't specifically link the fight to Christianity.

Fortunately, not all the stories have weighty themes. **"Simple Sentences"** concerns a vulgar pickpocket and his pompous victim, neither of whom can speak straightforwardly. The Devil gives them "the simplest sentence" he can think of: to stay together in a tiny room "till it all freezes over down here."

Although this amusing tale reveals Ms. Babbitt's facility with language, she is just as adept at making her point without words. Her illustrations for these stories easily capture their wit, particularly on the cover, where the Devil is shown contentedly reading this collection. Although the book hardly makes him a hero, it does have a charm he would find hard to resist.

NELLIE: A CAT ON HER OWN (1989)

Ilene Cooper

SOURCE: A review of *Nellie: A Cat on Her Own,* in *Booklist,* Vol. 86, No. 4, October 15, 1989, pp. 447-48.

Babbitt, long admired for her fiction, enters the picture-book genre with this story of a cat marionette lovingly fashioned from wood, yarn, and broom straws by the woman with whom she lives. Although Nellie delights in her afternoon leaps and spins to the tune of a music box, she is urged by Big Tom, a real cat, to dance without the manipulations of her mistress. Knowing her limitations, Nellie demurs, yet when the old woman dies, the marionette is faced with decisions about her future. "Belong to yourself, like me," Big Tom tells her, and, after stripping away her strings, he takes her with him to the countryside to meet other cats. Everything seems strange and risky to Nellie, but when she attends a late-night gathering of the cats, the magic of the moonlight allows her to dance alone. Babbitt subtly yet surely weaves a strong message about self-reliance into this charming fantasy lined with the same graceful and precise language as *Tuck Everlasting.* Working in strong colors, Babbitt creates evocative outdoor backdrops and spare interior scenes that heighten the story's impact. She also strikes the right note in her depiction of the various cats, especially in an imaginative two-page spread showing the felines' nighttime revelry. Babbitt's many fans will welcome her entry into picture books, which will give children a chance to make her acquaintance early.

Zena Sutherland

SOURCE: A review of *Nellie: A Cat on Her Own,* in *Bulletin of the Center for Children's Books,* Vol. 43, No. 3, November, 1989, p. 50.

When their owner dies, the cat Big Tom convinces the cat-puppet, Nellie, to come away with him. He escorts her to a moonlit session of dancing cats, a diversion in which Nellie, feeling a stirring in her wooden limbs, takes part. Nellie decides she'd rather stay there, tucked into a hollow in a tree, than search with Big Tom for a "new old woman." Not Babbitt's best fantasy, but a pleasant if insubstantial story, this has beautifully detailed illustrations, a bit softer than the paintings of William Pène du Bois, but often like them in composition and even more in the clear colors of a restrained palette.

Susan Perren

SOURCE: A review of *Nellie: A Cat on Her Own,* in *Quill & Quire,* Vol. 56, No. 1, January, 1990, p. 18.

Nellie the cat is a marionette, constructed of wood, yarn, and broom straws by a clever old woman. Every afternoon Nellie is taken down from her peg to dance. The old woman pulls Nellie's strings so that she leaps and dips and spins "just like a dancer on stage." When the old woman dies, Nellie wails in despair to Old Tom, the real cat of the household, that she will never dance again. Old Tom tells her it's time she pulled her own strings and belonged to herself, like him: "That way when changes come, you'll always be ready to hold your tail high and move along." With Old Tom's help Nellie takes the leap, literally and figuratively.

This perfectly paced book is a gavotte of prose and pictures that moves step by step toward a graceful finale. As always, the kernel of Babbitt's story is encased in plain but elegant language and her full-colour illustrations—spare, explicit, and sweet but never sugary—are in harmony with her prose.

Kay E. Vandergrift

SOURCE: A review of *Nellie: A Cat on Her Own,* in *School Library Journal,* Vol. 36, No. 1, January, 1990, p. 74.

Babbitt's illustrations are as carefully wrought and as flowing as her prose in this charmingly cozy story about friendship and independence. Two cats live in a cottage with an old woman: Nellie, the marionette cat, and Big Tom, the real cat. Each evening Tom leaves the house,

while Nellie stays on her comfortable, safe peg. When the old woman dies, Tom uses her ribboned hat as a cart, and takes Nellie out into the world to meet his friends. When all the cats gather in the moonlight, Nellie's wooden limbs come to life, and she and Tom dance until moonset. The soft hues of the illustrations and the perfectly balanced page layouts capture the gentle magic of this tale. Rosy browns and greens predominate, but the pale lavender of the book jacket is carried into the moonlit night skies to create a special time when truly wondrous things might occur. Children open the book to meet an appealing but hollowed-eyed Nellie hanging from her strings above a few lines of text on a white page, and leave the final page with a slightly larger bright-eyed Nellie dancing stringless on a spaciously open page. In between there are other subtle changes as Nellie's rigid body takes on life and expression, highlighted by the scene in which she, with a grin and shining blue eyes, steps out of her hat cart to dance in the moonlight. The cats' gathering is reminiscent of a gentler "wild rumpus" and, like Sendak's *Where the Wild Things Are,* this is the story of a small creature finding comfort in a big, often frightening, world.

Margery Fisher

SOURCE: A review of *Nellie: A Cat on Her Own,* in *Growing Point,* Vol. 29, No. 2, July, 1990, p. 5378.

When the 'clever old woman' dies who has made and manipulated the little wooden cat-marionette, Nellie is freed from her strings by Big Tom, who is ready to find a new home for the two of them and resourcefully drags the puppet (in the old woman's hat turned into a cart) to a clearing in a forest where the neighbourhood cats dance all night and where Nellie finds she can dance too and make a new life for herself. Quiet landscapes and very personable cats move and talk in a way any cat-addict would accept because of the warm mixture of observation and affection which Natalie Babbitt has achieved in a genre unusual for her but most skillfully employed.

Valerie Caless

SOURCE: A review of *Nellie, a Cat on Her Own,* in *The School Librarian,* Vol. 38, No. 4, November, 1990, p. 141.

Nellie is a cat. Not a fluffy one, not a sleek one, but a wooden marionette. She loves nothing better than to dance on her strings when her old mistress pulls them. When the old woman dies, it seems that Nellie may never dance again; but Tom, the live cat who lives in the house, knows better. He carries Nellie out into the world to the place where cats meet to dance in the full moonlight. Moonshine or magic? Either way, Nellie finds that she can dance alone and thereafter, like all cats, she is her own creature. Natalie Babbitt offers the young reader a timeless tale of growing up, of safe adventure and a touch of magic. The softly coloured pictures perfectly complement the text. This is a book to be read on laps. It certainly deserves a place in the infants reading corner.

BUB, OR THE VERY BEST THING (1994)

Kirkus Reviews

SOURCE: A review of *Bub, or the Very Best Thing,* in *Kirkus Reviews,* Vol. LXII, No. 3, February, 1, 1994, p. 137.

The King and Queen are at odds: *he* says "too many toys" will make the Prince "soft and silly"; *she* says the many lessons with the King will leave him "dry and dusty." Still, they agree on one thing: "I only want what's best for him." And what is that? Dressed in medieval splendor, they take a thoroughly modern palace poll, with predictable results: the nursemaids recommend vegetables and sleep, the gardener sunshine, and so on through a list of indispensables; only the cook's daughter has the sense to suggest asking the royal toddler, who responds "Bub"—a mystery to his parents, but not to the girl, who hears "Love." The meaning is delivered rather directly, but Babbitt lightens it with wit in her slyly honed dialogue, and with a jester—a perfectly observed golden retriever sporting cap and bells—tagging along to clown appealingly in each of the pertly ironic illustrations. "Not to mention the dog," says Babbitt in dedicating the book to her human models, and she doesn't; all the same, it's a delight and steals the show, as she doubtless intended.

Ilene Cooper

SOURCE: A review of *Bub, or the Very Best Thing,* in *Booklist,* Vol. 90, No. 12, February 15, 1994, pp. 1091-92.

Bub's parents, the king and the queen, have different ideas about raising their child, so they decide to find out just what *is* the best thing in the universe for him. After interviewing everyone in the castle and coming up with answers as diverse as vegetables and conversations, the cook's daughter asks the little prince himself. His parents aren't quite sure what his answer—"bub"—means, but the cook's daughter is. "The Prince was right, Mama. Love is the very best thing." The story itself, heavy on message, is static, leaving the art as the part of the book most attractive to kids, but even the pictures are a bit stiff. Enlivening things is the presence of a handsome golden retriever, topped with a joker's cap, who cavorts throughout the lavish full-page pictures and the charming cameos that decorate the opposite text pages. For larger collections or libraries that want their Babbitt collections complete.

Hanna B. Zeiger

SOURCE: A review of *Bub, or the Very Best Thing,* in *The Horn Book Magazine,* Vol. LXX, No. 3, May-June, 1994, pp. 305-06.

A parenting dispute arises between a young king and queen over the care of the toddler prince. Should he be given soft, silly toys or dry, dusty lessons? The royal couple both want "the one and only very best thing" for their son, but what would that be? While the king and the prime minister look for the answer in books, the queen and the prince, along with his stuffed toy dragon and the family dog, set out on a search through the castle. From various sources the queen hears that the prince needs vegetables, sleep, sunshine, and songs; the king's research is equally inconclusive. Unsatisfied with their results, the royal couple wanders into the kitchen and asks the cook's daughter her opinion. To their surprise, she suggests they ask the prince himself, and, after a whispered exchange with him, she announces, "'The one and only very best thing is bub.'" Since the king and queen haven't a clue as to what the prince means when he says "'bub,'" they decide that their best strategy will be to show him how much they both care for him until he's old enough to explain it to them himself. Meanwhile, the cook's daughter tells her mother, "'The Prince was right. . . . Love is the very best thing.'" Babbitt's elegant writing style and the totally engaging characterizations in her illustrations combine to create a memorable picture book. In the end, however, the royal dog and the toy dragon steal the show.

Betsy Hearne

SOURCE: A review of *Bub, or the Very Best Thing,* in *Bulletin of the Center for Children's Books,* Vol. 47, No. 10, June, 1994, pp. 312-13.

After an argument about what's "the one and only very best thing" for their toddler, the King goes off to look for the answer in his books and the Queen walks the Prince through the castle asking whomever she meets. It's a regular parade, with the old family dog following them around and snatching a favorite toy dinosaur whenever he can. Of course, everyone has a different prescription for "the one and only very best thing," from sunshine to songs; but, when the cook's daughter suggests asking the Prince himself, he repeats the only word he's spoken since the beginning of the story, "Bub," an echo of his mother's endearment to his father, "my love." The parents remain puzzled, but "the Cook's Daughter said to the Cook, 'The Prince was right, Mama. Love is the very best thing.'" It's a fine book for new parents, whose point of view it reflects entirely, but children themselves may fidget a bit at the Socratic abstractness of it all. Babbitt's studied watercolor scenes feature almost photorealistically literal characters and show limited variation of value, so that the contrasting hues sometimes appear flat despite carefully defined perspective and modelling. White muzzle notwithstanding, the dog is the liveliest element here—and, at the stage of a picture-book audience's development, the most likely suspect for the true meaning of the Prince's one and only word.

📖 *OUCH!* (retold by Babbitt, 1998)

Kirkus Reviews

SOURCE: A review of *Ouch!*, in *Kirkus Reviews,* Vol. LXVI, No. 21, November 1, 1998, p. 1596.

A fine, comfortable storyteller's voice meets up with sly and elegant illustrations in this tale from the Brothers Grimm. A baby boy who is "nobody special" is born with a crown-shaped birthmark, so the local fortune-teller predicts he will marry a princess. The king, father of a newborn daughter, bribes the parents to surrender their son, on the pretext that he will raise the boy. Instead, he puts him in a box and drops the box in a river. The baby is rescued and named Marco, and grows up tall and sweet and confident. Re-discovered by the king, he is saved by mischievous bandits, marries the princess, then is sent off by his new father-in-law mid-celebration to get three golden hairs off the devil's head. Now the story gets interesting, as Marco rides off to Hell, meets the devil's grandmother, and brings back the three hairs—the "ouch!" of title—while also doing away with the king and relieving a bored ferryman of his duties. The illustrations are rich in Renaissance pattern in architecture and clothing, chivied by [Fred] Marcel-lino's round-headed, puckish figures. Street, forest, and water vistas share the rosy golden light of fairy tale; the whole is quite satisfying.

Publishers Weekly

SOURCE: A review of *Ouch!*, in *Publishers Weekly,* Vol. 245, No. 44, November 2, 1998, p. 80.

In this abbreviated version of the Grimms' "The Devil with the Three Golden Hairs," a crown-shaped birthmark heralds a boy's bright future. Based on this omen, a fortune-teller predicts that Marco will marry a princess, and this comes to pass in short order: "So the two were married, with plenty of joy and noise, and that should have been the end of it, but it wasn't." The youth still must placate his evil father-in-law, the king, who demands three golden hairs from the head of the Devil. Marco ventures forth to Hell, where he meets the Devil's impish grandmother, who agrees to yank the three hairs. ("Ouch!" is the Devil's exclamation as she does the deed.) Thus, he keeps the princess, and then exacts revenge on the king. Babbitt rewrites the classic story in a casual voice infused with wry wit, paring it down to its essentials (e.g., leaving out the magical golden apples and the wine-flowing fountain), while Marcellino paints the characters in picturesque Renaissance-era garb. He constructs scenes of architectural grandeur: readers become spectators at the wedding, looking up at the starry ceiling, and stand alongside the newly married prince at the steps of Hell, which appears as a desolate castle with firelit bricks and oversize wooden furniture. The Devil himself is a slim, none-too-threatening figure in a red unitard decorated with ruffles at the wrist. The inventive layout, based on a rectangular grid, features creatively cropped and overlapping color images and blocky text. Although things come together a bit too easily in this Grimm tale, readers will likely lap up Babbitt's intelligent retelling, mixed with a dash of sly humor and dressed in Marcellino's signature finery.

Additional coverage of Babbitt's life and career is contained in the following sources published by Gale Research: *Contemporary Authors,* Vol. 49-52; *Contemporary Authors New Revision Series,* Vol. 38; *Dictionary of Literary Biography; Junior DISCovering Authors; Major Authors and Illustrators for Children and Young Adults; Something about the Author Autobiography Series,* Vol. 5; and *Something about the Author,* Vol. 68.

Sook Nyul Choi

1937-

Korean-American author of fiction, autobiography, and picture books.

Major works include *Year of Impossible Goodbyes* (1991), *Echoes of the White Giraffe* (1993), *Halmoni and the Picnic* (1993), *Gathering of Pearls* (1994), *The Best Older Sister* (1997).

INTRODUCTION

Recognized for bringing Korean history to the forefront of her works, Choi is celebrated for the heartfelt, graceful style and steadfast purpose of her writing. Rich with cultural and autobiographical details of her Korean heritage, her work has been praised as a powerful contribution to multicultural literature in the United States. Appealing to an audience of primary graders, young adults and adults, Choi's works are recognized for their global significance. At the center of her stories radiates an ardent optimism and unchained belief in the goodness of humanity. Her storytelling bears witness to the struggles and triumphs of the human spirit, speaking the "universal language of the heart," noted Carolyn Phelan. The honest observations and vivid characterizations in her stories expand the reader's vision of the world while relating the details of Choi's life as a young child in Korea. Readers recognize this small, far away country because she puts a human face on it. Choi shares her Korea in its war-torn state, and when she comes stateside she brings her homeland with her, giving us pictures of Korean immigrants having difficulties adjusting to a new country. Her principle themes—the importance of family, and the hopeful belief that goodness prevails even under the worst conditions—fervently repeat throughout her writing, but most especially in her memoir trilogy, which includes *Year of Impossible Goodbyes, Echoes of the While Giraffe,* and *Gathering of Pearls.* At the core of Choi's three-part story is her relationship with her mother who provides enduring hope to a family that experiences loss and separation across many years of war. "When our country was suffering," Choi told *Publishers Weekly,* "[mother] made me feel that this was not the way things were all over the world. She always saw good in people."

Choi once commented that she writes to share the culture of her homeland: "I hope that through my books Americans can gain insight into this very different and interesting culture." Korean customs and culture are interwoven throughout all of her stories, but nowhere is their significance more evident than in *Year of Impossible Goodbyes,* Choi's first novel and heart-warming memoir of her early childhood, which relates her family's survival of war, Japanese domination, and the Russian communist takeover of Korea. *Year of Impossisble Goodbyes* depicts a Japanese-occupied Korea that forbids any expression of the Korean language and culture. These national treasures are forced underground and behind darkened windows until, with the defeat of the Japanese, the Korean way of life resurfaces, rising like a precious jewel and restoring meaningful texture to the lives of Koreans. But renewal is short-lived when Communist Russia takes over, suppressing Koreans once more. With a gripping sense of truth and purpose, Choi writes from the heart, no matter how painful or bitter the experience. Speaking of *Year of Impossible Goodbyes,* she told *Publishers Weekly,* "I want my book to be received as a celebration of human spirit, of the ability to go on and forgive."

Biographical Information

Born in Pyongyang, North Korea, Choi was a passionate reader. She once explained in *Something about the Author (SATA),* "As a young girl growing up in Korea, I loved collecting books. I loved the feel and the smell of books; I liked the sound of pages turning; and I liked arranging them on my bookshelf. Sitting under the trellis of grapevines in our backyard, I would sit and read for hours as I snacked on the bitter green grapes. Through books, I could travel to the far corners of the world and meet people from distant lands and cultures." She later emigrated to the United States to advance her education. Always a serious student, she became even more so at Manhattanville College where she studied French, art, and European history. *Gathering of Pearls,* her third autobiographical novel, speaks of her intensity as a student, the language barriers she encountered, and the pressures from home. Margaret Cole described the mood of the novel as, "quiet" and "introspective," reflecting her educational experience. After receiving a bachelor of arts degree, Choi taught for twenty years in New York City elementary schools and also taught creative writing to high school students. Recalling her early writing experiences in *SATA*, Choi said, "as a grammar school student in Korea, I began writing short stories and poetry. I loved to write, for through writing, I could express my dreams and visions of the fantastic." Thirty years after emigrating to the United States, Choi began writing the story of her life. The first novel of her three-part memoir, *Year of Impossible Goodbyes,* was published in 1991.

Major Works

Year of Impossisble Goodbyes is Choi's first novel in her memoir trilogy. Through the voice of Sookan, Choi powerfully describes her childhood in Kirimni, Pyongyang, during the Second World War when Japanese troops occupied the country, separating and destroying families and suppressing the Korean culture and language. Her father and three older brothers, forced to work in labor camps, leave Sookan, her mother, younger brother, grandfather, and aunt to struggle on their own. Sookan and her grandfather study secretly behind covered windows while Sookan's mother runs a sock factory that employs other Korean women. The factory's production, constantly under the inspection of Japanese Captain Narita, closes down near the war's end, sending the women workers to the Japanese front to "comfort" the soldiers and leaving the family without means of an income. The relief and hope that follow the end of the war is short-lived when Communist Russia takes over—dividing and destroying the country even further. With her mother and brother, Sookan eventually escapes to the American-occupied South. Sookan's mother, a medial figure in the novel, holds onto hope and a belief in a better life and passes this spirit on to her daughter. Interweaving authentic details within a sympathetic, narrative voice, Choi produces a true-to-life picture of the war and those who experienced it, narrowing the distance between the reader and the people and culture of a remote country. Laura L. Lent applauded Choi's novel as a "historically accurate tale of the plight of the Korean people" that offers the reader "fresh insight into how another country was affected by the war." Joanne Schott noted, "Characterization is strong," as the author gives "authenticity of experience, detail, and emotion," while Michael Shapiro

called it a "glimpse into a young girl's mind and into a nation's heart—a tale of bearing witness to the plight of a people." Finally, Betsy Hearne praised the novel as "both artless and artful, both revealing of a complex culture and moving in its statement of human rights. Most of all, it proves that powerful fictional effects derive from subtle scenes and patient pacing, even in the case of dramatic situations. Readers will find themselves back in time and forward in spirit."

A reviewer for *Publishers Weekly* pointed out that Choi, in *Echoes of the White Giraffe,* "once again succeeded in putting a very human face on a tragic episode of world history" and judged it to have "universal reverberations." In this second autobiographical novel, bombing raids in Seoul, a result of war between North and South Korea, force Sookan, her younger brother, and her mother to abandon their home and flee to Pusan. The family now make their home at the top of a mountain filled with makeshift houses for refugees. Every morning a loud voice from the height of a mountain across from them calls out, "Hello, all you refugees on these mountains. Rise and shine." This shouting poet, as Sookan calls him, is the "White Giraffe" who "echoes" hope for her. In the midst of loss and separation from their family, Sookan, her mother, and little brother help build a new school; furthermore, romance blossoms as Sookan experiences a culturally forbidden, but very comforting and close relationship with a boy two years older than her. Ellen Levine viewed the novel not only as a story of "dislocation" but also one of "Sookan's personal growth, indeed her triumph," and concluded that "Ms. Choi's books may help American children wonder and understand." Along the same vein, Susan Middleton predicted that Choi's "authentic voice" would give readers a "deeper understanding of Korea's past."

Gathering of Pearls concludes Choi's memoir trilogy. Sookan, now nineteen, attends Finch, a small Catholic college in the United States. Departing from war-torn Korea, *Gathering of Pearls* shifts to quiet introspection as Sookan contends with low funds, language barriers, and a heavy class load. Separated by distance, family members are unable to relate to Sookan's circumstances, and the students at Finch, who seem to balance study with extracurricular activities, do not understand her intensity. As in the first two novels, Sookan's understanding mother comes through with loving support. Margaret Cole described the novel as an "intimately rendered narrative" with "soul-searching prose."

In her picture books for children, Choi continues to share the Korean culture and break down cross-cultural barriers by using characters who bring familiar human conflicts and emotions to her stories. With universal themes that appeal to younger readers, *The Best Older Sister* introduces Sunhi, a young Korean girl whose jealousy erupts when her new baby brother receives more attention, and her sensitive grandmother, who helps Sunhi understand the importance of being the older sister. Traditional Korean clothes worn by the children on the baby's first birthday give the story its cultural color. April Judge noted how Choi weaves Korean culture throughout the story while she "realistically and accurately portrays . . . sibling rivalry." In *Halmoni and the Picnic* Yunmi's third grade classmates invite her "Halmoni," or grandmother, to chaperon their picnic in Central Park. Newly emigrated to the United States, Halmoni does not know English and plans to take a Korean food called kimbap to the picnic. Worried that cultural differences might spoil her fun, Yunmi is surprised when her classmates enjoy the food and invite Halmoni back for next year's picnic. Halmoni relaxes with the children and tries out new English words. A *Kirkus Reviews* critic described *Halmoni and the Picnic* as a "sensitive exploration of difficulties facing immigrants, particularly older people." The "subtle text" "displays a fine sensitivity," noted Ilene Cooper, who recommended the book be used to initiate discussion about different cultures.

Awards

Choi was honored with five writing awards for her first novel, *Year of Impossible Goodbyes*. For this work, Choi received the Bulletin Blue Ribbon citation from the *Bulletin of the Center for Children's Books* and the Judy Lopez Book Award, both in 1991. Choi also won the Young Adults Library Services Association best book for young adults citation, the New York Public Library best book for the teen age citation, and the American Library Association notable book citation. In 1992 the Cambridge YWCA recognized Choi with the Women of Achievement Award.

GENERAL COMMENTARY

Lynda Brill Comerford

SOURCE: "Flying Starts: Sook Nyul Choi," in *Publishers Weekly,* Vol. 238, No. 56, December 20, 1991, pp. 22-3.

It is difficult to imagine that someone exuding as much warmth and exuberance as Sook Nyul Choi could have experienced all the horrors set down in her autobiographical book set in North Korea in the year 1945. Focusing on the day-to-day hardships of one family, *Year of Impossible Goodbyes,* relates how young Sookan, her little brother and mother endure routine humiliations from Japanese officers, mourn the death of Sookan's grandfather, survive their country's invasion by Russian soldiers and attempt a dangerous escape to the south.

Choi, whose earliest writing was published in Korean newspapers, had always felt compelled to write her life story, especially after American friends and students pressed her to talk about her past. But for years, other activities—attending college, teaching, school, raising a family and attaining American citizenship—took precedence over the time-consuming task of translating memories into English, her second language. It was not until 10 years ago, during a return trip to her homeland shortly after her husband's death, that Choi felt the time was right to begin *Year of Impossible Goodbyes.*

Initially, her decision was not met favorably by members of her family still living in Korea. "When I asked my father to tell me about some of his experiences in jail, he said, 'Why do you want to bring back the devils long gone? Why do you want to make people cry?'" But Choi is quick to explain that her purpose in creating the book was never to make people sad (a taboo of Korean culture). "I want my book to be received as a celebration of human spirit, of the ability to go on and forgive."

Eventually, Choi's massive undertaking evolved into a 400-page manuscript which her grown-up daughters and Houghton editor Laura Hornik helped trim to a more manageable size. Choi admits it was hard to "cut back," but she may be able to work some of the leftover material into the sequel she is planning. She has already completed a second novel, *Halmoni* (Grandmother), due out in 1993 from Houghton Mifflin, which explores the relationship between a Korean woman and her American-born grandchild.

Choi's faith in essential goodness, which is embodied in heroine Sookan, may be inherited from the author's mother, whose optimism was never shaken. "When our country was suffering," Choi recalls, "she made me feel that this was not the way things were all over the world. She always saw good in people."

In closing, Choi relates a story that her mother told her as a child: "My mother used to say that every time you go through horrible times, every time you suffer, a thin gold leaf will come out of your heart, pass through your mouth and go up to heaven. As a child, I used to imagine that when I died I would go up to heaven and see all those gold sparkles and go crunching through the gold leaves that came from my heart."

TITLE COMMENTARY

📖 *YEAR OF IMPOSSIBLE GOODBYES* (1991)

Publishers Weekly

SOURCE: A review of *Year of Impossible Goodbyes,* in *Publishers Weekly,* Vol. 238, No. 28, June 28, 1991, p. 102.

In 1945, 10-year-old Sookan's homeland of North Korea is occupied by the Japanese. Left behind while her resistance-fighter father hides in Manchuria and her older brothers toil in Japanese labor camps, Sookan and her remaining family members run a sock factory for the war effort, bolstered only by the dream that the fighting will soon cease. Sookan watches her people—forced to renounce their native ways—become increasingly angry and humiliated. When war's end brings only a new type of domination—from the Russian communists—Sookan and her younger brother must make a harrowing escape across the 38th parallel after their mother has been detained at a Russian checkpoint. Drawn partly from Choi's own experiences, her debut novel is a sensitive and honest portrayal of amazing courage. In clear, graceful prose, she describes a sad period of history that is astonishing in its horror and heart-wrenching in its truth. Readers cannot fail to be uplifted by this account of the triumph of the human spirit in an unjust world.

Kirkus Reviews

SOURCE: A review of *Year of Impossible Goodbyes,* in *Kirkus Reviews,* Vol. LIX, No. 16, August 15, 1991, p. 1087.

A moving fictionalized account of Choi's last months as a child in Pyongyang under the brutal Japanese rule that oppressed Korea for more than 30 years before 1945, and her harrowing escape with her seven-year-old brother south across the 38th parallel.

Choi describes the Japanese persecution in an even tone that makes it even more chilling: deliberate destruction of everything of value or beauty, even Grandfather's favorite pine tree; interdiction of religions other than Shinto and of the Korean language; indoctrination of children; systematic starving of the population; the forcing of young women to serve as "spirit girls" for the Japanese troops' pleasure. Despite all, Choi's family preserved dignity, familial love, and loyalty to their heritage. When the Russians arrived (not the hoped-for Americans), they proved less vicious but even more effective propagandists than the Japanese. Choi's father, who had spent the war in Manchuria, arranged an escape that was partially successful, even though their guide turned out to be a double agent: the two children, who had already demonstrated their intelligence and mettle, made their way on their own after their mother was detained (miraculously, she joined them later); other relatives left behind to cover for them were executed in retribution.

A vividly written, compellingly authentic story that complements Yoko Watkins's fine *So Far from the Bamboo Grove* (1986), which details a Japanese family's suffering en route from Korea to Japan during the same period.

Hazel Rochman

SOURCE: A review of *Year of Impossible Goodbyes,* in *Booklist,* Vol. 88, No. 2, September 15, 1991, pp. 140-41.

There's drama but no romantic adventure in this autobiographical novel about a child in war-torn North Korea—first, under Japanese military oppression; then, after 1945, under Russian occupation; and, finally, on the run across the border. The last third of the book is the most gripping, as 10-year-old Sookan, her little brother, Inchun, and their mother flee from their town to try and reach Sookan's father in South Korea. Their guide turns out to be a double agent, and their mother is captured. The two children wander alone through the rain and mud of the rice paddies, filthy, hungry, bruised, sobbing. A few adults help them and show them the way past the dogs and searchlights. To cross the tracks, Sookan and Inchun crawl under a train while it's in the station. To cross a rushing river, they drag themselves across the rungs of a dangerous railway bridge. They tear their backs on the frontier barbed wire. Choi communicates the overwhelming physical experience of these once-protected small children, who find themselves suddenly alone. We feel their dazed terror, their exhaustion and weakness, as well as the astonishing determination that somehow gets them across. A good book to recommend with the Holocaust refugee stories and with Watkins' *So Far from the Bamboo Grove,* about a Japanese girl's flight from Korea after the war.

Betsy Hearne

SOURCE: A review of *Year of Impossible Goodbyes,* in *Bulletin of the Center for Children's Books,* Vol. 45, No. 2, October, 1991, p. 34.

A gripping first-person narrative recounts ten-year-old Sookan's survival of the Japanese occupation of North Korea and the Communists' subsequent takeover in 1945. Even after Grandfather's death, Mother holds the family together in the absence of her husband and three oldest sons, but when she is detained at the 38th parallel guard station, Sookan and her little brother must escape to the south alone. Tragedies are not masked here, but neither are they overdramatized; the story has the same impact as Holocaust fiction that depicts a people caught between forces demeaning their lives, as in the case of the Korean "sock girls" who are rounded up at their knitting factory and herded to the front to serve as whores for the Japanese soldiers. The observations are honest, the details authentic, the characterizations vividly developed. This is a novel both artless and artful, both revealing of a complex culture and moving in its statement of human rights. Most of all, it proves that powerful fictional effects derive from subtle scenes and patient pacing, even in the case of dramatic situations. Readers will find themselves moved back in time and forward in spirit.

Lydia Champlin

SOURCE: A review of *Year of Impossible Goodbyes,* in *School Library Journal,* Vol. 37, No. 10, October, 1991, pp. 120, 122.

Ten-year-old Sookan tells of her Korean family's experiences during the Japanese occupation as World War II ends. The Japanese commit cruel, fear-provoking acts against this proud, hopeful family and against the young girls who worked in a sweatshop making socks for the Japanese army. Relief, hope, and anticipation of the return of male family members after the Japanese defeat is short lived as the Russians occupy the country, bringing their language, their customs, and communism to the village. Equally as insensitive to the pride and possessions of the Koreans, they are as bad as the Japanese. Plans are made for Sookan, her mother, and younger brother to escape to South Korea. However, their guide betrays them, causing the children to be separated from their mother, and the two begin a daring and frightening journey to cross the 38th parallel to safety. Through Sookan, the author shares an incredible story of the love and determination of her family, the threatening circumstances that they endured during occupations by two totalitarian governments, and the risks they took to escape to freedom. Readers will get a double bonus from this book—a good story, well told, and the reaffirmation of our faith in the human spirit against incredible adversities.

Laura L. Lent

SOURCE: A review of *Year of Impossible Goodbyes,* in *Voice of Youth Advocates,* Vol. 14, No. 5, December, 1991, pp. 307-08.

In this book, Choi poignantly describes her childhood in Kirimni, Pyongyang during the Second World War. During this time, the Japanese occupied Korea, and Choi's family suffered as a result of Japanese oppression. Her writing transports the reader back to her childhood home in 1945. She describes the family's day-to-day routine—including such things as her secret studies of the Chinese and Korean languages with her grandpa, and her family's operation of a sock factory in the shed on their property. Along with tales of their mundane life, Choi relates specific instances of brutality that she, her family, and their friends experience at the hands of the Japanese.

Choi recollects her countrymen's collective sigh of relief as the Japanese withdraw from Korea and their hope that all will get better soon. However, their hope for Korean independence is dashed when the Japanese are immediately replaced by the Communist Russians. As the realization sets in that life in North Korea will never improve, Choi's mom plans a daring escape to the South where the Americans are. Thus, the last part of her story focuses on the escape that her mother, her brother, and she make across the thirty-eighth parallel.

Choi's descriptive, frightening, yet historically accurate tale of the plight of the Korean people during the Second World War and immediately thereafter provides the teen reader—and anyone else who would like to read a fantastic book—with fresh insight into how another country was affected by the war. Most American teens have been exposed to information (via video, lecture-discussion, and/or books) on the death camps in Nazi-occupied areas; however, they have no idea that other nationalities (like the Koreans being oppressed by the Japanese and later by the Russians) also suffered at the same time. With Choi's book, another part of the war becomes public knowledge, and history is more fully told.

In addition to the book's historical merits, it should be noted that Choi is a tremendous author. Her memoirs evoke one emotion after another. For instance Choi describes how her grandfather is punished by Captain Narita, the Japanese policeman, because her grandfather had created a brush painting and written Chinese characters upon it. One feels first the humiliation that the old man must have felt when Captain Narita verbally abused him. More powerful emotions follow. One can feel life ebb from Choi's grandfather after Captain Narita orders the grandfather's pine tree—his final place of refuge and solitude—cut down. And when Choi ends this particular tale by describing her grandfather's eventual death, one feels a myriad of emotions ranging from anger to futility and helplessness. She evokes emotions from the reader because she vividly writes about the past so that the reader gets a picture of the events as they happened.

Because of the ease with which this story unfolds (Chinese, Japanese, and Russian words are defined within the narrative), I feel anyone, including young adults, can have an enjoyable experience reading this book. In sum, Choi's entertaining, yet informative writing style should win her a best book nomination.

Martha V. Parravano

SOURCE: A review of *Year of Impossible Goodbyes,* in *The Horn Book Magazine,* Vol. LXVIII, No. 1, January-February, 1992, p. 69.

Born during the thirty-six-year Japanese military occupation of Korea, ten-year-old Sookan has never known any other life. She receives glimpses of a proud past through her gentle, scholarly grandfather, who still keeps the old Korean ways, and through her staunch, brave mother, who reluctantly runs a factory that produces knitted socks for the Japanese army. Sookan's father and older brothers have been away for years, fighting in the resistance movement or held in Japanese labor camps. When World War II ends and the Japanese are finally driven out of Korea, the rejoicing is premature: the Russians are equally as oppressive as the Japanese. Sookan and her seven-year-old brother flee their northern Korean village, heading south to the safety of the 38th parallel, and are almost immediately separated from their mother. The children's subsequent journey is harrowing, but the entire family is finally reunited—except for Sookan's aunt and cousin, who are shot as traitors for helping Sookan and her family escape. The book lacks the pacing and power of Yoko Kawashima Watkins's *So Far from the Bamboo Grove* (Lothrop), but there are poignant, vivid moments that will stay with the reader: the children bathing their dying grandfather's feet and discovering that his toenails had been pulled out under torture by the Japanese; the "sock girls" frantically pushing themselves to impossible production levels, vainly hoping that it will save them from being sent to be raped by Japanese soldiers; the mortification of small Korean children as they urinate at their desks because they are not allowed a break from reciting Japanese propaganda. The author's love for her family and homeland was the inspiration for the novel; it shines through every word of her moving account.

ECHOES OF THE WHITE GIRAFFE (1993)

Publishers Weekly

SOURCE: A review of *Echoes of the White Giraffe*, in *Publishers Weekly*, Vol. 240, No. 12, March 22, 1993, p. 80.

Sookan, the heroine who fled war-torn Seoul with her mother and younger brother in Choi's *Year of Impossible Goodbyes*, returns in this haunting sequel to tell of life as a refugee in South Korea. Now 15, Sookan tries to establish a sense of normalcy during turbulent times as she attends a makeshift school, worries about her missing father and older brothers, and contends with living in a mountaintop shack on the outskirts of Pusan. But perhaps most confusing of all, Sookan experiences her first romance. She takes comfort in her blossoming yet forbidden friendship with the handsome Junho, sharing with him her hopes and dreams of a happy, peaceful future. The end of the war brings still more upheaval when Sookan and the other refugees make their way back to the North and pick up the rubble of their former lives. Sookan's first-person narrative sustains a level of emotional intensity befitting the often dire events that swirl around her. Choi's graceful writing sews the disparate catastrophes into a satisfying, almost cathartic whole. She has once again succeeded in putting a very human face on a tragic episode of world history. This inspirational work possesses a confidence and quiet triumph with universal reverberations.

Hazel Rochman

SOURCE: A review of *Echoes of the White Giraffe*, in *Booklist*, Vol. 89, No. 15, April 1, 1993, p. 1424.

This is a disappointing sequel to Choi's autobiographical novel *Year of Impossible Goodbyes* with little of the dramatic immediacy of that acclaimed refugee story. This time the historical facts are just as compelling: Sookan, now 15, has escaped with her mother and younger brother from the bombing of Seoul during the Korean War of the 1950s, and they're living in a rough refugee mountain community in Pusan; as the war ends, they return to rebuild their gracious home in Seoul. However, the first-person narrative is overemotional, and the characterization is thin. Sookan sighs a lot (pensively, sadly, and with resignation), hot tears keep flooding her

eyes, and her heart pounds—whether she's remembering the bombs, or helping build a school for the refugees, or listening to a poet, or developing a romantic (and forbidden) relationship with a sensitive young man, who also sighs gently. Despite all the intense talk, the suffering and the joy seem distant, almost abstract, and the romance is patched on. However, the death of Sookan's father is handled with restraint, and readers will get some sense of the war from the civilians' point of view. They also will be moved by Sookan's struggle for independence within the restrictions of her society.

Kirkus Reviews

SOURCE: A review of *Echoes of the White Giraffe*, in *Kirkus Reviews*, Vol. LXI, No. 7, April 1, 1993, p. 453.

In a sequel to the autobiographical *Year of Impossible Goodbyes*, Sookan, now 15, is again a refugee. After 1945, the family was reunited in Seoul and established a comfortable home. But as the story opens, Sookan is in coastal Posan, studying at a refugee school. Separated from Father and her older brothers—whose fate they won't know for two years—by the bombing of Seoul, Sookan and her mother and youngest brother are living high on a mountain where she's awakened each morning by a poet shouting on a nearby peak. The earlier book hinged on political events and the cruelties and injustices of war; more quietly, this one examines war's sorrows and the courage and compromises of those growing up in its shadow. Sookan comforts an orphaned friend; mourns the Shouting Poet, though they've never met; and, despite her shyness, defies tradition to rendezvous with a male friend. Though each plans to enter holy orders, their love for poetry and music draws them into a poignant, chaste accord that reveals a great deal about the culture and their own character. Their parting, as Sookan heads for college in the US, leaves much unspoken, and is just one of the many separations and losses composing this book. Except for Sookan, the characters are less fully realized than before; instead, wonderfully telling scenes evoke the time, the place, and—more subtly—the deep-running emotions that these people, bound by custom and besieged by troubles, were so rarely free to acknowledge.

Susan Middleton

SOURCE: A review of *Echoes of the White Giraffe*, in *School Library Journal*, Vol. 39, No. 5, May, 1993, p. 104.

Having narrowly escaped oppression in their native North Korea in *Year of Impossible Goodbyes*, Sookan and her younger brother were reunited with their mother and their long-missing father and three older brothers. In this, the sequel, the family is again separated, this time by the Korean War. Fleeing falling bombs, Sookan, Inchun, and their mother arrive safely in Pusan, uncertain of the whereabouts of the men. They establish themselves in a shack at the top of a mountain where, along with other refugees, they try to subdue their doubts and grief as they tackle daily routines, face their memories, and dare to hope for a secure future. Singing in the church choir, Sookan, now 15, meets Junho, a young man whose kindness and sympathetic nature deeply impress her. Incredibly tame by today's standards, their friendship leads to a few daring encounters, such as having a photograph taken together and having an un-chaperoned conversation. After the truce is signed ending the war, the surviving family members are reunited. Sookan immerses herself in her schoolwork and achieves her goal of attending college in the U.S. While it lacks the action of the first book, this is a poignant story in which Choi speaks with an authentic voice, both in describing a young girl's coming of age and a war-weary nation where, even today, people are uncertain about the fate of family members. Readers will finish the book with a deeper understanding of Korea's past.

Betsy Hearne

SOURCE: A review of *Echoes of the White Giraffe,* in *Bulletin of the Center for Children's Books,* Vol. 46, No. 10, June, 1993, p. 311.

In this sequel to Choi's dynamic *Year of Impossible Goodbyes,* teenaged Sookan recounts her experience as a refugee for two and a half years in Pusan, where she and her mother and younger brother have fled after the bombing of Seoul. Separated again from her father and older brothers, Sookan helps her mother get enough food, water, and supplies to eke out their existence in a barren shack high atop a mountain so slick with mud that they can barely manage to climb it every day. To some extent, the author has abandoned the storytelling style that casts such a spell in the first book; this one relates a situation without developing it consistently as fiction or decisively as nonfiction. For instance, the three older brothers who are introduced near the end of the book appear too briefly to become familiar despite their importance to the main character; we know that they are real in a factual sense and that she knows them, but we don't know them because their activities are summarized rather than detailed. Of course, the pace of waiting is always more technically difficult to sustain than the pace of survival. Like Siegal's *Grace in the Wilderness,* this must abandon wartime drama for a kind of post-traumatic stress syndrome that is inherently less forceful. There are, however, some powerful scenes, along with a well-realized romance that is doomed by religious commitment and social differences; Sookan's total sense of displacement will offer young readers a natural point of empathy.

Laura L. Lent

SOURCE: A review of *Echoes of the White Giraffe,* in *Voice of Youth Advocates,* Vol. 16, No. 3, August, 1993, p. 149.

Choi's second book about her adolescent experiences in the war-torn country of Korea measures up to the fine quality of her first book *Year of Impossible Goodbyes.* In this work Choi provides the reader with a realistic glimpse of how refugees of war cope with their losses and struggle emotionally with the futility that they feel. A second theme presented by the author is how she, as a self-reliant, female adolescent, overcomes traditional barriers to achieve her lifetime goals.

The story opens with Sookan and her best friend, Bokhi, putting the finishing touches on a makeshift school (similar to the one they had left behind in Seoul). For the second time in Sookan's young life, her family has had to flee—this time from Seoul to Pusan. Like other Korean refugees, Sookan, her mother, and her brother Inchun, live in a shack on one of the mountains bordering the city of Pusan. Through Choi's description of these shacks, the reader is able to feel some of the loss that the refugees have suffered. They have lost, quite literally, everything. As such, they are looked upon with disdain by the citizens of Pusan.

Since Sookan's family was separated when the bombing of Seoul began, Sookan, Inchun and their mother anxiously await word that their loved ones are still alive and hope that some day their family will be reunited. Throughout the book, Choi shows the emotional instability that war refugees feel. On the one hand, the refugees want to hope for the best and continue to put their lives back together. Nevertheless, they are not totally free to do this until they know whether or not their loved ones are alive. In other words, their emotions and their lives stay in disarray.

The author also shows the despondency felt by the refugees when they learn that they have lost someone dear to them. When Bokhi discovers that both of her parents were killed while trying to escape from the Communists, she tells Sookan that life is like a sand castle that is easily washed away by the tides. Depression sets in, and it is only through Sookan's persistency that Bokhi is able to go on.

Although many of the refugees in Pusan's camps feel that life is totally futile, one person remains optimistic. His name is Baik Rin (meaning White Giraffe). Even though he is dying of tuberculosis, the White Giraffe awakens each morning as the sun rises and yells from the top of his mountain a good morning greeting to everyone exhorting the refugees to rise and shine because it is a brand new day. His greeting reverberates across the mountains, and is a symbol of hope to many.

The other prevailing theme in this work is about the author coming of age in the postwar world. Sookan's first dilemma begins when she and the choir director's brother, Junho, start talking together without a chaperon being present. Sookan is torn by what she knows is the traditional, accepted Korean way to fall in love, and her heart. In the end, her heart wins, and she agrees to meet with Junho to have a picture taken together before she leaves to go home to Seoul. Unfortunately, their picture is discovered and Junho's parents forbid the two from meeting again. Their love remains unrequited showing the respect paid to both tradition and parents in Korean culture. Furthermore, Sookan is determined to attend college in the United States. In order to do this, she must pass a test, which is typically only taken by men. Filled with determination, she devotes her life to preparing for this test. Eventually, she is rewarded by attaining one of the coveted positions to study abroad.

Choi has once again touched this reviewer's heart. Her writing style is so succinct and informative that this book can easily and enjoyably be read in a day. She gives the reading audience a chance to learn more about Korean culture and about life for the Korean people during the Korean War. This, like Choi's first book, is an outstanding novel that many people from all age groups will enjoy. As such, I would highly recommend this work to teenagers because it will not only provide them with entertaining reading, but it will also broaden their perspectives of the world and deepen their understanding of the Korean War.

📖 *HALMONI AND THE PICNIC* (1993)

Publishers Weekly

SOURCE: A review of *Halmoni and the Picnic,* in *Publishers Weekly,* Vol. 240, No. 27, July 5, 1993, pp. 71-2.

In her first picture book, Choi tackles the sensitive topic of an immigrant's adjustment to life in the United States. Yunmi's grandmother Halmoni has just moved to New York City from Korea and she's having a tough time getting acclimated. She doesn't speak much English, she doesn't understand the customs and she misses her homeland and her friends. In an effort to reach out to the old woman, Yunmi's friends ask Halmoni to chaperon the class picnic in Central Park. Yunmi is both excited and scared at the prospect—maybe the other kids will make fun of Halmoni's clothes and the traditional kimbap (rice/vegetable rolls) that she insists on bringing to the outing. But the children turn out to be fine ambassadors, and Halmoni feels pleased and welcome. Choi's text, sentimental but never saccharine, captures a jumble of emotions, both Halmoni's and Yunmi's. Both must find a common ground where pride, love and tolerance can coexist. With a light hand Choi delivers a happy ending. [Karen M.] Dugan's serviceable pencil and watercolor illustrations are warm in spirit and accurate in their detail, as in depictions of Halmoni's dress. Bright Korean-inspired borders framing each painting provide an authentic flavor. This gentle intergenerational book should appeal on many levels, and will be especially appreciated by those seeking contemporary Asian American fare.

Ilene Cooper

SOURCE: A review of *Halmoni and the Picnic,* in *Booklist,* Vol. 89, No. 22, August, 1993, p. 2069.

Yunmi's grandmother Halmoni has recently arrived in New York from Korea, and her adjustment isn't easy. She doesn't want to speak English, especially around Yunmi's friends, though she endears herself to them by bringing them fruit. Yunmi is worried her grandmother won't ever get into the swing of things, so when her class needs a chaperon for a picnic, she volunteers Halmoni. Yunmi almost regrets her invitation when Halmoni insists on bringing *kimbap,* a sushi-looking dish made of rice, carrots, eggs, and green vegetables wrapped in seaweed. But the food is a hit, and so is Halmoni, who tries out her English for the first time with the kids in Yunmi's class. Nothing unexpected happens here; in fact, this is a story that's probably been told as long as there have been immigrant grandmothers. But it is pleasing nonetheless, thanks to the lovely bordered watercolor art and the subtle text, both of which display a fine sensitivity. A good jumping-off place for discussion about cultures and/or generations.

Kirkus Reviews

SOURCE: A review of *Halmoni and the Picnic,* in *Kirkus Reviews,* Vol. LXI, No. 15, August 1, 1993, p. 999.

Yunmi, a Korean-American third-grader in a NYC parochial school, worries about her grandmother Halmoni, who's been in the US only two months and is having a hard time with the English language and American customs. When Yunmi's friends invite Halmoni to chaperon a class picnic and Halmoni insists on bringing special Korean food, Yunmi fears her classmates may turn up their noses at the *kimbap* or make fun of Halmoni's traditional clothing. But thanks to Halmoni's gentle, generous ways and the children's good-natured curiosity, the day is a great success—and Halmoni is even emboldened to say goodbye in English. Manhattan looks clean and picturesque in color illustrations that fill alternate pages, bordered in beautiful Korean textile designs. A sensitive exploration of difficulties facing immigrants, particularly older people who don't get the crash course in American culture provided by school or a job.

Diane S. Marton

SOURCE: A review of *Halmoni and the Picnic,* in *School Library Journal,* Vol. 39, No. 11, November, 1993, p. 78.

Two months earlier, Yunmi's *Halmoni,* or grandmother, arrived from Korea to live with her family in New York City. She is lonely, hesitant to speak English, and unused to American ways. Yunmi's friends like the woman, so they suggest that she be the chaperon for their class picnic in Central Park. The girl is worried that the food her grandmother prepares will be unappreciated, but her classmates like it so much that they invite her to make it again next year. By the end of the day, Halmoni is murmuring a few words in English and has picked up some American customs. Dugan's realistic, full-page, full-color illustrations are set within borders reminiscent of the silk edgings on Oriental paintings. The story is predictable and ordinary, but with its descriptions of Korean food, clothing, and culture, it deserves a place in library collections.

The Reading Teacher

SOURCE: "Finding Ourselves as People and as Learners," in *The Reading Teacher,* Vol. 48, No. 1, September, 1994, pp. 64-74.

Field trips are always an exciting school event. In Sook Nyul Choi's *Halmoni and the Picnic,* Yunmi is afraid that her classmates will make fun of her grandmother's traditional Korean clothing and food when Halmoni is invited to the class picnic. At the picnic one of Yunmi's friends cautiously tries a dish of Halmoni's kimbap, which she finds to be delicious. "If you're going to be taught something new, you have to trust the person teaching you" (Eugene, age 10). Halmoni also comes to trust her granddaughter and begins to learn American customs. Karen Dugan's borders give the effect of oriental silks and surround paintings of intricate detailings and formally posed figures.

GATHERING OF PEARLS (1994)

Publishers Weekly

SOURCE: A review of *Gathering of Pearls,* in *Publishers Weekly,* Vol. 241, No. 32, August 8, 1994, p. 440.

Sookan, the young Korean heroine of *Year of Impossible Goodbyes* and *Echoes of the White Giraffe,* has arrived in the United States to attend a women's college at the start of Choi's latest novel, set in 1954-1955. Having survived the war in her homeland, Sookan now faces the challenges of learning English and adapting to a new culture while keeping up with her studies and making friends during her freshman year. She works harder than anyone else and endears herself to her classmates, roommate and professors. But the pressures of too much work, combined with homesickness, lead to exhaustion—and a more relaxed approach to the college experience. When she receives bad news from her family in Seoul, she struggles to "turn her pain into pearls of wisdom and understanding," as her mother has always urged. Despite some poignant scenes, this novel lacks the emotional depth and clear, exciting story lines of its predecessors. Sookan plays an almost martyrly role here, and the first-person narration shows her continually praising herself or being praised by others for her kindness and good deeds; her strength and spunk are conspicuously absent. Admirers of the earlier works may find this pristine, cheery world rather dull.

Kirkus Reviews

SOURCE: A review of *Gathering of Pearls,* in *Kirkus Reviews,* Vol. LXII, No. 16, August 15, 1994, p. 1123.

In this sequel to Choi's autobiographical *Year of Impossible Goodbyes* (1991) and *Echoes of the White Giraffe* (1993), 19-year-old Sookan continues her journey—this time leaving Korea to study at Finch, a Catholic women's college in White Plains, N.Y. Although frightened by the enormity of her adventure and confused by the strangeness of American culture, Sookan is determined to excel at her studies, work for her keep, *and* serve as unofficial ambassador for her country. She has little time to enjoy what her bubbly roommate Ellen calls "college life"—parties, football games, and young men. Sookan makes friends but feels guilty whenever she has fun; she has a responsibility to her family, as her older sister Theresa keeps reminding her, that her American classmates cannot begin to understand. Sookan rebelliously feels that many of the American customs are good, although she can never lead Ellen's carefree life. When tragedy comes to her again, Sookan recalls what her mother used to tell her: Just as oysters make pearls out of grains of sand, women create something precious from their suffering. Preparing to face life alone, Sookan gathers her strength—her pearls—and resolves to succeed.

Sookan is sometimes annoyingly good, but the story of her struggle with her Korean heritage makes her more than just an ethnic Pollyanna.

Hazel Rochman

SOURCE: A review of *Gathering of Pearls,* in *Booklist,* Vol. 91, No. 1, September 1, 1994, pp. 33-4.

In this sequel to *Year of Impossible Goodbyes* (1991) and *Echoes of the White Giraffe* (1993), Sookan Bak has left her Korean home to attend a Catholic women's college in New York in 1954. This semiautobiographical account of her freshman year is very much a docu-novel about the new scholarship girl caught between two cultures, trying to fit in. Everything is overarticulated. Sookan and her friends speak like therapists ("You need to live your own life"). She writes long letters home about her cultural conflicts ("Here they do not place so much emphasis on patience, humility"), and her first-person narrative repeats all the analysis. Mostly, the U.S. is better than Korea, freer for the individual, though she does come to see that sometimes her American friends feel like outsiders and have problems with their families' expectations, just as she does. The last section of the book is the most immediate: her beloved mother dies, and Sookan is not told till long after the funeral. Her grief is heartfelt. We feel her distance from home.

Margaret Cole

SOURCE: A review of *Gathering of Pearls,* in *School Library Journal,* Vol. 40, No. 10, October, 1994, p. 142.

This novel completes the autobiographical trilogy begun

in *Year of Impossible Goodbyes* and continued in *Echoes of the White Giraffe.* Here the story begins with Sookan's arrival in White Plains, New York, in 1954 to start college, where she is the only Korean student at a small Catholic school for women. She confronts all the problems of adjustment normal to freshmen, plus the added burdens of absorbing a foreign culture and earning extra money. It is easy to fall in love with this gentle girl. She combines a delicate sweetness with a fierce determination to fulfill her dreams. She works hard to produce her own blend of cultures and values—she delights in the new, and tempers it with the traditional. She also attempts to maintain a correspondence with family members struggling to rebuild their lives in postwar Korea, but they see her as a deserter. Only her mother understands her yearnings and conflicts. The soul-searching quality of Choi's prose is at least as important to this beautiful novel as the plot line. It is not essential to have read the previous books to appreciate this one, but its full impact will be diminished for those unfamiliar with Sookan's experiences growing up in her war-torn homeland. On the other hand, those who responded to the suspense, hardship, and emotional tensions of the first two novels may be disappointed by the quiet, introspective mood of this intimately rendered narrative. However, readers who share in this emotional journey with Sookan will grow along with her in wisdom.

Sue Krumbein

SOURCE: A review of *Gathering of Pearls,* in *Voice of Youth Advocates,* Vol. 17, No. 4, October, 1994, p. 206.

Gathering of Pearls is the third book by Choi, who immigrated to the United States from Korea. It is set at a small Catholic college in New York where Sookan, an eighteen-year-old from Korea, has been awarded a scholarship to attend school in the United States. This is Sookan's dream, to be educated in the United States, but she brings with her a past unlike that of any of her classmates.

The reader would definitely benefit from first reading *Year of Impossible Goodbyes* and *Echoes of the White Giraffe,* where Sookan's story from the age of six is told. The earlier books make clear why Sookan works so hard at school and doesn't allow herself the pleasures of a social life. This third title is very revealing of life in the 1950s in the United States, particularly in a small college for women, as seen through the eyes of a Korean student. Add this if the first two books are in the collection; it doesn't really stand alone.

Roger Sutton

SOURCE: A review of *Gathering of Pearls,* in *Bulletin of the Center for Children's Books,* Vol. 48, No. 3, November, 1994, p. 83.

Continuing the autobiographical story begun in *The Year of Impossible Goodbyes* and *Echoes of the White Giraffe* Sookan leaves Korea to attend Finch College, a Catholic women's school in New York. She finds the adjustment to a brash new culture difficult but exhilarating, and for the first time she begins to question the future her older sister Theresa has planned for her, that Sookan will come back to Korea after graduating and become a nun. Bossy, disapproving letters from Theresa arrive with depressing regularity, as well as loving, encouraging ones from Sookan's mother, but Sookan feels she can tell neither of them about her difficulties with the language, the workload, and a continuing shortage of funds. While Choi's style is sometimes flat and overexplanatory ("When I was in Korea, I thought everything my sister said was right. But now I find that I don't always agree with her, and I resent the way she tries to control every aspect of my life"), the figure of outsider Sookan is a potent if somewhat saintly one, set against an appealing, girls'-story background of dates, dances, friendly roommates, and caring professors that provide an innocent picture of a 1950s college campus that younger teens will find engrossing. Though there is sadness, this hasn't the drama and tragedy of the first book; still, followers of the series will be reassured that Sookan, who has seen so much terror, successfully gets through a difficult but rewarding freshman year.

THE BEST OLDER SISTER (1997)

Publishers Weekly

SOURCE: A review of *The Best Older Sister,* in *Publishers Weekly,* Vol. 244, No. 5, February 3, 1997, p. 107.

This first choice chapter book by the author of *Year of Impossible Goodbyes* reprises a topic frequently visited in picture books: an older child's resentment of the attention a younger sibling receives. Kiju has undeniably usurped Sunhi's focal position in her loving Korean American family. Her grandmother, Halmoni, is too busy caring for the baby while her parents work to meet the girl after school each day with a snack; and visitors ignore Sunhi while they make a fuss over Kiju. Even worse, some guests think boys are more important than girls. Not surprisingly, all is resolved happily, but not without some redundant exposition of Sunhi's feelings. The book's greatest asset is [Cornelius Van] Wright and [Ying-Hwa] Hu's (illustrators of *Zora Hurston and the Chinaberry Tree*) resonant, realistic art. Featured on most spreads, their well-lit watercolors neatly convey the key characters' changeable emotions, from Halmoni's concern at Sunhi's initial anger to the newly placated girl's delight in making her brother smile for the camera.

April Judge

SOURCE: A review of *The Best Older Sister,* in *Booklist,* Vol. 93, No. 17, May 1, 1997, p. 1504.

Sunhi is jealous of all the attention that is being showered on her new baby brother; Halmoni, Sunhi's loving and understanding grandmother, helps the girl put aside her negative feelings as she realizes that being a big sister is an important job. This realistically and accurately portrays the all-too-familiar situation of sibling rivalry. Descriptions of several Korean customs and traditions are subtly interwoven throughout, and the full-color illustrations capture the expressions of sorrow and joy of Sunhi and her family as well as their friends, who represent various cultures. Young readers will enjoy the story's compassion and resolution.

Gale W. Sherman

SOURCE: A review of *The Best Older Sister,* in *School Library Journal,* Vol. 43, No. 6, June, 1997, p. 85.

Sunhi struggles with jealously toward her young brother just before his first birthday. However, her sensitive grandmother helps the child understand more about the demands of babies and gives Sunhi some special attention. Choi tells a balanced, sensitive story that incorporates some Korean family traditions. The important first-birthday celebration with a traditional outfit for the baby and silk dresses for Sunhi and her two best friends showcases multicultural understanding as a natural part of life. The realistic watercolor and pencil illustrations on each double-page spread complement the text and provide a visual break for early chapter-book readers.

YUNMI AND HALMONI'S TRIP (1997)

Carolyn Phelan

SOURCE: A review of *Yunmi and Halmoni's Trip,* in *Booklist,* Vol. 94, No. 2, September 15, 1997, p. 240.

As readers of Choi's *Halmoni and the Picnic* (1993) know, Yunmi is a Korean-American girl whose grandmother, Halmoni, has come to stay with Yunmi and her parents in New York City. In this sequel, Halmoni goes home to Seoul for a visit, taking Yunmi for her first trip to see Korea and to meet extended family there. In the first book, Halmoni felt insecure in a strange country; here the tables are turned, as Yunmi visits a country foreign to her. They do a little sightseeing and observe different customs, but the heart of the story is Yunmi's growing fear that Halmoni will decide to stay in Korea. Like Guback's *Luka's Quilt* (1994) and Kellogg's *Best Friends* (1986), this book portrays a likable child confused and sometimes overwhelmed by her mixed emotions. The text is longer than in most picture books, but the story flows well and the expressive watercolor paintings [by Karen Dugan] will hold children's attention. This book transcends Korean or English, speaking the universal language of the heart.

Margaret A. Chang

SOURCE: A review of *Yunmi and Halmoni's Trip,* in *School Library Journal,* Vol. 43, No. 10, October, 1997, p. 89.

In *Halmoni and the Picnic,* Yunmi's grandmother went to New York City to take care of her while her parents worked, and charmed Yunmi's classmates during a class trip. Now Halmoni is taking the girl back to Korea for a memorial celebration of her late husband's birthday, and it is Yunmi's turn to feel like an outsider. Halmoni, who was so isolated and lonely in New York, is greeted by a large and loving family. Even her cat and dog welcome her back. Yunmi's cousins act as tour guides to the sights of Seoul, and the girl helps prepare Korean dumplings for the picnic at Grandfather's grave. At the memorial, worries overwhelm her. Halmoni seems so happy here that she may not want to return to New York. Not surprisingly, the woman reassures her American granddaughter, "We're lucky because we both have two families." This gentle, predictable story is more an introduction to Korean customs than a plot-driven narrative. Realistic illustrations of Yunmi's family, framed with borders suggesting Korean fabric design, add greatly to the book's appeal. Dugan's carefully composed paintings, glowing with color, convey the warm affection between granddaughter and grandmother.

Additional coverage of Choi's life and career is contained in the following source published by Gale Research: *Something about the Author,* Vol. 73.

Sonia (Wolff) Levitin

1934-

German-born American author of fiction and picture books.

Major works include *Journey to America* (1970, reprinted, 1993), *Roanoke: A Novel of the Lost Colony* (1973), *The No-Return Trail* (1978), *The Return* (1987), and *Incident at Loring Groves* (1988).

INTRODUCTION

Levitin's writing output has covered a wide range of subjects, including picture books for elementary graders based on Jewish folktales, and humorous fiction about high school life. Levitin is, however, most recognized for her fiction that takes place in actual historical settings, narrated by imaginary participants in the events. One theme that recurs in Levitin's historical fiction is the importance of her Jewish heritage. Three of her books—*Journey to America, Silver Days* (1989), and *Annie's Promise* (1993)—though fiction, are semi-autobiographical accounts of her own family's emigration from Nazi Germany to the United States, and the subsequent difficulties they encountered as they settled into their new life as Americans. Likewise, *The Return* focuses on Operation Moses, a Jewish-sponsored rescue in which Ethiopian Jews were smuggled to Jerusalem from refugee camps in Sudan. Levitin researched this book so well, speaking to many of the rescued Ethiopian Jews and their supporters, that a rabbit from Los Angeles could not believe Levitin had not been there herself. "How did you ever do it?" the rabbi once wrote to Levitin. "The stark accuracy, the mores, ways, feelings, practices, beliefs of an esoteric people— . . . I have grasped many an Ethiopian shoulder in alternate embrace, looked into a lot of eyes and listened to a lot of confidences, and all the little grains of information that clung to me in the process attest and confirm that you did it and did it just right." Levitin's other historical novels are equally well researched and based on actual events: *Roanoke: A Novel of the Lost Colony*, based on stories of the lost colonists, *The No-Return Trail,* about the first woman to travel to California by wagon train, and *Escape from Egypt* (1994), based on the story in Exodus. Critics have praised Levitin's authentic portrayal of historical events, her "direct, unsentimental prose," and her evocation of Jewish culture. Sheila Klass declared *The Return,* a novel that won major awards in both the United States and Europe, to be "crammed with history, as Sonia Levitin, the author of other distinguished books for young people about Jewish history, here tells the story of an entire people."

While some of Levitin's books for young adults are pure fun, the bulk of her work stresses serious themes of

mutual respect among all races and religions, and each person's moral obligation to look out for his or her fellow human beings. The thread that runs through Levitin's fiction, in both historic and contemporary settings, is the perspective she gives to her young protagonists. By and large, the viewpoints are those of teenagers on the verge of adulthood who are trying to make sense of the people and the world around them. Critics have commended Levitin's ability to create realistic characters that experience universal coming-of-age dilemmas. Of *Incident at Loring Groves,* Elizabeth Mellet commented, "This is a disturbing and all too believable look at teenagers growing up today." Levitin's young protagonists examine their relationships with family and friends, and explore the values they have been taught as they try to decide what to believe in and how to focus their lives. These themes are evident in all her books for young adults. Lisa in *Journey to America* and *Silver Days,* Annie in *Annie's Promise*, William in *Roanoke*, Nancy in *The No-Return Trail*, Cassie and Ken in *Incident at Loring Groves*, Mark in *The Mark of Conte* (1976), and Desta in *The Return* are all teenagers facing new challenges and difficulties, sometimes funny, sometimes tragic, that pull them out of the comforts of childhood and into the world of adult decisions and responsibility. Their common condition is like that of Lisa, who has just arrived in America, "The problem now is to assimilate without compromising her own identity." Nor does Levitin give pat answers or solve all the youngsters' problems. Questions are often left hanging as to what is the best choice, but readers are always left confident that these young people will come through with lessons well learned and their identities intact. In a paper she presented at the International Symposium on Jewish Children's Literature, Levitin wrote, "We have enough stories about bunnies and pine trees and talking toys to last a lifetime—we need books about real people having real problems and solving them with a mind to reverence, freedom, and justice." Interested in people and their past, their desires and goals, Levitin writes with a mission, as she explained in *Something about the Author,* "to be a mind-bridge between people of various colors, types, and persuasions. . . . I admit it, persuasion is surely the aim of the writer. Mine is to persuade beautifully, with clarity and in honesty. This demands self-examination and self-knowledge, both of which are attained only through a lifetime of effort—and then one is ever doubtful."

Biographical Information

Levitin was born in 1934 in Berlin. Her family was prosperous, but when Sonia was four years old, they left all they owned to flee the Jewish persecutions of Hitler's Nazi Germany and come, after many difficulties, to the United States. "The Holocaust experience left its deep mark on me," Levitin recalled in an account of her life that she wrote for *Something about the Author Autobiography Series (SAAS)*. "It is agonizing for me as a Jew to realize that our people were almost exterminated; it is equally agonizing, as a human being, to have to admit to the evil that humans can do to one another." Levitin's father and mother worked menial jobs to survive, and, in time, moved the family from New York City to Los Angeles, where Sonia grew up. Young Sonia became an avid reader and at age eleven wrote to Laura Ingalls Wilder, beloved author of the "Little House on the Prairie" novels, to confess that she wanted to become a writer. "To my great joy," she recalled in *SAAS*, "[I] received a reply, which remains among my treasures to this day." As Levitin progressed through school she continued to be drawn to the arts, writing poems and short stories and learning how to paint and play the piano. She later attended the University of California, Berkeley, where she met her husband, Lloyd Levitin. She received a bachelor of science degree in 1956 from the University of Pennsylvania and taught school for a year until she became pregnant and decided to stay home to raise her family. To make full use of her time she resolved to become a writer in earnest, and with encouragement from her husband, she became a part-time writing student at San Francisco State College. Levitin's career as a writer began modestly. To gain experience, she contributed articles to newspapers and periodicals. As an exercise, she eventually began writing a longer narrative based on the tribulations that her family experienced when she was very young. This story, which she originally intended only for her own children, grew over the course of several years into *Journey to America,* published in 1970. "With *Journey to America,*" Levitin wrote in *SAAS,* "I felt that my career was launched, and that I had found my niche. I loved writing for young people. I felt that in this genre I could be both gentle and serious, idealistic and pragmatic. I realized that I happen to possess a wonderful memory for the details of my own childhood, for smells and sights and sounds, how faces looked, how feelings felt, and what childhood was really all about."

Major Works

Journey to America, Levitin's first book, is a fictionalized account of her own family's escape from Nazi Germany. Papa, anticipating a worsening of already frightening conditions in Berlin, decides to go to America to prepare a place for his family's refuge. Life is very dangerous for Jews in Germany. Those who travel are considered highly suspicious, but Papa gets to New York City, and soon after, Mama and the three girls leave for a "vacation" in Switzerland. They bribe officials and former colleagues for their help, carrying what they can, and leaving behind their valuables, their friends, and the prosperous life they have known. As tourists, they cannot bring money out of Germany, nor obtain work permits for Switzerland, so they become poor refugees who must face hunger, humiliation, separation, and illness while they wait for Papa to send for them. However, they also find kind and compassionate people who help them until they are finally reunited with Papa in America. Told in the first person by Lisa Platt, the middle daughter, the story evokes not only a personal history of World War II, but the very real thoughts and emotions of a teenager coming into her adulthood. Of *Journey to America,* Ruth P. Bull commented in *The Booklist,* "The first-person narrative reflects the middle girl's experience with a crumbling world in which friends and families are scattered or killed, hunger and illness threaten, and people show unexpected cruelty or kindness. Commendably, neither issues nor ideals intrude on the reader abstractly, but emerge naturally from the human condition portrayed in the story."

Levitin's most highly acclaimed book is *The Return.* Like *Journey to America,* it presents a true historical event in the fictionalized account of a family of Jewish refugees escaping persecution in their homeland, told from the perspective of an adolescent girl. The dramatic difference is that these refugees are from Ethiopia, and the escape is "Operation Moses," a secret undertaking that rescued over 8,000 Ethiopian Jews in 1984-85 by smuggling them out of a refugee camp in Sudan and airlifting them to Jerusalem. The orphaned Desta, a young Ethiopian Jewish girl on the verge of womanhood, tells the story. Hated and feared by their fellow Ethiopians, who call them *falasha* (stranger) and *buda* (evil eye), Desta's people, descended from King Solomon and the Queen of Sheba, are kept imprisoned in their mountain villages by the Communist government and peasant soldiers who exploit and abuse them. When soldiers begin to descend upon their village, Desta, her older brother, and younger sister leave quickly, neglecting to bring food and unable to meet Desta's betrothed, Dan, and his family, who were to escape with them. As the siblings make their way to the refugee camp in Sudan, tragedy and misfortune befall them. Bandits kill Desta's resourceful brother, and she is left to bury him and take charge of her sickly younger sister. Villagers, who recognize her as *falasha* when she tries to buy food, stone Desta. The foul water they are forced to drink sickens her and her sister. They meet up with Dan to find that his father has been arrested, and Dan is proceeding to take his elderly grandmother to Jerusalem as his father would have wished. Dan is himself arrested as the party is sneaking across the border into Sudan, and when they at last reach the refugee camp, hunger, sickness, and death meet them. Eventually Desta, her sister, Dan's grandmother, and a cousin are taken in by the other Jews in the camp, given a precious place on the mysterious night bus that takes them to an airplane and at last to Jerusalem, where they are welcomed home. Desta is reunited with Dan, who she finds is as unready for marriage as she is, and the family they have become begins its new life in Israel. Marcus Crouch said of *The Return*, "[It] is one of Ms. Levitin's triumphs that we accept without question the immediacy and fluency of a narrative from an illiterate adolescent. So tense is the drama, so grave its physical and moral implications, that there is no place for a reader's skepticism. . . . Here is an important novel, for its subject certainly and also for the tone, free both of anger and self-pity, in which it is told."

Roanoke: A Novel of the Lost Colony and *The No-Return Trail* are also historical fiction with teenage protagonists. Set in 1587, *Roanoke* follows the story of an orphaned apprentice, sixteen-year-old William Wythers, who travels to Virginia with Governor John White and a group of English colonists. When the ship's captain refuses to sail to Chesapeake, the colonists land on Roanoke Island where they are met by Manteo, a Native American who has met Queen Elizabeth and feels friendship towards the English. The colonists build houses and start farms, a baby girl is born, William's friendship with Manteo's tribe develops, and he eventually falls in love with Manteo's cousin, Telana. This friendship saves William's life. When a hostile tribe attacks the colonists, Manteo's early warning allows William to escape the slaughter with the baby, his godchild, Virginia Dare. William marries Telana, and disappears into the North American wilderness. Nancy Berkowitz observed, "The plot moves swiftly, but the characterizations and the descriptions of 16th-century English life, colonialism in American, and Indian culture are the backbone of this fascinating look at early North American history."

Set on the western frontier of the United States in 1841, *The No-Return Trail* is told by seventeen-year-old Nancy Kelsey, the only woman to complete the trip from Missouri to California on the first wagon train. As with *Roanoke*, Levitin strove to make the book as historically accurate as possible, adding only the fictional elements necessary to flesh out the story. The novel begins as Nancy and her husband, Ben, make plans to join the wagon train that leaves Sapling Grove, Missouri, in 1841. Although the group of pioneers is small, they are all determined to discover for themselves the riches they have heard exist in California. The trip starts off well, with an experienced party of missionaries and their guide, but when the majority turn off the trail to head for Oregon, the remainder, heading for California, become subject to overwhelming hardship. They abandon their wagons and livestock, their horses are stolen by Indians, and they face illness, quicksand, and hunger. At last they reach their longed-for destination, with Nancy declaring her love for her husband and her life.

With *Incident at Loring Groves,* Levitin tries a new genre, although she continues to explore coming-of-age themes. This book is a mystery set in contemporary Loring Groves, an upscale California town. A group of teenagers, who exemplify a variety of relationships, decide to indulge in an after-prom party at a deserted summerhouse. Not everyone is happy to be there, but group mentality takes over and no one wants to go against the crowd. Drugs and alcohol appear and are passed around, but things turn sour when the group discovers the murdered body of a classmate who has been missing for several days. Levitin focuses the story on one of the school's most popular couples, Ken and Cassidy, who are trying to work out their relationship. When the other kids decide to keep the body a secret to avoid getting themselves in trouble, both Cassidy and Ken are disturbed. The book follows their thought processes as they try to sort through their guilt about doing the wrong thing and their fears about doing the right thing. Ken and Cassidy figure out who the murderer must be, and, in the end, they tell the police investigator everything they know and suspect. Along the way, these young people must make difficult and often ambiguous decisions as they try to figure out who they are as people, what is important, and what they believe in. Reviewing *Incident at Loring Groves*, Hazel Rochman noted, "[The] moral conflicts are presented with complexity and drama. What Levitin makes convincing are how easy it is to rationalize ('We didn't kill her . . . It isn't our responsibility') and how evil grows not only from action but also from not caring enough to get involved." A *Publishers Weekly* contributor further praised the work as "a searingly honest portrayal of adolescent society."

Awards

A prolific writer, Levitin has won many awards over her long career including, in 1981, the Southern California Council on Literature for Children and Young People Award for distinguished contribution to the field of children's literature. Her first book, *Journey to America*, won the National Jewish Book Award in children's literature and the American Library Association (ALA)

Notable Book citation in 1970. *Journey to America* was also a Junior Literary Guild selection. *Who Owns the Moon?* received an ALA Notable Book citation in 1973. *Roanoke: A Novel of the Lost Colony* was nominated for the Dorothy Canfield Fisher Award, the Georgia Children's Book Award, and the Mark Twain Award. *The Mark of Conte* received the Southern California Council on Literature for Children and Young People Award for fiction in 1976 and was nominated for the California Young Readers Medal in the junior high school category in 1982. *The No-Return Trail* received the Golden Spur Award from Western Writers of America and the Lewis Carroll Shelf Award in 1978. This book was also a Junior Literary Guild selection. *The Return* won the National Jewish Book Award in children's literature, the PEN Los Angeles Award for young adult fiction, the Association of Jewish Libraries Sydney Taylor Award, Austrian Youth Prize, the Catholic Children's Book Prize (Germany), a Parent's Choice Honor Book citation, an ALA Best Book for Young Adults citation, and a nomination for the Dorothy Canfield Fisher Award, all in 1988. *Incident at Loring Groves* received the Edgar Allan Poe Award from the Mystery Writers of America and nominations for the Dorothy Canfield Fisher Award and the Nevada State Award, all in 1989. *Silver Days* was named a Sydney Taylor Book Award Honor Book in 1989.

AUTHOR'S COMMENTARY

Sonia Levitin

SOURCE: "'The Return': Sonia Levitin, Children's Book Award Winner," in *Judaica Librarianship*, Vol. 4, No. 2, Spring, 1988 & Winter, 1989, pp. 171-73.

Who knows exactly when a book is born? I remember being in the second grade, learning about the animals of Africa, and I was intrigued. I imagined going to Africa; I was excited at the thought of all those people, so different from me, yet also alike—for aren't people everywhere basically the same? I've always thought so—one of the reasons I write is to proclaim this idea. We are all alike in our needs, our desires, our capacities for good and for evil. The conflict between good and evil interests me profoundly. *The Return* is such a story.

I was led to it one Rosh Hashanah about five years ago, when our rabbi spoke about the existence of a desperately poor community of Jews living in Ethiopia. Black Jews, who followed Torah to the letter, who have been isolated from mainstream Judaism since Biblical times. Jews who claim to be the descendants of King Solomon and the Queen of Sheba. I was intrigued. Then, I was frustrated, as my attempts to learn more about these people were thwarted. But I've learned in my career that frustration is often the impetus to a book. Frustration and anger and concern all combine into a growing cauldron of energy—and then it usually takes one more

catalyst to set the book free. The catalyst this time was Operation Moses.

Operation Moses was a heroic and remarkable feat that took place in 1984-1985. In secret, some eight to ten thousand Ethiopian Jews were airlifted out of Africa and brought to Israel, their ancestral homeland, the land of their prayers and dreams.

The moment I heard about Operation Moses, I knew this was my book to write, and that it would be the most difficult and also the most thrilling book of my career. Because this story brought together so many elements of my own past and my own yearning, it was a story so rich with potential to show the best in people, to inspire us and give us courage. Operation Moses is the antithesis to much we hear that is wrong with the world. Operation Moses showed us that there are still people who will save, who dream bold dreams and have the determination to make them come true. On paper, Operation Moses was impossible. In reality, Operation Moses happened in our own time, among our own people, and it must never be forgotten.

Africa is a continent steeped in tragedy. Famine. War. Disease. Drought. Flood. All these have taken their toll along with the human scourges of exploitation, interference, and neglect. For years I have been concerned about Africa, that beautiful land so rich in variety and possibility, so horribly neglected. It is neglect that called me to write this book. As a child of the Holocaust, I know well the fruits of neglect. The Holocaust memory is something I have had to live with every day of my life. And I have also lived with the guilt—both individual and collective, of seeing evils all around me today and lacking the commitment or energy or courage to make a difference. Maybe my power lies in the pen; maybe I am to be a witness to events, a bridge between cultures. I only know that this book cried out to be written, and it was mine to write. Why mine? Because I knew what it was to be persecuted. To be poor. To be hounded out of the country of my birth. To want freedom and security. And I knew, also, what it is to long for Eretz Yisrael, to want and need to put my feet on that soil, to feel my face pressed against the Western Wall, to see the Jews of the world mingled there, to come home.

That was the personal part. The writer in me saw this as the story of the decade, if not of the century; I was so intense and fired up about writing it that I was sure every author in the free world would rush to do this novel before I could get started. In 1985, I made two trips to Israel. The first was to see for myself the Beta Yisrael. I was not yet committed to the book, but wanted to reach out, to say to them in effect, Welcome.

I took a taxi to a hotel in Netanya where the Ethiopians were temporarily housed; I begged to see them, and was probably taken for a crazy person. But after about an hour of negotiating and convincing the officials of my honorable intentions, I finally got an interview with the director of the place. After twenty minutes of explaining the Ethiopians' plight and the reasons for keeping curious writers away, he invited me to visit the nursery. There I saw the black babies. Sabras. There I saw an Ethiopian mother, already speaking Hebrew, wearing Western clothes, in every way emulating the Israelis. As she bent over to pick up her baby, I saw that around her neck was tattooed a necklace of dark welts, African style. The paradox and the juxtaposition of cultures settled it; I had to write this story.

Back home, I began researching in the library, learning all I could about Ethiopia, its history, language, culture. I made plans to return to Israel, and I began the search for people who had traveled to Ethiopia, which resulted, finally, in dozens of interviews. For once, I would get the story immediately and first-hand. So often stories come to a writer through the filters of time and other people; this time I would be there. I could not make myself black, I could not become an Ethiopian Jew—but I could immerse myself in their lives. Total immersion for months and months is for me not only the best way to write, but the most interesting way to live.

To that end, I contacted everybody I had ever heard of in Israel who might be involved with the Ethiopian immigrants—and when I got to Israel on my first research trip, I had twenty-five appointments for interviews in the space of nine days. It was an absolutely exhilarating experience. In Jerusalem, I needed but five hours of sleep a night. The rest of the time I worked. I spoke to government officials, social workers, reporters, rabbis, teachers, counselors, doctors. I visited schools, absorption centers, homes. And I got so many stories, that when I got home, Desta was already a reality, her adventures borrowed from the many true experiences, both victorious and tragic, that I had heard about.

People ask me, have you been to Ethiopia? No. I studied everything I could on film and videotape and in magazines, watching the same bit of film again and again, so that I felt I'd memorized the look, the feel, the smell of the country—what grows there—how a mud hut is built—plowing, pottery smithing, Amharic words, songs. I read scholarly works and doctoral theses on the culture of the Ethiopians, so that when I came to write their story, I felt that I knew their thoughts, the cadence of their speech, their preoccupations, their ways. Presumptuous? Maybe—but when the book was done, a woman in Los Angeles who had made many missions to Ethiopia said to me—"Have you really never been there? It is impossible to believe, because you brought it back to me in a thousand ways." A rabbi who worked with the Ethiopians in the various stages of absorption wrote me: "How did you ever do it? The stark accuracy, the mores, ways, feelings, practices, beliefs of an esoteric people—and Desta, so intensely Jewish in such a strange way . . . I have grasped many an Ethiopian shoulder in alternate embrace, looked into a lot of eyes and listened to a lot of confidences, and all the little grains of information that clung to me in the process attest and confirm that you did it and did it just right . . . "

But of course, the praise for this story rightly belongs with the people who made the true escape happen. All over the free world there were people who worked quietly, tirelessly, to bring it about. Our own State Department was involved to the highest echelons. People took incredible risks. One man I tried to contact, who was responsible for organizing the transport from Sudan to Israel, had disappeared. He had been spirited away to South America, because his life was in danger after Operation Moses became public knowledge. In Europe, America, and Israel, small groups of Jews held endless meetings, raised money, plotted and planned how to save a beleaguered community of black Jews, not from famine or political persecution, but from religious extinction.

The Ethiopians cried out to world Jewry, not because of their poverty, but from despair at not being allowed to teach Torah to their children. They were a dying race. Once a million strong, they were reduced to about 25,000 souls in the 1980s. And now people responded. That was the story I had to tell. Because what happened in 1984 confirmed to me that our Passover reading of the exodus from Egypt, and the return to Jerusalem from Babylon—these are not something esoteric or distant, but valid for us, today. There are still people to save, and the risks are no different now than they were in ancient times. Freeing the captives is always complex. It is always difficult. It is always costly.

Imagine the rescue. What could be more complex? Someone had to go to Ethiopia, to communicate to these distant villagers that the time for their return to Jerusalem, that time longed for and prayed for these past 2000 years, had come now. Now. Avoiding the secret police, giving encouragement without running afoul of the government—these were some of the complexities. And then there was the further risk that the Ethiopian Jews would actually respond, for they had been tricked before, had been led out only to be robbed or killed by unscrupulous people.

The Ethiopian Jews responded. They piled their few possessions onto their backs, walked down cliffs, through the desert into that hell-hole called Sudan. This trek took weeks. They traveled at night to avoid bandits, soldiers, and hostile tribes. Secretly they crossed the border into Sudan. There they waited for the rescue that God had declared in the Book would someday come. Who among us would do what the Ethiopian Jews did, risking everything as an act of faith?

Difficulties? Imagine the difficulties of putting this plan in motion—contracting for airplanes, bribing officials, of keeping the Ethiopian Jews alive in those camps in Sudan, where they had to hide the fact that they were Jewish. Some waited for months until they were brought secretly to Israel. Imagine their arrival in Israel. I cried when I wrote about it. Imagine the further difficulties of helping them to adapt to their new lives.

Was it costly? You bet it was. There is always a price

on the head of every captive person—man, woman and child—and to think otherwise is foolish and naive. But the price was paid. Nothing was too complex, too difficult, too costly. And lives were saved. That is why I wrote **The Return.** Because it shows what can happen when people of courage are allied with people of conscience. Nothing we write or say can equal the achievement of saving even a single life.

There are still lives left to save in Ethiopia. Operation Moses ended too soon, because the secret airlift became known. Now families are split; the Ethiopian government does not allow the remaining Jews to leave and join their families in Israel. As before, the situation is complex. Difficult. Costly.

The good part of the story is that these people, just out of the stone age, today in Israel are living productive lives, have joined the twentieth century, have indeed come home. Boys less than a year out of African mud huts have already begun to work on computers. I have seen Ethiopian boys repairing autos, working in woodshops, making tools. I have heard the children talking Hebrew and English. I have visited with their mothers and fathers who are students, factory workers, nurses, teachers. Are they having problems? Yes. Aren't we all? Israel isn't heaven. They'll have problems. But they are alive, and Israel has let them in. Israel has no quota. Ten and twenty years from today, we will see the magnificent harvest that this aliya has brought.

On a personal level, this book was my deepest experience as a writer. In looking for the story line, I met wonderful and remarkable people from all over the world. And the story isn't over. I have gone back again and will return, I hope, many times. Someday I will write a sequel; I'm not in a hurry. My last trip to Israel confirmed my desire to write another adult novel, this time with a Jewish theme. Certainly, writing **The Return** will have helped prepare me for this. Because as I was writing **The Return,** something new happened in my work. Early on, I made a decision. I would begin each writing session with meditation and prayer. I would pray to God to release me from my ego, to let me feel and live this story. To turn away from all thoughts of myself, or what the book might do for me. This book was for them. About them. About Desta—whose name means "happiness"—and all the people in her life. And so, I let go of myself, and I became Desta, and as the incidents of the story unfolded, I could be true to *her* experience, her desires. When Desta and Joas and Almaz escaped, I knew how she would quake at having to light a match on the Sabbath. When her brother died, Desta still carried herself with dignity, and did not cry out against God. She wept, and she covered her brother's naked body, and then she prayed to find a place to bury her brother. She finds a ledge, a rocky outcropping, and she does what must be done, after which she takes charge of her little sister who wants to go home. "We are going home," Desta says, "Home to Jerusalem." And when Desta and Almaz are desperate, hungry and unable to buy food because they are Jews, they meet

a Moslem family, and they help each other. That small scene meant a great deal to me; it expanded Desta's humanity, it was a reaching out beyond Judaism, beyond one's own problems, to the universal and the eternal.

These things are not planned in writing a novel. They happen out of the emotional impact of the work, the combination of research and yearning. Desta's reunion at the Wall is purely my own. At first I thought it too highly personal ever to share. Then I realized that since I had invented Desta, was her mother and her creator, I could not hold anything back. I gave her my supreme moment and my vision.

How can I thank you enough for honoring my book? To be here with you, with so many familiar faces, all of you so warm and so caring about Jewish literature, is not only an honor, but a great joy. You and I are partners. We love the same traditions. We hope for the same kind of future. We believe that through heroic stories we are inspired, emboldened, kept free.

TITLE COMMENTARY

JOURNEY TO AMERICA (first novel in the "Platt Family" trilogy, 1970; reprinted, 1993)

Sidney D. Long

SOURCE: A review of *Journey to America,* in *The Horn Book Magazine,* Vol. XLVI, No. 2, April, 1970, p. 162.

In the Berlin of 1938 the handwriting was already clearly on the wall. But not all Jewish families could read it; and many that could, still felt bound to Germany by bonds too strong to break. The tension and the heartache of the time are caught in this story of one family's escape. Arthur Platt, realizing the danger, secretly leaves Berlin for America—planning to send for his wife and three daughters. For Lisa Platt, who tells the story, the months that follow are filled with excitement and anxiety. Frau Platt is almost denied her passport; the baby, four-year-old Annie, senses the "vacation" to Switzerland is really an escape, and her knowledge threatens the secrecy of the plan. Once in Switzerland they are refugees and eventually must separate—dependent upon the kindness and help of others. But Frau Platt's courage never falters, and for Lisa and her older sister Ruth it is a time of growing awareness and maturity. The illustrations [by Charles Robinson] in soft pencil give an added dimension to the text.

Gloria Levitas

SOURCE: A review of *Journey to America,* in *The New York Times Book Review,* May 24, 1970, pp. 26-27.

Narrated by Lisa Platt, the middle daughter of a middle-class Jewish family, *Journey to America* describes the Platts's escape from Nazi Germany in direct, unsentimental prose.

The author briefly sketches the humdrum background of Lisa's life: the ballet lessons, skating parties and schoolgirl pranks. Firmly anchored to reality by the warmth and devotion of her family, the girl succeeds in transforming fear into action, pain into humor as she is plunged into a nightmare world of storm troopers, indifferent bureaucrats and extortionists who prey on the misfortune of others. Escape to Switzerland, at first proves little better. Separated from her mother, she is sent to a home for refugee children run by a vicious, unfeeling profiteer—a woman who excels in the creation of petty misery. Lisa's subsequent adoption by a Christian family is a joyful prelude to the family's ultimate reunion in America.

Although Mrs. Levitin has done little to camouflage the tragedy of the Hitler years, today's children—so often overwhelmed by a sense of pervasive moral and environmental crisis—will find this story of a family's courage and devotion more thrilling than terrifying.

Ruth P. Bull

SOURCE: A review of *Journey to America,* in *The Booklist,* Vol. 66, No. 19, June 1, 1970, pp. 1214-15.

A quiet story that nevertheless sustains the suspense of a Jewish family's escape from Berlin in 1938. Three girls and their mother live in fear of Nazi harassment during their last days in Germany; once in Switzerland, they suffer poverty and frustration while waiting for tickets and passports from their father in America. The first-person narrative reflects the middle girl's experience with a crumbling world in which friends and families are scattered or killed, hunger and illness threaten, and people show unexpected cruelty or kindness. Commendably, neither issues nor ideals intrude on the reader abstractly, but emerge naturally from the human condition portrayed in the story.

Kay Weisman

SOURCE: A review of *Journey to America,* in *Booklist,* Vol. 90, No. 1, September 1, 1993, p. 61.

This reissue of Levitin's 1970 novel tells the story of a courageous Jewish family that flees Hitler's Germany in 1938. After Papa books passage to America, Mama and her three daughters travel to Switzerland for a "vacation." There, for 10 long months, they exist on practically nothing (as tourists, they can neither take money out of Germany nor obtain Swiss work permits) and wait for Papa to be able to send for them. Levitin's fine prose has not dated in the years since the book's first appearance. Libraries that need a new copy or that may

have missed the original will want to purchase this. Two sequels, *Silver Days* and *Annie's Promise,* are also available.

📖 *RITA THE WEEKEND RAT* (1971)

Janet French

SOURCE: A review of *Rita the Weekend Rat,* in *School Library Journal,* Vol. 17, No. 8, April, 1971, pp. 107-08.

TV watchers will recognize eight-year-old Cynthia and her family as typical suburban situation-comedy types: nice, wholesome people with small, wholesome problems. Bland in conception and undistinguished in delivery, the adventures of Cynthia (who calls herself a tomboy) and her white rat are not likely to generate much enthusiasm among readers who are hoping to find another "Ramona." The format militates further against the book: the type face is too small for most third graders, and older children will find the heroine's callow youth beneath their dignity.

The Booklist

SOURCE: A review of *Rita the Weekend Rat,* in *The Booklist,* Vol. 67, No. 18, May 15, 1971, p. 799.

Second-grader tomboy Cynthia has problems. She must prove to her father that she is responsible enough to keep Rita the kindergarten rat on a permanent rather than a weekend basis; she has to keep thinking up such projects as a rat race and a moneymaking paper drive to maintain her status as the only girl in the Boys' Club; she worries about her older brother's inability to learn to tie knots; and she must choose between Boys' Club and Brownies. Although its heroine is too young for its readership the lively story with laughable situations and natural dialog has much the same appeal as the Henry Huggins books.

📖 *ROANOKE: A NOVEL OF THE LOST COLONY* (1973)

Kirkus Reviews

SOURCE: A review of *Roanoke: A Novel of the Lost Colony,* in *Kirkus Reviews,* Vol. XLI, No. 13, July 1, 1973, pp. 691-92.

The word *Croatoan* carved on a tree was the only clue left by the vanished Roanoke colony, and Levitan projects into this cryptic message a happy ending for orphaned apprentice William Wythers who finds the New World of his dreams living among his Indian friends on Croatoan. While Governor White, his son-in-law Ananias Dare and the other leaders of the expedition debate the colony's proper relationship to Roanoke's "savages," William makes friends with Manteo—an Indian who has returned from England where he met the English "Weroance" Elizabeth—and falls in love with Manteo's cousin Telana. The young "pauper" feels more at home with the Indian way of looking at things than he does among his fellow Englishmen who have brought their ideas of class with them into the wilderness. William's ability to slip peacefully into the ways of Croatoan after the destruction of Roanoke—through hunger and measles and Indian attacks—is no doubt overly romanticized, but the English settlers have a kind of warty individuality that makes them both realistic and ultimately dispensable to William, while his observations—though influenced by his own isolation—are often strikingly acute.

Nancy Berkowitz

SOURCE: A review of *Roanoke: A Novel of the Lost Colony,* in *School Library Journal,* Vol. 20, No. 2, October, 1973, pp. 126-27.

In 1587, 16-year-old William Wythers, an orphaned runaway apprentice, joins the small band of colonists who are to found the first English settlement in America. Many of the group are convinced the New World will be filled with gold and jewels, and even temperate John White, the designated governor, is unprepared when wily Captain Ferdinando refuses to sail to Chesapeake and puts the travelers off on Roanoke Island. There, they are welcomed by Manteo, an Indian who was taken by Sir Walter Raleigh to Elizabeth I's court. The colonists build houses and begin to farm the land, and a baby, Virginia Dare, is born to John White's daughter. William befriends Manteo and finds himself drawn to Manteo's tribe, especially when he falls in love with the latter's cousin, Telana. His closeness to the Indians causes mistrust among some of the settlers and, after John White returns to England, the spirit of the colony disintegrates. Manteo's friendship eventually saves William and the baby Virginia from an attack by the hostile Wingos, and William marries Telana, never learning the fate of any survivors of the settlement. The author presents a logical explanation for the disappearance of the Lost Colony and states the recorded facts in an epilogue. The plot moves swiftly, but the characterizations and the descriptions of 16th-Century English life, colonialism in America, and Indian culture are the backbone of this fascinating look at early North American history.

Publishers Weekly

SOURCE: A review of *Roanoke: A Novel of the Lost Colony,* in *Publishers Weekly,* Vol. 204, No. 15, October 8, 1973, p. 96.

In 1587 William Wythers, a 16-year-old runaway apprentice, joins Governor John White's party. The group is bound for Virginia with supplies for the original 15 Roanoke Island settlers, whom they never find. White's party is threatened by the hostile Wanchese, leader of the Wingos, an Indian who had been taken to London by earlier voyagers and hates the white man. Manteo, a friendly "native," tries to mediate between the settlers and their enemies, but peace is short lived. In the end, the only survivors are Wythers, Telena, the half-breed he loves, and a baby, Virginia Dare. The book, based on actual people and events, can add a valuable dimension to the young reader's understanding of this tragic period.

Zena Sutherland

SOURCE: A review of *Roanoke: A Novel of the Lost Colony,* in *Bulletin of the Center for Children's Books,* Vol. 27, No. 7, March, 1974, p. 113.

A convincing and well-written fictionalized account of the Roanoke colony is told by one of the younger members, sixteen-year-old William Wythers. William describes the long and arduous journey, the futile attempts to build a permanent settlement, the dissent among the colonists, and the lack of understanding between the settlers and the Indians. In love with an Indian girl, William has become friendly with the members of her tribe and warns the other colonists that he has heard of an impending attack from another, hostile tribe—but they take no heed. All save William and the baby who is his godchild, Virginia Dare, are killed. A lively adjunct to a historical unit on colonial settlement, and an excellent adventure story. . . .

WHO OWNS THE MOON? (1973)

Denise Murcko Wilms

SOURCE: A review of *Who Owns the Moon?* in *The Booklist,* Vol. 70, No. 7, December 1, 1973, p. 387.

An engaging tale of three good friends who farmed the same mountain every day and argued together every night. Abel, Nagel, and Zeke fought about whose cow was best and whose wife was worst and, having exhausted all other subjects, began to argue about who owned the moon. When they continued to bicker instead of farm, their wives insisted that they go to a wise teacher, who not only settled the question of ownership, but put a satisfactory end to all their disputes. The story is appealing in itself, and [John] Larrecq's four-color illustrations wittily picture the peasant characters and their surroundings.

Zena Sutherland

SOURCE: A review of *Who Owns the Moon?* in *Bulletin of the Center for Children's Books,* Vol. 27, No. 5, January, 1974, pp. 80-81.

A tale in the folk tradition is told in sprightly style, the illustrations (very handsome indeed) capturing both the earthy peasant flavor and the noodlehead humor of the story. Three farmers who argued incessantly about everything claim ownership of the beautiful full moon; when it wanes they are furious: a piece has been stolen! Even when it completes its phases and is full again the three foolish men dispute ownership. Their harassed wives hatch a scheme; each convinces her husband to talk to the sage of the village, the Teacher. He decides that the moon will belong to each man for two days a week, and that on Sundays it will belong to everyone; each man must stay home on the nights he owns the moon and on Sundays they must all sit together in peace. Result: contented wives, pacified farmers, and an engaging story to read or tell.

JASON AND THE MONEY TREE (1974)

Publishers Weekly

SOURCE: A review of *Jason and the Money Tree,* in *Publishers Weekly,* Vol. 205, No. 3, January 21, 1974, p. 86.

This is a refreshing whimsy, a fairy tale with overtones of very real economic absurdities. With a ten dollar bill inherited from his grandfather, Jason discovers he can *grow* 10 dollar bills in a flower pot in the backyard. But the bonanza turns into a nightmare as he tries to conceal his multiplying wealth. His efforts exhaust him and damage his relations with family and friends. Finally, his sister Dinah, a toddler, resolves the situation when she finds the hidden harvest and flushes it down the toilet—a fixture which fascinates her. Ms. Levitin is a versatile writer. Her **Roanoke: A Novel of the Lost Colony** was also a good read. No history here, but lots of fun.

Kirkus Reviews

SOURCE: A review of *Jason and the Money Tree,* in *Kirkus Reviews,* Vol. XLII, No. 6, March 15, 1974, p. 300.

We never quite figured out exactly what lesson Grandfather hoped to teach when he left Jason a ten dollar bill that sprouts into an honest-to-goodness money tree, but all that seed money causes Jason nothing but anxiety from the start. Jason wonders whether the tree's fruit is really legal tender and frantically seeks odd jobs so that he will be able to account for his growing wad of bills. His preoccupation neatly parallels his father's worries over the approaching bar exam and the family's overburdened budget, and his sense of guilt makes one wonder whether Jason knows more than we do about the money missing from his storekeeper friend's cash register which he secretly replenishes. After the tree dries up from several days without care, Jason realizes that his negligence was not entirely accidental. But that's only one articulated example of the free-floating psychological insights that make this more than just another dig at the root of all evil.

THE MARK OF CONTE (1976)

Robert Unsworth

SOURCE: A review of *The Mark of Conte,* in *School Library Journal,* Vol. 22, No. 8, April, 1976, p. 90.

Levitin's wacky story will appeal to any students who have ever been hassled by a school computer. Conte Mark, a High Intelligence Child (HIC) in a Southern California high school, discovers that the computer has him registered as Mark Conte as well. Frustrated in his attempts to explain the error to Mr. Rhinefinger, his counselor, ("Read your Freshman Orientation Booklets. Everything will be *crystal* clear"), Conte declares war on the computer and Vista Mar High School. He devises an intricate scheme that will have him remain registered under both names and graduate in two years. How he manages to keep the scheme afloat with the help of his neighbor Greg Gaff and band manager Charlotta Jones ("A nice girl—but too generous") is the plot in toto. Every character is a caricature—the paranoid school counselor, scheming students, programmed computer science teacher, liberated artist mother, and psychologist father—but this zips along at a remarkably brisk pace.

Virginia Haviland

SOURCE: A review of *The Mark of Conte,* in *The Horn Book Magazine,* Vol. LII, No. 3, June, 1976, pp. 289-90.

The sprightly pen-and-ink sketches [by Bill Negron] that depict young people in a contemporary California high school are a key to the character of the story in which the school computer generates the action. Because of faulty registration printouts, Conte Mark, a freshman with high intelligence and versatility as well as an unusual name, decides to assume the all-but-impossible responsibility of two class schedules, one assigned to *Mark Conte* and one to *Conte Mark.* He hopes that he can thus graduate in two instead of four years. However, after a year of frenzy, he finds he has amassed not seventy-two but a mysterious one hundred forty-four credits and is therefore ready for a diploma. Never at a loss, he makes the necessary computer input to reassign the graduation credits under the name of his dog, *Dane Great.* The story, full of verve and spirited conversation, presents an exaggerated assemblage of conniving students and faculty members and reveals a keen understanding of school power factors. Conte's juggling enables him to cope with many activities at the same time—to manage playing in the band, sports, art, and social life; on the other hand, he is normally susceptible to physical and psychological stress.

Zena Sutherland

SOURCE: A review of *The Mark of Conte,* in *Bulletin of the Center for Children's Books,* Vol. 29, No. 11, July-August, 1976, p. 177.

Conte Mark had just moved to California, had just entered the freshman class at Vista Mar high school, and had just discovered that the computer had made a mistake. He had two program cards, one for Conte Mark and one for Mark Conte. Since he was a good student and a hard worker, Conte came up with the brilliant idea of taking a double course and graduating in two years. This is a spoof, of course, but it's a spoof just this side of reality, because all of the daft, hilarious things that happen and the people in Conte's life could be true. The author writes with zest and vitality, poking fun at everything in sight, but doing it with affection, and while Conte's rocky path is strewn with some peculiar stony obstacles, the problems he and his friends cope with are very real concerns for most adolescents.

A SINGLE SPECKLED EGG (1976)

Publishers Weekly

SOURCE: A review of *A Single Speckled Egg,* in *Publishers Weekly,* Vol. 210, No. 25, December 27, 1976, p. 60.

The author and illustrator [John Larrecq] earned critical praise with the appearance of an earlier book, **Who Owns the Moon?**, and their new publication features the same cast. Farmers Abel, Nagel and Zeke vie with each other in tales of ill fortune, apprehensions of coming calamities and other miseries. When Abel's hen lays one speckled egg, Nagel says that is surely bad luck; the hen might stop laying altogether. Zeke says the egg could mean that the hen house will burn down and Abel might have to sell his farm. Other omens convince Nagel and Zeke that they too are threatened. The wives of the three men grow impatient with their mutterings and seek advice from the local wise man, Teacher. His counsel is sound and, following it, the ladies convert their spouses from pessimism and superstition. Larrecq's pictures are handsome additions to a well-told, droll tale.

Anne A. Flowers

SOURCE: A review of *A Single Speckled Egg,* in *The Horn Book Magazine,* Vol. LIII, No. 1, February, 1977, pp. 40-41.

Abel, Nagel, and Zeke, the three heroes of **Who Owns The Moon?**, appear again with their witless antics. This time they are worrying about bad luck striking their farms and are driving their wives mad with doleful prognostications of doom. After Abel's hen lays a speckled egg, Abel says "A speckled egg is not a little thing. . . . It is bad luck. Next the hen house will burn down, and I will have to sell the farm." The wives consult the Teacher, whose homespun advice returns the three sillies to their right minds. The story . . . is an amusing example of folk wisdom. The warm, cheerful illustrations, each framed in a distinctive arch, reflect medieval peasant life in an individual style but with hints of Brueghel and Wanda Gág.

BEYOND ANOTHER DOOR (1977)

Barbara Elleman

SOURCE: A review of *Beyond Another Door,* in *Booklist,* Vol. 73, No. 15, April 1, 1977, p. 1170.

With the winning of a dish at the local carnival, the extrasensory perceptions that Daria has always known she's had develop into a psychic ability to communicate with her long-dead grandmother. Visions and voices result, leaving Daria frightened and unsure of what is happening to her. Kelly, her longtime friend, is revulsed after witnessing one of the strange visitations; although hurt, Daria finds a new friendship (which seems too mature for their 13 years) with Rob, who also admits to having an occult experience. Her always precarious relationship with her mother is further damaged when Daria learns through her grandmother that she was a "love child." Too many themes and personal implications crowd the plot; and Grandmother's appearances, "looking very much like white cheesecloth a trifle damp" and accompanied by silvery angels, push the credibility factor. However, Daria's search for expression through art and her troubled situation with her mother are perceptively drawn, while the subject ensures the book's popularity.

Publishers Weekly

SOURCE: A review of *Beyond Another Door,* in *Publishers Weekly,* Vol. 211, No. 22, May 30, 1977, p. 45.

Levitin's latest novel is a beautiful, evocative tale of a 13-year-old's journey into the supernatural. Unlike some works of this nature (exploitive and ghoulish), Daria's story is rooted in reality and in the troubling emotions of adolescence. Daria feels like a freak when she wins a dish at a carnival and it reflects her dead grandmother's face instead of her own. The girl needs someone to confide in but her mother is unapproachable. Her best friend, Kelly, is frightened by evidence of Daria's ESP and shuns her. As the narrative advances, the beset heroine luckily establishes a relationship with Rob, a kindly boy. Rob's father is a student of psychic phenomena and Daria's problems become easier to cope with as she learns from him (and from experience) facts which help her to establish her identity.

Sally Holmes Holtze

SOURCE: A review of *Beyond Another Door,* in *The Horn Book Magazine,* Vol. LIII, No. 3, June, 1977, p. 315.

Thirteen-year-old Daria is an artist and a dreamer, given to occasional instances of precognition that seem to alarm her down-to-earth mother. One night she is frightened by an apparition in her room; she smells a familiar perfume and hears a voice but concocts a rational explanation for her own satisfaction. The presence returns, however; finally, a ghostly form appears and the girl realizes it is her dead grandmother. The woman says that Daria is illegitimate and talks about her mother, telling the girl to "Take care of her. . . . give her love. For both of us." Trying to discuss the experiences with Kelly, her constant companion, Daria only succeeds in ending their friendship; then she meets new people with whom she can share her interest in psychic phenomena. A visiting aunt offers the information that the grandmother had been a well-known medium who had predicted the death of her mother's lover, causing an absolute rift between the two women. With new insight, Daria understands that her overly practical mother is apprehensive about the possibility that Daria has inherited psychic powers; she muses, "she is completely separate from me. . . . We can come together or grow far apart." The treatment of psychic phenomena is never heavy-handed but is used as an effective device enabling the author to explore the relationship between the girl and her mother and to bring Daria an awareness of herself. The reader can easily identify with the mature, individualistic protagonist as she probes the complexities of love and friendship.

📖 *THE NO-RETURN TRAIL* (1978)

George Gleason

SOURCE: A review of *The No-Return Trail,* in *School Library Journal,* Vol. 24, No. 8, April, 1978, pp. 94-5.

The story of the first wagon train to travel from Missouri to California in 1841 is told from the viewpoint of Nancy Kelsey, a young wife of about 17, who really was the first woman to make the journey. Unfortunately, what should be rattling good historical fiction comes off as only modestly interesting due to a few improbabilities (jelly made of crabapples and chokecherries in May; poor travelers having rubberized sheets and matches) and a lot of talk taking the place of suspense.

Kirkus Reviews

SOURCE: A review of *The No-Return Trail,* in *Kirkus Reviews,* Vol. XLVI, No. 11, June 1, 1978, p. 600.

Drawing on memoirs of participants, and concentrating on Nancy Kelsey, a 17-year-old wife and new mother who was the only woman to make the entire trip, Levitin has constructed a fictionalized account of the first wagon train journey from Missouri to California. Heading West is about all the Kelseys and their companions know about reaching the land of oranges and ocean; luckily they make most of the trip with an experienced party of missionaries and their guide. But when the priests head off for Oregon, and with them go many of the original resettlers (including the only other women in the band), the last stragglers plod on, ditching wagons and then

mules and oxen, losing horses to Indians and wearing through their shoes, and at last stumble upon an earlier pioneer's fabled ranch—their first inkling that they are "already there—in Californ-y." On the trail the travelers have faced quicksand, illness, hunger, dissension; but none of this is dramatized, and in fact there's a disappointing tameness to the whole narrative. Similarly Nancy, despite being "strong as an ox" (her husband's boast) and "spunky" too, and despite ending the trip with an almost ecstatic love for life and for her husband, comes across as oddly bland.

Denise M. Wilms

SOURCE: A review of *The No-Return Trail,* in *Booklist,* Vol. 74, No. 20, June 15, 1978, pp. 1618-19.

Rigors of the trail are the storytelling mainstay for Levitin's re-creation of the Bidwell-Bartleson expedition that set out for California in 1841. The reactions of 17-year-old wife and mother Nancy Kelsey provide emotional substance as she watches the struggling group dwindle and worries over her strained relationship with husband Ben. The mood is generally intense, particularly near the conclusion when illness and approaching winter threaten to finish the weakened travelers. A sober undertone encourages respect for the enormity of the task these settlers undertook. Nancy Kelsey is said to be the first white woman to travel overland to California. It's unfortunate that occasional derogatory references to Indians—indigenous to these Kentuckians' views—aren't offset by multidimensional portrayals of the not-always-hostile Indian groups encountered along the trail. Absorbing, if conventional, historical fiction in spite of the ethnic omission.

📖 *REIGNING CATS AND DOGS* (1978)

Kirkus Reviews

SOURCE: A review of *Reigning Cats and Dogs,* in *Kirkus Reviews,* Vol. XLVI, No. 7, April 1, 1978, p. 417.

When Baron, their long-haired black German shepherd, was aging, Levitin's family acquired a shepherd puppy, quick-sale merchandise they named Barney. Unlike his royal predecessor, Barney turned out to be a clown prince, urinating like a female, running the other way when called, and going "wild" at the sight of young blondes wearing jeans. He also dug up Baron's bones and brought home a distressing variety of decomposing rodent carcasses and, mysteriously, the tiny bodies of two newborn kittens. From the first eyedropper feeding, Jinxie and Jessie were destined to complete this menagerie, even though Levitin never considered herself the cat-mother type. A YMCA training course extinguished Barney's less endearing behaviors (actually, he had to repeat the course), Baron was mercifully put to sleep, and the two cats secured their own household niches—

Jinxie as breakfast table centerpiece, Jessica as queen bee. Within the genre, slight but bright rather than treacly.

Zena Sutherland

SOURCE: A review of *Reigning Cats and Dogs,* in *Bulletin of the Center for Children's Books,* Vol. 32, No. 4, December, 1978, p. 66.

What better combination for a book [illustrated by Joan Berg Victor] about personal experiences with animals than a love for them, a no-nonsense approach that eschews sentimentality, a sense of humor, and a yeasty writing style? The author and her family had one dignified and aging German Shepherd and decided to get a pup of the same breed; little did they know that the pup would be beset with fears, disobedient, wilful, hostile, and in dire need of discipline (finally acquired at obedience school, where he flunked and had to take the course over) or that the two newborn kittens that were to stay for one night would become permanent and dominating members of the household. What Levitin does is make rueful fun of herself as a soft-hearted dupe, an easy mark whose facile rationalizations are easily seen through by her affectionate family, all of whom are almost as easy marks as she. Delightful for animal lovers and even for those who aren't, but who appreciate effervescent humor.

Ruth M. Stein

SOURCE: A review of *Reigning Cats and Dogs,* in *Language Arts,* Vol. 56, No. 2, February, 1979, pp. 188-89.

We learn about a family through a first-person look at its pets—Baron, the German shepherd in his tenth year, Barney, the cowardly clown of a puppy brought in as a hedge against Baron's death, and the two newborn kittens whom Barney deposits on the doorstep. The author takes her pets seriously, but herself lightly, as seen in tongue-in-cheek writing that keeps the book from turning maudlin. For animals and family lovers concerned about the care and feeding of prima donna pets through fair and less fair weather.

A SOUND TO REMEMBER (1979)

Kirkus Reviews

SOURCE: A review of *A Sound to Remember,* in *Kirkus Reviews,* Vol. XLVII, No. 17, September 1, 1979, p. 1001.

Some balm for the spirit, here, and a rustling, tingling evocation of the Jewish High Holy Days. "Long ago, in the distant land of our fathers" . . . the rabbi, incomprehensibly, chooses slow, clumsy Jacov for the singular honor of blowing the shofar, the ram's horn, on Rosh Hashanah. Villagers intercede: "Wouldn't the rabbi reconsider?" "No, thank you. Jacov was going to blow the shofar." He has practiced; but on Rosh Hashanah only a tiny crackling sound comes out the first time, then some weak trembling notes, then nothing. Jacov is "too miserable even to weep." That evening, however, the rabbi comes and confides a secret to Jacov; and on Yom Kippur, after the rabbi's devout reference to Jacov's earlier "moment of silence" ("Love for each other and for God is more important than ritual"), the two hold shofars to their lips . . . "and none could say which shofar it was that gave the call so clearly." Told with dignity and quiet animation, and illustrated—as is this artist's [Gabriel Lisowski] wont—with tender amusement.

Helen Gregory

SOURCE: A review of *A Sound to Remember,* in *School Library Journal,* Vol. 26, No. 3, November, 1979, p. 67.

On the feast of Rosh Hashanah, the Jewish New Year, and ten days later on Yom Kippur, the Day of Atonement, a member of the congregation of the temple holds the honor of blowing the ceremonial ram's horn, the shofar. This particular year, long ago in the old country, the rabbi selects the boy Jacov, despite misgivings of the elders who feel that Jacov is too slow and clumsy for such an important role in the ritual. Sure enough, on Rosh Hashanah, Jacov is too nervous to make the shofar sound. The rabbi, however, has a plan to save Yom Kippur and restore Jacov's faltering self-respect. A simple, pleasant holiday story, well told and sensitively illustrated in pencil.

Virginia Haviland

SOURCE: A review of *A Sound to Remember,* in *The Horn Book Magazine,* Vol. LVI, No. 1, February, 1980, p. 51.

The artist's expressive pencil drawings give a pleasant rustic feeling to the important scenes and characters in the story, which takes place in "the distant land of our fathers." Women in kerchiefs and men in caps and heavy boots belong to an eastern European village. The young boy Jacov, the butt of whispering and teasing, was a bit clumsy and slow of speech. Nevertheless, the rabbi chose to give him the honor of blowing the ram's horn on Rosh Hashanah. Jacov had imagined the notes would sound "almost like living things, with bodies and spirits of their own," but when the day arrived, he first brought forth only a faint crackling tone, then only a weak and trembling one, and after that, nothing. But on Yom Kippur, the rabbi himself played a shofar along with Jacov, and the two together achieved a beautiful harmony. A story told as though remembered with feeling.

NOBODY STOLE THE PIE (1980)

Barbara Elleman

SOURCE: A review of *Nobody Stole the Pie*, in *Booklist*, Vol. 76, No. 14, March 15, 1980, pp. 1058, 1060.

A giant pie made from the village's lollyberry tree is ready for the evening's festivities when everyone will dance, celebrate, and share a piece of the tasty treat. A bird, however, pecks out a berry and a cat nibbles on the crust, beginning a chain of tasters that nearly empties the pan. When the mayor discovers the loss, he thunders, "Who stole the pie?" Receiving no answer, he declares, "It is clear that if nobody stole the pie, it must still be here. . . . As is our custom, the Mayor shall have the very first piece." And he ate "the one, the last, the only piece" there was. This moral is cleverly anchored in a surprise-ending, funny story that leaves room for thoughtful discussion. [Fernando] Krahn, who usually illustrates his own wordless, small-format books, uses the large pages effectively and ably expands the humor with cartoon line drawings, which are highlighted in crayon shades of red and yellow.

Kirkus Reviews

SOURCE: A review of *Nobody Stole the Pie*, in *Kirkus Reviews*, Vol. XLVIII, No. 7, April 1, 1980, p. 436.

"A little bit, a little bit, a little bit won't hurt." This fallacious reasoning, expressed by every villager who steals a nibble from the huge communal pie, is something that small children can relate to; and so, of course, is the offense. The implications can be stretched as far as anyone wants to take them. Levitin starts with a lollyberry tree in the center of a distant town. "Was it magic? you will want to know. I will have to answer no, not magic in the way of granting wishes or producing ice-cream cones instead of flowers. But it was a *very good* tree." She takes us through the villagers' annual ritual of picking the lollyberries and baking the tremendous pie, which then waits on a platform for the night's big celebration. And she has us witness helplessly as first a bird, then a cat, then one baker, another baker, and finally countless people from far and near, each following the previous one's example, sneaks a bit of the pie. Krahn takes a delightfully dim view of them all, from the mayor on down. We end up without much pie, but with an entertaining, tangy fable that sticks to the ribs.

Ethel L. Heins

SOURCE: A review of *Nobody Stole the Pie*, in *The Horn Book Magazine*, Vol. LVI, No. 3, June, 1980, p. 288.

In the town of Little Digby stood a remarkable tree—a "lollyberry" tree, which bore "luscious and juicy, sweet and tangy" berries. At harvest time a joyous festival was always held when the berries were picked and baked into a tremendous pie shared by all the townsfolk. But one year a strange disaster struck: Plucking a single delicious berry from the great pie cooling in the town square, a bird set in motion a sequence of furtive nibblers murmuring, "A little bit, a little bit, a little bit won't hurt." In the evening the whole populace was shocked and saddened by the almost total disappearance of the pie. Everyone denied stealing it—("It's one thing to take a taste . . . but the *whole pie!* That is a terrible crime")—and only the mayor was wise enough to perceive the truth. Constructed like one of the "noodlehead" folk tales, the story is entertaining though at times somewhat wordy. But the color-washed drawings with droll caricatures and exaggeration add a broad, earthy humor and make a decidedly funny picture book.

THE FISHERMAN AND THE BIRD (1982)

Publishers Weekly

SOURCE: A review of *The Fisherman and the Bird*, in *Publishers Weekly*, Vol. 221, No. 7, February 12, 1982, p. 99.

Prize-winner Levitin could renew anyone's faltering faith in humanity with the unfolding of her singular story. It is illustrated by [Francis] Livingston's soaring, breathtaking pictures in vivid hues of a fishing village and the sea. Here Rico lives apart from people he despises as false and foolish. One day, Rico discovers a bird and its mate nesting on the mast of his boat and fumes as the villagers twit him for his "catch." He's about to destroy the nest when the schoolteacher intervenes. The birds belong to a rare, almost extinct species, the teacher insists, and begs Rico to leave the boat at anchor until the eggs hatch and the nestlings are on their own. But if Rico can't fish, he will starve, a problem worked out in the author's moving account of the blessings arising from cooperation and kind hearts.

Ilene Cooper

SOURCE: A review of *The Fisherman and the Bird*, in *Booklist*, Vol. 78, No. 20, June 15, 1982, p. 1369.

Rico, a lonely and embittered fisherman, is disgruntled when a bird lights on his ship's mast and builds a nest. Once ashore, Rico wants to destroy it, but he is persuaded by the village teacher and the townspeople to leave the eggs of this almost extinct species alone so that they can hatch. Rico agrees, but when he learns he must not take the boat out for 33 days to ensure the hatching, he almost changes his mind. Because the people offer to share their catch and food with him, he decides to stay on shore and protect the eggs. On the day they hatch, he's amazed and elated. At the church, the priest allows him to ring the bell so he can share the good news with the villagers—who are now his friends. Rico's transformation borders on the didactic, but the story's ecological aspect fares better. Teachers doing a primary-grade unit on ecology will find this a good starting point. The full-color pencil and watercolor washes gracefully depict a beautiful sun-washed countryside and the simple seafaring life of the village.

THE YEAR OF SWEET SENIOR INSANITY (1982)

Stephanie Zvirin

SOURCE: A review of *The Year of Sweet Senior Insanity,* in *Booklist,* Vol. 78, No. 14, March 15, 1982, p. 950.

Excited yet scared at the prospect of finishing high school, Leni Pressman and her two girl friends decide to top off their senior year with a trip to Hawaii. But as the school year progresses, travel plans recede into the background with Leni finding herself at constant odds with her mother, acting as confidante to a pregnant friend, disillusioned by much she has always taken for granted, and desperately in love with handsome college student Blair Justin. When her parents take off on vacation, Leni invites Blair to move in, anticipating an idyllic week and looking forward to an initiation into sex. Things quickly go awry, however, and the sex turns into a real fiasco when her waterbed collapses during lovemaking, and Leni comes to the painful realization that Blair's love and sense of loyalty stop with himself. A believable and often humorous first-person record of teenage first love as well as a sure-footed, thoughtful rendering of that magical passage into adulthood when confused emotions begin to clarify and things familiar take on sharper hues and new directions.

Zena Sutherland

SOURCE: A review of *The Year of Sweet Senior Insanity,* in *Bulletin of the Center for Children's Books,* Vol. 35, No. 10, June, 1982, pp. 191-92.

Leni and her two best friends, Angie and Rhonda, plan to work and save money all through their senior year of high school so that they can take a celebratory trip to Hawaii when they graduate. It doesn't work out, just as other aspects of Leni's life don't work out; she is deeply in love with Blair and invites him to stay with her when her parents go away for a week, but her plans for an ecstatic union end with a broken waterbed and a quarrel. By the time of graduation, each of the three girls has decided—for different reasons—to cancel the trip. Leni tells the story, which has a good balance in the attention given to the various aspects of her life, and tells it in a flowing, natural style that has bittersweet, humorous, or intense passages, the changes giving pace to a story that is sharply evocative of the end of adolescence and its turbulent emotional conflict.

Randy Pastor

SOURCE: A review *The Year of Sweet Senior Insanity,* in *Voice of Youth Advocates,* Vol. 5, No. 3, August, 1982, p. 33.

This revolves around Leni, a high school senior, her two friends, Angie and Rhonda, her family, and her college boyfriend Blair. All three girls get jobs in order to go to Hawaii at the end of high school. Leni finds herself pulled between Blair's demands, her friends' problems, school, her family, and working. "Senior insanity" builds throughout the year and comes to a head during senior week. Leni's parents are away and she invites Blair to spend the week. She loses her virginity and somehow it's just not what she expected it to be. With her mother gone and her grandmother old-fashioned, she has no one with whom to talk over her extremely mixed-up feelings. A crisis with a broken waterbed lets her see Blair as he truly is [and] takes all of her Hawaii money to resolve it. The cover art is attractive and the story moves well; the book should be of interest to most high school girls. Because of the semi-explicit sex scene, I would only recommend for high school and young adult collections where censorship is not a problem.

ALL THE CATS IN THE WORLD (1982)

Kirkus Reviews

SOURCE: A review of *All the Cats in the World,* in *Kirkus Reviews,* Vol. L, No. 15, August 1, 1982, p. 864.

"Can you feed all the cats in the world?" the elderly lighthouse keeper taunts also-elderly Mikila, who faithfully feeds the promontory's hungry horde each day. She has thumbed her nose (literally) at his taunting; she has persevered in foul weather to prove her mettle. Now, feverish and despairing, she takes to her sickbed . . . only to rise, on the fourth day, newly determined— and discover the lighthouse keeper himself feeding the cats. His goat, he says "with a grin," heard the cats making a racket. And he's had the same thought as she: feeding the cats is much like "tending the lighthouse." (You can't, that is, save every ship either.) A modest, not particularly prepossessing book (in sandy beige and gray-blue) with two clear attractants—the cats and the squabbling pair—as well as an unusually genuine argument.

Ann A. Flowers

SOURCE: A review of *All the Cats in the World,* in *The Horn Book Magazine,* Vol. LVIII, No. 6, December, 1982, pp. 641-42.

Although they were very poor, Mikila and her friend Nella fed the homeless cats who lived at the seaside in the shadow of the lighthouse. But one day Nella died, and Mikila was left to do it alone. It was hard, but she went every day with her poor bag of scraps. The lighthouse keeper, gruff and scornful, came out to taunt her with the futility of her efforts: "Don't you know there are millions of hungry cats in the world? Can you feed all the cats in the world?" Mikila was faithful, however, until she fell ill and was forced to miss a few days. When she returned, she found the lighthouse keeper feeding the cats, and they became friends. A thoughtful picture book, fresh and human, on the value of responsibility. Lively illustrations [by Charles Robinson], mostly double-page line drawings washed in two colors, add a pleasant atmosphere to the story and show a typical coastal village, a rocky shore, and many grateful cats.

Denise M. Wilms

SOURCE: A review of *All the Cats in the World,* in *Booklist,* Vol. 79, No. 7, December 1, 1982, pp. 500, 502.

As old Mikila goes about feeding the wild seaside cats who need her help, she finds herself in a running battle of words with the lighthouse keeper who belittles her actions. "'How stubborn you are,'" he taunts; "'I am faithful,'" Mikila yells back. But then illness keeps Mikila from her self-appointed duties. When she worriedly returns some days later with supplies for her cats, she discovers they've been well kept, courtesy of the old lighthouse keeper. The verbal sparring is friendlier this time, though Mikila's tart tongue lets the old man know his rudeness hasn't been forgotten. There is an understanding between them now, however, and the makings of a solid friendship. Levitin's satisfying short story is in picture-book format but will appeal to a slightly older audience, who will be more attuned to the personality differences between the two main characters. The pen-and-ink drawings, washed in lavender and tan, have an agile look that suits the crustiness of the story's characters.

SMILE LIKE A PLASTIC DAISY (1984)

Zena Sutherland

SOURCE: A review of *Smile Like a Plastic Daisy,* in *Bulletin of the Center for Children's Books,* Vol. 37, No. 8, April, 1984, pp. 150-51.

Claudia, the narrator, is a high school senior who has always been quiet, academically competent if not outstanding, and generally conforming. What she does that upsets her parents is to get irritated, while at a school swim meet, at some boys' taunting of her because they can strip to the waist in the heat and she can't. So she does. In addition to the disciplining Claudia gets at school, she must face her parents' anger, and the taunts of classmates, and her own realization that the incident

may make it impossible to get into the college of her choice. Championed by a woman lawyer who is an activist, Claudia must decide what stance to take at the suspension hearing; readers may be divided as to the logic (given her own experience) or wisdom of her choice, but there is little question that Levitin uses the incident to focus on a substantive issue. And that is to some extent the weakness of the book, for the issue takes precedence over both the character development and the story line.

Ruth K. MacDonald

SOURCE: A review of *Smile Like a Plastic Daisy,* in *School Library Journal,* Vol. 31, No. 2, October, 1984, p. 168.

This book treats, in an open-minded fashion, the problems of taking any political persuasion too far. Claudia is a high-school senior who is all-around normal and not distinguished in any way until she confronts her nascent feminism. While attending a school athletic meet on a hot day, she finds the boys taking off their shirts. When taunted, she takes off her own. The result is suspension from school, a hearing before the school board, much publicity and a possible lawsuit. Encouraged by a teacher and a feminist lawyer, Claudia pursues her defiance, but gradually realizes that adults who are interested in her situation are using her for ends which do not coincide with her own. Throughout the story, the writer's balanced, mature point of view leads the heroine to realize the consequences of her actions and the reasonable limits to which she can pursue her principles. A valuable lesson cloaked in a story with a credible heroine.

Becky Johnson Xavier

SOURCE: A review *Smile Like a Plastic Daisy,* in *Voice of Youth Advocates,* Vol. 7, No. 4, October, 1984, p. 197.

Claudia and her friends are high school seniors who plan to coast through their senior year, but a charismatic high school teacher forces Claudia to question her values. After reading a number of feminist books, Claudia takes off her blouse at a swim meet, partly as an act of defiance against mores that prohibit women from going without tops. Her act sets off a series of events including a near riot for which she is held responsible. Claudia learns to use her own judgment after she makes the painful discovery that there are people who want to use her fight for a principle only to further their own ends. This book offers no pat characters or easy answers but it is quite thought-provoking and would be a good choice for YASD Best Books. It will not be read without some encouragement as the cover is a confusing jumble of images that seems more suited to a younger audience than the senior high school audience for which the book seems intended.

📖 *A SEASON FOR UNICORNS* (1986)

Kirkus Reviews

SOURCE: A review of *A Season for Unicorns*, in *Kirkus Reviews*, Vol. LIV, No. 5, March 1, 1986, p. 390.

While trying to grapple with her parents' weaknesses, 14-year-old Ingrid (Inky) learns to conquer her own fears.

When Inky discovers that her handsome, hearty father is involved in a series of affairs whenever he's away from home (he's a pilot), it throws her for a loop. School-work suffers as she tries to repair relationships, urging her agoraphobic mother to make herself more attractive, eventually confronting her with evidence of her father's misdemeanors, only to find that Mother already knows and has made her own accommodation: men have different needs, after all, and he's a good provider. Meanwhile, Inky has made friends with a mother and son, Gus, who have a business giving balloon rides. At first lying about her own family out of her grief at their situation, she later realizes, when she hears about Gus' family problems (his dead father was an abusive alcoholic), that any relationship must be based on truth and that while she cannot change her parents, she can change herself.

Levitin writes well. Her characters are complex mixtures of faults, talents, foibles and virtues, their revelations staged with a care that raises this above the run-of-the-mill coming-of-age novel.

Publishers Weekly

SOURCE: A review of *A Season for Unicorns*, in *Publishers Weekly*, Vol. 229, No. 26, June 27, 1986, pp. 92-3.

This is an affecting story of a girl's discovery of the truth about her parents and their life together, and her decision to break away. Ingrid—Inky—and her family (her mother, younger sister Becca and her grandmother), have always kept her father, Peter, as the focal point of their lives. A dashing airline pilot, Peter brings home exotic presents, buys the girls ice cream, praises Inky's art, while Inky's mother stays at home, frequently in bed because of her "bad back." When Inky finds out about her father's infidelities, she turns to a family that owns a hot air balloon. Mary and Gus McMurphy are completely different from Inky's own family. They have been through hard times, but have pulled together through communication. Inky attempts that approach at home. But when she confronts her mother, the woman reveals a truth Inky would never have suspected: acceptance of Peter's deceptions and "needs." Although Inky's mother is a little too harshly drawn and the story tends toward the melodramatic, Inky and Becca are both realistic and poignant in their attempts to make their family work. And Inky's resolution to the situation is quite moving.

Ann A. Flowers

SOURCE: A review of *A Season for Unicorns*, in *The Horn Book Magazine*, Vol. LXII, No. 4, July-August, 1986, pp. 455-56.

Fourteen-year-old Ingrid Stevenson, known as Inky, lives in the town of Seven Wells on the edge of the California desert. Her father is an airline pilot and gone a good deal, so Inky and her younger sister are alone much of the time with their rather withdrawn mother and elderly grandmother. Inky adores her handsome, glamorous father; the times when he is at home are filled with gaiety and happiness. So she is completely devastated when she accidentally discovers evidence that he has been repeatedly unfaithful for many years. Torn apart by her knowledge and uncertain as to what course to take, Inky strikes up a friendship with Gus McMurphy and his widowed mother who have just opened a hot air balloon launch on the desert. Gus, too, has a secret that he can't bear to discuss—his father was an abusive alcoholic. Inky finally tries to tell her mother about her father's behavior. But her mother, aware of the situation, has retreated into semi-invalidism and agoraphobia and tells Inky not to interfere. So Inky decides to work on her own problems, one of which is fear of heights, and in the end triumphantly takes a flight in the balloon with Gus. In essence, the book is about how we deal with our problems; Inky doesn't get a lot of help, but she's a sturdy character and manages pretty well in contrast to her mother, who has simply retreated. The characterization is somewhat uneven, although Inky's parents are very clearly drawn. The plot seems quite contrived with Gus and the balloon as a deus ex machina.

📖 *THE RETURN* (1987)

Diane Manuel

SOURCE: "Tales of Courage and Love: Here's Quality for Children," in *Christian Science Monitor*, April 3, 1987, p. B6.

Another new title with a conscious message is *The Return*, by Sonia Levitin. Drawing on her own experience as a Jewish child who escaped from Nazi Germany, author Levitin gives us a fictionalized account of a young Ethiopian girl who flees the religious persecution of her homeland and eventually makes her way to Israel.

It's a story that's based on "Operation Moses," the 1984-85 secret airlift of more than 8,000 Ethiopian Jews out of Sudan to Israel, and it doesn't gloss over the suffering of those who waited for help in the refugee camps—and those who still wait.

But for all its stark realism, *The Return* represents another believable triumph of the individual human spirit over great challenges.

Desta, the likable young heroine, dreams of skipping to

school along the golden streets of Jerusalem, but she has only a vague concept of the trek that lies between her mountain village and the Promised Land. As it turns out, her older brother is killed by bandits en route to Sudan, and Desta and her younger sister have to make the tortuous journey on their own. They've always been devout Jews, but they soon begin to discover spiritual resources they'd never known before.

Levitin has a sure, rhythmic touch, and her characters' conversations come from the heart. They're also full of wit and fun—much needed here. What's more, the atmospheric setting that's painted in the opening pages—a small village high in the misty, blue-green mountains, where the smell of freshly ground coffee beans hangs in the air and the blacksmiths' bellows wheeze—has a haunting refrain in the closing pages, when Desta finally arrives at Jerusalem's Western Wall:

> Slowly I approached the wall. High are the stones, and worn with time, the color of ochre, the color of dull clay with a hidden haze of gold . . . this wall I approached, my hands clasped, my eyes upon the stones. . . . I had returned.

Sheila Solomon Klass

SOURCE: "Waiting for Operation Moses," in *The New York Times Book Review,* May 17, 1987, p. 36.

Told as the firsthand experience of a young Ethiopian Jewish girl, *The Return* is a remarkable fictional account of the escape and flight of the Ethiopian Jews to Israel in 1984-85.

Desta, an orphaned adolescent, lives with her young sister and her elder brother in a remote, impoverished mountain village. These black Jews are beset by other Ethiopians who call them "falasha" (stranger) and "buda" (evil eye), and hate and fear them. The Communist Government pressures them to abandon their religion; marauding rebel bands rob and rape the Jewish villagers and forcibly recruit the young men. Nevertheless, they are forbidden to migrate.

Following the prophetic dream of a wise old woman that white Jews will soon come to their community, and that then there will be ultimate freedom for them—a return to Israel—Desta, her sister and brother, along with Dari, to whom she has been betrothed since childhood, and his family, start the illegal and dangerous pilgrimage to the Sudan. From there, they have been promised, they will be flown to Israel.

The journey on foot through Ethiopia and across the border is perilous; Desta and her small sister lose the others and, hungry, thirsty and terrified, they have to manage on their own. Desta sustains them both by her faith and courage until they meet up again with their small group, only to lose Dan in a violent confrontation. When they arrive at the Sudanese refugee camp, disease and starvation are rampant and refugees are dying all around them. There they wait along with thousands of others for Operation Moses, the secret Israeli airlift, to bring them to Israel. Tragically, only a limited number can go.

For those who make it there is comfort and hope, a new beginning, but readers are reminded in the somber epilogue that there are still some 10,000 Jews in Ethiopia who cannot get out.

The Return is rich in ethnographic detail about the Ethiopian Jews, their rural way of life and their unique faith. Elders are venerated; a youth kisses an old woman's knee in respect; parents arrange betrothals for their very young children; girls are brought up solely to be wives and mothers. During menstruation, females are segregated in the village House of Blood and not allowed to work or touch food; kinswomen feed them.

These isolated people know few Hebrew words; their fragmentary religious books are written in Geez, the classical (dead) Ethiopic language. They slaughter their animals ritually, observe the dietary laws and keep the Sabbath. On Passover they eat unleavened bread. They identify with their forebears imprisoned in ancient Babylon, who hung their harps on willows, refused to sing for their captors and wept for Zion. A particularly lovely, lengthy passage describes Segid, their holiday celebrating the deliverance from Babylon, when all of them, festively dressed, climb single file up a mountain—some elders carrying large stones, representing their sins, to be discarded at the summit—to celebrate the giving of the Torah and listen to the Ten Commandments. The long day of prayer ends in exultant dancing and feasting in the village. *The Return* is crammed with history, as Sonia Levitin, the author of other distinguished books for young people about Jewish history, here tells the story of an entire people.

Plot and character development are not this novel's strong points; nonetheless, it is a memorable work that calls for a sequel to describe what has happened to these Ethiopian Jews now that they are in their Promised Land.

Marcus Crouch

SOURCE: A review of *The Return,* in *The Junior Bookshelf,* Vol. 58, No. 2, April, 1994, pp. 70-71.

One of the few really heartening events of recent years was Operation Moses by which thousands of oppressed black Jews (the Falasha, a derogatory term much disliked by these descendants of the Queen of Sheba's people) were airlifted to a new life in Israel. Sonia Levitin's remarkable novel records how one family survived the ordeal and came safe home to stand at the Western Wall of Jerusalem. Here the story ends, avoiding anticlimax and a measure of disillusionment.

This is Desta's story. Desta stands between childhood

and womanhood, clinging to the past and reluctant to face the prospect of marriage to her long-promised betrothed Dan, the serious, very adult son of the priest of a neighbouring village. When Desta, with her brother and her child sister, begin their perilous journey to the Sudan, Dan and his father and grandmother make an earlier start, and in the haste to catch up Desta's resourceful brother is killed by bandits, leaving her to take charge of her sister and eventually to join the other party. Here Desta's responsibilities do not end. At the frontier Dan and his father are arrested, and it is Desta who has to negotiate for a place on one of the overcrowded and illegal flights to Israel.

The moving story is told throughout by Desta, and it is one of Ms Levitin's triumphs that we accept without question the immediacy and fluency of a narrative from an illiterate adolescent. So tense is the drama, so grave its physical and moral implications, that there is no place for a reader's skepticism. Desta may be a girl kept in poverty and ignorance of the world by the deliberate policy of the Government; she is nevertheless clear-sighted and uncompromisingly honest in her reporting of the terrible events she experiences during a dreadful odyssey. She also has the gift of bringing clearly before us the friendly and hostile people she encounters by the way, from the village children who drive away the wanderers with stones to Hagos, a little boy of the refugee camps who has learnt to live with squalor and starvation and who takes pride in smoothing the path of those even worse off than himself. Here is an important novel, for its subject certainly and also for the tone, free both of anger and self-pity, in which it is told.

Reva Klein

SOURCE: A review of *The Return,* in *Times Educational Supplement,* No. 4061, April 29, 1994, p. 15.

Operation Moses was one of those audacious actions undertaken by the Israeli government that both impressed the world and made us squirm. In six months during 1984-85, the Israelis carried out secret airlifts of thousands of Ethiopian Jews.

The justification was twofold: Jews, or falashas (strangers) as they are derogatorily known, were being persecuted on a wide scale. Anti-semitism was not new to that region of the Horn of Africa, but the Marxist Dergue, successors of Haile Selassie, had thrown the country into civil war. The common enemy of government, the opposing People's Liberation Army and the civilians suffering in the midst of it all were the falashas, the "strangers" who had lived there for as many generations as anybody could remember.

The second reason for the evacuations, and this is where the squirm factor comes in, was that Ethiopians were starving to death on a mass scale because of drought and famine. The Israelis would not sit back and watch Jews starve to death. They engineered countless top secret

missions to deliver their people to the land of milk, honey and freedom from religious persecution. These were literally the chosen people, snatched away from the jaws of death while the majority were left behind. And the world watched.

Sonia Levitin's *The Return* is the fictionalised story of an adolescent girl and her family who were caught up in those events. Orphaned Desta, her older brother and younger sister escape an African-style pogrom, unwillingly leaving their surrogate parents to their fate. On foot and with no food or water, they make the arduous, perilous journey to Sudan, where they have heard they will be delivered "home" to Zion.

Just short of the border, Desta's older brother is killed by bandits and she and her enfeebled sister Almaz are forced to continue their trek alone, sometimes accompanied by other refugees. Eventually, she is reunited with other people from her village, including her intended, at a vast refugee camp where life is a living hell of rampant epidemics, suffering and death all around.

It is from there that this modern day Exodus is staged. The story ends with Desta and Almaz in Jerusalem, learning a new culture, a new language, a way of existing in a new world. It is a deeply engaging story, following Desta's development from a dreamy sort of girl who makes lovely pots to a brave and, eventually, uncompromising young woman who has to take responsibility for her own and her sister's survival. It is moving, too, to enter the strange world of the isolated mountain Jews of Ethiopia, who follow many of the same practices as Jews on the other side of the world. I would be interested in a sequel about Desta and Almaz in Israel and their experiences with the spiritual brethren, some of whom see them as outcasts—indeed, as falashas.

📖 *INCIDENT AT LORING GROVES* (1988)

Publishers Weekly

SOURCE: A review of *Incident at Loring Groves,* in *Publishers Weekly,* Vol. 233, No. 19, May 13, 1988, p. 278.

Levitin creates an ordinary suburban world populated by typical teenagers. Cassidy Keaton knows how to play by the rules; then following a thought-provoking experience at summer camp, she's no longer confident that the rules are always right. Her new boyfriend Ken is on the fast-track to high-school stardom, pushed by an ambitious father. Ken, too, is discovering that he may want different things for himself. At a party gone wild, Cassidy, Ken and their friends stumble upon the body of a long-missing acquaintance. Because they had broken into an empty cabin, and were using marijuana and alcohol, they take a vow of silence and pretend they never saw the body. But both Cassidy and Ken are torn apart by this inaction. The point-of-view is consistently portrayed from these adolescents' perspectives: they are hard on their struggling parents; their thinking does not always follow through to logical consequences. A grim, gritty novel that closes on a bitterly ironic note, *Incident at Loring Groves* is a searingly honest portrayal of adolescent society.

Zena Sutherland

SOURCE: A review of *Incident at Loring Groves,* in *Bulletin of the Center for Children's Books,* Vol. 42, No. 1, September, 1988, pp. 13-14.

Cassidy and Ken are among the high school group that comes across the body of one of their classmates, Mary Lou, who has been reported missing. Since they all know they may get in trouble for being in a Park Service summer house (supposedly locked) at night, and that an inquiry may bring out the fact that some of them were using dope, they agree to keep silent. After all, they can't do Mary Lou any good, right? Although purposive, the theme is so effectively developed, and at such a good pace, that this novel about moral responsibility makes a dramatic impact. In the course of the story, which ends with Ken and Cass meeting at the police station where each comes to confess despite being ashamed of having kept silent, Levitin explores a range of attitudes. Most perceptive, and most damning, is that of Ken's father; he'd been furious when his son announced that he was going to the police ("You tell the cops and that's it. I'm through with you") but after television publicity that praises Ken, his Dad, just starting what looks to be a promising political career, states: "My sons know where I stand when it comes to telling the truth. And I've always encouraged them to get involved. Children learn by example. Children learn what they live." Uh huh.

Hazel Rochman

SOURCE: A review of *Incident at Loring Groves,* in *Booklist,* Vol. 85, No. 1, September 1, 1988, p. 68.

High school leaders Cassie and Ken are getting to like each other, and they seem bound for success in life, just like their affluent go-getter families. Ken's even in line for his California high school's Young Humanitarian Award. Then one night after a school dance, partying with drugs in the hills with some of their friends, they find the body of their murdered classmate Mary Lou. The group decides to keep quiet about it, to avoid trouble. But as it becomes clear that Wayne, a disturbed classmate and marijuana dealer, is the killer, and that he isn't going to be caught, Cassie and Ken find it more and more difficult to still their consciences. In a climactic encounter, Ken admits his shame to his father—who warns Ken that he'd be a fool to ruin his future by breaking the silence. But despite his father's threats and fierce peer pressure, Ken finally joins Cassie in going to the police. The message is heavy, and there's a clumsy attempt to make a mystery of the killer's identity, but

the moral conflicts are presented with complexity and drama. What Levitin makes convincing are how easy it is to rationalize ("We didn't kill her . . . It isn't our responsibility") and how evil grows not only from action but also from not caring enough to get involved.

SILVER DAYS (second novel in the "Platt Family" trilogy, 1989)

Kirkus Reviews

SOURCE: A review of *Silver Days,* in *Kirkus Reviews,* Vol. LVII, No. 5, March 1, 1989, pp. 379-80.

In a sequel to the author's autobiographical novel about fleeing Nazi Germany (*Journey to America,* 1970), the reunited Platt family arrives penniless in New York and later moves on to California.

As middle daughter Lisa continues the story from 1940 to 1943, the family sometimes faces fierce American prejudice against Jews, but begins to achieve economic stability as Papa's English improves and he is able to resume his trade of manufacturing coats. However, though Los Angeles provides a mostly friendly haven, there are reminders of a crueler world; the price of Lisa's chance to resume her beloved ballet is enduring the teacher—a martinet, and German; the Platts' Japanese neighbors are interned; Lisa is humiliated by having the hand-me-down clothes she's wearing to school pointed out by their original owner; older sister Ruth falls in love with a young man as he is going off to war; Mother is plunged into severe depression when the Red Cross destroys her hopes that her own mother is still alive in Germany. Through it all, Lisa grows, observes, and reports with immediacy and affection on these bittersweet years—not gold, but at least silver.

Authentic and involving.

Zena Sutherland

SOURCE: A review of *Silver Days,* in *Bulletin of the Center for Children's Books,* Vol. 42, No. 8, April, 1989, p. 200.

Once prosperous, a Jewish family that has fled Nazi Germany finds life difficult in Manhattan and moves to California, where Papa insists that he will be able to make a decent living. The story is told by the middle daughter (Lisa, 13) and the narration is punctuated by her italicized journal entries. The focus is on family life, family finances, and the reactions of each member of the Platt family to a new way of life, to the war effort, and to the bitter knowledge that Mama's mother, left behind in Germany, may have died. At the end, Mama is silent and morose, making an apathetic recovery from surgery, and hearing that her mother was sent to Auschwitz. There are minor plot threads: the oldest sister's love affair, Lisa's success as a budding dancer, but the emphasis is on the family, as it was in *Journey to America* to which this is a sequel. Although the plot is weakened slightly by a too-neat ending, it is still an effective story of the Platts' assimilation into a new culture, with sturdy characters, warm family relationships, good pace, and period details that are realistic but that never seem purposively introduced.

Hanna B. Zeiger

SOURCE: A review of *Silver Days,* in *The Horn Book Magazine,* Vol. LXV, No. 3, May, 1989, pp. 376-77.

The story of Lisa Platt and her family who escaped from Nazi Germany in *Journey to America* continues with their arrival in New York to be with their father. The joy of their reunion is soon overshadowed, however, by their extreme poverty. They live in a dilapidated, noisy tenement with orange crates for furniture and donations of cast-off clothing. While their parents work long hours at menial jobs, the three sisters struggle to learn a new language and new mores. After an encounter with an anti-Semitic neighbor, Lisa decides, "I'm going to learn English so well that nobody will ever know I was German." Papa, hoping for greater opportunities and a better life, painstakingly gathers money to move the family to California. In her diary Lisa records America's entry into the war, the internment of Japanese neighbors, and the family's concern about the grandmother left in Germany, along with the color of a new lipstick, Lisa's dreams of becoming a professional dancer, and speculation about her first kiss. When news from the Red Cross of their grandmother's probable death at Auschwitz precipitates a physical and emotional crisis for Mother, the family realizes that in working so hard to become totally American, they have drifted away from the things they really value. Papa tells the girls, "Our future must have room in it for the past." When Mother is able to venture from her room, the family gathers around her for the blessing of the Sabbath candles and the sense of peace it brings. Through Lisa's sometimes funny and often poignant experiences, the author has given us insight into the special problems of a young woman growing up as a refugee in America during World War II.

Laura L. Lent

SOURCE: A review of *Silver Days,* in *Voice of Youth Advocates,* Vol. 12, No. 2, June, 1989, pp. 103-04.

Levitin does an outstanding job depicting life as it was for Jewish immigrants who came to the United States in the 1930s and 1940s. She tells about the Platt family's struggles as Jews who emigrated from Germany and settled in New York City. The book is told from Lisa Platt's perspective, and provides a great deal of insight into what it was like to be a Jewish teenager in New York, and later on in California. The scenes which Levitin

describes are so poignant that they will bring tears to the reader's eyes, as if the reader is experiencing the prejudice and hatred. In addition, I enjoy how Levitin inserts excerpts from Lisa's diary. In those excepts, one can see how a teenager, in this case, Lisa, views events that occur daily, how Lisa questions people's actions and prejudice, and how she eventually comments on the irony of the prejudice and the way she actually lives. These excerpts show Lisa's gradual awareness of what it means to be a Jew during World War II. One example of this is the following:

> Lester's dad beat him badly this afternoon, just for playing with Annie and me. How could he do that to his own son? Lester's not supposed to play with us because we are Jews. Is something really wrong with Jews . . . Ruth says that some people . . . think all Jews are rich. Rich! That's a laugh.

This stereotype does not apply in any way to Lisa's family which is constantly scrounging for food and money.

There are several reasons why I highly recommend this book to any junior or senior high reader. First of all, the reader will gain an historical feel for the era and what life was like during World War II. Second, the reader will begin to understand the prejudice American Jews were exposed to during the war. This topic can be used by a teacher to initiate a classroom discussion on prejudice and stereotypes. Finally, the book is written in an easy-to-read style which all types of readers can understand. This is one book that a reader will not be able to put down once it is begun.

THE MAN WHO KEPT HIS HEART IN A BUCKET (1991)

Publishers Weekly

SOURCE: A review of *The Man Who Kept His Heart in a Bucket,* in *Publishers Weekly,* Vol. 238, No. 30, July 12, 1991, p. 65.

Love is always worth the risk—that's the message pulsing through this thoroughly captivating story firmly rooted in the folktale tradition. Jack is a lad whose heart was once broken, and he now keeps it in a bucket, safe from harm. Fearful of rejection, he holds himself aloof from friends and neighbors, allowing nothing—neither delicious food generously shared, a lilting melody, a baby—to move or engage him. Magic cracks his resolve, though, when a carp is transformed into a maiden who steals his heart, promising to return it only when he's solved a riddle. He does so, losing his heart to the maiden but thereby gaining the richness of spirit he lacked. Levitin (*Incident at Loring Groves; The Return*), is in fine form here; her eloquent, fluid story is a celebration of life and of love. [Jerry] Pinkney's dreamy, evocative watercolors, as subtly shaded as the dawn, are brimming with vitality and joy, though some readers may find his rather toothy characters—all of whom bear a curious resemblance to one another—a bit off-putting.

Hanna B. Zeiger

SOURCE: A review of *The Man Who Kept His Heart in a Bucket,* in *The Horn Book Magazine,* Vol. LXVII, No. 5, September-October, 1991, pp. 586-87.

In Levitin's original tale, Jack carries his heart in a bucket to prevent it from being broken. As he sets out one day to find work, he finds no joy in the taste of fresh-baked pies, the sound of happy music, or the touch of a young couple's baby. When he stoops by a pool to add water to his bucket, a golden carp leaps up and is transformed into a beautiful maiden. She steals Jack's heart and, laughing, offers to return it only when he solves her riddle and finds "three different scales of gold." The next day, the taste of the baker's pie thrills him, and he sees the baker's scales glowing gold in the sunlight. The piper's music sets him dancing, and Jack recognizes the golden scale of the notes. He holds the young farm couple's baby lovingly and wishes for one of his own. When they pay him with a gleaming, fresh-caught fish, he finds the last of the golden scales of the riddle. Now that his "heart is in the right place," he answers the riddle and asks the beautiful young woman to marry him, and "all of them celebrated love." The scenes of a village nestled among hills glow with jewel-like colors; Pinkney's illustrations, rendered in colored pencils and watercolors, are full of dramatic action.

Robert Strang

SOURCE: A review of *The Man Who Kept His Heart in a Bucket,* in *Bulletin of the Center for Children's Books,* Vol. 45, No. 5, January, 1992, p. 131.

"Jack's heart had once been broken," so now Jack keeps it safe in a bucket that he carries along while plying his trade as a metalsmith. Safe, but useless—Jack can't work up any enthusiasm for the baker's bread, the piper's music, or the holding of a baby that "squirms and cries," all three of which are offered to him in exchange for his work. But when Jack stops at the lake to get water for his heart, the story shifts from a reasonable parable to a confusing hash of the fictive and the folklike, the literal and the symbolic. A carp jumps into the pail, turns into a beautiful maiden, and steals Jack's heart, literally, and, as it turns out, figuratively, as we discover when Jack goes back into town in search of the answer to the maiden's riddle, an answer demanded for return of the heart. For some reason, Jack then melts down the bucket he had held his heart in; for some other reason the melted bucket turns into a golden heart. And, in gathering the answers to the maiden's three-part riddle, Jack discovers that he has a heart and that it is, as the townspeople point out, "in the right place after all." The riddling is irrelevant, the two hearts are confusing, the story's conclusion is filled with contradictions that have none of the mystery of paradox—they're just bewildering. Pinkney's watercolors feature his familiar rural landscapes; the facial distortions of the characters further confound the mixed messages of the story.

ANNIE'S PROMISE (third novel in the "Platt Family" trilogy, 1993)

Hazel Rochman

SOURCE: A review of *Annie's Promise,* in *Booklist,* Vol. 89, No. 11, February 1, 1993, p. 977.

Set during the last months of World War II, this fine sequel to *Silver Days* (1989) focuses on 13-year-old Annie's break from her overprotective Jewish immigrant parents. Reluctantly, they allow her to spend the summer in an idyllic Quaker camp in the mountains near her Los Angeles home. The rite-of-passage stuff is overstated at times, but Levitin is never simplistic about what it means to break away. Annie makes friends (and enemies) at camp and discovers surprising strength (and wickedness) in herself and her family. She does some ugly things, and she's sorry, but she can't always go back and put things right. People change in this book, and yet some things stay the same. At the beginning and at the end, Annie hates it when her parents "jabber" in German. Her relationships with her older sisters, Ruth and Lisa, are also drawn with candor, and there's a painful scene when Ruth's soldier fiancé returns from Europe transformed: he breaks with her and with Judaism. Annie's critical of her parents, especially when they are racist toward a black friend she meets at camp, but she also sees their bitter daily struggle as refugees; and when she runs away and returns, she learns that loving families can forgive each other, again and again. Annie's growing sense of herself is compelling precisely because she knows her meanness as well as her courage.

Deborah Stevenson

SOURCE: A review of *Annie's Promise,* in *Bulletin of the Center for Children's Books,* Vol. 46, No. 7, March, 1993, pp. 216-17.

It's 1945, and German-Jewish refugee Annie Platt (of the Platt family featured in *Journey to America* and *Silver Days*) is twelve going on thirteen in an America blown by "the howling winds of change." Annie's adventures, however, are more local: despite her family's initial reluctance, they allow her to accept an offered (and free) place at a coed and multiracial Quaker summer camp. At camp, Annie makes a good friend, has a serious crush, finds a few idols, and develops a serious enmity with a girl who's a bigoted bully. It may sound like fairly traditional camp-story fare, but this is a thoughtful book about blossoming and independence that possesses a particular poignancy due to its characters and time. Levitin has the integrity to leave in loose ends and sad truths without making them the point of the book: there's no rapprochement between Annie and the bully (upon whom Annie plays a truly nasty trick), Annie and her African-American camp friend have a disastrous post-camp encounter, after which they never see each other again, and there are occasional reminders that the war has taken its toll on Annie's relatives (her father's family have all perished in the Holocaust). Readers will empathize with Annie's struggle to define herself in the face of her strong family, and they'll enjoy this well-written account of her summer adventures.

Kirkus Reviews

SOURCE: A review of *Annie's Promise,* in *Kirkus Reviews,* Vol. LXI, No. 6, March 15, 1993, p. 374.

In a third book about the Platts, who fled Germany in *Journey to America* (1970) and built a new life in L.A. in *Silver Days* (1989), youngest daughter Annie, 13, is attending a Quaker camp in WWII's last weeks. Still weak from an appendectomy, Annie blossoms at camp, easily making friends (especially with Tallahassee, an African-American in her cabin); enjoying a crush on a junior counselor; becoming a favorite of the director; and starting a camp newspaper. Troubles echoing the world outside don't loom large, but, still, after Annie plays a cruel prank on an obnoxious, racist camper, her conscience troubles her. Home again, Annie finds her family in disarray: Ruth's soldier, traumatized by seeing the death camps, jilts her; rebelling at Papa's close supervision, Lisa moves out; and when Tallahassee visits, Papa—already in turmoil because of his daughters' new independence—reveals his own racism. The conclusion—Annie confronts Papa ("You are just like the Nazis. This is why there are wars!"), then runs away, back to camp, where she realizes her own limitations before coming home for a reconciliation—is over-tidy (Annie does have a lot of epiphanies at once); still, the lessons are valuable and the end is satisfyingly dramatic. Not as strong as its predecessors, but Platt family friends won't want to miss it.

THE GOLEM AND THE DRAGON GIRL (1993)

Sharon Grover

SOURCE: A review of *The Golem and the Dragon Girl,* in *School Library Journal,* Vol. 39, No. 3, March, 1993, p. 198.

Moving to a new house has Laurel Wang worried. She is nervous about living with the Chinese grandparents she has never met, and she is afraid that the spirit of her great-grandfather, which has always protected her, will not leave the old house with her family. Jonathan does not want to move into Laurel's old house because it will take him away from all that is familiar and force him to deal with his resentment toward his mother and his new stepfather. When Laurel tries surreptitiously to lure her great-grandfather's spirit out of the house, she causes an accident that results in a strong friendship between the two teenagers and their families. Ghosts, music, and poltergeists blend in this satisfying story, rich in Chinese and Jewish culture. Although Levitin's writing is a bit inconsistent, and readers unfamiliar with klezmer bands will miss much of the musical thread, the characters are well developed and the cultural information is presented in an interesting, nondidactic fashion. The theme of knowing one's own heritage in order to know and appreciate others is handled nicely, and the ghostly elements should make it easy to sell.

Kirkus Reviews

SOURCE: A review of *The Golem and the Dragon Girl,* in *Kirkus Reviews,* Vol. LXI, No. 7, April 1, 1993, p. 459.

There's a lot going on in this offering from a dependable author whose books range from the comic (*The Mark of Conte,* 1976) to the serious (*The Return,* 1987, about Jewish Ethiopian refugees) to picture books. The subject here is a friendship between Chinese-American Laurel and Jewish Jonathan, who has just moved into her former house. Both families are in flux: Jonathan has yet to make peace with a new stepfather; Laurel's normally equable mother is cranky and apprehensive about the arrival of her parents from China—she hasn't seen them since she was 11 years old. And, as they approach adolescence, both Laurel and Jonathan are reassessing their cultural heritages. The action centers on some mildly supernatural activity triggered by the move and the kids' transitional status—the uneasy spirit of Laurel's great-grandfather, still, apparently, in Jonathan's house; a model, constructed by Jonathan, in some ways akin to a golem. Among the many subplots (music plays a strong role; Jonathan's new dog epitomizes Laurel's fears; his uncle, a pleasantly quirky pivotal character, falls implausibly in love with a librarian), the Chinese grandparents steal the show. Their correspondence over the years may have been cursory; but in person they're lovely, kind, sensible people. The key is understanding: in each of the several tangles, it blows away fear, distrust, or anxiety. Levitin's entertaining, well-written story is a bit overneat but, still, it deals creatively with a number of significant themes.

Joanne Schott

SOURCE: A review of *The Golem and the Dragon Girl,* in *Quill & Quire,* Vol. 59, No. 6, June, 1993, p. 40.

In order to entice the protective spirit of her great-grandfather to follow her to her new home, Laurel must first find a way to return to her old one. So when she learns that Jonathan, whose family bought the house, will be getting a puppy, she begs to come and see it. In truth, though, she is afraid of dogs—and the deception costs Laurel dearly.

Unexplained happenings in the house make Laurel think she has disturbed the spirit; Jonathan believes he has released a golem. In looking for answers to the mystery, they explore their differing cultural traditions, Chinese and Jewish, and become friends. As they begin to understand the role of heritage in their lives, many of the things that have been troubling them are resolved.

Levitin has included more than one subplot in her story of being true to yourself, and leaves a few ragged edges. The spirit, pivotal to the plot, is not always handled satisfactorily. But she is a good storyteller, and the children's growth is presented with sincerity while the events and characters grip the reader's interest.

📖 ESCAPE FROM EGYPT (1994)

Kirkus Reviews

SOURCE: A review of *Escape from Egypt,* in *Kirkus Reviews,* Vol. LXII, No. 6, March 15, 1994, p. 398.

In her most ambitious novel since **The Return** (1987), Levitin follows the events in *Exodus* through two young people: Jesse of the tribe of Benjamin and Jennat, an Egyptian/Syrian orphan he meets in the house where both are slaves. Caught in a petty theft, Jesse is condemned to the quarries but saved from certain death by Jennat's intervention. Her mistress gives Jennat as a concubine to her cruel husband; after the plagues, Jennat is among many non-Jews who follow Moses. The great leader, however, remains offstage, while significant events such as the bloodbath that followed the worship of the golden calf and the proclamation of the rigorous new laws are dramatized in the experiences of his followers: questioners, idolators, and unbelievers as well as the obedient (and sometimes fanatically) devout. Like Jesse, readers may find God's will hard to fathom: His violent retribution sweeps away bystanders along with sinners, and the righteous seem to suffer gratuitously. But in the end—after Jesse kills a kid that's been mauled by predators (a symbolic antithesis to the actions of the Good Shepherd)—he makes peace with both Jennat (their mutual attraction and bitter strife have figured throughout) and a God whose "ways are not our ways." Jennat, too, accepts the one God who "asks that you live well and do justice"—though His ways are mysterious, His moral superiority to other gods is clear. In a last chapter, the two recall the past for their children: " . . . only those who remember their slavery will appreciate their freedom." A deeply felt novel, underlining the philosophical complexity of the story of the Jews' great covenant and their first return to their homeland.

Publishers Weekly

SOURCE: A review of *Escape from Egypt,* in *Publishers Weekly,* Vol. 241, No. 13, March 28, 1994, p. 98.

Not even the amply gifted Levitin (**Journey to America;**

The Golem and the Dragon Girl) can quite pull off this one, a coming-of-age/love story set against the Israelites' exodus from Egypt. As usual, Levitin's characterizations are superb; here, she draws particularly complex, believable portraits of a half-Egyptian, half-Syrian slave girl and a Jewish slave boy striving to reconcile integrity and passion. But the unusual verisimilitude of her writing may be at cross purposes with the attempt to convey the powerful themes of the Passover story. Taken literally, the mythic qualities of the biblical plagues and miracles shrink ("The raging green-and-gray waters were pulled back and back as if by invisible hands. The sea was raised up into two walls. Now the seafloor lay exposed"). On the other hand, Levitin's exploration of questions of conscience and faith is startling and searching. Nobody in her novel mouths pieties; religious convictions are the fruits of hard and dramatic struggle. Her rigorous approach, however uneasy its combination of the divine and the day-to-day, will spur her audience to fresh appraisals of sacred history.

Ilene Cooper

SOURCE: A review of *Escape from Egypt,* in *Booklist,* Vol. 90, No. 17, May 1, 1994, p. 1595.

Levitin is certainly courageous. At a time when authors are steered away from writing controversial books and when stories are presifted to make them palatable to the lowest common denominator, she has written a book that is troubling, moving, and sensual—and that forces its readers to think. Quite a combination, especially when presented in that much-maligned genre, historical fiction.

The story Levitin tells is hardly new. It is the biblical tale of the Exodus, the Israelite flight from Egypt, here seen from the point of view of two teenagers, Jesse, a Hebrew slave, and Jennat, a half-Egyptian, half-Syrian girl. The pair meet when they work together learning jewelry-making, but their burgeoning relationship is dwarfed by momentous events. Moses has come to gather the Jewish people; he is going to make Pharaoh let them go.

The biblical setting provides the wider context for a drama that is primarily a human one. Plagues and miracles swirl around real people who are so enmeshed in their own lives and passions that, at times, they seem almost oblivious to the spectacle threatening to engulf them. This human scale is the great strength of the novel. Levitin makes myth manageable, bringing it right into the lives of modern-day readers.

She accomplishes this formidable task in several ways. First, through her fully realized characters: Jesse, with all the longings of a modern-day teenager; Jennat, who risks the life she has known to follow a strange god; and Jesse's parents, Nathan and Devorah, one a skeptic who believes only in himself, the other a believer whose faith is challenged when her daughter is killed.

Once Levitin has established that her characters are made of flesh and blood, she is able to dramatize their struggle with the cosmic questions that have plagued humanity since time immemorial: Why is there evil? What is God's will? What do I believe? What am I willing to risk? Totally uncompromising in her depiction of Adonai, the god of Moses, Levitin starts each chapter with a long quotation from Exodus. The Bible's own words show Adonai to be a god who is willing to smite down the stranger and the Israelite alike to accomplish his goals. To the individual, however, no grand design is apparent in God's actions, only random suffering.

We believe in the spiritual struggles of Levitin's characters because we see their physical lives grounded in the everyday. We recognize in them what W. H. Auden called the "human position" of suffering: "how it takes place / While someone else is eating or opening a window or just walking dully along."

There are never easy answers to big questions, of course, and Levitin never pretends there are. Even an episode at the conclusion of the story, in which Jesse gets a glimmer of how it must feel to Adonai to make decisions for his flock, does not satisfy our need to make sense of the seemingly senseless. For Jesse and for the reader, more questions remain. But by refusing to tidy matters up, Levitin allows her readers an opportunity they are too seldom offered in contemporary fiction: To ponder the largest of questions; to understand that confusion, pain, and, yes, love span the ages; and to realize that to wonder—in both senses of the word—is to be alive.

Elizabeth Bush

SOURCE: A review of *Escape from Egypt*, in *Bulletin of the Center for Children's Books*, Vol. 47, No. 11, July-August, 1994, pp. 365-66.

Jesse, a Hebrew teenager, has had the good fortune to be apprenticed to an Egyptian goldsmith, a position that assures him security, status, and escape from the near-certain early death of Pharaoh's quarry laborers. But Jesse's ill-concealed attraction to Jennat, a half-Egyptian servant who has been given to her master as concubine, has prompted his parents to arrange an unwelcome engagement with his beautiful and devout cousin Talia. Self-absorbed, Jesse pays little attention as his elders discuss the rise of an upstart leader named Moses. But when the destruction of the Egyptian first-born sons impels Pharaoh to grant the Hebrews' release, they must decide whether to abandon the stability of life in Egypt to follow zealot Moses and his harsh god Adonai into the desert. Jesse and his extended family leave their homes for compelling reasons—faith, family duty, lure of better land, fear of Egyptian retaliation. Wandering in his own psychic wilderness, Jesse now plans his future in light of the miracles, carnage, idolatry, religious frenzy, and xenophobia that whirl around him. While reducing mythic events to human-scaled drama, Levitin illuminates those enduring themes that drive the Pentateuch

epic—theodicy, faith versus reason, power politics, nation-building. The death of Jesse's baby sister breaks his mother's faith; Moses' miracles are always subject to doubt; long-standing clan leader Uncle Rimon questions Moses' leadership; loose tribal organization must yield to the centralized authority of Adonai's demanding law. Jesse's marriage choice (which Levitin skillfully leaves in doubt until the final pages) effectively synthesizes themes of personal desire and commitment to Adonai and the Hebrew nation, as he claims Jennat with the quote, "Justice and compassion you shall show to the stranger, for ye were strangers in Egypt." Although some basic knowledge of the Exodus story may enhance a reader's enjoyment of the novel, well-chosen (but uncited) passages which introduce most chapters provide adequate Scriptural background.

ADAM'S WAR (1994)

Nancy Menaldi-Scanlan

SOURCE: A review of *Adam's War*, in *School Library Journal*, Vol. 40, No. 6, June, 1994, p. 132.

A disappointing effort. Adam and Hector are discouraged about their club, the Angels, for its members lack a sense of purpose. Everything changes when the boys discover an abandoned shack in the park and decide to make it their clubhouse. Unfortunately, the Terrestrials have the same idea, and the Angels decide to have a "war" to settle ownership. At the height of the war, one of the Terrestrials appears with a rifle. When Adam jumps him, the gun goes off, killing the dog of an emotionally disabled veteran. The gangs disperse, and Adam and Hector apologize to the man. Later he offers them a picture of his pet, giving them the hope of forgiveness. The theme is a powerful one, but Levitin's story [illustrated by Vincent Nasta] lacks depth. With the exception of Adam, the characters are flat caricatures. The Terrestrials are stereotypical bad guys, the Angels are wishy-washy braggarts, and Adam's parents are dysfunctional to say the least. Events seem contrived, unmotivated, and without consequence. Levitin's book gives mixed messages and doesn't allow readers much opportunity to reflect on the seriousness of the situation. "What had happened had simply happened, that was all." It's a scary way to explain a senseless act of violence to impressionable readers.

Publishers Weekly

SOURCE: A review of *Adam's War*, in *Publishers Weekly*, Vol. 241, No. 24, June 13, 1994, p. 65.

Levitin (*Journey to America; Escape from Egypt*) offers another unusually thought-provoking novel, this time tackling the irresolvable problem of how best to answer violence and aggression. Adam is having a hard time motivating the other members of his club, the Angels, but when he comes across an empty shack in the local park, he thrills the others with his idea to claim it as their clubhouse. But the Angels' rivals, the Terrestrials, usurp the shack, threaten to beat up the Angels and, finally, throw rocks to chase them off. Adam rallies the Angels by planning a "war" against the Terrestrials, but almost immediately he begins to question the use of force. Levitin introduces Adam's doubts subtly: he recoils when one of the Angels feeds his pet snake a live baby mouse; Adam's parents quarrel about whether it is ever appropriate to fight ("People should learn to talk over their differences," says Adam's mother, to which his father replies, "Then how come you're taking that course—self-defense for women."). As is typical for Levitin, the characters are as complex and commanding as the issues. The outcome of the war is dramatic and unforeseen, and the author gives her story an extra dose of staying power by leaving it up to the reader to judge the wisdom and ethics of Adam's decisions.

Kirkus Reviews

SOURCE: A review of *Adam's War,* in *Kirkus Reviews,* Vol. LXII, No. 12, June 15, 1994, p. 848.

The Angels are desperate for a meeting place; Adam and Mike can't have friends in while their parents are at work, Hector's sisters are too bossy, Brendan lives far away. The shack in the park looks like a perfect clubhouse, but no sooner have they claimed it than they're challenged by the bigger, more numerous, and less principled Terrestrials. But honor must be served; despite misgivings, Adam tries to enlist new members and urges his troop to "war." In the eventual battle, the Angels are betrayed by a hoped-for recruit, and the arsenal includes rocks, sticks, and a rifle brought by a Terrestrial. When Adam tackles him, a dog is shot and killed—the beloved pet of a troubled old veteran, a handsome animal the boys had hoped to make their mascot. Levitin's easily read narration is carefully framed to present issues—the boys' need for place and purpose, how trying to prove themselves imposes decisions, the war's escalation from game toward tragedy. Characters aren't realized with any depth in the simplistic result; still, questions of deep concern to boys like Adam are accessibly addressed and left realistically unresolved.

📖 *EVIL ENCOUNTER* (1996)

Kirkus Reviews

SOURCE: A review of *Evil Encounter,* in *Kirkus Reviews,* Vol. LXIV, No. 7, April 1, 1996, p. 533.

After her parents' divorce, Michelle and her mother, Sandra, move from Philadelphia to the Los Angeles area. Michelle is miserable, blaming her mother for the divorce without confronting her about it, hating her new school, and watching her grades drop. Sandra signs Michelle up for group encounter sessions run by the handsome, charming, fortyish Luke. Immediately

Michelle begins to heal, believing that Luke understands her, that he sees into her soul and accepts her even as he begins to uncover her weaknesses. She also feels herself falling in love with him, but rejects his advances during an encounter weekend at a desert spa. When Luke is murdered and Sandra is arrested as the killer, Michelle calls on her new resources to solve the crime.

Levitin starts out with a good premise that begins to unravel when Luke enters the scene. His psycho-babble won't get far with mystery fans, who also have to tolerate manipulative character development, sloppy melodrama, and preposterous plot twists. There are minor missteps that will drive careful readers crazy, e.g., Michelle's hair gets frizzy in the "dry desert air." It all requires more suspension of disbelief than most of Levitin's fans will be willing to muster.

Cindy Darling Codell

SOURCE: A review of *Evil Encounter,* in *School Library Journal,* Vol. 42, No. 5, May, 1996, pp. 132, 135.

Michelle, a high school junior, blames her mother for her parents' divorce and hates southern California because it is so far from the father she has always adored, but who never seems to be available anymore. When her school suggests professional counseling, Michelle's mother signs her up for group sessions. The young woman becomes intrigued with Luke, the charismatic therapist. While attending his special seminar in an isolated Palm Springs villa, she is terrified when he encourages her to take peyote and when he makes advances toward her. Later, when Luke is revealed to be a fraud, and her mother is accused of being both his lover and his murderer, Michelle realizes she is the only one who can solve the crime. From perky J. Peterman catalog fans to burned-out, aging flower children, Levitin knows California cool. She understands how adults with unresolved issues can lose themselves in pursuit of career and libido only to be mystified when they find they have lost their children, too, in some indefinable way. The portrayal of a pop-therapy group dominated by a gifted con artist is riveting. Luke is very believable as he wins confidences, probes pain, and uses vulnerability to maintain his grip. Smooth dialogue and a tension-filled plot will make readers eager to finish the story. Although more sophisticated YAs may challenge the denouement, and the drug scenes don't ring completely true, most will find it satisfying. An exciting story, sure to promote much-needed discussion about psychological practice and ethics.

Ilene Cooper

SOURCE: A review of *Evil Encounter,* in *Booklist,* Vol. 92, No. 17, May 1, 1996, p. 1498.

Floundering after her parents' divorce and a subsequent move to California, 16-year-old Michelle Morrow joins a New Age-ish therapy group led by the charismatic Luke. Luke has also drawn her mother into his magic circle, and when Luke is murdered, Mrs. Morrow is arrested, and it's up to Michelle to find the real killer. This is the bare bones of the story, and if Levitin had just added some flesh, it might have worked better. Instead, there is so much going on here the strongest story line gets buried in the bloat. Mentioned, but never really developed, are subplots about infidelity, eating disorders, father-daughter relationships, mental retardation, and first romance. One story line, concerning a relationship Michelle has with a druggie, takes place entirely offstage and never really fits in. What keeps readers turning pages is the strong character of Michelle and her push-pull liaison with Luke, whose magnetism won't be lost on the audience. Exploring that relationship should have been enough for any book.

📖 *NINE FOR CALIFORNIA* (1996)

Linda Greengrass

SOURCE: A review of *Nine for California,* in *School Library Journal,* Vol. 42, No. 9, September, 1996, p. 184.

When Pa writes from the California gold fields to say he's lonely, Ma resolves to take her five children and join him. Young Amanda tells about their 21-day journey west from Missouri, cramped into a stagecoach with three other adult passengers. Levitin has used travelers' journals and letters from the late 1800s to concoct an event-filled adventure. Slowly but surely, Ma's sack full of "everything we'll need" for the trip empties out as its contents saves more than one tense moment from erupting into a disaster. The long route is at times tedious for the travelers, but not so for readers. Every time Amanda begins to become bored, something exciting happens: hungry Indians surround the stage; a torrential rainfall causes it to get stuck in the mud; buffalo stampede toward the coach; and so on. The characters are all well drawn. The language makes the story come alive. The bright, colorful cartoons lend an amused, tongue-in-cheek tone to the story, making this exaggerated, composite narrative almost believable, and distinguishing it from many of the others covering the same experience.

Publishers Weekly

SOURCE: A review of *Nine for California,* in *Publishers Weekly,* Vol. 243, No. 37, September 9, 1996, p. 83.

This lighthearted picture book puts a uniquely human face on the Gold Rush era, one with which any kid who's endured a long car trip will identify. Mama and her five kids, including narrator Amanda and Baby Betsy, leave Missouri to meet Pa in far-off "Californ-y," where he's been working in the gold fields. They join persnickety Mr. Hooper and dainty Miss Camilia in a crowded stagecoach for the 21-day trip. The group groans as Mama insists on bringing a huge, bulging sack that makes the coach all the more cramped. But when her bag of tricks saves the passengers from Indians, a buffalo stampede, robbers and even boredom, everyone stops complaining. Levitin (*The Man Who Kept His Heart in a Bucket*) crafts a text balanced with humor, rambunctious read-aloud language and a bounty of factual information about westward travel in the mid-1800s. [Cat Bowman] Smith's characteristically rowdy watercolors are often funny, but they also exude a sweetness and sensitivity to the difficult conditions. And like the text, the illustrations provide clear frontier detail and fun facts, too, such as the "anatomy of a stagecoach" that appears on the back jacket. A solid-gold nugget of a history lesson.

Janice M. Del Negro

SOURCE: A review of *Nine for California,* in *Bulletin of the Center for Children's Books,* Vol. 50, No. 4, December, 1996, p. 141.

Amanda, her mother, and her sister and brothers (Baby Betsy, Billy, Joe, and Ted) pack up their belongings and head for the California gold mines via stagecoach to join Papa. Squeezed on board with Cowboy Charlie, banker Mr. Hooper, and schoolteacher Miss Camilla, they are a tight fit and are like to die of boredom on the twenty-one day trip, as Amanda's repeating refrain attests: "The long road never ended. I wished that something would happen. It did." Problematic encounters with hungry Pawnee, a freezing hailstorm, a buffalo stampede, and stagecoach robbers are all resolved with something out of Mama's big sack, and everyone arrives safe and sound in Californ-y. Levitin's tale borders on the tall, with the humorous text enlivened even further by Bowman's jolly, slapsticky watercolors.

📖 *A PIECE OF HOME* (1996)

Hazel Rochman

SOURCE: A review of *A Piece of Home,* in *Booklist,* Vol. 93, No. 6, November 15, 1996, p. 594.

A contemporary Russian American immigration story—the leaving, the plane journey, the arrival—is told from the viewpoint of a young boy in this tender picture book about family parting and reunion. Gregor is not sure he wants to go to America, but his father will find work there, and his mother cannot wait to be united with her sister's family. They don't have room to take more than essentials, but Mama packs a small samovar, Papa takes his garmoshka accordion, and Gregor insists on taking his blanket that Great-Grandmother made. The blanket comforts him on the journey, but when he gets to America, he worries that his cousin Elie will think him babyish. The realistic watercolor pictures focus on the people and show the heartfelt emotion at the airport and in the relatives' home, especially between Mama and her sister. The scene in which Mama brings the brass samovar to the table is as moving as the sisters' tears when they remember the story of the blanket.

Publishers Weekly

SOURCE: A review of *A Piece of Home,* in *Publishers Weekly,* Vol. 243, No. 47, November 18, 1996, p. 74.

When Gregor's family emigrates to the United States from Russia, he is allowed to take one item. The "piece of home" he chooses is his baby blanket—a surprising choice for a school-age boy, and indicative of Gregor's anxiety. But his dicey choice only compounds his trepidation: Will his American cousin Elie think he is a baby for bringing a blanket? Levitin (*Nine for California*) tells this tale with great empathy, steering clear of sentimentality. Gregor's divided feelings ring true, as do those of his anxious and excited parents. [Juan] Wijngaard's realistic watercolor renderings, perceptive and expressive, virtually tell the story on their own. He captures moments so clearly—Gregor's skeptical inspection of American airplane food, for example—that young readers will feel they are sharing these characters' experience.

Janice M. Del Negro

SOURCE: A review of *A Piece of Home,* in *Bulletin of the Center for Children's Books,* Vol. 50, No. 5, January, 1997, p. 179.

Gregor and his family are emigrating from Russia to America. He is understandably anxious, and he chooses his security blanket, part of a quilt made by his great-grandmother, as the one "treasure" he can take with him. When the family finally arrives in America, Gregor is sorry he brought it, certain that Elie, a cousin his age, will laugh at him. But Elie has a blanket just like it, and Aunt Marissa explains the similarity, saying, "We cut the blanket in half, so I could bring a piece of home with me to America." Levitin's story is message-driven, but it makes a specific immigrant experience universal by concentrating on the moving anxiety of one little boy. Gregor's uncertainty is evident in both text and illustrations as he huddles beneath and clings stubbornly to his old blanket. Though inclined to be flat and stodgy, Wijngaard's watercolors have a photo-documentary feel to them; focusing on the faces and reactions of the reunited family, they concretely chronicle the journey from Russia to America.

YESTERDAY'S CHILD (1997)

Gerry Larson

SOURCE: A review of *Yesterday's Child,* in *School Library Journal,* Vol. 43, No. 6, June, 1997, pp. 120, 122.

With skill and suspense, Levitin unveils a family's dark secrets. After her mother's sudden death, Laura, 16, is determined to discover why the two of them were never close. Searching through her mother's personal possessions, she finds a "Friends Forever" bracelet, a photograph of two teenage girls labeled "Megan and me," and an unmailed letter, written the day before the woman died, addressed to Megan. Laura mails the letter adding an explanation and hopes for a response. She then leaves on a class trip to Washington, DC, drawing close to her mother's hometown of Birch Bend, VA. With her friend Kim in tow or covering for her absence from scheduled events, Laura makes repeated visits to the town looking for the truth. Her obsessive investigation propels her to make a secret, one-day round-trip flight to Toronto to meet Megan. Piecing together the woman's disturbing reminiscences of Laura's mother with newspaper files in the Birch Bend library, Laura makes a shocking discovery: Megan and her mother killed Megan's parents. Laura's gripping quest will captivate teen readers. Although several chance encounters and repeated violations of school-trip rules seem improbable, the two girls create believable alibis. Tension builds steadily as Megan is slowly revealed as a psychopath who will kill again to keep the past buried. The complexities of friendship, loyalty, and honesty are fully explored. Wary of adults but yearning for parental love and understanding, Laura is a daring, resourceful, and introspective heroine.

Stephanie Zvirin

SOURCE: A review of *Yesterday's Child,* in *Booklist,* Vol. 93, Nos. 19 & 20, June 1 & 15, 1997, p. 1686.

Although never close to her mother, Laura is nonetheless thrown for a loop by her parent's sudden death. To ease the pain of loss, she begins going through her mother's things, but instead of giving her a better understanding of her distant, mercurial mom, her snooping opens a Pandora's box full of secrets. Even her mother's name seems to be a lie. Levitin starts out strongly here, examining Laura's confused feelings about her parents and her relationship with her friend Kim; and the Nancy Drew-like investigations are intriguing. The author strays off course and into melodrama, however, when she suddenly enters the villain's consciousness and when she has Laura fall in love (at first sight) with the boy who turns out to be the villain's son. As is true of Levitin's recent novel *Evil Encounter* (1996), there are some nice touches here, with the heroine somewhat more dimensional than is usual in this genre, but it's an uneven, not entirely satisfying read.

Deborah Stevenson

SOURCE: A review of *Yesterday's Child,* in *Bulletin of the Center for Children's Books,* Vol. 50, No. 11, July-August, 1997, p. 401.

Sixteen-year-old Laura is just beginning to realize how little she knew her mother, who recently died and whose privacy Laura's distant father still guards. When Laura's class takes a trip to Washington, DC, Laura determines to hunt down her mother's past in the little Virginia town where she was born. Soon she realizes she's stumbled onto her mother's dark mystery: back in high school, she and her best friend, Megan, deliberately burned up Megan's house with Megan's parents in it. What's more, Megan, now the mother of a boy whom Laura loves, is prepared to kill to protect the secret of her past. Impossible as the plot is, a sinewy, atmospheric writer of the Lois Duncan ilk might have been able to pull it off. That unfortunately doesn't happen here: Levitin's story is baggy rather than taut, with sloppiness (Laura's mother's death is sometimes attributed to an aneurysm and sometimes heart failure; at least one of the included songs is titled erroneously) and contrivance (Laura happens immediately onto her mother's high-school class reunion) both interfering with the smooth progression of the plot. Nor is Laura a particularly interesting heroine: her distress is authentic, but her indifference to the feelings of everyone but herself seems to be greater than the plot demands.

BOOM TOWN (1998)

Anne Scott MacLeod

SOURCE: "And No Television, Either," in *The New York Times Book Review,* May 17, 1998, p. 23.

Boom Town, by Sonia Levitin, is about a town created by the California gold rush and the awesome energies of a little girl named Amanda. On the first two pages, Amanda's family goes to California so Pa can prospect in the gold fields. By the third page, "after the water was fetched and the wash was done, after the soap was made and the fire laid, after the beds were fixed and the floor was swept clean," Amanda is bored. She wants to make pie.

And pie she makes, first for family, then for hungry gold miners. She sets up a bakery, enlisting several brothers to help. When an itinerant peddler stops by, she buys more pans and persuades him to settle down and start a store. Soon a cooper, a tanner, a miller and a blacksmith come for pie and stay to sell their skills. A livery stable and a bank, side-walks, a teacher and a preacher, and there: the settlement is a real town, all because of Amanda's enterprising spirit.

The pictures, by Cat Bowman Smith, are as spirited as Amanda. They are watercolors in earthy tones, loose, energetic, cheerful and full of accurate detail. The clothing is right and so are the tools and trappings of the time and place. Nobody in this book is beautiful—our heroine has a funny nose and a gap-toothed smile—but everyone is full of life and good will. *Boom Town* includes blacks and Asians; everybody works, and so does this warm-hearted book. An endnote says that there was such a young pie maker in California's history; unfortunately, no dates are mentioned anywhere in the book.

THE SINGING MOUNTAIN (1998)

Publishers Weekly

SOURCE: A review of *The Singing Mountain,* in *Publishers Weekly,* Vol. 245, No. 36, September 7, 1998, pp. 96-97.

Levitin contributes an unusually intelligent, thought-provoking novel about faith. Mitch Green, a suburban Californian bound for UCLA in the fall, is on a summer tour of Israel with his temple's youth group when he meets someone from an Orthodox yeshiva—and decides to stay on and study at the yeshiva himself. Mitch's cousin Carlie, an orphan who is being raised by Mitch's parents, describes the reaction at home: the Greens, Reform Jews, are horrified and certain Mitch has been brainwashed. Mitch's letters, saying that before he felt "parched" and now feels "nourished," sound to the family "almost as if someone else were dictating [them]." By Christmas, Carlie and her aunt are bound for Israel, to spend time with Mitch and see if they can bring him home. As they grapple with weighty issues—e.g., belief in God in the face of tragedy, and putting principles above personal relationships—Levitin's own touch is light. She maintains a remarkable evenhandedness with all her characters, major and minor, as she presents conflicting points of view without favoring any one of them or insisting that they ultimately converge. She unfolds bits of the characters' pasts with precision timing, creating little revelations that illuminate both the characters and the challenges they confront. Some of the religious matters are simplified—appropriately, given a general readership—but the fundamental issues will touch teens of all persuasions.

Additional coverage of Levitin's life and career is contained in the following sources published by Gale Research: *Authors and Artists for Young Adults,* Vol. 13; *Contemporary Authors,* Vol. 29-32R; *Contemporary Literary Criticism,* Vol. 17; *Junior DISCovering Authors; Major Authors and Illustrators for Children and Young Adults; Something about the Author,* Vol. 68; and *Something about the Author Autobiography Series,* Vol. 2.

Albert Marrin

1936-

American author of nonfiction.

Major works include *1812: The War Nobody Won* (1985), *Hitler* (1987), *Cowboys, Indians, and Gunfighters: The Story of the Cattle Kingdom* (1993), *"Unconditional Surrender": U. S. Grant and the Civil War* (1993), *The Sea King: Sir Francis Drake and His Times* (1995).

INTRODUCTION

A history professor and celebrated author of over twenty-five nonfiction titles, Marrin introduces middle graders and young adults to the fascination and enthusiasm that he so fervently feels for world history. Marrin lends dramatic appeal to his work by focusing on some of the most significant personalities and moments in U.S. and world history. As many reviewers have pointed out, Marrin brings history to life for young readers with his talent for relaying detail and anecdote. While a recognized expert at keeping meticulously true to documented facts, Marrin is also praised for conveying drama and excitement in his nonfiction. This rare combination of skills, which Zena Sutherland described as the ability to "infuse the facts of history with the drama of fiction," has resulted in Marrin's well-deserved reputation "as one of the best writers of history for YAs," Margaret Miles once wrote. Marrin's detailed and vivid descriptions, which Stephanie Zvirin accused of "com[ing] perilously close to the lurid," are intriguing to young adults, making his books eminently readable. Further increasing his books' appeal to young adults are Marrin's choices of interesting subject matter. *Cowboys, Indians, and Gunfighters: The Story of the Cattle Kingdom,* for example, is about that ever-fascinating period of U.S. history—the nineteenth-century Old West. Marrin also focuses on specific wars, including the American Civil War, the War of 1812, the Vietnam War, and various events of World War II, from the invasion of Europe by the Allies to a history of spies and a study of the air war. Marrin further explores military campaigns through biographies of their leaders, such as in *"Unconditional Surrender": U. S. Grant and the Civil War, Virginia's General: Robert E. Lee and the Civil War* (1994), *Napoleon and the Napoleonic Wars* (1990), and *Stalin: Russia's Man of Steel* (1988). In these biographies, as in all of his books, Marrin's sugar is his lucid, skillfully constructed prose, which conveys drama and excitement to help the medicine, or historical facts, go down easily. Whether writing about an event or a person, Marrin is recognized for creating a complete context, providing detail and real-life anecdotes, and striking a balance between perspectives of participating groups and individuals. *Cowboys, Indians, and Gunfighters* explores the Old West from the beginning—from the

earliest Spanish settlers who introduced horses and cattle to the Great Plains—and exemplifies Marrin's unique style of presenting a complete picture of history. As Deborah Stevenson observed, Marrin "succeed[s] particularly well in linking famous episodes in history to a broader view of the time." Marrin also incorporates gruesomely detailed descriptions of atrocities to illustrate the violence perpetuated by all sides, such as the cavalry's massacre of Native Americans, the resulting vengeance sometimes taken in scalps, and the troops' senseless slaughter of buffalo herds that are depicted in *Cowboys, Indians, and Gunfighters.* In addition to promoting balanced accounts of violent incidents, Marrin gives narrative voices to minority groups that are not often heard, such as African-American and Mexican cowboys. Although sometimes criticized for oversimplification or heightened dramatic effects, Marrin more often has been acclaimed for his well-documented research and his ability to make the past accessible to young readers.

Biographical Information

Born in New York City, Marrin later attended City

College (now City College of the City University of New York), and received a bachelor of arts degree in history in 1958. He began his teaching career at William Howard Taft Middle School in New York City. While teaching social studies, Marrin was also doing graduate work at Yeshiva University and preparing for his wedding to Yvette Rappaport in 1959. Completing a master's degree in education, Marrin went on to Columbia University, where he eventually received a master of arts degree in 1961 and a doctorate in 1968. While completing his graduate coursework and teaching middle school, Marrin became a visiting professor at Yeshiva University in 1967 and an assistant professor of history in 1968. During the early 1970s, he served as a visiting professor at Touro College in New York, and first began writing nonfiction for an adult audience. Marrin launched his career as an author for young adults with the publication of *Overlord: D-Day and the Invasion of Europe* in 1982. Currently a professor and chairman of Yeshiva University's history department, Marrin lives in the Bronx, New York, and enjoys travelling throughout Europe.

Major Works

1812: The War Nobody Won, Marrin's accessible overview of the War of 1812, is brought to life by facts, details, and anecdotes of daily life in the early nineteenth century. Marrin intentionally shows that the English, Americans, and Native Americans all had their foolish as well as their valiant moments, portraying each as complex and realistic, rather than vilified or idealistic. The account's balanced perspective is further aided by Marrin's recognition of the role of black sailors and soldiers during the war. Readers of *1812: The War Nobody Won* may be amused by anecdotes, such as the story of a commander who split his pants during battle, but they also learn historical facts, such as what sailors ate, and meet influential personalities of the time, including Tecumseh and Andrew Jackson.

Hitler is one of a quartet of biographies that Marrin has written on world leaders, including Stalin, Mao Tsetung, and Napoleon. True to his reputation, Marrin pays close attention to context. The work focuses on Hitler's childhood, describing factors such as his father's brutality and his experiences during World War I, which predisposed him to anger and arrogance. Marrin also examines the greater world context, looking at historical events that contributed to the world's willingness to accept Hitler's policies. The tragic impact of those policies and the pain suffered during World War II are described through facts, photographs, and personal accounts of the people who survived the war. A *Kirkus Reviews* critic appreciated Marrin's inclusion of topics of recent interest, including the White Rose resistance group and the fate of Josef Mengele. Mary A. Burns described the work as a "riveting account that is informative, illuminating, and inescapably painful." Acknowledging that many books have been written about the Second World War, Shirly Wilton remarked, "Marrin's book stands out for its lively writing, its emphasis on personal an-

ecdote, its value as a reference source, and its insight into the nature of totalitarianism."

Cowboys, Indians, and Gunfighters: The Story of the Cattle Kingdom is an account of life on the Great Plains in the Western United States during the 1800s, from the earliest Spanish settlements to the struggle between buffalo and cattle for the open range. Divided into six chronological chapters, the book includes descriptions of a diverse group of cowboys, including African-Americans and Mexicans. Julie Halverstadt praised *Cowboys, Indians, and Gunfighters* as "a dynamic look at one of the most exciting and dangerous periods in U.S. History."

Marrin's approach to the American Civil War resulted in two titles that profile generals on opposing sides: *Virginia's General: Robert E. Lee and the Civil War* (1994) and *"Unconditional Surrender": U. S. Grant and the Civil War.* Using each general's point of view to chronicle the war years, Marrin lures readers into Civil War history by presenting the positive and less commonly revealed negative character traits of these historical personalities. In *"Unconditional Surrender,"* for example, neither Grant's racism nor his drinking are glossed over. Deborah Stevenson wrote that the detailed accounts of battles combined with a plethora of facts and anecdotes make *"Unconditional Surrender"* a "history of living men and women who are complete with faults and contradictions."

With a focus on a "flamboyant figure," wrote a *Kirkus Reviews* critic, *The Sea King: Sir Francis Drake and His Times,* investigates "an extraordinary time of chaos and change." Through Sir Francis Drake, England's larger-than-life pirate, explorer, and privateer, readers are exposed to emotional events of the entire Elizabethan era—the development of the African slave trade, the Protestant Reformation, the Spanish Inquisition, and Prince Philip II's attempt to invade England. Marrin's detailed description of the Spanish Armada's defeat has been termed by Ann A. Flowers as "breathtaking in its tension and excitement." The extensive exploration of historical events, however, does not detract from Marrin's attention to the character of Sir Francis Drake, who is portrayed, Flowers concludes, as "complex and surprising . . . courteous and considerate . . . but also ruthless and ambitious." Characteristically, *The Sea King* is full of graphic descriptions of executions, battles, and ruthless behaviors that promise to hold the attention of even reluctant young historians. "Hero or villain," a *Kirkus Reviews* critic observed, "Drake emerges as an unforgettable persona in a masterly work."

Awards

Marrin's *1812: The War Nobody Won* was named a Notable Children's Trade Book by the National Council for Social Studies and Children's Book Council, and an Honor Book by *Boston Globe/Horn Book,* both in 1985. Marrin received the Western Heritage Award for best juvenile nonfiction book from the National Cowboy Hall of Fame, and the Spur Award from the Western Writers of America, both in 1993, for *Cowboys, Indians, and Gunfighters: The Story of the Cattle Kingdom.* "Unconditional Surrender": *U. S. Grant and the Civil War* was named an Honor Book by *Boston Globe/Horn Book* in 1994, and received the Dorothy Canfield Fisher Children's Book Award as well as the Association of Christian Public School Teachers and Administrators Honor Award, both in 1995. *The Sea King: Sir Francis Drake and His Times* was named a Best Book by *School Library Journal.* Marrin won the Children's Book Guild and *Washington Post* Nonfiction Award in 1995 for his contributions to children's literature.

TITLE COMMENTARY

📖 *OVERLORD: D-DAY AND THE INVASION OF EUROPE* (1982)

Publishers Weekly

SOURCE: A review of *Overlord: D-Day and the Invasion of Europe,* in *Publishers Weekly,* Vol. 222, No. 10, September 3, 1982, pp. 59-60.

Overlord was the code name for British and American landings in German-occupied France, 6 June 1944, that made the Allied victory possible. After sketching the World War II background, Marrin swings into a narrative of mounting excitement. Preparations for the mammoth invasion were perfectly kept secrets, helped by dummy armies and fake guns positioned to mislead the enemy's attention. As told here, the drama of the landings is deeply moving: paratroopers snagged in trees and quickly shot; heavily equipped troops slipping and drowning in the choppy sea; soldiers pinned on the beach by enemy fire suddenly pushing forward, the only way to go. There is pathos in the long-oppressed French offering gifts of welcome and British paratroopers behind Nazi lines roaring greetings to bagpipe-playing comrades fighting their way up from the landings to a miraculously on-schedule rendezvous. Young readers of Marrin's book (with nearly 50 graphic photos) will learn well about D-Day. Older readers, lucking into a copy, may cry.

Shirley Wilton

SOURCE: A review of *Overlord: D-Day and the Invasion of Europe,* in *School Library Journal,* Vol. 29, No. 3, November, 1982, p. 88.

Marrin has a special talent for nonfiction writing and, as evidenced by his recent book *The Airman's War,* for military history. *Overlord,* his account of the landing of 175,000 assault troops on the beaches of Normandy on June 5, 1944 and of the subsequent liberation of France,

is equally successful. He weaves together the planning of the invasion and the coordination of naval, intelligence and air forces with the roles and reactions of individual participants in the invasion. The result is an informational book that is highly exciting reading and that blends sound interpretation and explanation with the noise and smell of the battlefield. Other factual accounts of D-Day are available, but Marrin's book is a small masterpiece in the "literature of fact" and should be added to library shelves.

Ethel R. Twichell

SOURCE: A review of *Overlord: D-Day and the Invasion of Europe,* in *The Horn Book Magazine,* Vol. LVIII, No. 6, December, 1982, pp. 667-68.

In a straightforward and eminently readable account of the D-Day invasion, the author provides a brief historical background and then describes the enormously difficult task of procuring and organizing both men and material, the equally difficult problem of hiding them from enemy eyes, and finally the actual assault. Although the focus is on American participation, particularly after the invasion begins, the British receive generous praise, as do Polish, French, and other resistance fighters. The broad scope of the assignment, the careful planning, the lucky and the unlucky mistakes are all well described and enlivened by small but telling details. The use of exclamation points, question marks, italics, and quotations makes the prose somewhat breathless, but it does lend excitement and brings to mind the unforgettable picture of British and American troops wading to shore through the bloody and shell-torn waters off the coast of Normandy.

Ilene Cooper

SOURCE: A review of *Overlord: D-Day and the Invasion of Europe,* in *Booklist,* Vol. 79, No. 11, February 1, 1983, p. 725.

In this companion to Marrin's excellent *The Airman's War: World War II in the Sky,* the author focuses on Operation Overlord and D-Day, June 5, 1942. Placing the reader squarely in the midst of the action, Marrin describes the massive undertaking in a sure, highly readable manner. It is difficult to imagine how students could resist being caught up in the action-filled presentation: the planning, the attack, the "actors," the denouement of the battle. Excellent black-and-white photos extend the text.

📖 *VICTORY IN THE PACIFIC* (1983)

Kate M. Flanagan

SOURCE: A review of *Victory in the Pacific,* in *The Horn Book Magazine,* Vol. LIX, No. 2, April, 1983, p. 184.

From the attack on Pearl Harbor to Japan's surrender the book follows major battles fought by the Navy and the Marines in the Pacific. Fast-paced accounts of Doolittle's raid on Tokyo and the air, land, and sea action at Midway, Guadalcanal, Iwo Jima, and Okinawa give a broad, dramatic overview of Japanese and American strategies. The author tells of the individual and collective courage of soldiers, sailors, and fliers on both sides of the war with vivid re-creations of the battles. But while the accounts of these events are absorbing, the book is even more interesting when it focuses on the complex fighting machines that changed the face of modern sea warfare—huge aircraft carriers and their fighter planes, stealthy submarines, and the venerable battleships. A feeling for life on board the ships is given through details of how the sailors slept, what they ate, and how they relaxed. And by describing the warfare from both sides, the author provides an understanding of the warrior heritage that made the Japanese such a formidable enemy and that ultimately gave rise to the suicide attacks of the tragic Kamikaze pilots.

David A. Lindsey

SOURCE: A review of *Victory in the Pacific,* in *School Library Journal,* Vol. 29, No. 8, April, 1983, p. 126.

Readable, breezy prose characterizes this overview of World War II's battles for control of the Pacific. With a minimum of background information, Marrin jumps right into his narrative and concisely covers the course of war from Pearl Harbor to Tokyo Bay, making stops along the way to discuss carrier warfare, Guadalcanal, and life in the "silent service" on American submarines. Emphasis is placed upon the part played by individuals and the horrendous hardships and dangers faced by them at sea, on minuscule coral atolls or in the air. This, along with a generous sprinkling of anecdotes and quotes, constantly remind the reader that it was human flesh, blood and courage that brought about ultimate victory. On the whole, the work makes a good introduction to the Pacific Theater of Operations and may encourage young people to go on to read . . . other works with more depth and less breadth.

Michael Wessells

SOURCE: A review of *Victory in the Pacific,* in *Voice of Youth Advocates,* Vol. 6, No. 4, October, 1983, p. 226.

The insatiable cadre of World War II aficionados will form a ready audience for this straightforward account of America's war in the Pacific. A graphic chronological narrative of battle action is interspersed with lucid capsule descriptions of selected topics, including the structure of aircraft carriers and life aboard a submarine. The 47 contemporary photographs and four diagrams are

appropriately placed in relation to the descriptive text. The book includes an index and a selected reading list, though most of its entries are on a considerably higher reading level. The writing is clear and simple, if a little folksy, which will appeal to hi/lo readers. The approach is primarily anecdotal, with minimal attention to strategic and tactical detail. . . . The single map is adequate only for general strategic understanding, and lacks labels for some places mentioned prominently in the text (e.g. Marshall Islands). There are no new facts or interpretations, but the treatment is a good one-volume summary for collections thin in this subject and a worthy marginal addition for full collections.

THE SEA ROVERS: PIRATES, PRIVATEERS, AND BUCCANEERS (1984)

Zena Sutherland

SOURCE: A review of *The Sea Rovers: Pirates, Privateers, and Buccaneers,* in *Bulletin of the Center for Children's Books,* Vol. 37, No. 9, May, 1984, pp. 169-70.

The evidence of research in a rather lively text is corroborated by the appended list of sources; Marrin incorporates vivid details of personalities and conflicts in a book that describes both such famous figures as Henry Morgan, Blackbeard, and the pirates of the Barbary Coast, and lesser known ones such as the Chinese woman who commanded a greater fleet than any pirate of all time, Ching Yih Saou. The material itself offers enough drama and excitement to compensate for the several weaknesses of the writing style, one of which is a tendency to use the non sequitur ("The boy grew into a lonely, silent man, except when his temper flared"), and another the awkward phrasing: "Having wronged him, he felt that everything he did to them from now on was right." Wrong.

Kate M. Flanagan

SOURCE: A review of *The Sea Rovers: Pirates, Privateers, and Buccaneers,* in *The Horn Book Magazine,* Vol. LX, No. 3, June, 1984, pp. 349-50.

Focusing on the "'golden age' of sea roving" that began with the discovery of the New World and ended with the United States Navy, the book vividly recounts the exploits of the colorful men and women who terrorized the seas. Sometimes working on their own and sometimes backed by various governments, the pirates helped shape history. Sir Francis Drake was considered a monster by the Spaniards, but with the Queen's blessings he plundered and later became a naval hero. The buccaneers, a wild breed of men that roamed the Caribbean, became the British colonies' defense against the strong Spanish Navy. And later, when the pirates moved their operations to the Atlantic, they helped the colonial seaports to prosper by circumventing the British monopoly on manufactured goods. The author rounds out the historical facts with numerous quotations, anecdotes, and bits of folklore, providing lively portraits of many legendary characters, from the fearsome Blackbeard to a Chinese woman called Ching Yih Saou, "the greatest pirate of all time." Details about clothing, weapons, shipboard conditions, and the pirates' harsh codes of behavior help bring to life a violent but fascinating era in seafaring history.

Elizabeth Mellett

SOURCE: A review of *The Sea Rovers: Pirates, Privateers, and Buccaneers,* in *School Library Journal,* Vol. 30, No. 10, August, 1984, p. 76.

Marrin introduces Sir Francis Drake, Henry Morgan and Blackbeard as well as lesser-known pirates and privateers who roamed the seas during a "Golden Age" for pirates that lasted for 300 years after Columbus discovered America. Emphasis is placed on the adventures and heroics of individuals like Drake (whom the author clearly admires) and Blackbeard, although there is some description of life at sea for the ordinary sailor or pirate. Marrin also devotes a brief chapter to three women pirates, two of whom posed as men throughout their careers. The book ends with a chapter on the beginnings of the U.S. Navy, and the Navy's fight against the Barbary pirates. The numerous black-and-white illustrations, diagrams and maps add to readers' enjoyment; however, most of the illustrations are not included in the index, which consists largely of the names of men and ships. An enjoyable introduction that should leave readers eager for more.

Ilene Cooper

SOURCE: A review of *The Sea Rovers: Pirates, Privateers, and Buccaneers,* in *Booklist,* Vol. 81, No. 1, September 1, 1984, p. 68.

In a lively, readable style punctuated with engrossing biographies, this [book] describes the "golden age" of sea roving that began with Columbus and ended 300 years later when America and some European nations banded together to wipe out the last vestiges of privateering. Marrin distinguishes between outlaw pirates and privateers or buccaneers who, though they could be just as nasty, had the law on their side. Among the individuals Marrin singles out are Sir Francis Drake, the British nemesis of Spain; Henry Morgan, a buccaneer who later became a judge and sent many pirates to the gallows; and the terrifying Blackbeard, who made other pirates seem meek and mild in comparison. Most fascinating is the chapter on women pirates, who disguised themselves as men and could be just as ruthless. A well-researched piece complemented by old prints, engravings, diagrams, and maps.

1812: THE WAR NOBODY WON (1985)

Cheryl Penny

SOURCE: A review of *1812: The War Nobody Won,* in *Booklist,* Vol. 81, No. 22, August, 1995, p. 1668.

Marrin's lively, readable history of the War of 1812 supplies not only the names, dates, and facts students need for their assignments, but also a variety of intriguing details, vignettes, and anecdotes that bring the participants to life. Balanced in terms of showing that the Americans, British, and Indians had their foolish or inglorious moments as well as their heroic ones, the book repeatedly points out the bravery of black sailors and soldiers throughout the conflict. Marrin deftly fills in the details of the everyday lives of those who fought on land and sea. Readers will learn what the common sailor ate, how his cannons worked, and what he feared, as well as why the British soldiers wore scarlet coats.

Elizabeth Reardon

SOURCE: A review of *1812: The War Nobody Won,* in *School Library Journal,* Vol. 32, No. 1, September, 1985, p. 136.

Marrin attempts to present the confusing events before and during the War of 1812 in a manner that will appeal and inform, and for the most part, he succeeds. He covers the war from its start, explaining the impressment of American sailors, to its bloody conclusion at the Battle of New Orleans. Along the way, readers meet the "characters" of the times—from the leaders, like Andrew Jackson and Tecumseh, to the legends, like Johnny Appleseed and the original Uncle Sam. Especially good is the information on the early Navy and its battles. Marrin is unbiased and pulls no punches; the early blunders of the Americans are fully discussed, as is the later overconfidence of the British. Marrin relates some amusing anecdotes (such as the American commander who split his trousers in the heat of battle) in telling his story. Although such tales will capture readers and perhaps bring history alive to them, one must question the sources of such information. Marrin has obviously done a great deal of research, for minute details crowd each page; yet there are no footnotes, and no primary sources are listed in the bibliography. Throughout, there are numerous reproductions, maps and some excellent diagrams. A good introduction and overview of this often confusing chapter in American history.

AZTECS AND SPANIARDS: CORTÉS AND THE CONQUEST OF MEXICO (1986)

Zena Sutherland

SOURCE: A review of *Aztecs and Spaniards: Cortés and the Conquest of Mexico,* in *Bulletin of the Center for Children's Books,* Vol. 39, No. 8, April, 1986, pp. 153-54.

As dramatic as fiction but well-grounded in fact, this account of the clash between Aztecs under Montezuma and conquistadors under Cortes gives vivid cultural background on each group, fine portraits of the leaders involved, and a well-organized tour through the action-packed events. Marrin includes telling quotes from observers and writers of the sixteenth century; his own style is readable, even in detailed battle descriptions, and his balanced perspective and respect for each side are clearly an asset. The unfamiliar names have pronunciation guides in parentheses after each one is introduced. A list of books for further reading is appended. An excellent resource for any study of Central American history or in conjunction with research into parallel developments in the U.S.

Ilene Cooper

SOURCE: A review of *Aztecs and Spaniards: Cortés and the Conquest of Mexico,* in *Booklist,* Vol. 82, No. 15, April 1, 1986, p. 1224.

In riveting fashion, Marrin describes the rise and fall of the Aztecs and brings clearly into focus the actions of Cortés and the Spanish conquistadors who helped change the face of the New World. Marrin begins his story in 1325, when a wandering Indian tribe saw a sign from their god and began settling the land now known as Mexico. In fascinating detail, Marrin tells readers how the Aztec culture evolved, with its strong points and its weaknesses. Among its flaws was the slavish devotion of the Indians to their gods, who demanded constant tribute in the form of human sacrifice. Marrin also takes readers to Spain, where the intrepid though egocentric Hernando Cortés is bound and determined to gather men and seek his fortune in the New World. Eventually, of course, these two groups clash, and, with a you-are-there sense of immediacy, the author makes readers feel as though they are living the events. Some of his reporting is so realistic, in fact, that squeamish readers may have a few problems. The description of the Aztec sacrificial ceremony in which ghoulish-looking priests tear the hearts from their victims is particularly horrific. This is an excellent choice for students who don't think they like nonfiction. They will find Marrin's book has the same page-turning drama, action, and full-bodied characters found in the best fiction; it is impossible not to be caught up in it. To be illustrated with black-and-white maps, diagrams [by Richard Rosenbloom], prints, and photographs.

Dennis C. Tucker

SOURCE: A review of *Aztecs and Spaniards: Cortés and the Conquest of Mexico,* in *School Library Journal,* Vol. 32, No. 10, August, 1986, p. 104.

On February 10, 1519, Hernan Cortes, anxious to avoid arrest, disobeyed orders and set sail from Havana with an army of 500 soldiers to conquer a golden land called Mexico. Marrin has distilled the best from several contemporary accounts of the expedition and condensed it into a palatable form. Under his skilled pen, Cortes and Montezuma become real people. The story begins with a historical perspective of the Aztecs and their origins, followed by the place of the "conquistadors" in their world. Readers travel with Cortes through a chronological account of the capture of Tenochtitlan and its reconstruction to the end of his life. Events are told with sufficient detail to add interest without bogging down. Sensitive readers may be bothered by graphic "blood and guts" descriptions; yet such description is unavoidable. One minor flaw is that the spellings of some Mexican words and their suggested pronunciations are not standard. The illustrative material is excellent. Many are photographs of artifacts now located in museums scattered throughout the world. Others are drawings that are based on ancient codices. An excellent account of the conquest of Mexico.

Elizabeth S. Watson

SOURCE: A review of *Aztecs and Spaniards: Cortés and the Conquest of Mexico,* in *The Horn Book Magazine,* Vol. LXII, No. 5, September-October, 1986, pp. 610-11.

Albert Marrin has written the grim history of the defeat of the Aztecs in a compelling work that reads like a novel while providing all the dates, people, places, and details necessary for a reference book. The first quarter of the book draws an unforgettable picture of the Aztec Empire from its early days to the height reached at the beginning of the sixteenth century. The coming of Cortes and his campaign against and eventual subjugation of the Aztecs constitute the largest part of the book, with the last few pages summing up Cortes's frustration in later life when he was denied the governorship of New Spain. The emphasis is on action—battles, sacrifices to the Aztec gods, and progress of the conquest. Yet Marrin manages to give the reader a sense of the personalities involved—Cortes, Montezuma, Doña Marina, even the distant King Charles in Spain. The illustrations, redrawn from historic sources, give an interesting feeling for the original creators, both Indian and Spanish, who were there. The drawings, diagrams, maps, and photographs are used sparingly and effectively to clarify and accentuate points and ideas in the text. The index includes a pronunciation guide to the Aztec names.

HITLER (1987)

Shirley Wilton

SOURCE: A review of *Hitler,* in *School Library Journal,* Vol. 33, No. 10, June-July, 1987, p. 110.

Hitler's life is inseparable from Hitler's Germany and Hitler's war, so it is not surprising that, after describing the dictator's childhood and youth in Austria, Marrin turns away from personal biography to describe life in Nazi Germany and then to recount the campaigns of World War II. Throughout the history of events, however, he points to the influence of the dictator, his increasingly irrational drive to consummate his racial policies, and his responsibility for major military decisions. Marrin brings to this biography a wealth of background information. The author is scrupulous in mentioning sources, and he makes liberal use of quotations, statistics, popular sayings, and other factual material. While not a complete biography, the book emphasizes facts that young readers should know about the impact of Hitler's policies on the lives of the German people, the controls exercised over a whole society, and the horrors of the Second World War. In comparison to available literature on this period of history, Marrin's book stands out for its lively writing, its emphasis on personal anecdote, its value as a reference source, and its insight into the nature of totalitarianism. It is an excellent addition to any library.

Ilene Cooper

SOURCE: A review of *Hitler,* in *Booklist,* Vol. 83, No. 21, July, 1987, p. 1681.

Marrin writes insightfully about the life of Adolf Hitler and attempts to ascertain the reasons for his fanaticism, as well as the motives of those who blindly followed him. The author forgoes sensationalism, and his matter-of-fact writing style and recitation of events are more than adequate to chronicle the horror. Step-by-step, he describes how Hitler, a seemingly shy, insecure, young man, was able to inspire a defeated nation that saw the extermination of many of its citizens as its salvation. The especially strong focus on Hitler's childhood—his life with a tyrannical father, his crushing rejection from art school, and his motivating experiences during World War I—will give readers a better understanding of the dictator, but even after all the cogent theories, the question of just how so many people could have been swayed by a madman lingers. Even Marrin at times seems perplexed. In the book's introduction he says Hitler wasn't "born evil," but later, that people who responded to Hitler were "bewitched." In the end, perhaps, there are no explanations.

Margaret A. Bush

SOURCE: A review of *Hitler,* in *The Horn Book Magazine,* Vol. LXIII, No. 5, September-October, 1987, p. 630.

Once again Marrin combines narrative flair with scholarship to recreate the life story of Adolf Hitler and the devastating effect of his life on world history. In the beginning chapters the author describes those factors in Hitler's early life which likely contributed to his arrogance and bitterness as well as the historical events which predisposed the Germans, and also the governments of other countries, to be gullible during Hitler's rise to power. Of course, the events of the war engineered by Hitler and his brutality are the major focus of the book. The accounts are told unflinchingly, with the author making good use of statistics; writing careful descriptions and explanations of political, military, and human aspects; and quoting occasionally from firsthand accounts. Marrin has drawn from a wide range of sources, several identified in the bibliography, and in turn he draws a riveting account that is informative, illuminating, and inescapably painful. The accompanying photographs share these characteristics, some being mercifully dark in tone. The need for remembrance, stated in the conclusion of this book and in many other books on the subject, is well served by this lucid, skillfully constructed chronicle.

STRUGGLE FOR A CONTINENT: THE FRENCH AND INDIAN WARS, 1690-1760 (1987)

Paula Nespeca Deal

SOURCE: A review of *Struggle for a Continent: The French and Indian Wars, 1690-1760,* in *Voice of Youth Advocates,* Vol. 10, No. 4, October, 1987, p. 189.

Often receiving minor coverage, the 70 years of struggle for control of North America by the combatants, the English, the French and the native Americans, was a prelude to our war for independence. Each group knew that the control of the vast, rich land was worth a fight to the death. This fascinating, easy-to-read overview clearly explains the political maneuverings and military history. The author, a well-known historian, brings this often misunderstood conflict to life with vivid details of the cultural and social background such as the hardships settlers and soldiers faced and the terror created by ruthless fighting that condoned scalping and torture. The factual account is enlivened with colorful descriptions and excerpts from primary sources. The contributions of women are included and the actions of the Indians put in their cultural context. The index and bibliography will make this useful for research for middle school through high school students although a lack of maps and illustrations may be a drawback. Any YA, however, who enjoys history, historical fiction or who must read a nonfiction book for an assignment will find *Struggle for a Continent* a pleasurable, even exciting choice.

Kirkus Reviews

SOURCE: A review of *Struggle for a Continent: The French and Indian Wars, 1690-1760,* in *Kirkus Reviews,* Vol. LV, No. 19, October 1, 1987, pp. 1465-66.

A rich feast of well-told facts brings a war—skirted hastily in almost every history text—to vivid life. Lasting 70 years, it dragged the people of Europe into a conflict in the American wilderness, pitted Indians against the power of England in a last-ditch effort to oust white people from the continent, and set the stage for the struggle for independence. Marrin gives the reader not only a history of Indians in America since the land bridge over the Bering Sea, but also a context for understanding the tenacity of the British and the French in the New World. Also, insights into Washington's first battles, the budding wisdom of [Benjamin] Franklin, the inspired bravery of Pontiac, and other details are told with a fine eye for historic trivia—Franklin writes, "Some seem to think that forts are as easy to take as snuff"; Washington rode with a pillow until he became accustomed to strenuous horseback forays; Pontiac invited Frenchmen to a feast of "young beef," which proved to be a fricasseed English soldier.

Altogether, then, a dense but very readable book, requiring thought and application. There is a lot of explicitly described gore (the Indians were not a mild bunch when angered; the white men also retaliated with some violence); and a chart or time-line would help, as would an index. But, still, for the student or the lover of history of any age, this is a clear and detailed account.

Mary Mueller

SOURCE: A review of *Struggle for a Continent: The French and Indian Wars, 1690-1760,* in *School Library Journal,* Vol. 34, No. 4, December, 1987, p. 108.

A detailed history of the four wars that led to English supremacy in colonial North America. The book opens with an excellent discussion of how differences in ways of life between the Indians, the French, and the English led to inevitable conflict. One of the book's many strengths is the way in which Marrin explains how many of the practices of the time, especially those of the Indians, are now considered barbaric, but were largely accepted at that time. He then describes the major military actions of the wars. It is clear that he considers the Indians, with their losses of population and land, the real losers in the conflicts. Many titles minimize the roles Indians played in the conflicts, and Marrin fills in gaps left by their lack of coverage. Maps and reproductions are well chosen and add greatly to the text. The book is well written and well researched. Profiles provide insights into the personalities of the people involved. All of these strengths would make this a good book, but Marrin's unbiased historical analysis makes it an excellent one. He does not show prejudice against any group, and he puts the actions of various people in historical perspective. Readers will come away from this book knowing why people acted as they did, why these wars were important, and how their outcome influenced history.

STALIN: RUSSIA'S MAN OF STEEL (1988)

Kirkus Reviews

SOURCE: A review of *Stalin: Russia's Man of Steel,* in *Kirkus Reviews,* Vol. LVI, No. 19, October 1, 1988, p. 1472.

An unrelenting portrait of the "greatest mass murderer of all time."

Abused as a child, Stalin grew up motivated by hate, an amoral, atheistic, hysterically suspicious killer with no ideological convictions. He rose to power on a tide of blood that, says the author, never ebbed; he created famines, set out to eliminate the entire class of free peasants, and had millions of people killed or transported. With the help of a corrupt bureaucracy, Stalin kept the standard of living at subsistence level and governed by terror. He had no sense of personal or political honor, ignored his family, and had definite plans for World War Three at the time of his death.

Marrin writes with authority (though his bibliography lists only English-language books, most of them secondary sources) and, as in *Hitler,* indulges in occasional dramatic phrases: after an NKVD [Soviet secret police] masked ball, "drooling drunks" chant Stalin's praises and the invasion of Finland becomes "a grim struggle of man against tank, flesh against steel." This technique is sometimes overdone but does give the narrative immediacy, suiting the author's cautionary purpose. Though conditions have improved since Stalin's death, Marrin contends that Soviet society is still structured along Stalinist lines, still susceptible to totalitarian rule.

This horrifying tale will leave shaken readers conscious that no crime is truly unthinkable.

Mary Mueller

SOURCE: A review of *Stalin: Russia's Man of Steel,* in *School Library Journal,* Vol. 35, No. 3, November, 1988, p. 138.

This excellent biography of Stalin follows the same pattern as Marrin's outstanding *Hitler.* He chronicles Stalin's early life and then turns to the history of the USSR and the influence Stalin had on it, emphasizing that Stalin *was* the USSR during his long regime. Marrin provides exceptional historical background, explaining how czarist Russia was ready for revolution and how the communists were able to seize power. He spends some time on Lenin and the communist consolidation of power, but most of the book is about the will of Stalin and how he imposed that will on the revolution and the entire country. His manipulations and purges are described in detail, as is his struggle with Hitler and Germany. Throughout the book, Marrin does a superb job of conveying the sheer horror of Stalin's totalitarian regime, describing for readers how one man can be the cause of millions of deaths and enormous suffering. He uses quotations, primary sources, statistics, and excellent writing to make a difficult subject understandable and interesting for intermediate readers. As the USSR enters the age of *glasnost,* this title is very timely and fills a need for material for this age group. It is better than *Joseph Stalin;* by Liversidge and completely replaces older titles such as Appel's *The Age of Dictators.* **Stalin** is an outstanding biography. It deserves a place in all libraries serving intermediate and young adult readers.

Publishers Weekly

SOURCE: A review of *Stalin: Russia's Man of Steel,* in *Publishers Weekly,* Vol. 234, No. 20, November 11, 1988, pp. 56-7.

Stalin, Marrin writes, was "among the two or three worst men who ever lived." The numbers bear this out— Stalin was directly or indirectly responsible for 14 million deaths in the famine of the 1930s, 12 million deaths in the gulag and 20 million deaths in World War II (an "unnecessarily high" price for victory). This biography of Stalin is gripping, however, because of its complexity and boldness as well as its horrors. The author of numerous books for young adults, Marrin explains the rise of Bolshevism, describes the tenets of socialist thought and shows Stalin's role in the creation of a totalitarian state. Stalin himself—his battered youth, his incapacity for expressing gratitude—is vividly presented. This is an agile history of a complicated subject, a breakthrough for readers not yet ready for the tomes on adult shelves.

📖 INCA AND SPANIARD: PIZARRO AND THE CONQUEST OF PERU (1989)

Kirkus Reviews

SOURCE: A review of *Inca and Spaniard: Pizarro and the Conquest of Peru,* in *Kirkus Reviews,* Vol. LVII, No. 14, August 1, 1989, p. 1162.

A companion volume to *Aztecs and Spaniards* tells the sad, bloody tale of another New World empire's brutal dismemberment.

Marrin presents the "Land of the Four Quarters" as an empire with impressive public works; a stern, efficient, totalitarian government; and a relatively homogeneous society that—thanks to gloomy prophecies, civil war, and Old World diseases—proved remarkably fragile. Using techniques developed by Cortés and cleverly exploiting his own strengths (horses, heavy armor, new weapons, reckless courage), Pizarro—an aging mercenary—quickly took control of major cities and hauled off enormous quantities of loot. Since the period is not well documented, Marrin generalizes extensively and can only suggest why Pizarro's small band was so easily able to overcome huge armies, often without a casualty; in his lurid narrative, Spaniards are depicted as cruel and treacherous ("Soldiers raped [Manco's] wives before his eyes, and the Pizarros chuckled"), the Inca as accomplished but weak.

Though Marrin does not cite specific sources for his research, he does, commendably, depart from the "March of Civilization" view of the conquest common to older

books. A long list of adult books is appended; illustrations and index not seen.

Ann Welton

SOURCE: A review of *Inca and Spaniard: Pizarro and the Conquest of Peru,* in *School Library Journal,* Vol. 35, No. 15, November, 1989, p. 132.

The conquest of Peru provides a story that is inherently dramatic, given the ruthless nature of both the Inca and the Spanish conquistadors. Francisco Pizarro, a penniless soldier from Spain, rose by dint of his craft and almost maniacal singlemindedness to be the Marquis of Atavillos, the most powerful man in Peru. Always serving his own interests, Pizarro reduced the powerful Inca kingdom of Atahualpa to rubble within a few years. Marrin does an admirable job of portraying the complex machinations that went on both within the Inca nation and among the squabbling Spanish. His prose is lucid and readable, despite the occasionally jarring colloquialism. The text is enhanced by black-and-white illustrations, many of which come from the contemporary accounts of Guaman Pomo, an Indian who served the Spaniards as a minor official. These line drawings have a piercing immediacy that poignantly communicates the suffering of the native population. Given the detail in the text, this is probably not the best source for quick information. . . .

What Marrin provides is enrichment material for students interested in either an unvarnished view of the conquistadors or the fate of the native populations of the Americas.

Kathryn Pierson

SOURCE: A review of *Inca and Spaniard: Pizarro and the Conquest of Peru,* in *Bulletin of the Center for Children's Books,* Vol. 43, No. 6, February, 1990, p. 142.

With his characteristically involving style, Marrin describes the devastation of the powerful Inca empire by a handful of Spaniards. The atrocities committed by both cultures during the sixteenth-century conquest produced enough blood and gore to fascinate the most reluctant history student ("After an enemy leader had been flayed alive, his skin was stuffed with straw and his stomach made into a drum. The thin, dangling arms were used to pound upon his belly. . . . "). Conscientiously, the author shows that the Spaniards and Incas matched each other, horror for horror, until the Spaniards got the upper hand and enslaved the Inca people. This readable text could be useful to interest a student and/or provide a quick overview on the subject, but it is not solidly documented. A map misspells Colombia; there are virtually no footnotes, with sources for quotes mentioned less than a dozen times in 197 pages. It is impossible to tell where research ends and legend or fiction begins (as Pizarro dies by assassination, he gasps "'Jesu,' tracing a cross on the floor with his own blood.") Choosing to write with the flair of a novelist rather than with the objectivity of a historian, Marrin has limited the research value of his book, but has probably enhanced its appeal.

MAO TSE-TUNG AND HIS CHINA (1989)

Kirkus Reviews

SOURCE: A review of *Mao Tse-Tung and His China*, in *Kirkus Reviews*, Vol. LVII, No. 16, September 1, 1989, p. 1330.

In the third of his biographies of 20th-century rulers (*Hitler*, 1987; *Stalin*, 1988), Marrin covers the Chinese leader's life—from his troubled youth through his patchy, hard-earned education to his emergence as a political figure—showing how early disappointments and resentments influenced Mao's later acts. Throughout, Marrin weaves in details of Chinese history, allowing these to take over as Mao becomes a public rather than a private figure. In the final chapters on life in Communist China and on the Cultural Revolution, Mao himself almost disappears, replaced by the effects of his rule.

Marrin's style here is more impassioned than elegant and, while readable, produces a less-than-balanced account. The result is a page-turner, useful for highlighting its subject, but not a definitive biography for young people.

Stephanie Zvirin

SOURCE: A review of *Mao Tse-Tung and His China*, in *Booklist*, Vol. 86, No. 8, December 15, 1989, pp. 823-24.

Marrin, a prolific and able writer of history, consistently produces exceptional nonfiction whether he's dealing with a particular event or an important historical person. His latest endeavor is, for the most part, no exception. It explores a great chunk of Chinese history while it reveals, at least to some degree, the driven and complicated man who orchestrated the political upheaval that helped spread Chinese communism among the masses, then nearly destroyed his country with the purges and rigid policies of the Cultural Revolution. Was he a brilliant, selfless leader, totally dedicated to his people and to his political philosophy, or was he (particularly in later years) misguided, deranged, or simply greedy for power? Marrin only speculates, but he covers a tremendous amount of China's bloody history, bringing it to life. In so doing, however, he treads too close to the line between the vivid and the sensational, with graphic descriptions of massacres and brutalized bodies beyond what seems necessary to demonstrate facts. That aside, however, his lucid and dramatic chronicle makes sense of a tumultuous period in China and introduces some of the men involved.

The New York Times Book Review

SOURCE: A review of *Mao Tse-Tung and His China*, in *The New York Times Book Review*, February 25, 1990, p. 33.

Albert Marrin's **Mao Tse-Tung and His China** is a vivid but inconsistent account, alternately demonizing and eulogizing Mao. In the prologue, the author, who is chairman of the history department at Yeshiva University, introduces his subject as "a dictator, a ruler greedy and concerned only for himself," a "fanatic" who was driven by hatred and was "eager to kill for the communist idea."

Yet more than half the book, covering the period 1919-49, offers a more sympathetic picture, showing how Mao shared both meals and hardships with the miserably equipped Communist Army. During the anti-Japanese and civil war years, the author casts Chiang Kai-shek, rather than Mao, in the role of corrupt tyrant. Mao emerges as a brilliant commander who inspires patriotic devotion among his peasant soldiers and teaches them to respect the people, deploy guerrilla tactics against a superior fighting force, and unite against Japan for the common good of China. There are accounts of heroic feats of endurance and courage during the early battles and the Long March.

In the post-1949 period, however, Mr. Marrin reverts to the view of Mao as an iron-handed totalitarian who maneuvers "stealthily, like a spider spinning a web." Here he is compared at least five times with two other 20th-century arch-villains, Hitler and Stalin (who happen to be the subjects of Mr. Marrin's two previous biographies).

This book is actually less a biography than a highly readable historical overview of modern China. In his treatment of the People's Republic, Mr. Marrin is most informative on the surveillance functions of work units, neighborhood committees and the secret police. His account of the Cultural Revolution focuses on the dramatic spectacle of masses of youthful Red Guards surging through Tiananmen Square although without explaining the movement's political causes or Mao's ideological and personal motivations.

Sadly, Mao himself never emerges as a clear historic personality, remaining lost in the alternately damning and idealizing hyperbole. Of course Mr. Marrin is not the only one who finds it hard to get a fix on Mao Zedong. He was widely criticized within China after his death in 1976 for the excesses of his later years, particularly his implicit responsibility for the fanaticism of the Cultural Revolution. Larger-than-life size statues of the Great Helmsman were toppled; copies of his "Little Red Book" disappeared from bookstores. Yet the myths of the early period of Communist organizing remained largely unchallenged. In recent years, more liberal Chinese intellectuals—in China and abroad—broadened their scope and began to criticize the entire political system Mao established. But all such criticism was crushed last June, and since then the Government has tried to re-establish the centrality of "Mao Zedong Thought." Even now some Chinese dissidents refer to Mao as "the greatest and the worst" of their leaders.

Though Mr. Marrin's account is generally accurate, there are numerous factual errors—Mao did not live in the Forbidden City and the Gate of Heavenly Peace is not south of Tiananmen Square—and he is also inconsistent in Romanizing Chinese names. Still, the narrative is lively and engrossing. But readers may be frustrated when the author manipulates their responses with his own biased judgments rather than allowing them to draw their own conclusions, and Mr. Marrin's facile reliance on cliched stereotypes is irritating. People from Hunan Province are "hot tempered and stubborn," "adult peasants believed things that would make today's youngsters hold their sides with laughter." Overlook such simplistic and sometimes confusing rhetoric, and enjoy the information about Mao and 20th-century China.

📖 *THE SPANISH-AMERICAN WAR* (1991)

Kirkus Reviews

SOURCE: A review of *The Spanish-American War,* in *Kirkus Reviews,* Vol. LIX, No. 4, February 15, 1991, p. 250.

A fresh (and timely) look at what one diplomat dubbed "a splendid little war," a triumph of yellow journalism and US imperialism.

Writing in his usual lurid style ("Chunks of steel buzz-sawed through the air, slicing through anything that stood in their way"), Marrin ably describes the harsh Spanish regimes in Cuba and the Philippines; the incidents, culminating in the (probably accidental) explosion of the *U.S.S. Maine,* which caused McKinley to dispatch his strong new navy and a hastily assembled army to war; and the course of both campaigns. The author misses none of war's ironies (in Cuba alone, 345 U.S. soldiers died in combat, 5,462 of disease), but he also describes many instances of heroism, especially in the black units. He concludes with a detailed account of the Philippine Insurrection, "the least-known of all our wars"—a bitter conflict he sees as having much in common with Vietnam. Excellent notes; lengthy bibliography; index.

David A. Lindsey

SOURCE: A review of *The Spanish-American War,* in *School Library Journal,* Vol. 37, No. 5, May, 1991, p. 122.

"A splendid little war!," exulted diplomat John Hay about the Spanish-American War of 1898. Marrin makes clear that this sentiment was shared by many—including the hero of San Juan Hill, Theodore Roosevelt—in this readable, fascinating account. In his usual taut, no-nonsense, research-based prose, Marrin delineates how American jingoists, expansionists, "big navy" advocates, yellow journalists, and filibusters manoeuvered the nation into taking part in the easy defeat of an outgunned Spanish fleet. He makes good use of relevant contemporary quotations, informative discussions of famous and not-so-famous participants, and incisive examinations of causes and results; he enables readers to understand how the war led directly to the bloody Philippine Insurrection and the many parallels that this anti-guerilla war had with the U. S. participation in Vietnam. The book goes beyond the older *The Spanish-American War* by Chidsey and is an important contribution to literature for young people.

Zena Sutherland

SOURCE: A review of *The Spanish-American War,* in *Bulletin of the Center for Children's Books,* Vol. 44, No. 11, July-August, 1991, p. 268.

As he has demonstrated in previous books, Marrin has the ability to infuse the facts of history with the drama of fiction. The result is an eminently readable account of the Spanish-American War, and it incorporates perceptive character sketches of major figures such as Theodore Roosevelt, William Randolph Hearst, and George Dewey. The text gives a broad background of events and those who influenced them, so that Marrin's description of the onset and progression of the war are given meaningful context. Chapter notes, a bibliography, and a full index are provided. Bully for you, Albert Marrin.

Margaret A. Bush

SOURCE: A review of *The Spanish-American War,* in *The Horn Book Magazine,* Vol. LXVII, No. 4, July-August, 1991, pp. 480-81.

The author sees bureaucratic bungling, luck, and incredible personal determination among military officers as major ingredients of the four years of bloody battles in Cuba and the Philippines. Teddy Roosevelt's thirst for war is a major theme: "All men who feel any power of joy in battle know what it is like when the wolf rises in the heart." Joseph Pulitzer and William Randolph Hearst also had a greedy yearning for war, using yellow journalism to raise popular support—and, of course, sell newspapers. In one of many intriguing vignettes capturing human moments of the war, Marrin recounts that marching troops in Cuba "were surprised to see a horseman in a black business suit watching them as they set out. . . . William Randolph Hearst had come to see the war in person. It was his war, something he'd created, and he was proud of it." Albert Marrin draws on copious sources, identified in the endnotes and a lengthy bibliography, and develops an informative, well-paced account beginning with the 1898 sinking of the *Maine* and following the two strands of war that ultimately turned the isolationist United States into a colonial power. The brutality with which the war was conducted is treated quite graphically. The enormous naiveté and lack of planning for clothing, feeding, and transporting troops or for providing medical care and supplies boggles the mind. One shudders at the words of John Hay, U.S. ambassador to England, at the end of the Cuban campaign, as he proclaimed it "'a splendid little war.'" The author creates a fine sense of immediacy in his lucid text, which is complemented by an excellent array of [black and white] photographs. The book is unabashedly antiwar and uncanny in its timeliness as it points out that some of the greatest suffering and loss occurred in the war's aftermath.

📖 NAPOLEON AND THE NAPOLEONIC WARS (1991)

Patricia Braun

SOURCE: A review of *Napoleon and the Napoleonic Wars,* in *Booklist,* Vol. 87, No. 21, July, 1991, p. 2039.

Controversial but brilliant, Napoleon Bonaparte remains, arguably, the greatest military figure of all time. In this light, Marrin interprets Napoleon's life in the context of his times, providing as much a history of the French Revolution and its aftermath as a biography that may lead readers to an understanding of how Napoleon came to such power. Profuse in his positive comments, Marrin offers an enlightening account of the Little Corporal that is recommended for world and French history collections. Further readings are appended.

Ann W. Moore

SOURCE: A review of *Napoleon and the Napoleonic Wars,* in *School Library Journal,* Vol. 37, No. 8, August, 1991, p. 205.

An outstanding book about Napoleon and his era. As the title indicates, Marrin—while not neglecting Napoleon's other accomplishments—focuses on his subject's military genius, with thorough descriptions of weapons, campaigns, battles, and opponents such as Nelson and Wellington. He gives a balanced analysis of Napoleon, does an excellent job of putting things in context, and provides a wealth of detail. Marrin's study is truly fascinating, not merely educational; it should become the definitive work on this period of French history.

Margaret Miles

SOURCE: A review of *Napoleon and the Napoleonic Wars,* in *Voice of Youth Advocates,* Vol. 14, No. 4, October, 1991, p. 265.

Napoleon remains one of the most fascinating as well as one of the most studied individuals in history: Marrin's introduction notes over 40,000 biographies to date! The complexity of that life, often simultaneously appealing and appalling, is well conveyed here. However, as the title suggests, Marrin has chosen a somewhat wider focus than individual biography. He describes the life of the period as well as the Emperor, focusing particularly on what the campaigns and battles were like for the ordinary soldiers and sailors of these wars. The achievement of Napoleon, Nelson, Wellington, and the other generals and admirals, Marrin reminds the reader, rested on the compliance of ordinary people in frequently horrible conditions.

Marrin continues to deserve his reputation as one of the best writers of history for YAs. As usual, his *Napoleon* is both insightful and a can't-put-it-down read. His battle scenes are especially gripping and might go far to convince the skeptical YA that reading history really can be exciting. It is this excitement that will probably make Marrin's book the first choice of those available for this age group. The visual appeal of Leslie McGuire's *Napoleon,* with the most illustrations by far, bogs down in the encyclopedia-style just-the-facts text. Manfred Weidhorn's *Napoleon,* probably the best until Marrin's, retains the geographical advantage with nine maps to Marrin's one, but can't quite equal Marrin's particular talent for selecting an incident or anecdote to convey an individual's character or the mood of the times.

📖 AMERICA AND VIETNAM: THE ELEPHANT AND THE TIGER (1992)

Juliann Tarsney

SOURCE: A review of *America and Vietnam: The Elephant and the Tiger,* in *Booklist,* Vol. 88, No. 13, March 1, 1992, pp. 1269-70.

After a historical overview that conveys the Vietnamese people's centuries-old passion for independence, Marrin chronicles the American record in modern Vietnam. His point of view tends to reflect the outlook of the American government. While occasionally critical of particular policy decisions, he never seriously questions the assumptions used to justify U.S. military intervention. Atrocities allegedly committed by the enemy are presented in grisly detail as documented fact, without analysis of their sources, and far more space is devoted to such accounts than to the corruption of the unpopular South Vietnamese government or to the war crimes that the author acknowledges were committed by the American military. Marrin sees opposition to the war among Americans as the "ultimate tragedy of Tet [the 1968 Tet Offensive]: a battlefield victory for the United States became a still greater political triumph for the enemy." While not wholly critical of the American antiwar movement, Marrin decries its more radical elements. His style is readable throughout, but he is at his best in the more fleshed-out passages that capture the personalities of such men as Ho Chi Minh and Lyndon Johnson and the hellish everyday experiences of the average "grunt." Ideally, his book should be read together with materials reflecting other viewpoints and by readers sophisticated enough to recognize the impossibility of being truly objective about so recent and painful a period in our history.

Mary Mueller

SOURCE: A review of *America and Vietnam: The Elephant and the Tiger*, in *School Library Journal*, Vol. 38, No. 6, June, 1992, p. 146.

This unflinching look at the Vietnam War is very different from the usual geopolitical histories often written for this age group. Marrin shows readers how the war affected both countries, opening with an excellent background history of Vietnam and a brief biography of Ho Chi Minh. He also describes the sights, sounds, and smells of war, as well as the endless horror of death and torture that was so characteristic of it. He takes readers on missions with both armies, and on bombing runs with the U.S. Air Force. All of this makes for fascinating reading; few books for YAs are as honest as this one. Many histories of this conflict set out to prove that one side or the other was good or evil; Marrin, in contrast, makes it very clear that in this war there were no such absolutes. In great detail and with objectivity, he exposes the brutality of both Vietnamese governments, the cruelty of the Communists, the unrealistic expectations and decisions of President Johnson, and the hypocrisy of the war protesters in the U. S. An excellent companion to the Hooblers' *Vietnam* (1990) and Warren's *Portrait of a Tragedy* (1990), this book deserves a place in every high school.

Margaret A. Bush

SOURCE: A review of *America and Vietnam: The Elephant and the Tiger*, in *The Horn Book Magazine*, Vol. LXVIII, No. 5, September-October, 1992, pp. 600-01.

Two theses undergird this informative and compelling account of "the longest, and in many ways the most bitter, conflict in American history." One is that history has ingrained in the Vietnamese character a deep yearning for independence from conquering nations; the other, that the Americans and Vietnamese alike were humane and heroic as well as immoral. Marrin's insightful narrative, based on extensive research, is remarkably even-handed as it moves through the political and military complexities of the war. He begins by describing the long centuries of Vietnamese village culture under the rule of China, as a free nation, and through growing domination by the French since the 1600s. A long account of the early life of Ho Chi Minh and his establishment of communism in the northern part of the country after World War II is provided. The defeat of the French at Dien Bien Phu, the American fear of communism, the

actual fighting of the war, and the different beliefs and tactics of the U.S. presidents in entering, prolonging, and ending the conflict are all discussed. The prose is often pungent as brutal events are described. As he moves along in his account, Marrin occasionally interjects anecdotal material from his own experiences with individuals who fought in the war; these anecdotes do not intrude on his objective account but nicely suggest personal experience with his subject. The book explores the profound effects of the war on both countries—the destruction of Vietnam and the demoralizing of American citizens, troops, and veterans. The title of the concluding chapter, "The Peace That Never Was," is a sad summation of the yet unfinished story. Source notes for each chapter, a substantial bibliography, and an index are included.

COWBOYS, INDIANS, AND GUNFIGHTERS: THE STORY OF THE CATTLE KINGDOM (1993)

Carolyn Phelan

SOURCE: A review of *Cowboys, Indians, and Gunfighters: The Story of the Cattle Kingdom*, in *Booklist*, Vol. 89, No. 22, August, 1993, p. 1993.

Beginning with the introduction of horses and cattle to North America, Marrin chronicles the changes brought to the Great Plains as ranchers encroached on the area, particularly during the 1800s. Debunking the romantic images, this discussion clarifies who cowboys were, what they did, and how they viewed their lives. While Marrin is graphic, perhaps too graphic, in describing scalping and other atrocities performed by Indians on pioneers, he balances the political scale by bluntly relating such brutal happenings as the massacres of Indians by cavalry troops, and the swift, senseless slaughter of the buffalo herds. Black-and-white reproductions of paintings, engravings, sketches, and photographs appear throughout the book, while full-color plates appear at intervals. A double-page-spread map of the Plains States will help readers get their bearings. Marrin's inclusion of concrete details and his engaging writing style make this an exceedingly readable account of a unique and turbulent period in American history.

Julie Halverstadt

SOURCE: A review of *Cowboys, Indians, and Gunfighters: The Story of the Cattle Kingdom*, in *School Library Journal*, Vol. 39, No. 8, August, 1993, p. 199.

Colorful, graphic language makes *Cowboys, Indians, and Gunfighters* an exciting account of the old West. Detailed descriptions of Comanche vengeance, buffalo hunts, and frontier law and lawlessness capture the period vividly. Marrin breaks the book into six chapters, each covering an important segment of the development and expansion of the frontier. He begins his history with the arrival of cattle, horses, and settlers from Spain, emphasizing this as the turning point in the area's history. He describes the cowboy's existence, life in frontier towns, the economic realities behind the near extermination of the buffalo species and the Native American population. He depicts the clash of wills between the land and the people trying to conquer it. Marrin includes minority viewpoints and details the contributions of African American and Mexican cowboys and soldiers. Prints by such notable artists as Frederic Remington and Charles M. Russell, as well as poignant period photographs bring the era to life. A dynamic look at one of the most exciting and dangerous periods in U.S. history.

Deborah Stevenson

SOURCE: A review of *Cowboys, Indians, and Gunfighters: The Story of the Cattle Kingdom,* in *Bulletin of the Center for Children's Books,* Vol. 47, No. 1, September, 1993, pp. 17-18.

Picking his way carefully through legends and skeletons, Marrin creates a detailed and vivid picture of the U.S.'s conversion of the Plains from grassy buffalo habitat to cattle-feeding, money-making (and money-losing) property. He succeeds particularly well in linking famous episodes in history to a broader view of the time so that the reader learns about barbed wire as well as Bat Masterson. Television and movie fictions are differentiated from fact, but the facts of hardship, violence, and adventure are certainly dramatic enough to make compelling reading in their own right. Chapters focus on subjects such as the introduction of the horse to America, the longhorn cow, and life in the frontier towns. Colorful and comprehensive, this has both appeal and worth for browsers (who will become readers) as well as report-writers. Period photographs and art, including several color inserts, appear on almost every attractively formatted page; an annotated bibliography, endnotes, and an index are included.

Mary M. Burns

SOURCE: A review of *Cowboys, Indians, and Gunfighters: The Story of the Cattle Kingdom,* in *The Horn Book Magazine,* Vol. 69, No. 5, September-October, 1993, pp. 625-26.

A large map serves as an appropriate introduction to a well-researched study of the cattle kingdoms, their development, the many wars fought for the territory which spawned them, and the principal players in the struggles for their domination. The story begins with the coming of the Spaniards in 1493 and the introduction of horses, "the noble beasts of Spain," into the Americas. As these animals multiplied, they emerged as a dominant force in the economic and social structure of the area. The Spaniards also introduced cattle, which by the late eighteenth and early nineteenth centuries mingled with the mainly British breeds brought by later settlers to become the

Texas longhorn. These two factors became the foundation of a huge industry as traced in subsequent chapters. It is a more fascinating than happy story for, from the very beginning, efforts to control the lands which later supported the vast cattle herds resulted in what seems to be almost continual conflict and the infliction of suffering by one opponent on the other—from the enslavement of the Native Americans to the quarrels between farmers and cattle barons. Certainly, the westward movement was not the romantic saga depicted in film, song, and story. And nowhere is that more evident than in the treatment accorded to the earliest inhabitants of these vast lands—the Native Americans—and in the callous destruction of the great buffalo herds upon which they depended. The period usually associated with the "cowboys and gunfighters" is not as long as the legends it inspired—mostly untrue, it seems. But it has influenced the way people remember history and, as a consequence, history itself. Through conscientious research, Marrin has tried to dispel the myths without dismissing their impact. The oversized book is attractively produced and generously illustrated; the selection of paintings by Catlin, Remington, and Russell add color and dimension. An extensive bibliography, notes for each chapter, and an index are appended.

"UNCONDITIONAL SURRENDER": U. S. GRANT AND THE CIVIL WAR (1993)

Deborah Stevenson

SOURCE: A review of *Unconditional Surrender: U. S. Grant and the Civil War,* in *Bulletin of the Center for Children's Books,* Vol. 47, No. 7, March, 1994, p. 227.

Although this book tells of the early and post-war life of Ulysses Grant, it's not a biography so much as a Civil War chronicle that very successfully uses General Grant as a focus. Especially after Ken Burns' *Civil War* PBS documentary, books on the subject need to meet some mighty high standards, and *Unconditional Surrender* does. You won't find tales of Gettysburg or Bull Run here, because Grant wasn't at those battles and was not yet in command of the army. What you will find are lucid accounts of military strategies, both successful and unsuccessful, at Shiloh and Petersburg; frightening visions of the force of Grant's subordinates such as Sherman and Sheridan as they cut swathes of destruction across the South; blood-soaked scenes of battle; and stirring—there's no other word for it—stories of effort, inspiration, and camaraderie (such as Sheridan shouting to his loyal men in the heat of battle, "God *damn* you, don't cheer me! If you love your country, come up to the front!"). Using extensive eyewitness accounts, Marrin has distilled copious research into a history of living men and women who are complete with faults and contradictions (the racism of many of the Northern commanders, including Grant, is made clear); Grant seems here to be a man splendid in wartime and floundering in peace, except in his happy family life. An evocation as well as a description of war, this also demonstrates how the quiet intimacy of the written word can carry a power greater than faster media such as television or film. Readers may find this book turning them into Civil War buffs or turning them onto history, leading them to Barbara Tuchman and others. Period photographs appear throughout; extensive notes and an index are included.

Carolyn Phelan

SOURCE: A review of *"Unconditional Surrender": U. S. Grant and the Civil War,* in *Booklist,* Vol. 90, No. 15, April 1, 1994, p. 1440.

Part history, part biography, this is a fine study of Grant and his pivotal role in the Civil War. Marrin points out the many ironies of Grant's life: educated at West Point and a soldier by trade, he hated war; he seemed a failure until the war drew him from obscurity and brought his best qualities into prominence; repelled by the sight of blood since childhood, he led forces into the Battle of Shiloh, still remembered as a bloodbath; the leader of the Union army and a man who had freed his slaves, he once said he was not an abolitionist or even antislavery; anything but a politician, he became president of the U.S. Using these paradoxes to explore who Grant was and how he shaped events, Marrin creates a detailed and lively picture of the man and those who fought under him throughout the war. Well researched and vividly written, the book includes many quotations as well as photographs from the period. Source notes and a bibliography round out this very readable biography.

Elizabeth M. Reardon

SOURCE: A review of *"Unconditional Surrender": U. S. Grant and the Civil War,* in *School Library Journal,* Vol. 40, No. 7, July, 1994, p. 112.

Marrin gives an interesting overview of the many phases of history through which Grant lived and places him within the context of his time. He presents the paradoxical aspects of his subject's life and is unflinching in recounting Grant's failures as a civilian and as president. The rumors of his drinking are fully disclosed, as are his triumphs in battle. Well-chosen and informative black-and-white photographs and reproductions add to the appeal of this handsome, oversized volume. An excellent bibliography is appended, as are detailed notes. A well-written, lively, and informative biography that fills a real need, and will be much appreciated by both history students and Civil War buffs.

Mary M. Burns

SOURCE: A review of *"Unconditional Surrender": U. S. Grant and the Civil War,* in *The Horn Book Magazine,* Vol. 70, No. 4, July-August, 1994, pp. 473-74.

"Without Ulysses S. Grant, there is no telling how the Civil War would have ended. By 1864, the struggle was his to win or lose. He won. And for that reason, Americans will remember his name so long as they fight wars." Dr. Marrin has not written a history of the Civil War but rather a study of one of its central figures. Through this intense focus, the war becomes more than history; it is transformed into an epic struggle the understanding of which is central to understanding the United States of America. What may be more surprising to some is that U. S. Grant—who, according to his great adversary Robert E. Lee, was unmatched as a military leader—hated war and sought peace, despite the association of his initials with the term "unconditional surrender" after the taking of Fort Donelson in the early days of the struggle. In developing this portrait of a remarkable human being who seemed a most unlikely candidate for fame, Marrin has translated a formidable array of sources into a readable and provocative narrative. His observations range from engaging glimpses of Grant as a devoted husband and father to haunting, horrific anecdotes of life in wartime. Marrin makes the enormous loss of life in the Civil War concrete by the reiteration of casualties after each engagement, together with comments on aspects of modem warfare first introduced during those battles. Detailed descriptions of equipment, weaponry, medical treatment, and diet are given immediacy through quotations from those who fought. Marrin also makes it clear that the war, although it preserved the Union and abolished slavery, did not abolish racism. Although fascinated with his subject, Marrin also manages to preserve a scholar's perspective, allowing readers to examine Grant's shortcomings as well as his triumphs.

A multi-faceted study, the book is attractively designed and thoroughly documented with notes and a selective bibliography.

VIRGINIA'S GENERAL: ROBERT E. LEE AND THE CIVIL WAR (1994)

Kirkus Reviews

SOURCE: A review of *Virginia's General: Robert E. Lee and the Civil War,* in *Kirkus Reviews,* Vol. LXII, No. 22, November 15, 1994, p. 1537.

After his recent *"Unconditional Surrender": Ulysses S. Grant and the Civil War* (1993), Marrin returns with it's companion volume about that other great Civil War general, Robert E. Lee. The two men couldn't have been more different. Grant was a slovenly alcoholic who was only successful in warfare; Lee, on the other hand, was perfection—at least he was to hear Marrin talk about him. But Marrin's adulation is excusable. Lee was truly an extraordinary man: outstanding in school, at the top of his class in West Point, a brave and cunning soldier. Lee also became one of the most brilliant generals America has ever known. With a small and pitifully undersupplied army, he ran rings around the stronger North until, his supply lines cut, he ran out of troops and provisions. Marrin describes Lee's decisive battles clearly and with excitement. Lee was also beloved by his men and respected by all, a loving husband and father. Marrin shows Lee to be a Southern gentleman in the finest tradition.

Comprehensive and coherent, a superb history.

Carolyn Phelan

SOURCE: A review of *Virginia's General: Robert E. Lee and the Civil War,* in *Booklist,* Vol. 91, No. 8, December 15, 1994, p. 746.

A good companion to Marrin's *"Unconditional Surrender": U. S. Grant and the Civil War,* this biography presents Lee as a gentleman and a soldier. Beginning with Lee's pivotal decision to refuse command of the U.S. Army, the book fills in the details of his childhood, education, marriage, and career, and then concentrates on the Civil War years. Quotations from Lee, his generals, and particularly his soldiers offer insight into the times. Source notes are appended. Period photographs and prints of people and battles illustrate the book, and maps show the location of significant places and battlefield positions. Although readers of both books will come away feeling they know Grant better than Lee, each volume contributes to a fuller understanding of the Civil War. Well researched and quite readable, this biography belongs in many library collections.

Deborah Stevenson

SOURCE: A review of *Virginia's General: Robert E. Lee and the Civil War,* in *Bulletin of the Center for Children's Books,* Vol. 48, No. 5, January, 1995, p. 173.

This is Marrin's counterpart to his excellent *"Unconditional Surrender"* about Ulysses Grant; here he takes on arguably the most beloved figure on either side of the Civil War, Robert E. Lee. Marrin chronicles Lee's upbringing and early career, but, as he did in the previous volume, really uses his subject as a lens through which to view the Civil War. There is limited overlap between the two books, since Lee's war differed very much from Grant's. Lee dominated the Confederate Army from the beginning of the war (after turning down command of the Union Army), his battles such as Sharpsburg/Antietam and Gettysburg, were often not Grant's, and finally he had to bear the crushing disappointment of loss and surrender. Again Marrin paints a vivid picture of the war, its participants, and its effects: he describes battle scenes where stampeding cows and swarms of angry bees played roles as pivotal as military strategy, soldiers of both sides writing home letters of halting spelling and tangible longing, and the moments when Union and Confederate soldiers pulled together in attempts to rescue wounded comrades of both. Over all the details is the constant, exhausting bloodshed, fight-ing over the same ground again and again, and the increasing inevitability of defeat for Lee's forces. Marrin makes it clear what a feat Lee accomplished by staving off the Union with its vastly superior resources as long as he did; he also makes it clear what a terrible price that prolongation of the war exacted. Throughout the book shines the portrait of General Lee, apparently respected by the Union army as well as nearly deified by the Confederate, as a principled and astute leader and a proud and honorable man. Black-and-white period art and photos appear throughout; endnotes demonstrate the wide variety of sources Marrin employed to paint this vivid picture; a necessarily selective bibliography and an index are included.

THE SEA KING: SIR FRANCIS DRAKE AND HIS TIMES (1995)

Kirkus Reviews

SOURCE: A review of *The Sea King: Sir Francis Drake and His Times,* in *Kirkus Reviews,* Vol. LXIII, No. 11, June 1, 1995, p. 783.

Marrin once again focuses on a complex, flamboyant figure as a way to introduce an extraordinary time of chaos and change.

The author marshals facts, period documents, and current historical interpretations into a vivid book about a larger-than-life man who was knighted for his crimes of piracy. The Elizabethan era was characterized by intense loyalties and rivalries, religious conflict, and powerful economic change; the author weaves these and more into a well-organized narrative that crackles with near-novelistic flourishes and dramatic intensity. Part of the picture: the developing African slave trade, the Protestant Reformation and the Inquisition, the pressures of almost indescribable and overarching greed, the subjugation and looting of native peoples in the Americas, exciting sea battles, courageous navigation, and near-constant exploration. Though lacking labeled diagrams of the Spanish and British ships that are so well-described, the handsome book is bolstered by maps and well-captioned black-and-white period illustrations.

Marrin presents Drake as a catalyst for and emblematic of this protean age. Hero or villain, Drake emerges as an unforgettable persona in a masterly work.

Carolyn Phelan

SOURCE: A review of *The Sea King: Sir Francis Drake and His Times,* in *Booklist,* Vol. 91, No. 21, July, 1995, p. 1872-73.

In this lively, detailed account of his adventurous life, Sir Francis Drake is firmly set within the context of his times—and what times they were! From his circumnavigation of the globe (1577-1580) to his days as a privateer to his part in the defeat of the Spanish Armada, Drake cuts a dramatic figure. Quotations, meticulously attributed in the source notes, bring an immediacy sometimes lacking in biographies. Not every reader, though, will appreciate the many scenes of "execution and torments," whether they appear in quotation marks or not. Numerous black-and-white reproductions of period paintings, engravings, and maps appear throughout the book. A handsome, informative edition.

Ann A. Flowers

SOURCE: A review of *The Sea King: Sir Francis Drake and His Times,* in *The Horn Book Magazine,* Vol. 71, No. 5, September-October, 1995, p. 621.

The legendary Sir Francis Drake, one of the great seafaring heroes of Britain, was a superb seaman. Almost any of his early adventures would have been enough to make him famous, but he was also the first Englishman to circumnavigate the globe and a prime mover in the defeat of the Spanish Armada. His character was complex and surprising: he was courteous and considerate of his crew but also ruthless and ambitious. He came from humble beginnings; his education was almost nonexistent. His brave and fascinating story is told with great attention to the complex historical background of the times. The many historical forces that were at work and especially the reasons for and the personalities concerned in Philip II of Spain's attempt to invade England are clearly laid out. The description of the defeat of the Spanish Armada is breathtaking in its tension and excitement. The author has an exceptional ability to present complicated history in an understandable yet not oversimplified way. A fine, readable biography—unfortunately marred by a few careless errors in production.

Carolyn Caywood

SOURCE: A review of *The Sea King: Sir Francis Drake and His Times,* in *Voice of Youth Advocates,* Vol. 18, No. 4, October, 1995, p. 254.

Although there have been over a hundred books about Drake, this one finds a niche of its own. The format and appearance are appropriate and the author uses primary source materials to explain all the cultures that came into conflict in Drake's time. To accomplish so much in a book this size, he risks creating misimpressions. For example, Drake accompanied [Sir John] Hawkins on an African slave raid, but the focus of the first hand accounts quoted is cannibalism. One specific error in the book is that the map on page 38 shows the city of Nombre de Dios on the Pacific coast while the text states it is on the Caribbean. Aside from these concerns, however, Marrin does an exemplary job of defining words in context, incorporating quotations, explaining both sides of a conflict, all while retaining the essential drama of Britain's most famous sailor. Marrin's Drake is not just a swashbuckling hero, but a complex character spanning

the transition from feudal authority to the emergence of self-made men. This Drake deserves to be read for more than just another explorer report.

PLAINS WARRIOR: CHIEF QUANAH PARKER AND THE COMANCHES (1996)

Deborah Stevenson

SOURCE: A review of *Plains Warrior: Chief Quanah Parker and the Comanches,* in *Bulletin of the Center for Children's Books,* Vol. 49, No. 9, May, 1996, p. 308.

Marrin has roamed the Old West before, literarily speaking *(Cowboys, Indians, and Gunfighters);* here he focuses on the Comanche and their losing nineteenth-century battle for their traditional life and lands on the Great Plains. The book starts with a prologue about the Comanche kidnapping of Cynthia Ann Parker, Quanah's mother; it then describes Comanche history and culture, the increasing hostilities between Indians and Europeans, and Quanah Parker's leadership during the bitterest last years of the struggle. While noting that "much of the history of the American West is, and must forever remain, one-sided," the author makes an impressive attempt to be even-handed about the behavior and attitudes of both sides, clearly depicting cultural differences and political wranglings and painting neither side as totally virtuous. His inclusion of detail and his reliance on first-hand sources help bring the period to life, and his careful analyses keep the images from becoming Western-movie simplistic. Kids may come for the adventure, but they'll leave with a deeper understanding of what it all meant. Black-and-white photographs appear throughout; endnotes, a reading list, and an index are appended.

Lisa Mitten

SOURCE: A review of *Plains Warrior: Chief Quanah Parker and the Comanches,* in *School Library Journal,* Vol. 42, No. 6, June, 1996, p. 161.

This biography is a throwback to the sensationalistic dime novel Westerns of the turn of the century. As much a recounting of Comanche/Texan warfare as a biography of the man who guided the Comanche transition from freedom to reservation life, the book is largely based on soldiers' memoirs and captivity accounts, which are noted for their frequent biases and misunderstanding of Native cultures. Author of many earlier titles on various military topics and battles, Marrin uses that perspective here. Beginning with the abduction of nine-year-old Cynthia Ann Parker, her adoption and subsequent marriage into the tribe, he then devotes nearly half of the book to various military activities in Texas, such as the formation of the Texas Rangers and daily life for the enlisted men. Interesting, perhaps, but peripheral to a biography of a Comanche leader. The second half of the book, beginning with Cynthia Ann's (now Naduah's) recapture by the Texans after 25 years, finally turns its focus back to the subject at hand, her son Quanah. But it is almost too little too late. The constant use of inappropriate vocabulary (women are always "squaws"; men are always "braves," "warriors," or "chiefs"); inflammatory descriptions; and just plain inaccurate information make it difficult to recommend this title for purchase.

Mary M. Burns

SOURCE: A review of *Plains Warrior: Chief Quanah Parker and the Comanches,* in *The Horn Book Magazine,* Vol. 72, No. 5, September-October, 1996, pp. 621-22.

More than a biography of a leader, this is also the story of a people, the land they considered their own, and their eventual defeat as the United States expanded westward. A prologue outlines the content of six succeeding chapters that present the story of Quanah Parker's birth to a white woman wedded to one of her Comanche captors, his emergence as a skilled leader in battle, and his role after hostilities had ceased. Included in this introductory material is an important observation: "Much of the history of the American West is, and must forever remain, one-sided . . . Indians did not have a written language. . . . Thus, the history we have is essentially the conqueror's story, seen through their eyes and told with their pens." Marrin does take care to indicate the major differences between the Comanche and the white points of view and the tragedy inherent in those differences. As told here, the story is often one of bloody brutality from whites and Indians alike, and Marrin's vivid writing occasionally strays into sensationalism. The repeated use of the word *squaw* is a disturbing element. Expected in quotes from the period, it is jarring in a present-day account, particularly as the term has acquired pejorative overtones. These aspects . . . detract from otherwise absorbing descriptions of the landscape and from accounts of the introduction of the horse in the sixteenth century and its later significance, the white-dominated attitude of the United States government, and the specific events that propelled Parker into a memorable historical figure—leader in war and peace, friend of presidents, successful businessman. Source notes, bibliography, and index.

📖 *EMPIRES LOST AND WON: THE SPANISH HERITAGE IN THE SOUTHWEST (1996)*

Kirkus Reviews

SOURCE: A review of *Empires Lost and Won: The Spanish Heritage in the Southwest,* in *Kirkus Reviews,* Vol. LXV, No. 8, April 15, 1997, p. 644.

Marrin retraces the Spanish conquest of the American Southwest in this distinctive, authentically illustrated volume. His approach capitalizes on the drama inherent throughout human struggle, providing a dense, compelling narrative inhabited by such dazzling figures as the 16th-century nobleman, Francisco Vásquez de Coronado, whose expedition resulted in battle with the Zuni and whose scouts were the first outsiders to stumble across the Painted Desert and the Petrified Forest. Marrin's clear-eyed research presents a three-dimensional portrait of General Antonio López de Santa Anna, easily the most despised figure of Mexico in the 19th century, who, after promising political reform, seized power as military dictator and subsequently led Mexico to defeat in the war against the U.S. and Texas. Although this history is enlivened by such personalities, it is also brimming with details of day-to-day living, e.g., the supplies a trader packed for the eight-week journey to the first stop on the Santa Fe trail.

Elizabeth Bush

SOURCE: A review of *Empires Lost and Won: The Spanish Heritage in the Southwest,* in *Bulletin of the Center for Children's Books,* Vol. 50, No. 9, May, 1997, p. 330.

Marrin breathes new life into the litany of explorers, conquistadors, and soldier-statesmen that comprise the textbook history of the Old Southwest. In his opening chapters he forges beyond simplistic accounts of a facile European rout of the natives, portraying complex men driven by gold fever, religious zeal, nationalistic fervor, and an adventurousness born of peacetime boredom who meet their match in the sometimes fierce, sometimes cunning resistance of indigenous cultures. In discussing political and military developments after Mexican independence (which, curiously, receives little attention here), however, Marrin loses some of his objectivity; his sarcastic take on Santa Anna, for example, sounds like a personal vendetta: "Preferring not to ride, he went about in a carriage fit for Napoleon himself. Heaven forbid that His Excellency, El Presidente, should raise saddle sores on his tender behind!" Still, the stirring battles scenes for which Marrin is noted (*"Unconditional Surrender," Virginia's General*) are much in evidence here, and history students will find this to be a rich and thought-provoking account. Period illustrations, extensive endnotes and bibliography, and an index are included.

Phyllis Graves

SOURCE: A review of *Empires Lost and Won: The Spanish Heritage in the Southwest,* in *School Library Journal,* Vol. 43, No. 6, June, 1997, p. 141.

A colorful narrative enriched by salient details. Beginning in A.D. 711 when Catholic bishops fleeing the Moors first told stories of cities of gold, inspiring Spanish exploration and conquest for 1000 years, this inclusive account stretches across centuries, all the way to the mid-1800s and the Mexican War. Marrin offers realistic descriptions of Spain in the late Middle Ages, the perils and hardships of seagoing travel, the everyday life of the Native Americans and their abuse at the hands of the explorers, Coronado's expedition, and more, all told with close reliance on clearly cited sources. After dealing extensively with 16th- and 17th-century events, the author moves quickly to the sweeping panorama of the 19th-century westward expansion and the inevitable confrontation between east and west. The powerful text, written by a gifted storyteller, is beautifully blended with vivid, carefully placed, firsthand accounts. Poems and songs of the various time periods clearly convey the moods of the ages, and frequent illustrations include helpful maps, original drawings, and portraits. This book has wide appeal, partly because the narrative is so engaging, and also because this information is not readily found in other sources. This is an excellent portrayal of life as it really was, and how the lust for gold, land, and riches so strongly affected human behavior and altered the course of history.

Additional coverage of Marrin's life and career is contained in the following sources published by Gale Research: *Contemporary Authors New Revision Series,* Vols. 30, 58; and *Something about the Author,* Vol. 90.

Jim Murphy

1947-

American author of nonfiction and fiction.

Major works include *Weird and Wacky Inventions* (1978), *Death Run* (1982), *The Boys' War: Confederate and Union Soldiers Talk about the Civil War* (1990), *The Long Road to Gettysburg* (1992), *Across America on an Emigrant Train* (1993), *The Great Fire* (1995).

INTRODUCTION

While Murphy has written a considerable amount of both fiction and nonfiction ranging from mechanical to zoological and ecological, his unique approach to United States history for middle graders and young adults has brought him attention and celebration. Using diaries, memoirs, journals, and letters, Murphy blends the words, thoughts, and feelings of people who lived through a particular moment in history with authentic details of the times and circumstances in which they lived. His works provide readers with a variety of deeply personal perspectives and viewpoints within the context of a given situation. Adding the vital element of human experience, he creates fascinating, involving, and memorable stories that remind readers just what history really is about—the intimate, personal accounts of those who lived before us. Murphy's writing also emphasizes the valuable contributions that children have made to and the perspectives they offer about our historical past. In a publicity release for Scholastic, he once commented, "One of my goals in writing about events from the past is to show that children weren't just observers of our history. They were actual participants and sometimes did amazing and heroic things." Reviewers have applauded Murphy's narrative technique of presenting factual information in a clear, unambiguous, and entertaining fashion. Through attention to detail, careful selection of material, and exacting research, Murphy has a talent for making history come to life. As Elizabeth M. Reardon said of *The Long Road to Gettysburg,* "The excellent use of quotes and descriptions from [personal] journals brings authenticity and immediacy to the narrative."

Murphy's ability to meld personal narrative into his presentation of a wider perspective makes his books informative and fun to read. Although Murphy encourages the reader to feel empathy with the diarist, he also sheds light on the context in which these stories took place, including the social conditions and prejudices of the time, the physical and geological surroundings, and how these factors affected the individuals involved. Of *Across America on an Emigrant Train*, the story of a transcontinental trip made by Robert Louis Stevenson in 1879, Ellen Fader commented, "Amid Stevenson's commentary about the other passengers, the scenery, and his

poor state of health, Murphy skillfully interweaves a general history of the growth of the transcontinental railroad and the emigrant experience." Likewise, Elizabeth Bush wrote in her review of *The Great Fire,* a book about the fire that destroyed Chicago in 1871, "This account offers not only the luridly enticing details disaster junkies crave, but also a more complex analysis of the causes of the conflagration than is usually offered in children's history books, and an examination of evolving fire apocrypha that introduces young readers to some rudimentary historiography." Murphy's enthusiasm and delight in his subject matter make his text all the more dynamic. "I thoroughly enjoy my work," Murphy once commented in *Something about the Author (SATA)*. "The nonfiction projects let me research subjects that I am really interested in; they provide me an opportunity to tell kids some unusual bits of information. The fiction lets me get out some of the thoughts and opinions that rattle around my head."

Biographical Information

Murphy was born in Newark, New Jersey, in 1947 and

raised in nearby Kearny, not far from New York City. His interest in reading was cursory until a high school teacher told him he could absolutely, positively NOT read Hemingway's *A Farewell to Arms*. "I promptly read it," Murphy explained in *SATA*, "and every other book I could get a hold of that I felt would shock my teacher." He began to write, mostly poetry, but occasionally short stories, and had a string of mechanical jobs that included repairing boilers, tarring roofs, putting up chain-link fences, and maintenance and construction work. In 1970, he received a bachelor of arts degree from Rutgers University, married later that year, and began graduate study at Radcliffe College. He eventually got an editorial job in the juvenile department of Seabury Press, later named Clarion Books, and became managing editor by 1977. One year later, Murphy published his first book, *Weird and Wacky Inventions*, which reflected his mechanical experience and set a pattern for several of his early nonfiction works. Murphy continues to work as a freelance author and editor.

Major Works

Murphy is best known for his books on specific periods of United States history. Two of these, *The Boys' War: Confederate Soldiers Talk about the Civil War* and *The Long Road to Gettysburg*, focus on the American Civil War. In what has become his signature method of presentation, Murphy uses excerpts from the letters and diaries written by people who actually participated in the events he narrates. In *The Boys' War*, the words expressing feelings of pride, horror, exhaustion, sadness, and numbness come directly from the boys, some as young as twelve years old, who enlisted, drilled, and fought as soldiers in what started for many as an exciting adventure, but became a shocking loss of innocence. With a liberal use of photographs, Murphy interweaves the boys' actual words into an account of the disheartening conditions endured by those living, fighting, and dying as soldiers on both sides of the conflict. As David A. Lindsey commented, "Their accounts bring to life, as no other versions can, the Civil War and all of its glories and horrors."

Murphy followed *The Boys' War* with *The Long Road to Gettysburg,* another book about the Civil War, but this time focusing on the most famous battle of the war, made so, in part, by the most famous Presidential speech ever delivered, the Gettysburg Address. He again uses excerpts from journals and reports, this time those of nineteen-year-old Lieutenant John Dooley from Virginia and seventeen-year-old Corporal Thomas Galway from Ohio, to bring an immediate and personal view to his factual analysis of the battle, the events leading up to it, and its aftermath. The text is augmented with maps, photographs, and Lincoln's address. Elizabeth M. Reardon noted, "By focusing on these two ordinary soldiers, readers get a new perspective on this decisive and bloody battle."

In *Across America on an Emigrant Train*, Murphy re-fined his formula. This book follows the emigration voyage of Robert Louis Stevenson from his native Scotland to America, and across the country to California to the woman who became his wife. On the journey, Stevenson kept a journal of astute observations about America, its people, his fellow emigrants, and the conditions of his trip. Murphy gracefully segues into information about building the transcontinental railroad, the devastation of the buffalo herds, treatment of Native Americans, and the social and physical conditions of immigrants from across both the Atlantic and Pacific Oceans. Commenting on *Across America on an Emigrant Train,* a critic for *Kirkus Reviews* observed, "A fascinating, imaginatively structured account that brings the experience vividly to life in all its detail: history at its best."

In his Newbery Award-nominated *The Great Fire*, Murphy uses four witnesses to tell four very different personal accounts of the 1871 Chicago fire. He then casts these accounts into an historical overview of the social and political ideologies of Chicago in the late nineteenth century and today. Supported by a series of maps and historic photographs, the book follows the course of the fire from its inception in Mrs. O'Leary's barn through all the mistakes, accidents, forces of nature, and general bad luck that turned it into a devastating three-day conflagration, ending only by the advent of a long-awaited rainfall. Murphy includes commentary about the class prejudices of the time, and how those prejudices skewed newspaper accounts and the public's view of the fire and of the poorer classes that were blamed in the popular press for starting it. Critic Elizabeth Bush stated, "Murphy makes an analytical leap at which children's authors often balk—he guides readers into considering circumstances and predispositions that influence the disparate accounts."

Murphy's interest in mechanical devices is evident in a number of his early nonfiction writings. *Weird and Wacky Inventions* first brought him into the public eye with an amusing book about real inventions that never became successful. Contraptions featured include a coffin with an escape hatch for people who have fear of being buried alive, training pants for dogs that are not housebroken, and a hammock for use on trains. Each invention is accompanied by a drawing based on an original patent diagram and an invitation for the reader to guess its use before being presented with the solution. Although the major focus of the book is the many strange contraptions that passed through the U.S. Patent Office, Murphy also includes information on inventions that have helped shape American history. The book is rounded out with essays on the inventing and patent process.

Several of Murphy's other works also examine mechanical devices. In *Two Hundred Years of Bicycles* (1983), Murphy traces the story of how bicycles changed from late eighteenth-century "celeriferes" to modern racers and dirt bikes. He also looks at the ways that human powered vehicles may become important for the future. *Custom Car: A Nuts-and-Bolts Guide to Creating One*

(1989) tells how Murphy bought a junk car and, with the help of mechanic Tom Walsh, rebuilt the engine and replaced the damaged interior and exterior parts. The book features step-by-step procedures for car repairs, including illustrations, explanations, and advice, sources for buying parts, and ideas on where to find further information.

While Murphy's nonfiction for middle graders and young adults is highly acclaimed, his fiction, both for young adults and juveniles, has also been well received. *Death Run* tells of how four high school age boys—Brian, Roger, Sticks, and Al—are accidentally involved in the death of another young man on a local suburban basketball court. Originally, public opinion has it that the death is from natural causes, but the boys, fearing that someone will accuse them, panic and flee. Detective Sergeant Wheeler recognizes their flight as a sign of guilty consciences, and he begins his own investigation into the death after the case has been officially closed.

Awards

Murphy has twice won the Orbis Pictus Award from the National Council of Teachers of English, for *The Great Fire* in 1996 and *Across America on an Emigrant Train*. *The Great Fire* also received a Newbery Honor Book citation, an ALA Notable Children's Book citation, an ALA Best Book for Young Adults citation, *Boston Globe/Horn Book* Award Honor Book, *Bulletin of the Center for Children's Books* Blue Ribbon Book, *Publishers Weekly* Best Book of the Year, Notable Children's Trade Book in the Field of Social Studies, and *Booklist* Editor's Choice citation, all in 1996. *Across America on an Emigrant Train* also received an ALA Notable Children's Book citation, an ALA Best Books for Young Adults citation, a *School Library Journal* Best Book of the Year citation, and a *Booklist* Editor's Choice citation. For both *The Long Road to Gettysburg* and *The Boys' War: Confederate and Union Soldiers Talk about the Civil War*, Murphy received the Society of Children's Book Writers and Illustrators Golden Kite Award for nonfiction and an ALA Best Books for Young Adults citation. *Death Run* received an ALA Notable Children's Book citation in 1982, and *Weird and Wacky Inventions* won the International Reading Association's Children's Choice Award in 1979.

TITLE COMMENTARY

📖 *WEIRD AND WACKY INVENTIONS* (1978)

Publishers Weekly

SOURCE: A review of *Weird and Wacky Inventions,* in *Publishers Weekly,* Vol. 214, No. 3, July 17, 1978, p. 168.

The reactions of kids to an aptly named book will range from smiles to giggles to guffaws. And any adult would find Murphy's work worth diving into, for instruction and merriment. The very professional and mind-boggling drawings of gadgets created by the hopeful during the last 200 years are presented first, for readers to guess their functions. You have to guess shrewdly when you behold the wildly complicated inventions, whose functions are described on succeeding pages. They are a machine to make dimples (they last for about eight hours), a portable fire escape, a terrifying gimmick to cut hair and many more. The author also provides information on some practical inventions—the essential safety pin, for example—plus a section on how to get a patent.

Barbara Elleman

SOURCE: A review of *Weird and Wacky Inventions,* in *Booklist,* Vol. 75, No. 1, September 1, 1978, p. 52.

Collected from the files of the U.S. Patent Office, these drawings depict some ingenious ideas dreamed up over many years. Numerous inventions such as an automatic hat-tipping machine, jumping shoes, sunbather's toe rings, grapefruit shields, used gum receptacles, snore-preventing mouthpieces, and portable bathtubs are presented in quiz format with clues and multiple-choice answers to titillate the reader. Line drawings of the item alone and in use supplement each presentation. A separate chapter discusses the variety of unusual patents surrounding the invention of two simple items—the bicycle and the bellows—and general procedures for applying for a patent are described in an afterword. A browser's delight.

Kirkus Reviews

SOURCE: A review of *Weird and Wacky Inventions,* in *Kirkus Reviews,* Vol. XLVI, No. 17, September 1, 1978, p. 952.

Mustache guard, dimple maker, automatic hat tipper, spaghetti fork, bird diaper, used gum receptacle. . . . All of these devices have been patented, but some look so peculiar that Murphy turns his offbeat catalog into a guessing game: first, he shows the patent diagram and offers one or more clues, with a choice of answers; then, overleaf, he identifies the gadget and tells a little more about it. Some items like the primitive washing machine were actually used at one time, and others never will be; let's hope the sunbather's toe rings patented in 1973 remain in the second category. As Murphy notes in explaining why such inventions are patented at all, "You never can tell what might or might not intrigue people." For a tinkerer's idle moments, this might do it.

Robert Unsworth

SOURCE: A review of *Weird and Wacky Inventions,* in *School Library Journal,* Vol. 25, No. 3, November, 1978, p. 66.

Murphy has brought together some of the oddest of the four million or so inventions granted patents by the U.S. Patent and Trademark Office since it opened in 1790. There are excellent black-and-white reproductions of the drawings which originally accompanied the patent requests for such items as a dimple maker, a bird diaper, a hair-cutting machine, a canine tooth brush, and a used-gum receptacle. The text is enlivened by having readers guess what the contraption was intended for, with the answer and some further explanation supplied on the page following. There are things to wear, things to make you look better, kitchen helpers, transportation aids, and self-improvement devices, all strange and unsuccessful. The final chapters discuss how one invention often leads to another and the how and why of getting a patent. The book is very nicely put together and should appeal to youngsters beyond the third to fifth grade levels for whom it is intended.

📖 *RAT'S CHRISTMAS PARTY* (1979)

Laura Geringer

SOURCE: "A Litter of Runts: Christmas Books '79," in *School Library Journal,* Vol. 26, No. 2, October, 1979, pp. 116-20.

This year's note of irreverence starts out well with a scrawny Gackenbach rat child in a "Three Penny Opera" slum setting, reprimanded for saying "please" vs. the proper "hand it over" or "gimme." But once the lesson takes hold and the gangster is grown, the saga degenerates into a snore. Rat is just a run-of-the-neighborhood brat, stealing fuel from Squirrel, tweaking Rabbit's soft nose, kicking Mole's cane out from under him. At last, his own vengeful zeal undoes him; he (literally) crashes a . . . *Christmas Party* and spends the evening stuck in a bowl of sour punch. There is plenty of spice and vinegar in the illustrations [by Dick Gackenbach] of a potbellied villain bursting his vest buttons, but Murphy's text is mischief pursued with no imagination.

Kirkus Reviews

SOURCE: A review of *Rat's Christmas Party,* in *Kirkus Reviews,* Vol. XLVIII, No. 3, February 1, 1980, p. 122.

Our sympathy is all with mean Rat in this cheerless Christmas story which begins by showing how Rat got his evil ways: his unkempt-looking parents threatened to wash his mouth out with soap if he ever said please, and threw out his potatoes to drive home the lesson. It's not surprising then when a grown-up, bullying Rat decides to sabotage the other animals' Christmas party. What is surprising after that childhood scene is the absence of Scrooge-like redemption. Instead, when Rat foils himself and gets stuck in a bowl of vinegar-spiked punch, the other animals leave him to stew while they take their party elsewhere. It's illustrated with gusto, but the vinegar galls.

📖 *HAROLD THINKS BIG* (1980)

Kirkus Reviews

SOURCE: A review of *Harold Thinks Big,* in *Kirkus Reviews,* Vol. XLVIII, No. 5, March 1, 1980, p. 287.

Harold (a pig, like the rest of the cast) is playing on the monkey bars with his friends Willy and Susie just before he sees the Poonton Bay Porkers practicing football and falls for cheerleader Esther. We know that he must be a little kid then, and presumably Esther and her football-player boyfriend Bruiser aren't, but the difference is not evident in the pictures. Perhaps pigs who play football and cheer-lead and fall in love are exempt from such considerations. Anyway, Harold's attempt to win Esther by thinking big is a big flop: at the next game he has the words "Harold and Esther" appear in lights on the scoreboard, rain down on balloons, and show up in the marching band formation; but Esther's understandable response is "Are you crazy?" And Harold, wasting little time in tears, finds happiness with old friend Susie, who likes the balloons and comes to cheer him up. [Susanna] Natti's pictures of funny little pigs with skinny legs (and in Harold's case) a Charley Brown appeal, add an absurd touch to the flighty goings-on. Perhaps that and the cut-to-size outcome are enough to qualify this for the second string.

Zena Sutherland

SOURCE: A review of *Harold Thinks Big,* in *Bulletin of the Center for Children's Books,* Vol. 33, No. 9, May, 1980, p. 179.

Boy pig meets girl, pig loses girl, pig finds girl. That is the plot of a lightly written picture book illustrated with casual line and wash drawings that have little subtlety or charm, but plenty of vitality. The story is written in a bland, easy-reading style that has humor, particularly in the scene in which Harold, besotted with the cheerleading pig who really prefers the star of the Poonton Bay Porkers' football team, pulls out all stops, flooding the field with balloons ("Harold and Esther Forever," they say) and arranging for the scoreboard to say "Harold thinks Esther is Wonderful." He's thought big, as advised by his lawyer, and it hasn't worked; happily, his old friend Susie thinks the whole thing was fun and says she likes balloons, so Harold is soothed.

Publishers Weekly

SOURCE: A review of *Harold Thinks Big,* in *Publishers Weekly,* Vol. 217, No. 19, May 16, 1980, p. 212.

Murphy's frolicking tale is zestfully illustrated by Natti's full-color pictures of the characters, an appealing cast of pigs. Harold falls hard for Esther, cheerleader for the Porkers football team. Abetted by his pals, Willie and Susie, Harold tries to get Esther's attention but

Bruiser, the Porkers' famous quarterback, thwarts the lovelorn youth. Lawyer Owl gives Harold the stupendous idea that is sure to make Esther notice him. At the next football game, the scoreboard declares Harold's love for the cheerleader, the band spells out "HAROLD AND ESTHER" and a blimp drops hundreds of balloons with the tender message onto the field. While the payoff is satisfactory indeed, it is quite different from what Harold and the giggling readers expect.

DEATH RUN (1982)

Kirkus Reviews

SOURCE: A review of *Death Run,* in *Kirkus Reviews,* Vol. L, No. 8, April 15, 1982, p. 496.

What happens when some malicious teasing by four teenagers ends in unintended death. Brian, younger than gang leader Roger and happy to be included, is one of the four drinking beer in the park when schoolmate Bill Janowski walks by with his basketball. They grab the ball, toss it back and forth . . . then Roger slams it against Janowski's face, knocking him down. What the horrified boys then witness, though they don't know it at the time, is an epileptic seizure followed by a burst aneurism that sends blood trickling from Janowski's nose and mouth. The four take off, and though Brian thinks they should report the incident, Roger talks him into keeping quiet. Later, after they know of Janowski's death, Roger and his sidekick set up Brian and another nervous and tenuous member of the group: If they tell, it will look like they did it. So Brian sweats it out, becoming more and more obsessed—and, to Detective Sergeant Robert Wheeler, more and more obviously obsessed—with avoiding detection. Murphy alternates the depiction of Brian's ordeal with passages from the viewpoint of Wheeler, who pursues the case when officials want it closed. Wheeler, we learn, has his own demon to lay: the panic shooting and killing of a fleeing kid years earlier, and the near repetition of that act as he closes in on Brian. That Murphy has us liking Wheeler before disclosing his past act is a neat trick, and throughout, he involves us in this standard plot with his empathetic projections of both hunter and hunted.

Stephanie Zvirin

SOURCE: A review of *Death Run,* in *Booklist,* Vol. 78, No. 17, May 1, 1982, p. 1153.

Four teenage boys looking for trouble find more than they bargained for when their harassment of a 17-year-old boy contributes to his death. Focusing on one of the group, sophomore Brian Halihan, and on police sergeant Wheeler, the officer obsessively determined to get to the bottom of the teenager's death, Murphy lays out a neat, fairly straightforward suspense plot threaded through with overtones of television drama. Guilt, fear, and loyalty to his friends keep Brian silent initially, but he becomes

increasingly alarmed and confused when one of his friends is ousted from the group's protection, Wheeler spots Brian outside the dead boy's home, and the detective's daughter is assaulted because of her independent efforts to investigate the case at school. Few stories of this genre are written specifically for a teenage audience, and Murphy handles his competently, keeping a firm hold on tough talk, including plenty of fast-action sequences, and providing just enough character motivation to fill out the plot.

Kate M. Flanagan

SOURCE: A review of *Death Run,* in *The Horn Book Magazine,* Vol. LVIII, No. 4, August, 1982, p. 415.

The newspaper said the boy whose body was found in the park had died of natural causes. High school sophomore Brian Halihan knew better; he and three friends had witnessed—and perhaps caused—the boy's collapse. Frightened, "Brian had chosen to flee with the others. And once you make a choice like that, you're welded to the action." Plagued by guilt, Brian tried to go about his daily routine, but his anxiety was soon fueled by the realization that at least one policeman suspected that the death was not accidental. Detective Sergeant Wheeler, the stereotype of a tough, determined cop bucking the system, continued to investigate, even though the case had been officially closed by the police department. Battling the bureaucracy and emotional strain that threatened his objectivity, Wheeler gradually moved in on the boys. By telling the story from different points of view—primarily Brian's and the detective's—the author creates tension and suspense. He does not delve too deeply into the psyches of his characters, and neither the hunter nor the prey inspires much sympathy. But the slow unfolding of the investigation as the detective doggedly mulls over the evidence, pursuing mundane details and his own instincts, lends the story a distinctly realistic flavor.

Tony Manna

SOURCE: A review of *Death Run,* in *The ALAN Review,* Vol. 10, No. 1, Fall, 1982, p. 21.

For Brian, Roger, Sticks, and Al, four ordinary high school students, the trouble begins in Van Bedford Park, a typical meeting place in a typical suburban town not far from New York City. Out to have a little fun, they mercilessly taunt an innocent bystander, the star basketball player on the high school team, accidently causing him to have a seizure which costs him his life. Enter Detective Sergeant Wheeler whose determination to prove to the powers at large that Janowski was a victim of foul play is complicated by a lingering personal conflict over an incident from his past, the fact that he shot and killed a young, unarmed prowler on the run. Wheeler's teenage daughter turns sleuth against her father's wishes and adds her evidence to the details and connections her father so painstakingly tracks down.

It is the psychology of detection and the anatomy of fear—mostly Brian's—which make Murphy's first novel such an enticing read. Despite his inclination to tell more than he shows, Murphy is a master at creating tension and sustaining the complex emotions of the hunter and the hunted.

📖 *TWO HUNDRED YEARS OF BICYCLES* (1983)

Connie Tyrrell

SOURCE: A review of *Two Hundred Years of Bicycles,* in *School Library Journal,* Vol. 29, No. 8, April, 1983, p. 116.

Murphy offers a comprehensive history of the slow change and experimentation in the development of the bicycle from before the early French "celeriferes" of the late 18th Century to the present day sleek ten-speed racers. Some speculation on the beginnings of the bicycle is included, as is speculation on the future of bikes, including HPVs, or human-powered vehicles. Antique black-and-white illustrations and photographs are a valuable inclusion. The text is clearly written, with enthusiasm. A detailed index, bibliography and a chart of the anatomy of a ten-speed bicycle are appended. Murphy's book focuses solely and comprehensively on the history of the bicycle, unlike others which include: safety tips and information on how parts work; do-it-yourself maintenance for owners; or information on purchasing, racing and hosteling, to name a few. Murphy's is a fine addition to the growing body of literature about bicycling.

Zena Sutherland

SOURCE: A review of *Two Hundred Years of Bicycles,* in *Bulletin of the Center for Children's Books,* Vol. 37, No. 1, September, 1983, p. 13.

Photographs and drawings illustrate the history of bicycles, from the drawings of Leonardo da Vinci to the celerifere (which the rider used by running) to the Michaux "boneshaker" which was the first machine to include foot pedals, through many variants and improvements to the sleek and powerful machines of today. The text is well-organized, crisply written, and carefully indexed. A one-page bibliography and a photograph of a contemporary bicycle, with parts labelled, are appended.

📖 *THE INDY 500* (1983)

Robert Unsworth

SOURCE: A review of *The Indy 500,* in *School Library Journal,* Vol. 30, No. 4, December, 1983, p. 87.

The earliest Indianapolis 500-mile race was run in 1911 and was won by a car that averaged 74.6 miles per hour, or just about the speed of half the cars that travel our highways today. This past year Tom Sneva averaged 162 miles per hour in winning this country's single most popular sporting event. Why do drivers risk life, limb and sometimes solvency to race at Indy? Part of the appeal, says author Murphy in this fine photo and story book, is the competitiveness, but he doesn't discount the lure of the money at all, for even the last car in the race, he notes, earns over $40,000. Written in a spare, careful style that characterized the author's *Death Run* and his *Two Hundred Years of Bicycles,* the book is very much enhanced by an excellent selection of clearly reproduced black-and-white photographs that closely accompany the text. A sure winner.

Linda Ward Callaghan

SOURCE: A review of *The Indy 500,* in *Booklist,* Vol. 80, No. 10, January 15, 1984, p. 754.

In charting how race car design has evolved in response to the difficult Indianapolis 500 track, Murphy gives a clear introduction to the race, the drivers, and the duties of each racing team member from designing the car through running the race. The driving skills and safety precautions necessary for traveling 200 mph are illustrated through discussions of specific crashes and near-crashes in past races. The excitement and challenge of the race is captured in the text and complemented by high-quality black-and-white photographs that both capture the action and illustrate points in the text. An index, limited glossary, and list of the winners from 1911-83 add to this fine overview.

📖 *BASEBALL'S ALL-TIME ALL-STARS* (1984)

Linda Ward Callaghan

SOURCE: A review of *Baseball's All-Time All-Stars,* in *Booklist,* Vol. 80, No. 21, July, 1984, p. 1554.

On the heels of *Tom Seaver's All-Time Baseball Greats* come Murphy's choices. Where Seaver divided his favorites into four teams, Murphy has selected only two from all of baseball history: National Leaguers and American Leaguers. Entries include places and dates of birth, career spans, nicknames, Hall of Fame election years, anecdotes, and professional and personal strengths and weaknesses, as well as full-page, black-and-white photographs. Each entry concludes with a full set of lifetime career statistics. An introduction defines the criteria used to evaluate players against others who played in the same position in an effort to find the 26 players whose all-around performance was consistently high. Murphy has put in considerable research, and his terse style has a steady flow while packing interesting details and insights into each thumbnail sketch. A list of statistical abbreviations, an index, and a bibliography are included.

Zena Sutherland

SOURCE: A review of *Baseball's All-Time All-Stars,* in *Bulletin of the Center for Children's Books,* Vol. 37, No. 11, July-August, 1984, pp. 209-10.

Save for the pitching staffs, Murphy has chosen one player for each position on two all-star teams (one for each league) and, as with any roster, individual readers may quibble about the inclusion or exclusion of individual players. With few exceptions, the baseball players who are each briefly described are included in most such compilations as well as in individual biographies, but die-hard fans will probably enjoy reading about them one more time. On the adulatory side, the book is adequately written; a bibliography and an index are included.

Jack Forman

SOURCE: A review of *Baseball's All-Time All-Stars,* in *School Library Journal,* Vol. 31, No. 3, November, 1984, p. 135.

Murphy has sifted through the batting, pitching and fielding records of American and National League baseball players to select what he calls his "all-time all-stars"— a first team of 13 players (including 4 pitchers) for each league. A two- to four-page narrative celebrates the playing virtues of each selection (and often includes comments on their off-field life); a statistical summary of playing performance is also provided. Murphy includes standard measurements but does not include slugging averages and many fielding measurements. His selections, as he admits, are strange and surprising, although few will agree on any such list. However, the teams are inexplicably weighted heavily toward older players—only three of the American League team played after 1946 (none are still playing) and the National League choices (except for the pitchers) are largely from the 1950s and before. Unfortunately, the short narratives can't and don't provide much information on each player. Young readers will be able to get more information from the many baseball histories and biographies of individual players available. The short and uninspired narrative makes this book a low priority purchase for sports collections.

📖 *TRACTORS: FROM YESTERDAY'S STEAM WAGONS TO TODAY'S TURBO-CHARGED GIANTS (1984)*

Denise M. Wilms

SOURCE: A review of *Tractors: From Yesterday's Steam Wagons to Today's Turbo-Charged Giants,* in *Booklist,* Vol. 81, No. 1, September 1, 1984, p. 70.

If you need a history of tractor development, this is it. Murphy, whose style is direct and not without humor, recounts how these machines evolved over the last 300 years. Something called Cugnot's fire carriage, a lumbering, steam-powered contraption, proved in 1765 that steam power could move large vehicles and pull heavy loads. Certainly the giant, locomotive-like steam engines that followed are nothing like either the small or large tractors we see today. Readers will find it interesting that farmers at first rejected tractors as too dangerous, too heavy, or too expensive (some insurance companies refused to cover farms with tractors), and it was not until the giant Great Plains wheat farms developed in the 1890s that tractors became profitable. Twentieth-century developments include both the affordable tractor (first built by Ford) and the giant, turbo-harged models of today's factory farms. Murphy covers his subject well; frequent photographs and reproductions of historic prints provide illustration.

Elizabeth Gillis

SOURCE: A review of *Tractors: From Yesterday's Steam Wagons to Today's Turbo-Charged Giants,* in *Appraisal: Science Books for Young People,* Vol. 18, No. 1, Winter, 1985, pp. 28-29.

The evolution of the steam wagon and plowing engine into our modern farm tractor does not appear to be a likely topic for interesting reading. But the author with judicious use of black-and-white illustrations of such machines and a clear entertaining style tells the story well. A French engineer named Cugnot is credited with the first step in this evolutionary process when he devised a cumbersome steam wagon to pull a cannon in 1765 (he even had the first traffic accident when he collided with a wall). Interesting tidbits are included. For example, when James Watts' assistant built a three-wheeled runabout the local clergyman seeing the steam and sparks at night was sure that he had seen the devil! The development of the internal-combustion engine, the gas tractor, and the diesel engine are described. Along with the successes are some delightful oddities. One in 1805 was amphibious with its creator able to drive from the street into the river in order to dredge it. My personal favorite is one with six legs in addition to the usual wheels to help get the bulky creature up a hill. A brief bibliography and index are included. A good picture of the inventive process with its failures and curiosities as well as its more durable accomplishments.

📖 *GUESS AGAIN: MORE WEIRD AND WACKY INVENTIONS (1986)*

Publishers Weekly

SOURCE: A review of *Guess Again: More Weird and Wacky Inventions,* in *Publishers Weekly,* Vol. 229, No. 26, June 27, 1986, p. 97.

The author of **Weird and Wacky Inventions** is back with

another collection of inventions almost too preposterous to believe. Only Murphy's assurances could convince the reader that someone really *did* invent a coffin with an escape hatch (to comfort those afraid of being buried alive by mistake), or the tapeworm trap (a spring-loaded, metal tube baited with food and swallowed whole). The list goes on and on, each more hilarious than the last, all illustrated with original patent or magazine drawings. Murphy includes true stories of creative problem-solving like the revelation that the modern centralized kitchen was invented by Catherine Beecher in 1869, and modeled after a ship's galley. *Guess Again* is just as wacky as its predecessor.

Margaret H. Hagel

SOURCE: A review of *Guess Again: More Weird and Wacky Inventions,* in *School Library Journal,* Vol. 33, No. 2, October, 1986, p. 180.

Guess Again, a sequel to *Weird and Wacky Inventions,* uses a lighthearted multiple-choice quiz to introduce more unusual inventions, such as a coffin with an escape hatch and training pants for dogs. A descriptive paragraph is accompanied by a pen-and-ink drawing, based on the original patent drawings. Readers are then given three or four possible choices of the invention's purpose; on the next page, along with the correct answer, is more information about the invention. Because the act of invention to fulfill a need is an important ingredient of the American spirit, the first and last chapter tell the stories behind other inventions that were more "needed" than those in the main body of the book. The afterword tells a little about the patent process. The game-like format and sometimes absurd inventions will hold readers' attention.

Arrolyn H. Vernon

SOURCE: A review of *Guess Again: More Weird and Wacky Inventions,* in *Appraisal: Science Books for Young People,* Vol. 20, No. 1, Winter, 1987, pp. 48-49.

Murphy's *Weird and Wacky Inventions* is an ALA Notable and *School Library Journal* Best Book. In *Guess Again,* he reproduces the same format with forty-five new thing-a-mag-jigs and contraptions. For each, he adapts its patent application sketch or a drawing that appeared in *Scientific American.* He accompanies the adapted illustration with a bit of enigmatical description and comment and a list of possible identifications. The reader/looker plays a multiple choice game. He can brainstorm a context or a purpose, make a choice, then turn the page and see the "real" invention, briefly described and shown in use or in context. Historical and sociological insights spring up. (The importance of scale and mindset in assigning identities is demonstrated, all in a spirit of near-trivia game-playing.)

A final chapter, more serious than the rest, tells a longer story of each of five different inventors and their successful or failed devices. The book should be fun for those who enjoy the cryptic, especially when imaginative visualization is exercised. It offers teachers a somewhat quirky change of pace in the subject of inventions. And some of what appears to be fluff could turn out to be grist for older students, considering the mysterious ways of creativity.

THE LAST DINOSAUR (1988)

Phillis Wilson

SOURCE: A review of *The Last Dinosaur,* in *Booklist,* Vol. 84, No. 17, May 1, 1988, p. 1527.

Murphy uses the perplexing questions of why and how dinosaurs died out to thoughtfully imagine the end of the age of dinosaurs. His story begins as a dwindling herd of Triceratops feeds at dawn 65 million years ago. Heat lightning starts a fire in the tangled forest of pine and poplar, and the animals move quickly to stay clear of the smoke. Later, as flames erupt again, forcing the one female to abandon her eggs to the foraging shrewlike mammals, something moves in the dark forest shadows; it is the menacing Tyrannosaurus. After they battle, only one Triceratops is left, seen lumbering off as the sun goes down. Murphy notes in an afterword that though no one knows which dinosaur was actually the last survivor, scientists believe that Triceratops' speed, power, and capabilities make it the best candidate. [Mark Alan] Weatherby's predominately green-gray watercolors portray the dense forest as hauntingly quiet, with shafts of sunlight just penetrating the lush foliage. Grim, to-the-death battle scenes and the concept of extinction make this a more appropriate offering for older dinosaur fans.

Betsy Hearne

SOURCE: A review of *The Last Dinosaur,* in *Bulletin of the Center for Children's Books,* Vol. 41, No. 10, June, 1988, p. 213.

Full-color illustrations characterized by a filmy photo-realism evoke the setting for this story of the last dinosaur, a female Triceratops whose remaining herd of two males is killed in a fight with a Tyrannosaurus Rex and whose eggs are eaten by small mammals when she abandons the nest to escape a forest fire. The scenario certainly renders the end of the Age of Dinosaurs more immediate than many non-fiction accounts, though the author seems to apologize for this in an afterword ("It's sad to think about the death of the Dinosaurs. But we shouldn't be too sad about their end"). A preface mentions the factors of disease, temperature change, and a comet explosion that may have contributed to the dinosaurs' disappearance. None of these appears as a factor in the story; in fact, the opening, in which a Triceratops charges an enormous tree to free its head of grapevines, may make readers wonder how creatures so dense survived as long as they did. Nonetheless, this will be appreciated by a picture-book audience as well as by students reading independently.

Janet Hickman

SOURCE: A review of *The Last Dinosaur,* in *Language Arts,* Vol. 65, No. 5, September, 1988, p. 500.

The Last Dinosaur, a fact-based fictional speculation about the fate of the very last dinosaurs on earth (Triceratops, the author posits), is surprisingly poignant and beautifully illustrated. It's quite an accomplishment to make a sixty-five-million-year-old setting seem immediate. The focus helps: a single female struggles to protect her eggs from forest fire and thieving small mammals (she doesn't succeed); she fights to save the two males left in her herd from the attack of a Tyrannosaurus (all three males die); she plods away on the last page in search of food and perhaps somewhere another herd. Illustrations bring life to the giant animals as individuals by showing movement and shifts in perspective on their great bodies. Background landscapes capture the drama of rugged terrain and deep forests, with careful portrayal of the era's plant life. This is a welcome companion for "straight" informational books that examine possible reasons for the dinosaurs' extinction.

Cathryn A. Camper

SOURCE: A review of *The Last Dinosaur,* in *School Library Journal,* Vol. 35, No. 1, September, 1988, p. 184.

A fictionalized story about what life was like for one Triceratops when the dinosaurs began to die off. The text and detailed illustrations tell the story of several Triceratops, describing their environment and how they found food, laid eggs, and defended themselves against carnivores. When T. Rex kills one of them, and another perishes in a forest fire, only a female Triceratops remains. At the end of the book, she sets off, in hopes of finding others of her kind. But the final illustrations, of her disappearing into the haze followed by a trail of small mammals, foreshadows a different ending. The gorgeous full-color illustrations realistically capture both the prehistoric beauty and the violence of these dinosaurs lives. However, in at least one instance, the text and picture don't jibe. The text describes the Triceratops's chosen nesting spot ("On the opposite side of the marsh she found a warm, sandy area with low-growing shrubs") but the illustration shows the nest just a few feet from the swamp, with no shrubbery in sight. And while the picture book format will attract readers, it makes it difficult for readers to differentiate between fact and anthropomorphism.

CUSTOM CAR: A NUTS-AND-BOLTS GUIDE TO CREATING ONE (1989)

Kirkus Reviews

SOURCE: A review of *Custom Car: A Nuts-and-Bolts Guide to Creating One,* in *Kirkus Reviews,* Vol. LVII, No. 7, April 1, 1989, pp. 551-52.

Two guys with a few tools and $5500 convert a junker Ford into a sleek street machine.

"Taking apart an engine is one of the easiest jobs imaginable." Suspend your disbelief: as the author says, "the people who build and repair engines aren't any smarter than you." With casual confidence, he describes how he and Tom Walsh—a mechanic and the book's "technical consultant"—breathed new, funky life into an old, rusty, fire-damaged car—rebuilding the engine, replacing much of the trim and interior, carefully shopping for bargains and ideas. Murphy has sound advice for prospective customizers (outline goals in advance; don't buy specialized tools that can be borrowed or rented; etc.), and plenty of b&w photos with chatty captions show the work in progress as well as sample-parts catalogs and specialty magazines. But this is not an instruction manual (neither text nor illustrations are specific) or even an "insider's" guide: Murphy doesn't go into how much time or room the project needed, and—except in cleaning the engine compartment—he barely mentions getting dirty. The "can-do" attitude is infectious, however, and readers will find the agenda, general suggestions, and price and tool lists helpful.

Despite the fairy-tale quality here—the car cost $75, the extensive bodywork and painting, including a hood scoop and racing strip, only $1800—this makes a breezy first book for both doers and dreamers.

Ann G. Brouse

SOURCE: A review of *Custom Car: A Nuts-and-Bolts Guide to Creating One,* in *School Library Journal,* Vol. 35, No. 11, July, 1989, p. 96.

Although not a step-by-step manual, this book uses photographs to follow the progress of a rusty victim of an engine fire through its interior and exterior renovation to the hot red-and-black custom car pictured on the book's jacket. The authors (and renovators) give actual costs for nearly all replacement parts, accessories, and cosmetic services used in the transformation. They encourage installing good used parts and accessories rather than always buying brand new. Suggestions and some addresses for sources of such items are included. Hints for the order of procedure lead to a smooth progression of work and the avoidance of inadvertent damage or extra work. The authors recommend looking at finished custom cars and reading up on the automotive work involved before deciding on a theme and course of action for customizing a particular vehicle, but there is no bibliography. . . . The three-page glossary defines some of the common and unfamiliar terms used in the text. Anyone who has not had considerable experience with car repair will need a greater familiarity with engine parts and automotive operating systems before attempting an actual customizing job.

THE CALL OF THE WOLVES (1989)

Betsy Hearne

SOURCE: A review of *The Call of the Wolves,* in *Bulletin of the Center for Children's Books,* Vol. 43, No. 1, September, 1989, p. 13.

With an involving text and arresting art, this is a nature narrative that commands attention without ever becoming sentimental or anthropomorphic. A young wolf is separated from his pack during a caribou hunt that is interrupted by illegal hunters shooting from a plane. Trapped, the wolf plunges over a cliff, injures a leg, and labors through a snowstorm in another pack's territory to return home. The story yields plenty of unobtrusive information, and an afterword explains how much modern research contradicts myths of the past. A brief list of important sources for further information is appended. Because the style is straightforward and the dramatically textured paintings—each a handsome composition unto itself—are so dynamic, this can be read by independent readers older than the picture book listeners for whom it's intended.

Kirkus Reviews

SOURCE: A review of *The Call of the Wolves,* in *Kirkus Reviews,* Vol. LVII, No. 22, November 15, 1989, p. 1674.

Set in the Arctic, a realistic story about a two-year-old wolf who is separated from his pack in the confusion caused by illegal hunters shooting at caribou from a small plane. The straightforwardly presented events are chosen to demonstrate characteristic behavior: the young wolf caring for younger cubs; wolves following the caribou pack and culling its weak members; the perils of straying into another pack's territory. [Mark Alan] Weatherby's beautiful, meticulously detailed paintings—generously extended across the gutter to almost 14"—make the wolves appealing without sentimentalizing them; he conveys the magnificence of the snowy mountain backgrounds and captures, without sensationalizing, the action's drama.

An effective plea for respect for and conservation of an often misunderstood fellow creature. A careful note adds more information about wolves' behavior; annotated bibliography, including the film of Mowat's *Never Cry Wolf.*

Deborah Abbott

SOURCE: A review of *The Call of the Wolves,* in *Booklist,* Vol. 86, No. 9, January 1, 1990, p. 919.

During the arctic winter a young wolf and his hungry pack stalk a herd of caribou. Unexpectedly, an airplane filled with hunters breaks up the herd, and the noise from the shots causes panic among the animals. The frantic young wolf, caught in the confusion, bolts, realizing too late his only choice is to leap over a cliff. A rough landing results in an injured leg, but the wolf's survival instinct helps him plow through a blizzard. He narrowly escapes a neighboring wolf pack, whose territory he has invaded while trying to find his mates. The dramatic, full-color paintings of snowy scenes, bathed in blues, whites, and grays, will draw readers into the arduousness and terror of the journey. The wolves, with strong, graceful bodies, heavily textured fur, and dazzling silver-blue eyes, add to the audience's respect for and fascination with this species. The taut story line, compelling illustrations, and recently renewed interest in wolves make this fictionalized account valuable. A short history of wolves and bibliography included.

Susan Wolfe

SOURCE: A review of *The Call of the Wolves,* in *The Booktalker,* Vol. 65, No. 1, September, 1990, p. 4.

What would you do if you suddenly found yourself all alone, far from friends and family, and unable to find your way home? In Jim Murphy's ***The Call of the Wolves,*** a young wolf finds himself in just this situation—separated from his pack and alone in the icy Arctic.

He and his pack have been following a herd of caribou for eight days over steep and dangerous terrain. They have traveled far; they are hungry. Finally, one of the caribou can go no further. In a snowy Arctic clearing, the wolves close in on the sick, weak animal that is no longer able to outrun them. Just as they are about to attack, a plane of illegal hunters zooms over the area. Wolves and caribou frantically scatter as gunshots break the silence of the snowy wilderness.

One young wolf, eager to escape, runs in the opposite direction from the others. He soon realizes he is being followed by the plane of hunters. As he runs, he comes face to face with his only route of escape—a plunge over a steep cliff. His instinct to survive is strong. He launches himself over the cliff, dropping into a mound of branches and snow. His rear leg crumples beneath him as he struggles to escape the plane that continues to pursue him. He scrambles on three legs into the protective trees that hinder the hunters' view. Alone, hurt and hungry, the young wolf curls up in the snow for a night of rest, knowing that the next day he must find his pack, even though he doesn't know where he is and has no trail to follow. Will he be able to do it? He will have to contend not only with cold and snow, but also with other animals who may attack him boldly now that he is alone.

What can one young wolf do, alone in the Arctic with no pack to help him? Will his instinct to survive be strong enough to overcome his confusion, his injury, and his weakened condition?

📖 THE BOYS' WAR: CONFEDERATE AND UNION SOLDIERS TALK ABOUT THE CIVIL WAR (1990)

Betsy Hearne

SOURCE: A review of *The Boys' War: Confederate and Union Soldiers Talk about the Civil War,* in *Bulletin of the Center for Children's Books,* Vol. 44, No. 5, January, 1991, p. 126.

Just in time to follow up on the interest stirred by the PBS series on the Civil War, this will serve long-term student research needs as well. Various chapters cover young soldiers' enlistment, battle experiences, living conditions, food supplies, medical and sanitary problems, and imprisonment. Drum and bugle corps boys get special attention, since they tended to be the youngest recruits. The author acknowledges that we have no statistics on how many underage boys fought or died in the war, but there were many; and some of their eyewitness accounts, here woven into background explanations, are vivid. Unfortunately, the sources for these are not directly documented, although readers could track a few of them from names cited in the text to names appearing in titles of the bibliography (*Private Elisha Stockwell, Jr. Sees the Civil War,* for instance). Numerous historical photographs, reproduced in sepia and well-placed in the text, add significant impact to the information.

David A. Lindsey

SOURCE: A review of *The Boys' War: Confederate and Union Soldiers Talk about the Civil War,* in *School Library Journal,* Vol. 37, No. 1, January, 1991, p. 120.

Making extensive use of the actual words—culled from diaries, journals, memoirs, and letters—of boys who served in the Union and Confederate armies as fighting soldiers as well as drummers, buglers, and telegraphers, Murphy describes the beginnings of the Civil War and goes on to delineate the military role of the underage soldiers and their life in the camps and field bivouacs. Also included is a description of the boys' return home and the effects upon them of their wartime experiences. Boys 16 years and younger, Murphy states, made up perhaps as much as 10-20 percent of the total number of soldiers who served in the Civil War. Little did these boys realize that they would become like young Pvt. Henry Graves, who was able to "—look on the carcass of a man with pretty much such feeling as I would do were it a horse or hog." Private Henry and his contem- poraries were direct and simple in their observations and possessed, says Murphy, "an eye for everyday details." Their accounts bring to life, as no other versions can, the Civil War and all of its glories and horrors. An excellent selection of more than 45 sepia-toned contemporary photographs augment the text of this informative, moving work.

Margaret A. Bush

SOURCE: A review of *The Boys' War: Confederate and Union Soldiers Talk about the Civil War,* in *The Horn Book Magazine,* Vol. LXVII, No. 1, January-February, 1991, pp. 86-87.

Twelve-year-old Johnny Clem, shown in full uniform just after the Battle of Shiloh in 1862, is an arresting figure on the jacket of this sobering account. Jim Murphy draws widely on actual letters and diaries in developing his examination of the participation and experiences of boys under the age of sixteen who fought in the Civil War, whether because of patriotism or a thirst for adventure. Dreams of glory most often gave way to a dreary and grim reality, well documented here in an impressive collection of photographs. Although the author does not dwell on suffering and death, they are an inescapable focus. In the early days of the war finding a proper uniform was difficult; one sixteen-year-old reports his unease at the solution. "—After each fight I would search the field for anyone . . . who did not require use of his equipment. I must confess to feeling very bad doing this, believing the dead should not be disturbed, but I had no other course." Murphy ranges over the bright expectations of enlistees, the realities of fighting, problems of foraging for food, life in the army camps, and experiences in prisons and medical facilities. Finally, he looks at the psychological effects of the war on these young men and at the shock of families being reunited at the war's end. It is startling to learn of the large number of very young soldiers whose lives were given to the war, and this well-researched and readable account provides fresh insight into the human cost of a pivotal event in United States history.

Joanne Johnson

SOURCE: A review of *The Boys' War: Confederate and Union Soldiers Talk about the Civil War,* in *Voice of Youth Advocates,* Vol. 14, No. 1, April, 1991, p. 60.

Between 1861 and 1865, an estimated 250,000-400,000 boys between 12 and 16 joined the Union and Confederate armies. Most did so because they wanted adventure and freedom from the boredom of farm life. What they received instead was a dose of reality and horror beyond their wildest imaginings. As one young man put it, "I thought what a foolish boy I was to run away and get into such a mess as I was in. I would have been glad to have seen my father coming after me." That young man's opinion came to be held by a large number of the underage drummer boys and soldiers who fought in the Civil War.

Murphy's account of the lives of these youngest soldiers is well done. The excerpts from the diaries and letters written home by this group of young men between 12 and 16 provide an insight for YAs not available in other books. Reading their reactions makes this war come alive in a way that the diaries and letters of adults may not. The author's commentary paints an excellent picture of what daily life was like for the ordinary soldier. The chapters on the winter encampments, prisons, and medical hospitals provide a grim but realistic picture of the conditions these young men endured. The accounts of the battles in which these boys participated completes the picture of soldiering during war time. While the subject matter may limit the popularity of the book, it should be in all libraries.

THE LONG ROAD TO GETTYSBURG (1992)

Kirkus Reviews

SOURCE: A review of *The Long Road to Gettysburg,* in *Kirkus Reviews,* Vol. LX, No. 9, May 1, 1992, p. 614.

Relying heavily on firsthand accounts plus uncredited (but apparently contemporary) photos, prints and sketches, Murphy opens and closes with the battlefield dedication ceremony, in which Edward Everett delivered a long, eloquent speech and President Lincoln was tentatively invited to give "a few appropriate remarks" (quoted in full); in between, the author analyzes Lee's strategy; points out the many ironies of timing and position that affected the battle's outcome; and, using brief extracts from the journals of a Union corporal and a Confederate lieutenant, captures a soldier's-eye-view of the exhausting marches, frantic firefights, and weary, poignant aftermath. Readers will get a good sense of what generals and privates, countryside and battle looked like from the many b&w illustrations, and a general idea of troop movements from a set of sketchy maps.

Carolyn Phelan

SOURCE: A review of *The Long Road to Gettysburg,* in *Booklist,* Vol. 88, No. 18, May 15, 1992, p. 1677.

Beginning and ending with the dedication ceremony at which Lincoln delivered the Gettysburg Address, Murphy's intriguing book presents the story of the battle from the points of view of two actual participants. Murphy introduces readers to a Confederate lieutenant, John Dooley, and a Union corporal, Thomas Galway, then follows their footsteps and relates what they see during the battle, often in their own words. Meanwhile, maps and background information give a sense of Gettysburg as a whole. Though some readers may have difficulty with the back-and-forth shifts of perspective, this method makes for a more evenhanded account of the divisive

war than Murphy could have achieved by giving one soldier's perspective along. In the end, Dooley, one of 42,000 wounded at Gettysburg, lies in the rain for two days and nights before being tended and sent to a Union prison. Galway helps with the burial detail's monumental task before moving out with Meade's forces. The firsthand accounts, drawn from Dooley's and Galway's own writings, give the narrative immediacy and personalize the horrors of battle. Like Murphy's *The Boys' War,* this volume is generously illustrated with period drawings, engravings, paintings, and, especially, photographs. An important addition to the Civil War shelf.

Elizabeth M. Reardon

SOURCE: A review of *The Long Road to Gettysburg,* in *School Library Journal,* Vol. 38, No. 6, June, 1992, p. 146.

As in *The Boys' War,* Murphy returns to the Civil War, this time focusing on the Battle of Gettysburg. He introduces two participants—19-year-old Lieutenant John Dooley, CSA, and 17-year-old Union army Corporal Thomas Galway—through whose eyes the action unfolds. Each is a fairly "typical" soldier: for Galway, who has experienced anti-Irish prejudice, the war is personal; Dooley is there to defend the honor and integrity of the South. Through alternating narratives, readers see the march northward through Virginia and Pennsylvania, and are present for Pickett's Charge. Murphy does not spare the grim details of battle, and the well-chosen, sepia-toned illustrations and their accompanying captions do much to illuminate the text. The maps are comprehensive and thorough in recording the troop movements. The book closes with Lincoln delivering his Gettysburg Address, and with an epilogue about the young men's postwar lives. The excellent use of quotes and descriptions from Dooley and Galway's journals brings authenticity and immediacy to the narrative. By focusing on these two ordinary soldiers, readers get a new perspective on this decisive and bloody battle. A first-rate addition to Civil War collections, especially where Murphy's previous book is popular.

Anita Silvey

SOURCE: A review of *The Long Road to Gettysburg,* in *The Horn Book Magazine,* Vol. LXVIII, No. 4, July-August, 1992, pp. 469-70.

Jim Murphy uses all of his fine skills as an information writer—clarity of detail, conciseness, understanding of his age group, and ability to find the drama appealing to readers—to frame a well-crafted account of a single battle in the war. He begins and ends the book with details of the speech Lincoln believed to be one of his greatest failures—the Gettysburg Address. The book focuses on the experiences of a Union soldier, John Dooley, and a Confederate soldier, Thomas Galway, who would take part in the battle in the sleepy Pennsylvania town. Although the text probably doesn't contain all of the detailed information about the actual fighting at Gettysburg that a budding military tactician would want, it does capture the drama—from the opening salvos to Pickett's immortal charge. Augmented by a clear design and enhanced by period photographs and numerous maps, the account provides something missing in the literature for young readers—a sense of what happened in an actual Civil War battle.

Alleen Pace Nilsen

SOURCE: A review of *The Long Road to Gettysburg,* in *English Journal,* Vol. 82, No. 8, December, 1993, p. 71.

Jim Murphy is an up-and-coming author of information books for young readers. Up to now, his most acclaimed book was **The Boys' War** based on Civil War letters, diaries, and news accounts of young soldiers. **The Long Road to Gettysburg** grew out of the same research and reflects how well steeped the author is in the period. Among the reasons for the book's success are that Murphy begins with something young readers know about (Lincoln's Gettysburg Address); he limits his topic (the battle of Gettysburg rather than the whole Civil War), and he focuses on young protagonists (an eighteen-year-old Southern lieutenant named John Dooley and a seventeen-year-old Union corporal named Thomas Galway, both of whom kept journals). Perhaps most important is the fact that Murphy searched through original sources until he found the kinds of details that he could use as explanatory background information as well as primary facts to move the story forward. For example, he explains how "straggling was considered a sign of weakness or, worse, laziness," and then quotes from the embarrassed Galway's journal in which he writes:

> My feet are very sore. Generally, I am one of the best marchers in our company which, by the way, is considered one of the best marching companies in the brigade. . . . I kept with my company for another couple of hours. Finally I could not put one foot before another. I was utterly done out, so telling my sergeant of my intentions, I stepped out from the ranks and lay down on a spot of grass.

Murphy's goal in putting this documentary together was to

> connect what many kids might consider a remote bit of speechmaking to an actual, dramatic event, making clear the human element of the battle and how it changed the course of the war and the United States.

He did exactly that through careful research and equally careful writing. Fortunately, his publishers supported his standard of excellence with a spacious layout and high-quality paper to enhance the reproduction of historical documents. Five maps are included as are forty-five drawings or paintings, and twenty-eight photographs. These visuals help make for quick reading.

Obviously, this is a book that history teachers will want to use, but we also encourage English teachers to use it in teaching young people to read and appreciate nonfiction. And it's a good example of how to make historical research interesting through a smooth blending of quotes with original writing. Speech and communication teachers might also make use of the book because it both begins and ends with a discussion of Lincoln's 269-word speech as compared to the one-hour-and-forty-five minute oration of Edward Everett, the main speaker.

DINOSAUR FOR A DAY (1992)

Denia Hester

SOURCE: A review of *Dinosaur for a Day,* in *Booklist,* Vol. 89, No. 4, October 15, 1992, p. 435.

Readers are invited to follow a dinosaur family for a day as it hunts for food on a lush green island. Mother hypsilophodon and her eight children search for tender leaves, shoots, and flowers for breakfast, all the while alert for any sign of predators. Their vigilance pays off when a deinonychus pack charges toward the clearing. The dinosaur mother must outrun the ferocious carnivores and divert attention from her babies. Because of the static narrative voice, the story lacks dramatic impact, but the book is well worth a look for its rich illustrations [by Mark Alan Weatherby]. The sunlit greens and browns of the acrylic washes make a stunning forest. Readers may be tempted to try to brush away raindrops from a thick frond.

Publishers Weekly

SOURCE: A review of *Dinosaur for a Day,* in *Publishers Weekly,* Vol. 239, No. 49, November 9, 1992, p. 84.

With its odd, sometimes uneasy mix of fact and fiction, this story of a neatly imagined, drama-filled day of a parent Hysilophodon may disappoint eager dinosaurophiles. Though creatively presented, Murphy and Weatherby's proficient collaboration doesn't quite deliver on its title's promise. While the Hysilophodon and its brood forage, a pack of sharp-clawed Deinonychus attack. The adult leads the predatory meat-eater away from the babies and rejoins them later, in time for the family to return safely to their inland nest. The gauzy, highlighted paintings look as if they were shot in soft focus, and provide an eery, often startling ground-level view of the action. Facts weigh heavily—pages of information book-end the story; there are listings of dinosaurs mentioned and books about dinosaurs (most more suitable for adults than for children). Jarring elements such as strange stone surfaces appearing as text backdrops, along with a didactic approach, may limit the audience for this team's second dinosaur book

Nicholas Hotton III

SOURCE: A review of *Dinosaur for a Day,* in *Science Books & Films,* Vol. 29, No. 6, August-September, 1993, p. 180.

This very attractive book is simple in concept, well executed, and gorgeously illustrated. It is an imaginative attempt to recreate a day in the life of the small herbivorous dinosaur *Hypsilophodon,* represented by a female and her eight chicks. The exposition is satisfactory and does not obtrude on the story, as it is restricted to sidebars on three pages. The action is low key and, with respect to the behavior of the protagonists, is consistent with current scientific opinion. The temporal context, however, is a disaster. *Hypsilophodon* lived during the Lower Cretaceous period, about 100 million years ago, but most of the organisms mentioned or illustrated as contemporaries are anachronistic by 20 to 90 million years. Two of five dinosaurs are from the Upper Cretaceous period, all of the birds are of middle to late Tertiary origin, and most of the plants are modern forms. Illustrations also include a bat, honeybees, vespid wasps, and swallowtail butterflies, none of which appeared earlier than about 45 million years after *Hypsilophodon* became extinct. Since time is an important factor of the book, these gaffes should have been avoided, and could have been without much effort. The presence of the errors drops the quality of the book from exceptional to marginally acceptable.

📖 *BACKYARD BEAR* (1993)

Kirkus Reviews

SOURCE: A review of *Backyard Bear,* in *Kirkus Reviews,* Vol. LXI, No. 1, January 1, 1993, p. 66.

Told mostly from a bear's point of view, a thoughtful, nonjudgmental, and scrupulously realistic depiction of people in uneasy confrontation with the wild. In a note, Murphy explains that human encroachments on bears' territory and the lure of easy food are making bear sightings in suburban neighborhoods more common. This story describes such an incident. Driven away by an older bear protecting some blackberries, a bear follows the smell of food into town, where he disturbs some raccoons and rouses a dog and its family who, when they realize it's a bear, call the police. In the confusion created by the interaction of the dog, a boy with a camera, his frightened parents, and a policeman about to shoot the cornered animal, the bear knocks down a fence, then hides out nearby until escaping to the woods at dawn. [Jeffrey] Greene's dark, dramatically posed paintings nicely capture the ambience of the peaceful, moonlit rural community and the confusion of an exciting encounter that could easily have ended in tragedy. Brief

but interesting bibliography, including books from several state agencies.

Deborah Abbott

SOURCE: A review of *Backyard Bear,* in *Booklist,* Vol. 89, No. 10, January 15, 1993, p. 923.

In his latest animal story. Murphy focuses his attention on the plight of the black bear in America. A hungry young bear flees from an alluring blackberry patch when an older male brutally stakes out the territory. Hoping to squelch his hunger pangs, the young bear ventures into civilization, attracted by the smells from garbage cans. The bear makes noise, waking a sleeping family. Before long, the bear is trapped in a backyard with a growling dog, surprised parents, their son with a camera, and the local police, who threaten to shoot the animal. Fright and survival instincts provide the bear with enough stamina and speed to escape into the woods, where he begins anew to search for food. Although this story is fiction, it is based on fact, according to the note and bibliography at the end. Greene's dark pastel drawings are extremely effective in showing the night scenes, with their shimmering cast of moonlight.

Publishers Weekly

SOURCE: A review of *Backyard Bear,* in *Publishers Weekly,* Vol. 240, No. 4, January 25, 1993, p. 87.

Borne on Greene's detailed, nocturnal pastel illustrations, this realistic tale rises above its matter-of-fact roots to take on hues of wonder and imminence. One night, a hungry black bear cub wanders innocently into a neighborhood, unaware of its sleeping inhabitants. As he searches for the food he smells, a chain reaction wakes a family and raises a sudden storm of police sirens and piercing lights. The bruin is saved from gunfire when a camera's blinding flash sends him crashing through a fence and out of range. After a fearsome night of hiding in nearby bushes he makes his way home in the dim, pre-dawn stillness. While the book's voice (narrative is in the present tense), layout and, in particular, illustrations call to mind the style and quality of Chris Van Allsburg's work, Murphy's account is distinctively naturalistic and down-to-earth. Its ending cleverly segues into a newspaper-style report on the encroachment of human civilization on wilderness habitats (this story, in fact, is based on an actual event). As a reportorial memoir emotionally enhanced by dramatic illustrations, this book embodies a rare hybrid tone.

Karen K. Radtke

SOURCE: A review of *Backyard Bear,* in *School Library Journal,* Vol. 39, No. 4, April, 1993, p. 101.

A young bear, forced out of his natural habitat by an

older, territorial bear, is lured into a suburban neighborhood by the smell of food. Through dramatic prose, readers follow his encounters with clotheslines, a raccoon, a barbecue grill, dogs, and people, including the police. He manages to elude all searchers, and at dawn lumbers back to the forest. Murphy concludes with information about bears and the news clipping that inspired the story. The pastel illustrations in deep blues, greens, and luminous whites are naturalistic in their portrayal of landscapes and figures. They span lengthwise across the book, offering a sense of open spaces and the atmosphere of the night. As the animal becomes entangled with civilization, the composition gets more crowded and off balance. An exciting story, and one that is becoming more common in real life all the time.

NIGHT TERRORS (1993)

Bruce Anne Shook

SOURCE: A review of *Night Terrors,* in *School Library Journal,* Vol. 39, No. 9, September, 1993, p. 252.

The narrator of these horror tales is an "old geek" who has made a career of digging graves. He tells stories that have been handed down to him through the years, and in between he gives an account of his own unusual life. This makes for a short-story collection with more cohesion than usual. Each selection includes a young person who is breaking some sort of rule and whose fate is somehow brought on by this transgression. These selections build suspense from the very beginning. The contemporary nature of the settings makes the twists that come at the end of each one all the more frightening. One story that begins as an account of a late night break-in to steal a mid-term science exam becomes a chilling vampire tale. Other equally scary yarns involve a boy's being buried alive, mummified animals that come to life to devour the one who resurrected them, cannibalism, and good witches who punish evil. This may sound like strong stuff for youngsters, but the narrative has a light touch and only enough detail to fire the imagination. Digger is an interesting character who is developed as a lovable if eccentric old guy who can certainly be trusted, even if readers don't really take him too seriously. This factor makes the surprise ending the most terrifying story of all. Overall, the collection evokes "night terrors" without being too explicit or gory. Buy this one for all the middle grade youngsters who long for a good horror story but can't yet manage Stephen King.

Stephanie Zvirin

SOURCE: A review of *Night Terrors,* in *Booklist,* Vol. 90, No. 3, October 1, 1993, p. 332.

Five unrelated horror stories are surrounded by episodes in the odd career of the narrator, known as Digger because he digs graves. Ostensibly told to Digger by various individuals he has encountered on the job, the tales are all of the gruesome (but not sensational) variety, populated with an assortment of vampires, mummies, and cannibals. Digger's expansive comments provide a glimmer of humor as well as atmosphere, the latter manifesting itself largely in the final chapters, in which Digger's own life takes a particularly ghastly turn. With the possible exception of the gruesome finales, there's little that horror buffs will find truly unexpected in the stories, but Murphy has a knack for evocative descriptions, which will probably be enough to keep readers happy.

Margaret Mary Ptacek

SOURCE: A review of *Night Terrors,* in *Voice of Youth Advocates,* Vol. 16, No. 5, December, 1993, p. 312.

Night Terrors is a collection of horror stories told by an old gravedigger named Digger. Digger has gathered these tales throughout the years by living and working in cemeteries. There are five stories within the story. In **"Like Father, Like Son"** Brian attempts to bring to life a mummy his father, an archaeologist, is trying to rise from the dead. Unfortunately, Brian brings back a different kind of mummified creature instead. In **"The Cat's-Eye"** Kirsten and Jessica house-sit six cats owned by Mrs. Hayward. Kirsten, a bold and unpleasant but popular young woman, is restless and starts to investigate the house. Jessica, her meek and mild companion, follows her and tries to dissuade her from the activity. They discover a closet with almost endless depth with a surprise at the end. Digger enjoys telling us about the stories and creatures of the night until you discover he might have more than entertainment in mind.

This is your better than average horror collection. The stories within a story is an attractive approach. Each tale has an interesting twist. They rely more on irony than gore. Horror is extremely popular with YAs, and this will prove to be a hit.

Kirkus Reviews

SOURCE: A review of *Night Terrors,* in *Kirkus Reviews,* Vol. LXI, No. 23, December 1, 1993, p. 1527.

An old gravedigger embeds five mild horror stories, all featuring young people, into an account of his peregrinations. In **"Catseye,"** Jessica and the malicious Kirsten discover a backless closet in a witch's house; the trip that three teens are making to a party is interrupted when their car breaks down near a hungry couple's isolated shack; Brian brings a large and famished collection of mummified Egyptian animals to life; a prospective grave-robber is seized and buried by a living watchman and an animate corpse, working together; and, in **"Just Say Yes,"** Kelly is invited by her science teacher—and, to her amazement, her bubble-headed best friend—to be a werewolf. The stories—nearly free of explicit gore or violence—follow predictable paths and are written in a conventional style that's at odds with the narrator's gruff, personal voice.

ACROSS AMERICA ON AN EMIGRANT TRAIN (1993)

Kirkus Reviews

SOURCE: A review of *Across America on an Emigrant Train,* in *Kirkus Reviews,* Vol. LXI, No. 22, November 15, 1993, p. 1465.

The 19th century's transcontinental railroads, explored via a delightfully effective narrative device: tracing the 1879 journey of Robert Louis Stevenson, who, at 29, was making an as-swift-as-possible journey from Edinburgh to Monterey, California, where his beloved Fanny was desperately ill. Murphy draws extensively on Stevenson's own account of his journey, by boat and a succession of trains of varying speed and discomfort, paraphrasing the gist of his experiences and including splendid quotes revealing RLS as a sharp observer—and extraordinarily gifted reporter—with an open mind and an unusually humane attitude toward people of all sorts. Meanwhile, in well-integrated tangents, Murphy discusses related topics: the building of the railroad, including the roles of different ethnic groups; the prevalence of collisions like one that delayed RLS's train; various immigrant groups; the real nature of the "Wild West." He ends with the joyful reunion (Fanny has recovered) and a summary of RLS's brief later life. A fascinating, imaginatively structured account that brings the experience vividly to life in all its detail: history at its best. Generously illustrated with period photos and prints; endpaper map; extensive bibliography, mostly of sources; index.

Diane S. Marton

SOURCE: A review of *Across America on an Emigrant Train,* in *School Library Journal,* Vol. 39, No. 12, December, 1993, pp. 129-30.

In 1879, Robert Louis Stevenson journeyed from Scotland across the Atlantic and then by train across the United States to join the woman he loved in Monterey, California. Murphy has drawn from the writer's journal to provide a fresh, primary-source account of transcontinental train travel at that time. Choosing by necessity the cheapest passage, Stevenson traveled with other newcomers to the U. S. who had not yet reached their final destination. He describes his companions, the passing countryside, the interior of the railroad cars, and daily life aboard a train. Into these journal entries, Murphy has woven meticulously researched, absorbing accounts of the building of the railroad and its effect on the territory it crossed: the disruption and destruction of Native American life, the slaughter of the buffalo, accidents, the development of the Pullman car, the towns

that quickly came and vanished as the construction crews moved on, the snowsheds built to protect the trains in the Sierra Nevada mountains. Abundant, carefully selected period photographs, engravings, and lithographs are every bit as intriguing as the text. Appended is a lengthy bibliography with some original source material. This work supplements Leonard Everett Fisher's more extensive *Tracks Across America;* it is a readable and valuable contribution to literature concerning expansion into the American West.

Ellen Fader

SOURCE: A review of *Across America on an Emigrant Train,* in *The Horn Book Magazine,* Vol. 70, No. 2, March-April, 1994, p. 220-21.

Murphy draws readers into the adventure of train travel in the late nineteenth century by recreating the trip Scotsman Robert Louis Stevenson took in 1879 as he traveled from Glasgow to New York to Monterey, California, to see the woman he loved. Stevenson had little money, since he not yet achieved fame as an author, so he traveled across America in the least expensive way possible: on so-called "emigrant trains." His traveling companions were emigrants from such places as France, Sweden, and Germany, and included African Americans from the South fleeing the ravages of the Civil War. Stevenson's trip from Scotland to California required twenty-four days and numerous transfers from one train to another, since no one company owned all the routes, and the tracks did not connect. Murphy's account of his journey is vivid, making extensive use of Stevenson's own words about the exhausting and often unpleasant experience. Amid Stevenson's commentary about the other passengers, the scenery, and his poor state of health, Murphy skillfully interweaves a general history of the growth of the transcontinental railroad and the emigrant experience. The narrative's frequent digression into such subjects as the working conditions of railroad laborers, the public's fascination with the luxury of the Pullman cars and the horror of train wrecks, and the impact of the railroad on Native-American life enhance the book's appeal. The volume's attractive design, with its wide margins and generous selection of well-chosen photographs, engravings, and lithographs, invites readers.

Elaine Aoki and others

SOURCE: "Bookalogues: Outstanding Nonfiction Choices for 1993," in *Language Arts,* Vol. 71, No. 6, October, 1994, pp. 453-59.

In 1879 Robert Louis Stevenson, then a little-known, struggling author, received a startling cable telling him that his beloved F. was gravely ill with brain fever. So begins this year's Orbis Pictus Award winner, *Across America on an Emigrant Train,* which traces Stevenson's journey from Scotland to America in pursuit of his love and future wife, Fanny Van de Grift Osbourne.

Stevenson's 24-day journey begins with a 3,000-mile trans-Atlantic crossing from Scotland to America in steerage class and ends in Monterey, California, after 3,000 additional miles of railroad travel. Using the narrative thread of Stevenson's journey, author Jim Murphy weaves in a great deal of information about the historical context. Readers learn about the workers who built the railroads; the frequent train disasters; the various levels of train accommodations, ranging from the bare bones "emigrant" trains to the lush Pullman cars; the emigrants who traveled the trains and settled in the West; the plight of the Buffalo; and the shameful treatment of Native Americans. Murphy shows how the mix of people and events occurring in the United States between 1850 and 1900 made it a time of "monumental changes." Excerpts from Stevenson's journal help the reader understand both the hardships and delights of train travel in the 1870s. Stevenson reports that as a result of one frustrating delay outside of Philadelphia, "We paid for this in the flesh, for we had no meals all day." In addition to these firsthand descriptions, more than 80 photographs and prints extend the reader's understanding and enjoyment. Illustrations are accompanied by informative captions that frequently point out details that might otherwise be overlooked. Readers who appreciate the engaging style of this book should not miss Murphy's *The Long Road to Gettysburg* and *The Boys' War.* Like *Emigrant Train,* each makes extensive use of first-person accounts and archival photographs to draw children closer to the people and events of the past.

📖 INTO THE DEEP FOREST WITH HENRY DAVID THOREAU (1995)

Publishers Weekly

SOURCE: A review of *Into the Deep Forest with Henry David Thoreau,* in *Publishers Weekly,* Vol. 242, No. 11, March 13, 1995, p. 69-70.

Presented as an account of one of Thoreau's three treks into Maine's wilderness, this is a thoroughly shuffled amalgamation of the philosopher/naturalist's quotes held in place by Murphy's fiction. Despite its mongrelization, the text is eminently approachable and generally faithful to Thoreau's spirit. The third-person narrative conveys Thoreau's fascination with nature: "Despite being lost in a mucky swamp, Henry still makes notes"—about round leafed orchids, dwarf raspberries, a red squirrel. And Thoreau's own words express the individualist's discomfort with society: "We live thick and are in each other's way." But sometimes Murphy's *(The Boy's War)* genteel text smothers his subject's accurate record of the wild. For instance, where Thoreau's moose are shot and killed, Murphy's "turn and bound into the cover of the trees." Debut artist [Kate] Kiesler's serene, atmospheric oil paintings, simply framed by wide white borders, depict Maine's diverse inland landscapes: swamp barrens, misty lakes, rock-strewn streams, charred forests and stony mountain tops. An introductory essay doubles as a thumbnail biography.

Carolyn Phelan

SOURCE: A review of *Into the Deep Forest with Henry David Thoreau,* in *Booklist,* Vol. 91, No. 16, April 15, 1995, p. 1496.

Following an introduction to Thoreau's life and works, this third-person narrative describes his journey with two companions to Mount Ktaadn (now Katahdin) in Maine and laces it with Thoreau's journal entries for three trips into the area. Action and reflection alternate as the naturalist observes moose from his canoe, slogs through a mucky swamp, discovers an advertisement for a Boston clothier on a tree deep in the woods, climbs to the mountaintop, and looks out on the landscape below. Murphy notes that he has made some changes in the journal entries for consistency and brevity, and the result is a text that is concise and readable, though the subject may have limited appeal at this age level. Appearing on each left-hand page, oil paintings illustrate the natural world as a beautiful, mysterious place. While some scenes include the shadowy figures of the three men, most focus on what they saw, from broad landscapes to minutely observed flowers. Small, delicately shaded pencil drawings illustrate the travelers' equipment as well as plants and animals.

Susan Scheps

SOURCE: A review of *Into the Deep Forest with Henry David Thoreau,* in *School Library Journal,* Vol. 41, No. 7, July, 1995, p. 90.

Murphy's brief introduction to the naturalist/writer, written as a third-person narrative, has been adapted from Thoreau's own journal entries and an article he wrote about his 1857 trip into the Maine wilderness, during which he climbed Mount Katahdin. Although Thoreau's entries have been condensed, the text is liberally sprinkled with quotes. Traveling with a friend and a Native American guide, he noted his observations of plants and trees, animals and birds, commenting on man's needless hunting of creatures such as moose " . . . merely for the satisfaction of killing" them. Several pages of biographical information are included. The format is journal-like. White-bordered oil paintings face full pages of text decorated with small pencil sketches of birds, berries, flowers, and tracks in the margins. Despite the brevity of the passages, Murphy ably conveys a sense of Thoreau's regard for nature and his need to escape civilization, but because his writings are usually studied in high school, this lovely production may be a shelf-sitter.

📖 THE GREAT FIRE (1995)

Elizabeth Bush

SOURCE: A review of *The Great Fire,* in *Bulletin of the Center for Children's Books,* Vol. 48, No. 9, May, 1995, pp. 297-98.

A peg leg wedged into the floorboards of a burning barn, a leather hat writhing in the heat, fireproof buildings gutted, beerhall carousers singing amid the blaze—the 1871 Chicago Fire has all the stuff a young pyrophile's dreams are made of. This account offers not only the luridly enticing details disaster junkies crave, but also a more complex analysis of the causes of the conflagration than is usually offered in children's history books, and an examination of evolving fire apocrypha that introduces young readers to some rudimentary historiography.

Murphy opens with a riveting portrait of a tinder town ready to ignite. Wooden buildings, roofed with tar, huddle together on small city lots. Commercial enterprises that run on volatile materials are interspersed throughout residential neighborhoods, and the city is girded with wooden sidewalks waiting to conduct flames through a "highly combustible knot." Add a lengthy spell of dry weather with high winds and the scene is set for disaster.

Why one particular barn fire in a season's worth of similar fires blazed out of control has been the subject of debate since the original inquest, and Murphy weighs the evidence as he describes events which, but for their consequences, could play as comedy. Human error undoubtedly contributes: no alarm bell sounds at the Courthouse; visual sightings are inaccurate and wagons are dispatched to the wrong street; one patrolman ignores a supervisor's signal order, while another turns in an inaccurate second alarm. Even nature conspires against containment as an updraft ignites a church spire, hurling embers across the river into another quadrant of the city.

But of course it's the human melodrama the audience expects, and as Murphy traces the fire's progress, he also deftly incorporates the testimonies of four eyewitnesses who observe the inferno from radically different vantage points. Joseph Chamberlin and Horace White, both newspapermen, initially savor their encounter with what is obviously a major news item. White describes a scene of orderly evacuation: "There was no panic, no frenzy, no boisterousness, but only the haste which the situation authorized." This is definitely not the experience of Claire Inness and Alexander Frear. Separated from her family by a panicking mob, twelve-year-old Claire is trapped in an alley and receives no aid from people in flight; Frear, attempting to move his in-laws to safety, encounters "a mob of men and women, all screaming and shouting . . . intercepting each other as if deranged."

Here Murphy makes an analytical leap at which children's authors often balk—he guides readers into considering circumstances and predispositions that influence the disparate accounts. Do Horace White's public statements reflect his role as civic booster? ("After all," Murphy points out, "a city that had gone wild would not instill much confidence in potential business investors.") Could a shift in the wind simply have bought White's neighborhood time to make an orderly retreat? Cham-

berlin's testimony concerning two drunken boys and "wretched female[s] . . . rushing out almost naked" should be weighed against his known distaste for the inhabitants of the De Koven Street area. In the concluding chapter, "Myth and Reality," Murphy demonstrates how similar attitudes, among members of White's and Chamberlin's class, would direct public outrage against society's easiest targets—Mrs. O'Leary, portrayed as an old hag who burned the barn for the insurance money, and "a drunken Fire Department," unable to respond to an emergency, creating a legacy of urban myth that lingers today.

Carefully credited and captioned period photographs and engravings, collected by the author, mirror the range of experiences presented within the text: calm spectators view the blaze from the river bank; a child is trampled by a fleeing crowd; booster spirit emerges in a "Laborers Wanted" sign perched on the portico of the burnt-out Insurance Exchange. Each chapter concludes with an identical base map, shaded to indicate the current extent of the fire; the tiny area of the fire's origin is pindotted on each map—a chilling visual reminder of the fragile infrastructure, bungled communications, and plain rotten luck that condemned a city to ashes.

Publishers Weekly

SOURCE: A review of *The Great Fire,* in *Publishers Weekly,* Vol. 242, No. 19, May 8, 1995, p. 297.

For more than a century, poor Mrs. O'Leary and her cow have shouldered the blame for Chicago's infamous Great Fire of 1871. Now Murphy (*The Boys' War, Across America on an Emigrant Train*) lays bare the facts concerning one of the biggest disasters in American history, in the process exculpating the maligned bovine and her owner. Murphy demonstrates that the fire could have been contained: he unfolds a tale of botched communication, class discrimination (the fire began in a working-class section of the city and only later spread to the wealthier areas) and plain old bad luck. Strategically quoting the written accounts of witnesses—who include a 12-year-old girl and a newspaper editor—Murphy both charts the 31-hour spread of the fire and conveys the atmosphere in the streets. This volume, beautifully printed in sepia tones, contains historic photos, engravings and newspaper clippings on nearly every page. Especially helpful are maps placed at intervals throughout the book that represent the progress of the fire. Engrossing.

Frances Bradburn

SOURCE: A review of *The Great Fire,* in *Booklist,* Vol. 91, Nos. 19 & 20, June 1, 1995, p. 1757.

The great Chicago fire has long been the stuff of folklore and legend. Yet separating fact from fiction in this major disaster has often appeared a secondary priority at best. Murphy sets the record straight through carefully selected documents, personal accounts, photographs, and illustrations. Beginning on that warm Sunday evening, October 8, 1871, in the O'Leary barn, Murphy traces the fire through its three horror-filled days as, fed by lusty prairie winds, cinders from a Saturday night blaze, and structures (even streets and sidewalks) built almost entirely of wood, it consumed block after block of homes, businesses, and bodies, eventually leaving 100,000 people homeless. The book's design complements the author's treatment of the subject. Six double-page spreads of Chicago street maps show the sweep of the flames from the little-known Saturday blaze until rain finally extinguished the fire on Tuesday. Photographs and illustrations of the conflagration and the damage it left behind only add fuel to the author's dramatic text, a riveting narrative that combines the details of the fire itself with personal anecdotes gleaned from newspaper accounts and books written during and immediately after the fire. *The Great Fire* will automatically draw readers with its fiery cover and illustrations of disaster, but the text will keep them reading.

Susannah Price

SOURCE: A review of *The Great Fire,* in *School Library Journal,* Vol. 41, No. 7, July, 1995, pp. 89-90.

A book that sparks excitement and interest from the picture of Chicago afire on the cover to the last well-written chapter. Murphy's text reads like an adventure/survival novel and is just as hard to put down. Adding to the interest are many newspaper quotes, woodcuts, labeled maps, etchings, and historical renderings. Though dark, their sepia-toned brown seems in keeping with the somber subject. Quotes and recollections have been incorporated from contemporary articles and letters to personalize the happenings and add to the vivid portrayal of fear, chaos, and destruction. By following several main characters of varying ages and walks of life, the author adds to the reality of the scenes at hand. This volume has more in-depth information regarding the problems of fighting the fire than Corinne J. Naden's *The Chicago Fire, October 8, 1871* and is much more riveting. At times, the language and concepts regarding class structure philosophy may be difficult for younger readers, but their inclusion make this volume well suited to high school students. Murphy makes a strong statement for understanding some of the architectural and human errors in thinking that contributed to the tragedy. He includes not only important facts and statistics, but also skillfully weaves pathos into the fabric of his scientific historical rendering of this tragic event. History writing at its best.

Elaine Aoki and others

SOURCE: "Bookalogues: Outstanding Nonfiction Choices for 1995," in *Language Arts,* Vol. 73, No. 6, October, 1996, pp. 436-44.

Jim Murphy's remarkable book, *The Great Fire,* is the 1996 Orbis Pictus Award winner. Murphy's entire book focuses on one event, the great Chicago fire that began on Sunday night, October 8, 1871. The fire burned until the following Tuesday morning, or for "thirty-one hours of terror," killing nearly 300 people and destroying 17,500 buildings. Meticulously researched by Murphy, the book provides readers with details on all aspects of the fire and its effects. *The Great Fire* reads like a too-good-to-put-down novel as we follow the paths of four individuals during the fire: Joseph E. Chamberlin, a 20-year-old reporter for the *Chicago Evening Post;* Horace White, editor-in-chief of the *Chicago Tribune;* Alexander Frear who was visiting relatives, and 12-year-old Claire Innes.

As Murphy points out, Chicago in 1871 was a city ready to burn with 59,500 buildings, two-thirds of them built entirely of wood. We learn how, once the fire started, everything went wrong and about all the missed opportunities to stop the fire in its opening minutes. We also learn how the fire was finally contained. Murphy sorts out the myths and reality about the fire. As he points out, "the origin of the fire was never in doubt: It had begun in a barn at 137 De Koven Street. Other than this, there was absolutely no other detail that suggested how the fire started or who was to blame". But the story of the O'Leary's cow kicking over a lamp in the barn became a convenient scapegoat. Maps trace the course of the fire, and the book is illustrated with photos, paintings, and documents from original sources. A bibliography and index are provided.

A YOUNG PATRIOT: THE AMERICAN REVOLUTION AS EXPERIENCED BY ONE BOY (1996)

Elizabeth Bush

SOURCE: A review of *A Young Patriot: The American Revolution as Experienced by One Boy,* in *Bulletin of the Center for Children's Books,* Vol. 49, No. 10, June, 1996, p. 347.

Enlisting at fifteen (underage) to avoid teasing by his friends, Joseph Plumb Martin served in many of the major engagements from New York to Virginia during the war for Independence; his memoirs, which he zestily recorded at age seventy, offer an intimate and sometimes humorous perspective on the battles and their participants, and Murphy weaves them carefully into this biography. Martin learned new military drill under von Steuben (who cursed in several languages), witnessed a cannonball pass between Molly Pitcher's legs ("She observed that it was lucky it did not pass a little higher"), and wryly commented on his commander's equivalent of a modern photo-op ("General Washington struck a few blows with a pickax . . . that it might be said —General Washington with his own hands first broke ground at the siege of Yorktown"). Martin and Murphy frequently remind readers that the soldiers were fighting for political liberties toward which their fellow countrymen were often hostile or apathetic; periods of deprivation and even starvation for the army occurred in times of plenty, as supplies were withheld by Tory sympathizers and tightwad allies. Period engravings are accompanied by caption commentaries that point out inaccuracies and romanticization in the images, and viewers can visually trace the development of Revolutionary legend. Report writers will appreciate the detailed index, and a chronology fixes Martin's experiences within the larger framework of wartime events. Bibliographical references are included.

Lisa Von Drasek

SOURCE: A review of *A Young Patriot: The American Revolution as Experienced by One Boy,* in *School Library Journal,* Vol. 42, No. 6, June, 1996, p. 163.

Murphy presents the life of Joseph Plumb Martin, a 15-year-old Connecticut farm boy who enlisted in the Continental Army in 1776. Through well-selected quotes from Martin's self-published memoir, *A Narrative of Some of the Adventures, Dangers and Sufferings of a Revolutionary Soldier,* readers experience the young soldier's excitement and fear during battle, his boredom while marching, and the deprivation of a winter encampment. The author's compelling writing intertwines major events of the American Revolution with Martin's own story, rendering historical events and military strategy readily comprehensible. The book is generously illustrated with black-and-white maps and reproductions; captions present information that complements rather than repeats the text. Unfortunately, there is neither a map of the colonies from the Hudson to Yorktown, nor a glossary of military terms. Important figures such as Burgoyne, Cornwallis, and Washington are portrayed as individuals as well as military leaders. The index is comprehensive. This volume compares favorably to Doris and Harold Faber's *The Birth of a Nation* and is certainly more accessible than *Yankee Doodle Boy,* an abridged version of Martin's memoir edited by George F. Scheer. An outstanding example of history brought to life through the experience of one individual.

Carolyn Phelan

SOURCE: A review of *A Young Patriot: The American Revolution as Experienced by One Boy,* in *Booklist,* Vol. 92, Nos. 19 & 20, June 1, 1996, p. 1723.

Murphy tells the story of the American Revolution through the eyes of Joseph Plumb Martin, who enlisted in the army in 1776, at the age of 15. Murphy frequently quotes Martin, evidently drawing from Martin's book *A Narrative of Some of the Adventures, Dangers, and Sufferings of a Revolutionary Soldier* (1830), listed in the extensive bibliography. The lively quotations give Murphy's account a feeling of immediacy, heightened by the many details of life in the army. For instance, few history books for children even mention the muti-

nies among the American troops, but Murphy vividly explains their causes and consequences, or lack of consequences. He quotes Martin on the mutinous soldiers: "venting our spleen at our country and government, then at our officers, and then at our selves for our imbecility in staying there and starving . . . for an ungrateful people who did not care what became of us, so they could enjoy themselves while we were keeping a cruel enemy from them." Many black-and-white reproductions of period engravings, paintings, and documents appear throughout the book. Although source notes would have been a welcome addition, young readers researching the military and social history of the American Revolution will find this an excellent resource.

Maeve Visser Knoth

SOURCE: A review of *A Young Patriot: The American Revolution as Experienced by One Boy,* in *The Horn Book Magazine,* Vol. 72, No. 5, September-October, 1996, p. 623.

Joseph Plumb Martin enlisted in the Connecticut militia in 1776 as a sixteen-year-old. Using Martin's first-person account of his participation in the Revolutionary War as his primary source, Murphy tells the story of one teenager's life as a soldier. Murphy weaves Martin's story into a broader tale, giving background about the causes of the Revolution and providing an account of the unfolding of the war, the significant battles, and the war's end. As he has in previous books, the author shows a talent for choosing and explicating details that make history both personal and fascinating. The description of the winter at Valley Forge includes the fact that the soldiers were too tired and hungry even to build themselves shelter from the cold; Washington had to bribe the soldiers by offering a prize of twelve dollars to the group who finished building a hut first. The informative text is peppered with quotations and illustrated with many period reproductions, maps, and diagrams. These, in conjunction with a chronology of the American Revolution and an extensive bibliography, complete Murphy's intriguing account.

WEST TO A LAND OF PLENTY: THE DIARY OF TERESA ANGELINO VISCARDI (1998)

Elizabeth Bush

SOURCE: A review of *West to a Land of Plenty: The Diary of Teresa Angelino Viscardi,* in *Bulletin of the Center for Children's Books,* Vol. 51, No. 7, March, 1998, p. 253.

"I Hate Poppa. And Momma—for letting him do this to us! And Uncle Eugenio—I hate him for seeing the advertisement and for making Poppa leave our street." Teresa vents to her diary her considerable displeasure with her family's move from New York City to the wilds of "THE WESTERN TERRITORY OF IDAHO, WHERE LAND IS CHEAP AND THE SOIL IS OF THE RICHEST KIND." As their train sluggishly chugs its way toward the frontier, younger sister Netta worms her own entries into the diary, and soon the two complementary (and occasionally bickering) voices paint a pretty complete picture of the rail/wagon train journey west. Outgoing Netta records the characters and pranks along the route; Teresa soon revels in the newfound opportunities, away from the watchful eyes of her family, to tackle "boys' jobs" and to pursue her first romance. What could have been merely another overland trail story is considerably enriched by Murphy's attention to the rapid and profound Americanization of these fictional Italian immigrants as they meet the exigencies of wagon train life—Teresa's father wiggles out from under the authoritarian thumb of his older brother Eugenio, and even superstitious, platitude-spouting Nanna relaxes some of her Old World attitudes. Newcomers to the series will find this an enticing selection, and readers who are already hooked will recognize it as one of Dear America's stronger entries.

Carolyn Phelan

SOURCE: A review of *West to a Land of Plenty: The Diary of Teresa Angelino Viscardi*, in *Booklist*, Vol. 94, No. 15, April 1, 1998, p. 1320-21.

West [to a Land of Plenty] tells of Teresa, a 14-year-old Italian immigrant whose family leaves its Jersey City home to cross the country by train and covered wagon, heading for a new community in the Idaho Territory. Her younger sister Antoinetta shares the diary, their entries differentiated by the typeface as well as their signatures. This technique offers two points of view, as well as a bit of sisterly tension along the way. [The] novel will reward [readers] with its picture of wagon train life and its sympathetic portraits of the main characters.

GONE A-WHALING: THE LURE OF THE SEA AND THE HUNT FOR THE GREAT WHALE (1998)

Randy Meyer

SOURCE: A review of *Gone A-Whaling: The Lure of the Sea and the Hunt for the Great Whale*, in *Booklist*, Vol. 94, No. 14, March 15, 1998, p. 1233.

Diary entries form the backbone of this fascinating look at whale hunting in America, from the nineteenth century to today. Murphy structures his tale like a whaling

voyage, beginning with the thrill of signing up for duty and ending with a grateful trip home. In between, he describes life and work aboard the ship, including the grisly techniques for killing, harvesting, and processing the enormous animals. Primary sources support an emotionally rich narrative, filled with the thoughts of the young men and boys as they move between excitement and boredom, boundless energy and exhaustion. Murphy also looks at women who went whaling and the number of vessels crewed or captained by African Americans. Two final chapters examine the slaughter made possible by the steam engine and the cruelly efficient factory ships of today. Murphy occasionally scolds nineteenth-century whalers for their harsh approach, rather than explaining their lack of knowledge about the sophisticated creatures they hunted. The book is beautifully illustrated with black-and-white photos and engravings, and a sprinkling of sidebars supplies details about the most hunted whale species.

Mary M. Burns

SOURCE: A review of *Gone A-Whaling: The Lure of the Sea and the Hunt for the Great Whale*, in *The Horn Book Magazine*, Vol. 74, No. 3, May-June, 1998, p. 363.

Whaling was a young man's game, or rather a young boy's. Using a variety of sources, Murphy makes it plain that the crews of whalers included a substantial number of youths barely out of childhood. Although presented from their perspective, the book is more than a collection of biographical vignettes. It is a substantive examination of the history of whaling, the socio-economic forces that supported it, the process by which whales were transformed into salable commodities—from oil to corset stays—and, finally, the environmental impact of reckless commercialism as technology increased the hunters' success. In this context, Murphy offers proof of the innate cruelty of the whale hunt, refutes legends of the whale's evil intent and vengeful nature—including that icon of American literature, Moby Dick—and comments on the decimation of many species through lack of regulation even today. Details of life aboard a whaler, including the ethnic composition of the crews, the role of the captains, families, and the development of the art of scrimshaw, add color and drama. The concluding chapter takes the reader into the twentieth century where cameras substitute for harpoons as spectators join whale watching expeditions. The book is enhanced by drawings, engravings, and photographs, and also features information about specific types of whales in boxed inserts. The appended bibliography is substantial, drawing on a variety of sources.

Additional coverage of Murphy's life and career is contained in the following sources published by Gale Research: *Authors and Artists for Young Adults*, Vol. 20; *Contemporary Authors*, Vol. 111; and *Something about the Author*, Vol. 77.

Dr. Seuss

1904-1991

(Born Theodor Seuss Geisel; has also written under the pseudonyms Theo. LeSieg and Rosetta Stone) American author and author/illustrator of picture books.

Major works include *And To Think That I Saw It on Mulberry Street* (1937), *Horton Hatches the Egg* (1940), *The Butter Battle Book,* (1984) *Oh, the Places You'll Go!* (1990), *Daisy-Head Mayzie* (1994).

For more information on Seuss's career prior to 1984, see *CLR* Vols. 1, 9.

INTRODUCTION

The Cat in the Hat, Horton the elephant, the Grinch who stole Christmas: these legendary characters, among the most beloved in all of children's literature, are only a few of the creations of Theodor Seuss Geisel, better known to generations of children as Dr. Seuss. Seuss's books have sold more than one hundred million copies and have been translated into almost every language on the globe, and the award-winning animated television specials based on his books are perhaps as popular as the books themselves. Not only is Seuss considered a children's literature icon, but many of his quirky characters are accepted as part of contemporary folklore. The guiding force behind Seuss's work is his innate understanding of children and genuine respect for their individuality and imagination. Seuss once told *U.S. News & World Report* that he kept getting asked if he liked children. His reply was, "I like children in the same way that I like people. . . . I like or dislike them as individuals." This statement reflects the philosophy that has made his works legendary. Seuss combined this profound respect for the child's mind with an artistic talent that was far from childlike to produce picture books that are loved by children and adults alike.

Seuss began most of his books with simple ideas, and then built them into fabulous concepts through repetition, suspense, and surprise. He combined words and pictures to fashion a series of complex situations that border on the lunatic but retain an integral logic. His language is distinguished by invented words that, as nonsensical as they sound, fit perfectly with his stories and pictures. In a *Publishers Weekly* interview, Seuss commented on the distinctiveness of his work: "I have a Seuss astigmatism in both eyes so that I see things as if they've been put through a Mixmaster or viewed through the wrong end of a telescope." At a time when Dick, Jane, and Spot were teaching children how to read, Seuss's use of absurd pictures and inventive rhymes represented a new type of children's literature—pleasure reading for beginning and reluctant readers. The now

classic *The Cat in the Hat* (1957) was the first work of this new, visionary style.

Even at his most extravagant, Seuss invested his works with positive values. Many of his books contain veiled moral statements that balance the zaniness of his characters and situations. Concerned thematically with creativity, tenacity, loyalty, and self-confidence, Seuss also treated political and social issues such as racial and religious prejudice, conservation, and the nuclear arms race. While critics have praised Seuss as an outstanding nonsense poet and storyteller, he has also been considered a natural moralist whose works offer children a positive and enthusiastic view of life. Some observers have viewed his involvement with beginning readers as limiting his creativity; others have disapproved of his unconventional English and unschooled art. The preponderance of reviewers, however, esteemed Seuss as an imaginative genius whose oeuvre has captured readers for generations.

Biographical Information

Born on March 2, 1904, in Springfield, Massachusetts,

Seuss grew up reading and drawing, but never intended to make illustration a career. He began nurturing his talent at an early age as he tagged along with his father, a superintendent of public parks, to the zoo six blocks away from their home. Every morning as his father practiced target shooting in a nearby park, Seuss would sneak off to sketch the zoo animals. Seuss told *Yankee* magazine that he learned everything he knew about animals from those trips to the zoo. Later, his high-school art teacher told him that he would never learn to draw. Despite this dismal prediction, Seuss's first published drawings appeared in the pages of Dartmouth College's humor magazine, *Jack-o'-Lantern,* of which he was the editor. After graduating from Dartmouth, Seuss moved on to Oxford University, where he planned to pursue a doctorate in English literature. However, both his professional and personal lives changed dramatically when he met fellow student Helen Palmer. She encouraged him to pursue a career in cartoon illustration, and the two were married in 1927. They returned to the United States, and soon Seuss was selling drawings and prose pieces to magazines such as *Vanity Fair, Life,* and the *Saturday Evening Post.*

Seuss got his first big break when one of his cartoons caught the attention of Standard Oil Company. He signed a contract to create grotesque, enormous insects to illustrate Standard Oil's famous slogan, "Quick, Henry! The Flit!" Those characters and others appeared on billboards nationwide and made a name for Seuss as an illustrator. His entry into the world of children's books was not far behind. The idea for his first picture book came from a rather mundane experience, but one which would characterize the writing style for which he is known and loved. While crossing the Atlantic on an ocean liner, Seuss became caught up in the monotonous pulse of the ship's engine. He began to put words to the rhythm, added illustrations, and the result was *And To Think That I Saw It on Mulberry Street.* Twenty-seven publishers rejected the manuscript. Ironically, they said the story was silly, the rhymes nonsensical. Finally in 1937 an editor agreed to take a chance with *Mulberry Street,* and Dr. Seuss the children's author was born.

By the time the Second World War interrupted his work, Seuss had published several well-received children's books, including *The 500 Hats of Bartholomew Cubbins* (1938), *The King's Stilts* (1939), and the ever-popular *Horton Hatches the Egg.* After the war, Seuss settled in La Jolla, California, and in quick succession released *McElligot's Pool* (1947), *Thidwick, The Big-Hearted Moose* (1948), *Bartholomew and the Oobleck* (1949), *If I Ran the Zoo* (1950), and *Horton Hears a Who!* (1954). Then, in 1957, Seuss wrote the book that would revolutionize the world of books for beginning readers. In May, 1954, *Life* magazine excerpted the report of a panel analyzing the teaching of reading in a Connecticut school system. One of the panelists, journalist John Hersey, implied that kids' reading could not develop sufficiently because they were being given dull texts on which to practice. The panelist, in effect, issued Seuss

a challenge, as noted in *Parents Magazine*: "Why should [children] not have pictures that widen, rather than narrow, the associated richness the children give to the words [the pictures] illustrate, drawings like those of the wonderfully imaginative geniuses among children's illustrators, Tenniel, Howard Pyle, 'Dr. Seuss'?" A publisher, learning of the challenge, contacted Seuss. Seuss accepted the challenge, and produced *The Cat in the Hat,* using 220 words from a list of 400 that his publisher had sent him. Decades later, in a *Parents* magazine article, Hersey credited *The Cat in the Hat* for forever changing the way in which children learned to read: "There's no question about Seuss's impact. He dealt 'Run, Spot, Run' a serious blow when he began providing things both real and unreal. His language was so lively and so full of explosive noises that it engaged the ear as well as the eye. Dick and Jane were deadly dull, and it was precisely the touch of mischief Seuss had that was so much more exciting."

The success of *The Cat in the Hat* led Seuss and his wife to found Beginner Books, a division of Random House dealing exclusively in books for beginning readers. Beginner Books published seventeen more of Seuss's limited-vocabulary books, including the immensely popular *Green Eggs and Ham* (1960), which contained only fifty words, and *One Fish, Two Fish, Red Fish, Blue Fish* (1960). Over twenty other books followed, including several with sometimes controversial, strong moral viewpoints, such as *The Lorax* (1971) and *The Butter Battle Book.*

After the death of his wife and business partner, Helen, Seuss married Audrey Stone Diamond in 1968. By his eightieth birthday, Seuss was considered the dean of humorous children's writers. Translations of his books are selling all over the world, some of his best-loved stories have been made into award-winning television shows, and almost every honor the publishing industry bestows has found its way onto his shelf. His alma mater, Dartmouth College, legitimized his "Dr." title in 1955 with the awarding of an honorary doctorate degree. On September 24, 1991, the world of children's literature said goodbye to a hero, when at the age of 87, Seuss died in his sleep at his California home.

Major Works

Seuss's first book, *And To Think That I Saw It on Mulberry Street,* embodies the rollicking, nonsensical rhyme and fantastic illustrative creations that are his trademarks. Set in his native Springfield, Massachusetts, the book tells the story of Marco, who has been chided by his father for neglecting the ordinary routines of life. On his way home from school one day, Marco determines to have a story to tell when he gets home, and soon his imagination transforms a simple horse-drawn wagon into a fabulous parade of exotic beasts and vehicles. The crazy cartoon animals that had made Seuss's Standard Oil advertisements so famous found their home in the picture-book medium. Seuss portrays the workings of Marco's imagination, as a horse turns into a zebra and a wagon into a chariot. In his *Pipers at the Gates of Dawn: The Wisdom of Children's Literature,* Jonathan Cott praises the hypnotic energy of Seuss's rhymes, observing "the unflagging momentum, feeling of breathlessness, and swiftness of pace, all together acting as the motor for Seuss's pullulating image machine. . ."

Seuss continued to give imagination free reign with the famous *Horton Hatches the Egg,* in which Horton the elephant is tricked into sitting in a nest and guarding the eggs of a vacationing mother bird. Seuss told an interviewer for *The New Yorker* that *Horton* was his favorite book, because it was the easiest to write and he had the most fun doing it. In characteristic Seuss fashion, *Horton* came about almost by accident. Seuss tells the story: "I was doodling around with drawings . . . and a sketch of an elephant on some transparent paper happened to fall on top of the sketch of a tree. I stopped, dumbfounded. I said to myself, 'That's a hell of a situation. An elephant in a tree! What's he doing there?'" Like Horton, many of Seuss's characters find themselves in unique situations, such as being presented with a meal of green eggs and ham, or with unusual features, such as the cat who wears a hat or the outlandish "flustards," "joats," and "tufted mazurka" in *If I Ran the Zoo.*

Some of Seuss's later works explore slightly more sophisticated themes. *You're Only Old Once!* (1986) addresses the elderly, whom Seuss dubs "obsolete children." The book pokes good-natured fun at the medical profession with a tongue-in-cheek look at one of the rituals of aging, the medical checkup. *Oh, the Places You'll Go!,* which chronicles its young protagonist's journey down the road of life, has ageless lessons for "upstarts of all ages," whether nursery-school or college graduates: "You have brains in your head./You have feet in your shoes./You can steer yourself/any direction you choose. . ." However, Seuss gives the story a moral by tempering its optimism with a healthy dose of reality, as well: "Alone will be something/you'll be quite a lot./And when you're alone, there's a very good chance/you'll meet things that scare you right out of your pants." Indeed, many of Seuss's works make serious statements while they entertain. *The Lorax* is a comment on ecology, and *The Butter Battle Book* is a parable of nuclear arms escalation. The latter chronicles the war between the Yooks, who eat their bread butter-side down, and the neighboring Zooks, who eat theirs butter-side up. The book's thinly disguised parodies of human military activity, including the "Snick-Berry Switch" and "Boys in the Back Room," make its message heard loud and clear. *The Butter Battle Book* sparked controversy, with its critics bemoaning the violence and the absence of Seuss's usual lighthearted approach. A *Publishers Weekly* article called it "the least carefree of all [Seuss's] books." Seuss downplayed the book's strong moral message in the same article: "I didn't want to be interpreted as a pacifist. . . . [The book is] simply a statement of a situation between the Yooks and the Zooks. If anyone wants to apply the story to the world, he can do it."

A testament to his timeless influence, several new books were published after Seuss's death from drawings and verses found among his papers. One of these, *Daisy-Head Mayzie,* is the story of a young girl who one day mysteriously sprouts a daisy from her head, prompting a flurry of confused activity from the adults around her. Critical reception of *Daisy-Head Mayzie* was lukewarm, as the book lacked the magical touch that only Seuss's own hand could give it. Despite this, the "good doctor" keeps his place in the world of children's literature as the master rhymer, the keeper of the delights of the child's imagination.

Awards

Seuss won an Academy Award in 1946 for his short-subject World War II film "Hitler Lives," another in 1947 for "Design for Death," and a third in 1951 for "Gerald McBoing-Boing." He received a Randolph Caldecott Honor Award in 1948 for *McElligot's Pool,* in 1950 for *Bartholomew and the Oobleck,* and in 1951 for *If I Ran the Zoo.* He won a Lewis Carroll Shelf Award in 1958 for *Horton Hatches the Egg* and in 1961 for *And To Think That I Saw It on Mulberry Street.* The animated cartoons "How the Grinch Stole Christmas" and "Horton Hears a Who" received a Peabody Award in 1971. "The Lorax" won a Critics' Award from the International Animated Cartoon Festival and a Silver Medal from the International Film and Television Festival of New York, both in 1972. Seuss received a Southern California Council on Literature for Children and Young People Award in 1974 for special contribution to children's literature, and was named "Outstanding California Author" by the California Association of Teachers of English in 1976. He also received an Emmy Award in 1977 for the cartoon "Halloween is Grinch Night" and a Laura Ingalls Wilder Award from the Association for Library Services for Children, American Library Association, in 1980. The week of March 2-7 was proclaimed "Dr. Seuss Week" by State Governers in 1981. Seuss won a Pulitzer Prize in 1984 for his "special contribution over nearly half a century to the education and enjoyment of America's children and their parents." *The Butter Battle Book* received a PEN Los Angeles Center Award for children's literature in 1985. Seuss was honored with a special program by the Academy of Motion Picture Arts and Sciences in 1989. In 1993, Random House established the Dr. Seuss Picture Book Award, a biannual award given in Seuss's honor to a children's book author/illustrator.

AUTHOR'S COMMENTARY

Dr. Seuss

SOURCE: An interview in *U.S. News & World Report,* April 14, 1986, p. 69.

Q Dr. Seuss, what prompted you to do a book for adults—*You're Only Old Once!*—about the trials of medical treatment?

I had some medical problems and found myself sitting in the vestibules of hospitals rather more often than at my drawing board. The waits were most unpleasant. I began to take sketch pads with me and amused myself by thinking of the horrible things they were going to do to me next. Gradually words came, too.

Now, kids are coming up with the book for autographs. I've said: "This isn't a book for you." But they say that they've had their experience in hospitals with tonsillectomies and the like. They think it's amusing.

Q Your books tend to have a moral message—

I seldom start with one, but when you write a kid's book, somebody's got to win. You find yourself preaching in spite of yourself. But sometimes people find morals where there are none. People have read all kinds of things into *Green Eggs and Ham,* including Biblical connotations. There's a teacher—and this one nauseates me—who says the book's message is that you shouldn't make up your mind against anything until you've tasted it. I'm getting blamed for a lot of stuff I haven't done.

Q Where did you get the idea for *Green Eggs and Ham?*

People write essays and deliver lectures about the meaning of that book. The only meaning was that Bennett Cerf, my publisher, bet me 50 bucks I couldn't write a book using only 50 words. I did it to show I could.

Q Are your books designed to introduce youngsters to only a limited number of new words?

My first book with a controlled vocabulary was *The Cat in the Hat,* but that was 30 years ago for an educational publishing house which said that it was impossible for a first-grader to comprehend more than 250 words at a time. They sent me a list, and I was forbidden to use any words beyond it. I almost threw the job up. I finally gave it one more chance and said, "If I find two words that rhyme and make sense to me, that's the title." That's how educationally wise I was. So I found *cat* rhymed with *hat.* And like a genius, I said, "That's the name."

I did only a few books after that from a controlled list. I changed the rules, based on my belief that a child could learn any amount of words if fed them slowly and if the books were amply illustrated. We began to concentrate our efforts on linking the artwork with the text.

Q How important is rhyming to your books?

Rhyming forces recognition of words. You also establish a rhythm, and that tends to make kids want to go on. If you break the rhythm, a child feels unfulfilled.

Q Do rhymes come easily to you?

The agony is terrific at times, and the attrition is horrible. If you're doing it in quatrains and get to the end of four lines and can't make it work, then it's like unraveling a sock. You take some of your best stuff and throw it away.

Q Does it take long to come up with a rhyme that works?

The Lorax was a son of a gun. I worked almost two years and got nowhere. And my wife said, "We'll get out of the country." She was finding me a little bit difficult to live with.

We went to Africa. We were at an inn in Kenya, and I was sitting near a swimming pool. About a mile away, a herd of elephants came over a hill. I don't know what happened. I grabbed a laundry list that I had beside me and wrote the whole book in 45 minutes.

I've looked at elephants ever since, but it has never happened again.

Q Do you first write the story and then draw the pictures?

There's no pattern. When I start a new book, I'll noodle things over and develop some characters. Most of them go in the wastebasket, but a couple get in conflict. Then words begin to come. If I get stuck mentally in a story, I'll draw my way out. Other times, as in the case of *The Lorax,* I wrote the whole thing without any illustrations.

Q What are your favorite children's books by others?

I'll give you one name, Maurice Sendak. I'm going to duck the rest because no matter how I do this I offend confreres by leaving them out. Sendak has the courage not to be influenced by editors. Everybody said his book *Where the Wild Things Are* would drive kids crazy, and they love it. Like me, he isn't writing for kids; he's writing for all people.

Q Do you try to stay in touch with kids?

Not especially, I keep getting asked the question, "Do you like children?" I like children in the same way that I like people. There are some stinkers among children as well as among adults. I like or dislike them as individuals.

In my early days, I was forced by the publisher to do a certain amount of dropping in at schools. I finally said "No" because youngsters expect you to be wearing a hat, and I'm a disappointment.

In an autographing line, it's different. You just have a short contact. But I had a horrible thing happen recently. A mother brought a child in who was about a year and a half. The child had his hand all the way in his mouth. And the mother said, "Take your hand out of your mouth and shake hands with Dr. Seuss." I looked around, and I tried to get out of the store. I was able to grab the child somewhere up on the arm. You get that about once every year or so.

There's a mother who will say, "Osbert, don't you want to kiss Dr. Seuss?"

Q And what do you do?

Usually I'm on a platform and can't escape. You sometimes get kissed.

GENERAL COMMENTARY

Jennifer Crichton

SOURCE: "Dr. Seuss Turns 80," in *Publishers Weekly,* Vol. 225, No. 6, February 10, 1984, pp. 22-3.

The Butter Battle Book is possibly the least carefree of all [Dr. Seuss's] books. It's hard to say which is the more absurd: the Dr. Seuss tale or the un-Seussified reality. The Yooks eat their bread with the butter side down. The Zooks eat theirs with butter side up. For this discrepancy in taste, the two groups hate each other with unflinching passion. The Yooks and Zooks parade past a wall that divides them to show off their increasingly elaborate, and, to the credit of Dr. Seuss, highly decorative, weapons.

At the end of the book the cunning Boys in the Back Rooms of both the Yooks and the Zooks invent an unnervingly realistic bomb called the Big Boy Boomeroo. It's a very unattractive, very powerful little bomb. The Yooks and the Zooks clench one as they glare across the Wall in a standoff and citizens march down into bomb shelters. "We'll see," the closing line reads. "We will see. . . . "

An old Seuss reader might shout, "Bring back the Cat in the Hat! Bring back a messy house picked up in a minute flat!" But the Cat in the Hat lives in a world different from the one he lived in back in 1953 when Dr. Seuss first introduced him. So does Theodor Geisel. So do kids.

"Since this is the hottest topic in the world, if kids are at all intelligent and read anything, of course they're facing it," Geisel says of the nuclear arms race. "I don't think *The Day After* scared any child in the United States. All this hoopla about not showing the program to children unless you're right there to hold their hands! Kids see worse things every week on Saturday morning television.

"Oddly enough, there's no violence in this book of mine. Tension is all. Nobody shoots anything. We're safe at

this point." The way Geisel emphasizes the last three words makes his meaning clear. "At this point" is the operative phrase.

Geisel's main fear in writing *The Butter Battle Book* wasn't that kids would be alarmed by the topic but that his intentions would be misread. "I didn't want to be interpreted as a pacifist—which I am not—or that the book is a plea to burn draft cards—which I am against," Geisel says. "It's simply a statement of a situation between the Yooks and the Zooks. If anyone wants to apply the story to this world, he can do it."

And, no doubt, readers will. This isn't the first Dr. Seuss book to express a barely disguised political or social message. *Yertle the Turtle* is Hitler, *The Sneetches* deals with racial prejudice, *How the Grinch Stole Christmas* focuses on greed, and *Horton Hears a Who* addresses social snobbery. *The Lorax*—Geisel's own personal favorite but not a favorite among his readers—cautions against the despoilment of nature.

"I have the reputation for being the worst didactic author since Elsie Dinsmore—does anybody remember Elsie Dinsmore?—but it isn't necessarily so," protests Geisel.

From The Butter Battle Book, *written and illustrated by Dr. Seuss.*

"I've done 44 books, and only six were message-oriented. So it's only a ratio of six to 36. That's not so bad, hmmm?"

Rare for a writer who is often held captive by his imagination, Geisel schemed out a plan for *The Butter Battle Book* and stayed faithful to his plan even when his instinct pulled at him to stray into fanciful digressions. "This was one of the few books that I started with a definite idea in mind. Usually I'll have a character who'll kind of lead the thing," Geisel explains. "I wasted months drawing different architecture and clothes, even different kitchen utensils for the Yooks and the Zooks. Then I realized that what I was trying to say was that the Yooks and the Zooks were intrinsically the same. The more I made them different, the more I was defeating the story.

"So I boiled it down to the butter thing—which was ridiculous—and the Yooks wearing orange suits and the Zooks wearing blue. I'm making the same point which I've made in all my speeches, which is: kids are pretty much the same with slight differences."

Geisel claims he didn't write his parable of arms escalation with a view toward the parents of kids digesting the meaning as they read the book aloud. "When I do a book, I have only one person in mind. I'm writing it for myself," he says. "Like all my books, I don't know if this is a children's book for adults or an adults' book for children. If I do it for myself, it usually comes out about halfway between the two groups."

The author believes that each of his books—even the silliest—is rooted, in some way, in reality. "I have a Seuss astigmatism in both eyes so that I see things as if they've been put through a Mixmaster or viewed through the wrong end of a telescope. It's not intentional. That's just the way I see things. That's why my books are satire rather than whimsy. Whimsy is based on nothing."

And that's why Geisel says he couldn't furnish readers of *The Butter Battle Book* with a happy ending, much as he generally likes to have a happy ending. "How else could you end it?" he asks. "I was tempted to give it a happy ending, but then I would have gotten into dishonesty. That's the situation as it is."

For his entire career, Geisel has searched for the chance to finish off a book with the lady-or-the-tiger gambit that has baffled and fascinated him since childhood. "Finally, this fell right in my lap," he says. "As for a sequel, I don't know that the time is right for a sequel. We'll let someone else do the sequel if they straighten things out—hmmm?"

Michael J. Bandler

SOURCE: "Seuss on the Loose," in *Parents Magazine,* Vol. 62, No. 9, September, 1987, pp. 116-20, 229-30.

Dr. Seuss was seething a mock seethe. "I just had the worst experience of my life!" he barked into the phone to a friend.

What happened? Was it more embarrassing than the time when he visited a school for a chalk-talk and found that the kids didn't think much of his artwork? Was it as humbling as the visit to a big-city department store for a book signing, where he was greeted by a grand audience of one small and totally innocent boy—who wandered in accidentally while looking for the bathroom?

What could be worse?

Well, it seems that the father of Zooks and Sneetches, the Grinch and the Lorax, Yertle and Bartholomew Cubbins was autographing books at a suburban New York store, when a woman came up to the table with a tot in her arms.

As Seuss tells it, "The kid's hand was down his throat up to his elbow. The woman pointed at me, looked at the boy, and said, 'George, take your hand out of your mouth and shake hands with Dr. Seuss.' And he did!!"

George, naturally, was too young to appreciate the fact that the bow-tied, bespectacled, courtly 83-year-old gentleman whose hand he had just covered with spittle is the most universally known children's book author of our day, with more than 100 million copies of his 46 books sold in twenty languages.

But he's more than that. . . .

It was in September, 1937, that a small boy named Marco stood on his city sidewalk and watched a parade that grew more and more wondrous and outlandish as it passed by. The book was entitled *And To Think That I Saw It on Mulberry Street,* and although it had been previously rejected by two dozen publishers, Vanguard Press took it on. For Geisel—then an advertising copywriter whose greatest claim to fame to date had been the phrase, "Quick, Henry, the Flit!"—a brand-new career had begun.

Twenty years later, Dr. Seuss, the zany fabulist, assumed his most meaningful role, that of a warrior against illiteracy. The problem hasn't gone away in the three decades since (" . . . must be some adults out there that I missed when they were kids," Geisel says). But that's not the good doctor's fault: he did his share, sending Dick, Jane, and Spot running into oblivion and replacing them with the Cat in the Hat.

How it happened has become legend, and as with most legends, the facts do tend to blur. We know, though, that it all began with John Hersey, the eminent journalist-novelist, who, in the early 1950's, was serving on a panel analyzing the teaching of reading in a Connecticut school system. In May, 1954, *Life* excerpted a segment of the panel's report, specifically some comments by Hersey, headlining the article, "Why Do Students Bog Down on

First R?" The implication was that kids' reading couldn't develop sufficiently so long as they were being given dull texts on which to practice.

"Why should they [children] not have pictures that widen, rather than narrow, the associated richness the children give to the words they [the pictures] illustrate"—Hersey wrote, "drawings like those of the wonderfully imaginative geniuses among children's illustrators, Tenniel, Howard Pyle, 'Dr. Seuss'?"

Was Hersey altogether serious at the time? "Absolutely," he says emphatically, more than a generation after the landmark article appeared in *Life.*

"There's no question about Seuss's impact. He dealt 'Run, Spot, Run' a serious blow when he began providing things both real and unreal. He also may have helped shift the approach back to phonics—his language was so lively and so full of explosive noises that it engaged the ear as well as the eye. Dick and Jane were deadly dull, and it was precisely the touch of mischief Seuss had that was so much more exciting."

Education at the time was still suffering from the effects of the death of phonics, which had been rejected years before as a teaching technique in favor of word recognition—a decision Geisel deplores to this day. An enterprising textbook publisher, learning of Hersey's sideswipe at "Run, Spot, Run" and his sounding the heraldic trumpets for Seuss, seized the opportunity, contacted Geisel, and sent him a list of 400 words. He was asked to whittle them down to 220—the most it was felt kids could absorb in one time frame at a particular age—and to build a book around them.

Geisel went through the list once, twice—and got nowhere. He decided to give it one more shot: if he could find two words that rhymed, they'd form the title and theme of the book. Within moments, "cat" and "hat" leaped off the page. But then it took him nine months to write the entire book!

Generally, it's next to impossible to get this self-effacing man—whose genuine sweetness is hidden behind a playful gruffness that's all an act—even to whisper his own praises. But he will acknowledge that his most lasting contribution to literature may have been to rid the world of Dick, Jane, and the dog.

Looking back, Geisel laments that there hasn't been even more visible progress.

"I have no idea whether we're winning or losing the battle. I used to say that I didn't think television hurt. Now I think it does. There was a time when I thought it would stimulate kids' minds—it still does, and I think they have a breadth of understanding, but not a depth of understanding. They know more things that are going on in the world, but not what the hell they're all about."

[In 1971], Seuss changed course again, becoming more issue-oriented than ever before in his career. His cause was the environment, and his spokesperson a walrus-like creature called the Lorax, who claimed to "speak for the trees," a voice crying in the wilderness against the ecological pollution that was threatening the Truffula Trees and the Brown Bar-ba-loots.

Geisel won't rank his peers or express preference for one writer over another, nor does he have a "top ten" among his own books. But he will readily admit that *The Lorax* is his favorite.

"I wrote it as a piece of propaganda and disguised the fact," he states forthrightly. "I was on the soapbox. I wasn't afraid of preaching—but I was afraid of being dull."

He needn't have worried. In 1984, he went back on the soapbox with *The Butter Battle Book,* a thinly veiled plea for nuclear disarmament, couched in a fantasy about two warring nations—one that preferred its bread buttered on top, the other advocating that the spreading be done on the bottom. [In 1986], he turned out a book directed to adults—"obsolete children," he calls them—that focused on the realities of aging. It was called *You're Only Old Once!,* and its broad-based popularity with kids, parents, and grandparents was so pervasive that it sold a million copies in less than a year, leading the combined fiction-nonfiction best-seller lists. It also has forced him to remain healthy after a decade of ailments, because, he says, his eyes twinkling, "I can't go back to doctors after what I did to them in the book." . . .

I Am Not Going to Get Up Today, illustrated by James Stevenson, builds in wackiness and incredulity as it progresses, à la *Mulberry Street.* The problem is how to get a kid out of bed one morning; potential solutions range from siblings' pesterings and horn honking to the enticement of a delicious breakfast and the arrival of the Marines.

Prepublication, Geisel traditionally assumes a conservative stance ("I do not like to brag and be caught with my pants down"). He's not normally a risk taker. But he's taking one with . . . *The Seven Lady Godivas.*

The risk is inherent in the book itself, a reprint of his only adult novel and, not coincidentally, his only resounding failure. This utterly ridiculous retelling of the story of Lady Godiva, her bareback ride through Coventry, and Peeping Tom had minimal impact on book audiences in 1939 and quickly was remaindered for 45 cents a copy at a small cigar store in New York City.

"Wouldn't it be embarrassing if it failed again?" Geisel mused with more than a touch of wariness. Of course, failure is relative: copies of that original edition now sell for upwards of $1,000 among collectors.

"It'll probably wow them in kindergarten," he said. "It'll be my best kindergarten book of all time, and I'll get to spend the rest of my life there lecturing on it." . . .

Geisel continues to hew to a work schedule he's followed for decades—eight-hour days of imagining and sketching. Experience has taught him the agony of waiting for ideas to surface, the significance of trial and error, the power and presence of fate. He can't forget the time a gentle breeze filtered into his study and blew one sheet of transparent tracing paper, featuring a sketch of an elephant, onto another that depicted a tree. Within minutes, the classic *Horton Hatches the Egg* was born. . . .

The ideas flow, swirl, become diluted, disappear, and sometimes return—just like the Pacific's blue waters down the incline. [At one time], Geisel was juggling two key ideas—a nonsense story called *The Square Blue Balloon,* and a melange of totally unrelated art that he was trying to fashion into a unit. "I'd never used any of the illustrations, but they all interested me," he noted. "Just for the hell of it, I put them up on the board. I'm in the middle of seeing if they can be used together." As for the nonsense tale, it's possible he was trying to repeat the decades-old success of *Green Eggs and Ham* ("the only book I ever wrote that still makes me laugh"), which actually resulted from a bet with the late Bennett Cerf, Random House's founder and publisher, that Seuss could write a book using only 50 words.

[Later] Geisel disclosed that *The Square Blue Balloon* "burst." He elaborated: "It was a piece of nonsense that wasn't jelling. Two ideas got mixed up in it. They contradicted each other, and the silliness was lost. So I took it down. But maybe it'll be up again in another year." The assorted sketches from different projects were still under active consideration as a book.

It's ironic, in considering Dr. Seuss the author and Ted Geisel the man, that his involvement with children is either vicarious—writing for an unseen audience of millions around the globe—or fleeting, at chalk-talks and other events. He and his first wife, Helen, who died [in 1967], had no children. His second wife, Audrey, whom he married in 1968, has two daughters from her first marriage, but no grandchildren. Still, Geisel believes he has a partnership of sorts with parents everywhere. His timeworn slogan: "You have 'em, I'll amuse 'em."

His fandom and its trappings run deep and wide. Little kids dress up in "cat in the hat" outfits when Geisel visits their schools. Others mail him green eggs and ham. College kids faithfully watch the annual telecast of *How the Grinch Stole Christmas* on one campus simply to observe the ritual of chug-a-lugging a beer each time the word "who" is used. Undergraduates are writing term papers on Seuss' books ("There are no doctoral dissertations yet—I'll have to die first"). And a group of students in Austin, Texas, have formed "The Seuss Co-op," which meets Wednesday evenings at nine to read Seuss's works and discuss them. By their own admission, the discussions often are as "downright ridiculous" as the nonsense verse itself.

Over the years, Geisel has certainly discovered *how* to be popular. He touches an emotion, a funny bone—and it registers. But does he have any clues to *why* he's popular?

"If I think in terms of the average fan letter, I have to say that nearly all of them use the word 'funny.' The next thing most of them refer to is 'rhyme.' And then come the pictures. It's strange that they don't mention 'ideas' before 'pictures,' though."

Perhaps it's a good sign that he is able to appeal to some purely on the basis of the charm of it all, and to others in terms of ideas. There's an air of escapism in coming in contact with the "collapsible frink" or Dr. Derring's singing herrings, or reveling in the mysteries of McElligot's pool and the simple goofiness of "fox in sox."

Despite that broad appeal, and the uniqueness of his art and texts, there are some Grinches about who've never warmed to his work. He knows they're out there (though he says he doesn't hear from them directly) and realizes they find his drawings overly outlandish and his vocabulary counterproductive for kids with SAT exams in their future. The fact is, though, that much of this subsurface criticism seems to be fading away. After all, you don't win a Pulitzer Prize or an award from the National Association of Elementary School Principals if you haven't made something of a contribution to language, literacy, the art of reading, and—most of all—to children.

Seated at his desk in his oceanside aerie, he voices his hope that *The Seven Lady Godivas* someday will become a part of Broadway musical history. A few attempts . . . to get the production on the boards have been postponed. Naturally, if the book—"reissued by multitudinous demand"—succeeds, the theatrical picture may brighten. Still, Geisel cautions, "I have to be awfully careful before going into it. I'd be committing myself to something for a couple of years. And at the age of 83, you don't commit yourself for a couple of years without thinking about it pretty carefully."

So what keeps him going?

"It's the fun of it, I think, and the feeling that I'm doing some good.

"And curiosity—about what's around the next corner."

Francelia Butler

SOURCE: "Seuss as a Creator of Folklore," in *Children's literature in education,* Vol. 20, No. 3, September, 1989, pp. 175-81.

On March 2, 1989, Dr. Seuss was 85, and it is time for a reassessment. Probably the best known writer and illustrator of children's books in the world, his very popularity hurts his reputation with some people, who regard his work as nothing more than simplistic jingles.

My own view is that it is not so simplistic as some people consider it. Indeed, it has many of the qualities of folk rhymes, that linger in the human psyche long after supposedly more sophisticated poetry is forgotten.

Much of his work has these characteristics of folk rhymes: the rhythms are rollicking and easily remembered, and the rhymes deal with universal concerns, such as protest, loneliness, love, nonsense, the future (including death), or, like folk rhymes, are mainly effective ways of developing physical and mental agility.

In the latter category are such stories as *Scrambled Eggs Super, On Beyond Zebra, The Foot Book, Mr. Brown Can Moo! Can You?* and *Marion K. Mooney, Will You Please Go Now?*

Since Seuss was once a prominent political cartoonist for such journals as *Judge, Liberty, Vanity Fair,* and *Life,* it is not surprising to find much political or social protest in his books. Seuss's favorite book, *The Lorax,* is a brilliant protest against industrial pollution. *The Sneetches* is a protest against discrimination. *Yertle the Turtle* (the protagonist is modeled after Hitler) is a protest against false pride and inhumanity. *Horton Hears a Who* is concerned with indifference on the part of the influential to the well-being of the little people (they don't "hear" them).

An analysis of *The Lorax* reveals the Lorax protesting all the damage the Once-ler is doing to the plants, water, and air:

> "What's more," snapped the Lorax (His dander
>   was up.)
> "Let me say a few words about Gluppity-Glupp.
> Your machinery chugs on, day and night without
>   stop
> making Gluppity-Glupp. Also Schloppity-Schlopp.
> And what do you do with this leftover goo? . . .
> I'll show you. You dirty old Once-ler man, you!

As in some folk rhymes ("Annie cum banny, tee alligo skanny," for example), Seuss uses onomatopoeia (suiting the sound to the sense) and alliteration (having words begin with the same letter, as the lines in the folk rhyme "Where the green grass grows"). The evil Once-ler "lerks in his Lerkim." He makes his clothes out of "miffmuffered moof." He wears a "gruvvulous glove." The whispered story of the Once-ler is carried down from his towerlike dwelling in a "snergelly hose." *Snergelly* is a wonderful coined word which combines twisting, twirling, and not being very attractive.

Seuss also uses similes, or comparisons, very adroitly. The Once-ler sounds as if he has "bees up his nose." The trees have "the sweet smell of fresh butterfly milk." And he uses metaphor, or having one word stand for another: his teeth sound "gray." The pond is "rippulous." Words are repeated for emphasis: "But those trees. Those trees. Those Truffula trees!"

The Lorax, representing outraged nature, emerges from the first tree that the Once-ler chops down. When he asks what thing that is that the Once-ler has made, the Once-ler sounds like a slick salesman, and Seuss parodies such a man: "It's a shirt. It's a sock. It's a glove. It's a hat. But it has other uses. Yes, far beyond that. You can use it for carpets. For pillows! For sheets! Or curtains! Or covers for bicycle seats!" We have all heard this kind of sales pitch on television, for certain kitchen tools, for instance.

When the Lorax doubts that anyone will want it, the materialistic Once-ler replies, "You never can tell what some people will buy." There is considerable irony in this and in the Once-ler's following comment on his destruction of nature, which reminds one of the fake tears shed by Lewis Carroll's walrus and carpenter over the death of the oysters they had eaten. Here is the Once-ler's delicious satire:

"I, the Once-ler, felt sad / As I watched them all go, / BUT . . . / business is business!" There is escalating satire in Seuss's parody of Big Business, as he professes to see things from the Once-ler's point of view:

> "I meant no harm. I most surely did not.
> But I had to grow bigger. So bigger I got.
> I biggered my factory. I biggered my roads.
> I biggered the wagons. I biggered the loads.
> I went right on biggering . . . selling more
>   Thneeds.
> And I biggered my money, which everyone needs.

Seuss's satire becomes even more bitter as he describes how the Once-ler sees the civic-minded Lorax as "a nuisance" (just as some factory owners feel about protesters over pollution). The Once-ler, in fact, becomes very angry and he protests that his rights are being invaded.

As for the illustrations in *The Lorax,* those connected with the Once-ler, including the first one depicting the coarse grass and old crows, are in somber shades of brown and black with a dull blue sky. The ramshackle house of the Once-ler is a dead pale purple with brown trim and touches of bilious green. By contrast, the land of the Truffula trees before it has been trashed by the Once-ler is a paradisiacal scene of red, white, yellow, and rose colors, with light blue sky. Pages sometimes face each other, with ugliness in the world of the Once-ler, shown in drab colors, and brightness and life in the colors of the world of the Lorax. At the end of the book, as at the beginning, the colors are sad and dark. For a while, hopefully not for always, the dead world of the Once-ler is all there is.

Loneliness is also one of the universal concerns dealt with in Dr. Seuss's world. One famous example is the protagonist in *Horton Hatches the Egg.* Poor Horton the elephant is up in a tree, guarding the egg of the lazy bird, Maisie, who has promised to return to relieve him of his baby-sitting job—he is doing it just as a favor—

but is too happy gallavanting around. Horton's friends laugh at him for his faithfulness:

> They laughed and they laughed. Then they all ran
>   away.
> And Horton was lonely. He wanted to play.
> But he sat on the egg and continued to say:
> "I meant what I said
> "And I said what I meant . . .
> "An elephant's faithful
> "One hundred per cent!"

As with folk rhymes, the unforgettable rhythm here is not so simple as some people might think. The first line of the above, for instance, consists of an iambic foot ("they laughed," an unaccented and an accented syllable), followed by an anapest (two unaccented syllables and an accented one: "and they laughed"). In the fourth line, "I meant" is a spondee, which consists of two syllables of equal weight, and in the sixth line, "faithful" is a trochee, consisting of an accented and then an unaccented syllable. The last line is a line of spondees.

Horton also has a lonely job defending the Whos in the sequel, *Horton Hears a Who.* But he sticks to the small ones through thin and through thick until he finally proves that a person's a person, no matter how small. (Seuss often uses inverted word order, as he does here. Most people say, "Through thick and through thin.")

Like the heroes in myth, Seuss's heroes are often pathetically lonely. The little boy in *And To Think That I Saw It on Mulberry Street* is left essentially alone, with his imagination. Bartholomew Cubbins in *The 500 Hats of Bartholomew Cubbins* is left alone with his hats to face the vanity of the king's court or, in *Bartholomew and the Oobleck,* the pride of a silly emperor, even sillier than the one in Hans Christian Andersen's story "The Emperor's New Clothes," for Seuss's emperor's demands not only concern himself but destroy the environment.

Perhaps the loneliest of all is the man in the amazing story *I Had Trouble in Getting to Solla Sollew,* who makes a Pilgrim's Progress through nightmarish difficulties until he finally arrives at a beautiful flower-filled place, "with a chap at a doorway [an angel?] that shimmered and shined" and finds the key doesn't work.

Then there is *Thidwick the Big-Hearted Moose,* oppressed by small animals who establish homes inside his horns. He is so weighed down by these ingrates that hunters are about to shoot him until nature intervenes and his horns drop off.

One of the best instances of love in Seuss's work is the story of the lonely Grinch who stole Christmas, and who discovers that it isn't material things but the love between people that makes the day meaningful. Then his heart grows three sizes.

Seuss also takes up the future, including death. This

occurs in *The Butter Battle Book.* Is the old grandfather right to teach his grandson that the Zooks on the other side of the wall are horrible and ought to be killed because they eat their bread butter-side-down? It is the old man who is promoting this silly reason for hating someone, but no sillier than the reasons gray-beard politicians still sometimes use to advocate war. Seuss makes his point.

The story begins when the old grandfather proudly tells his grandson how he used to be part of the border patrol that watched the Zooks. The conflict is between the Yooks, who eat their bread butter-side-up, and the Zooks, who eat theirs butter-side-down. The action escalates as the Yooks and the Zooks keep making bigger and more terrible weapons to frighten and attack each other. This moves the story forward until the climax, when the weapons are so terrible that they would kill everybody on both sides. At the end, both sides are poised, ready to press the button:

> "Grandpa," I shouted. "Be careful! Oh, gee!
> "Who's going to drop it?
> Will you . . . ? Or will he . . . ?
> "Be patient," said Grandpa. "We'll see.
> We will see . . . "

I especially like this story because I have made a tax-exempt Foundation for Contributed Thought on Peace, with the hope of instituting study of conflict resolution in courses in secondary schools across the country. Perhaps they can all make peace games, where peace with honor wins and war is averted.

Perhaps the best examples of nonsense rhymes are the tongue twisters in *Fox in Socks.* It is full of them:

> Who sews crow's clothes?
> Sue sews crow's clothes.
> Slow Joe Crow
> Sews whose clothes?
> Sue's clothes.

And:

> Through three cheese trees
> Three free fleas flew.
> While these fleas flew,
> freezy breeze blew.
> Freezy breeze made
> these three trees freeze.
> Freezy trees made
> these trees' cheese freeze.
> That's what made these
> Three free fleas sneeze.

And:

> When a fox is
> in the bottle where
> the tweetle beetles battle
> with their paddles

in a puddle on a
noodle-eating poodle.
THIS is what they call . . .
. . . a tweetle beetle
noodle poodle bottled
paddled muddled duddled
fuddled wuddled
Fox in Socks, sir!

You will note that many of the words begin with the same letter, as *paddles, puddle,* and *poodle,* for example.

Now for the illustrations, particularly Seuss's amazing animals. Since his father was a zoo keeper, his interest in exotic animals was well motivated, but wildly imaginative animals have a long history. The hydra in ancient Crete is supposed to have had nine snake heads. Medusa's hair was all twisting, writhing snakes. Polyphemus, the giant whom Ulysses blinded, had one eye in the middle of his forehead. The minotaur had the body of a man and the head of a bull. It used to eat boys and girls before the hero, Theseus, killed it. Then there are the gods of the Hindus with their many arms and the various gods of the native Americans, the Eskimos, and other cultures.

Six hundred years ago, an English traveler, John Mandeville, claimed he had seen in faraway places people with no heads, but with eyes on their shoulders, and other people with great ears hanging down to their knees. Even a biologist, Edward Topsell, about the same time claimed to have seen monsters with the bodies of animals and the heads of men and women, as well as ducks growing on bushes.

More recently, in nineteenth-century literature of fantasy, Alice in Wonderland developed a neck a yard long, and a baby in the same story turned into a pig. Edward Lear also drew weird forms of life: people enveloped in bushy hair and so on. But Seuss's imaginative creatures are unsurpassed.

Even Seuss's rhymes concerned with physical and mental agility have a special depth to them, as in his most popular book, *The Cat in the Hat:*

"Now look what you did!"
Said the fish to the cat.
"Now look at this house!
Look at this! Look at that!
You sank our toy ship,
Sank it deep in the cake.
You shook up our new house
And you bent our new rake.
You should not be here
When our mother is not.
You get out of this house!"
Said the fish in the pot.

The fish is the conscience of the children, their shadow.

Hop on Pop is supposed to be "the simplest Seuss for youngest use," but it still shows Seuss's genius as a writer. In fact, his simplest things are sometimes the deepest. The story has the eerie quality of Gertrude Stein's "The World Is Round." Compare, for instance, Seuss's lines:

Hill Will
Will went up hill.
Will Hill Still
Will is up hill still.

with those in Stein's classic:

A little boy upon a hill
Oh Will oh Will
A little boy upon a hill
He will oh Will
Oh Will oh Will.

Like most folk rhymes, most of Seuss is so rhythmic it can be skipped to.

When Shakespeare was a boy, his teacher in grammar school would say to him (and to other children his age): "Now when you write, you must imitate a famous and successful writer who wrote before you. You must promise me that not a thing you do will be original."

We know this because the grammar-school books still exist from that time. Everyone back then, from Shakespeare to Milton, was taught to write by mimesis, or imitation. Shakespeare's plays were imitations of old plays written before him, except that his imitations are better than the originals. Even now, many successful writers learn to write by imitating a previous writer whom they admire.

But teachers say, "Everything you do must be original. Nothing can be imitated from anybody else." So students of writing are almost in the position of having to reinvent the wheel, to start in again from the beginning. And as a result, their writing has no roots. It is like cut flowers stuck in sand.

It would be good for everybody to become Seuss imitators, to make up rhymes about their own concerns and illustrate the rhymes with crazy animals of their own invention. And if they want to add the ritual of rope skipping to the exercise, so much the better. Within the invisible world of the whirling rope, they might well come closer to the universal soul. Or, at least, lose some weight!

Alison Lurie

SOURCE: "The Cabinet of Dr. Seuss," in *The New York Review of Books,* Vol. XXXVII, No. 20, December 20, 1990, pp. 50-2.

Theodore Seuss Geisel, known to millions as Dr. Seuss,

is the most popular . . . juvenile author in America today. Almost everyone under forty was brought up on his books and cartoons, and even those who didn't hear the stories read aloud or see them on TV probably met his fantastic characters at school. Beginning with *The Cat in the Hat* in 1957, Seuss revolutionized the teaching of reading. managing to create innovative, crazily comic tales with a minimum vocabulary (*The Cat in the Hat* uses only 220 words). The inventive energy of these books and their relative freedom from class and race norms made middle-class suburban Dick and Jane look prissy, prejudiced, and totally outdated.

What made it all the more wonderful was that Dr. Seuss's life was a classic American success story. He began as a cartoonist and advertising artist; his "Quick, Henry, the Flit!" drawings showing a citizen attacked by giant insects, half-comic and half-threatening, were widely reproduced. But his first children's book, *And To Think That I Saw It on Mulberry Street,* was rejected by forty-three publishers; it was finally printed in 1937 only as a favor by a friend.

Why didn't editors see at once what a winner Seuss would be? Partly because of his artistic style, which was unabashedly cartoon-like and exaggerated in an era when children's book illustration was supposed to be pretty and realistic. Perhaps even more because of the content of his stories, especially their encouragement of wild invention and, even worse, the suggestion that it might be politic to conceal one's fantasy life from one's parents. Children in the Thirties and Forties were supposed to be learning about the real world, not wasting their time on daydreams, and they were encouraged to tell their parents everything.

Marco, the hero of *And To Think That I Saw It on Mulberry Street,* is warned by his father at the start of the book to "stop telling such outlandish tales" about what he sees on the way home from school. Yet the very next day his imagination turns a horse and wagon, by gradual stages, into a full-blown parade with elephants, giraffes, a brass band, and a plane showering colored confetti—all portrayed by Seuss with immense verve and enthusiasm. Marco arrives home in a state of euphoria:

> I swung 'round the corner
> And dashed through the gate,
> I ran up the steps
> And I felt simply GREAT!
> FOR I HAD A STORY THAT NO
> ONE COULD BEAT!

Then he is quizzed by his father about what he has seen. His reply is evasive:

> "Nothing," I said, growing red as a
> beet,
> "But a plain horse and wagon on
> Mulberry Street."

The message that it is sometimes, perhaps always, best

to conceal one's inner life reappears in *The Cat in the Hat.* Here "Sally and I," two children alone and bored on a rainy day, are visited by the eponymous Cat. He proceeds to totally destroy the house, causing first excitement and then panic (What will their mother say?). Finally he puts everything back in place. The kids—and not only those in the story, but those who read it—have vicariously given full rein to their destructive impulses without guilt or consequences. When their mother returns and asks what they've been doing, there is a strong suggestion that they might not tell her:

> Should we tell her about it?
> Now, what SHOULD we do?
> Well . . .
> What would YOU do
> If your mother asked YOU?

In these tales the children whose imagination transforms the world are abashed or secretive when confronted with possible adult disapproval. More often, however, Seuss lets fancy run free without equivocation or apology. A whole series of books from *McElligot's Pool* through *On Beyond Zebra!* and *If I Ran the Circus* celebrates the wildest flights of fantasy. They usually begin in familiar surroundings, then move into an invented world where the scenery recalls the exotic landscapes of *Krazy Kat* comics. There, just as Seuss's Elephant-Bird, Tufted Gustard, and Spotted Atrocious defy natural history, so his buildings and roads and mountains defy gravity, seeming always to be on the verge of total collapse.

Though these stories are full of euphoric vitality, there is occasionally something uneasy and unsatisfying about them. Seuss's verbal inventions can become as shaky and overblown as the structures in his drawings. At the end of these books the elaborate language always does collapse. There is an abrupt return to simple diction, and a simple, realistic illustration implicitly declares that Seuss's protagonist was only fantasizing.

Innovative as he was, Seuss can also be seen as squarely in the tradition of American popular humor. His strenuous and constant energy, his delight in invention and nonsense recall the boasts and exaggerations of the nineteenth-century tall tale, with its reports of strange animals like the Snipe and the Side-Winder. Seuss brought this manner and these materials up to date for a generation raised on film and TV cartoons. And, though most of the time he addresses himself almost exclusively to children, he includes occasional jokes for adults. In *If I Ran the Zoo,* for instance, the hero plans to bring a Seersucker back alive; he will also "go down to the Wilds of Nantucket / And capture a family of Lunks in a bucket." According to the illustrations, the Seersucker is a foolish, shaggy, flower-eating animal with what looks like a red bow tie, while Lunks are pale, big-eyed creatures with blond topknots, captured with the help of beach buggies.

Parents as well as children seem to be addressed in *One*

Fish Two Fish Red Fish Blue Fish (1960), in which two kids find a very large uncomfortable-looking tusked sea monster. They exult:

Look what we found
in the park
in the dark.
We will take him home.
We will call him Clark.

He will live at our house.
He will grow and grow.
Will our mother like this?
We don't know.

But Seuss is not only in favor of the free-ranging imagination; in many of his books there is a strong liberal, even anti-establishment moral. As in the classic folk tale, pride and prejudice are ridiculed, autocratic rule overturned. In *Yertle the Turtle,* Mack, who is bottom turtle on the live totem pole that elevates King Yertle, objects to the system:

I know, up on top you are seeing
    great sights,
But down at the bottom we, too,
    should have rights. . . .
Besides, we need food. We are
    starving!

So he burps and upsets the whole stack, turning Yertle into King of the Mud. In *Bartholomew and the Oobleck* another overreaching ruler, dissatisfied with the monotony of the weather, commands his magicians to cause something more interesting than rain or snow to fall from the sky. He gets a sticky, smelly substance which, though it appears as green, is clearly excrement ("You're sitting in oobleck up to your chin"); it does not disappear until he admits that the whole thing was his own fault.

In *Horton Hatches the Egg* and *Horton Hears a Who* a charitable and self-sacrificing elephant protects the rights of the unborn and of small nations and obscure individuals in spite of the ridicule and scorn of his friends, because "A person's a person, no matter how small." There are limits to charity in Seuss, however. *Thidwick the Big-Hearted Moose* allows his horns to become the refuge of an overwhelming number of immigrant animals and bugs, repeating wearily that "A host, above all, must be nice to his guests." Luckily, just when he reaches the limits of his endurance and is being pursued by hunters, his antlers moult and he escapes. His guests end up stuffed and mounted on the wall of the Harvard Club, "as they *should* be."

For years Seuss's tales were hailed by experts as a wonderful way to teach children not only reading but moral values. Recently, however, a couple of them have run into opposition. [In 1989], loggers in northern California went after *The Lorax* (1971). In this story, a greedy Once-ler and his relatives move into an area of natural beauty and proceed to chop down all the colorful

Truffula Trees in order to manufacture Thneeds, which resemble unattractive hairy pink underwear. Soon the sky is choked with smog and the water with something called Gluppity-Glup. Though Seuss said the book was about conservation in general, the loggers saw it as blatant propaganda and agitated to have it banned from the school's required reading list. "Our kids are being brainwashed. We've got to stop this crap right now!" shouted their ad in the local paper, taking much the same belligerent anti-environmentalist tone as the Once-ler himself does when criticized:

I yelled at the Lorax, "Now listen
    here, Dad!
All you do is yap-yap and say 'Bad!
    Bad! Bad! Bad!'
Well, I have my rights sir, and I'm
    telling you
I intend to go on doing just what I
    do!
And for your information, you
    Lorax, I'm figgering
    on biggering
        and BIGGERING
            and BIGGERING
                and BIGGERING
turning MORE Truffula Trees into
    Thneeds
which everyone, EVERYONE,
    EVERYONE needs!"

The Butter Battle Book (1984), a fable about the arms race, also provoked unfavorable comment. Like Swift's tale of the Big- and Little-Endians who went to war over how to open an egg, it begins with a meaningless difference in domestic habits. Two groups of awkward-looking flightless birds, the Yooks and the Zooks, live side by side; the Yooks eat their bread butter side up, the Zooks prefer it butter side down. They become more and more suspicious of each other, and finally a member of the Zook Border Patrol with the rather Slavic-sounding name of VanItch fires his slingshot. Escalation begins: more and more complicated weapons are developed by the Boys in the Back Room ("TOP-EST, SECRET-EST, BRAIN NEST" says the sign on their door), until both sides possess the means of total destruction. Unlike most of Seuss's books, this one doesn't end reassuringly, but with the child narrator asking anxiously, "Who's going to drop it? / Will *you* . . . ? Or will *he* . . . ?" *The New York Times Book Review* considered the story "too close to contemporary international reality for comfort," while *The New Republic,* somewhat missing the point, complained that the issues between our real-life Zooks and Yooks were more important than methods of buttering bread.

Other, perhaps more relevant criticisms might be made today of Seuss's work. For one thing, there is the almost total lack of female protagonists; indeed, many of his stories have no female characters at all. The recent *You're Only Old Once!,* a cheerfully rueful tale about the medical woes of a senior citizen, which was on the best-seller list for months, is no exception. It contains one female receptionist (only her arm is visible) and one female nurse, plus a male patient, a male orderly, and twenty-one male doctors and technicians. There is also one male fish.

The typical Seuss hero is a small boy or a male animal; when little girls appear they play silent, secondary roles. The most memorable female in his entire *oeuvre* is the despicable Mayzie, the lazy bird who callously traps Horton into sitting on her egg so that she can fly off to Palm Beach. Another unattractive bird, Gertrude McFuzz in *Yertle the Turtle and Other Stories,* is vain, envious, greedy, stupid, and fashion-mad. She gorges on magic berries to increase the size of her tail, and ends up unable to walk.

Seuss's little girls, unlike his boys, are not encouraged to exercise and expand their imagination very far. In "The Gunk that Got Thunk," one of the tales in *I Can Lick 30 Tigers Today!,* this is made clear. The narrator relates how his little sister customarily used her "Thinker-Upper" to "think up friendly little things / With smiles and fuzzy fur." One day, however, she gets bored; she speeds up the process and creates a giant Gunk:

> He was greenish.
> Not too cleanish.
> And he sort of had bad breath.

She tries to unthink him, but fails; meanwhile the Gunk gets on the phone and runs up a $300 long-distance bill describing recipes. Finally he is unthunk with the help of the narrator, who then gives his sister

> Quite a talking to
> About her Thinker-Upper.
> NOW . . .
> She only
> Thinks up fuzzy things
> In the evening after supper.

Moral: Woman have weak minds; they must not be ambitious even in imagination.

Seuss's most recent book . . . also has a male protagonist. But in other ways *Oh, the Places You'll Go!* is a departure for him. "The theme is limitless horizons and hope," Seuss . . . told an interviewer, and the blurb describes the book as a "joyous ode to personal fulfillment": but what it really reads like is the yuppie dream—or nightmare—of 1990 in cartoon form.

At the beginning of the story the standard Seuss boy hero appears in what looks like a large clean modern city (featureless yellow buildings, wide streets, tidy plots of grass). But under this city, as an urbanite might expect, are unpleasant, dangerous things—in this case, long-necked green monsters who put their heads out of manholes. Seeing them, Seuss's hero, "too smart to go down any not-so-good street," heads "straight out of town."

At first everything goes well; he acquires an escort of four purple (Republican?) elephants, and rises in the world, joining "the high fliers / who soar to high heights." The narrative is encouraging:

> You'll pass the whole gang and
> you'll soon take the lead.
> Wherever you fly, you'll be best of
> the best.
> Wherever you go, you will top all
> the rest.

In the accompanying illustration Seuss's hero is carried by a pink and yellow balloon high over fields and mountains; his competitors, in less colorful balloons, lag behind at a lower altitude.

Then comes the first disaster: the balloon is snagged by a dead tree and deflated. The boy's "gang" doesn't stop for him—as presumably he wouldn't for them—and he finds himself first in a Lurch and then in a Slump, portrayed as a dismal rocky semi-nighttime landscape with giant blue slugs draped about. Doggedly, he goes on and comes to a city full of arches and domes which looks rather Near Eastern,

> where the streets are not marked.
> Some windows are lighted. But
> mostly they're darked.

Turning aside (in the light of recent events, an excellent choice), he continues "down long wiggled roads" toward what Seuss calls The Waiting Place. Here the sky is inky black and many discouraged-looking people and creatures are standing about:

> . . . waiting, perhaps, for their Uncle
> Jake
> or a pot to boil, or a Better Break.

For the energetic, ever-striving young American, this is a fate worse than death, and it is vigorously rejected:

> NO!
> That's not for you!
>
> Somehow you'll escape
> all that waiting and staying.
> You'll find the bright places
> where Boom Bands are playing.

Seuss's hero is next seen riding another purple elephant in a procession of elephants, on his way to further solitary triumphs.

> Oh, the places you'll go. There is
> fun to be done!
> There are points to be scored. There
> are games to be won. . . .
> Fame! You'll be famous as famous
> can be,

From Oh, the Places You'll Go!, *written
and illustrated by Dr. Seuss.*

with the whole wide world watching
    you win on TV.

In the accompanying picture, some kind of fantasy football or lacrosse is being played—our hero kicking off from the back of his elephant, the other contestants on foot. But almost immediately this success is undercut:

Except when they don't
Because, sometimes, they won't.

I'm afraid that some times
you'll play lonely games too.
Games you can't win
'cause you'll play against you.

The most dangerous enemy of the celebrity is his own doubt and self-hatred. The illustration shows a totally insecure-looking fantasy version of a Hollywood hillside mansion, where the protagonist is shooting baskets alone. Seuss assumes, no doubt quite properly, that in any career devoted to success, competition, and fame, "Alone will be something / you'll be quite a lot," and that often "you won't want to go on."

But his hero, of course, does go on, meeting a number of comical and/or frightening monsters.

You'll get mixed up
with many strange birds as you
    go . . .

Seuss predicts. The strange birds, who all look alike, are shown against another totally black background, some marching upward to the right with smiles, others plodding downward to the left with depressed expressions. The message here seems to be that it is a mistake to commit oneself to any organization; instead one must

Step with care and great tact
and remember that Life's
a Great Balancing Act.

This is followed by the happy climax, in which Seuss's hero, is even more triumphant than before:

And will you succeed?
Yes? You will, indeed!
(98 and ¾ percent guaranteed.)

KID, YOU'LL MOVE MOUNTAINS!

This promise is depicted literally in the illustration; if we chose to take it that way, we might assume that Seuss's "kid" has become a property developer, like so many California celebrities.

In one or two of Seuss's earlier books, similar dreams of money and fame occur. Gerald McGrew, for instance, imagines that

The whole world will say, "Young
    McGrew's made his mark.
He's built a zoo better than Noah's
    whole Ark! . . .

"WOW!" They'll all cheer,
"What this zoo must be worth!"

    (If I Ran the Zoo)

This was written in 1950, when Seuss's own imaginary zoo had just begun to make his fortune. Today life has wholly imitated art; his wild inventions, like those of his boy heroes—and of course in the end they are the same thing—have made him fantastically rich and famous. It is difficult to estimate what Seuss's own zoo must be worth now.

Elizabeth B. Moje and Woan-Ru Shyu

SOURCE: "The Places You've Taken Us, Dr. Seuss!" in *Education Digest,* Vol. 58, No. 4, December, 1992, pp. 26-30.

When Theodor Seuss Geisel died on September 24, 1991,

in his California home at age 87, he left many sad hearts, but he also left a rich legacy of "great sights and high heights," of the spirit and optimism he offered to children of all ages for the last half-century. And he left us encouragement to explore life's journey with the same enthusiasm he had.

Dr. Seuss lived in a converted lighthouse with a sign that read, "Beware of the Cat." He created such well-loved characters as Bartholomew Cubbins, the Lorax, Sam-I-Am, and the Cat in the Hat. . . .

Born in Springfield, Massachusetts, on March 2, 1904, he was known by his given name until he was involved in a minor infraction of school rules at Dartmouth College. After being dismissed as editor-in-chief of the college humor magazine for his shenanigans, he started using his middle name, Seuss, in order to continue writing for it. When he dropped out of Oxford University in 1927, where he studied English literature, he added "Dr." to his middle name, not wanting to disappoint his father. Although he assumed various nicknames in the 1920s, such as Theo Seuss 2nd and Dr. Theophrastus Seuss, the name Dr. Seuss brought the most fame.

While he was attending Oxford, classmate Helen Palmer urged Geisel to pursue an art career. Her advice motivated him to leave the university and travel through Europe in 1926-27, during which he produced drawings representative of what he called his "Roman and Florentine Period." His travels completed, he returned to the United States in 1927 and married Palmer, who remained his wife and business partner until her death 40 years later.

When he returned to the U.S. in 1927, his exotic animals doing the cocktail-party circuit were an uncommon subject for cartoons. A genius at creating a page crowded with images and spiced with a telling line of dialogue, he insightfully recorded the mores of society in popular humor magazines. He also expressed a political sensibility in his work, from his earliest Dartmouth drawings of the 1920s to his explicit political cartoons of the early 1940s.

When his work was spotted by an advertising executive, Seuss was contracted to develop an ad campaign for an oil company. He also created other ad campaigns.

Seuss stumbled on writing children's books when he illustrated *Boners* (1931), a collection of schoolboy cartoons he worked on to circumvent his advertising contract, which prohibited him from most commercial publishing ventures. Seuss did not want to be limited to illustrating, however, and in 1937 wrote, for his own amusement, his first full-length book *And To Think That I Saw It on Mulberry Street.* In the atmosphere of 1930s children's books, it became an instant hit, once Seuss managed to convince publishers to accept it.

With the publication of *The Cat in the Hat* (1957), Random House (publisher of all the Dr. Seuss books

since 1939) created a special division, Beginner Books, with Seuss as president. Best seller followed best seller; prize followed award. In 1968, Seuss launched another learn-to-read concept with *The Foot Book,* and pioneered a new Random House division for preschool and kindergarten readers: Bright & Early Books.

Seuss created some of his most language-conscious works during the 1970s. These books helped establish that children could experiment with language by reading humorous and appealing stories.

In 1984, Dr. Seuss made headlines when *The Butter Battle Book* set a world's record by appearing for six months on *The New York Times* adult best-seller list; it offered readers a clearer understanding of issues surrounding nuclear war. And Seuss's final work, *Oh, the Places You'll Go* (1990) approached life the way Geisel did, as a journey in which one could "move mountains."

How did Dr. Seuss start writing? Why did he draw such wild pictures? And how did he think up those crazy places and names? Seuss said, "My animals look the way they do because I can't draw." Seuss also claimed he could think up and draw such unusual places with such crazy animals because he had been to most of those places. The animals' names were no problem to spell, he said, because he kept a special dictionary with each animal listed in it for quick reference.

As for his stories, Palmer explained, "Ted doesn't sit down and write for children. He writes to amuse himself. Luckily, what amuses him also amuses them." Such amusement was usually inspired by conversations, overheard phrases, or as an accompaniment to some of his doodling. Sometimes rhythms would pop into his head.

The Cat in the Hat was, in contrast, the result of a concerted effort to write a particular kind of book. In the mid-1950s, author John Hersey wrote an article in *Life* magazine condemning the Dick-and-Jane type of writing found in elementary school readers. Hersey challenged Dr. Seuss to use his skill to create books with controlled vocabulary which could still appeal to children. Seuss took up the challenge. He received a contract and a public school word list from a publishing company, and he started to write.

Writing such a book was apparently so difficult that Seuss almost gave up. The popular story says that, in frustration, Seuss was looking through discarded sketches when he happened to spot one of a cat. Seuss took another look at the word list and two words which rhymed jumped out at him: cat and hat. At that moment, the infamous cat in the stovepipe hat was born.

The number-one selling Seuss book, *Green Eggs and Ham,* resulted from a bet with his Random House publisher, Bennett Cerf, who bet Seuss he could not write a book using only 50 words. Not only did Seuss manage, but he wrote a best seller! Seuss once said that

Green Eggs and Ham was the only book he had written that still made him laugh.

Although Dr. Seuss described his work as being written for children, the meanings and purposes behind his books have long been a source of speculation. Seuss claimed he never wrote with a moral message in mind, but he did admit that morals developed naturally from the plots of his stories. He said, "Kids . . . can see a moral coming a mile off and they gag at it. But there's an inherent moral in any story."

One popular Seuss book often cited for its allegedly moral purpose is *Horton Hatches the Egg.* According to Seuss, however, the book was written as a result of his doodlings of an elephant on a piece of transparent paper. The paper had been shifted about on his desktop when Seuss noticed it lying atop a sketch of a tree. "I stopped, dumbfounded. I said to myself, 'That's a hell of a situation. An elephant in a tree! What's he doing there?'" Almost a month later, Seuss was creating a story about an elephant playing surrogate for a duck.

Dr. Seuss was adamant about writing to have fun, which usually helped him produce books that children could have fun with, too. "My books don't insult their [children's] intelligence. Maybe it's because I'm on their level. When I dropped out of Oxford, I decided to be a child, so it's not some condescending adult writing."

While Seuss denied sending moral messages, he never denied writing about issues: "It's impossible to write anything without making a statement in some way." Seuss wrote *Yertle the Turtle* (1958) as a reaction against the fascism of World War II, *The Lorax* (1971) in response to environmental concerns, and *The Butter Battle Book* (1984) to reflect on nuclear proliferation.

The Lorax (which Seuss listed as his favorite) stirred up such negative feelings in the lumber industry in the north western United States that some schools considered banning it from school reading lists. Seuss argued that while the book was political, "propaganda with a plot," he also stated that it was a result of his frustration with the waste of natural resources in the world in general, not a direct attack against specific U.S. industries.

Regardless of the meanings critics extended to Seuss books, his personal reason for writing was clear: Seuss wanted to write so children could have fun reading. "I'm trying to capture an audience. Most every child learning to read has problems, and I am just saying to them that reading is fun."

Whenever Seuss was asked why he remained childless throughout his life, he consistently responded, "You make 'em, and I'll amuse 'em." And amuse them, he did. All 47 Dr. Seuss books he wrote and illustrated in his 54-year career are still in print. In addition, Geisel published several other books under the pseudonym "Theo LeSieg" ("LeSieg" is "Geisel" spelled backward).

Young fans were frequent, albeit uninvited, visitors at the Seuss home in La Jolla, California, and letters of admiration poured in by the thousands. One 9-year-old once wrote Seuss that "This was the funniest book I ever read in nine years," while another declared, "Dr. Seuss, you have an imagination with a long tail!"

Maurice Sendak, author of such children's favorites as *Where the Wild Things Are,* saw Seuss as a "mischief-maker and revolutionary" who was "on the side of the kids." Sendak called Seuss "the big papa," saying that the inspiration for his own books was drawn from the early work of Dr. Seuss. Charlotte Zolotow, author and publisher of children's books, said of Seuss, "He went straight to the most elemental feeling that people had, and the characteristics of certain personalities, and he caught it with a sense of mischief and fun and compassion and understanding." Such sentiments are heard not only from fellow writers and children's literature critics, but from children, parents, and teachers who have spent time with Dr. Seuss over the last half-century.

Theodor Seuss Geisel worked diligently at his craft of entertaining children and adults with fun stories that often carried important messages, intended or not. Writing was a struggle for him because he had such a high regard for children. "Children have as much right to quality as their elders," he said. Perhaps Seuss realized the importance of amusing, exciting, exuberant literature for children because he was still a child at heart.

Judith Morton, Seuss's friend and biographer, said, "Ted never grew old. He never even really grew up. Each of our visits . . . was a joyful, mischievous revelation with his wonderfully skewed view of the world which was also his defense against its pomposity and foolishness." Morton's statement leaves us with an optimistic feeling. Although Dr. Seuss is gone from our world, he has not, like the fickle cat he created, simply disappeared with a tip of his hat. Dr. Seuss has left us a treasury of literature through which we can visit and journey with him for generations to come.

Oh, the places you've taken us! Thanks, Dr. Seuss.

TITLE COMMENTARY

THE BUTTER BATTLE BOOK (1984)

Betty Jean Lifton

SOURCE: A review of *The Butter Battle Book,* in *The New York Times Book Review,* February 26, 1984, p. 37.

[W]e have only to turn a few pages [of *The Butter Battle Book*] before realizing that the intolerant Yooks, who eat their bread butter side up, and their stubborn neighbors, the Zooks, who eat theirs butter side down, are caricatures too close to contemporary international reality for comfort as they glare at each other over the wall they have built to separate their two lands.

When a "very rude" Zook with a slingshot zaps part of the Yook Border Patrol, we are in an arms race that escalates rapidly from such weapons as "Jigger-Rock Snatchems" to the "Eight-Nozzled, Elephant-Toted Boom-Blitz" which has the power to shoot "explosive sour cherry stone pits." It's only a flying leap from there into the space age with outlandish flying machines. And, of course, you've guessed it, it doesn't take long for the Boys in the Back Room on both sides to "figger" out a bomb, the Bitsy Big-Boy Boomeroo, filled with "mysterious Moo-Lacka-Moo" that can blow everyone to "Sala-ma-goo."

The book closes with both populations in their underground shelters as the young narrator's grandfather stands poised on the wall with his bomb, confronting a Zook with his. "Be careful!" the boy cries out. "Oh, gee! / Who's going to drop it? Will *you* . . . ? / Or will *he* . . . ? To which his grandfather replies: "Be patient. We'll see."

But dear Dr. Seuss, we want to protest—you can't leave us hanging like this. Can't the Boys in the Back Room come up with some equally clever peace machines, or the Cat in the Hat come back to save the day, if not the world? No use. Our concerned doctor—much like our real Dr. Spock—offers no placebos this time. He wants his children to know what the adults are up to, and that in devising bigger and more destructive armaments neither Yooks nor Zooks know which side their bread is buttered on.

It's not an easy task, this trying to find a way to tell children the nuclear facts of life. Thank you, Dr. Seuss, for attempting this cautionary tale. We hope, if we're patient, we'll see a colorful sequel in which the Yooks and Zooks have "figgered" a "walloping wizz-zinger" way to coexist. We need it, too.

Kirkus Reviews

SOURCE: A review of *The Butter Battle Book*, in *Kirkus Reviews*, Vol. LII, Nos. 1-5, March 1, 1984, p. J-9.

A parable of armaments escalation—from the Snick-Berry Switch to the Big-Boy Boomeroo—whose high-level meaning no child can miss. This anti-nuke message in Seussian terms has one point of difference with such earlier anti-war picturebooks as William Wondriska's *The Tomato Patch:* it doesn't end in amity, but with the enemy Yooks and Zooks both poised to drop their bombs—and the grandson of the bomb-wielding Yook looking aghast. But, like previous embodiments of the theme, this one reduces the rivalry to a petty, nonsensical difference—the titular Butter Battle. Yooks, that is, spread their bread with the butter side up; Zooks, with

the butter side down. (A perverse notion, the pictures demonstrate.) The actual weapons escalation involves some wild Seussian creations and some characteristic manic glee. Says Zook-rep VanItch (note the name): "My wonderful weapon, the Jigger-Rock Snatchem, will fling 'em right back as quick as we catch 'em./ We'll have no more nonsense./ We'll take no more gupp/ from you Yooks who eat bread with the butter side up!" But in the aftermath of wide exposure to *The Day After* and other 1980s arousals, all this seems, however well-intended, a little simplistic, a little out-of-date, even a little out-of-keeping.

YOU'RE ONLY OLD ONCE! (1986)

Kirkus Reviews

SOURCE: A review of *You're Only Old Once!* in *Kirkus Reviews,* Vol. LIV, No. 5, March 1, 1986, p. 379.

Over the past 30 years, Dr. Seuss has endeared himself to millions of youngsters (and harried older types) with his tales of such giggle-producing creatures as "The Cat in the Hat" and "Yertle the Turtle." Now, finally, he's written a book for those he calls "obsolete children." It's the nicest thing to happen to "senior citizens" since Medicare.

This time around, the Doctor enlists his jaunty rhymes and sprightly illustrations to present a not altogether tongue-in-cheek look at that unnerving ritual of aging, "the medical check-up." His reactions to the whole demeaning (and distinctly expensive) process are so wryly knowing, he might well have entitled his opus "The Cynic in the Clinic." The medical profession, under Seuss's steady gaze, comes in for some hilarious—and pointed—joshing.

The action takes place at the "Golden Years Clinic on Century Square for Spleen Readjustment and Muffler Repair." Here, after first undergoing an "Eyesight and Solvency Test" (the chart reads "Have you any idea how much money these tests are costing you?"), the grey-mustachioed hero meets a battery of specialists including "Von Crandall, the World-Renowned Ear Man" and "Dr. Pollen, the Allergy Whiz." These worthies pinch, prod and poke about in search of such maladies as "Prune Picker's Plight" and "Chimney Sweep's Stupor." Diets are devised—"What you like . . . forget it!" Seuss has a great deal of fun with the "Pill Drill," in which the hero must memorize the dosages of a bewildering medicinal array: "I take the pill with zebra stripes to cure my early evening gripes . . . This long flat one is what I take if I should die before I wake." Having mastered that challenge, he goes from being "properly pilled" to being "properly billed." Finally, socks, coat and pants restored, necktie back under his chin, he's pleased to assure himself, "You're in pretty good shape for the shape you are in."

Seuss, is in better than "pretty good shape"; he's in top

form with this book that's sure to delight "obsolete children," and even those of us who are merely obsolescent.

Ilene Cooper

SOURCE: A review of *You're Only Old Once!* in *Booklist,* Vol. 82, No. 14, March 15, 1986, p. 1043.

For almost 40 years Dr. Seuss has been writing nonsensical stories for children. Now, as he turns 82, he has decided to address his own set in the same wacky verse and with the same amusing, cartoon-style illustrations that generations of children and their parents remember fondly. His story follows an intrepid senior citizen through a check-up at the Golden Years clinic, where he gets poked and pushed, "properly pilled and properly billed." Though most of the action is intentionally absurd in vintage Seuss fashion, it will look all too familiar to patients who have sat in more than a few hospital waiting rooms themselves. The humor may sting a little, but that won't stop the good doctor from finding a whole new audience with this likely best-seller.

David W. Dunlap

SOURCE: "Waiting in Fotta-Fa-Zee," in *The New York Times Book Review,* March 23, 1986, p. 39.

Once you know that *You're Only Old Once!* is autobiographical, you might be misled into thinking that Dr. Seuss is a timorous and slightly wilted type who wears a bow tie and would accept any indignity that a Golden Years Clinic cared to dish out.

He does wear a bow tie. And in the more recent of his 82 years, Theodor Seuss Geisel has had "a series of everything," including a heart attack and cataracts. But the mischievous smile that crinkles his white beard and glows from his penetrating gaze betrays a man who will suffer none of it quietly. Including a clinic's tedium.

"Frankly," he said, "it was a matter of sitting in waiting rooms being bored. I began sketching what I thought was going to happen to me for the next hour and a half. I had no idea of doing a book. I just began drawing hospital machinery. It is autobiographical, which makes it different, of course, from anything I've ever done. It got very heavy at times. I probably wrote 200 pages and had to throw away the real unpleasant ones. I got that out of my system and didn't print it."

"In the interest of commerce, there's a happy ending," Mr. Geisel said. "The other ending is unacceptable."

There is only a glimpse of the familiarly exotic Seuss terrain when the patient picks up a waiting-room copy of the National Geographic ("from 1907—I tried to get that in but the rhyme wouldn't accommodate it"). Suddenly, briefly, the reader is transported to Fotta-fa-Zee, whose most prominent denizen is a smiling, yellow, long-necked, pointy-toed, camellike creature. Mr. Geisel explained, "Putting that animal in there says, 'This is a Seuss book. . . .'"

Edward Sorel

SOURCE: "The Shape That He's In," in *The New York Times Book Review,* March 23, 1986, p. 39.

Illustrated with his characteristic verve and imagination, the book follows an elderly Mr. Everyman as he is forced to endure the boredom, anxiety and humiliation of a basic medical check-up from "Doctors Schmidt, Smoot, Sinatra, Sylvester, and Fonz," who in the Internal Organs Olympics "won fifteen gold medals, nine silver, six bronze!" There's also "Dr. Pollen . . . [the] Allergy Whiz, / who knows every sniffle and itch that there is," and Dr. Van Ness, specialist in, of course, stress. My own favorite was Dr. Von Eiffel.

> Dietician Von Eiffel controls the Wuff-Whiffer,
> our Diet-Devising Computerized Sniffer,
> on which you just simply lie down in repose
> and sniff at good food as it goes past your nose.
> From caviar souffle to caribou roast, from
>   pemmican patties to terrapin toast
> he'll find out by Sniff-Scan the foods you like
>   most.
>
> And when that guy finds out
> what you like
> you can bet it

From Daisy-Head Mayzie, *adapted from the textual dramatization and thumbnail sketches for an animated TV special, written and illustrated by Dr. Seuss.*

won't be on your diet.
From here on, forget it!"

All ends well when the old-timer is told, "You're in pretty good shape for the shape you are in!"

Aging, or better yet, dying, is just the kind of dreaded experience that can be rollicking good fun when described by, say, Moliere, Evelyn Waugh, Harold Pinter, Robert Benchley or Ogden Nash. There's nothing wrong with the topic, but there's something amiss in the blithe assumption that the sort of rhymes which delight a 4-year-old (or an adult reading to a 4-year-old) will still entertain when read alone through bifocals. For that to be, one has to believe that old people invariably pass through a second childhood.

Clearly, *You're Only Old Once!* is not my cup of Geritol, but then I've never been described as being young in heart. Others will no doubt be charmed by this reprise of Dr. Seuss' jolly rhymes and spirited cartoons, especially when it's read to them by their own—very precocious, of course—grandchild.

📖 THE TOUGH COUGHS AS HE PLOUGHS THE DOUGH (edited by Richard Marschall, 1986)

Ray Olson

SOURCE: A review of *The Tough Coughs as He Ploughs the Dough,* in *Booklist,* Vol. 83, No. 5, November 1, 1986, p. 451.

Before he took to scribbling his glorious children's books, Dr. Seuss was a successful adult humorist whose ridiculous beasts and silly puns delighted readers of a host of popular humor magazines of the 1920s and 1930s. Here, resurrected from the pages of those long-defunct journals, is a selection of 20 sketches, 60 cartoon essays, 30 full-page cartoons, and 21 advertisements for Flit insecticide ("Quick, Henry, the Flit!"). They are quite often crashingly innocuous, but many still amuse. The doctor's forte, then as now, was neither satire nor even comedy, really, but whimsy—fanciful wordplay and gently energetic cartooning, not a hint of malice in either. Editor Richard Marschall, who has also compiled S. J. Perelman's early work, adds a slight introduction tracing Seuss's early years. Unfortunately, dates are not provided for any of the selections, hampering the book's usefulness for studious Seussians.

George Garrett

SOURCE: "Young Dr. Seuss: Early Wit and Whimsy from a National Treasure," in *Chicago Tribune—Books,* January 18, 1987, p. 6.

Back in the lively 1920s and early 1930s, before he became a national, indeed an international, treasure as Dr. Seuss, Ted Geisel worked as a writer and an illustrator and cartoonist for a number of the popular humor magazines, including *College Humor, Life, Liberty, Vanity Fair* and, especially, *Judge.*

At *Judge* he wrote and drew, working cheek by jowl with the inimitable likes of Milt Gross and S. J. Perelman, all members-in-good standing of a clique or club of artists who, as editor Richard Marschall puts it in his excellent introduction, "employed zaniness, irreverence, iconoclasm, universal parody, and, sometimes, a literary approximation of anarchy."

Marschall, possessor of one of the world's great archives of comic books and humor magazines, has selected 13 representative essays, a large number of pieces combining illustrations and text and a wonderful grab bag of cartoons, including an entire final section of Geisel's "Quick, Henry, the Flit!" cartoon-advertisements which led to a 17-year hitch during which he did the Flit ads for Standard Oil of New Jersey.

Jokes, whether as plain and simple as a whoopee cushion or as elaborate as an artificial spider web, date very quickly. The best of them light up the sky, brief and sudden as summer lightning, and are gone for good. But, then, time—enough time, in this case 50 years—refines away the purely ephemeral and leaves, intact, the essential. Words, which once were dated, are now old-fashioned, which is a very different thing. Some of the things here, all composed between 1927 and 1937, have the shine of new-minted coins, are as fresh and funny now as can be. Others, inevitably, have seen their better days. All are interesting in a variety of ways, not the least of which is the clear demonstration of a developing genius. It's a pleasure to see where our Dr. Seuss came from.

Selma G. Lanes

SOURCE: A review of *The Tough Coughs as He Ploughs the Dough,* in *The New York Times Book Review,* April 12, 1987, p. 27.

For those curious about the man whose 45 children's books have sold more than 100 million copies to date, . . . these collected essays cum pictures, educational charts (from one of which the work's title was lifted) and early cartoons lay bare [Dr. Seuss's] first decade (1927-1937) as a paid humorist. Theodor Seuss Geisel began his career by writing and illustrating for adults, in such publications as *Judge, Liberty,* and the old *Vanity Fair.* The nom de plume Dr. Seuss was there from the start. So were dead ringers for the yet-to-be-conceived Cat in the Hat, as well as early denizens of the Seuss zoo: the Absorbent-Pawed Dingo, the Nelp, the Plodoplutt and the Scotch Dilemma ("with six-passenger horns"). During these tyro years preceding publication of his first children's book, ***And To Think That I Saw It On Mulberry Street*** (1937), Dr. Seuss's medium was prose; there's not so much as a single couplet of his inspired doggerel here. Yet the poetry is there. Take his description of a frigid evening: "Many poor people were caught that night with their marrow unprotected and were severely chilled to it." Or his ringing advertising catch phrase that swept the nation in the 30s: "Quick, Henry! The Flit!" True Dr. Seuss aficionados will surely regret that neither the dates of the pieces nor the names of the publications in which they appeared are listed. On balance, however, while a thing of beauty may be a joy forever, Dr. Seuss's zany pictures and cockeyed prose—in which beauty plays no part—are brimful of fleeting pleasures. And who'd be dumb enough to knock that?

I AM NOT GOING TO GET UP TODAY! (1987)

Kirkus Reviews

SOURCE: A review of *I Am Not Going to Get Up Today!* in *Kirkus Reviews,* Vol. VI, No. 21, November 1, 1987, p. 1580.

In the familiar Seuss pattern of a simple premise exaggerated to comic effect, a boy declares, "My bed is warm. My pillow's deep. Today's the day I'm going to sleep"—regardless of his mother, various arguments, successive waves of reinforcements, including the Marines, and a TV crew filming the momentous event. Actually, the development of the idea is a little tame compared with Seuss's other extravaganzas (and such determined all-day slumber is more the province of teen-agers and the good doctor's contemporaries than of readers at this level); but the book is delightfully enlivened by [James] Stevenson's vigorous illustrations, which considerably augment the text by showing the full extent of the consternation caused by the hero's stubborness.

Though there is plenty of the repetition required by learning readers, there are also some unusual words like Memphis, suggesting that this is not the *easiest* easy reader; but it has enough appeal to keep beginners entertained.

Publishers Weekly

SOURCE: A review of *I Am Not Going to Get Up Today!* in *Publishers Weekly,* Vol. 232, No. 20, November 13, 1987, p. 69.

Part of the Beginner Books series, this light piece of whimsy is narrated by a boy in striped pajamas who, with closed eyes, proclaims that under no circumstances will he be getting out of bed and going anywhere. "I don't choose to be up walking. I don't choose to be up talking. The only thing I'm choosing is to lie here woozy-snoozing." The Marines can't raise him, nor can a big brass band. In this everychild's fantasy, the boy takes charge of his own destiny on this particular morning. Stevenson shows the surrounding madcap lunacy, as well

as the neat, sublime smile of the narrator recounting his plans. Easygoing and funny fare, not only for beginning readers.

Betsy Hearne

SOURCE: A review of *I Am Not Going to Get Up Today!,* in *Bulletin of the Center for Children's Books,* Vol. 41, No. 5, January, 1988, p. 100.

The master rhymester catches that moment of morning rebellion when it's just too hard to get up. "My bed is warm. / My pillow's deep./ Today's the day I'm going to sleep," declares the boy portrayed in Stevenson's bouncy watercolor cartoons. The lad elaborates his ultimatum with an exaggerated energy that belies his intent. Not food, nor noise, nor prodding, nor police can move him, and his mother finally gives his breakfast egg to the arresting officer. The unrhymed ending is a bit of a textual letdown, but it serves well enough as a joke. Readers won't protest practicing their skills on this one.

Laura McCutcheon

SOURCE: A review of *I Am Not Going to Get Up Today!* in *School Library Journal,* Vol. 34, No. 6, February, 1988, pp. 64-5.

There is no arguing the rich contributions and enduring popularity of both Dr. Seuss and James Stevenson in the world of children's literature. Despite (or, perhaps, because of) their individual credentials, *I Am Not Going to Get Up Today* is a disappointment. The story of a little boy who refuses to get out of bed holds promise, but Dr. Seuss's rhymes are uneven and forced, lacking the natural cadence and choice of terms so necessary for the success of a beginning reader format. Stevenson's identifiable watercolor and ink illustrations are loose and fluid but border on messy. There is not a positive meshing of text and illustration in this book; readers never get the feeling that they belong together. All factors combine to make this book less than satisfying.

OH, THE PLACES YOU'LL GO! (1990)

Publishers Weekly

SOURCE: A review of *Oh, the Places You'll Go!* in *Publishers Weekly,* Vol. 236, No. 20, November 24, 1989, p. 69.

As familiar as Mulberry Street, as warmly optimistic as Horton, and as wise as the reformed Grinch on Christmas morning, *Oh, the Places You'll Go!* seems old and new at the same time. This is Dr. Seuss at his best, his message expressed in language and illustrations that could charm the socks off a fox.

A miniature Everychild dressed in yellow follows the narrator's advice: "You have brains in your head. / You have feet in your shoes. / You can steer yourself / any direction you choose. . . . OH! THE PLACES YOU'LL GO!" The child struts toward a castle under a canopy held by purple elephants, and flies over a pastel patchwork in a striped balloon. And then, like Bunyan's pilgrim in a Slough of Despond, he ends up, balloon burst, hanging from a scraggly tree. "I'm sorry to say so/ but, sadly, it's true / that Bang-ups / and Hang-ups / *can* happen to you," cautions the narrator.

Unlike *You're Only Old Once,* which was directed at an adult audience, Seuss here returns to images and pithy language that are accessible to children as well as adults. Even when the plucky hero feels "in a Slump" or when his sneakers leak or when he's scared "right out of [his] pants," he continues on his way because he's "that kind of a guy!"

In many ways a compendium of his previous books, this sanguine allegory of "Life's Great Balancing Act" advises readers to "step with care and great tact," and "*never* mix up your right foot with your left." Although Seuss's hero confronts loneliness, confusion and fears, the ultimate message is one of hope. Will he succeed? He "will indeed! / (98 and 3/4 percent guaranteed.) / KID," says Seuss to children of all ages, "YOU'LL MOVE MOUNTAINS!"

Kirkus Reviews

SOURCE: A review of *Oh, the Places You'll Go!* in *Kirkus Reviews,* Vol. LVIII, No. 1, January 1, 1990, p. 52.

Lightly disguised as one of the old versifier's fantastical journeys, a rueful survey of the pleasures and pitfalls along the road of life—a sort of commencement address for tots and their elders.

The clever, tripping rhymes and whimsical creatures and landscapes here will draw the faithful as usual, though the illustrations are subtler than the good doctor has produced at his most ebullient—there are pages where the wide world looks as placid as a counterpane, and some of the beasts that lurk in wait look as though they have their own troubles. Most beguiling, however, is the artful phrasing of the gentle message: caught in life's waiting games, we wait for "the mail to come, or the rain to go / or the phone to ring, or the snow to snow . . . or a string of pearls, or a pair of pants / or a wig with curls, or Another Chance." And, while there will be fun and fame, "you'll play lonely games too. / Games you can't win / 'cause you'll play against you." There is, of course, an upbeat conclusion: "You're off to Great Places! . . . / So . . . *get on your way!*"

Montaigne pointed out that it's the journey that matters, not the arrival; here, Seuss explores the same philosophical message in his own inimitably wise and witty style.

Diane Manuel

SOURCE: A review of *Oh, the Places You'll Go!* in *The New York Times Book Review,* March 11, 1990, p. 29.

Fuchsia zebra stripes and curlicue castles leap as preposterously as ever from neon-colored pages, and there are a few neat rhymes that have to do with "Bang-ups" and "Boom Bands." But it takes a searching eye and ear to find a ton of fun in Dr. Seuss's latest rendition of life's "Great Balancing Act," called *Oh, the Places You'll Go!*

The celebrated whimsicalist who has given young readers and gigglers so many outrageous adventures over the years has opted for a more purposeful stroll in his latest outing. A little "guy" (sorry, girls) headed for "Great Places" hops an occasional balloon and rowboat, but mostly he hoofs it, with his "shoes full of feet."

The publisher's jacket copy suggests that the book is for "upstarts of all ages," nursery-school grads or medical-school achievers, which raises quizzical questions about the story's intended audience. One 7-year-old acquaintance, raised on green eggs and ham, brought up another concern: "He might be traveling through different planets and worlds, but he's not having much fun. I think he just wants to find his way home."

Heading "straight out of town," clearly determined to make his mark in the world, the little guy is assured that he'll be "best of the best" and "top all the rest." Granted, there are a few "Hang-ups," he's left in one "Lurch" and even bumps into a "Slump," but mostly it's a straight-ahead, arm-pumping power walk for this "mind-maker-upper." After all, "There are points to be scored. There are games to be won." And he's apparently been told that if he faces up to his problems, "whatever they are," he'll move whatever mountains he chooses.

But seriously now, who's got the punch line? Where's the sly beastie waiting to toss a big dollop of gooky green oobleck on this path to success? Horton, old pal, can you hear us?

No answer? Okay, we can wait. This has happened before, you know, when Dr. Seuss has shushed us and rapped on his desk for attention and tried to teach us all the lesson of the day. There was *Hunches in Bunches,* about decision making, *The Butter Battle Book,* about the desperation of war, and *The Lorax,* about greed.

We've tried to learn the significant and meaningful stuff. Really, we have. But all we can remember is Horton in his tree, hatching his egg. Or the Cat in the Hat, tossing fish into a bowl. Or Yertle the Turtle getting bumped off the ladder of success by a burp.

If an elephant's faithful, 100 percent, we can be, too. We'll simply sit here and wait for Dr. Seuss to tell us another wondrously silly tale, as only he can tell them. In fact, we'll sit ourselves down in "The Waiting Place" he's provided on the way to "Great Places," where everyone's "waiting around for a Yes or No / or waiting for their hair to grow," or "waiting, perhaps, for their Uncle Jake / or a pot to boil, or a Better Break / or a string of pearls, or a pair of pants / or a wig with curls, or Another Chance." We can wait.

Ann A. Flowers

SOURCE: A review of *Oh, the Places You'll Go!* in *The Horn Book Magazine,* Vol. LXVI, No. 3, May/June, 1990, p. 329.

What appears to be a standard, jolly, cheerful Dr. Seuss picture book has disquieting undertones of pessimism and depression—even the colors seem gloomy and dark. In the story, one of Dr. Seuss's generic young persons is starting out in life, urged on by whoops and halloos of encouragement but also cautioned against going down dangerous streets and warned that failure and loneliness are bound to occur. *All Alone! / Whether you like it or not, / Alone will be something / you'll be quite a lot. / And when you're alone, / there's a very good chance / you'll meet things that scare you right out of your pants. / There are some, down the road between hither and yon, / that can scare you so much you won't want to go on.* Admittedly, life is full of pitfalls, and the book returns to its reassuring message at the end, but whether the picture book audience is ready for so much discouragement is dubious. Such a tempered outlook on life is perhaps better reserved for those old enough to profit by it.

📖 *DAISY-HEAD MAYZIE* (adapted from Dr. Seuss's dramatization and sketches for an animated TV special, 1994)

Publishers Weekly

SOURCE: A review of *Daisy-Head Mayzie,* in *Publishers Weekly,* Vol. 242, No. 4, January 23, 1995, p. 31.

Not long after Seuss's death in 1991, his widow, Audrey Geisel, began the daunting process of sorting through and cataloging her husband's belongings in their La Jolla, California home. Several months later she discovered a treatment and a series of thumbnail sketches for a screen dramatization entitled **Daisy-Head Mayzie,** the tale of a girl who one day sprouts a daisy from her head, touching off a media frenzy. The executor of Seuss's estate, Geisel has remained in close contact with the staffers at Random House, the author's longtime publisher, and, as a matter of course, she mentioned her discovery to people there. Mayzie soon found a welcoming home on the Random House list with her various Seuss "siblings."

Though fans and colleagues were excited about the new book, the publishing process without Seuss—known for being very "hands on"—at the helm was intimidating. "We're always glad to have any Seuss project," [said] Cathy Goldsmith, [then] vp and executive art director

for Random House Books for Young Readers. "But of course, the difference between working with Ted and without him is like night and day."

[Then] vp and Random House BFYR editor-at-large Janet Schulman [agreed] that working on Mayzie was a "strange experience." She and Goldsmith had edited Seuss for many years and jointly shepherded this new title as well.

"I have as good an understanding as anyone about how Ted would have wanted things done," Goldsmith [said]. "But I felt a little tenser than usual because I knew I was responsible for keeping Ted's high standards. We tried very hard to be consistent about things he would and would not do." Audrey Geisel also had approval over everything, and viewed the book in its various stages.

The main difference this time out, according to Schulman, was that "Ted had written Mayzie as a dramatization, so it was all dialogue. He had never made a book out of a dramatization before; it had always been the other way around," To accommodate such an adaptation, Schulman [said] she had to change some things slightly so they would work on the printed page.

"It was hard for me to know if what we did was something he would have liked," she [added]. "But I hope he would have liked it." She [added] that working on a Seuss book was always a joyful experience. "Being the editor to Dr. Seuss was like a gift from God," she [said]. "We had discussions about one word here or there, or some punctuation, but his manuscripts required almost no work at all."

While the book publishing process had begun, work was already underway developing the thumbnail sketches into an animated special from Hanna-Barbera. . . . For the book's artwork, Random House worked from storyboards for the special to render an accurate adaptation. Goldsmith [said] she and her in-house group regularly consulted with another creative team at Hanna-Barbera.

Publishers Weekly

SOURCE: A review of *Daisy-Head Mayzie,* in *Publishers Weekly,* Vol. 242, No. 5, January 30, 1995, p. 100.

More than three years after his death comes a new work from bestselling and beloved Seuss (Theodor Geisel). While fans are sure to be tickled by the prospect of Seussian entertainment, they are likely to be disappointed in the "also-ran" flavor of this picture book, adapted from an animated TV special. The Cat in the Hat, jauntylooking as ever, introduces and narrates the tale of young Mayzie McGrew, who one day mysteriously sprouts a daisy from her head. The phenomenon is followed by a lengthy and predictable scramble of adults rushing in to solve the problem. The attendant media buzz makes a celebrity of Mayzie and her daisy, and she learns the hard way about the high cost of fame. While the premise and concluding moral are all Seuss, the posthumous execution falls flat. Much of the text lacks the snap and panache of standard Seuss verse, and the artwork—extrapolated from Seuss sketches—seems off-kilter too. The economy of line of his best work gives way here to clutter, and the colors combine heavily and sometimes even harshly. One great success is the daisy itself, which conveys much human emotion through its stalk, leaves and petals.

Deborah Stevenson

SOURCE: A review of *Daisy-Head Mayzie,* in *Bulletin of the Center for Children's Books,* Vol. 48, No. 7, March, 1995, pp. 233-34.

Flap copy states that the good doctor wrote this story in the 1960s and it was found posthumously among his papers. Certainly the story of Mayzie McGrew, who is startled one day in school when a daisy grows out of the top of her head, has the galloping rhythm and rollicking rhyme that Dr. Seuss was so good at and others so often feebly imitated. Soon various adults realize that Mayzie and her floral topping could be a feather in their own caps, so a politician, a doctor, and a movie agent sow their own plans around her; Mayzie, however, soon tires of fame and embraces love (with a little guidance from the petals of the daisy), whereupon the daisy disappears. The plot weakens considerably at its resolution, finishing the story with more fuzz than fizz and making the classic Seuss didacticism seem rather forced, but the silliness of the situation is enjoyable enough to carry the story off nonetheless. More problematic are the illustrations, "inspired by Dr. Seuss's sketches": the colors are garish and the lines unimaginative and cartoonish (the book is in fact released simultaneously with an animated TV version), so that the cast has none of the raffish charm usually found in a Seuss book, looking more like *The Jetsons* than, say, the Whos. Kids who see the cartoon will probably clamor for the book and they'll enjoy it as a lively readaloud; its best use, however, would be in serving as a bridge to classic—dare one say genuine?—works of the master.

Liz Waterland

SOURCE: A review of *Daisy-Head Mayzie,* in *Books for Keeps,* No. 97, March, 1996, p. 7.

Dr Seuss is either liked or loathed. I have colleagues who won't have his books in the room because they can't bear the burden of either reading him or hearing him read, whilst others (including me) find his silliness and reeling rhyme irresistible. Personally, I thoroughly enjoyed this unusual tale of Mayzie who suddenly sprouted a daisy out of her head, found it brought her fame and fortune, but missed her friends, finally finding them again after the daisy had performed the ultimate sacri-

From Hooray for Diffendoofer Day!, *written by Jack Prelutsky and illustrated by Lane Smith, from the unfinished manuscript and sketches of Dr. Seuss.*

fice. Well, yes, it is silly and long and all in doggerel. If you like Dr Seuss, you'll love it. Otherwise, leave it to the children, who'll probably adore it.

MY MANY COLORED DAYS (1996)

Publishers Weekly

SOURCE: A review of *My Many Colored Days,* in *Publishers Weekly,* Vol. 243, No. 30, July 22, 1996, pp. 240-41.

The archives of many a late author, from Margaret Wise Brown (*Four Fur Feet*) to Sylvia Plath (*The It-Doesn't-Matter Suit*), often yield unpublished manuscripts. Theodor Geisel, aka Dr. Seuss, is no exception: he wrote but did not illustrate this rhyme, which assigns colors to moods. The effort is pleasant but lightweight: "You'd be / surprised/ how many ways / I change / on Different / Colored / Days," announces a child, portrayed as a flat, gingerbread-man shape of yellow, then blue, then purple. Spread by spread, the character metamorphoses into animals of varying hues, from an energetic red horse to a secretive green fish to a droopy violet brontosaur ("On Purple Days / I'm sad./ I groan./ I drag my tail./ I walk alone"). Husband and wife Johnson and Fancher *(Cat, You Better Come Home)* do not mime the author's pen-and-ink creations but work in pasty, expressionistic brushstrokes and blocky typefaces that change with the narrative tone. The characteristically catchy Seussian rhyme could help turn a Gray Day into a "busy, buzzy" (Yellow) one, and the snazzy die-cut jacket gives this volume an immediate lift above the competition. But the pointed message of *Oh, the Places You'll Go!* and the genius of Seuss's early work go missing.

Kirkus Reviews

SOURCE: A review of *My Many-Colored Days,* in *Kirkus Reviews,* Vol. LXIV, No. 16, August 15, 1996, p. 1246.

Pairing emotions with colors is nothing new to poetry (e.g., Mary O'Neill's *Hailstones and Halibut Bones*), but pairing impressionistic full-color paintings to the text of Dr. Seuss is a first. His formerly unpublished manuscript becomes the basis for a simple color concept book; children will easily identify primary colors and enter into the feeling and mood depicted by the creature in every spread: "On Bright Red Days/how good it feels / to be a horse / and *kick* my heels!" Broad strokes of thick paint on canvas create basic forms with texture, sometimes dark and weighty, sometimes bold and breezy. Those who can set aside preconceived expectations— there is no butter-side-up Seuss here—will find that some of the spreads gracefully elevate poetry that often has feet but no wings.

Hazel Rochman

SOURCE: A review of *My Many Colored Days,* in *Booklist,* Vol. 93, No. 5, November 1, 1996, p. 510.

Thirty years ago, Dr. Seuss wrote this active rhyming verse connecting colors with moods and feelings. The new illustrations are glowing and lively; for each color, a different animal jumps with energy. Pink flamingos dance; a bright red horse kicks its heels; a green fish glides quietly. Why, though, in a book for children, are brown and black only associated with sadness and anger? Would Dr. Seuss have written this today? In the words of Langston Hughes, "The night is beautiful / So the faces of my people."

Ronald Jobe

SOURCE: A review of *My Many Colored Days,* in *School Library Journal,* Vol. 42, No. 12, December, 1996, pp. 105-06.

An amusing look at how color affects children's lives and especially their behavior: red days are good for kicking up one's heels and blue ones for flapping one's wings. Purple days are sad, pink are happy, black are mad, and mixed up—watch out! There is an unevenness and unfinished quality to the text, as the patterned flow appears to be interrupted many times and the word choice gets lost in the rhyme. The artists obviously had fun with this book—an enormous gray owl watchfully peers out at readers, busy bees buzz across a yellow page, a cool fish glides in a green sea, a purple dinosaur sadly drags his tail, and pink leggy flamingos just don't think. Simplistic stylized illustrations, initially reminiscent of children's snow angels or gingerbread cookies, help to create the fantasy by letting the colors speak and have a memorable impact. In fact, they far outshine the words. Youngsters will want to talk about how they feel color, and even the unevenness of the text will not deter them— they will quickly set the book aside and get into their own ideas.

HOORAY FOR DIFFENDOOFER DAY! (written by Jack Prelutsky and illustrated by Lane Smith; from the unfinished manuscript and sketches of Dr. Seuss, 1998)

Publishers Weekly

SOURCE: A review of *Hooray for Diffendoofer Day!* in *Publishers Weekly,* Vol. 245, No. 7, February 16, 1998, p. 211.

Dr. Seuss's name towers over the title on the jacket here, setting up readers to measure the book within— extrapolated from scanty manuscript and sketches—against the late artist's classic works. While such a comparison is almost certain to disappoint, it also distracts from an appreciation of the fruitful collaboration between the ebullient [Jack] Prelutsky *(The Dragons Are Singing Tonight)* and the innovative [Lane] Smith *(The Stinky Cheese Man).* Given some rough art and verses and a list of characters that were compiled by Seuss in 1988 or 1989, Prelutsky and Smith fashion a plot, message and visual milieu. Zesty rhymes, some of them Seuss's own, catalogue the eccentric staff of Diffendoofer School. Then trouble threatens: the students must take a standardized test to prove Diffendoofer's worth, lest the school be closed and everyone sent to Flobbertown ("And we shuddered at the name,/ For *everyone* in Flobbertown/ Does *everything* the same"). The valiant Miss Bonkers inspires her troops. Balancing a globe on one finger, she proudly declaims: "We've taught you that the earth is round,/ That red and white make pink,/ And something else that matters more—/ We've taught you how to think." Smith pastes in some Seuss sketches and invites Seuss characters and book jackets into his collages. The look, however, is very much Smith's; his style is so strong that it subsumes the Seussian elements in evidence (not just the collaged art but the typeface, the colored pages, the tilt of a given character's nose, etc.). Perhaps the richest reward—for adults if not for children—is the absorbing, meaty afterword by editor Janet Schulman, which allows readers a view of Seuss's draft and gives rare insight into the creative process.

From the original sketches for Hooray for Diffendoofer Day!, *illustrated by Dr. Seuss.*

Deborah Stevenson

SOURCE: A review of *Hooray for Diffendoofer Day!* in *Bulletin of the Center for Children's Books,* Vol. 51, No. 10, June, 1998, p. 374.

Students at the very silly Diffendoofer School are faced with the prospect of a test; failure of that test means that they'll have to attend classes in dreary Flobbertown (where "their lunches have no taste at all" and "their dogs are scared to bark"). Fortunately, the students' eccentric education has fitted them perfectly for the exam, which they ace, and the previously worried principal is sufficiently gleeful to abandon his former frown and declare a holiday. This is a fairly entertaining idea, and the rhymes contain some energetic particulars. Unfortunately they also go on rather longer than the story and its elements warrant, and the lines sometimes creak rather than gallop and rely on too-obvious filler for scansion. A multipage afterword (on matte paper to distinguish it from the story proper) includes Geisel's early sketches and text for the story, and it reveals that the clunkiest parts of the text came from the master himself and that Prelutsky has done noble labor not only in expanding the story but in minimizing the flaws of his source material. Smith's art achieves a more effective blend, with cutout Seuss characters (and their creator) mingling with the sharper-edged Smith creations in a bubbling illustrative stew that resembles an MTV homage to Seuss's original plans—young viewers will enjoy identifying those characters who've graced previous Seuss books and matching the newer ones to the sketches in the afterword. This will probably appeal most to kids ready to be retro about their Dr. Seuss experience, especially if they're coveting their siblings' stories of Sachar's Wayside School.

Joanna Rudge Long

SOURCE: A review of *Hooray for Diffendoofer Day!* in *The Horn Book Magazine,* Vol. LXXIV, No. 4, July-August, 1998, pp. 479-81.

After Dr. Seuss's death, editor Janet Schulman retrieved the unfinished manuscript on which this book is based: fourteen pages of sketches, snippets of verse, and jottings of names—but no plot. With becoming respect for both Seuss's unique creativity and their own, Prelutsky and Smith have brought this fragment to fruition in a style that does credit to all three artists. Prelutsky's was the easier task. Long a master of the kind of rib-tickling verse that Seuss pioneered, he has come up with a satisfying conflict: if the kids at freewheeling Diffendoofer School don't pass a demanding test, they'll be sent to school in dreary, regimented Flobbertown. Fortunately, their wacky teachers have taught them how to *think* (a worthy message, though it's hard to fathom just how the pictured classroom activities would have that result, but never mind); therefore, they pass with a resounding "10,000,000%." Since Seuss's entire manuscript is reproduced here as an endnote, it's possible to see how Prelutsky has folded it into his own deliciously Seussian text, which features a preposterous school staff ("Miss Twining teaches tying knots / In neckerchiefs and noodles, / And how to tell chrysanthemums / From miniature poodles," while librarian Miss London " . . . hides behind the shelves / And often cries out, 'LOUDER!' / When we're reading to ourselves"). Illustrations were a greater challenge. Though the absurdity of Smith's art has always been akin to Seuss's antic spirit, his mixed-media collages, with their smoothly rounded forms, complex textures, and subtle palette, are a far cry from the deceptive simplicity of Seuss's deft, airy cartoons. Smith's illustrations here are like translations: satirical renditions, in his own distinctive, sophisticated style, of such zany folk and weirdly expressive settings as Seuss might have dreamed up to finish this book. As an additional tribute, Smith tucks a number of Seuss drawings (e.g., a surprised Horton) into his pictures. It works, and it's fun, though comparing the whimsical energy of Seuss's sketches with Smith's polished art is a telling reminder of what made the good Dr.'s work so popular, and so great. Grown-ups will enjoy figuring out who's responsible for what here. Kids will simply delight in the teachers' outlandish capers. What better honor could be paid to the memory of Dr. Seuss?

Additional coverage of Seuss's life and career is contained in the following sources published by Gale Research: *Contemporary Authors,* Vol. 13-16R; *Contemporary Authors New Revision Series,* Vol. 13; *Dictionary of Literary Biography; Dictionary of Literary Biography Yearbook, Major Authors and Illustrators for Children and Young Adults;* and *Something about the Author,* Vol. 75.

David Small

1945-

American illustrator and author/illustrator of picture books.

Major works include *Eulalie and the Hopping Head* (1982), *Imogene's Antlers* (1985), *Paper John* (1987), *Ruby Mae Has Something to Say* (1992), *George Washington's Cows* (1994), *Fenwick's Suit* (1996).

INTRODUCTION

A respected author and illustrator of picture books for preschool and elementary readers, Small's works are cherished for their positive messages, offbeat characters, and rich watercolor illustrations. Praised for the wit and cleverness of his text, Small notably places his colorful characters—typically human and animal protagonists—in highly unusual circumstances, and then leads readers to delightfully surprising endings. His detailed illustrations are recognized for bringing his stories and humor to life, and have been described as "wonderfully imaginative and inventive," "jolly caricatures" which "brim with humorous details." In his review of *George Washington's Cows,* a *Publishers Weekly* critic praised Small's "opulent and expansive" illustrations and noted the verse as "witty and silly in equal measure." Combining quirky, eccentric characters with positive, traditional lessons has been a successful marriage for Small. Reviewing *Ruby Mae Has Something to Say,* Emily Arnold McCully observed in *The New York Times Book Review,* "David Small tackles the universals—greed, evil, folly, peace and understanding—in a clear-eyed, puckish celebration of personal integrity, eccentricity, even barminess."

Biographical Information

Small was born in Detroit, Michigan, but spent many of his summers in rural Indiana, giving him an appreciation for urban as well as country life. A shy child, he spent much of his free time playing alone. He also was ill for long periods and spent time bedridden. These perimeters encouraged a life of imagination, and he began drawing at an early age. His mother supported his creativity and took him for lessons at the Detroit Institute of Arts. "How I loathed those lessons," Small once commented in *Sixth Book of Junior Authors and Illustrators.* "They never taught me anything I was interested in, such as cartooning or drawing animals." But the lessons introduced him to the galleries of the Institute—the art of the Mexican muralist Diego Rivera, and in general to another world where the "work of the artist is noble and worthy," Small continued. Small had a difficult time in school. "I was a terrible student," he noted in *Something About the Author (SATA),* "painfully shy, much abused by the world around me and unable for many years to be comfortable in it." High school English class was the exception, and he later found his niche in the Art Department at Wayne State University. He went on to earn a master of fine arts degree at Yale and then began his decade-long career as an assistant professor of art, first at Fredonia College at State University of New York and then at Kalamazoo College in his home state of Michigan. Small's first children's book, *Eulalie and the Hopping Head,* was published in 1982. He then began not only writing and illustrating his own works, but providing the pictures for other authors as well. Small has illustrated the texts of such notable writers as Jonathan Swift, Eve Merriam, Milton Meltzer, Beverly Cleary, and his wife, Sarah Stewart. His editorial drawings appear in newspapers in New York, Boston, and Chicago. "Of all things I do now as an artist," Small remarked in *Sixth Book of Junior Authors and Illustrators,* "the creation of children's books is the most pleasurable."

Major Works

Small's goal in creating his books is "to make a real

contribution to children's literature, not simply add to the growing heap." Small stated in *Sixth Book of Junior Authors and Illustrators,* "In my books I have spoken to the concerns I had as a child—those of being different from others, of being an outsider. . . . I think of my books as a kind of dog whistle pitched high above normal human hearing, sending their signal of acceptance to the strange ones out there, telling them to hold on." Small's desire to relay this message is clearly demonstrated in *Imogene's Antlers.* When young Imogene wakes one day to find she has grown antlers, she realizes that not only is there nothing wrong with being different, but there may be some advantages. Her surprising new appearance evokes mostly helpful suggestions from other members of the household, who find creative ways to put the antlers to practical use. Imogene herself takes it all in stride, although the same cannot be said for her mother, who faints regularly at the sight of Imogene's antlers. "Hilarious," reviewer David Gale observed, "with a subtle lesson in acceptance." Small's memorable characters also come to life in *Eulalie and the Hopping Head,* a story in which a toad, Mother Lumps, is impressed by the good behavior of a doll she found when out walking one day with her daughter, Eulalie. A neighbor suggests that the doll's actions could serve as a role model for Eulalie, who often misbehaves. Under the impression that the doll is a human child, they all are puzzled when the doll's head falls off, and even more puzzled when Eulalie slips inside the head and begins rolling around in it. The pages of Small's third picture book, *Paper John,* brim with a "candy-color palette" as he creatively depicts the simple, gentle soul of a character who delights children with his origami. However, John's paper creations are challenged by a devil that threatens to destroy the village by using his mastery over the wind to blow the town into the sea. The devil's plan backfires when the wind he planned to use for evil turns on him, blowing him back to where he came from, and the village is saved when Paper John folds his paper house into a ship and sails the people back to safety. "Small is one of the most inventive illustrators around today," Ilene Cooper acknowledged. "His work, filled with charm and nuance, has a certain quaintness that is uniquely his own. . . . Naturally . . . young eyes will want a second and third look at the rows of paper dolls, angels, and snowflakes that adorn John's one-room house."

Another of Small's eccentric characters, Miss Ruby Mae Foote, has an honorable message of peace she intends to deliver to the United Nations in *Ruby Mae Has Something to Say.* Unfortunately, the only words Ruby Mae delivers are unintended insults and absurdities. She is saved by the clever engineering of her nephew, Billy Bob, who creates an elaborate headpiece that accurately translates Ruby Mae's message for the dignitaries. Her clear speech is short-lived, however, as a passing hawk seizes her large hat, leaving her speechless. After Billy Bob raids the UN kitchen and rigs a second headpiece, Ruby Mae's response to her snickering audience once again demonstrates Small's intent to relay a positive message—it is better to speak plainly and look foolish

than to talk nonsense and look good. "Small has a wonderful way with words," remarked Janice Del Negro. "His text is full of clever touches, and his watercolors are full of energy and vigor." Silliness abounds in *George Washington's Cows,* as Small wittily pokes fun at daily life at Mount Vernon by featuring cows who dress in gowns, scholarly sheep, and pigs who take over for absent servants. Luann Toth noted that "the only thing funnier than this book's lighthearted, irreverent rhyme is its marvelous watercolor artwork." Small's earlier themes of overcoming the obstacles of being an outsider are revisited in *Fenwick's Suit,* whose offbeat character feels that his lack of friends is perhaps due to his image, which he sets out to change by overhauling his wardrobe. His new suit, however, is so popular that his co-workers fail to notice that there is anyone inside of it. A *Kirkus Reviews* critic observed, "Small renders extraordinarily witty watercolors of a bristling, bustling New York City and a suit that just won't quit."

Awards

Eulalie and the Hopping Head was cited on the Library of Congress Children's Books of the Year list and *School Library Journal*'s Best Books for Spring list, both in 1982; it further was honored that year as a Parent's Choice Remarkable Book from Parent's Choice Foundation. *Mean Chickens and Wild Cucumbers* was recognized by the National Council of Social Studies as a Notable Book for Children in the Field of Social Studies in 1983. *Anna and the Seven Swans* appeared on the *School Library Journal* and *Booklist* Best Books lists in 1984, and *The Christmas Box* was cited on the Child Study Association of America's Children's Books of the Year list in 1985. *Imogene's Antlers* received the Parents' Choice Award for literature from the Parents' Choice Foundation in 1985. *Company's Coming* received the Redbook Award, and was recognized as a Notable Book from the American Library Association, both in 1988. *As: A Surfeit of Similes* and *Box and Cox* both received the Parents' Choice Award for picture books in 1989 and 1990, respectively.

TITLE COMMENTARY

📖 *EULALIE AND THE HOPPING HEAD* (1982)

Publishers Weekly

SOURCE: A review of *Eulalie and the Hopping Head,* in *Publishers Weekly,* Vol. 221, No. 10, March 5, 1982, pp. 70-1.

A first in more ways than one, Small's little book is a frolic, enticingly illustrated by ingenious woodland scenes in pretty shades and witty depictions of the anthropomorphic cast. Mrs. Lumps (a toad) takes her toddler Eulalie for a stroll and they meet lofty Mrs. Shinn (a fox), who says her nine children are perfect, a model for Eulalie (who sometimes misbehaves). Mrs. Shinn suggests that Mrs. Lumps take home an abandoned child, lying in the grass, whose exemplary conduct can teach the toad girl lessons in decorum. The lost one is a doll, as readers will recognize, but the mothers believe it's a person like themselves, even when its head keeps coming off and rolling about. One day, Eulalie slips inside the doll's head and sends it leaping all over the Lumpses' yard, creating a dilemma for the motherly toad and the high point of Small's high-larity.

Richard Smith

SOURCE: "A Toad is to Kiss?" in *The New York Times Book Review,* April 25, 1982, p. 45.

This macabre title had me picturing a head, guillotined from its body, hopping around in search of a Vincent Price movie, especially since the copy on the jacket flap asked, "What type of child is this whose head falls off occasionally, and when given the opportunity, hops about the garden on what appear to be two strong little toad legs?" This is the stuff of which nightmares are made. The story is actually cheerfully simplistic. While strolling through the park, Mother Lumps, a toad with an inexcusable name, and her little daughter, Eulalie, find a doll, which they think is a genuine child. They are somewhat puzzled, though, because the doll doesn't walk or talk. To make matters worse, the head keeps falling off, a malfunction the toads attribute to the inherent imperfections of the human race. The next day they take the doll's head out for a walk. Unbeknownst to Mother Lumps, mischievous Eulalie climbs inside the head and begins to hop around. Mother Lumps, though confused at first, finally discovers it is Eulalie who is making the head hop, and they all live happily ever after. The illustrations, by the author, are lovely.

Ilene Cooper

SOURCE: A review of *Eulalie and the Hopping Head,* in *Booklist,* Vol. 78, No. 20, June 15, 1982, p. 1370.

It's offbeat, but those whose senses of humor are slightly askew will appreciate this. The toad Mother Lumps, her irrepressible daughter Eulalie, and Mrs. Shinn, a fox, are out for a stroll when they spy a doll resting against a tree. Assuming it is a real child, they are amazed at its docility, ever-smiling face, and good manners. Mrs. Shinn comments that perhaps Eulalie would do well to emulate its behavior. Indeed. Mischief begins when the doll's head falls off and unbeknownst to her mother, Eulalie crawls inside. She talks through it, eats through it, and eventually hops away. When the trick is finally discovered, Mother Lumps just kisses her errant daughter and says that although one of her two daughters is perfect, she loves the noisy, troublesome

one a thousand times more. Children will have a fine time feeling superior to the characters because they know what's going on while the adult characters do not. The sweet, pastel watercolors are deceiving; seemingly demure, they are really full of comic asides. The piece de résistance is the sight of a doll's head hopping insouciantly through the flowers. It will not easily be forgotten.

Nancy K. Johansen

SOURCE: A review of *Eulalie and the Hopping Head,* in *Language Arts,* Vol, 59, No. 7, October, 1982, p. 747.

After a funny, delightful encounter with a doll believed to be a quiet, apathetic, perfect child, Mrs. Lumps discovers she really prefers Eulalie, her slightly noisy, forgetful daughter, and so does her fastidious friend, Mrs. Shinn, a fox, and mother of nine. The illustrations give a sense of intimacy with color, acting almost as a supplement to the delicate type and detailed pencil drawings. Hilarious characterizations are nicely balanced between full page illustrations and vignettes. Primary readers should enjoy reading, or hearing, or even just looking through this book.

IMOGENE'S ANTLERS (1985)

Publishers Weekly

SOURCE: A review of *Imogene's Antlers,* in *Publishers Weekly,* Vol. 227, No. 8, February 22, 1985, pp. 157-58.

Fully as frolicsome as *Eulalie and the Hopping Head,* Small's new picture book pokes fun at Imogene's hoity-toity family, aghast when she appears at breakfast one morning with antlers growing out of her head. Imogene has problems dressing and getting through doorways. On the whole, though, she enjoys the imposing appendages. So do the kitchen help. They find the antlers handy for drying towels, for hanging doughnuts that Imogene takes outside to feed the birds. "You'll be fun to decorate, come Christmas!" says the cook. But the magic growths vanish as inexplicably as they had appeared, to the momentary relief of Imogene's mother. That distressed woman's fainting spells become worse during the days when Imogene is sporting a glamorous peacock tail. The swift fairytale and its colorful, silly pictures are a dazzling attraction.

David Gale

SOURCE: A review of *Imogene's Antlers,* in *School Library Journal,* Vol. 31, No. 8, April, 1985, pp. 82-3.

Imogene realizes that there's nothing wrong with being different—and that there may even be some advantages—when she awakens one morning with antlers. And what an elaborate pair they are! Undaunted after surmounting the problems of dressing and getting downstairs, Imogene (and the cook and the kitchen maid) realize the merit of antlers as a drying rack, a bird feeder and a candelabra. Her hefty mother, not quite so liberal, reacts to her daughter's predicament by fainting repeatedly. The matter appears to resolve itself the next morning, when an antler-less Imogene appears at breakfast—proudly displaying her new peacock tail. This is one of those special books. Its silliness will entice young listeners to beg for more, while its cleverness will coax adults to reread it willingly. The few words per page, in a large, clear typeface, also make it suitable for the youngest independent readers. Small maximizes the inherent humor of the absurd situation by allowing the imaginative possibilities of Imogene's predicament to run rampant. The brief text is supported by Small's expansive watercolors. They brim with humorous details. His jolly caricatures—whether fatter, more elongated, more egg-headed or more content than the norm—delight with their exaggerated comic reactions. Hilarious, with a subtle lesson in acceptance.

Zena Sutherland

SOURCE: A review of *Imogene's Antlers,* in *Bulletin of the Center for Children's Books,* Vol. 38, No. 9, May, 1985, p. 176.

The members of a very large household react in different ways when young Imogene appears one day with a pair of enormous antlers on her head, an overnight phenomenon. As the day passes, one of the servants finds the antlers useful for drying towels, and another uses them as a multiple feeding station for birds. Imogene's mother faints periodically; Imogene's doctor is baffled. Everyone is delighted, next day, when Imogene pokes her head around the dining room door, antler-free. They're delighted, that is, until they see the rest of Imogene. This ebullient fantasy in the tall tale tradition is told with pace and flair, and it's illustrated with pictures that are as deft as they are funny.

Ilene Cooper

SOURCE: A review of *Imogene's Antlers,* in *Booklist,* Vol. 81, No. 18, June 1, 1985, p. 1406.

Small, who ably demonstrated his talent for writing about the unusual in *Eulalie and the Hopping Head,* has written and illustrated a neat little story that is equally quirky. Young Imogene wakes up one morning to find she has sprouted antlers. Unflappable, Imogene takes the whole thing in stride; the same cannot be said for her mother, who faints every time her daughter comes into view. Perhaps the most practical reaction comes from Mrs. Perkins, the cook, who gives Imogene a doughnut, trims her antlers with a dozen or so more, and comments, "You'll be lots of fun to decorate, come Christmas!" The next morning Imogene awakes to find her antlers

gone, but on the last page, the reader will see that she has grown peacock feathers instead. Small's quaint drawing style is put to good use. The effervescent, softly colored illustrations incorporate all the humor inherent in the tale. A laugh-aloud read-aloud.

Ethel R. Twichell

SOURCE: A review of *Imogene's Antlers,* in *The Horn Book Magazine,* Vol. LXI, No. 4, July-August, 1985, p. 444.

Not many people would treat the appearance of enormous antlers on their heads with the cheerful aplomb of Imogene. Quite unperturbed by the unusual protuberance, the young girl blandly contends with the problems of dressing and the difficulty of maneuvering through her bedroom door. Her mother, quite understandably, faints at the sight, but the rest of the household placidly suggest ways to put the unwanted encumbrance to work. Imogene finds it pleasant to read by the warm oven while dish towels dry on her many prongs, and it is even more fun to be covered with the cook's freshly baked doughnuts and sent into the garden to feed the birds. She has a thoroughly exciting and eventful day, but both Imogene and her family rejoice the next morning to find that the awkward antlers have disappeared. Do not be deceived. Imogene has another surprise in store. The absurd predicament is treated with pleasant tongue-in-cheek humor in the text, and the lively illustrations amusingly bring to life Imogene's swooning mom, mild-mannered dad, and bookish younger brother whose practical responses give the book an endearing and zany logic.

PAPER JOHN (1987)

Kirkus Reviews

SOURCE: A review of *Paper John,* in *Kirkus Reviews,* Vol. LV, No. 8, April 15, 1987, p. 643.

The imaginative creator of *Imogene's Antlers* and *Eulalie and the Hopping Head* presents a benevolent character who can make anything he needs from paper, in a parable concerning the triumph of the creative imagination over the mean-spirited.

John, who resembles Leslie Brooke's Simple Simon, comes to a seaside, cobble-stoned, Victorian town where he sells paper flowers and builds a lacquered paper house adorned with pinwheels and other fanciful paper constructions. He folds boats for the children, and is so good-natured that people say he could even get along with the devil. But when John catches a little gray devil instead of a fish, the ungrateful devil demands food and lodging, and then picks pockets in the market square before escaping via John's golden sunburst kite. After John sends a paper falcon to puncture the kite, the devil invokes the four winds to destroy the town, but John rescues everyone by quickly refolding his house into a ship, and the winds blow the devil back wherever he came from.

Small's illustrations—full of entrancing detail including not only his cut and folded confections but a multitude of animals and the bulbously stupid-looking winds—are as good as he's done. A good choice for sharing aloud or for children to read on their own.

Betsy Hearne

SOURCE: A review of *Paper John,* in *Bulletin of the Center for Children's Books,* Vol. 40, No. 10, June, 1987, p. 197.

Paper John is a gentle, good-humored man of whom "it was said he could get along with the devil himself. And . . . he soon had the chance." While John is making a kite in his lacquered paper house by the sea one night, the fishing poles he has hung out the window hook a devil who demands food and a bed, then follows John to the market place and pick-pockets the populace. When the devil tries to escape via John's kite, however, John folds a paper falcon to bring it down; and when the devil causes a great storm, John folds his house into a boat and rescues the townsfolk. Paper John has all the makings of a folk hero, and the story has a quixotic yet solid quality that's well substantiated by the author's watercolor art. Some of the characters and scenes depicted through vividly sequenced illustrations are Dickensian in tone, especially the devil and the town setting. Paper John will hook, along with his devil, any youngster's imagination.

Ilene Cooper

SOURCE: A review of *Paper John,* in *Booklist,* Vol. 83, No. 20, June 15, 1987, p. 1608.

Paper John is a gentle soul who arrives in the village and delights children and adults with his origami. Paper flowers, masks, and birds are among his creations; he even makes a paper house for himself—lacquered to keep the water out. John's kindness is well known, so not surprisingly, when he sees a crabby gray-colored man tangled in his fishing line, he pulls him out and gives him shelter and food. But this little man is no ordinary fellow. A devil in the true sense of the word, he repays John's kindness by stealing the villagers' money and escaping in John's magnificent paper kite. When the wicked one is shot down by one of John's paper falcons, he uses his mastery over the wind to destroy the village. But in performing its evil deed, the gusty wind also turns on the devil, blowing him back to where he came from. John, in his paper boat, saves the townsfolk, who want to reward him by appointing him mayor. John declines, however, content to live his simple life, surrounded by his friends and paper creations. Small is one of the most inventive illustrators around today. His work,

filled with charm and nuance, has a certain quaintness that is uniquely his own. The candy-color palette he uses to depict the village life contrasts well with the nasty little gray devil and the leaden sky that is home to the multi-headed wind. Naturally, paper figures and shapes are strewn liberally throughout the pictures, and young eyes will want a second and third look at the rows of paper dolls, angels, and snowflakes that adorn John's one-room house.

Ethel R. Twichell

SOURCE: A review of *Paper John,* in *The Horn Book Magazine,* Vol. LXIII, No. 5, September-October, 1987, p. 603.

Fortunate is the village where John has chosen to settle. An amiable, gentle soul, he quickly endears himself to young and old with the enchanting flowers and boats he folds out of brightly colored paper. Even more beguiling is his paper house, complete with a paper chimney and paper smoke. The brightly lit pictures perfectly mesh the busy, bustling life of the small seaside town with the fantasy of John's creations and the appearance of a particularly nasty little devil who is caught in John's fishing lines. When the devil calls up a violent storm and the villagers and their cats, dogs, and tea sets are blown into the sea, John brings everyone safely to shore by simply refolding his little house into a sturdy rescue boat. All the fun and nonsense are brought to life in the lively, sun-washed illustrations. Pigs and geese, rollicking children, and bonnet-clad women frolic across the pages, adding even more zest and enjoyment to a well-paced highly original story.

Margery Fisher

SOURCE: A review of *Paper John,* in *Growing Point,* Vol. 27, No. 5, January, 1989, p. 5104.

Tall and meditative, Paper John takes up residence in a seaside town where in his paper house, lacquered against weather, he makes boats for the children to sell but brings danger to the town when he fishes up the Devil in a most injudicious rescue. The bizarre story, with its traditional flavour, is illustrated in idiosyncratic scenes crowded with small details; there is a vaguely Victorian feeling in costume and physiognomy and a subtle sense of the entrance into a real world of a strangely alien personage.

Donnarae MacCann and Olga Richard

SOURCE: "Picture Books for Children," in *Wilson Library Bulletin,* Vol. 64, No. 10, June, 1990, pp. 114-15.

[In *Paper John,*] John is a paper sculptor who secures a lodging, a livelihood, and numerous young friends by means of his craft. Lacquered paper suffices as home-building material. Paper ornaments and toys are sold on market days. John even resorts to folding paper sheep when the devil's snores keep him awake. The devil enters the story as a two-bit criminal who picks pockets and possesses just one supernatural trick: the power to command the four winds. He imposes upon John's hospitality because the most notable thing about John is his good nature. As rumor has it, "he could get along with the devil himself." When Paper John upsets the devil's escape plan, the winds are unleashed upon the seaside town and only John's quick conversion of his paper house into a paper boat saves the drowning townsfolk.

David Small uses a third-person narration almost exclusively, yet the main characterization is so original that the quieter storytelling style (in contrast to the dramatic method in the Christelow book) is not a drawback. Moreover, we do hear the devil and John in one exchange that underscores their differences:

> As soon as he was set free of the lines, [the devil] cried in a whining voice, "I'm hungry!"
>
> "Hungry? Why then, you shall eat!" exclaimed Paper John.
>
> "Where shall I sit?" the devil demanded.
>
> "Sit here," said Paper John, quickly making a seat and a table, on which he served a supper of bread, cheese, and fish.
>
> The devil ate greedily, then yawned. "I'm tired," he announced. "Where shall I sleep?"

The relationship between this devil and the villagers comes to a hair-raising climax, but throughout most of this period piece we see an assortment of children befriending Paper John and serving as a calm, folksy background for the more vigorous confrontation. The relaxed style accentuates this element of warmth and affection.

COMPANY'S COMING (written by Arthur Yorinks, 1988)

Publishers Weekly

SOURCE: A review of *Company's Coming,* in *Publishers Weekly,* Vol. 233, No. 4, January 29, 1988, p. 429.

When a flying saucer lands in the yard, and two aliens emerge, Shirley promptly invites them in for dinner. Her husband, less sanguine, phones the FBI, and they call in the military. By the time the visitors return, the house is surrounded by soldiers and tanks. As her relatives faint with apprehension, Shirley unwraps the gift the aliens offer. Her trust is rewarded, for the box contains a quite harmless blender ("And we don't even have one," she exclaims). Now assured of the aliens' peaceful intentions, everyone sits down together for a homemade meal. [Arthur] Yorinks displays his talent for droll, surprising humor in this offbeat tale about trust and hospitality. Through deliberate exaggeration and

absurdity, he pokes fun at paranoid and militaristic responses to perceived threats from those different from ourselves—a timely message indeed. Small's illustrations reflect the story's quirkiness and humor, from Shirley and Moe's broad gestures and shrugs, to the bug-like aliens who understand the value of a nice appliance and a warm welcome.

David Gale

SOURCE: A review of *Company's Coming,* in *School Library Journal,* Vol. 34, No. 6, February, 1988, p. 66.

Two aliens land in Moe and Shirley's backyard on the same day that Shirley has invited the cousins for dinner. Out of nervousness, Shirley invites the aliens to join them. Moe, fearing that they will be atomized, calls in the FBI, the Pentagon, and the military as Shirley prepares the potato salad. The house is surrounded with tanks, jets, and helicopters when the aliens return—carrying what cousin Etta fears is a laser, but which is actually a blender ("We thought you'd like it. And it was on sale!"). The dry humor and deadpan telling of this suburban science fiction tale will delight young readers and listeners. Small's watercolors show wonderful idiosyncracies of the caricatured cousins and small, round bug-like aliens. These pictures extend the hilarity of the text, as in the slap-stick fainting reactions and the scene of a huge missile—on the dining room table—aimed at the box. This thoroughly enjoyable picture book view of faulty assumptions and over-reacting will be a welcome guest.

THE MONEY TREE (written by Sara Stewart, 1991)

Publishers Weekly

SOURCE: A review of *The Money Tree,* in *Publishers Weekly,* Vol. 238, No. 39, August 30, 1991, p. 83.

From the window of her cozy farmhouse, Miss McGillicuddy notices "an unusual shape" poking through the snow. By spring it has grown into an oddly configured tree the branches of which are laden not with leaves but with dollar bills. Word of this extravagant foliage spreads fast and far, and all summer long the woman watches quietly as townsfolk and strangers greedily pick money from her tree. After its leaves drop to the ground and winter arrives once again, Miss McGillicuddy decides to chop down the tree, and she is left with something very valuable indeed: wood that will keep her warm during the coldest months. Though its message may be beyond the reach of some readers, [Sarah] Stewart's first book will raise worthwhile questions for both children and adults. Yet more exceptional than the story are Small's (*Paper John*) paintings. Often reminiscent of the art of Carl Larsson, these evocative, pastel-filled watercolors echo the hushed, mysterious tone of the tale.

Hanna B. Zeiger

SOURCE: A review of *The Money Tree,* in *The Horn Book Magazine,* Vol. LXVIII, No. 1, January-February, 1992, p. 62.

Miss McGillicuddy leads a rich and purposeful existence. In January, she makes a quilt; in February, she flies a kite; and in May, she invites the neighborhood children to dance around a Maypole. She plants vegetables, tends her flowers, and cares for the farm animals. Paralleling her activities through the seasons is the growth of a strange tree on her land. She first notices the strange shape in January and in February decides the small tree is a "'gift from the birds.'" By spring the tree has grown large, and, as the children circle the Maypole, she gently picks some of the tree's green foliage—shaped like dollar bills of many denominations—to give as party favors. Soon the children's parents appear to see the tree, and Miss McGillicuddy offers them cuttings. Next, town officials arrive to ask for greenery for special projects. Soon there are complete strangers carrying bags and baskets away from the tree, and by harvest time crowds surge around the tree night and day. Miss McGillicuddy is seemingly unconcerned as she observes this frenetic activity; but in autumn, when the strange leaves turn brown, she sighs with relief. In December, she and some neighborhood boys chop the tree down for firewood. As she sits beside her cozy, roaring fire, she smiles to herself. David Small's charming and detailed illustrations portray a strong, independent woman whose life is graceful and meaningful—the kind of person who would be friends with Barbara Cooney's Miss Rumphius. Though the book can be enjoyed as a portrait of a life with a touch of fantasy, it could also lead to some interesting discussions about contemporary values.

📖 *FIGHTING WORDS* (written by Eve Merriam, 1992)

Carolyn Phelan

SOURCE: A review of *Fighting Words,* in *Booklist,* Vol. 88, No. 18, May 15, 1992, p. 1688.

Leda lives in the city, and Dale lives across the river on a farm. Jealous of each other's life-style, they meet for a fight. Chasing each other through cityscape and countryside, they hurl insults: "Leda strikes. NINCOMPOOP / NUMSKULL / NITWIT. Dale counterattacks. BUFFOON / BLUNDERBUSS / BLOCKHEAD," until they lose their voices and call it quits, agreeing to fight again soon. Illustrating the power of words as well as the richness of the dictionary, the late poet Eve Merriam indulged in the sort of anarchic wordplay that will delight kids. After all, this picture book is devoted to the words that teachers really don't want to hear, no matter how much they urge children to use words rather than fists. Merriam must have considered contemporary kids' insult repertoire limited; certainly readers will learn a few new invectives like *poppycock, piffle,* and *dolt.*

Small's captivating ink-and-watercolor artwork sets the war of words in a variety of entertaining settings. An original.

Luann Toth

SOURCE: A review of *Fighting Words,* in *School Library Journal,* Vol. 38, No. 6, June, 1992, p. 99.

Dale and Leda are best enemies. Since the grass is indeed always greener . . . the children are each envious of the very things that the other perceives as misfortune. They meet halfway between Dale's country and Leda's city home, square off to do battle, and let the insults fly. The two larger-than-life cartoon figures proceed on an energetic romp through the city streets, a sports stadium, the zoo, across the river, and into the countryside hurling hilarious and often outrageous epithets back and forth. While the invectives are truly inventive and amusing, they are all harmless and in good fun. Merriam shares with readers that "All these fighting words live happily, harmoniously together in the Oxford English Dictionary and in Webster's Unabridged." The youngsters take center stage in the quirky pen-and-ink and watercolor drawings with perfect facial expressions to match each verbal assault; the miniature urban and rural landscapes seem to be populated with action figures and littered with matchbox vehicles. Of course, the combatants shake hands, compliment one another on "' . . . a good fight,'" and agree to meet again soon. A sly and silly salute to the power of words.

📖 *RUBY MAE HAS SOMETHING TO SAY* (1992)

Janice Del Negro

SOURCE: A review of *Ruby Mae Has Something to Say,* in *Booklist,* Vol. 88, No. 21, July, 1992, p. 1945.

Miss Ruby Mae Foote wants to deliver a message of peace to the United Nations, but nothing she says comes out the way she intends it. To the rescue comes her young nephew Billy Bob, who invents the "Bobatron," a gadget made from kitchen equipment. When placed on his aunt's head, the device (usually hidden under a hat) transforms her into a silver-tongued orator. Unfortunately, on her visit to the [United Nations] a bird seizes both hat and gadget, shattering Ruby Mae's confidence. Her message comes out garbled—until Billy Bob races to the UN kitchen, reconstructs the Bobatron, and puts it back on his aunt's head. Small has a wonderful way with words. His text is full of clever touches, and his watercolors are full of energy and vigor. While Ruby Mae's message (it is better to speak plainly and look foolish than to talk nonsense and look good) is something of an anticlimax after the frenetic buildup Small gives it, words of wisdom are often much plainer than we'd like.

Kirkus Reviews

SOURCE: A review of *Ruby Mae Has Something to Say,* in *Kirkus Reviews,* Vol. LX, No. 13, July 1, 1992, p. 855.

A satirical parable, buoyed up by delicious visual whimsy. Ruby Mae lives in tiny Nada, Texas, where her home is "World Headquarters for Universal Peace and Understanding." Unfortunately, she's so tongue-tied that she can't even get a neighborly greeting right, much less realize her dream of delivering her message to the United Nations. Then young Billy Bob—using a colander and other kitchen paraphernalia—is able to engineer an extraordinary headpiece that frees his aunt's powers of speech. Wearing giant hats over Billy Bob's contraption, Ruby Mae is elected governor and is finally invited to the UN—where a passing hawk seizes her huge hat (ornamented with doves), leaving her literally speechless. Raiding the UN kitchen, Billy Bob quickly rigs an alternate that makes Ruby Mae a figure of fun, sending the delegates into giggles but also nicely setting up her punch line: " . . . you have only to speak plainly, even though you may look foolish. This is a thousand times better than looking good and talking nonsense." Small's deftly limned illustrations, bursting with witty caricatures and details (including Ruby Mae's final Statue of Liberty pose), make it easy for readers to lighten up, too. Sensible message; good fun.

Publishers Weekly

SOURCE: A review of *Ruby Mae Has Something to Say,* in *Publishers Weekly,* Vol. 239, No. 30, July 6, 1992, pp. 55-6.

Small's *(Imogene's Antlers)* keen sense of fun and comic flair infiltrate both the text and the cartoony pictures that tell this winning story of Ruby Mae Foote, whose Texas home is the World Headquarters for Universal Peace and Understanding. Because the speech of this tongue-tied, engagingly disheveled woman often sounds like gibberish, it seems unlikely that she will ever fulfill her dream of delivering a message of peace at the United Nations. But her nephew, Billy Bob, wires some kitchen utensils onto an old colander, thus creating the "Bobatron"—a hatlike device that enables Ruby Mae to speak articulately and intelligently. Billy Bob comes to his aunt's rescue when a bird flies off with her Bobatron, and Ruby Mae at last gets her chance to share her important message with the world. Even the youngest readers will benefit from the wisdom of Ruby Mae's simple declaration, and they will be highly amused by the goings-on leading up to it.

Kate McClelland

SOURCE: A review of *Ruby Mae Has Something to Say,* in *School Library Journal,* Vol. 38, No. 9, September, 1992, p. 212.

Ruby Mae Foote, whose dream of delivering a message of "universal peace and understanding" before the United Nations, is thwarted by her inability to speak clearly without garbling and mixing up her words. Her nephew's wacky invention, the "Bobatron," which is assembled from kitchen gadgets and worn on the head, gives Ruby Mae the confidence to conquer public speaking. When she loses the Bobatron just before her speech, she is unable to carry on until her young nephew rushes to the UN kitchen to construct another, enabling her to declaim that it is better to speak clearly even though you look foolish than to look good while talking nonsense. While Small excels in blending whimsy with wisdom, both may elude young readers. Some of Ruby Mae's garbled gabble is quite funny when read aloud, but much of the humor will be lost on children who do not "get" the wordplay or grasp the abstractions. Unfortunately, when the hapless Ruby Mae is faced with the necessity of speaking without her support mechanism, she cannot. Furthermore, her declaration that " . . . to achieve universal peace and understanding on this planet, you have only to speak plainly" is simplistic in the extreme and may be downright misleading. . . . Still if children have never heard of the UN or considered the meaning of "universal peace and understanding," this may be a lighthearted place to begin.

Patricia Riley

SOURCE: A review of *Ruby Mae Has Something to Say,* in *The Horn Book Guide to Children's and Young Adult Books,* Vol. IV, No. 1, Spring, 1993, p. 46.

When tongue-tied Ruby Mae wears her nephew's contraption on her head, she speaks eloquently and is invited to the United Nations to deliver a "message of universal peace and understanding." Although Small's watercolors are whimsical and energetic, his use of a speech defect is not particularly amusing, and Ruby Mae's message doesn't live up to expectations.

PETEY'S BEDTIME STORY (written by Beverly Cleary, 1993)

Publishers Weekly

SOURCE: A review of *Petey's Bedtime Story,* in *Publishers Weekly,* Vol. 240, No. 28, July 12, 1993, p. 80.

Petey is a kid who actually likes bedtime—even if he never quite gets to bed. The energetic boy splashes wildly in his bath before bounding into the lap of his sleepy mother for a bedtime story. After his yawning father reads him yet another one, the boy induces his patient parents to search under the bed for monsters and to listen to an endless recitation of prayers in which he blesses everyone he knows and says good night to each object in his room. And then he demands that they recount the events of the night he was born. When his father suggests that Petey tell the story this time, the child embellishes it with made-up details that young readers will relish—when he was born, he reports, he "was wearing a bow tie and cowboy boots." Because his parents are sound asleep when he finishes his tale, Petey climbs out of bed, heads to the kitchen for a box of cookies and devours them all in his parents' bed, leaving plenty of crumbs. Cleary's text is as buoyant and amiable as its hero, and both his real and fabricated antics are captured cleverly in Small's (*Imogene's Antlers*) stylized pen-and-ink and watercolor pictures, which have an appealing 1950s flavor.

GEORGE WASHINGTON'S COWS (1994)

Publishers Weekly

SOURCE: A review of *George Washington's Cows,* in *Publishers Weekly,* Vol. 241, No. 35, August 29, 1994, p. 78.

Witty and silly in equal measure, Small's (*Ruby Mae Has Something to Say*) cheeky expose about the real reason the father of our country went into politics works on a number of conceptual levels. George Washington's farm is home to a host of precocious animals, including some secretive, moody cows ("They had to be dressed in lavender gowns / and bedded on cushions of silk / . . . / Begged every hour in obsequious tones, / Or they just wouldn't give any milk"); house-servant hogs ("Always polite and impeccably dressed, / They were certainly well-bred swine"); and a crew of scholarly sheep bent on mastering the mysteries of the universe. Illustrations are opulent and expansive, with both the overall conceits and the characters' costumes wonderfully imaginative and inventive. Buoyant rhymed couplets have an across-the-board appeal, while the sly political joke that doses the tale will satisfy adults primarily: George, stymied by the animals ("My cows wear dresses, my pigs wear wigs / And my sheep are more learned than me"), is last seen in a famous pose, being ferried across the Delaware, and saying, "Sell the Farm . . . I'll try Politics!" Smart entertainment.

Kirkus Reviews

SOURCE: A review of *George Washington's Cows,* in *Kirkus Reviews,* Vol. LXII, No. 18, September 15, 1994, p. 1281.

The night they drove poor George Washington into politics. His fussbudget cows demand to be swaddled in lavender gowns and bedded on silk. His hogs have all the cultivated solicitude of Jeeves. His sheep pretend to great knowledge. All this is way too much for George, who decides it's better to brave the perils of revolution than stay home on the farm. Small's rhymes are a delight—fun, smart, quick. His illustrations have the same measure of sharp humor: The animals very much take on their roles as dowdy frumps or amiable hoteliers or pathetic, self-important scholars. Everything is turned on its head—clod to preciousness, slob to Mrs. Grundy, idiot to savant—with such good humor that every character emerges as a hero. And, in the process, history is rewritten, fashioned to a reality more compelling than a list of the places George slept.

Small may be on to a brand of you-were-there history that could yield some important understandings.

Kathy Broderick

SOURCE: A review of *George Washington's Cows,* in *Booklist,* Vol. 91, No. 5, November 1, 1994, p. 510.

With his usual flair and sense of humor, Small spoofs daily life at Mount Vernon. A rhyming text introduces the ridiculously pampered life of Washington's cows: "They had to be dressed in lavender gowns / and bedded on cushions of silk, / Fed on a diet of jam and cream scones, / Frequently sprayed with expensive colognes, / Begged every hour in obsequious tones, / Or they just wouldn't give any milk." Small's watercolors immeasurably extend his zany poem and make maximum use of the double-page spreads. Cleverly designed and well-executed scenes are filled with silly details that children will love (like the anthropomorphised farm animals dressed in historical garb and the facial expressions that reveal just what the various human characters are thinking). Small continues his tale with visions of gracious, helpful pigs and serious, scholarly sheep. All of this is very trying for [George Washington], so he takes off across the Delaware. And who could blame him?

Luann Toth

SOURCE: A review of *George Washington's Cows,* in *School Library Journal,* Vol. 41, No. 1, January, 1995, p. 94.

You may very well wonder how a man who could not tell a lie ever found his way into the political arena. Well, according to this outlandish historical tall tale, it all began at Mount Vernon. In description befitting the larger-than-life legend, Small relates the trials and tribulations that face gentleman farmer George Washington. As he is forced to cope with extraordinarily fussy cows, dandified pigs, and intellectually superior sheep, it soon becomes apparent that the man is simply not cut out for country living and he jumps at the chance to make a career change. The only thing funnier than this book's lighthearted, irreverent rhyme is its marvelous watercolor artwork. In accurately rendered detail, the artist's engaging double-spread cartoons depict the interiors and grounds of the historical site, and deftly incorporate the engaging, decidedly eccentric cast of characters, all in period costume. The future father of our country laments, "My cows wear dresses, my pigs wear wigs,/ And my sheep are more learned than me./ In all my days on the farm I've seen/ nothing to equal such tricks." Washington takes a backseat here, but, as is often the case, the forces that motivate greatness are many, varied, and wide open for speculation.

📖 *THE LIBRARY* (written by Sarah Stewart, 1995)

Ilene Cooper

SOURCE: A review of *The Library,* in *Booklist,* Vol. 91, No. 14, March 15, 1995, p. 1338.

Although there is no author's note, this picture book is dedicated to the memory of the real librarian who inspired it. The story begins with young Elizabeth Brown, who doesn't like dolls or skates but instead prefers to spend her time reading. She reads through childhood and college, and as an adult, she spends her money on books, books, and more books. It's a little difficult to incorporate some of the concepts into the pithy, rhyming text. For instance: "The form was for donations. / She quickly wrote this line: 'I, E. Brown, gives to the town / All that was ever mine.'" The next page shows a library with her name on the sign. Did she donate the books to a library, which was then named after her, or did she actually help build the building? It's a testament to [Sarah] Stewart and Small's collaboration that the book works as well as it does. The story of a spinster who does nothing but read isn't the most scintillating of topics, but Elizabeth's life takes on gentle humor as she is shown reading while standing on her head or trying to vacuum and read at the same time. Small's framed pastel artwork uses wonderfully unique perspectives, showing rooms with roaring fireplaces and books piled high to the ceiling. Reading has never looked quite so delicious.

Publishers Weekly

SOURCE: A review of *The Library,* in *Publishers Weekly,* Vol. 242, No. 15, April 18, 1995, p. 61.

The creators of *The Money Tree* paint a blithe yet affectionate portrait of a woman whose life centers on reading. Elizabeth Brown's obsession begins in childhood: "She didn't like to play with dolls, / She didn't like to skate. / She learned to read quite early / And at an incredible rate." Stewart's nimble verse follows the bibliophile through the years as she fills her home with books. Finally, "when volumes climbed the parlor walls / And blocked the big front door, / She had to face the awful fact / She could not have one more." Elizabeth then decides to share her wealth: she donates her collection to the town, turns her home into a library and—of course—continues to read voraciously. Attuned to the story's humor and period setting, Small's (*George Washington's Cows*) airy illustrations charm with historical touches and soothing pastel hues. Triple-ruled black borders and filigreed corners suggest a family album of old, while black-and-white spot art highlights details of a singular life.

Rebecca Pepper Sinkler

SOURCE: A review of *The Library,* in *The New York Times Book Review,* June 4, 1995, p. 25.

Everybody knows an Elizabeth Brown. She's the little girl who was born with a library card, was reading before she was out of diapers and got her first pair of Coke-bottle glasses in kindergarten. In *The Library,* Sarah Stewart rhymes her way through Elizabeth's entire life, a dozen jaunty lines to a page at most, just enough to put a small reader happily to bed, where, if she's like Elizabeth, "with a flashlight under the sheet . . . she'd make a tent of covers and read herself to sleep."

David Small's pale watercolors are splashed with occasional bright accents—as vibrant and quirky as Elizabeth Brown herself. Parents may worry about their own little bookworms, but you won't waste a moment fretting about how this small redhead will turn out. She may be "skinny, nearsighted and shy," but public opinion 'means nothing to our Lizzie. And she learns early what many of us come to late: it's a rare social occasion that bests staying up reading.

Every addiction has its downside, of course. With compulsive readers it's a tendency to bump into doors, not to mention a life-threatening accumulation of volumes. And so it is with Elizabeth: "Books were piled on top of chairs. / And spread across the floor. / Her shelves began to fall apart. / As she read more and more." (A double spread of Elizabeth's teetering stacks may hit a little too close to home for some of us.) But she finally comes out of denial, faces her powerlessness and quits—buying books, not *reading*.

And what would a savvy single woman in latish middle age do with a lifetime's collection of literature? The title gives it away. In a cathartic move, she renounces all material goods—except, if you look closely, her cat, her teacup and her reading lamp.

No one familiar with Mr. Small's work will be surprised by the way he amplifies the quite simple verses. He never dominates Ms. Stewart's text; instead, the author and illustrator of *Imogene's Antlers* and *George Washington's Cows* grounds the action of this story in time and place. This is quintessential small-town America beginning in, say, the 1930s and running up till right now, judging by the backward baseball caps worn by youngsters outside the library. It's those touches that have won Mr. Small his deserved reputation and that earn this book its rightful designation "for all ages." It's a joy to look at, from its delicately framed full-page illustrations to the witty doodads that fill the white spaces around the smaller ones. The pacing seems perfect and there is just enough detail to linger over, never so much as to slow the story. After the fifth reading or so, a young child should love counting cats—one on practically every page.

As for Elizabeth, her renunciation pays off: unburdened

of possessions, she now acquires a nice bookish companion, visiting rights to her precious books, the gratitude of an entire small town and a chance to read her way through the rest of her years. You could do worse than be Elizabeth Brown.

Ann A. Flowers

SOURCE: A review of *The Library,* in *The Horn Book Magazine,* Vol. 71, No. 4, July-August, 1995, p. 454.

As in *The Money Tree,* the author and illustrator have created another strong, independent, iconoclastic heroine. *The Library* follows the life of omnivorous reader Elizabeth Brown, who learns to read early and stays up reading until late. She scorns dates and keeps trysts with good books. Finally settling down as a tutor, Elizabeth Brown tries to read her way through all the books in existence. Her house grows more and more crowded until finally, in desperation, she gives her house and its contents to the town for a library. This deeply satisfying story is told in simple rhyme; the illustrations of glorious piles of more and more books and of happy, red-headed Elizabeth Brown and a friend reading by the fire, each with a cat in her lap and a cup of tea, depict the acme of utter bliss for bibliomaniacs.

Peggy J. Latkovich

SOURCE: A review of *The Library,* in *School Library Journal,* Vol. 42, No. 9, September, 1996, p. 156.

When Sarah Stewart's *The Library* was published librarians across the country looked at the endearing character of Elizabeth Brown and shouted "That's me!" Anyone who grows up with as intense a love of books as Elizabeth is bound to bond with libraries in one way or another. This sweet, simple story has now been issued in video and audio formats. The female narrator gives a warm, approachable reading to Stewart's gently humorous verse. The sprightly cello soundtrack suits the text perfectly. A few subtle sound effects enhance the story. In the video version, David Small's softly shaded line drawings are panned to pick out the details which best describe the text. The whimsical, yet not altogether unrealistic story is a good choice for story hours and a pleasant introduction to the library for young or library-phobic children.

📖 *HOOVER'S BRIDE* (1995)

Kirkus Reviews

SOURCE: A review of *Hoover's Bride,* in *Kirkus Reviews,* Vol. LXIII, No. 17, September 1, 1995, p. 1288.

More rhymed foolery from Small, with an ending that may seem cold-hearted to some, and subtexts that don't bear too much scrutiny. When Hoover, a balding, mid-

dle-aged bachelor, sees Elektra the vacuum cleaner sweeping up mountains of dust, he falls rapturously in love. They are soon married ("While this seems like the strangest alliance,/I now pronounce you Man and Appliance"), but their honeymoon at the posh Hotel Dunes is interrupted when Elektra runs off with a newlywed power mower from across the hall. Hoover and the mower's spouse have their marriages annulled and live happily ever after; the eloping machines meet a harsher fate at the city dump. The moral: "It's good to have humans aboard/When you run out of gas, or run out of cord." In the cleanly drawn watercolors Elektra, a small canister model, peeps coyly up from the floor as genteel humans react with comically exaggerated gestures and expressions. As usual, Small displays both sharp wit and a lively imagination, but this is flat next to his other books, which are mostly about the value of being different rather than its perils.

Publishers Weekly

SOURCE: A review of *Hoover's Bride,* in *Publishers Weekly,* Vol. 242, No. 43, October 23, 1995, p. 68.

Kids who appreciate the preposterous will giggle over this rhyming romp by the author of *Ruby Mae Has Something to Say.* After a vacuum cleaner rids his home of mountains of dust, a man named Hoover falls madly in love with it. Draped with a bridal veil, Elektra rolls down the church aisle alongside her groom; a priest says, "While this seems like the strangest alliance,/ I now pronounce you Man and Appliance." Alas, the union is short-circuited when the honeymooners encounter another odd couple: a woman and a lawn mower. When the machines disappear (together, perhaps?), Hoover sets his sights on the mower's jilted wife. After viewing the newly hitched humans happily sprucing up their grand home (she mows, he cleans), readers turn the page to find mower and vacuum rusting in a junkyard: "They learned that it's good to have humans aboard / When you run out of gas, or run out of cord." Enticingly droll visuals include Hoover placing a diamond ring on the end of Elektra's hose, and a chef pulling the mechanical bride's plug after she sucks up all the goodies on the buffet table.

Virginia Golodetz

SOURCE: A review of *Hoover's Bride,* in *School Library Journal,* Vol. 41, No. 11, November, 1995, p. 107.

The front cover of this book is in the form of a formal wedding invitation and it invites readers to the marriage of man and machine at the swanky Dunes Hotel. How Oliver Hoover and his bride Elektra, a Vac-U-Lux model #O-U-QT vacuum cleaner, met and were married is told in amusing rhyming couplets. When Mr. Hoover finds his bride missing, he quickly takes steps to find her, but gets off the track when he meets a woman in similar

While taking his usual solitary walk at lunch, Fenwick was stopped in his tracks by the sight of a fabulous suit in a tailor's window.

"Why not?" he said, and stepped down into the quiet shop.

From Fenwick's Suit, *written and illustrated by David Small.*

distress. Her husband, a power lawn mower, is also missing. The human couple fall in love immediately, are married, and live happily ever after, she pushing a hand mower and he flitting about with a feather duster. And the machines? They are seen rusting in the city junk yard, unable to go anywhere without humans to provide the power. The moral: Humans shouldn't depend solely on machines because they can't get anywhere by themselves. The witty cartoon illustrations in watercolor, pen, and black ink are well suited to the nonsense verse. Even though the couplets don't scan perfectly, the humor carries them. This story may be outrageous for some, but it's all in fun and the moral makes it worth considering in these machine-dominated times.

Leone McDermott

SOURCE: A review of *Hoover's Bride*, in *Booklist*, Vol. 92, No. 11, February 1, 1996, p. 939.

This exuberantly loopy romance will delight the silly. Hoover is a bachelor whose slovenliness has led to mountainous piles of dust inside his home. Following an interior avalanche, he is reformed by the timely loan of a vacuum cleaner. In this case, cleanliness is next to amorousness, and Hoover falls head over heels in love with the gleaming machine: "Her name was Elektra. He bought her a ring—/ And he didn't buy her just any old thing./ A grapefruit-size diamond was what Hoover chose / In a size that would fit on the end of her hose." After being pronounced Man and Appliance, the two head for a honeymoon by the sea, where they encounter another mixed couple, a woman with a lawnmower for a husband. Alas, mechanical love proves fickle, as lawnmower and vacuum cleaner shortly run off with each other. But Hoover and his new lady friend soon find annulments and a more conventional life together. Family values triumph again.

FENWICK'S SUIT (1996)

Publishers Weekly

SOURCE: A review of *Fenwick's Suit*, in *Publishers Weekly*, Vol. 243, No. 30, July 22, 1996, p. 240.

Clad in bow tie and hitched-up trousers, nerdy Fenwick muses that perhaps his dress is responsible for his lack of friends. He spies a solution in a tailor's window: a flashy yellow-and-red windowpane-check suit ("It's you!" the tailor insists), which propels him to strut, strike humorous poses and leap around. The next day, while Fenwick recuperates at home from his taxing day, the suit takes off on its own and becomes the life of the office, exuding so much personality and confidence that Fenwick's co-workers don't notice that no one is inside. Feeling more inadequate than ever, Fenwick tries to stuff the suit in a box: "The suit threaded its way through the crowd . . . Fenwick collared the suit and hemmed it in." But the suit escapes, swells to 20 times its size and, wearing Fenwick like a handkerchief in its pocket, sails over the city until the desperate fellow "grabbed an errant thread and bailed out." Small's (*The Library*) animated, comical illustrations, which have a cartoonish, '30s quality, add visual wit, but they aren't enough to compensate for an abrupt, almost arbitrary ending:

like Fenwick's suit, the story unravels just when it begins to sail.

Kirkus Reviews

SOURCE: A review of *Fenwick's Suit,* in *Kirkus Reviews,* Vol. LXIV, No. 16, August 15, 1996, p. 1243.

A punny cautionary tale about a nondescript office drone who mistakenly believes that the clothes make the man.

Bored, friendless, and invisible in his busy city office, Fenwick studies a magazine and decides, "Maybe it's the way I'm dressed." At a tailor shop, he happens upon a bright yellow suit with a windowpane check; once dressed, Fenwick begins to strut with self-confidence. In fact, the suit wears him out. The next morning, it leaves for the office without him. On the third day, Fenwick follows his suit to the office and discovers just how insignificant his role is in the suit's fabulous life. Determined to capture his wayward clothing, Fenwick gives chase through the streets: "Legging it up the street the suit threaded its way through the crowd . . . Fenwick collared [it] . . . and hemmed it in, but just when he thought he had things all buttoned up, the suit cuffed him back. Both were panting for breath." In a spectacular finale, Fenwick escapes the suit's clutches, returning to his dull life sadder but no wiser. Small renders extraordinarily witty watercolors of a bristling, bustling New York City and a suit that just won't quit. It's too easy to deem this book—with its puns and wry tone—as aimed at adults; the plot depends on readers believing that having an animated suit is a problem. Actually, it looks like fun.

Susan Pine

SOURCE: A review of *Fenwick's Suit,* in *School Library Journal,* Vol. 42, No. 9, September, 1996, p. 192.

Fenwick, lonely at work, determines to change his image and allows a slightly disreputable-looking tailor to fit him with a splashy yellow suit. The transformation is immediate. Fenwick now strides and struts with confidence through his congested urban environment, only to fall asleep that night totally exhausted. The next morning he stays in bed, but his suit goes off to work on its own and hangs itself neatly in the closet in the evening. The next day, Fenwick follows it and observes the sad truth. His coworkers are so dazzled that they don't even notice there is no one inside. Fenwick follows the garment and boxes it up, only to see it reshape itself as a giant balloon and find himself trapped in the pocket. Flying high over the city, Fenwick finally pulls on a loose thread, unravels the suit, and lands in a laundry cart. But he hasn't learned his lesson. He's last seen looking at hair magazines. Small tells his tall tale with humor, verve, and tongue-in-cheek sauciness. On one page alone he manages to use the words "threaded," "collared," "hemmed," "buttoned," "cuffed," and "panting" without straining at the seams. The watercolor art nicely conveys the frantic tone. Altogether, this is a funny fable for readers who appreciate an offbeat story that speeds along with the acceleration of a Harold Lloyd movie short.

Stephanie Zvirin

SOURCE: A review of *Fenwick's Suit,* in *Booklist,* Vol. 93, No. 2, September 15, 1996, p. 242.

Here's a new addition to the burgeoning crop of picture books that sidestep the usual picture-book crowd. This time, the most appreciative audience will be older readers (including a few high-schoolers) who can savor the period flavor of the cartoon artwork, the sophisticated theme, the grown-up protagonist, and Small's witty wordplay. Fenwick, roundly ignored by his coworkers, decides to change his image by buying a new suit. And what a difference! He struts, he poses, he entertains—and people love it. But he soon realizes that it's really his yellow-and-orange suit that's doing the acting out and that the energetic garment has a mind of its own. Both Small's art and his storytelling are equally good: his pictures are alive with movement and filled with exuberant physical comedy—even the errant suit has character—and his telling is brisk and funny: "Fenwick collared the suit and hemmed it in, but just when he thought he had things all buttoned up . . . " It is just right for easing into a discussion of self-image and will be great fun for the right audience.

Pat Mathews

SOURCE: A review of *Fenwick's Suit,* in *Bulletin of the Center for Children's Books,* Vol. 50, No. 2, October, 1996, p. 76.

What can you do about a yellow and red plaid three-piece suit that takes over your life? In this slapstick comedy the clothes don't make the man, the clothes nearly do the man in. Fenwick, the local office nerd, is dissatisfied ("I don't have any friends. Maybe it's the way I'm dressed"). Thus Small takes us on an improbable, hilarious escapade with Fenwick and his garish new ensemble. Sharp, exaggerated angles, a few bony felines, and the suit's sophisticated strut through bustling cityscapes capture the flamboyant spirit of the story, while mottled tones provide appropriate background for the garment, itself swathed in a pristine white aura. The cartoonish art agreeably matches the fast-paced text, which leads readers into a fantastic adventure when Fenwick's threads become combative, inflate like a hot-air balloon, and tuck Fenwick in their pocket ("'How humiliating! My clothes are wearing me!' he exclaimed"). The caper literally unravels, concluding Fenwick's humorous exploits—or perhaps not concluding them ("Maybe it's the way I wear my hair, he told himself"). This is a story which could engender some lively discussions on what does make a man (or woman), and it's tailor-made for laughs.

THE GARDENER (written by Sarah Stewart, 1997)

Stephanie Zvirin

SOURCE: A review of *The Gardener,* in *Booklist,* Vol. 93, No. 19-20, June 1 & 15, 1997, p. 1722.

[Sarah] Stewart's quiet story, relayed in the form of letters written by a little girl, focuses on a child who literally makes joy blossom. Small's illustrations are a bit more softly focused than usual, but they're still recognizably his, with wonderfully expressive characters, ink-line details, and patches of pastel. Their muted backgrounds convey perfectly the urban 1930s setting where most of the story takes place. When hard times hit her family, Lydia Grace is shipped off to stay with her somber, undemonstrative uncle who owns a city bakery. She makes the best of her stay by helping out and by pursuing her favorite pastime, gardening, a talent she uses to make her uncle smile—in a very unusual way. In the end, she receives not simply one reward for her kindness but two.

Susan P. Bloom

SOURCE: A review of *The Gardener,* in *The Horn Book Magazine,* Vol. 73, No. 6, November-December, 1997, p. 673.

Elizabeth Brown from *The Library* (Stewart and Small's previous collaboration) would certainly appreciate Lydia Grace Finch: each of these red-headed, spirited protagonists has a true passion—the one for books, the other for flowers. But Depression times determine that Lydia Grace put aside her love for growing things when she must join her baker uncle in the dreary city to ease the burden on her unemployed parents. This epistolary picture book catalogs Lydia Grace's correspondence home, from her departure in early September 1935 to her return in July of the following year. Her ivory letter paper both complements the dull brown and yellow hues of trying times and sets off the vibrant pencil-colored washes of impressionistic, Dufy-like flowers that begin to sprout from windowboxes and assorted pots and pans in Lydia Grace's city life. Return letters from her grandmother spill out seeds, dirt, baby plants. All the illustrations are double-page spreads; three dramatize Lydia Grace's situation without any accompanying text: Lydia Grace's arrival in the cavernous, coal-black railroad station, whose gloom eclipses even the highlighted heroine; her discovery of the litter-strewn rooftop alive with possibilities; and its later transformation into a resplendent roof garden. David Small controls the action with dramatic angles as we look down on the busy street in front of Uncle Jim's bakery or up at the looming fire escape; objects placed close up, such as an iron or a flowerpot, afford deep perspective to a page bustling with detail. Stewart introduces further action in her plot line: Uncle Jim is kind, but dour, and Lydia Grace intends her surprise rooftop garden to elicit a smile from her gruff uncle. Yet Stewart and Small do not resort to the predictable; Uncle Jim never does smile, but in the end shows his love for Lydia Grace with an enveloping hug.

Additional coverage of Small's life and career is contained in the following source published by Gale Research: *Something about the Author,* Vols. 50, 95.

Jonathan Swift

1667-1745

(Also known as Isaac Bickerstaff, M. B. Drapier, and Simon Waystaff) Anglo-Irish author of fiction, nonfiction, and poetry.

Major works include *A Tale of a Tub, Written for the Universal Improvement of Mankind. Diu multumque desideratum. To Which Is Added, An Account of a Battel between the Antient and Modern Books in St. James's Library* (1704), *Travels into Several Remote Nations of the World. In Four Parts. By Lemuel Gulliver, First a Surgeon, and Then a Captain of Several Ships* (1726), *A Modest Proposal for Preventing the Children of Poor People from Being a Burthen to Their Parents, or the Country, and for Making Them Beneficial to the Publick* (1729), *The Lady's Dressing Room. To Which Is Added, A Poem on Cutting Down the Old Thorn at Market Hill* (1732), *Verses on the Death of Dr. Swift. Written by Himself: Nov. 1731* (1739).

Major works about the author include *Remarks on the Life and Writings of Dr. Jonathan Swift, Dean of St. Patrick's, Dublin, in a Series of Letters from John, Earl of Orrery, to His Son, the Honourable Hamilton Boyle* (by John Boyle, 1752), *The Life of the Rev. Dr. Jonathan Swift, Dean of St. Patrick's Dublin* (by Thomas Sheridan, 1784), *The Mind and Art of Jonathan Swift* (by Ricardo Quintana, 1936), *Jonathan Swift and the Age of Compromise* (by Kathleen Williams, 1958), *Swift: The Man, His Works, and the Age* (by Irvin Ehrenpreis, 1983), *Jonathan Swift, A Hypocrite Reversed: A Critical Biography* (by David Nokes, 1985).

The following entry presents criticism on *Gulliver's Travels*.

INTRODUCTION

Called "the English Rabelais" by Voltaire, "the English Lucian" by Henry Fielding, and "the greatest genius of the age" by Joseph Addison, Swift is considered one of the most important figures in the history of English literature as well as one of the most outstanding men of his time. Often regarded as the foremost satirist in the English language as well as Ireland's most distinguished man of letters, he is also praised as an accomplished poet, a leading patriot, a master of political journalism, and a recognized leader of the Irish Anglican church. Swift was a prolific author, writing satires, essays, histories, and poetry as well as autobiography. In his day, his work was both extremely influential and extremely controversial. Currently, he is perhaps best known as the creator of *Travels into Several Remote Nations of the World. In Four Parts. By Lemuel Gulliver, First a Surgeon, and Then a Captain of Several Ships,* a work published in 1726 that is now commonly referred to as

Gulliver's Travels. Written in the form of a travel journal, *Gulliver's Travels* describes the four journeys of Lemuel Gulliver, an English physician who signs on as a ship's surgeon when he is unable to provide his family with sufficient income. After being shipwrecked, Gulliver arrives at Lilliput, an island whose inhabitants are six inches high. Gulliver is pressed into service by the Lilliputians in a war against a neighboring island, Blefuscu; after escaping from Lilliput, he returns briefly to England before embarking on a second voyage. This adventure takes Gulliver to Brobdingnag, a land peopled by giants who are sixty feet tall. His size puts Gulliver in danger—for example, he encounters huge rats and a curious toddler—and his pride leads him to incur the scorn of the kindly Brobdingnagians. Housed in a miniature box, Gulliver abruptly departs Brobdingnag when a giant eagle flies off with him and drops him in the ocean. A third voyage takes him to the land of Laputa, a mysterious flying island that is inhabited by scientists and magicians who conduct ill-advised experiments. While in Laputa, Gulliver also visits Glubbdudrib, a place where it is possible to summon the ghosts of the dead, and Luggnagg, an area peopled by immortals whose bodies are feeble and decrepit. After returning home, Gulliver journeys to the land of the Houyhnhnms, a superior race of intelligent horses, and the Yahoos, a vile, depraved race of apelike creatures. After the Houyhnhnms gently insist that Gulliver return to his own kind, he comes back to England; however, Gulliver has trouble adjusting to everyday life, since everyone he meets reminds him of a Yahoo.

Written in simple yet vividly descriptive prose and a direct style noted for masking the complexity of the author's irony, *Gulliver's Travels* is Swift's most discussed work. Critics have provided an enormous variety of interpretations of his motives and the objects of his satire as well as the moral tendency of the novel, the meaning of each of the four voyages, and the character of Gulliver. The book is viewed as a complex study of human nature as well as Swift's analysis of the philosophical, scientific, political, and religious thought of his time. Often linked to John Bunyan's *Pilgrim's Progress* and Daniel Defoe's *Robinson Crusoe* as a touchstone in the development of the English novel, *Gulliver's Travels* has been called a travelogue, an allegory, a treatise, and a tale for children; it is in the latter category that the work is now most often placed. Thematically, the book is alternately considered a vicious attack on humanity, one that exposes the author's misanthropy, and an accurate assessment of human strengths and weaknesses. Swift uses his narrator—a scientist who makes close observations and takes precise measurements—to comment matter-of-factly on what he sees; in addition, Gulliver embodies some human vices of his own, such as vanity. Through Gulliver's observations and what the reader discovers about him, Swift is credited with attacking the baseness of human beings while suggesting their greatest virtues. He questions the degeneracy and tyranny to be found in modern civilization while interpreting symbolically the dual nature of humanity. He also skewers educational and political systems while implying the appropriate functions of art, science, and government. Believing that it was difficult to correct the moral complacency of humankind, Swift used the perspectives of Gulliver to mirror the qualities of his age; the popularity of *Gulliver's Travels* since that time suggests that his observations have resonated deeply among readers. As Roger D. Lund noted in *Dictionary of Literary Biography,* with *Gulliver's Travels,* Swift makes "us recognize, however reluctantly, that the face in his satiric glass is none other than our own."

Biographical Information

Born in Dublin to English parents, Swift lost his father at the age of seven months. While still an infant, his nurse took him across the Irish channel to Whitehaven, where they stayed for a three-year period during which Swift learned to read; he later wrote that by the time he returned to his family, he "could read any chapter in the Bible." At age six, Swift entered Kilkenny School, considered the best in Ireland, and at fifteen was admitted to Trinity College, Dublin, where he received a bachelor of arts degree. In 1689, he became the secretary of

Sir William Temple, a courtier, statesman, and writer who served as the model for the gracious king of Brobdingnag in *Gulliver's Travels*. In 1690, Swift wrote his first poem, a congratulatory ode to King William. In 1692, he received his master's degree from Oxford University, and in 1695 took orders as a priest of the Church of Ireland (Anglican). Later that year, he proposed marriage to the sister of one of his college friends; the woman refused him, and Swift never forgave her. In 1699, he wrote what is considered his first masterpiece, *A Tale of a Tub,* a satirical work that is considered a precursor to *Gulliver's Travels*. At around the same time, Swift met Esther Johnson, nicknamed Stella, a ward of Sir William Temple whom Swift tutored and who became his lifelong companion. Swift received his doctor of divinity degree in 1700 and began writing church pamphlets and polemical papers for the Tory government. Although he hoped to be named a bishop of England, the appointment never came, and in 1713, he became the dean of St. Patrick's Cathedral in Dublin. Evidence suggests that he married Stella secretly in 1716, insisting that they remain platonic friends.

Swift had become a member of the Scriblerus Club, a group of Tory writers that included Alexander Pope, John Gay, Thomas Parnell, Dr. John Arbuthnot, and other literary luminaries. The group met weekly to write satires on modern education, writings that formed the nucleus of *Gulliver's Travels*. In 1720, Swift began writing the first of Gulliver's adventures; for the next five years, he worked on the book while continuing his work as a clergyman, poet, and polemicist. In 1725, he wrote, "I have employd my time . . . in finishing, correcting, amending, and Transcribing my Travells, in four parts Compleat, newly Augmented, and intended for the press when the world shall deserve them, or rather when a Printer shall be found brave enough to venture his Eares. . . ." The next year, *Gulliver's Travels* was published anonymously. In his essays, Swift typically adopted a literary persona; he wished to leave no clues regarding his authorship of *Gulliver's Travels* until he was assured that it was rightfully understood. However, Swift's identity was soon made public, since ten thousand copies of *Gulliver's Travels* were sold within three weeks of its publication. In a letter to Swift two days after the book was issued, John Gay wrote, "From the highest to the lowest it is universally read, from the Cabinet to the Nursery. . . . [T]he whole town, men, women, and children are quite full of it." In a letter to Swift written later that year, John Arbuthnot wrote, "I will make over all my profits to you, for the property of *Gulliver's Travels,* which, I believe, will have as great a Run as John Bunian [sic]. Gulliver is a happy man that at his age can write such a merry work. . . . I lent the Book to an old Gentleman, who went immediately to his Map to search for Lilly putt." However, Swift's joy in the success of *Gulliver's Travels* was tempered by news of Stella's illness; she died less than two years later. Swift continued to write political commentary, essays, satire, and poetry until his last years, when his health began to deteriorate. Throughout his life, Swift had suffered from what is known today as

Meniere's Syndrome, or labyrinthine vertigo, a disease of the inner ear that causes nausea, dizziness, pain, and temporary deafness. He also suffered a paralytic stroke in 1740 that caused aphasia and memory loss. In the years before his death, Swift's failing health caused his detractors to label him insane. In 1742, he was placed in the custody of guardians. Swift died in 1745 and was buried beside Stella in St. Patrick's Cathedral, Dublin.

Critical Reception

After its initial public acceptance, *Gulliver's Travels* quickly became one of the most controversial titles in English literature. Although many of them enjoyed Gulliver's first two journeys, critics complained about the acidic satire of the book and labeled Swift a misanthrope. Negative reactions to the book increased when Dr. Samuel Johnson, an influential literary figure in the second half of the eighteenth century, called Swift an author whose hatred of humanity drove him to terminal insanity. Reviewers in the eighteenth and nineteenth centuries were mainly concerned about the personal aspects of Swift's life, such as his perceived immorality, and concentrated on such aspects as his treatment of women and use of scatology; *Gulliver's Travels* was often considered filthy and obscene because of its inclusion of sexual incidents and waste elimination. Although sympathetic critical analyses appeared in the years before the twentieth century, *Gulliver's Travels* was often considered the work of a distorted, enigmatic writer. Observers in this century reevaluated Swift's career and dispensed with the salacious stories that often accompanied previous criticism. In their assessments of *Gulliver's Travels,* reviewers have come to perceive the character of Gulliver as an everyman, a flexible persona that Swift uses to present the complex nature—and ultimate indefinability—of human nature. Since he challenged assumptions about the superiority of political and social institutions and questioned the high place of rational animals in the chain of existence, Swift is generally considered a man out of time, a writer who transcended the prevalent philosophies of his age. Twentieth-century critics generally concur that Swift—who once wrote that he would sooner "vex the world. . . than divert it"—did not detest humanity; in fact, contemporary reviewers believe that his works reflect a sensitive man who attempted to change humanity by exposing its less than noble aspects. Swift is now most often regarded as a brilliant and original writer who created lasting works filled with truths about the human condition.

Throughout its publication history, *Gulliver's Travels* has been beloved by children. Young readers who ignore the social and philosophic implications of the book are delighted by the humor and invention of Gulliver's fantastic journeys as well as by the exactness and consistency of the imaginary worlds that Swift describes. Appearing when children's literature consisted mostly of didactic, instructive tales used by adults to improve the young, *Gulliver's Travels* was considered an antidote to this dull fare. Consequently, young people adopted it as their own. It also influenced the works of writers for children who followed Swift, such as John Newbery, who named his juvenile periodical *Lilliputian Magazine,* and Lewis Carroll, whose character Alice, like Gulliver, participates in a series of strange and wonderful adventures. Although *Gulliver's Travels* is sometimes considered unsuitable for children, especially in its original form, the many expurgated and adapted versions of the book, which include retellings, textbook editions, and pop-up books, are mostly directed to a youthful audience. *Gulliver's Travels* is now considered a classic of childhood; it is also a staple of popular culture, with terms such as "lilliputian" and "yahoo" becoming part of everyday use. Contemporary reviewers praise the book as one of literature's most precious creations; for example, George Orwell, who first read it at eight, claimed that *Gulliver's Travels* should be one of the six books preserved when all others were destroyed. Writing in the *Times Educational Supplement,* Harry Ritchie concluded, "Few novels, in fact, have had such power to haunt, enchant, and disturb. . . . Rarely has a novel produced so many episodes and scenes that have entered the collective imagination. And rarely has a novel provoked such violently different reactions—so much so that *Gulliver's Travels* acts as a literary lit-mus test to the principles, attitudes, and fears of its readers. . . . [As William] Hazlitt pointed out, the distinguishing feature of Swift's satire is his ability to 'tear off the mask of imposture from the world; and nothing but imposture has a right to complain of it.' In *Gulliver's Travels* Swift tore off that mask with such aplomb that, 250 years after his death, his inventions enjoy as vigorous a life as ever. . . ."

COMMENTARY

Jonathan Swift

SOURCE: A letter to Alexander Pope on September 29, 1725, in *The Writings of Jonathan Swift: Authoritative Texts, Background, Criticism,* edited by Robert A. Greenberg and William Bowman Piper, W. W. Norton & Company, Inc., 1973, pp. 584-85.

[The following letter was written to Alexander Pope, September 29, 1725, and contains Swift's famous remarks on the nature of his work and temperament. Both denigrators and defenders of Swift have utilized this letter when discussing Swift's misanthropy. Those who would believe that Swift detested human beings point to his remarks regarding the "foundation of Misanthropy" upon which **Gulliver's Travels** *is erected and to his desire to vex the world; those who deny that Swift was a misanthrope note that he hated the general foibles of humanity but not the individual.]*

I have employd my time (besides ditching) in finishing

correcting, amending, and Transcribing my *Travells,* in four parts Compleat newly Augmented, and intended for the press when the world shall deserve them, or rather when a Printer shall be found brave enough to venture his Eares. . . . The chief end I propose to my self in all my labors is to vex the world rather then divert it, and if I could compass that designe without hurting my own person or Fortune I would be the most Indefatigable writer you have ever seen without reading. I am exceedingly pleased that you have done with Translations. Lord Treasurer Oxford often lamented that a rascaly World should lay you under a Necessity of Misemploying your Genius for so long a time. But since you will now be so much better employd when you think of the World, give it one lash the more at my Request. I have ever hated all Nations, professions and Communityes and all my love is towards individualls. For instance, I hate the tribe of Lawyers, but I love Councellor such a one, Judge such a one, for so with Physicians (I will not Speak of my own Trade), Soldiers, English, Scotch, French, and the rest; but principally I hate and detest that animal called man, although I hartily love John, Peter, Thomas and so forth. This is the system upon which I have governed my self many years (but do not tell) and so I shall go on till I have done with them. I have got Materials Towards a Treatis proving the falsity of that Definition *animal rationale;* and to show it should be only *rationis capax.* Upon this great foundation of Misanthropy (though not Timons manner) the whole building of my *Travells* is erected: And I never will have peace of mind till all honest men are of my Opinion: by Consequence you are to embrace it immediately and procure that all who deserve my Esteem may do so too. The matter is so clear that it will admit little dispute. Nay I will hold a hundred pounds that you and I agree in the Point. . . .

Mr Lewis sent me an Account of Dr Arbuthnett's [sic] Illness which is a very sensible Affliction to me, who by living so long out of the World have lost that hardness of Heart contracted by years and generall Conversation. I am daily loosing Friends, and neither seeking nor getting others. O, if the World had but a dozen Arbuthnetts in it I would burn my *Travells* but however he is not without Fault. There is a passage in Bede highly commending the Piety and learning of the Irish in that Age, where after abundance of praises he overthrows them all by lamenting that, Alas, they kept Easter at a wrong time of the Year. So our Doctor has every Quality and virtue that can make a man amiable or usefull, but alas he hath a sort of Slouch in his Walk. I pray god protect him for he is an excellant Christian tho not a Catholick and as fit a man either to dy or Live as ever I knew.

John Arbuthnot

SOURCE: A letter to Jonathan Swift on November 5, 1726, in *The Writings of Jonathan Swift: Authoritative Texts, Background, Criticism,* edited by Robert A. Greenberg, W. W. Norton & Company, Inc., 1973, pp. 586-87.

[Arbuthnot addressed the following letter to Swift, November 5, 1726, in response to his reading of **Gulliver's Travels.***]*

I will make over all my profits to you, for the property of *Gulliver's Travells,* which I believe, will have as great a Run as John Bunian. Gulliver is a happy man that at his age can write such a merry work.

I made my Lord ArchBishop's compliment to her R[oyal] Highness who returns his Grace her thanks. . . . when I had the honor to see her She was Reading *Gulliver,* & was just come to the passage of the Hobbling prince, which she laughed at. I tell yow freely the part of the projectors is the least Brilliant. Lewis Grumbles a little at it & says he wants the Key to it. . . .

Gulliver is in every body's Hands. Lord Scarborow who is no inventor of Storys told me that he fell in company with a Master of a ship, who told him that he was very well acquainted with Gulliver, but that the printer had Mistaken, that he livd in Wapping, & not in Rotherhith. I lent the Book to an old Gentleman, who went immediately to his Map to search for Lilly putt.

Alexander Pope

SOURCE: A letter to Jonathan Swift on November 16, 1726, in *The Writings of Jonathan Swift: Authoritative Texts, Background, Criticism,* edited by Robert A. Greenberg and William Bowman Piper, W. W. Norton & Company, Inc., 1973, p. 587.

[In the following letter dated November 16, 1726, Pope records some reactions of his contemporaries to **Gulliver's Travels,** *alluding to the unnecessary efforts made by Swift and his publisher, Benjamin Motte, to conceal Swift's authorship.]*

I congratulate you first upon what you call your Couzen's wonderful Book [*Gulliver's Travels*], which is *publica trita manu* at present, and I prophecy will be in future the admiration of all men. That countenance with which it is received by some statesmen, is delightful; I wish I could tell you how every single man looks upon it, to observe which has been my whole diversion this fortnight. I've never been a night in London since you left me, till now for this very end, and indeed it has fully answered my expectations.

I find no considerable man very angry at the book: some indeed think it rather too bold, and too general a Satire: but none that I hear of accuse it of particular reflections (I mean no persons of consequence, or good judgment; the mob of Criticks, you know, always are desirous to apply Satire to those that they envy for being above them) so that you needed not to have been so secret upon this head. [Benjamin] Motte receiv'd the copy (he tells me) he knew not from whence, nor from whom, dropp'd at his house in the dark, from a Hackney-coach:

by computing the time, I found it was after you left England, so for my part, I suspend my judgment.

John Gay

SOURCE: An excerpt from a letter to Jonathan Swift on November 17, 1726, in *The Correspondence of Jonathan Swift: 1724-1731, Vol. III,* Oxford at the Clarendon Press, Oxford, 1963, pp. 182-84.

[The following excerpt was taken from a letter addressed to Swift on November 17, 1726. A friend of Swift's, Gay was a popular poet and dramatist of the eighteenth century who specialized in humorous and satiric works. He discusses with tongue-in-cheek some contemporary reactions to **Gulliver's Travels** *and sustains the pretense that the author is unknown and that the work has no specific political references. Lord Bolingbroke, whose reaction Gay notes, is considered by many critics to be one of the principal subjects of satire of the voyage to Laputa.]*

About ten days ago a Book was publish'd here of the Travels of one Gulliver, which hath been the conversation of the whole town ever since. The whole impression sold in a week; and nothing is more diverting than to hear the different opinions people give of it, though all agree in liking it extreamly. 'Tis generally said that you are the Author, but I am told, the Bookseller declares he knows not from what hand it came. From the highest to the lowest it is universally read, from the Cabinet-council to the Nursery. The Politicians to a man agree, that it is free from particular reflections, but that the Satire on general societies of men is too severe. Not but we now and then meet with people of greater perspicuity, who are in search for particular applications in every leaf; and it is highly probable we shall have keys published to give light into Gulliver's design. Your Lord [Bolingbroke] is the person who least approves it, blaming it as a design of evil consequence to depreciate human nature, at which it cannot be wondered that he takes most offence, being himself the most accomplish'd of his species, and so losing more than any other of that praise which is due both to the dignity and virtue of a man. Your friend, my Lord Harcourt, commends it very much though he thinks in some places the matter too far carried. The Duchess Dowager of Marlborough is in raptures at it; she says she can dream of nothing else since she read it; she declares, that she hath now found out, that her whole life hath been lost in caressing the worst part of mankind, and treating the best as her foes; and that if she knew Gulliver, tho' he had been the worst enemy she ever had, she would give up all her present acquaintance for his friendship. You may see by this, that you are not much injur'd by being suppos'd the Author of this piece. If you are, you have disoblig'd us, and two or three of your best friends, in not giving us the least hint of it while you were with us; and in particular Dr. [John] Arbuthnot, who says it is ten thousand pitys he had not known it, he could have added such abundance of things upon every subject. Among Lady-critics, some have found out that Mr. Gulliver had a particular malice to maids of honour. Those of them who frequent the Church, say, his design is impious, and that it is an insult on Providence, by depreciating the works of the Creator. Notwithstanding I am told the Princess hath read it with great pleasure. As to other Critics, they think the flying island is the least entertaining; and so great an opinion the town have of the impossibility of Gulliver's writing at all below himself, that 'tis agreed that Part was not writ by the same Hand, tho' this hath its defenders too. It hath pass'd Lords and Commons, *nemine contradicente;* and the whole town, men, women, and children are quite full of it.

Jonathan Swift

SOURCE: A letter to Mrs. Henrietta Howard on November 27, 1726, in *The Correspondence of Jonathan Swift: 1724-1731, Vol. III,* Oxford at the Clarendon Press, Oxford, 1963, pp. 187-88.

[In the following letter, dated November 27, 1726, Swift responds to a correspondent who considered him the author of the anonymously published **Gulliver's Travels***. Swift suggests that Gulliver's viewpoint is not consistent with his own beliefs, a point that would later be much debated by critics. Henrietta Howard, Countess of Suffolk, was the Bedchamber Woman to the Princess of Wales.]*

When I received your Letter I thought it the most unaccountable one I ever saw in my Life, and was not able to comprehend three words of it together. . . . But I continued four days at a loss for your meaning, till a Bookseller sent me the *Travells* of one Cap[tain] Gulliver, who proved a very good Explainer, although at the same time, I thought it hard to be forced to read a Book of seven hundred Pages in order to understand a Letter of fifty lines; especially since those of our Faculty are already but too much pestered with Commentators. The Stuffs you require are making, because the Weaver piques himself upon having them in perfection, but he has read Gulliver's Book, and has no Conception of what you mean by returning Money, for he is become a Proselyte of the Houyhnhnms, whose great Principle (if I rightly remember) is Benevolence. And as to my self, I am rightly affronted with such a base Proposall, that I am determined to complain of you to her Royall Highness, that you are a mercenary Yahoo fond of shining Pebbles. What have I to do with you or your Court further than to show the Esteem I have for your Person, because you happen to deserve it, and my Gratitude to Her Royall Highness, who was pleased, a little to distinguish me; which, by the way is the greatest Compliment I ever made, and may probably be the last. For I am not such a prostitute Flatterer as Gulliver; whose chief Study is to extenuate the Vices, and magnify the Virtues, of Mankind, and perpetually dins our Ears with the Praises of his Country, in the midst of Corruptions, and for that Reason alone, hath found so many readers; and probably will have a Pension, which, I suppose, was his chief

Jonathan Swift

design in writing: As for his Compliments to the Ladyes, I can easily forgive him as a naturall Effect of that
Devotion which our Sex always ought to pay to Yours.

Jonathan Swift

SOURCE: A letter to Alexander Pope on November 27,
1726, in *The Writings of Jonathan Swift: Authoritative
Texts, Background, Criticism,* edited by Robert A. Greenberg and William Bowman Piper, W. W. Norton &
Company, Inc., 1973, p. 590.

*[Swift addressed the following letter to Alexander
Pope on November 27, 1726, in response to the
letter he received from Mrs. Howard.]*

I am just come from answering a Letter of Mrs. Howard's
writ in such mystical terms, that I should never have
found out the meaning, if a Book had not been sent me
called *Gulliver's Travellers,* of which you say so much
in yours. I read the Book over, and in the second volume observe several passages which appear to be patched
and altered, and the style of a different sort (unless I am
much mistaken). Dr. Arbuthnot likes the Projectors least,
others you tell me, the Flying island; some think it

wrong to be so hard upon whole Bodies or Corporations,
yet the general opinion is, that reflections on particular
persons are most to be blamed: so that in these cases,
I think the best method is to let censure and opinion take
their course. A Bishop here said, that Book was full of
improbable lies, and for his part, he hardly believed a
word of it; and so much for Gulliver.

Anne Liddell

SOURCE: A letter to James Clavering on November 29,
1726, in *Notes and Queries,* n.s. Vol. 14, No. 5, May,
1967, p. 172.

*[Anne Liddell, née Clavering, a strong Whig and
sister-in-law of Lord Chancellor Cowper, records
her reaction to* **Gulliver's Travels** *in the following
letter, dated November 29, 1726, to her kinsman,
James Clavering.]*

If you have not read two volumes of ficktitious voyages
of fairys, giants, flying islands &c., said to be Dean
Swift's, and (which) have had a great run here you may
peruse them at leisure, for now the fashion of praising
them is almost ov[e]r. My natural stupidity, which coud
not be moved by education coud not penetrate the deep
design of the author, save to ridicule the deprived (sic)
taste of mankind in general. Once in an age my fashion
(and) dress come in vogue tho' here no hope of success.

Abbé Desfontaines

SOURCE: "Abbé Desfontaines and *Gulliver's Travels,*"
translated by Kathleen Williams, in *Swift: The Critical
Heritage,* edited by Kathleen Williams, Barnes & Noble
Books, Inc., 1970, pp. 77-89.

*[Desfontaines was a French man of letters who free-
ly and inaccurately translated* **Gulliver's Travels** *to
conform to his ideas of French taste and propriety.
Although the 1727 preface to his translation,* **Voyages de Gulliver, Vol. I,** *from which the following
excerpt is taken, is often inaccurate or derogatory,
it is nevertheless one of the earliest examples of
thoughtful critical discussion of the work. Desfontaines later wrote a popular imitation of* **Gulliver's
Travels.**]*

At the end of last year, Mr. Swift published in London
the *Travels of Captain Lemuel Gulliver,* which I am to
deal with now. An English nobleman living in Paris,
having received the *Travels* almost immediately after
publication, did me the honour of speaking to me about
them as an agreeable and witty work. The opinion of
this nobleman, who has himself a great deal of wit,
taste, and literary knowledge, predisposed me in favour
of the book. Some other Englishmen of my acquaintance, whose intelligence I esteem equally, had the same
opinion of it; and as they knew that I had been learning
their language for some time they urged me to make this

ingenious work known in France, through a translation that could come up to the original.

All that made me, at the beginning of February this year, not only desire to read it, but even to plan to translate it, if I felt myself capable of it and if I found it to my taste. I read it and found no difficulty in it. But I admit that the first thirty pages gave me no pleasure. The arrival of Gulliver in the Lilliputian empire, the description of that country and of its inhabitants, of six inches high, and the circumstantial detail of their feelings and conduct towards a stranger who to them was a giant, all that seemed to me rather frigid and mediocre, and made me afraid that the whole work would be of the same kind.

But when I had read a little further, my ideas changed, and I recognized that people were right to praise the book to me. I found in it entertaining and judicious things, a well sustained fiction, fine ironies, amusing allegories, a sensible and liberal morality, and, throughout, playful and witty satire. In a word, I found a book quite new and original in its kind. I hesitated no longer; I set to work to translate it purely for my own advantage, that is to say to perfect my knowledge of the English language, which is beginning to be fashionable in Paris and has lately been learned by several people of merit and distinction.

Nevertheless I cannot conceal here the fact that I found in this work of Mr. Swift some weak and even very bad parts; impenetrable allegories, insipid allusions, puerile details, low thoughts, boring repetitions, coarse jokes, pointless pleasantries: in a word things which translated literally into French would have appeared indecent, paltry, impertinent, would have disgusted the good taste which reigns in France, would have covered me with confusion, and would certainly have drawn just reproaches on my head if I had been so weak and imprudent as to expose them to the eyes of the public. . . .

I know that some people will reply that all these passages which shock us are allegorical, and are witty to those who understand them. For me, who have not the clue (any more than have those gentlemen who defend them) and who neither can nor will find the explanation of all these fine mysteries, I confess that I believed it proper to take the course of suppressing them entirely. If I have by any chance left any of this kind of thing in my translation, I beg the public to consider that it is natural for a translator to let himself be won over, and to feel sometimes too much indulgence for his author. For the rest, I thought myself capable of making good these deficiencies and replacing the losses by the help of my imagination, and by certain turns that I gave to things which displeased me. I have said enough about this to make clear the nature of my translation.

Certain people of serious, solid, and weighty mind, who are enemies of all fiction or who condescend, at most, to tolerate ordinary fictions, will perhaps be put off by the audacity and novelty of the inventions they will see

here. Pigmies of six inches, giants of a hundred and fifty feet, a flying island inhabited by geometricians and astronomers, an academy of systems and fancies, an island of magicians, immortal men, finally horses endowed with reason in a country where animals in human shape are not reasonable creatures—all this will disgust solid minds who want above all truth and reality, or at least verisimilitude and possibility.

[But] one should not censure *Gulliver's Travels* precisely because its fictions are not believable. They are, it is true, fantastic fictions, but they provide exercise for the imagination and give a good opportunity to the author, and on this count alone they must be enjoyed if they are handled with judgment, if they are entertaining, and above all if they lead to a judicious moral. For it is this that, it seems to me, is found here.

The first two voyages are based on the idea of a very sure principle of natural philosophy, the knowledge that there is no absolute size, and that all measurement is relative. The author has worked on this idea, and has drawn from it all that he could, to entertain and instruct his readers, and to make them feel the vanity of human grandeur. In these two voyages he seems in a way to regard men through a telescope. First he turns the object-glass to his eye, and consequently sees them as very small: this is the voyage to Lilliput. Then he turns the telescope around, and then he sees very big men: this is the voyage to Brobdingnag. This furnishes him with pleasing images, allusions, reflections.

As for the other voyages, the author intended here, still more than in the first two, to censure various customs of his country. The flying island of Laputa seems to be the English court, and can have no reference to any court elsewhere.

In all voyages, and above all in that to Houyhnhnmland, the author attacks man in general, and makes us aware of the absurdity and the wretchedness of the human mind. He opens our eyes to enormous vices that we are accustomed to regard as, at most, slight faults, and makes us feel the value of a purified reason, more perfect than our own.

All these great and serious ideas, however, are here treated in a comic and burlesque way. They are not fairy tales, which commonly contain no moral conclusions and which in that case are good only to amuse children: indeed we ought to prevent even children from reading them for fear of familiarising their minds with frivolous things. In general all fiction is insipid when it leads to nothing useful. But this will not be said, I think, about the fictions now under discussion. Intelligent men will find them witty, and the common run of readers will be entertained by them.

It is clear that this book was written not for France, but for England, and that what it contains of direct and particular satire does not touch us. Next, I protest that if I had found in my author any sharp strokes which seemed to me to carry a marked and natural allusion, and whose bearing I had felt to be injurious to anyone in this country, I would have suppressed them without hesitation, just as I have struck out everything that seemed to me gross and indecent.

What pleased me in the original was that I have perceived nothing in it that could be prejudicial to true religion. What the author says of Big-Endians, High-Heels, and Low-Heels in the Empire of Lilliput clearly refers to the unfortunate differences which divide England into Conformists and Nonconformists, into Tories and Whigs. This is an absurd spectacle in the eyes of a profane philosopher; but it excites compassion in a Christian philosopher attached to true religion and to unity which is only to be found in the Roman Church. I do not press this reflection, which is too serious for the preface to a book such as this.

I think, moreover, that no one will be upset by certain details to do with seafaring, or by some small indifferent circumstances which the author relates and which I have left in my translation. He seems in this to have affected to imitate real travellers, and to have intended to mock their scrupulous exactitude, and the minute details with which they load their accounts.

The way in which Gulliver ends the relation of two of these voyages is a natural portrayal of the effects of habit. On leaving the Kingdom of Brobdingnag all men seem to him pigmies; and when he has left Houyhnhnmland, where he heard so much that was bad about human nature, he could no longer tolerate it when he returned among men. But he makes us feel at last that all impressions wear away in time.

Although I have done all I could to adjust this work of Mr. Swift to the taste of France, I do not claim to have made of it quite a French work. A foreigner is always a foreigner; whatever wit and polish he may have, he always retains something of his own accent and manners. . . .

Jonathan Swift

SOURCE: A letter to Abbé Desfontaines in July, 1727, in *The Writings of Jonathan Swift: Authoritative Texts, Background, Criticism,* edited by Robert A. Greenberg and William Bowman Piper, W. W. Norton & Company, Inc., 1973, p. 591.

[In response to the omissions, Swift sent the following reply, a translation of the French original, to Desfontaines in July, 1727.]

We may concede that the taste of nations is not always the same. But we are inclined to believe that good taste is the same everywhere that there are people of wit, of judgment, and of learning. If, then, the writings of Gulliver were intended only for the British Isles, that traveller must be considered a very contemptible author.

The same vices and the same follies reign everywhere; at least, in all the civilized countries of Europe: and the author who writes only for a city, a province, a kingdom, or even an age, warrants so little to be translated that he deserves not even to be read.

The partisans of Gulliver—they number a good many amongst us—maintain that his book will endure as long as our language, because it draws its merit not from certain modes or manners of thought and speaking, but from a series of observations on the imperfections, the follies, and the vices of man. . . . You will no doubt be surprised to learn that [some] consider this ship's surgeon a solemn author, who never departs from seriousness, who never assumes a role, who never prides himself on possessing wit, and who is content to communicate to the public, in a simple and artless narrative, the adventures that have befallen him and the things that he has seen or heard during his voyages.

Lord Orrery (John Boyle, Earl of Cork and Orrery)

SOURCE: A series of letters to Hamilton Boyle in 1752, in *Swift: The Critical Heritage,* edited by Kathleen Williams, Barnes & Noble Books, Inc., 1970, pp. 115-31.

[Orrery was a friend of Swift's. The series of letters excerpted below, addressed to Hamilton Boyle in Orrery's Remarks on the Life and Writing of Dr. Jonathan Swift, Dean of St. Patrick's, Dublin, 1752, *largely attack Swift's personality and are characterized by inaccurate biographical details and personal spite. Unfortunately, this work served as a source of information for many eighteenth- and nineteenth-century critics. Orrery believed that although Swift's intent in* **Gulliver's Travels** *was to correct vice and folly by holding it up to ridicule, the work actually displays his misanthropy and blasphemous beliefs.]*

[*The travels of LEMUEL GULLIVER into several remote nations of the world*] is intended as a moral political romance, in which SWIFT seems to have exerted the strongest efforts of a fine irregular genius. But while his imagination and his wit delight, the venomous strokes of his satyr, although in some places just, are carried into so universal a severity, that not only all human actions, but human nature itself, is placed in the worst light.

To correct vice, by shewing her deformity in opposition to the beauty of virtue, and to amend the false systems of philosophy, by pointing out the errors, and applying salutary means to avoid them, is a noble design. This was the general intent, I would fain flatter myself, of my hieroglyphic friend.

GULLIVER's travels are chiefly to be looked upon as an irregular essay of SWIFT's peculiar wit and humour. Let us take a view of the two first parts together. The inhabitants of *Lilliput* are represented, as if reflected from a convex mirror, by which every object is reduced to a despicable minuteness. The inhabitants of *Brobdingnag,* by a contrary mirrour, are enlarged to a shocking deformity. In *Lilliput* we behold a set of puny insects, or animalcules in human shape, ridiculously engaged in affairs of importance. In *Brobdingnag* the monsters of enormous size are employed in trifles.

LEMUEL GULLIVER has observed great exactness in the just proportion, and appearances of the several objects thus lessened and magnified: but he dwells too much upon these optical deceptions. The mind is tired with a repetition of them, especially as he points out no beauty, nor use in such amazing discoveries, which might have been so continued as to have afforded improvement, at the same time that they gave astonishment. Upon the whole, he too often shews an indelicacy that is not agreeable, and exerts his vein of humour most improperly in some places, where (I am afraid) he glances at religion.

The seventh chapter of the voyage of *Brobdingnag* contains such sarcasms on the structure of the human body, as too plainly shew us, that the author was unwilling to lose any opportunity of debasing and ridiculing his own species.

It is with great reluctance, I shall make some remarks on GULLIVER's voyage to the *Houyhnhnms.* In this last part of his imaginary travels, SWIFT has indulged a misanthropy that is intolerable. The representation which he has given us of human nature, must terrify, and even debase the mind of the reader who views it. His sallies of wit and humour lose all their force, nothing remaining but a melancholy, and disagreeable impression: and, as I have said to you, on other parts of his works, we are disgusted, not entertained; we are shocked, not instructed by the fable. I should therefore chuse to take no notice of his YAHOOS, did I not think it necessary to assert the vindication of human nature, and thereby, in some measure, to pay my duty to the great author of our species, who has created us in a very fearful, and a very wonderful manner.

We are composed of a mind, and of a body, intimately united, and mutually affecting each other. Their operations indeed are entirely different. Whether the immortal spirit, that enlivens this fine machine, is originally of a superior nature in various bodies (which, I own, seems most consistent and agreeable to the scale and order of beings) or, whether the difference depends on a symmetry, or peculiar structure of the organs combined with it, is beyond my reach to determine. It is evidently certain, that the body is curiously formed with proper organs to delight, and such as are adapted to all the necessary uses of life. The spirit animates the whole; it guides the natural appetites, and confines them within just limits. But, the natural force of this spirit is often immersed in matter; and the mind becomes subservient to passions, which it ought to govern and direct. . . .

In painting YAHOOS he becomes one himself. Nor is

the picture, which he draws of the *Houyhnhnms,* inviting or amusing. It wants both light and shade to adorn it. It is cold and insipid. We there view the pure instincts of brutes, unassisted by any knowledge of letters, acting within their own narrow sphere, merely for their immediate preservation. They are incapable of doing wrong, therefore they act right. It is surely a very low character given to creatures, in whom the author would insinuate some degree of reason, that they act inoffensively, when they have neither the motive nor the power to act otherwise. Their virtuous qualities are only negative. SWIFT himself, amidst all his irony, must have confessed, that to moderate our passions, to extend our munificence to others, to enlarge our understanding, and to raise our idea of the Almighty by contemplating his works, is not only the business, but often the practice, and the study of the human mind. It is too certain, that no one individual has ever possessed every qualification and excellence: however such an assemblage of different virtues, may still be collected from different persons, as are sufficient to place the dignity of human nature in an amiable, and exalted station. We must lament indeed the many instances of those who degenerate, or go astray from the end and intention of their being. The true source of this depravity is often owing to the want of education, to the false indulgence of parents, or to some other bad causes, which are constantly prevalent in every nation. Many of these errors are finely ridiculed in the foregoing parts of this romance: but the voyage to the *Houyhnhnms* is a real insult upon mankind.

Deane Swift

SOURCE: An excerpt from *A Letter to Deane Swift on His Essay,* Garland Publishing, Inc., 1974, pp. 218-21.

[Deane Swift, a cousin of Jonathan, wrote the following refutation of Lord Orrery's Remarks *(1752) to defend his family's honor. He attacks Orrery's statement that Swift was a misanthrope, noting that Swift attempted to combat vice and corruption by subjecting them to ridicule. In the following excerpt of that reply, from* An Essay upon the Life, Writings and Character of Dr. Jonathan Swift, *1755, Deane Swift defends his cousin's presentation of the Yahoos, concluding that they are not blasphemous caricatures of humanity but represent an attempt to expose those elements of human nature that Christian teaching finds abominable, a position consistent with Swift's ecclesiastical vocation.]*

I have been told that some others, beside the grand remarker upon the works of DR. SWIFT [see excerpt by Lord Orrery, 1752] have thought proper to censure GULLIVER'S voyage to the HOUYHNHNMS. But whether indeed their animadversions proceeded from the infirmity of their judgment, or from some YAHOO depravity in their own nature, I shall not vouchsafe to enquire; as the daily occurrences of this wretched world prove, illustrate, and confirm all the sarcasms of the Doctor. Shall we praise that excellent moralist, the humorous HOGARTH, for exposing midnight revels, debaucheries, and a thousand other vices and follies of humankind, in a series of hieroglyphicks, suited to the improvement and the correction of the wild, the gay, the frolick, and the extravagant? And shall we condemn a preacher of righteousness, for exposing under the character of a nasty unteachable YAHOO the deformity, the blackness, the filthiness and corruption of those hellish, abominable vices, which inflame the wrath of GOD against the children of disobedience; and subject them without repentance, that is, without a thorough change of life and practice, to everlasting perdition? Ought a preacher of righteousness; ought a watchman of the Christian faith, (who is accountable for his talents, and obliged to warn the innocent, as well as terrify the wicked and the prophane) to hold his peace, like a dumb dog that cannot bark, when avarice, fraud, cheating, violence, rapine, extortion, cruelty, oppression, tyranny, rancour, envy, malice, detraction, hatred, revenge, murder, whoredom, adultery, lasciviousness, bribery, corruption, pimping, lying, perjury, subordination, treachery, ingratitude, gaming, flattery, drunkenness, gluttony, luxury, vanity, effeminacy, cowardice, pride, impudence, hypocrisy, infidelity, blasphemy, idolatry, sodomy, and innumerable other vices are as epidemical as the pox, and many of them the notorious characteristicks of the bulk of humankind? I would ask these mighty softeners, these kind pretenders to benevolence; these hollow charity-mongers; what is their real opinion of that OLD SERPENT, which, like a roaring lion, traverseth the globe, seeking whom he may devour? Was he not created by the ALMIGHTY pure, faultless, intelligent? but is there now throughout the whole system of created existences, any BEAST, any YAHOO, any TYRANT so vile, so base, so corrupted? And whence originally proceeded the change? was it not from the abuse of that freedom, without which no created INTELLIGENCE can be reputed faithful, wise, brave, or virtuous, in the eyes of his CREATOR? And surely, if this once great, once glorious spirit hath been reduced for many thousands of ages, for aught we know to the contrary, below all the several gradations of created beings, whether intelligent, animal, or insensible; and exposed to the fury of that avenging, although merciful GOD, who is the fountain of all wisdom, goodness, and virtue; are we not to conclude by an exact parity of reason, that every moral agent is equally accountable to GOD for that degree of intelligence and perfection, which determine the nature of his existence? And upon this very principle, which cannot be denied without running into the last of absurdities; and which in fact is the reasoning of ST. PETER throughout his whole second chapter of his second epistle; that creature man, that glorious creature man, is deservedly more contemptible than a brute beast, when he flies in the face of his CREATOR by enlisting under the banner of the enemy; and perverts that reason which was designed to have been the glory of his nature, even the directing spirit of his life and demeanour, to the vilest, the most execrable, the most hellish purposes. And this manifestly appears to be the groundwork of the whole satire contained in the voyage to the HOUY-HNHNMS.

Francis Jeffrey

SOURCE: "Scott's 'Edition of Swift,'" in *The Edinburgh Review*, Vol. XXVII, No. LIII, September, 1816, pp. 1-58.

[Jeffrey was a founder and editor of the Edinburgh Review, *an influential magazine that helped raise the standards of periodical reviewing in early nineteenth-century England. Jeffrey promoted a personal approach to literature that was sympathetic to the general principles of the Romantic movement. He felt that literature should be judged by a criterion of beauty—a beautiful work being one that inspired sensations of tenderness or pity in the reader—rather than by considerations of structure, composition, or metaphysics. A liberal Whig, he supported the inclusion of the middle class in government and believed in principles of moderate social progress. Jeffrey was thus politically, philosophically, and temperamentally opposed to Swift's work and all that it stood for. The following review of Sir Walter Scott's edition of* The Works of Jonathan Swift *was published in the* Edinburgh Review, *September, 1816.]*

The voyages of Captain Lemuel Gulliver is indisputably [Swift's] greatest work. The idea of making fictitious travels the vehicle of satire as well as of amusement, is at least as old as Lucian; but has never been carried into execution with such success, spirit, and originality, as in this celebrated performance. The brevity, the minuteness, the homeliness, the unbroken seriousness of the narrative, all give a character of truth and simplicity to the work which at once palliates the extravagance of the fiction, and enhances the effect of those weighty reflections and cutting severities in which it abounds. Yet though it is probable enough, that without those touches of satire and observation the work would have appeared childish and preposterous, we are persuaded that it pleases chiefly by the novelty and vivacity of the extraordinary pictures it presents, and the entertainment we receive from following the fortunes of the traveller in his several extraordinary adventures. The greater part of the wisdom and satire at least appears to us to be extremely vulgar and common-place; and we have no idea that they could possibly appear either impressive or entertaining, if presented without these accompaniments. A considerable part of the pleasure we derive from the voyages of Gulliver, in short, is of the same description with that which we receive from those of Sinbad the sailor, and is chiefly heightened, we believe, by the greater brevity and minuteness of the story, and the superior art that is employed to give it an appearance of truth and probability, in the very midst of its wonders.

That the interest does not arise from the satire but from the plausible description of physical wonders, seems to be farther proved by the fact, that the parts which please the least are those in which there is most satire and least of those wonders. In the voyage to Laputa, after the first description of the flying island, the attention is almost exclusively directed to intellectual absurdities; and every one is aware of the dulness that is the result. Even as a satire, indeed, this part is extremely poor and defective; nor can any thing show more clearly the author's incapacity for large and comprehensive views than his signal failure in all those parts which invited him to such contemplations. In the multitude of his vulgar and farcical representations of particular errors in philosophy, he nowhere appears to have any sense of its true value or principles; but satisfies himself with collecting or imagining a number of fantastical quackeries, which tend to illustrate nothing but his contempt for human understanding. Even where his subject seems to invite him to something of a higher flight, he uniformly shrinks back from it, and takes shelter in commonplace derision. . . . For the rest, we have observed already, that the scope of the whole work, and indeed of all his writings, is to degrade and vilify human nature; and though some of the images which occur in this part may be rather coarser than the others, we do not think the difference so considerable as to account for its admitted inferiority in the power of pleasing. . . .

William Hazlitt

SOURCE: "On Swift, Young, Gray, Collins, Etc.," in *Lectures on the English Poets,* Oxford University Press, London, 1924, pp. 160-89.

> [Hazlitt is considered one of the most important critics of the Romantic age. In the following excerpt from Hazlitt's lectures, 1818, he praises Swift's genius for irony and the power of his attack upon false pride and empty grandeur.]

Whether the excellence of **Gulliver's Travels** is in the conception or the execution, is of little consequence; the power is somewhere, and it is a power that has moved the world. The power is not that of big words and vaunting commonplaces. Swift left these to those who wanted them; and has done what his acuteness and intensity of mind alone could enable any one to conceive or to perform. His object was to strip empty pride and grandeur of the imposing air which external circumstances throw around them; and for this purpose he has cheated the imagination of the illusions which the prejudices of sense and of the world put upon it, by reducing everything to the abstract predicament of size. He enlarges or diminishes the scale, as he wishes to show the insignificance or the grossness of our overweening self-love. That he has done this with mathematical precision, with complete presence of mind and perfect keeping, in a manner that comes equally home to the understanding of the man and of the child, does not take away from the merit of the work or the genius of the author. He has taken a new view of human nature, such as a being of a higher sphere might take of it; he has torn the scales from off his moral vision; he has tried an experiment upon human life, and sifted its pretensions from the alloy of circumstances; he has measured it with a rule, has weighed it in a balance, and found it, for the most part, wanting and worthless—in substance and in show. Nothing solid, nothing valuable is left in his system but virtue and wisdom. What a libel is this upon mankind! What a convincing proof of misanthropy! What presumption and what *malice prepense,* to show men what they are, and to teach them what they ought to be! What a mortifying stroke aimed at national glory, is that unlucky incident of Gulliver's wading across the channel and carrying off the whole fleet of Blefuscu! After that, we have only to consider which of the contending parties was in the right. What a shock to personal vanity is given in the account of Gulliver's name Glumdalclitch! Still, notwithstanding the disparagement to her personal charms, her good nature remains the same amiable quality as before. I cannot see the harm, the misanthropy, the immoral and degrading tendency of this. The moral lesson is as fine as the intellectual exhibition is amusing. It is an attempt to tear off the mask of imposture from the world; and nothing but imposture has a right to complain of it. It is, indeed, the way with our quacks in morality to preach up the dignity of human nature, to pamper pride and hypocrisy with the idle mockeries of the virtues they pretend to, and which they have not: but it was not Swift's way to cant morality, or anything else; nor did his genius prompt him to write unmeaning panegyrics on mankind! . . .

Samuel Taylor Coleridge

SOURCE: "Coleridge on *Gulliver's Travels,*" in *The Athenaeum,* Vol. 108, No. 3590, August 15, 1896, p. 224.

> [The following notes by Coleridge were discovered on the flyleaf of a volume of Swift's works in William Wordsworth's library and were published for the first time in the Athenaeum in 1896. No date for their composition has been fixed, but it is assumed to be around 1834. Coleridge denies that Swift was a misanthrope, and discusses the symbolic meaning of the Houyhnhnms and Yahoos. Coleridge's reservations about the Houyhnhnms as models of virtue foreshadow the interpretations of many twentieth-century critics.]

The great defect of the Houyhnhnms is not its misanthropy, and those who apply this word to it must really believe that the essence of human nature . . . consists in the shape of the body. Now, to show the falsity of this was Swift's great object; he would prove to our feelings and imaginations, and thereby teach *practically,* that it is Reason and Conscience which give all the loveliness and dignity not only to Man, but to the shape of Man; that deprived of these, and yet retaining the Understanding, he would be the most loathsome and hateful of all animals; that his understanding would manifest itself only as malignant cunning, his free will as obstinacy and unteachableness. And how true a picture this is every madhouse may convince any man; a brothel where highwaymen meet will convince every philosopher. But the defeat of the work is its inconsistency; the Houyhnhnms are not rational creatures, *i.e.,* creatures of perfect reason; they are not progressive; they have servants without any reason for their natural inferiority or any explanation how the difference acted (?); and, above all, they—*i.e.,* Swift himself—has a perpetual affectation of being wiser than his Maker . . . , and of eradicating what God gave to be subordinated and used; *ex, gr.,* the maternal and paternal affection. . . . There is likewise a true Yahooism in the constant denial of the existence of Love, as not identical with Friendship, and yet distinct always and very often divided from Lust. The best defence is that it is a Satyr; still, it would have been felt a thousand times more deeply if Reason had been truly pourtrayed, and a finer imagination would have been evinced if the author had shown the effect of the possession of Reason and the moral sense in the outward form and gestures of the Horses. In short, critics in general complain of the Yahoos; I complain of the Houyhnhnms.

William Makepeace Thackeray

SOURCE: "Swift," in *The English Humorists of the Eighteenth Century: The Four Georges, Etc.,* Macmillan and Co., Limited, 1904, pp. 1-32.

[Thackeray was a novelist known for his satires of upper-class English life. The following essay, originally published in 1853, presents one of the most extreme examples of eighteenth- and nineteenth-century attacks upon Swift's character and the immorality of Gulliver's Travels.*]*

In the famous Lilliputian kingdom, Swift speaks with approval of the practice of instantly removing children from their parents and educating them by the State; and amongst his favourite horses, a pair of foals are stated to be the very utmost a well-regulated equine couple would permit themselves. In fact, our great satirist was of opinion that conjugal love was unadvisable, and illustrated the theory by his own practice and example—God help him—which made him about the most wretched being in God's world.

As for the humour and conduct of [*Gulliver's Travels*] I suppose there is no person who reads but must admire: as for the moral, I think it horrible, shameful, unmanly, blasphemous; and giant and great as this Dean is, I say we should hoot him. Some of this audience may not have read the last part of Gulliver, and to such I would recall the advice of the venerable Mr. Punch to persons about to marry, and say, 'Don't.' When Gulliver first lands among the Yahoos, the naked howling wretches clamber up trees and assault him, and he describes himself as 'almost stifled with the filth which fell about him.' The reader of the fourth part of *Gulliver's Travels* is like the hero himself in this instance. It is Yahoo language: a monster gibbering shrieks, and gnashing imprecations against mankind—tearing down all shreds of modesty, past all sense of manliness and shame; filthy in word, filthy in thought, furious, raging, obscene.

And dreadful it is to think that Swift knew the tendency of his creed—the fatal rocks towards which his logic desperately drifted. That last part of Gulliver is only a consequence of what has gone before; and the worthlessness of all mankind, the pettiness, cruelty, pride, imbecility, the general vanity, the foolish pretension, the mock greatness, the pompous dulness, the mean aims, the base successes—all these were present to him; it was with the din of these curses of the world, blasphemies against heaven, shrieking in his ears, that he began to write his dreadful allegory—of which the meaning is that man is utterly wicked, desperate, and imbecile, and his passions are so monstrous, and his boasted powers so mean, that he is and deserves to be the slave of brutes, and ignorance is better than his vaunted reason. What had this man done? what secret remorse was rankling at his heart? what fever was boiling in him, that he should see all the world blood-shot? We view the world with our own eyes, each of us; and we make from within us the world we see. . . .

Edmund Gosse

SOURCE: "From A History of Eighteenth Century Literature," in *A Casebook on Gulliver among the Houyhnhnms,* edited by Milton P. Foster, Thomas Y. Crowell Company, 1961, pp. 83-4.

[The following excerpt was originally published in Gosse's A History of Eighteenth Century Literature, *1889.]*

In all these miscellaneous excursions there is little or nothing which displays to us the darker side of Swift's genius. That side is, however, exemplified to excess in the final part, the Voyage to the Country of the Houyhnhnms. It is difficult not to believe that this was written during the last illness of Stella, when Swift was aware that his best companion was certainly leaving him, and when that remorse which he could not but feel for his conduct to the woman who had so long loved him was turning what milk remained in his nature to gall. In the summer of 1726 the loss of Stella's conversation made him, he tells us, weary of life, and he fled from Ireland in a horror lest he should be a witness of her end. Delany tells us that from the time of her death, and probably from a few months earlier, Swift's character and temper underwent a change. His vertigo became chronic, and so did his misanthropy, and it seems probable that the first literary expression of his rage and despair was the awful satire of the Yahoos. It was with the horrible satisfaction of disease that Swift formed a story which could enable him to describe men as being, though "with some appearance of cunning, and the strongest disposition to mischief, yet the most unteachable of all brutes," and there is something which suggests a brain not wholly under control in the very machinery of this part of the romance. In Lilliput and in Brobdingnag we are struck by the ingenious harmony of the whole design, there being no detail which is not readily credible if we admit the possibility of the scheme; but among the Houyhnhnms probability is ruthlessly sacrificed to the wild pleasure the author takes in trampling human pride in the mire of his sarcasm. Of the horrible foulness of this satire on the Yahoos enough will have been said when it is admitted that it banishes from decent households a fourth part of one of the most brilliant and delightful of English books.

W. L. Phelps

SOURCE: "A Note on Gulliver," in *Twentieth Century Interpretations of 'Gulliver's Travels': A Collection of Critical Essays,* edited by Frank Brady, Prentice-Hall, Inc., 1968, p. 97.

[The following excerpt was originally published in The Yale Review, *1927.]*

[Swift] may have taken horses as the ideal [in Book IV] because England—much more than any other country—is the land of horses, where this animal is understood and appreciated. There is an enormous difference between England and America in the respective attention paid to these quadrupeds. There is not a single horse-race in America that is in any sense a national event, like the Derby in England. Nor does anyone—outside of those few specially interested—ever hear horse-racing discussed, as one hears baseball, tennis, football, and prize-fighting. I have never heard anyone in any American club mention horse-racing. George Moore's "Esther Waters" was a revelation to Americans of the English obsession.

Perhaps it is not too fanciful for me to suggest that another reason for taking the Houyhnhnms is because their language and inflection are so similar to the speech of English gentlemen. H. G. Wells in "Christina Alberta's Father" mentions an Englishman with one of these "whinnying voices," an absolutely accurate description, the voice beginning high and hesitating, and descending in cascades of sound.

J. R. Moore

SOURCE: "The Geography of *Gulliver's Travels,*" in *Twentieth Century Interpretations of 'Gulliver's Travels': A Collection of Critical Essays,* edited by Frank Brady, Prentice-Hall, Inc., 1968, pp. 102-04.

[The following excerpt was originally published in Journal of English and Germanic Philology, *1941.]*

It is a commonplace that *Gulliver's Travels* is patterned after the real voyages of Swift's age, which it either travesties or imitates. It lacks the supplement, describing the flora and fauna, so often appended to voyages; but it has the connecting links of detailed narrative, the solemn spirit of inquiry into strange lands, the factual records of latitude and coasts and prevailing winds, and (most of all) *the maps.* . . .

According to a letter to Swift, written November 8, 1726, Dr. Arbuthnot "lent the book to an old gentleman, who went immediately to his map to search for Lilliput." That old gentleman is now presumably dead; the results of his investigation are long overdue. . . . In the latest critical edition of *Gulliver's Travels* the editor informs us that

> Swift took a great deal of pains to make these sections of the narrative as plausible and circumstantial as possible. . . . Swift was bold enough to supply fairly exact data concerning the positions of these countries, although two errors (in the first chapter of the first voyage and the first chapter of the third voyage) and an insufficiently detailed paragraph in the next to the last chapter of the fourth voyage have led to some misunderstanding. . . . If this initial error is corrected all the rest of the geographical data which have caused confusion fall neatly into place. . . . the geography, was carefully worked out, . . .

These assumptions of the essential accuracy of the geography of *Gulliver's Travels* are groundless. Not only are the fanciful regions of Brobdingnag and Laputa quite unlike those shown on the maps of the First Edition; even if we allow for all possible errors from slips of unsupervised printers in faraway London, and for the probability of still greater errors from editorial attempts to correct the text, the geography of the book is so incredible that we must assume (1) that Swift intended an extravagant burlesque on voyages, or (2) that he was ignorant of geography, or (3) that he intended a burlesque and knew too little geography to carry it out accurately. . . .

Gulliver reported that the dominions of Brobdingnag reached "about six thousand miles in length, and from three to five in breadth." Mr. G. R. Dennis annotated this with a very cautious remark that "It will be noticed that on the map Brobdingnag is made very much smaller; but, as Sir Henry Craik suggests, this may be due to the engravers."

Precisely so. On leaving Brobdingnag Gulliver was picked up by a vessel which had reached a longitude of 143° E. and a latitude of 44° N., and he was told that he was at least a hundred leagues from any land. The eagle which had carried him southward from the southern extremity of Brobdingnag had presumably brought him from a latitude of approximately 50°. At that latitude the lessening of the earth toward the North Pole has become so considerable that *a degree of longitude* (which amounts to 69 statute miles at the equator) *has lessened to approximately 45 miles.* Six thousand miles, at 45 miles to the degree, would extend for about 133° of longitude, or considerably more than a third of the way around the globe on the fiftieth parallel. The ship's captain had reached a longitude of 143° E. before rescuing Gulliver. If the eastern end of Brobdingnag lay directly north of there, the western extremity would lie due north of Hamburg. If the western end of Brobdingnag lay in a longitude of 143° E., the eastern limit would be somewhere north of Saginaw, Michigan. . . .

As the other voyages do not lead to Brobdingnag, they cannot be expected to furnish such Gargantuan dimensions; but all were, in their way, incredible enough. The piratical crew of the fourth voyage, who sailed on past the Cape of Good Hope for the explicit purpose of marooning their captain, were not satisfied with putting Gulliver off at one of the usual landing places for pirates on or near Madagascar. They went on and on, out of any known course, until they confessed that they had no idea where they were, and put him off some 4,000 nautical miles or more (or, if we accept the suggestion that he was marooned near the southeast end of Tasmania, some 6,000 miles) east of the Cape, by far the longest voyage of the sort in the annals of piracy. If the land of the Houyhnhnms was where Gulliver *seemed* to place it, west of the southwestern extremity of Australia, he was able, in leaving the country, to travel 1,500 or 2,000 nautical miles eastward in a canoe of stitched Yahoo skins, *in an actual sailing time of sixteen hours at a speed which he estimated at no more than a league and a half an hour.* To be sure, Gulliver had a "very favourable wind," but his "little sail" was obviously some sort of magic carpet.

> # TRAVELS
> ### INTO SEVERAL
> ## Remote NATIONS
> ### OF THE
> # WORLD.
> ### In FOUR PARTS.
> By *LEMUEL GULLIVER*,
> Firſt a Surgeon, and then a Cap-
> tain of ſeveral SHIPS.
> ## Vol. I.
> ### *LONDON:*
> *Printed for* Benj. Motte, *at the*
> *Middle* Temple-Gate *in* Fleet-ſtreet.
> Mdccxxvi.

Half-title page from Travels into Several Remote Nations of the World, *written by Jonathan Swift, 1726.*

George Orwell

SOURCE: "Politics vs. Literature: An Examination of *Gulliver's Travels,*" in *Shooting an Elephant and Other Essays,* Harcourt Brace Jovanovich, 1950, pp. 53-76.

Orwell is significant for his unwavering commitment, both as a man and an artist, to personal freedom and social justice. His controversial essay on Swift, "Politics vs. Literature," originally published in Polemic, *1946, displays one great political satirist commenting on another. In the following excerpt from that work, Orwell expresses admiration for* **Gulliver's Travels,** *but professes abhorrence for Swift's temperament, which he characterizes as authoritarian and reactionary, and for Swift's belief that any form of social improvement was impossible.]*

[No] one would deny that **Gulliver's Travels** is a rancorous as well as a pessimistic book, and that especially in Parts I and III it often descends into political partisanship of a narrow kind. Pettiness and magnanimity, republicanism and authoritarianism, love of reason and lack of curiosity, are all mixed up in it. The hatred of the human body with which Swift is especially associated is only dominated in Part IV, but somehow this new preoccupation does not come as a surprise. . . .

Swift's disgust, rancor and pessimism would make sense against the background of a "next world" to which this one is the prelude. As he does not appear to believe seriously in any such thing, it becomes necessary to construct a paradise supposedly existing on the surface of the earth, but something quite different from anything we know, with all that he disapproves of—lies, folly, change, enthusiasm, pleasure, love and dirt—eliminated from it. As his ideal being he chooses the horse. . . . [But the Houyhnhnms] are unattractive because the "Reason" by which they are governed is really a desire for death. They are exempt from love, friendship, curiosity, fear, sorrow and—except in their feelings towards the Yahoos, who occupy rather the same place in their community as the Jews in Nazi Germany—anger and hatred. . . . They lay store by "Friendship" and "Benevolence," but "these are not confined to particular Objects, but universal to the whole Race." They also value conversation, but in their conversations there are no differences of opinion, and "nothing passed but what was useful, expressed in the fewest and most significant Words." . . . Their marriages are arranged for them by their elders, on eugenic principles, and their language contains no word for "love," in the sexual sense. When somebody dies they carry on exactly as before, without feeling any grief. It will be seen that their aim is to be as like a corpse as is possible while retaining physical life.

Happiness is notoriously difficult to describe, and pictures of a just and well-ordered Society are seldom either attractive or convincing. Most creators of "favorable" Utopias, however, are concerned to show what life could be like if it were lived more fully. Swift advocates a simple refusal of life, justifying this by the claim that "Reason" consists in thwarting your instincts. The Houyhnhnms, creatures without a history, continue for generation after generation to live prudently maintaining their population at exactly the same level, avoiding all passion, suffering from no diseases, meeting death indifferently, training up their young in the same principles—and all for what? In order that the same process may continue indefinitely. The notions that life here and now is worth living, or that it could be made worth living, or that it must be sacrificed for some future good, are all absent. The dreary world of the Houyhnhnms was about as good a Utopia as Swift could construct, granting that he neither believed in a "next world" nor could get any pleasure out of certain normal activities.

From what I have written it may have seemed that I am *against* Swift, and that my object is to refute him and even to belittle him. In a political and moral sense I am against him, so far as I understand him. Yet curiously enough he is one of the writers I admire with least reserve, and *Gulliver's Travels,* in particular, is a book which it seems impossible for me to grow tired of. . . . Its fascination seems inexhaustible. If I had to make a list of six books which were to be preserved when all others were destroyed, I would certainly put *Gulliver's Travels* among them. This raises the question: what is the relationship between agreement with a writer's opinions, and enjoyment of his work?

If one is capable of intellectual detachment, one can *perceive* merit in a writer whom one deeply disagrees with, but *enjoyment* is a different matter. . . . If a book angers, wounds or alarms you, then you will not enjoy it, whatever its merits may be. If it seems to you a really pernicious book, likely to influence other people in some undesirable way, then you will probably construct an aesthetic theory to show that it *has* no merits. And yet the opposite process can also happen: enjoyment can overwhelm disapproval, even though one clearly recognizes that one is enjoying something inimical. Swift, whose world-view is so peculiarly unacceptable, but who is nevertheless an extremely popular writer, is a good instance of this. Why is it that we don't mind being called Yahoos, although firmly convinced that we are *not* Yahoos?

Millions of people, in many countries, must have enjoyed *Gulliver's Travels* while more or less seeing its antihuman implications: and even the child who accepts Parts I and II as a simple story gets a sense of absurdity from thinking of human beings six inches high. The explanation must be that Swift's world-view is felt to be *not* altogether false—or it would probably be more accurate to say, not false all the time. Swift is a diseased writer. He remains permanently in a depressed mood which in most people is only intermittent, rather as though someone suffering from jaundice or the after-effects of influenza should have the energy to write books. But we all know that mood, and something in us responds to the expression of it. . . . Swift falsifies his

picture of the world by refusing to see anything in human life except dirt, folly and wickedness, but the part which he abstracts from the whole does exist, and it is something which we all know about while shrinking from mentioning it. Part of our minds—in any normal person it is the dominant part—believes that man is a noble animal and life is worth living; but there is also a sort of inner self which at least intermittently stands aghast at the horror of existence. In the queerest way, pleasure and disgust are linked together. The human body is beautiful: it is also repulsive and ridiculous, a fact which can be verified at any swimming pool. The sexual organs are objects of desire and also of loathing, so much so that in many languages, if not in all languages, their names are used as words of abuse. Meat is delicious, but a butcher's shop makes one feel sick: and indeed all our food springs ultimately from dung and dead bodies, the two things which of all others seem to us the most horrible. A child, when it is past the infantile stage but still looking at the world with fresh eyes, is moved by horror almost as often as by wonder—horror of snot and spittle, of the dogs' excrement on the pavement, the dying toad full of maggots, the sweaty smell of grown-ups, the hideousness of old men, with their bald heads and bulbous noses. In his endless harping on disease, dirt and deformity, Swift is not actually inventing anything, he is merely leaving something out. Human behavior, too, especially in politics, is as he describes it, although it contains other more important factors which he refuses to admit. So far as we can see, both horror and pain are necessary to the continuance of life on this planet, and it is therefore open to pessimists like Swift to say: "If horror and pain must always be with us, how can life be significantly improved?" His attitude is in effect the Christian attitude, minus the bribe of a "next world"—which, however, probably has less hold upon the minds of believers than the conviction that this world is a vale of tears and the grave is a place of rest. It is, I am certain, a wrong attitude, and one which could have harmful effects upon behavior; but something in us responds to it, as it responds to the gloomy words of the burial service and the sweetish smell of corpses in a country church.

It is often argued, at least by people who admit the importance of subject-matter, that a book cannot be "good" if it expresses a palpably false view of life. We are told that in our own age, for instance, any book that has genuine literary merit will also be more or less "progressive" in tendency. This ignores the fact that throughout history a similar struggle between progress and reaction has been raging, and that the best books of any one age have always been written from several different viewpoints, some of them palpably more false than others. In so far as a writer is a propagandist, the most one can ask of him is that he shall genuinely believe in what he is saying, and that it shall not be something blazingly silly. Today, for example, one can imagine a good book being written by a Catholic, a Communist, a Fascist, a pacifist, an anarchist, perhaps by an old-style Liberal or an ordinary Conservative: one cannot imagine a good book being written by a spiritualist, a Buchmanite or a member of the Ku Klux Klan. The views that a writer holds must be compatible with sanity, in the medical sense, and with the power of continuous thought: beyond that what we ask of him is talent, which is probably another name for conviction. Swift did not possess ordinary wisdom, but he did possess a terrible intensity of vision, capable of picking out a single hidden truth and then magnifying it and distorting it. The durability of *Gulliver's Travels* goes to show that, if the force of belief is behind it, a world-view which only just passes the test of sanity is sufficient to produce a great work of art.

Edward A. Block

SOURCE: "Lemuel Gulliver: Middle-Class Englishman," in *Modern Language Notes,* Vol. LXVIII, No. 7, November, 1953, pp. 474-77.

That Gulliver was intended ultimately to represent, and to be recognized as, an average human being of no particular nationality and of no particular age was pointed out by Swift himself in his letter to Abbé Desfontaines, the translator of the *Travels* into French. However, by the very scheme of the *Travels,* Swift was compelled to give his universal and timeless hero a "local habitation and a name"; he therefore presented him in such a way that the reader's awareness of Gulliver's universality and timelessness stems out of his prior recognition that he represents the average Englishman.

What I believe has not hitherto been noted is the care with which Swift in the opening lines of *Gulliver's Travels* indelibly places the middle-class stamp upon Gulliver to the end that from the very outset the reader shall recognize him for exactly what, at the primary level, his creator intended him to represent, namely, the average Englishman. Deceiving in its simplicity, but pregnant with meaning, the opening sentence reads as follows: "My father had a small estate in Nottinghamshire; I was the third of five sons." It is immediately obvious that Gulliver is the middle son in the sense that he could never have been if his father had had 2, 4, or 6 sons. Again, his father has a small estate. If he had a large estate he would have been a member of either the upper class or the upper-middle class; if he had had no estate, he would have been a member of the lower class or the lower-middle class. As the owner of a small estate he is evidently a member of the middle-middle class. Finally, a casual glance at a map of England reveals the fact that Nottinghamshire is geographically a middle county: it is almost equidistant from the North Sea and the Welsh border, on the one hand; it is exactly equidistant from the Scottish border and the English Channel, on the other.

The opening words of the next sentence are also, I think, significant. There we read that "he (Gulliver's father) sent me to Emmanuel College in Cambridge. . . . " From the information contained in the opening pages of the *Travels* it is a simple matter to calculate that Gulliver was in residence at Emmanuel College during the three years 1675-1678. Founded by Sir Walter Mildmay in 1584, in order to train ministers who would later become preachers in various parts of the country, Emmanuel became closely connected with the Puritan movement and, in fact, adopted certain Puritan customs, such as sitting at Communion, using an unconsecrated chapel, and making its own deviations from the Prayer Book. "Puritan families flocked there," writes A. L. Rowse, who adds that "by far the largest contingent of any college, and the most influential, came from this (Emmanuel College) to become pastors in the new England across the Atlantic." Indeed, for the first 50 years of its existence, Emmanuel was marked by its extreme Puritanism. If Cambridge was, as is generally agreed, the intellectual centre of Puritanism, then Emmanuel must properly be regarded as the intellectual centre of Cambridge Puritanism. Furthermore, if Puritanism was "the reasoned expression of the middle-class state of mind" its centre was very definitely in the middle class, and its leading spirits were middle-class men. In short, during the 50-year period 1584-1634, Emmanuel College was the symbol *par excellence* of a middle-class education.

Much happened at Emmanuel between 1634 and 1675, when Gulliver took up residence there. As we have seen, its early history reflects the rise of Puritanism; its later history, however, just as certainly reflects the decline of Puritanism, for by 1660 Emmanuel College had, with the rest of the country, swung over to the King's side at least to the extent that it was prepared to accept the religious and political changes involved in the Restoration. Actually, the Restoration marked a turning point in the College's history. No longer enjoying the advantage that it had so long derived from its position as the favored seed-bed for ministers of a triumphant religious sect, it became the home of undistinguished conformity, "of sound loyalty and Churchmanship." Thus, just about the time Gulliver was attending Emmanuel College it was entering upon a long period of comparative insignificance and mediocrity, which persisted through the years when Swift was writing the *Travels.* I hazard the suggestion that, in sending Gulliver to Emmanuel, Swift had a double motivation. In the first place, on the basis of its early history, Emmanuel was the symbol of middle-class education; in the second place, on the basis of its history from 1634 to 1675 and later, it symbolized the change that came over the nation at large, and particularly over the middle class, as the tide of Puritanism ebbed and Anglicanism surged in. On both counts, or on either, the fact that Gulliver attended Emmanuel would seem to have a significance; it was, I think, intended to show that he obtained a typical middle-class education in a way that he could not have, had he gone to Oxford, which had remained staunchly Anglican and Royalist, or to another Cambridge College which, lacking Emmanuel's Puritan background, was unable to reflect the changing religious and political sympathies of the middle class.

As we have seen, Gulliver stalks into the pages of the *Travels* as the middle son in a family of five sons; is brought up by a middle-middle class father in a county

' I roared.'

From Travels into Several Remote Nations of the World. By Lemuel Gulliver, First a Surgeon, and Then a Captain of Several Ships. *Written by Jonathan Swift. Illustrated by Charles E. Brock, 1894.*

that lies as nearly as it is possible for a county to lie at the very geographical centre of England; and then proceeds to receive an education which seems, in one way or another, intended to represent the quintessence of a middle-class education. These details are cumulatively impressive; so much so that I find it difficult to believe that they were inserted unintentionally. Actually, I am suggesting that the opening lines of the *Travels* not only play an important part in establishing Gulliver's middle-class role, but that they do so designedly, and therefore constitute one more interesting and significant example of Swift's scrupulous attention to detail in the interest of achieving a larger purpose.

Lillian H. Smith

SOURCE: "The Lineage of Children's Literature" and "Fantasy," in *The Unreluctant Years: A Critical Approach to Children's Literature,* American Library Association, 1953, pp. 23, 158.

Dean [Jonathan] Swift never intended his stinging, biting

satire, *Gulliver's Travels,* for children. It is interesting to speculate what he would have said, had someone told him that the book he worked at so savagely, night after night, in his big lonely house in Ireland, would be the delight of many generations of boys and girls. There is much in *Gulliver's Travels* that children cannot understand. They take what they like from it; and what they like best is the inexhaustible imagination that pictured and peopled the Lilliputian world in which Gulliver has such entertaining adventures, and the equally surprising and laughable predicaments of Gulliver in Brobdingnag among the giants. To them it is a story, as alive today as when it first appeared in 1726. . . .

"How did the children happen to get hold of Swift?" asks Paul Hazard. Like *Pilgrim's Progress* and *Don Quixote, Gulliver's Travels* owes its place as one of the immortal classics of childhood to the fact that children stumbled on it in an age which produced little else from which children could obtain the imaginative sustenance they craved. *Gulliver's Travels* proved an antidote to the dreary moral and didactic tales with which their elders strove to improve the young.

Children have always refused to be bored by what does not interest them. They excel in the gentle art of skipping. It is the miniature world of Lilliputia and the reverse world of the giants that beguile them in *Gulliver's Travels.* As Paul Hazard says "They like its wild inventions that are not only comical but concrete." The rest of the book is forgotten.

Marjorie Nicolson and Nora Mohler

SOURCE: "The Scientific Background of Swift's 'Voyage to Laputa,'" in *Science and Imagination,* by Marjorie Nicolson, Great Seal Books, 1956, pp. 110-54.

[Nicolson and Mohler examine the scientific background of Swift's "Voyage to Laputa," suggesting the Philosophical Transactions of the Royal Society as the specific source for the general idea of the travels of Gulliver and of Swift's Laputans, his projectors of the Grand Academy of Lagado, and his Flying Island. The following excerpt probes the eighteenth-century context of the Laputans' fear of the sun and of a comet.]

The widespread interest in scientific discovery among English men of letters was in large part a natural effect of the rapid strides made by science during the seventeenth and eighteenth centuries. More specifically, it was the result of the attendance at meetings of the Royal Society by men of letters, many of whom claimed the title of *virtuosi,* and of the publication of the *Philosophical Transactions,* which were widely read. In addition to the complete *Transactions,* various abridged editions were published in the early eighteenth century. In 1705 many of the papers were made still more accessible in an edition in three volumes under the title *Miscellanea Curiosa.* Reports of discoveries, inventions and experiments were therefore available in various ways to Jonathan Swift in Ireland, and even more after his return to England, where he "corrected, amended, and augmented" his voyages. The influence of the *Philosophical Transactions* upon Swift appears in two ways. These volumes were storehouses of such accounts of travel as those imitated by Swift in *Gulliver's Travels.* In addition they offered him specific sources for his scientific details in the "Voyage to Laputa."

The various sources of the general idea of such voyages as those of Gulliver have been traced so often and are so obviously part of the great interest in travel that had persisted in England since the time of the earliest voyagers that it seems almost a work of supererogation to suggest the *Philosophical Transactions* as still another source for the main idea of *Gulliver's Travels.* Yet it is at least interesting to see the space devoted in the *Transactions*—particularly between 1700 and 1720—to accounts of travel. From them Swift may well have gleaned many a suggestion not only for the proper style of Captain Lemuel Gulliver, but also for the pattern of such tales of travel and observation, for such a pattern there was in the actual accounts. The newly discovered islands of the Philippines, reported in the *Transactions,* must have appealed to the creator of Gulliver, who discovered so many islands, some inhabited, some desolate; the Hottentots, as they appear in the accounts sent to the Royal Society, are as curious a people as any discovered by Gulliver.

More specifically, Swift may have picked up from these voyages a hint for his "men who never die," the Struldbrugs. The authors who reported this particular group of travels to the Royal Society showed an almost morbid interest in "antient" men who live too long. Mr. G. Plaxton, a clergyman, who seemed to have an uncanny affinity for livings in remote districts, reported from the parsonage of Kinnardsey: "I took the Number of the Inhabitants, and found that every sixth Soul was sixty Years of Age, and upwards; some were 85, and some 90." His next incumbency proved even more remarkable; the number of the aged was much greater and the parishioners lived so long that the Reverend Mr. Plaxton seldom had the pleasure of burying a member of his flock. . . . Like the Struldbrugs, [these men] have passed beyond curiosity, and beyond interest in life. With Tithonus they seem to have found immortal life but not immortal youth. Gulliver saw the Struldbrugs as "the most mortifying sight I ever beheld. . . . Besides the usual deformities in extreme old age, they acquired an additional ghastliness in proportion to their number of years, which is not to be described. . . ."

Whether such voyages as those in the *Philosophical Transactions* combined in Swift's mind with literary sources already well established to lead him to the general idea of the travels of Gulliver, we may conjecture, though not prove. That the *Philosophical Transactions,* together with more complete works of the *virtuosi,* were the specific source of Swift's Laputans, his projectors of the Grand Academy of Lagado, and his Flying Island can be proved beyond the possibility of doubt.

The section of the "Voyage to Laputa" which deals with the mathematical peculiarities of the Laputans has been generally recognized to be of a piece with others of Swift's pronouncements upon mathematicians. Although several of the critics incline to think that such satire is peculiar to Swift, there is little in the main idea of this section that is unique. Behind the Laputans lay the rapidly growing interest of the seventeenth century in mathematics, embodied in the work of Kepler, Descartes, Leibniz and many others, and a persistent attitude of the seventeenth-century layman toward the "uselessness" of physical and mathematical learning. . . .

More specific satire with [a] more immediate source is found in the sections in which Swift discusses the two predominant prepossessions of the Laputans—their fear of the sun and of a comet. In spite of Swift's suggestion that the Laputans still share astrological fears, he has made them a people whose dread is founded less upon tradition than upon celestial observation. They possess "glasses far excelling ours in goodness," by means of which they have extended "their discoveries much further than our astronomers in Europe." They have made important discoveries with their telescopes, none more remarkable than that of the two satellites of Mars—which actually remained hidden from all eyes but those of the Laputans until 1877! They are careful observers, among whom one would expect to find science rather than superstition. Yet their dread of the sun and of a comet is greater than had been their ancestors', for their fear is more deeply rooted in contemporary science.

Three ideas of the sun particularly disturbed the Laputans:

> that the earth, by the continual approaches of the sun towards it, must in course of time be absorbed or swallowed up. That the face of the sun will by degrees be encrusted with its own effluvia, and give no more light to the world. . . . That the sun daily spending its rays without any nutriment to supply them, will at last be wholly consumed and annihilated; which must be attended with the destruction of this earth, and of all the planets that receive their light from it.

Such fears were in no way original with the Laputans. Behind the fear that their planet might fall into the sun lay the potent influence of "Britain's justest pride, the boast of human race." Newton's analysis of planetary motion showed that there must exist a nice balance between the velocity with which the earth is falling toward the sun and its tangential velocity at right angles to that fall. Any disturbance of this "due proportion of velocity" would be disastrous. The most obvious possibility of disturbance is the gradual decrease of our tangential velocity, for then the earth's orbit would no longer repeat itself year after year, but would approach the sun with ever-increasing speed, eventually to fall into it. This possibility is recognized in the *Principia* by general calculations of the time required for such falls, and by an estimate of the density of the material in space through which the earth spins and the retarding effect to be expected from it. While Newton's conclusion was, on the whole, an optimistic one that the loss of velocity would be quite inappreciable even for "an immense tract of time," other conclusions were drawn from the same premises. The Laputans might well have found reason for their doubt in Robert Hooke, who, opposing his wave-theory to Newton's theory of light, recognized clearly that there is difficulty in describing the medium which carried these waves and that any imaginable medium would have a retarding effect upon the earth's motion.

Die we must, it would seem, if we are fearful eighteenth-century Laputans. Even if we follow the conclusion of Newton in regard to our earth's falling into the sun, there still remains the warning of the sun-spots and of the consumption of the sun's energy. From the time of Galileo's first observation of sun-spots, astronomers had been concerned to explain these phenomena. During the early years of the eighteenth century the *Philosophical Transactions* devoted much attention to the problem of these phenomena. A letter of "Mr. Crabtrie," written in 1640, was revived and republished, and his theory

debated, that the spots were "fading Bodies . . . no Stars, but unconstant (in regard of their Generation) and irregular Excrescences arising out of, or proceeding from the Sun's body." At the least, these spots indicated "a Smoak arising out of the Body of the Sun." At the worst, the "Smoak" suggested volcanic action. . . .

The Laputans, it would seem, were incorrigible pessimists. Granted we escape falling into the sun, and granted too that the sun-spots indicate only "Smoak," not "Vulcano," our fate will be as surely sealed, if the sun cools or dwindles to a vanishing point. The natural explanation of the heat of the sun, that it is a tremendous burning mass, had been made even more plausible by the discovery of those spots on the sun, which look suspiciously like smoke. . . .

Fear of the sun was not all; even greater was the Laputan dread of comets and of one comet in particular. "The earth very narrowly escaped a brush from the tail of the late comet, which would infallibly have reduced it to ashes," Gulliver learned in Laputa. It is not however the "last comet" that terrifies the Laputans so much as one that is to come "which will probably destroy us." Is this mere pointless satire? Swift's imagination here, as so often, is making of the real something apparently unreal. His reference, as every reader of his day must have realized, was not merely to a comet, but to "Halley's comet"—the first comet whose period of return was definitely predicted, with resultant excitement both to literary and to scientific imagination. Thomson, writing only a year later than Swift, shows the same interest when he writes in "Summer":

> Lo! from the dread immensity of space
> Returning with accelerated course,
> The rushing comet to the sun descends:
> And as he sinks below the shading earth,
> With awful train projected o'er the heavens,
> The guilty nations tremble. . . .
> While, from his far excursion through the wilds
> Of barren ether, faithful to his time,
> They see the blazing wonder rise anew.

In this passage Swift has told us the date of composition of at least part of the "Voyage to Laputa." The Laputans calculated the return of their comet in "one and thirty years"; thirty-one years after 1726—the date of the first publication of *Gulliver's Travels*—English laymen expected the return of Halley's comet. True, Halley himself had predicted that the comet of 1682 would return not in 1757, as Swift's passage implies, but in 1758; but Halley's prophecy left some reason for doubt. Laymen, then as now, grasped the main point, but neglected the careful mathematics in which Halley corrected a generalization. Seventy-five years had elapsed between the appearance of the comet in 1607 and its reappearance in 1682; years, not days, are important to the layman. The "Mean period" Halley himself calculated at "75 Years and a half." The general public was not at all concerned with the careful table of Halley's "inequalities" nor with his masterful application to his theory of comets of the explanation he had earlier proposed for the deviation from equality in the case of Jupiter and Saturn. As he had suggested that that inequality was the result of the attraction of these planets for each other, in addition to the attraction of the sun for both, so he concluded that the inequalities in the comet's return might arise from a similar cause. The layman understood only that the comet would appear in approximately seventy-five years; and he vaguely recognized that, if it did, it would put beyond question Newton's theory of gravitation.

In the period of the Renaissance, "Comets importing change of time and states" had brandished their bloody tresses, and predicted "disasters in the sun." But during the seventeenth century, under the impact of the new astronomy, the attitude toward comets began gradually to change, as men questioned whether these strange phenomena too might not prove to have a natural place in the great cosmic scheme. There are indications in almanacs and other popular literature of the day that this was one result of Newton's discoveries. Nevertheless, old beliefs still largely dominated popular imagination. As Swift himself wrote: "Old men and comets have been reverenced for the same reasons; their long beards, and pretenses to foretell events."

The dread of the Laputans rested however less upon such superstition than upon scientific discovery. With their telescopes they had "observed ninety-three different comets, and settled their periods with great exactness." If therefore they feared that a comet "one and thirty years hence" would destroy them, they must have had scientific grounds for their belief. The basis for their fear was implied even in Halley's earlier *Synopsis,* in connection with his discussion of the approach of various comets to the earth. His paper concluded with the statement: "But what might be the Consequences of so near an appulse; or of a contact, or, lastly, of a shock of the Celestial Bodies, (which is by no means impossible to come to pass,) I leave to be discussed by the Studious of Physical matters." In his later amplification of the *Synopsis,* Halley went further and expanded this section in connection with the comet of 1680:

> Now this Comet, in that part of its Orbit in which it descended towards the Sun, came so near the paths of all the Planets, that if by chance it had happened to meet any one of the Planets passing by, it must have produced very sensible effects, and the motion of the Comet would have suffered the greatest disturbance. In such case the plane and species of its Ellipsis and its periodic Time would have been very much changed, especially from meeting with Jupiter. In the late descent, the true path of this Comet left the Orbits of Saturn and Jupiter below itself a little towards the South: It approached much nearer to the paths of Venus and Mercury, and much nearer still to that of Mars. But as it was passing thro' the plane of the Ecliptic, viz., to the southern Node, it came so near the path of the Earth, that had it come towards the Sun thirty one days later than it did, it had scarce left our Globe one semidiameter of the Sun towards the North: And without doubt by its centripetal

> force . . . it would have produced some change in the situation and species of the Earth's Orbit, and in the length of the year. But may the good GOD avert such a shock or contact of such great Bodies moving with such forces (which however is manifestly by no means impossible), lest this most beautiful order of things be intirely destroyed and reduced into its antient chaos.

Although this suggestion alone would have been sufficient to explain the Laputans' dread of the comet, there is little doubt that popular imagination was even more deeply stirred by another paper which Halley presented to the Royal Society—on the subject of Noah and the Flood. This was one of many papers published in the period by important men of science in which an attempt was made to explain difficult passages in Scripture in such a way as to keep the reverence for the Bible, yet make it consistent with modern scientific thought. Straining at the gnat, Halley and others swallowed the Deluge. In an earlier version of the paper, read before the Royal Society [December 12, 1694], Halley had suggested "the casual Choc of a Comet, or other transient Body" as "an Expedient to change instantly the Poles and Diurnal Rotation of the Globe." But in the later paper he went further: "At that Time," he says, "I did not consider the great Agitation such a Choc must necessarily occasion in the Sea." Halley's description of the probable consequences of such a "Choc" was sufficient to strike terror into braver hearts than those of the Laputans. He visualizes the Deluge

> raising up Mountains where none were before, mixing the Elements into such a Heap as the Poets describe the Old Chaos; for such a Choc impelling the solid Parts would occasion the Waters, and all fluid Substances that were unconfined, as the Sea is, with one Impetus to run violently towards that Part of the Globe were [*sic*] the Blow was received; and that with Force sufficient to rake with it the whole Bottom of the Ocean, and to carry it upon the Land; heaping up into Mountains those earthy Parts it had born away with it, in those Places where the opposite Waves balance each other, *miscens ima summis.*

Thus Halley, discovering that the comets, like the stars in their courses, obey the universal law of gravitation, established in 1705 the point of view that was to free men from their long dread of "those stars with trains of fire and dews of blood": but through a few sentences in a paper in which he announced the law of comets, and, most of all, through republishing in 1724 a paper largely written thirty years before on the subject of that Deluge weathered only by an ark, put into the minds of the Laputans—and many of Swift's contemporaries—a greater dread, of the complete annihilation of this globe which we inhabit. Small wonder that in the morning the Laputans exchanged no trivial greetings. "The first question is about the sun's health, how he looked at his setting and rising, and what hopes they have to avoid the stroke of the approaching comet." Like children who have listened to tales of hobgoblins, the Laputans "dared not go to bed for fear."

Paul Fussell

SOURCE: "The Frailty of Lemuel Gulliver," in *Twentieth Century Interpretations of 'Gulliver's Travels': A Collection of Critical Essays,* edited by Frank Brady, Prentice-Hall, Inc., 1968, pp. 106-07.

[The following excerpt was originally published in Literary History, *edited by Rudolf Kirk and C. F. Main, 1960]*

Gulliver's clothing and personal property are perpetually suffering damage, and, when they are not actually being damaged, Gulliver is worrying that, at any moment, they may be. Of course, mindful of Crusoe's pathetic situation, we are not surprised that a shipwrecked mariner suffers damage to his clothing and personal effects. But we may be surprised to hear Gulliver go out of his way to call careful attention to the damages and losses he suffers. In the first voyage, for example, Gulliver circumstantially lets us know that his scimitar has rusted, that his hat has been sorely damaged by being hauled through the dust all the way from the sea to the capital, and that his breeches have suffered an embarrassing rent. The boat in which Gulliver escapes to Blefuscu is, we are carefully told, "but little damaged." Once off the islands and, we might suppose, secure from losses and accidents until his next voyage, Gulliver loses one of his tiny souvenir sheep—it is destroyed by a rat aboard ship.

Presumably outfitted anew, Gulliver arrives ashore in Brobdingnag with his effects intact, but the old familiar process of damage and deterioration now begins all over again. Wheat beards rip his clothes; a fall into a bowl of milk utterly spoils Gulliver's suit; his stockings and breeches are soiled when he is thrust into the marrow bone which the queen has been enjoying at dinner; his clothes are again damaged by his tumble into the mole hill; and his suit (what's left of it) is further ruined by being daubed by frog slime and "bemired" with cow dung. Likewise, in the third voyage, our attention is called to the fact that Gulliver's hat has again worn out, and in the fourth voyage we are informed yet again by Gulliver that his clothes are "in a declining Condition."

At times, in fact, Gulliver's clothes and personal effects seem to be Gulliver himself: this is the apparent state of things which fascinates the observing Houyhnhnm before whom Gulliver undresses, and this ironic suggestion of an equation between Gulliver and his clothing, reminding us of the ironic "clothes philosophy" of Section II of *A Tale of a Tub,* Swift exploits to emphasize that

From the NBC television movie, "Gulliver's Travels," starring Ted Danson, 1994.

damage to Gulliver's naturalistic garments is really damage to the naturalistic Gulliver. The vulnerability of Gulliver's clothing, that is, is a symbol three degrees removed from what it signifies: damage to Gulliver's clothes is symbolic of damage to Gulliver's body, which, in turn, is emblematic of damage to Gulliver's self-esteem.

Jim W. Corder

SOURCE: "Gulliver in England," in *Twentieth Century Interpretations of 'Gulliver's Travels': A Collection of Critical Essays,* edited by Frank Brady, Prentice-Hall, Inc., 1968, pp. 107-09.

[The following excerpt was originally published in College English, *1961.]*

The land of the Houyhnhnms is after all a familiar setting—England, seen by a distorting eye. In Chapter Eight, wherein Gulliver relates "several Particulars of the Yahoos," and describes the virtues, education, and exercise of the Houyhnhnm youth, he has occasion to speak of the quarterly tests which the youth of the land undergo:

> Four times a Year the Youth of certain Districts meet to shew their Proficiency in Running, and Leaping, and other Feats of Strength or Agility; where the Victor is rewarded with a Song made in his or her Praise. On this Festival the Servants drive a Heard of *Yahoos* into the Field, laden with Hay, and Oats, and Milk for a Repast to the *Houyhnhnms;* after which, these Brutes are immediately driven back again, for fear of being noisome to the Assembly.

Horse show, horse race, or what have you—this is England, with men tending to the horses before the exhibition. The Houyhnhnms are horses, not Utopians, and certainly one of the finest comic effects in the entire work is the eagerness with which the happy gull seizes on the life of the horse as ideal.

Other passages also reveal these fleeting images of England. Gulliver, speaking to his Master, mentions the horses that are kept in England, "where *Yahoo*-servants were employed to rub their Skins smooth, comb their Manes, pick their Feet, serve them with Food, and make their Beds." The Houyhnhnm Master immediately understands that there is after all no difference between England and his own land—except, as the reader knows, for that point of view which reverses the position of master and servant and makes the English groom the horse's inferior. At another point, the Houyhnhnm mentions the repulsiveness of the Yahoo's diet: "Herbs, Roots, Berries, corrupted flesh of Animals"—the diet of humans, of course; or "all mingled together"—a good English stew. Later in his discussions, the Master's description of the behavior of the female Yahoo is, if we remember whom we are hearing and under what conditions we hear him, an almost literal description of a belle in St. James Park. He describes, in fact, such a scene as we have often encountered in Restoration comedy:

> . . . a Female *Yahoo* would often stand behind a Bank or a Bush, to gaze on the young Males passing by, and then appear, and hide, using many antick Gestures and Grimaces; at which time it was observed, that she had a most *offensive Smell;* and when any of the Males advanced, would slowly retire, looking often back, and with a counterfeit Shew of Fear, run off into some convenient Place where she knew the Male would follow her.

If one looks closely here, he can see the gestures of a lady with a fan, looking flirtatiously over her shoulder. He can also observe in the "offensive Smell" not just the sexual implication, but also, quite simply, the presence of perfume.

One last passage must be noted. Again in Chapter Eight Gulliver speaks of marriage among the Houyhnhnms:

> In their Marriages they are exactly careful to chuse such Colours as will not make any disagreeable Mixture in the Breed. *Strength* is chiefly valued in the Male, and *Comeliness* in the Female; not upon the Account of *Love,* but to preserve the Race from degenerating: For, where a Female happens to excel in *Strength,* a Consort is chosen with regard to *Comeliness.*

Gulliver is impressed, as he is by most Houyhnhnm practices. Here the thing that impresses him is simply English horse breeding methods, seen the wrong way.

W. B. Carnoghan

SOURCE: "Some Roles of Lemuel Gulliver," in *Texas Studies in Literature & Language,* Vol. 5, No. 4, Winter, 1964, pp. 520-29.

The "character" of Lemuel Gulliver offers only a little help to an understanding of his *Travels;* and the attempt to read the *Travels* as a careful psychological novel is a critical habit properly going out of fashion. Recurrent episodes and imagery give unity to the satire. So does the central theme of pride, which seems to fulfill a supposed requirement of classical satire, defined by [John] Dryden: "The Poet is bound, and that *ex Officio,* to give his Reader some one Precept of Moral Virtue; and to caution him against some one particular Vice or Folly." But Gulliver the man is sometimes inconsistent and in general lightly sketched. Only in his fourth voyage does he acquire anything like a fully developed character—a character which suggests a painful self-portrait of Swift the satirist, who thoroughly mistrusted the value of his motivations and his satiric art. Yet Gulliver's change from innocent to misanthropic satirist, abrupt though it seems, is anticipated not only by some of the "rhythmic" devices which control the structure of the book— for example, Gulliver's increasing difficulty in adjusting to life at home after voyages I, II, and IV—but also by some important and interlocking roles which he plays. Indeed Swift prepares for Gulliver's last role as a disillusioned reformer in ways that often deepen the ironies of his tale.

Even in Gulliver's occupation Swift hints at the part his protagonist is eventually to take; for Gulliver is a surgeon, with training also in "physick," and the metaphor of the critical observer as the anatomist of mankind is a commonplace in the history of satire, especially so in the satire of the English Renaissance. If imaginative literature, in the well-worn analogy, is the physician's cup of truth honeyed over with sweet embellishments (or his sugared pill), satire is the most extreme form of literary medicine, effecting its cures less often by physick than by cutting. . . . Even more common is the image of the scourge or flail—sometimes implying that the sickness is past cure. In this case the satirist-surgeon becomes custodian of the madhouse, controlling the diseased world by violent punitive measures. In **"The Legion Club"** Swift tells the keeper of the madhouse, here the Irish parliament, how to handle two especially unruly inmates:

> Both are apt to be unruly,
> Lash them daily, lash them duly,
> Though 'tis hopeless to reclaim them,
> Scorpion Rods perhaps may tame them.

Swift evokes some pointed associations, therefore, when he tells us, in the opening lines of Book I, about Gulliver's professional training. He has been four years an apprentice to Mr. James Bates, "an eminent Surgeon in *London*"; and, knowing that physick "would be useful in long Voyages," he has studied for two years and seven months at Leyden, perhaps with the famous Boerhaave ("so loudly celebrated, and so universally lamented through the whole learned world," as Samuel Johnson was to write after his death in 1738). But the point, of course, is that in the world of moral understanding Gulliver is unprepared for the long voyage that he is about to take. Although he is a man of scruples and fails in his business (with the result that he has to go to sea) because "my Conscience would not suffer me to imitate the bad Practice of too many among my Brethren," his case is proverbial: he has still to heal himself.

If Gulliver's case is typical, however, the cure may be more painful than the disease—and not wholly a cure at that. At the end of his travels he ministers to the world, or tries to. He resolves to instruct the Yahoos of his family "as far as I shall find them docible Animals." He publishes his adventures with a mixture of hope and uncertainty. But the world will have little to do with this would-be anatomist of man's moral ills, who now attempts a different sort of "Surgeon's Employment" on land, having grown weary even before his last voyage of that employment at sea. The only "cure," it seems, is to confront the radical sickness of one's own nature and to recognize that human remedies are no more than palliative—a conclusion that Gulliver comes partly and reluctantly to accept at last. (Naturally, the unfallen Houyhnhnms suffer no diseases and have no need of physicians. Gulliver's master cannot understand that "Nature, who worketh all things to Perfection, should suffer any Pains to breed in our Bodies"; and Gulliver's subsequent account of human diseases makes clear the direct relationship between moral and physical sickness.) Gulliver can hardly avoid nostalgia, however, for the days of his innocence; and, like the hack writer of the **Tale of a Tub,** he is ready to identify the appearance of health with the reality, at least on one occasion. At the start of Book IV, he describes his earlier felicity: "I continued at home with my Wife and Children about five Months in a very happy Condition, if I could have learned the Lesson of knowing when I was well"—"well" in the double sense, perhaps, of "well-off" and "sound of body and mind." This lament for the loss of innocence reverberates through the pages of Gulliver's last voyage.

As Gulliver's profession colors the fabric of his travels, so does a role that he assumes, to some extent willingly, in the kingdoms of Lilliput and Brobdingnag: the role of court fool. In Lilliput, of course, he takes on other duties also; he becomes a Nardac, he tells us proudly, as a reward for his military services. But he first earns his freedom by playing the part of court entertainer. He allows the children of Lilliput to play in his hair. He has the good fortune, as he calls it, to "divert" the emperor and the nobility "after a very extraordinary Manner," converting his handkerchief to a battlefield where the Lilliputian armies can exercise their valor. And he is exposed (in the most literal sense) to laughter when he stands astride "like a *Colossus*," for the amusement of the emperor, who watches his legions march between Gulliver's legs. Some of the soldiers cannot forbear an upward glance, despite the explicit order that they should "observe the strictest Decency, with regard to my Person." And "to confess the Truth," says Gulliver, "my Breeches were at that Time in so ill a Condition, that they afforded some Opportunities for Laughter and Admiration." Ernst Kris observes that "the strongest incentive to playing the fool is [sexual] exhibitionism," and the incident seems contrived to give Gulliver the chance of exhibiting himself: it is hard to imagine what special pleasure the emperor derives from parading his armies between the legs of his giant visitor. As Gulliver says, the emperor has taken a "fancy of diverting himself in a very singular Manner"; but Gulliver confesses to the soldiers' laughter and—more important—admiration with evident satisfaction.

In Brobdingnag, Gulliver's function as a *"Lusus Naturae,"* literally a joke of nature, is even more obviously and more exclusively to provide amusement. "Every Day," he furnishes the court "with some ridiculous Story"; and he seems almost to pride himself on his humiliations. With a suggestion of surreptitious pleasure he tells of his ill-fated effort to leap over a patch of cow-dung and the delight of the court when the misadventure becomes known: "I was filthily bemired, and my Nurse confined me to my Box until we returned home; where the Queen was soon informed of what had passed, and the Footmen spread it about the Court; so that all the Mirth, for some Days, was at my Expence." The malicious dwarf who torments Gulliver has a better reason for doing so than Gulliver realizes: supplanted by a greater freak of nature than himself, the dwarf is understandably vindictive.

Even in Houyhnhnmland Gulliver retains something of his identity as an entertainer. His master is at pains to instruct him in the ways of the Houyhnhnms, and Gulliver profits so much from the instruction that his master "brought me into all Company, and made them treat me with Civility, because, as he told them privately, this would put me into good Humor, and make me more diverting." There is no logical reason why the self-sufficient Houyhnhnms require this sort of diversion; they lack the frailty that needs the solace of greater and less inhibited frailty than one's own. The implication that the Houyhnhnms might *not* treat Gulliver with civility is also surprising; Gulliver resembles a Yahoo, of course, yet none but his master knows how close is this physical resemblance; and the trait of "incivility" is otherwise unknown among the Houyhnhnms. To maintain a pattern established in Books I and II, Swift casts a momentary shadow on the horses' ideal nature. And later in the book we hear that the female Yahoo's attack on Gulliver provides "Matter of Diversion to my Master and his Family." The significant word is "Diversion," for it reminds us of the many times before when Gulliver has "diverted" his masters.

Gulliver the fool, like Gulliver the surgeon, is a stock character who lacks the wisdom conventionally ascribed to his office. He has neither the plain man's insight nor the madman's inspired perceptions—the extremes of wisdom attributed to "folly." Gulliver the fool is utterly foolish. And it is only at the end of his adventures once again that the possibilities of his role are partly realized. Kenneth Tynan's characterization of Alceste—"Nearly everything he does is silly; nearly everything he feels is immensely serious"—applies equally to Gulliver when he comes home. He tells us "that in speaking I am apt to fall into the Voice and manner of the *Houyhnhnms,* and hear myself ridiculed on that Account without the least Mortification." And the absurdity of his actions has led some critics to discount the seriousness of his feelings. But Gulliver's folly is now of a different kind, for he no longer plays the fool willingly. Despite his assurance, it is unlikely that he hears himself ridiculed "without the least Mortification." He has seen the Yahoos exhibit themselves; he has no further desire to exhibit himself in any way. He hides from men and would be free, if he could, from the universal madness: "we are, *ad unum omnes,* all mad, *semel insanivimus omnes,* not once, but always so." This is "Democritus Junior" (borrowing from Mantuan); and it is Gulliver's anatomy of his own melancholy, perhaps, that leads him finally to hope for a reconciliation with the "Yahoo-kind." His hope is a virtual admission that "we are, *ad unum omnes,* all mad" and a realization that "sanity" (impossible though it may be to achieve) is to admit yet not be overwhelmed that this is so.

Associated with Gulliver's role as court fool and (less directly) with his occupation as surgeon and physician is still another part he plays—a part which [Paul Fussell, Jr.] has described as that of "archetypal victim." Like *Huckleberry Finn, Gulliver's Travels* fulfills a common requirement if a book is to become persistently popular with children: it is filled with pain, cruelty, violence, and the possibility of death. And Gulliver, the healer of other men, discovers that he is himself especially vulnerable to pain and to physical danger. In his first adventure, he awakes to find himself bound by the Lilliputians and manages to loosen the strings that tie his hair on one side, but only "with a violent Pull, which gave me excessive Pain." The Lilliputians fire their arrows at him, and he falls "a groaning with Grief and Pain." He nearly loses his eyes in the war with Blefuscu. And finally the Lilliputians sentence Gulliver to have his eyes put out, at the same time conspiring to rid themselves of their expensive guest by means of gradual starvation. At this point a friend at court lets Gulliver know the deliberations of the council and tells him also the advance preparations for disposing of his corpse: " . . . five or six Thousand of his Majesty's Subjects might, in two or three Days, cut your Flesh from your Bones, take it away by Cartloads, and bury it in distant Parts to prevent Infection." The preliminary matter-of-factness ("five or six Thousand of his Majesty's Subjects," "two or three Days") and the subsequent macabre images call to mind the inhumanity of the **"Modest Proposal"**; but the possibility of such a symbolic indignity as this—having his flesh cut off and carried away by cart-loads—is not much more monstrous than the other indignities which threaten Gulliver or those which he has to endure.

In Brobdingnag he is even more frequently in danger, exposed to the malice of the Queen's dwarf and all the hazards of nature; among others, hailstones which give him "cruel Bangs all over the Body, as if I had been pelted with Tennis-Balls"; the mole-hill into which he falls and the snail-shell on which he absent-mindedly breaks a shin; the flies which he cuts in pieces as they buzz about his ears; the frog which smears him with its "odious Slime"; and the monkey which takes him for one of its own, in an episode which anticipates the assault of the female Yahoo. Gulliver describes as "ridiculous and troublesome" the accidents which he suffers in Brobdingnag: they are "troublesome" to him but "ridiculous" to others, and it is here that Gulliver's role as victim most closely coincides with his role as court jester. His accidents are the symbol and source of his office as fool. As he confesses to his unhappy experience with the monkey: " . . . the Sight was ridiculous enough to every Body but my self." If ever a text seemed to illustrate the Hobbesian theory of laughter—the theory that the motive for laughter is a sense of personal superiority: a "sudden glory"—that text is Book II of *Gulliver's Travels.* And Gulliver's misanthropic seclusion [according to Fussell] at the end of his adventures would be almost logical, even without the events of Book IV. In the light of his final role, Gulliver, so assaulted by physical circumstance, may remind us of the satirist in *his* conventional role as victim, assaulted, almost physically, by all the fools and parasites of the day. . . .

When he comes to Houyhnhnmland, however, Gulliver finds relief from physical suffering. One of the two horses who discover him squeezes his hand so hard that "I was forced to roar"; but thereafter "they both touched me with all possible Tenderness." And later Gulliver describes the felicity of his stay with the Houyhnhnms: "I enjoyed perfect Health of Body, and Tranquility of Mind." Here Gulliver is telling only a partial truth. He enjoys perfect health of body, so far as we know, but not perfect tranquility of mind. The physical dangers of Books I and II are no longer a threat, but Gulliver, long the victim of external accident and the observer of other men, now is forced as seldom before (the process began in Brobdingnag, is completed in Houyhnhnmland) to observe himself, and his pains become those of introspection. Only a few pages after describing his tranquility of mind, he contradicts himself entirely: "When I happened to behold the Reflection of my own Form in a Lake or Fountain, I turned away my Face in Horror and detestation of myself; and could better endure the Sight of a common *Yahoo,* than of my own Person." And the natural mirrors where Gulliver sees his reflection are an image that has appeared before in the *Travels* and is to appear again—an image linked (we shall see) with the theme of Gulliver's physical dangers and, finally, an image that suggests one of Gulliver's most important roles.

Gulliver, at the beginning of his narrative, is the myopic hero whose lack of understanding is symbolized by the weakness and vulnerability of his eyesight. In Lilliput the only items which escape the inventory of his captors are his "Pocket Perspective" and the pair of spectacles "which I sometimes use for the Weakness of mine Eyes." And these are evidently the possessions by which he sets the most store. He keeps them in a secret pocket, and he explains with a trace of guilt that he did not surrender them to his captors because they were of "no Consequence" to the emperor; therefore, "I did not think my self bound in Honour to discover [them]; and I apprehended they might be lost or spoiled if I ventured them out of my Possession." Gulliver's caution turns out to be well advised: his spectacles later shield his eyes, which otherwise "I should have infallibly lost," from the arrows of Blefuscu. But the only way for Gulliver to shield his eyes—"and consequently my Liberty"—from the lenient workings of Lilliputian justice is by flight; and the official sentence of the council is the climax to the theme of sight and understanding in the first Book. Reldresal, who first proposes the idea of blinding the Man-Mountain as a humane alternative to capital punishment, defends his plan with these arguments (as reported to Gulliver by his informant from the court): "That the loss of your Eyes would be no Impediment to your bodily Strength, by which you might still be useful to his Majesty. That Blindness is an Addition to Courage, by concealing Dangers from us; that the Fear you had for your Eyes, was the greatest Difficulty in bringing over the Enemy's Fleet; and it would be sufficient for you to see by the Eyes of the Ministers, since the greatest Princes do no more." At first Reldresal speaks quite literally, although the metaphorical meaning of sight is always latent; in his last argument he lapses into pure metaphor, as though unawares. And his sophistries remind us of the links between weak sight and weak understanding. Since Gulliver is not a tragic figure, how-

ever, he is spared the purgative blindness that sometimes brings insight in the world of tragedy. In time, and with experience, Gulliver comes to see more clearly; or, as some would argue, to think he sees more clearly. In any case, it is himself he sees. The spectacles and pocket perspective of Book I, which Gulliver uses to examine the external world, give way in Brobdingnag and Houyhnhnmland to reflecting surfaces in which Gulliver looks upon his own features—first with chagrin, then with loathing, and finally with the hope of accepting what he sees.

Gulliver first glimpses himself early in his voyage to Brobdingnag, and he joins the Brobdingnagians in their amusement at the sight: "Neither indeed could I forbear smiling at my self, when the Queen used to place me upon her Hand towards a Looking-Glass, by which both our Persons appeared before me in full View together; and there could be nothing more ridiculous than the Comparison." The result of this first confrontation is to make Gulliver think that he is no longer what he was before: "So that I really began to imagine my self dwindled many Degrees below my usual Size." Like Alice, in Wonderland, Gulliver has found that "being so many different sizes . . . is very confusing;" and, like Alice, Gulliver would find it hard to answer the Caterpillar's question: "Who are *you?*" Self-abasement has begun, and Gulliver tries now to avoid his reflection; it is painful, he discovers, to be laughable—a reminder, once more, of the Hobbesian theory of laughter. When Gulliver is rescued from the sea, he tells the ship's captain of his experiences in Brobdingnag and of his increasing self-contempt, adding in an aside to the reader: "For, indeed, while I was in that Prince's Country, I could never endure to look in a Glass after mine Eyes had been accustomed to such prodigious Objects; because the Comparison gave me so despicable a Conceit of my self."

Gulliver's feelings in Houyhnhnmland—his "Horror and detestation" when he catches sight of himself in a lake or fountain—are an intensification, therefore, of feelings that he has first experienced in Brobdingnag. Now Gulliver is taught by the Houyhnhnms to distrust the powers of human reason; his master comes to the conclusion that "instead of Reason, we were only possessed of some Quality fitted to increase our natural Vices"; and he likens this quality to a troubled stream that gives off distorted images of objects mirrored there—"as the Reflection from a troubled Stream returns the Image of an ill-shapen Body, not only *larger,* but more *distorted*"—. . . . Then the assault of the female Yahoo causes Gulliver to see himself as a "real Yahoo, in every Limb and Feature"—a conclusion that first seems unjustified. Might Gulliver not have concluded equally well that he was a monkey in every limb and feature after the parallel incident in Book II? But there is a difference. Gulliver admits that he has stimulated the Yahoos to look on him as one of their species by frequently "stripping up my Sleeves, and shewing my naked Arms and Breast in their Sight." His exhibitionism in this case is overtly sexual (there seems no other interpretation); and, despite his humiliation, Gulliver apparently feels some reciprocal attraction to his Yahoo assailant: he remarks that she "did not make an Appearance altogether so hideous as the rest of the Kind." Thus bereft of pride of mind and pride of body, Gulliver understandably prefers the sight of a common Yahoo to the sight of himself. When he returns home, however, his loneliness leads him eventually to look for ways of coming to terms with mankind, and he decides that he can no longer avoid the sight of what he is. He decides "to behold my Figure often in a Glass, and thus if possible habituate my self by Time to tolerate the Sight of a human Creature."

Folklore has it that the reflection of oneself is the soul and that it is hazardous to see oneself reflected, for then the soul is exposed to external dangers. Certainly the experience is hazardous for Gulliver, for other reasons; and his travels are an emblem of that universal journey in which man sometimes catches sight of his soul. They are also a fable of Lockean man who turns from examination of the outer world to examination of the world within, from "sensation" (Gulliver's physical afflictions are relevant again) to "reflection." [John] Locke defines the process in the *Essay Concerning Human Understanding:*

> Children when they come first into it, are surrounded with a world of new things, which, by a constant solicitation of their senses, draw the mind constantly to them; forward to take notice of new, and apt to be delighted with the variety of changing objects. Thus the first years are usually employed and diverted in looking abroad. Men's business in them is to acquaint themselves with what is to be found without; and so growing up in a constant attention to outward sensations, seldom make any considerable reflection on what passes within them, till they come to be of riper years.

(And, as Locke adds, "some scarce ever at all.") The parallel with *Gulliver's Travels* is exact. But the question remains: are the reflections of Gulliver's "riper years," which culminate in his perception of the soul, are these accurate? No doubt they are not *precise.* If the human understanding is indeed like a rough mirror or a troubled stream, Gulliver's image of himself is like that image of an ill-shapen body which the stream returns, "not only *larger,* but more *distorted.*" But the implication is clear: the body and soul of man *are* ill-shapen—hardly an original conclusion, however misanthropic it has seemed to some. . . . Alice travels into the world of the looking-glass, where she loses her name and identity and is eventually reborn a queen. Gulliver looks into the glass and finds he is a Yahoo, though an uncommon one. In each case the mirrors are intended to heighten reality but not to falsify it; and Gulliver's resolve to look often into his mirror is a resolution to confront the unbearable if he can. He does not succeed at all well, if we take the letter to Cousin Sympson as evidence of his later history; the thing is impossible for him as it is for Swift. *Gulliver's Travels,* finally, is an ironic version of the myth in which the hero at last comes face-to-face with the monster. And the only release available to Swift and Gulliver is perhaps this: to hold up the mirror, in the fashion of the artist, for all to see what is reflected there.

Kenneth Rexroth

SOURCE: "Gulliver's Travels," in *Saturday Review,* Vol. LII, No. 12, March 22, 1969, pp. 12, 16.

The critical literature on *Gulliver's Travels* is immense, contradictory, and exhausting. It is as though Swift had written an additional "Voyage to the Land of Pihsralohcs," a land governed by the iron rule of Publish or Die. In all this vast mass of paper to which beautiful trees have been sacrificed, there is scarcely a mention of the greatest mystery attending *Gulliver's Travels.* Why has it been for more than two hundred years one of the most popular of all children's books? If the critics are right, especially about the fourth book, it is an obscene and immoral rejection of the weak but striving, falling but trying human race, the work of a psychotic who hated all men, especially women, who was impotent, paranoid, and fixed in a clinging and cloying anal eroticism. This, it would seem, is reading matter for adults only. Even if the critics are wrong, the fact that they can make such deductions would make the book dangerous or incomprehensible, or both, to children. Yet children love it, quite innocently, and see nothing bad or even nasty about it. So likewise do very common people. A good measure of this was the immense popularity among peasants and simple workers of the classic Russian motion picture made of *Gulliver's Travels* long years ago.

On his voyage to the continent of Balnibarbi and the flying island of Laputa, Gulliver learned, long before they were ever seen by real astronomers, that Mars had two moons. Swift describes them with considerable accuracy. This has fascinated many a science fiction writer. There are stories that describe Swift's visit to Mars or the Martians' visit to him, but the best is one based on the hypothesis that Swift himself was a Martian—an engineer who had planned to put two large satellites in orbit about Mars (the moons were not discovered until later because they were not there), but had been swept away in his space ship, and forced to land on Earth. The science fiction writers are sounder critics than the scholars. Like the children who love *Gulliver's Travels,* Swift is an Outsider, one of the first and greatest. He was horrified by the condition of humanity and dumbfounded that he was a human being.

Superficially, there is nothing extraordinary about the satire of *Gulliver's Travels.* Swift uses the standard classical formula that goes back to Aristophanes, Menander, and Plautus, and survives to this day in all plays based on the Italian Comedy. In his own day, in Molière or Aphra Behn or the disciples of Ben Jonson, the formula dominated the popular stage. Each character in the classic comedy is assigned one of the vices or follies of mankind and acts out its consequences in absurdities or incongruities that follow logically from a given situation. What Swift did was simply use whole peoples, instead of individuals, as personifications. Starting with an assumption—men six inches or 60 feet high, the roles of horses and humans reversed, literal physical immortality—he deduced all the consequences he could think of, with relentless logic and realism, from an initial absurdity. But the absurdity is the only vesture of a vice or folly or major defect of ordinary people. The Lilliputians are petty; the Brobdingnagians are gross; the Struldbrugs are senile; the Houyhnhnms are endowed only with rationality; the Yahoos lack it. Taken altogether, the nations of *Gulliver's Travels* make up a well-rounded human character—seen from the outside.

So children, like Martians, see the adult world. Who did not dream as a child that some day, after he was grown up, he would meet the real adults—so unlike those he saw about him—who would be rational, just, and large of vision and who would keep the world from collapsing? Somewhere they must exist, a little conspiratorial committee of the sane in ice caves in Tibet or in the undersea palaces in Atlantis or the Land of Oz. Certainly the world a child sees about him and judges by the simple values of innocence, or the equally simple ones he has been taught—"Don't do as I do, do as I say"—could not endure overnight unless somewhere the responsibles were keeping it going. The perspective of Swift is no different. His "savage indignation" is just outraged innocence. The point of view assumed by all satirists was not with him an assumption or a pose; it was congenital and incorrigible.

It is his innocence that distinguishes Swift from Franz Kafka and those who have come after him in the Theater of the Absurd or the novels of the blackest Black Comedy. The squeamish and sheltered academicians of an older generation, like the critics of earlier times from Sam Johnson on, have been outraged and nauseated by the fourth voyage. In our day it seems mild indeed. The Houyhnhnms, except for their rationalism, differ little from horses. In fact, the only difference is that they can take care of themselves at the standard of living of rather pampered racehorses. The conclusion that this was in fact the status of the philosophers of the Enlightenment is easily drawn. As for the terrible Yahoos, they behave pretty much like human beings unable to think up excuses for their behavior. Neither species is evil. Swift was himself a man of the first half of the eighteenth century in his conception of evil. He did not know what it was. Nowhere does he give any indication of comprehending that human beings of the greatest intelligence can deliberately live out a rationally organized evil or that whole societies can operate in decency and order for the most vicious ends. To Swift, as to Aristophanes, war, treachery, and exploitation are follies. Vice may be disgusting, but it is never reasonable. So Swift is outside the human condition in a way that Choderlos de Laclos or Balzac or Proust is not. This is innocence.

It is his innocence that endears Swift to children. As he logically draws out the details of Lilliputian or Houyhnhnmian behavior, he is inexhaustibly playful, he is never whimsical. Uncorrupted children loathe whimsy because it is one of the final manifestations of corruption. *Gulliver's Travels* is at the opposite esthetic pole to *Winnie the Pooh*.

Bernard J. Lonsdale and Helen K. Mackintosh

SOURCE: "Adventure and Mystery: Gulliver's Travels," in *Children Experience Literature,* Random House, 1973, pp. 377-78.

Jonathan Swift, one of the great English satirists, wrote *Gulliver's Travels* for adults as a satire of the human race. Published in 1726, the original title was *Travels into Several Remote Nations of the World in Four Parts by Lemuel Gulliver.*

The first-person narrator gives this imaginative story a ring of authenticity for young readers. The authenticity is furthered by Gulliver's giving the exact time of day and date of happenings as well as exact locations in terms of latitude.

At the beginning of Part I, Gulliver swims ashore after a shipwreck and finds himself in the land of the Lilliputians, where one situation after another charges the imagination and brings humor to the story. Gulliver's second journey in Part II takes him to Brobdingnag. In contrast to the little people of Lilliput, the inhabitants of Brobdingnag are giants. Not all of Gulliver's experiences with the people of Brobdingnag are as pleasant as his experiences with the people of Lilliput, but young readers thoroughly enjoy the elaborate exaggerations about the giants. The last two parts of the book continue with surprises, adventure, and humor, taking Gulliver to the flying island of Laputa and the country of the Houyhnhnms, the wise, talking horses. Very often the editions for young readers are limited to Gulliver's voyages to Lilliput and Brobdingnag.

Margaret Blount

SOURCE: "Four Satires," in *Animal Land: the Creatures of Children's Fiction,* William Morrow & Company, Inc., 1975, pp. 62-9.

True satire, like *Gulliver's Travels,* . . . uses animal disguises only to show the human race to itself in caricature. At first sight, Gulliver's voyage to the Houyhnhnms is a tables-turned story in which the functions of animal and man are neatly reversed, as in *The Jungle Book;* the horses are disguised people, the people disguised animals. But the difference is that here there is no real disguise—the horses *are* people, of a specialised sort. They are reasoning beasts, and the Yahoos are people too. The black streak of bitterness that makes this last book of *Gulliver's Travels* so bleak an experience that even Gulliver is irreversibly changed by it, colours all human nature, the best and the worst. The best is too good to be portrayed in human terms, and horses, the noblest of beasts, embody it. The worst parts of human nature, the meanest and most degraded, are given human form. For an even sharper lesson the two species could have been two different kinds of ape, but Swift's dislike and disgust for the human body perhaps led him to choose, as the rational and speech-using leaders, the one animal that cannot be humanised. The equine form and face are as far from the human kind as one can get; even a reptile does not look too odd on its hind legs, but to imagine a horse like this is impossible.

One can't help comparing Gulliver's first meeting with the horses to Ransome's encounter with the Hross in *Out of the Silent Planet*. Both men are expecting an animal and find a human intelligence—yet while C. S. Lewis (not writing satire) manages to make his account of that meeting one of the most moving passages in the book, Swift's hero, seeing a familiar animal, is at first less wary and at the end less filled with wonder and awe; satire has no numinosity. 'I did not much like my present situation,' notes Gulliver, 'and I at last concluded they must needs be magicians,' and he produces the gifts he had in readiness for savages. These are naïve reactions, and the idea that (being conjurors) the animals are conversing does not surprise him. Perhaps the difference is that Ransome's mind is full of the idea of an unattainable Eden in which humans and animals are equal—which is, in a way, what he finds in Malacandra—while Gulliver, a seasoned traveller, is an objective observer and has to be unemotional. The transition from concluding that the rational horses are 'all necromancy and magic' to the realisation that they are the masters and the humans are dumb and bestial, is hardly noticed.

The horses are a singularly innocent society, as inhuman as the Yahoos are sub-human, yet each *is* human in intention. The horses do not steal or fight and cannot understand a lie; it is 'the thing which is not,' a phrase also used among the Hrossa who are similarly innocent. The horses are almost too perfect, they have no weaknesses, they live in clean spacious stables among fields full of oats, share their children in Platonic amity, do not fear or mourn for death, do not blame the Yahoos for being miserable, dirty and incorrigible.

As fantasy, the fourth voyage falls short of Gulliver's other three travels. Who built the stables, and why do the horses live in this odd, semi-human way? And who planted the oats, made the pottery and did the cooking? The explanation of the hoof and pastern used as a kind of finger and thumb does not overcome horse resistance to human likeness. The horses' manner of sitting back on their haunches recalls a fallen cabhorse or Tom Cobley's old mare writing her will; but as a satiric device for undermining European confidence, the horse, the least human, or the ape, the most human, are admirable.

Gulliver (as soon as he has learned horse language)

makes the great mistake common to many science-fiction heroes who visit alien cultures: he starts to tell the truth about his own society and unleashes the contempt and incomprehension of the inhabitants. Professor Cavor made this mistake with the Selenites; explaining human institutions never goes well. The scene is set for the simple, Spartan virtues of the horses and the hopeless vices of the Yahoos: the drawbacks of the human frame, the soft, useless feet, awkward placing of the eyes, inability of the mouth to eat without having food put in it by the hands, and the whole body's need for artificial covering; the defects of the reason which make for wars, the misapplied intelligence, which gives rise to the profession of lawyer; the miseries which cause criminality, disease and drink. Self-disgust can go no further. The horses' suspicions are confirmed; the Yahoos, when wild, are not even good monkeys—when allowed power, they get out of hand. The reader's shame at being a Yahoo almost makes him regard horses with superstitious dislike for ever.

Margery Fisher

SOURCE: "Who's Who in Children's Books: Gulliver," in *Who's Who in Children's Books: A Treasury of the Familiar Characters of Childhood*, Holt, Rinehart and Winston, 1975, pp. 130, 132.

Gulliver's adventures have been adopted by children because of the fantasy element which became more prominent in the many chapbook versions, as indeed it is also in the expurgated versions published for children today. 'Gulliver's sojourn in Lilliput' has always been the most widely known and liked of the four sections. The flattering idea of being a giant among pygmies has been used in countless children's stories, most often in a fanciful spirit. A few authors have stressed the responsibility of the large for the small; Pauline Clarke, for example, describes in *The Twelve and the Genii* the attitude of Max Morley to the lively wooden soldiers he has discovered. The most direct and the most interesting echo of Swift's satire, T. H. White's *Mistress Masham's Repose*, is an adult book which has rightly been made available to young readers. Maria lives in a huge country house, her life governed by her repulsive governess and the sadistic vicar, her only friends the cook and an old professor living in the rambling grounds of the estate. When one day Maria finds that a colony of Lilliputians has been established on the shore of a lake, her instinct is to treat them as dolls; the professor not only explains their history to her but also helps her to find her own independence and freedom in respecting the claim of the Lilliputians to the same human rights. The humanity and humour of the story wholly justify its derivation.

Swift's second theme, of a pygmy among giants, is also, perhaps understandably, treated most often in a fanciful way for the young, although Mary Norton's books about the Borrowers and Jane Curry's *The Housenapper* and *The Lost Farm* suggest strongly enough to an imaginative child the emotional fears which go deeper than the actual dangers of such a situation. Erich Kastner in *The Little Man* and *The Little Man and the Little Miss* hid his obvious concern so deeply in slapstick and social satire that we end with the impression that Maxie Pichelsteiner enjoyed most of his life as a circus freak and at least suffered little psychological harm from it. . . .

Only E. B. White in *Stuart Little* has tried to convey something of the horror and disgust which fill Swift's description of Gulliver's life in Brobdingnag. When the mouse-boy hides 'in a grove of celery' in the dustbin to escape a dog, the author comments 'It was a messy spot to be in. He had egg on his trousers, butter on his cap, gravy on his shirt, orange pulp in his ear, and banana peel wrapped around his waist.'

Donna E. Norton

SOURCE: "History of Children's Literature: Defoe and Swift—Great Adventure Writers," in *Through the Eyes of a Child: An Introduction to Children's Literature*, Charles E. Merrill Publishing Company, 1983, pp. 44-5.

Children love adventure stories. . . .

Two adventure books that appeared in the early eighteenth century were written for adults but were quickly embraced by children.

A political climate that rewarded dissenters by placing them into prison molded the author of the first great adventure story, *Robinson Crusoe*, in 1719. [Daniel] Defoe was condemned to Newgate Prison after he wrote a fiery pamphlet responding to the political and religious controversies of his time. His prison experiences, however, did not deter his writing; he wrote constantly even while in jail.

Defoe was motivated to write *Robinson Crusoe* when he read the personal accounts of a Scottish sailor, Alexander Selkirk, who had been marooned on one of the Juan Fernandez islands, located off the coast of Chile. . . . The resulting tale first appeared in serial publication and then in a book. Children and adults enjoyed the exciting and suspenseful story about Robinson Crusoe and how he coped with his problems. . . .

The second major adventure story written during the early eighteenth century also dealt with the subject of shipwreck. Jonathan Swift's *Gulliver's Travels*, published in 1726, included realistic adventures with strange beings encountered in mysterious lands. Like Defoe, Swift did not write for children. In fact, Swift wrote *Gulliver's Travels* as a satire about the human race. Children, however, thought of the story as an enjoyable adventure. Gulliver was considered a hero when he was captured by the Lilliputians, the tiny people who lived in the land of Lilliput, whom he rescued from a series of mishaps. Nineteenth-century children enjoyed Gulliver's other adventures: he went into the land of the Brobdingnag, the realm of giants; onto the flying island of Laputa; and finally, into the land of the Houyhnhnms, the talking horses.

These adventure stories must have seemed truly remarkable to children surrounded otherwise by literature written only to instruct or to moralize. The impact of these eighteenth-century writers is still seen today, as twentieth-century children enjoy versions of these first adventure stories.

J. Paul Hunter

SOURCE: "*Gulliver's Travels* and the Novel," in *The Genres of Gulliver's Travels*, edited by Frederik N. Smith, University of Delaware Press, 1990, pp. 56-74.

[Hunter's essay discusses **Gulliver's Travels** *as a cutting-edge transitional text that uses satire to parody the subjective, first-person narrative, thus anticipating the rise of the novel as a narrative form. In the following excerpt, Hunter examines how Swift uses parody to delineate an erroneous episode in Daniel Defoe's* Robinson Crusoe].

Gulliver's Travels is not a novel in any meaningful sense of that slippery term that I know, yet its generic status would be difficult to establish without having the novel in mind. Swift's masterpiece is, in fact, so conceptually dependent upon the novel that it is almost impossible to imagine the existence of the *Travels* outside the context of the developing novelistic tradition. The relationship of *Gulliver's Travels* to the novel has been obscured, however, by two contextual matters, one historical, the other generic. The historical issue involves the fact that the *Travels* appears when the English novel had barely begun, and it is difficult for us to think of it as involved in the tradition. With only Defoe, among major English novelists, having yet tried the waters, with the issue of definition still two decades away from even being broached, and with the great craze for novel-reading and novel-writing also still well in the future, how can it be meaningful to think of there yet being a *tradition* of the novel even though there are some few discernible examples? Unless one regards the *Travels* as a kind of paradigm—positive or negative—for the tradition, how can one think of it as involved in a tradition-to-be? The second issue, although generic, does not involve the genre of the novel; rather it involves parody and the assumptions we make about its strategy of working from, imitating, and trying to tease or embarrass a particular writer or work. Because of the way we define parody, we do not usually think of Swift as a parodist, and I think we miss something about both Swift and the possibilities of parody by the standard definition. I shall, then, . . . try to suggest in what sense Swift is a parodist and show how some of his parody works; . . .

Gulliver's Travels has generally resisted efforts to consider it parodic, and some Swift critics lurch toward apoplexy when the very idea of parody is broached within reaching distance of *Gulliver's Travels.* And yet Swift's consciousness of contemporary writing is nearly as apparent there as in *A Tale of a Tub,* and if passages that specifically echo another writer . . . are rare, a large awareness of contemporary writing habits and the prevailing tastes of readers is visible at nearly every turn. Swift's awareness of contemporary travel writers—William Dampier, for example—has been often remarked, and much of the fun in the book's first appearance had to do with its solemn title page: *Travels into Several Remote Nations of the World,* it advertised, promising something quite other than what is delivered. Swift, in one of his letters, has something of a lark in imagining literal-minded readers who are gulled by such an expectation: he speaks of an Irish bishop who, after reading *Gulliver's Travels,* concluded that it was "full of improbable lies, and for his part, he hardly believed a word of it."

But quite beyond its evocation of travel literature, *Gulliver's Travels* engages a whole tradition of fiction that was then in the process of developing, and Swift saw that this new kind of writing was beginning to codify a "modern," significantly new way of perceiving the world. Contemporary narratives of personal experience—scandalous memoirs and chronicles of personal and public political intrigue, as well as books that charted personal travel to far-off places or new experiences—were increasingly sought by a public that wanted material, intellectual, and psychological satisfaction in the conquest of space and the accrual of experience. Because of its new popularity, this subjective writing, whether genuine or fictional, seems to offer a personal yet universal key to reality and, like [Robert] Boyle's *Meditations,* can only deliver on its promise by exaggerated and distorted emblematicism and by verbal sleight-of-hand. The assumptions, values, and forms that seem to be implicitly attacked in *Gulliver's Travels* would be easy enough to defend on their own terms, and in fact in our time most of us find it easier to understand them than we do Swift's objections; but the *Travels* offers us persuasive evidence that Swift perceived the brave new literary world of the 1720s much as Pope did, with the significant difference that Swift merges its personalities and consciousnesses into composite figures who anonymously participate in the creation of a single work that expressed their values and outlook, rather than being named and even individuated by their antagonist. Even in their monotonous sameness, though, some identifiable characteristics emerge, and in the choral voice one can pick out a few distinctive, personalized tones that remind us of a voice insistent on being subjective, authoritative, and modern.

Because Swift's parody works through an accretion and absorption of particulars, it is difficult to illustrate his method without a detailed consideration of the text and its contexts, but here I will be only suggestive through brief attention to one episode and its surrounding circumstances. The suggestive place I want to examine may at first seem a bit unlikely—Lemuel Gulliver's pockets as he empties them for his interrogation in Lil-

liput. Here is an inventory of what turns up concealed on Gulliver's person:

a handkerchief

a snuffbox

a diary

a comb

a razor

a set of eating utensils

a watch

a set of pistols

a pouch of gunpowder and another pouch of bullets

silver and copper money and several pieces of gold

a pair of spectacles

a pocket perspective and "several other little Conveniences."

To appreciate the full effect of this pocketful, we have to remember that Gulliver is supposed to have swum ashore—in dangerous stormy waves—with his pockets jammed like that, and he is also wearing a full set of clothes, a hat, and a large sword.

Because this information is not all presented at once, one might read the *Travels* several times and not notice Gulliver's rich and varied cargo. Gulliver, being Gulliver, does not tell us that his swimming was impeded by his load, nor does he tell us why he hung onto the material things that connect him to his past when, buffeted by waves that threaten to scuttle him, it would have seemed sensible to discharge himself of some of his burdens. The things are, to be sure, useful to Swift in initiating Gulliver's dialogue with the Lilliputians, but they are not necessary, as subsequent voyages show. Swift pretty clearly is having some fun at Gulliver's expense in making him such a dull-witted freighter, and his point seems crucially connected, on the one hand, to a contemporary joke, and, on the other, to Swift's perceptions about first-person narrative and the mind-numbing absurdities it sometimes offered to readers of contemporary narrative.

The joke was seven years old in 1726. It had involved a slip of Defoe's pen in *Robinson Crusoe*—a slip that, when corrected, still exposed a lapse in memory or lack of factual knowledge. When Defoe has Crusoe swim to the shipwreck at one point, he allows him to strip off his clothes to make the journey easier, but a little later we see Crusoe on shipboard stuffing his pockets with biscuits. Defoe later explains that Crusoe had left on his seaman's britches, but as a contemporary, Charles Gildon, pointed out, Defoe didn't thus improve his marks as a purveyor of information about seamen, for seaman's britches usually do not have pockets, and even when they do, the pockets are tiny ones, much too small for biscuits: Defoe's explanation had only pinpointed and elaborated his ignorance. For Gildon, Defoe here makes Crusoe perform unlikely, even absurd actions, and his attack is on the false realism in Defoe, just as in *Gulliver's Travels* the thrust is to demonstrate what the realism and pseudofactuality of contemporary travel accounts and fictional narratives come to at last. Gildon's joke on Defoe was, by the way, well enough known and remembered in 1725—six years after *Crusoe* and a year before *Gulliver*—that the *London Journal* can speak of the pocket episode as "a most notorious *Blunder,*" which had given "Abundances of Pleasure [to] many of his Readers."

Gulliver's pockets, then, work something like this: they remind us of Defoe's mistake and how authors who try to pass off genuine memoirs often are tripped by simple facts. The pockets also remind us of larger points quite beyond the comical allusion—that first-person narrators, in their haste to make a point and glorify themselves, are hopelessly inaccurate, obtuse, and pretentious; that long lists and particular details do not necessarily add up to some larger truth, and that attempts to read the world and its purpose through the recording of sense impressions and the imparting of symbolic qualities to things and events (as done in *Robinson Crusoe* and in the emblematic tradition represented by meletetic meditators like Robert Boyle) is finally an arrogant, self-serving, even solipsistic way of regarding the world. *Robinson Crusoe* comes up for examination in *Gulliver's Travels* quite often in various ways: in the opening paragraph in which the particulars of Defoe's life (his career as a hosier, his imprisonment as a debtor, his prudent marriage to a woman with a large dowry) are alluded to; in the preparatory events that preface each voyage proper; in the vague motivation for Gulliver's decisions to go repeatedly to sea because of "rambling Thoughts" and an unaccountable sense of destiny; in the habitual phrases that fall from Gulliver's lips and link him repeatedly but not constantly to the consciousness of Crusoe; in the ending in which Swift provides a sharp contrast to Crusoe's homecoming. Defoe, exploring what man can do to achieve salvation and deliverance within a providential pattern, has Crusoe readjust to the company of human beings and society generally with relative ease, giving no hint that lack of conversation, human companionship, sexual relationship, and exile from the familiar for more than a quarter century offer any obtrusive problems in readjustment, and Crusoe returns to find himself remembered, beloved, and provided for by partners and well-wishers who have preserved and improved his property and investments so that he is now a rich plantation owner, soon to be a happy new husband and father. Alexander Selkirk, often said to be the prototype of Crusoe and in any case an island castaway who lived in isolation only a fraction of Crusoe's tenure, found

postvoyage life far otherwise, returning to his home a silent misanthrope who avoided all company, living altogether by himself, some say in a cave he himself dug as an emblem of his psychological space. Swift's portrait of Gulliver neighing quietly to himself in his stable, unable to stand the company of his wife and children, his nose stopped with lavender, tobacco, and rue so that he cannot smell human smells, stands in sharp relief to Crusoe's homecoming and tacitly reminds us realistically of historical figures like Selkirk and of civilization and its discontents.

The example of the allusive pockets suggests that *Gulliver's Travels* is, among many other impressive things, an accreting generic or class parody not only of travel narratives per se but also of a larger developing class of first-person fictional narratives that make extraordinary claims for the importance of the contemporary, the knowableness through personal experience of large cosmic patterns, the significance of the individual, and the imperialistic possibilities of the human mind—a class parody, in short, of what we now see as the novel and the assumptions that enable it. . . .

M. Sarah Smedman

SOURCE: "Like Me, Like Me Not: *Gulliver's Travels* as Children's Book," in *The Genres of 'Gulliver's Travels,'* edited by Frederik N. Smith, University of Delaware Press, 1990, pp. 75-100.

Gulliver's Travels, like *Pilgrim's Progress* and *Robinson Crusoe,* has for more than two and a half centuries been a book read for pleasure by children. How a religious allegory or adventure novel underlaid with social, economic, and philosophic implications can appeal to children is a question rarely asked. On the other hand, how and why a bitter satire aimed at eighteenth-century political, religious, and cultural targets has attracted child readers is a question that has continually puzzled scholars. . . . It is . . . *Gulliver's Travels* as children's literature, the appeal of the book to the child reader, that interests me.

Consideration of children's literature as a genre is problematic, for, like literature in general, that for children comprises many genres, each of which is defined by the elements of the literary work itself, not in terms of its audience. Although many have grappled with the question of what constitutes children's literature, none have been able to confine it within the popular conception that there is a kind of writing suitable only for children: a literature limited to child characters, restricted in subject matter, range of emotion, nature and quality of language. Good writers for children have never subscribed to such limitations. . . .

Readers, writers, and critics agree that the best children's literature has characteristics that may or may not be found in adult literature, qualities that enrich rather than impoverish the works: a good and comparatively simple story; a strong moral theme (to be sharply distinguished from didacticism); honesty; a sense of wonder; an appreciation for the world; and a hopeful resolution, not to be confused with wish-fulfillment and happily-ever-after. Discussions of the nature of children's literature point, finally, to the inference that while no inherent qualities distinguish it exclusively from adult literature, the closure of a good children's book intimates something positive, "something which turns a story ultimately toward hope rather than resignation."

Measured by the preceding criteria for children's literature, *Gulliver's Travels* fits well. The book has many qualities to delight child readers, qualities deriving from the child always alive in the Swift whose favorite maxim was *vive la bagatelle,* and from the comic Swift, who for many adult readers gets buried under the bitterness of the misanthropic Gulliver, whose realistically hopeful creator dramatizes the dangers of staring too fixedly at human folly. Swift's dramatic vision seems one with his moral vision, an idealistic though not optimistic vision that admits of the coexistence, sometimes precarious, of irony and hope. Whatever else *Gulliver* is, it is an adventure story told with precision and logic in straightforward, unadorned prose, neither inflated nor magniloquent; Swift's logic delights children, whose own thought processes are so direct. Set in fantasyland, always the province of children, the story evokes wonder, is inventive and rich in detail and infused with the writer's passionate concern for his subject.

Swift's narrative perspective is in some ways that of a child. Like a child, Swift was possessed of an intensity born of the ability to see things clearly, "as if for the first time, in their original radiance and darkness." Like a child, Swift wished to bring what he saw up close for examination. Not only did he discover Lilliput and the other countries of his imagination, he mapped them, described them, limned their inhabitants and their culture. Young readers, still sorting out the relationship between story and truth, are quite capable of perceiving the authenticity of Swift's vision, exaggerated as it may become in the telling. As George Orwell so graphically reminds us:

> A child, when it is past the infantile stage but still looking at the world with fresh eyes, is moved by horror almost as often as wonder—horror of snot and spittle, of the dog's excrement on the pavement, the dying toad full of maggots, the sweaty smell of grown-ups, the hideousness of old men, with their bald heads and bulbous noses. In his endless harping on disease, dirt, and deformity, Swift is not actually inventing anything, he is merely leaving something out.

Samuel Holt Monk was wont to say that Swift's only insanity was his terrible, unbearable sanity, a state comprehensible perhaps only to those with unclouded, childlike vision.

An inherent problem with criticism of children's books is that adults must presume to speak for children. Because adults write, edit, publish, purchase, and review books for children, their opinions tend to override those of children themselves. What children do or do not like to read is not equivalent to what adults believe is or is not appropriate for them. Although histories and anthologies of children's literature invariably cite *Gulliver's Travels* as a classic and hundreds of editions have been published for juveniles, from the date of the book's publication adults have disagreed over its fitness as a companion for youth. Diverse points of view reflect adults' various preconceived notions of childhood and the proper education of children. John Gay, responding to the fun in the *Travels,* tacitly approved it for children in his letter to Swift dated 17 November 1726, just two days after the anonymous publication of the book: "From the highest to the lowest it is universally read," Gay wrote, "from the Cabinet-council to the Nursery." He added that although lady-critics might construe it as an "insult on Providence, by depreciating the works of the Creator," the book "hath pass'd Lords and Commons *nemine contradicente;* and the whole town, men, women, and children are quite full of it." By 1728, however, Jonathan Smedley, Dean of Clogher and a Whig, impervious to irony and disgusted by Swift's satires on religion and government, published *Gulliveriana,* in which he venomously attacks *Gulliver's Travels* as an "Abominable Piece," a "Book made up of Folly and Extravagance." Unable to perceive the reverence beneath the impious veneer of Swift's book, Smedley painstakingly emphasizes its pernicious effects upon impressionable young minds and judges it "Wicked, for a Man whose Vocation it is to preach the Holy Gospel, to spend so much precious Time purely to tempt Youth to misspend it." Similarly, in the mid-nineteenth century, when it was the presupposition that all literature for children should be solemnly didactic, Thackeray, who admired the "fable" of *Gulliver,* misconstrued its moral as "horrible, shameful, unmanly, and blasphemous," and accused Swift of lacking "softness," of entering "the nursery with the tread and gayety of an ogre"; Thackeray believed no one but Swift could have found it possible to write **"A Modest Proposal"** because most people melt at the thought of childhood, fondle and caress it. A century after Thackeray, George Orwell's assessment of Swift's masterpiece sounds more like John Gay's. *Gulliver's Travels,* Orwell declared, ought to be included among six books to be preserved when all others were destroyed. "I read it first when I was eight," he says, "and I have certainly not read it less than half a dozen times since. Its fascination seems inexhaustible."

The controversy over whether or not *Gulliver's Travels* is suitable for children would seem to derive from two misconceptions: (1) an imprecise and often erroneous conception of children's literature; and (2) paradoxically, a single-minded focus on the complexities and bitterness of the book. The tenet, evinced in the statements of Smedley and Thackeray, that children's literature is simplistic moral pap, limited in subject matter to sweetness and light, limited in mode to romance or comedy, continues to be prevalent. Children themselves, of course, have never restricted their reading to the vacuous, which accounts for their adoption of *Gulliver's Travels.*

When *Gulliver's Travels* was published, the cultural ethos was conducive to its wide reception. Jonathan Smedley notwithstanding, children and their elders who were part of the society that Gulliver took by storm in November of 1726 would have understood children's ability to see the truth and the fun in the book. The popular audience for books in the early eighteenth century was still largely a single audience, as that for television is today. Not until midcentury did Thomas Boreman, followed by John Newbery, begin to publish specifically for children. Children were familiar with the same stories as their parents, heroes often familiar to them through both the oral and written traditions. Three of these stories widely known through popular chapbooks were particularly relevant to the immediate acceptance of Gulliver by children: *The History of Tom Thumbe, The History of Jack and the Giants,* and *The World Turned Upside Down.* These stories of pygmies amidst giants and of a topsy-turvy world—both situations universally appealing to children—had prepared young people for Swift's situations and inversions. Of the three stories, none is so relevant in its particulars to *Gulliver's Travels* as is that of *Tom Thumbe.*

In his preface to the 1621 prose version of *The History of Tom Thumbe,* Richard Johnson addresses at some length various constituents of the single audience for whom he had chosen to write Tom's story:

> This is the Subject that my Pen means to make you merry with, and the only Story that (at noone dayes) may in time become the awaker of Sleepy Youth, prone to sluggishnesse: The ancient Tales of Tom Thumbe in the olde time, have been the only revivers of drouzy age at midnight; old and young have with his Tales chim'd Mattens till the Cocks crow in the Morning. . . .

Although Johnson explicitly names Gargantua's story as one he eschewed in favor of Tom Thumbe's, Michael Patrick Hearn states in his preface to the Garland reprint that Johnson not only depended heavily on Rabelais's giant Gargantua, but "borrowed liberally" from the host of legends about Tom. Hearn enumerates many similarities between the stories of Tom and Gulliver: Gulliver in Brobdingnag, like Tom, can be picked up by the middle between forefinger and thumb; just as Tom falls into his mother's pudding, Gulliver tumbles into a bowl of cream; both are attacked by animals, birds, and insects larger than themselves; from his perspective each finds the persons of court ladies physically offensive; King Arthur gives Tom a gold ring, which he wears as a girdle, whereas the Brobdingnagian queen gives Gulliver one he wears as a collar. A "huge blacke Raven" carries off Tom while he is attempting "to scarre away crowes . . . with a cudgell made of a Barley straw"; Gulliver is snatched by "some Eagle [who] had got the Ring of my Box in his Beak." Hearn attributes both Tom's boast that he "can drowne a whole Towne with

[his] pisse" and Gulliver's extinguishing the fire in the queen's palace with his urine to Gargantua's drowning of 260,418 people by the same means. Hearn, however, takes no notice of the similarity between Swift's Yahoos, who climb trees to shower Gulliver with their excrement, and the giant in *Tom Thumbe,* who, to relieve the indigestion caused by Tom's "rumbling and tumbling in his guts . . . hyed he up to the toppe of his Castle wall, where he disgorged his stomacke, and cast out his burthen, at least three miles into the Sea."

My point here is not to trace possible sources of *Gulliver's Travels* but to offer evidence that the book found a ready audience prepared by popular chapbooks. Citing also crude, scatalogical verses unabashedly published for children—the kind of rhymes that Francelia Butler has demonstrated are still part of skip-rope culture of children around the world—Hearn states what by today is a truism among students both of the eighteenth century and of children's literature:

> Adults of this period apparently thought nothing of giving their young unexpurgated editions of such popular literature as *Gulliver's Travels* . . . with its many references to bodily functions.

Once having the book in hand, what do children find that has kept them coming back to *Gulliver's Travels* for more than 250 years? The strongest attraction, say most historians of children's literature, is the adventure in the book. Ahead of that I would put Swift's relationship to his material exhibited in the playfulness pervading the *Travels,* untainted by sentimentality or nostalgia. Sentimentality, never playful, cannot peacefully coexist with irony and is corrosive of common sense. Perhaps precisely because nostalgia, that entirely adult emotion, never intrudes into *Gulliver's Travels,* children of any century find easy access into the book, identifying with Gulliver as a person who sees things as they do. Since John Newbery's *Lilliputian Magazine* (1752) and such publications as John Harris's twelve-volume miniature *Cabinet of Lilliput: Instructive Stories* . . . (1802), children, because of their relative size, have been associated with the Lilliputians. In reality, children, often more sensible than adults, revel in Gulliver's benevolent power in Lilliput and share the troubles his size brings upon him in Brobdingnag.

The first two voyages, particularly, are imbued with Swift's childlike spirit, which evokes in young readers a sense of kinship. Not only the subjects Swift treats in many episodes but also his point of view, reasoning, and tone attest to his keen recollection of what it means to be a child. Consequently, he is able both to capture the essence of childhood and to speak its language. Most representative of the child still alive in the mature Swift is the understanding, lacking in many subsequent adapters of his work, that learning language, with its attendant frustrations and delight in sheer sound, is childhood's greatest task and triumph. Children appreciate the many incidents dramatizing failure to understand or be understood because of linguistic ignorance, learning the language, and consequent ability to communicate. In Lilliput children understand and enjoy the logic, as well as the naughtiness, of doing what comes naturally to extinguish the palace fire and are as baffled as Gulliver by his ostracism for having accomplished the feat. Statements like Gulliver's about the Lilliputian king—"He was then past his Prime, being twenty-eight Years and three Quarters old"—capture children's exactness about their own ages, the childish inability to recognize that "grown-up" does not mean "old," and the conception that everyone existing before their frames of reference belongs to the past, all of which is equally ancient history. For children, who quarrel and quickly make up, the causes of war might not seem so petty had Swift not taken such great care to trivialize them; they will wonder at the longevity of the discord. With their innate sense of justice, they will stand with Gulliver in his refusal to enslave a courageous people, just as, in their craving to be the center of attention, they will share his pleasure in the attendance of the Blefuscudian ambassadors. With Gulliver they will learn the pain of ingratitude. The voyage to Brobdingnag combines a clear reflection of what it means to be a child among big people and the child's desire to be seriously listened to by adults. Swift captures children's ambivalent attraction to and fear of other inhabitants of their world—rats, dogs, wasps, and bigger children who bully them. To timid children, all aliens are ogres. Children seeking independence sympathize with Gulliver's wish to deal with the frog who climbs aboard his boat by himself; his success will give them courage. Frequently the object of unwanted attention and inane remarks from strangers, young readers will squirm with Gulliver displayed as a freak in a circus. Especially, they will empathize with his having been able to live "happy enough in that Country if my Littleness had not exposed me to several ridiculous and troublesome Accidents," as well as with the effort it costs him to read and to play the piano. They will also laugh at Gulliver in these predicaments and thereby learn to laugh at themselves.

From the publication of *Gulliver's Travels,* the voyage to Laputa has been considered the weakest part of the book. [Dr. John] Arbuthnot and [John] Gay wrote Swift, respectively, that it was the "least brilliant" and the "least entertaining," although Gay added that "this hath its defenders too." Among the defenders will be those children fascinated by a flying island and its flappers, by the detailed directions on how to drive it, by the opportunity to summon dead heroes, and by the picture of what it might be like to live forever. Children are curious about, fascinated with, and fearful of death from a very early age; the misery of the Struldbruggs' existence should quell any desire to live forever, though the full impact of that vivid narrative may remain half-submerged until the child is old enough to believe in his or her own mortality. It is impossible to believe that Natalie Babbitt's novel for young readers, *Tuck Everlasting,* does not at least in part derive from her desire to counterbalance the Struldbruggs with the Tucks, destined to live forever a pleasant life without aging. Babbitt's point, however, like Swift's, is that being cut off from the natural wheel of life-death is an undesirable fate.

Young people, too inexperienced to be cynical, are more likely to read Gulliver's fourth voyage as comedy than malevolent cynicism. Amused by the topsy-turvydom of a world where horses behave like passionless but perfect humans and humans behave like Yahoos, the average child, having persevered to the end, cannot miss the blatant ironies of the final chapter:

> Thus, gentle Reader, I have given thee a faithful History of my Travels . . . wherein I have not been so studious of Ornament as of Truth. I could perhaps like others have astonished thee with strange improbable Tales: but I rather chose to relate plain Matter of Fact in the simplest Manner and Style; because my principle Design was to inform, and not to amuse thee.

Through the irony, the average child will also glimpse the truth. Swift wrote "to vex the world," yes, but the ingenuousness of his hero, his childlike delight in games, verbal and physical, the clarity of his view of life and his exaggerated expression of it—these not only amuse but were designed to do so.

Since 1726, there have been innumerable editions of *Gulliver's Travels* for children in English—including abridgments, expurgations, retellings, textbook editions, shorthand editions, some which can only be called prostitutions. Each abridgment or retelling reflects an adult's conception of childhood and of what is or is not suitable material for children, both in content and in difficulty of language. To see what changes have occurred in the real *Gulliver's Travels* and in attitudes toward childhood through the years, I examined fifty-five versions published between 1727 and 1985 in the United States and Great Britain in a survey that does not pretend to be comprehensive but does intend to be representative. The survey includes editions that have been published specifically for children or have been recommended for them by specialists in children's literature: editions that include only part 1 or part 2, parts 1 and 2, parts 1 through 3, as well as those which include all four parts. I examined all eighteenth-century abridgments to which I had access—including the first (1727)—and tried to locate at least one edition meeting my specifications from each decade of the nineteenth and twentieth centuries. The books surveyed range in format from cheap chapbooks, like Redpath's Books of the Campfire and the tiny paperback from Ross's Juvenile Library series, to artistically designed, expensively bound copies, such as the Excelsior Edition of Standard Juvenile Fiction and the Oxford Illustrated Classics edition included in *British Book Design 1956.* Of the fifty-five editions studied, twelve include only the first voyage; one, only the second voyage; eighteen, both the first and second; one, the first three; and twenty-three include all four voyages, two of the latter (1947, 1963) combining the third and fourth in one. These figures provide some basis for questioning the statement appearing in most histories of children's literature that children's editions contain only the first two voyages. It is more difficult to contest the assumption that children read only the first two voyages, but an educated conjecture is that those youngsters to whom the four voyages have been available, having read the first two, would not stop there.

Other general discoveries prove interesting. Of the fifty-five editions in the sample, forty-three retain the first person in which *Gulliver's Travels* was originally written, many of these retellings as well as abridgments; twelve are retold in the third person. No editor comments on his or her reason for the change, so one can only infer that it may have been to approximate more closely the style of the fairy tale, an inference that seems valid in light of the fact that most of the third-person versions are for young children. Similarly, thirty-eight editions retain the word *Travels* in the title, while twelve use *Adventures* and four, *Voyages*—that is, *The Adventures of Gulliver in . . . ,* or *Gulliver's Voyages to. . . .* Most editors decided that Swift's prefatory letters were too topical or subtle for young people, for few children's editions contain either of them, though the letter from Richard Sympson appears occasionally. Many of those not in cheap paper bindings contain biographical sketches of Swift, most of them to some degree antipathetic to Swift as a person. They tend to emphasize his eccentric temperament, to attribute to him a vision of despair, and to credit him as a brilliant stylist. The abridgments rarely alter Swift's diction or syntax except to modernize terms—for example, substituting *Australia* for *Van Diemen's land* and *pumpkin* for *pompion.* Even many of the versions that change the narrative to third person retain much of Swift's language. Retellings for younger children, such as Edith Robarts's and John Lang's, simplify as they delete.

To chart all the variations in the fifty-five editions is not possible here. However, it is possible to point to several incidents that may serve as touchstones in a brief survey of the process of editing for children: namely, Gulliver's observation upon the nurse's breast as she suckles the baby; Gulliver's frolics with the maids-of-honor; his harmless sport of jumping cow dung; the Lagadan experimenter's attempt to return human ordure back into food and Gulliver's fit of colic; descriptions of male and female Yahoos and the attack of the female Yahoo upon Gulliver. These touchstone passages tend to be ribald and scatological but are not exclusively so.

What has happened to the story of Gulliver's putting out the palace fire, in the context of comparable incidents in Lilliput, illustrates something of the nature of emendations in children's versions of *Gulliver's Travels.* From the fifty-four editions that include the voyage to Lilliput, eighteen retain Gulliver's vindication of the reputation of Flimnap's wife, but only five retain any mention of his natural need for elimination, though all describe in some detail what Gulliver eats and drinks. Thirty-four editions excise the extinguishing of the fire in the queen's palace, the first of which in my sample did not occur until 1829; the second, in 1840; the third, in 1886. Not

From Gulliver in Lilliput, *retold by Margaret Hodges from* Gulliver's Travels *by Jonathan Swift. Illustrated by Kimberly Bulken Root, 1995.*

until the late 1880s did that deletion occur almost as a matter of course. Fifteen editions retain the story of the fire just as Swift told it. One merely reports, "most unfortunately, at this time, that Gulliver had offended the Queen by a well-meant, but badly-managed effort to do her a service, and thus he lost also her friendship." Four editions retain the incident, portraying Gulliver as victimized hero, but alter the manner in which he puts out the fire. The first, the Excelsior Edition of Standard Juvenile Fiction, published in the 1870s, supplies an adjoining palace with a "reservoir of water kept for the especial use of the empress." For any other person to use the water was a capital crime. "But, necessity, [Gulliver] thought,

> had no law; so reaching over I lifted the tank, which might contain about four gallons of water, and applied it so well to the proper places that in three minutes the fire was wholly extinguished and the rest of that noble pile, which had cost so many ages in erecting, preserved from destruction.

Gulliver in Lilliput, retold by Edith Robarts, provides Gulliver an additional occasion for heroism and finds a use for his retrieved hat, which he wears to the fire although he forgets his coat:

> It seemed a very dreadful thing that this beautiful palace should be burnt to the ground, and just as I was fearing this might happen, an idea suddenly occurred to me. This was to use my hat for a bucket, and by filling it at the lake in the palace garden, I emptied the lake and soon put out the fire! But to my horror I also nearly drowned the Queen and her royal children. The water quite filled the rooms in which the royal family were, and I had the greatest difficulty to pick them out at the windows. They were quite insensible, but soon after became conscious again, and were unhurt.

Like the anonymous adapter of the Excelsior Edition, W. B. Scott works an altered expedient into the framework of Swift's prose:

> In consequence of the great difficulty of providing me with washing accommodation inside the temple, a brewer's vat had been assigned to me. This, for the convenience of obtaining a sufficient supply of water, was placed by the side of a well, near the entrance to the city, and, therefore, at no great distance from the palace. Coming home late the previous night I had washed myself before retiring to rest; and by great good fortune, as I thought, the suds had not been thrown away. I lost no time in carrying the vat to the palace, and as it contained nearly an English gallon of water, I was able to use it with such good effect that in three minutes the fire was wholly extinguished. . . .

Not nearly so convoluted is the Usborne/Hayes Picture Classics *Gulliver's Travels,* which simply states: "Gulliver helped out and within minutes he had put out the fire. The palace was saved and he went back home to bed."

Each interesting in its own way, every edition of *Gulliver's Travels* for young readers seems worthy of comment; some, however, have one or another feature that ought not go unremarked. For example, 1) a prefatory statement of motivation for abridgment of the original, which usually reveals a particular attitude toward children and their literature; 2) the very nature of the edition or its significance in the history of children's publications; 3) inventive interpolations or substitutions; or 4) simply a uniqueness which eludes classification.

The first abridged edition, pirated in 1727 by Stone and King, was apparently published with no thought of children as a special audience. Its stated purpose is to "lessen the Expence" of the original, thus making the bestseller available to a greater number of readers. The publisher promised that the abridgment would be "faithful," would answer "the intention of the Author," and would not deprive "the Original of those Ornaments which recommend it to the Judicious." "It is true," the introduction acknowledges, "that some Passages in the Original, which the Generality of Mankind have thought immodest and indecent, are entirely omitted." For the

most part, however, the touchstone passages remain intact. What is "contracted into a very narrow Compass" are the lengthy descriptions of the lands, their customs and laws, and the philosophical disquisitions between Gulliver and various rulers.

The first abridgment of *Gulliver's Travels* published in America was for children, that by Young and M'Culloch in Philadelphia in 1787: *The Adventures of Captain Gulliver in a Voyage to the Islands of Lilliput and Brobdingnag.* According to A. S. W. Rosenbach, this first juvenile edition goes back to a John Newbery original. A retelling in the third person, its various printings by different publishers keeps much of Swift's language, including:

> Mr. Gulliver could not help wondering at the intrepidity of those diminutive mortals who [ventured to mount and] walk upon his body, while one of his hands was at liberty, without trembling at the sight of so prodigious a creature as he must appear to them.

The vocabulary was apparently quite within the range of nearly seven-year-old Thomas Dow, who, according to an inscription in a 1794 copy, was presented with the book on 4 December 1811. A second inscription reads: "Thomas Dow was born February the 2 Day A.D. 1805."

In a Smedleyan vein, though milder, Edwin O. Chapman in the introduction to his "New Edition, Edited for Young Readers" (1888) damns Swift with the faint praise that he was "an able writer and a great scholar" but never "a good man nor a happy man." Chapman grants that though there is much in *Gulliver's Travels* that is "of no interest to" or "unsuitable for" children, the "romantic adventures of Gulliver will always have for young readers the attractions of a fairy tale." Chapman concludes:

> This editor has faithfully preserved these attractive features and as mercilessly cut out the objectionable portions. His only excuse for taking such liberties with the author's text is that the work may with propriety be placed, where it has so long been improperly classed, among books for children.

Chapman's is properly an edition, preserving Swift's prose but deleting or sanitizing all touchstone incidents.

In his "Introductory Sketch" to the 1896 Riverside Literature Series edition of *The Voyages to Lilliput and Brobdingnag,* Horace Scudder, of landmark significance in the history of children's magazines, addresses children as intelligent and literate but betrays his prejudice against Swift, occasionally propounding factual inaccuracies. The "Sketch" begins:

> It is curious fortune for a book to be written as a political satire and to come finally to be read by the young for their entertainment, with no thought at all of the satire except as it is pointed out by students of literature.

Unlike Defoe's mind, Scudder suggests, Swift's was perverted: he had "an imperious intellect," which tyrannized over his sense of "natural play, and life, instead of being humanized by it, was rendered more cruel and passionate." Scudder does pay tribute to Swift's genuine love of "language used skillfully and exactly," not only in word but by retention of the original prose in his edition. He justifies his categorical judgment—"the greatest interest centred on Lilliput, for it appealed to people much as fairy tales appeal to children"—by reference to the eighteenth century as a time when "people had little abundance of imagination, and not much faith in supernatural life." Comparing himself with "all editors who have prepared these *Travels* for popular reading," Scudder, too, omits "such passages as show an unseemly coarseness." He equates "popular reading" with reading for children.

William Dean Howells's introduction to the 1913 Harper publication illustrated by Louis Rhead is interesting because he says that before he read the book when he was "ten or twelve years old," he knew from his father that *Gulliver's Travels* was one of the great books among different literatures. Howells recognizes the personal and cultural satire but also "the far more subtle and sanative irony which plays through these most delightful studies of human Nature"; but he does not

> expect the boys, or even the girls, who more than grown people, will delight in the witchery of one of the most amusing fables ever invented, to feel the play of undercurrent in it.

On the contrary, the entire design of the Macmillan Classics 1919 *Gulliver's Travels* edited by Padraic Colum assumes that children are aesthetically sensitive and intelligent readers. Beautiful as an object, the book has powerfully fine and funny illustrations by Willy Pogany. In the 1962 reissue, Clifton Fadiman, in his pointed afterword, tells young readers that "this particular edition is a kind of compliment to you":

> Your editor, Padraic Colum, is a man who knows something about youth. He is confident that you are capable of reading all of Swift's masterpiece in a form very little different from the original version.

Colum indeed compliments young readers: his introduction contains an excellent, objective biographical sketch of Swift, which places the author in human perspective and literary context, and also an analysis of *Gulliver's Travels* focusing on Swift's "one idea firmly held." Colum clearly explains satire and its function in the book, Swift's love of language and its impact on the *Travels,* and the place of affection and wonder in readers' responses to the stories. Differing markedly from Howells, Colum addresses children as capable of understanding many of the layers of meaning and literary techniques in Swift's book and possesses the Swiftian skill of conveying penetrating insights in terse and lucid prose. While many commentators liken *Gulliver's Travels* to fairy tales, and Andrew Lang includes a simplified re-

telling in his famous collection of folktales from many cultures, the 1889 *Blue Fairy Book,* it is the differences which interest Colum:

> *Gulliver's Travels* is a fairy tale inverted. In the fairy tale the little beings have beauty and graciousness, the giants are dull-witted, and the beasts are helpful, and humanity is shown as triumphant. In *Gulliver* the little beings are hurtful, the giants have more insight than men, the beasts rule, and humanity is shown, not as triumphant, but as degraded and enslaved.

In 1962, after twenty years of successful publishing, Golden Press released *Gulliver's Travels* as one of its Illustrated Classics. This retelling by Sarel Eimerl deletes all references to political discussions, to scatological and sexual incidents, and to humans as diminutive, contemptible animals, and it greatly abbreviates parts 3 and 4. Sentence patterns tend to be simple and syntactically repetitive. The pictures by Maraja in brilliant primary colors are profuse, many of them decorative as well as illustrative. Because of Golden Press's philosophy of publishing well-written stories by reputable authors and illustrators in durable but cheap format, the Golden Books edition undoubtedly reached a wider audience than more authentic but expensively bound books.

Textbook editions of the *Travels* include an abridgment of Lilliput and Brobdingnag published by Ginn in 1886, and also an adaptation "retold" by Frank L. Beals, assistant superintendent of the Chicago schools, and published by Sanborn in 1946. Beals thought *Gulliver's Travels* "interesting and fascinating" but "too difficult" to be read by children in the middle grades. Humbler in tone than Chapman, having fewer expectations of children than Colum, Beals notes that the "present rewriting is not an effort to improve upon *A Voyage to Lilliput,* but to simplify it and make it available to the young people of today." Too pedestrian to excite wonder, each of the fourteen short chapters is followed by questions calling for recall, interpretation, or opinion, plus vocabulary words. Brief definitions accompany a "word list" at the end of the text. Several passages are explicitly didactic, appropriate perhaps to a textbook, never to a good story, and certainly not worthy of Swift's subtlety. What the original Gulliver thinks about the Lilliputian emperor's desire to enslave the Blefuscudians and his own refusal to cooperate, Beals spells out in wooden, moralizing dialogue.

Perhaps taking its cue from Laputa's school of languages where the professors' "first Project was to shorten Discourse by cutting Polysyllables into one," in 1895 A. L. Burt published the *Travels* in "Words of One Syllable" by Mrs. J. C. Gorham. Interesting if only because it evinces the challenge posed by a clever game, the book has a liveliness of style derived from varied sentence patterns and apt diction. Gorham cheats only a little when she divides the months of the year into hyphenated words. Another attempt of a similar kind, the Dolches' *Gulliver's Stories for Pleasure Reading* (1960) is one of their series of classics rewritten in language limited to their famous basic list of the first thousand words for children's reading. Unlike Gorham's, the Dolches' adaptation is a travesty, stifling rather that stimulating the imagination.

The Macmillan edition illustrated by Charles E. Brock (1894, 1923) displays an eagerness to uphold the integrity of the legal profession and its practioners. Into Gulliver's account of lawyers and the adjudication of the case of his cow, the anonymous adapter reinserts a lengthy passage from the original 1726 edition which Swift had deleted in 1735:

> The numerousness of those that dedicated themselves to this Profession were such that the fair and justifiable Advantage and Income of the Profession was not sufficient for the decent and handsome Maintenance of the Multitudes who followed it. Hence it came to pass that it was found needful to supply that by Artifice and Cunning which could not be procured by just and honest methods. . . . [Dishonest] practi[tion]ers were by Men of discernment called Pettifoggers . . . and it was my ill Hap as well as the Misfortune of my suffering Acquaintance to be engaged only with this Species of the Profession.

The ensuing account of the practice of following legal precedent is extended to emphasize that not all lawyers are crooked. Nowhere else does this editor, whoever he was, attempt to justify a class of people, a custom, or a law that Swift vilifies. This passage with a few changes in diction and capitalization appears again in the editions of W. B. Scott (1911) and Rand McNally's Windemere Series (1912).

Patrick Bellew is one among several editors and retellers of Gulliver's adventures who injudiciously delete the language Swift fabricates for the inhabitants of his fantasy lands, particularly the Lilliputians. However, Bellew's edition (1945) is unique in that it creates his own nonsense language in which the Lilliputian king and Gulliver converse:

> *Schmoz garumph kabob!* said the little man.
>
> *Wazzat?* said Gulliver.
>
> *Kiwee galurki chimpoo!* replied the midget.
>
> Neither understood the other, but from Gulliver making chewing motions and swallowing, the little man finally appeared to understand, although at first he thought Gulliver wanted to eat him.

Later, when the king's horse shies before the Man-Mountain, the following conversation takes place: "*Nok urak goydoo!* [the king] cried." Not understanding, Gulliver "tried the only other language he knew."

> *Parlez-vous Français?*
>
> *Novak prum bagoz yewohee-hee,* was all he got in exchange.

Je ne vous comprends pas, he replied.

As this seemed likely to go on forever, Gulliver tried sign language, which seemed more successful, and soon he began to gather what the King wanted.

Once Gulliver can speak a bit of Lilliputian, Bellew translates an occasional phrase into English. When Gulliver visits Mildendo, the inhabitants shout, "*Helugi galumph!* meaning *Hail and Welcome!*" Gulliver replies, "*Yugosi pizzu,* that is The same to you." Bellew also changes Flimnap's name to Floogumph, probably because the combination of the roundly hollow and thudding sounds better match his own "little language" than the thinner, lighter Flimnap. Purists may castigate Bellew as a corruptor, but he captures something of Swift's spirit of fun and love of language.

An unusual, jolly *Gulliver in Lilliput* is a British pop-up version illustrated by Vojtech Kubasta and printed by Artia in Prague. The cover is a puppet theater with royalty in the audience and a little girl holding her doll by one hand at stage edge. Gulliver appears in the proscenium arch, hand to his hat. When the book is opened, Gulliver, inside the front cover, doffs his hat and bows:

> Hello, children!
>
> Allow me to introduce myself. My name is Lemuel Gulliver and I am a ship's surgeon. . . .

Through the slim volume, Gulliver speaks cozily to the children, the anonymous narrator attributing to him details that not only increase merriment but, like Swift's, poke fun at contemporary culture. A few samples convey the flavor. During the noisy astonishment of the Lilliputians when Gulliver stands to his full height, Gulliver confesses that it was "a wonderful feeling— something like being born a second time"; then he records:

> local police tried in vain to keep order. The official news agency published a report that ten people were trampled to death by the crowd, but two hours later it denied this.

More specifically directed to children are Gulliver's accounts of boys' and girls' games:

> Children played hide-and-seek in my hair, finding it extremely good fun, for nowhere else did they have so many hiding places. Once a little girl got lost there and could not find a way out. She cried and cried until I helped her disentangle herself and set her down on the ground again.

On the day of the parade of the royal troops between Gulliver's legs,

> . . . drummers drummed, the emperor's jester outdid himself in being funny, flags and banners fluttered from the towers, and the sun looked down in surprise

at all this unusual activity. The boys, who in Lilliput just as elsewhere, painted all kinds of signs on the wall, waved their little flags, and one of them even climbed on the top of the Castle parapet, although this was strictly forbidden.

Despite the fact that at least from the time John Newbery published the *Lilliputian Magazine,* children have been associated with Swift's little people, this Artia version of the story is the only one in the sample in which children may identify with the Lilliputians rather than with Gulliver.

The texts and formats of the four 1980s editions recapitulate trends in the publication of *Gulliver's Travels* during its long lifetime. Both the two retellings and the two reissues differ from each other in nature and quality. The Usborne/Hayes Picture Classics retelling of the voyage to Lilliput is a glossy, garish paperback, only a cut above the comic book in design and quality of illustration. The text is insipid. By contrast the 1983 version of the first two voyages illustrated by David Small has a verve of its own, enhanced by its brevity. Certainly the text pales by comparison with Swift's, but it has more regard for the sound and sense of words than most retellings. Unfortunately, nothing in the book corrects the title-page indication that Swift wrote the text as it appears; the storyteller remains anonymous. The oversize book has strong, expressionistic, heavily-lined illustrations. Sadly, because of its fine bookmaking, it will not have the mass market appeal of the Usborne/Hayes "Classic."

Schocken's 1984 one-volume, moderately priced issue of the *Travels* illustrated by Rex Whistler makes available to a wide audience an example of book illustration that had previously been limited to an edition of only two hundred copies (1930). The text is that of the 1735 edition. Nonetheless, the book is marketed for children, and Lawrence Whistler, the illustrator's brother, in his preface refers to the story as "inescapably, a splendid children's book," wisely commenting that the author "probably enjoyed arousing wonder in minds that as yet had no grasp of the satirical." The artist's preliminary colored sketch of the frontispiece is on the book jacket, though the final illustrations are in pen and ink, for Whistler is "not in favour of colour, as destroying unity even while it added charm." The 1985 edition illustrated by Arthur Rackham is a version of a book printed in various formats since its appearance in 1900. A new edition, including additional colored illustrations, was published in 1909; another, in 1952. In contrast to the attractively designed volume of 1909 bound in gilt-engraved covers, the 1985 book is cheap, with all the colored plates lumped together in the middle of the book, a caricature of both Rackham as illustrator and of quality children's books.

A complete history of the editions of *Gulliver's Travels* for children might well prove to be a paradigm of the history of children's books, for even my sample includes a wide variety of publications passed off as children's

literature: (1) pop-up books for toddlers, complete editions for adolescents, and editions aimed at every age in between; (2) texts of *Gulliver's Travels* in syntax and vocabulary ranging from paraphrases in short, simple sentences composed of words from the Dolches' basic list, to editions retaining Swift's prose unaltered; (3) texts reflecting the belief that stories for children must be cute, sentimental, and didactic; (4) sanitized texts reflecting the belief that children must be sheltered not only from what is political, violent, and vulgar but also from anything that has to do with natural bodily functions; and (5) unexpurgated texts reflecting the belief that though young people may be inexperienced, they are intellectually and emotionally capable of coping with several levels of meaning in stories. Of course, neither writers, critics, nor young readers would consider every edition of equal merit. Like other books marketed for children, some editions of *Gulliver's Travels* have literary significance; others are pulp.

Children's expectations for a good story are basic and stringent: it should have a single trajectory along which the story develops; it should have clearly delineated characters and settings; it should have adventure beyond the actual; and it must be true, "real." Good literature for children should simultaneously enlarge and enrich their imaginations and extend their insights into the patterns and meaning of life. *Gulliver's Travels* satisfies those expectations as well today as it did in 1726—or in 1927, when William Lyons Phelps wrote in *The Yale Review:* "'*Gulliver's Travels*' is the most terrible satire ever aimed at humanity; and it has diverted hundreds of thousands of children." Perhaps Padraic Colum, in that fine introduction to his edition of the book, has best expressed the reason why Gulliver's story has so strong a hold upon children's—and adults'—imaginations. In contrast to modern writers, Colum says, Swift and his contemporaries referred to few ideas but illustrated them prodigiously. Swift's book has "abundance in power," for

> It is an illustration of one idea firmly held: Swift looks from above, down upon men, he looks from below up at them and then he looks at them from behind. He breaks into no complexity of idea. But he puts so much power into his statement that we know as much about the Lilliputians and the Brobdingnagians and the Houyhnhnms as if we had read our twelve volumes on each by the Gibbon of their respective empires.

Undoubtedly this power is one reason Clifton Fadiman places *Gulliver's Travels* among the ten books he predicts will still be read by children in five hundred years.

Swift's forceful representation of strange exterior worlds and the relationships that exist within them enables readers—children and adults—to understand their interior landscapes. Consequently, even today's children who adventure with Gulliver learn through the Lilliputians, Brobdingnagians, Houyhnhnms, and others much about human nature. Though they neither know nor care about topical or personal allusions, they will understand that people and their institutions can be corrupt; but they will realize, too, that they need not be so. Correctives are at hand, one of which children may imbibe (if their editions leave them the third and fourth voyages, as many do) is that we should not too proudly aspire to perfection and happiness through reason and technology. That way lies·madness, as Gulliver portrays but never learns.

More important, young readers learn from Gulliver because they are intrigued and amused by his exploits. According to the study by Carleton Washburne and Mable Vogel, eighty-nine percent of the boys and seventy-five percent of the girls who reported reading the book for pleasure ranked it in interest value somewhere between "a good book; I like it," and "one of the best books I ever read." Surely a major cause of the continued viability of *Gulliver's Travels* is that children have always enjoyed it. Perhaps Fadiman is not far wrong when he claims, "Whether by accident or design . . . the gods tend to grant immortality to those books which, in addition to being great, are loved by children."

John F. Sena

SOURCE: "*Gulliver's Travels* and the Genre of the Illustrated Book," in *The Genres of 'Gulliver's Travels,'* edited by Frederik N. Smith, University of Delaware Press, 1990, pp. 101-38.

Although we tend to think of the illustrated book as a nineteenth-century phenomenon, immortalized by Dickens and Thackeray, virtually all the major works of prose fiction published during the eighteenth century were illustrated. Of these no work was more frequently or more exhaustively illustrated in that period and throughout the nineteenth and twentieth centuries than *Gulliver's Travels*. This should not be surprising when one considers the nature of Swift's artistry. *Gulliver's Travels* is a highly visual work: we are constantly being encouraged to picture in our mind's eye the appearance of people, buildings, and objects. Each part abounds with specific measurements and precise numbers: we know, for instance, that four yards to the right of the prostrate Gulliver a stage was erected eighteen inches from the ground, capable of holding four Lilliputians; that his body is equal to 1728 of theirs; that a Brobdingnagian·breast is sixteen feet in circumference. Swift often describes the physical pose struck by a character, the expression on his face, as well as Gulliver's numerous gestures and those of the people he encounters. He is also careful to delineate in all four voyages the precise physical settings for Gulliver's adventures; we know literally where our hero stands. In addition to making a conscious effort to create verbal pictures, Swift's prose style contributes to the visual atmosphere of the work. His language is, for the most part, nonmetaphoric; sentences are filled with concrete nouns, adjectives appear in clusters to achieve a precise description, parenthetical statements and apositives are employed for further clarity and definition. In short, *Gulliver's Travels* lends itself to pictorial illustration. . . .

Although he was willing, even desirous, to have *Gulliver's Travels* illustrated, [Swift] did not collaborate with any illustrator. In fact, a number of his opinions communicated to Benjamin Motte concerning possible illustrations have been largely ignored, even rejected, by graphic artists for the past 250 years. He thought, for instance, that part 2 did not lend itself to illustration as well as part 1 because Gulliver would have to be too "diminutive a figure" to be seen. Historically, part 2 has been illustrated as often as part 1; in fact, illustrators have not only failed to have the difficulty Swift predicted in maintaining the proper proportions, I do not think that any book of *Gulliver's Travels* has been more imaginatively illustrated. Several of the scenes from part 1 that Swift thought should be illustrated—"The Ladyes in their Coaches driving about his table. His rising up out of his Carriage when he is fastened to his House . . . His Hat drawn by 8 Horses"—have rarely been illustrated. Although Swift remarked to Motte that he did not know how the projectors could be drawn, they have been by far the most frequently illustrated group of characters from part 3. He thought, on the other hand, that part 4 would "furnish many" scenes for illustration; in reality, it has been the least illustrated book of *Gulliver's Travels* and the one that appears to have given illustrators the greatest difficulty. It is ironic that a writer whose work lends itself so well to illustration seems to have been unable to evaluate more perceptively the problems and potential of his narrative for illustration.

Within a year of its publication, illustrated editions of *Gulliver's Travels* appeared in England, Holland, and France; the illustrations from these editions were reproduced in subsequent editions throughout the century. Illustrated editions also appeared in Germany and Spain. The illustrations in all of these early editions are few in number and generally undistinguished in conception and execution. Of the three illustrated editions that appeared in 1727, for instance, each contains only one picture per book, and that illustration is generally a literal visualization of the text. There is also a remarkable similarity in the selection of scenes to illustrate: all three depict Gulliver in part 1 with Lilliputians swarming over him and Gulliver about to board the Flying Island in part 3. Even the work of the best-known eighteenth-century illustrator of *Gulliver's Travels*, Thomas Stothard, fails to alter or mold significantly our understanding of or reaction to the text. Stothard, . . . designed four pictures in 1782—one for each book—for a popular edition of *Gulliver's Travels* that appeared in the widely read series, *The Novelist's Magazine*. He selected scenes that are inherently interesting and lend themselves to visual depiction; however, he succeeds in offering little more than an uninspired literal rendering of the text. His illustration, for instance, of Gulliver being pulled up to the Flying Island, by contrast with the fanciful depictions of that scene in nineteenth- and twentieth-century illustrations, is unimaginative and flat. The Flying Island appears merely as a large box floating in mid-air, with Gulliver being hoisted by a simple pulley and chain while sitting on a horizontal piece of wood. Gulliver's face, here as in Stothard's other illustrations of him, is totally without expression. Unfortunately, the illustration detracts from the text, for we are likely to have conceived of the island as a much more complex and elaborate place, filled with miraculous devices, and Gulliver as experiencing at this moment fear or awe or confusion or a combination of all three. Furthermore, Stothard's practice of placing an ornate border around each illustration has the effect of separating it from the text; it appears as a picture in a frame—suitable for hanging—rather than as an illustration to be integrated into our reading of the narrative.

Ironically, the most imaginative and artistically accomplished of the early illustrations of *Gulliver's Travels* was in part a literary hoax. In 1726, just two months after the publication of *Gulliver's Travels,* William Hogarth drew an illustration for the work titled: "The Punishment Inflicted on Lemuel Gulliver" and tried to create the illusion that the picture was commissioned by Swift or his publisher to serve as a frontispiece for the first edition. He wrote at the bottom of the engraving: "The Punishment inflicted on Lemuel Gulliver by applying a Lilypucian fire Engine to his Posteriors for his Urinal Profanation of the Royal Pallace at Mildendo which was intended as a Frontispiece to his first Volume but Omitted." Neither Swift nor his publisher, however, commissioned the work; in fact, Swift was at this time scarcely acquainted with the twenty-nine-year-old artist. . . .

A number of competently illustrated editions of *Gulliver's Travels* appeared in the first three decades of the nineteenth century. The illustrations of W. H. Brooks in 1808, T. Uwine in 1815, Henry and George Corbould in the 1820s, and McLean in 1823 stress the romantic and fanciful nature of Gulliver's journeys to exotic lands— the strange customs and unusual clothing he observed— rather than the satiric and moral dimensions of his travels. Their illustrations are generally few in number and derivative. All this was to change in 1838 with the appearance of J. J. Grandville's illustrations for *Gulliver's Travels.* Jean Ignace Isidore Gerard (J. J.) Grandville, a French political cartoonist and book illustrator, produced the most important, influential, and artistically brilliant illustrations of *Gulliver's Travels* ever published. His four hundred illustrations have never been surpassed in their imaginative and graphic quality, their ability to intensify, transform, and interpret Swift's text, and their power to delight, excite, and move the reader. Not only have his illustrations been widely reproduced—a total of fourteen times, including a 1935 edition of *Gulliver's Travels* published in Moscow and more recently in a facsimile edition published in this country—Grandville's influence on other illustrators of the *Travels* is ubiquitous in the nineteenth and twentieth centuries. When his illustrations appeared in a two-volume edition of *Gulliver's Travels* in England in 1840, where it was an immediate popular and critical success, Thackeray proffered perhaps the finest compliment that could be given to Grandville: he referred to him as "the Swift of the pencil."

While most illustrators up to this point were satisfied with illustrating fairly predictable episodes—Gulliver being captured by the Lilliputians, the dwarf shaking apples on him in part 2, the appearance of the Flying Island, Gulliver's initial encounter with a Houyhnhnm— Grandville goes beyond the predictable and commonplace to illustrate virtually all aspects of Swift's text. The articles, for instance, that Gulliver is required to swear to in Lilliput in order to gain his liberty are presented as a scroll with an elaborate border placed along both sides of the page, creating the illusion that one is actually reading an unfurled official document. The border contains iconography that highlights Lilliputian life: two shoes, one with a high, one a low, heel; three eggs in egg cups; a quiver filled with arrows laid next to a bow. In part 3 we see one of several attempts Grandville makes to narrate through a rapid succession of pictures: in the school of political projectors, for instance, he describes the process of deciphering secret messages concealed in seemingly innocuous words by providing us with twenty illustrations, each separated by a brief phrase, a strategy that allows us to observe the movement of the satire rather than restricting us to a single static image. He also begins each chapter in all four books with illuminated letters that are so delicately and imaginatively executed that they alone would have brought this edition of *Gulliver's Travels* widespread acclaim. . . .

Grandville's illustrations almost never simply reflect the text; as a creative artist he is constantly exploring the satiric possibilities that lie dormant in Swift's narrative, continually seeking to create his own statement by redefining, altering, or intensifying the text. An example of this may be found in his illustration of the dispute between the Big-Endians and the Little-Endians. Swift satirizes the contentiousness between Catholics and Protestants by employing the literary technique of diminution; sublime religious doctrines are transformed into a common, material object—an egg—while theological debates over those doctrines are reduced to a trivial and meaningless argument over which end of the egg to break. Grandville takes Swift's reduction and diminishes it even further. In his rendering of the episode, the participants in the debate *become* eggs; that is, he combines the object of the debate and the protagonists in the controversy, both of which remain separate in Swift's narrative, by personifying the eggs and attributing to them openings at either their large or small end. In doing so, he is able to satirize not only religious controversy but also the degree of commitment of partisans in religious struggles: they literally become what they believe. Furthermore, while Swift's text makes religious zealots appear foolish by having them fight over inconsequential matters, Grandville's illustration makes them even more absurd by depicting them as warmongering eggs. The fight, of course, is portrayed in mock-heroic terms, carried out on a table top instead of a battlefield, using common, everyday eating utensils instead of implements of war. While one Big-Endian and one Little-Endian have fallen, it is doubtful that it is the result of combat. Given the fact that their weight is concentrated in their heads, it is more likely that they simply toppled over. Although Swift uses a highly imaginative metaphor in this passage, he keeps us rooted in historical reality by alluding in allegorical fashion to Henry VIII's break with the Roman Catholic Church, the death of Charles I, the forced abdication of James II, and the Test Act. Grandville, however, creates in his illustration a bizarre scene, devoid of historical grounding, populated by grotesquely comic figures. His figures are literally eggheads; in fact, their egg heads are the same size as the rest of their body, while their torso and legs are parts of an eggcup.

By personifying the eggs, Grandville has significantly altered Swift's text; he has transformed an historical allegory into the realm of fantasy. . . .

Grandville's illustrations were followed by another extraordinary pictorial edition of *Gulliver's Travels* illustrated by Thomas Morten in 1865. Morten's illustrations, while indebted to Grandville, rival the pictures of the French master in both their comprehensive coverage of the *Travels* and their popularity: he designed almost four hundred plates, which were reprinted thirteen times in the nineteenth and early twentieth centuries in England and America. While each of Morten's illustrations reveals his attention to detail and skillful use of perspective, the strength of his artistry lies not merely in depicting individual scenes but in presenting a "progress piece," a series of illustrations that elucidate the development of a theme or a character and thus provide the reader with an interpretation of an entire book. In his illustrations for part 4, for instance, he presents us with his view of the "progress" of Gulliver: Morten's Gulliver begins as an arrogant and haughty Englishman who is transformed into a humble and disillusioned creature, one who perceives the folly and evil in himself and his countrymen.

From Gulliver's Travels into Several Remote Nations of the World, *written by Jonathan Swift. Illustrated by Arthur Rackham, 1909.*

In the first of Morten's fourteen plates for this book, Gulliver is depicted as a prideful colonizer who has landed in a strange country and is patronizingly greeting a Houyhnhnm. His self-esteem and self-importance may be seen not only in his pose and facial expression but in his clothing: he is impeccably adorned in a fashionable jacket with his sword hanging from his belt and his hat securely on his head. After becoming acquainted with the Houyhnhnms in the first three plates, his relationship to them undergoes a change, and Gulliver is seen in the next three illustrations as a curiosity, a strange animal that must be inspected and examined. Throughout these plates the superiority of the Houyhnhnms is emphasized. Their heads are held high, which conveys a sense of condescension toward Gulliver, while their eyes, which are disproportionately large, create the impression of intelligence, perceptiveness, and intensity. They are almost always drawn as taller than Gulliver, even when they are sitting, so that we see them as continuously looking down on him, literally as well as metaphorically. Gulliver's subordination to them may be seen in the fifth picture in Morten's series, in which a group of Houyhnhnms gather to inspect him. Morten's use of

light and shadow in this plate is representative of his technique throughout his illustrations. The body of the large horse behind him and of the two colts to his right are heavily shaded. This dark background serves to direct our eyes to the one point of light in the center of the darkness: Gulliver's face. Morten further emphasizes Gulliver's face as the focal point of the picture by placing the horses around him in a semicircular fashion; the straight lines formed by the noses of three horses and their line of vision point directly to Gulliver's face. The expression on his face suggests a significant change in his attitude toward the Houyhnhnms. He now looks upon them not with condescension but with a mixture of awe, deference, and fright. Morten underscores this change by removing Gulliver's hat, which in the first picture helped to convey his self-confidence and dignity, and placing it on the ground. The stripping of Gulliver's pride, symbolized by the stripping of his clothing, continues in Morten's sixth picture, in which the Houyhnhnms have forced him to remove his pants. . . .

While Morten's illustrations achieved a universal appeal, a number of illustrated editions in the late nineteenth century failed to transcend contemporary tastes. A. D. Lalauze designed a set of aquatints in 1875, for instance, in the pre-Raphaelite style, while V. A. Poirson reflected in an 1884 edition the interest of the period in orientalism. Arthur Rackham, however, returned to the satiric spirit and moral concerns of Swift's text in his 1899 illustrations. The success of his line drawings encouraged Rackham to revise some of his illustrations, to add new pictures, and to water color all but two for a highly acclaimed edition published in 1909. His twelve illustrations are graphically sophisticated and aesthetically pleasing: the pencil lines clearly show through the watercolor to define facial and physical features with precision, while the muted shades of red, green, yellow, and brown add a sense of realism and freshness to his depictions. The illustrations were so well executed, in fact, that the publisher conceived of this edition largely as a vehicle for Rackham's pictures: in a prefatory note he stated that he makes "no apology for a new edition since the fine drawings of MR. ARTHUR RACKHAM are a sufficient *raison d'etre.*"

While most of Rackham's illustrations attempt to capture the serious elements of Swift's satire, especially of the plight of Gulliver in part 2, he is one of the few illustrators to reflect Swift's spirit of playfulness as well. In his illustration of a Laputan deep in thought, for instance, he depicts the eyes as not simply turned inward but as crossed, while the complex mathematical problem the Laputan contemplates is being solved by counting on his fingers. The poor man is so absorbed in abstract speculation that his next step will submerge him in a duck pond. . . .

One of Rackham's most colorful and imaginative creations is his illustration of the attack on Gulliver in part 2 by giant wasps. While most illustrators have provided a fairly literal visualization of this scene, Rackham has altered the thrust of Swift's satire, ultimately presenting us with a Gulliver who is more vulnerable and threatened than Swift's character. In Swift's description of the attack by the wasps, it will be recalled Gulliver emerges victorious; . . . In Rackham's illustration . . . Gulliver's bravura and success in the episode are undermined. Gulliver is depicted as a victim of the wasps, as a frail creature who is being mercilessly victimized by insects. . . . While Gulliver may have been successful in warding off Brobdingnagian flies with his knife in the episode immediately before this one, he appears totally unable to protect himself from the wasps with his sword, for that weapon is held in a contorted manner with the back (rather than the inside) of his hand facing the reader. The billowing of his loose-fitting garment creates the impression of a bloated stomach that is being gnawed on by a wasp. This predatory aspect is emphasized by Rackham's placing the wasp on Gulliver's stomach at the structural center of the picture and having Gulliver's eyes direct our vision to his tormentor. Gulliver's body has also undergone a metamorphosis. In all but one other picture in this edition—that of Gulliver's being nearly crushed to death by apples—the narrator is depicted as a young man with a full face and smooth skin.

Here he appears as an old, decrepit man. His face is drawn and wrinkled; his arms, wrists, and legs are emaciated; the subcutaneous fat in his hands has receded so that his hands and fingers appear shriveled. His aged and withered appearance, which has no basis in Swift's text, increases our sense of Gulliver's helplessness as well as our sympathy for him.

Rackham's selection of this particular episode to illustrate from chapter 3, as opposed to several other scenes that lend themselves equally well to graphic depiction, also affects our conception of Gulliver. Chapter 3 is filled with events that establish the physical inferiority of Gulliver in Brobdingnag: he is examined by three Brobdingnagian scholars; a dwarf drops him in cream; he is forced into the marrow of a bone; he is attacked by flies. Rackham could have illustrated any of these events, but by selecting the final episode of the chapter, the attack by the wasps, he has provided us with a sense of climax, a finale, to the crescendo of abuse experienced by Gulliver. While Swift ends this chapter in a more positive fashion with Gulliver warding off the wasps, Rackham has transformed the episode into the final and most dangerous assault on Gulliver's body and dignity in the chapter, leaving us with a firm and lasting impression of his—and, by extension, our—weakness and frailty and alienation. Man cannot protect himself physically, according to Rackham, even from those creatures below him on the great chain of being. The reader is forced, after examining this illustration, to seek solace in the fact that it is man's reason and not his body that has given him dominance over animal life. Rackham has prepared us for Swift's attack on the abuses of man's intellect in part 3.

Three years after Rackham's illustrations appeared, Louis Rhead produced one of the most notable illustrated editions of *Gulliver's Travels* published in the twentieth century. For the 1913 edition of the *Travels,* published by Harper Brothers and containing an introduction by William Dean Howells, Rhead provided sixty-one illustrations, thirty-three of which are full-page pictures, and illuminated letters at the beginning of each chapter. His illustrations of part 1 abound in detail; they are generally filled with Lilliputians, frequently between fifty and one hundred, who are so carefully and precisely drawn that we may observe objects in their hands as well as their physical gestures. His illustrations of part 2 are remarkable for his depictions of the animals which attack Gulliver: they are generally disproportionately large, even for the scale established by Swift, and resemble the drawings one would find in an early twentieth-century biology textbook. His illustration of the Struldbruggs in part 3 vividly captures the grotesquerie and tragedy of their plight through their facial ugliness and bodily deformities, while his portrayal of the experiments at the Grand Academy are among the most imaginatively conceived and precisely drawn in any illustrated edition. Throughout his work, Rhead employs contrasts between light and dark as well as shades of black, creating effects not unlike those of a mezzotint, to highlight characters. . . .

While the illustrations of Rackham and Rhead were probably the most popular, influential, and accomplished drawings of the early twentieth century, there has not been a shortage of sophisticated and imaginative illustrations of *Gulliver's Travels* in the past fifty years. Rex Whistler, for instance, produced twelve large color pictures for an edition of the *Travels* published by the Cresset Press, which, unfortunately, has not been widely circulated. While Whistler pays a great deal of attention to clothing and physical poses in his illustrations, it is in the frames for his pictures that his imagination and creativity may best be seen. The frames or borders are themselves elaborate pictures filled with iconography that comments on the action which is enclosed. One frame of an illustration for part 1, for instance, consists of mythological figures, columns, and various structures from classical architecture that are decayed and in disarray, suggesting the decline from the classical ideal in both Lilliput and Augustan England. . . . W. A. Diggins's illustrations, on the other hand, which are all done in shades of green, are exceptional in their use of perspective. . . . While Whistler's and Diggins's illustrations have a significant effect on our perception and interpretation of the text, probably the most compelling and moving illustrations of *Gulliver's Travels* in the past fifty years have been done by Luis Quintanilla in the 1947 edition issued by Crown Publishers. Many of his 184 drawings tend toward caricature, which heightens our response to even minor characters. His illustration of the maids of court in part 2 fondling Gulliver is dominated by voluptuous young women who are semi-nude; here, as in several other pictures that contain nude bodies, he captures the eroticism of Swift's text, a quality that has been generally ignored by Swift's illustrators. Following in the tradition of Blake, he engraved twenty-three of the printing plates himself. While not as compelling as Quintanilla's drawings, James Millar's illustrations for the Appletree Press edition, which celebrated the two-hundred-fiftieth anniversary of the publication of *Gulliver's Travels,* are undoubtedly the most unusual recent illustrations of Gulliver and the people he encounters. Using a method of painting over linoleum in which thin lines are cut in the shapes and forms he wishes to reproduce, Millar created eighteen illustrations in which figures are defined by thin white lines over a black background. . . .

Finally, though the art work may not be as sophisticated or the text as reliable as the editions we have been examining, probably no illustrated edition of *Gulliver's Travels* has had a more profound influence on an entire generation of readers than the version published by Classics Illustrated, better known as Classic Comics. Classics Illustrated chose the voyage to Lilliput for one of its earliest issues; published in 1946, this popular comic book probably provided many American readers with their first contact with Gulliver's adventures. The illustrations are detailed, imaginative, and colorful. The clothing of Gulliver and the Lilliputians ranges in style and period from the English Renaissance to the eighteenth century, while the illustrations of Gulliver capturing the Blefuscudian fleet, the naval battle between Lilliput and Blefuscu, and the Lilliputians preparing redhot pokers to be used to blind Gulliver fill the reader with excitement, suspense, and a sense of adventure. . . .

It is evident, I believe, from the works we have examined that illustrated editions of *Gulliver's Travels* differ significantly from the text of Swift's satire without illustrations. The illustrations we have seen are constantly commenting on the text, clarifying a theme, shaping our response to a character, recasting a scene so that we can see it anew. One final, brief example of this may be seen in [the] well-known illustrations—by Lefebvre [and] C. E. Brock—of the episode from part 2, chapter 5, in which Gulliver is brought to the chambers of the maids of honor. In Lefebvre's illustration of this scene, the women scrutinize Gulliver as one would examine an unusual artifact or a rare curiosity. The woman holding him and gazing at him through a magnifying glass has a studious aspect, while the facial expressions and gestures of her cohorts suggest a mixture of inquisitiveness, surprise, and wonder. Although in Swift's text Gulliver is described as an erotic toy, a source of sexual gratification for the young women, Lefebvre's depiction of the scene is decidedly nonsexual. The semiscientific examination, the manner in which Gulliver is being held, and his spread-eagle pose suggest that he exists for these women more as a specimen than as a human, more as an object of intellectual inquiry than as a sex object. The reader is inclined to recall the earlier examination of Gulliver by the king's scholars rather than to dwell on the suggestive description in Swift's text. C. E. Brock's illustration of the same scene also departs from Swift's text. Rather than depicting the women as nude or semi-nude, Brock presents them elaborately dressed in clothing that resembles a mixtures of oriental and occidental designs. Gulliver's kissing of one woman's finger, the gracious appearance of all three women, and their modest demeanor suggest that Brock wishes the reader to conceive of the relationship between Gulliver and the maids of honor to be one of mutual respect and courtliness; etiquette and civility have replaced the eroticism and exploitation present in Swift's text. . . .

In offering widely different interpretations of a text, illustrations may, then, function as a form of critical commentary. . . . The commentary on the text provided by illustrations is no less serious or compelling or informative than a prose essay. At the same time, illustrations have a life of their own; they are acts of the imagination which have an autonomy apart from the text.

Hazel Rochman

SOURCE: A review of *Gulliver's Travels,* in *Booklist,* Vol. 89, No. 6, November 15, 1992, p. 599.

[The following review discusses James Riordan's 1992 adaptation of **Gulliver's Travels**, *illustrated by Victor G. Ambrus.]*

Focusing on the two adventures of Gulliver that have

always appealed to children—the story of Lilliput, where the human is a giant among dwarves; and the story of Brobdingnag, where the human is a dwarf among giants—Riordan and [Victor G.] Ambrus have adapted Swift's satiric fantasy into a romp for young readers. The play with size and perspective makes for vastly entertaining stories and pictures. Right at the start we see, stretched across two pages, the eighteenth-century gentleman tied firmly with ropes while at least 40 tiny men run all over him and attack him with bows and arrows that feel like sharp needles. His handkerchief is a carpet large enough to cover the state room at the palace; when he's freed, he has 300 cooks to prepare his food. The opposite happens in Brobdingnag, where the lice are the size of pigs rooting in the mud, Gulliver is horrified to see people as though through a magnifying glass ("It made me realize how ugly people are, with spots, pimples, and freckles that normally the eye does not see"), and the noise of a palace concert nearly deafens him. Particularly in Brobdingnag, Riordan keeps some of the sharpness of Swift, but Ambrus' sunny watercolor-and-ink illustrations are a bright counterpoint, mischievous more than grotesque, with lots of smiling, energetic creatures of all sizes staring at each other in amazement.

Hazel Rochman

SOURCE: A review of *Gulliver's Adventures in Lilliput,* in *Booklist,* Vol. 90, No. 1, September 1, 1993, pp. 71-2.

[The following two reviews discuss Ann Keay Beneduce's 1993 retelling of **Gulliver's Travels,** *illustrated by Gennady Spirin.]*

The Lilliput adventure is the one episode in the eighteenth-century classic *Gulliver's Travels* that has enduring appeal for children. This handsomely illustrated, simplified retelling captures the fantasy of the traveler who finds himself a giant prisoner in the land of people no bigger than his middle finger. Reminiscent of old maps and prints, the soft-textured, intricate pencil-and-watercolor pictures in warm shades of brown feature elaborately detailed miniature humans, animals, and objects. In keeping with the story, the illustrator has fun with perspective: when Gulliver first stands upright, the vertical double-page spread shows armies on horseback round his ankles; in another scene, he stands with legs apart, like a colossus, while the general parades the troops through the archway. Gulliver defeats the kingdom's enemies and then—like people everywhere—the Lilliputians get power hungry. The satire is gentle, the humor never condescending: Gulliver [is] a dreamy giant, like a child playing with toys.

Kathleen Whalin

SOURCE: A review of *Gulliver's Adventures in Lilliput,* in *School Library Journal,* Vol. 39, No. 10, October, 1993, p. 132.

Swift's satire has elements that have always appealed to children—high adventure, detailed fantasy, and scatological humor. The challenge in adapting an edition is to somehow keep the author's cynical, political voice and not reduce the story to a series of merry sea adventures. The best of the 17 versions now in print, James Riordan's *Gulliver's Travels* does exactly that. In contrast, Beneduce's book, however lushly illustrated, retains too little of the original to offer readers an adequate introduction. She omits Gulliver's shame at his body excretions, which Riordan includes; more importantly, she omits plot details that are basic to explaining the story's events. For example, readers are told that Lilliput is about to be invaded by Blefescu, but they are not told why. The serious dispute of the big and little enders is not mentioned. Beneduce has made an attempt to maintain the book's original tone, but has edited out its heart. In contrast to the spare text, [Gennady] Spirin's illustrations are a beautiful celebration of Lilliput. His fantastic paintings seem drawn from 17th century court life—the clothing, buildings, and ships have a dreamlike quality as well as a sense of historic accuracy. But the illustrations are not enough to salvage a text that is a barebones travelogue, not an early introduction to a rich novel.

Nancy Menaldi-Scanlan

SOURCE: A review of *Gulliver in Lilliput,* in *School Library Journal,* Vol. 41, No. 6, June, 1995, p. 114.

[The following two reviews discuss Margaret Hodges's 1995 retelling of **Gulliver's Travels,** *illustrated by Kimberly Bulcken Root.]*

Told as Gulliver might have recounted his adventures to young children, Hodges's adaptation of Part I of *Gulliver's Travels* is a masterful retelling of the 18th-century classic. While condensing the story considerably, she has retained not only the important details of the involved plot, but also the flavor of Swift's rich, descriptive language; she even includes occasional expressions in the Lilliputian tongue that, as in the original, are explained in the text. Furthermore, Hodges has divided the narrative neatly into nine "chapters," allowing the story to be read in logical installments while also clarifying the progress of the plot. Root's stunning pen-and-watercolor illustrations do much to bring the fanciful tale to life. Her fine details add a wonderful touch of realism, providing a feast for the eye to accompany the well-chosen words. As with Hodges's wonderful retelling of the medieval tale *The Kitchen Knight,* her latest work will find its way into the hearts of adventure-loving young readers and listeners, serving as an outstanding introduction to Swift's literary treasure.

Ann A. Flowers

SOURCE: A review of *Gulliver in Lilliput,* in *The Horn Book Magazine,* Vol. 71, No. 4, July-August, 1995, p. 450.

Gulliver's Travels was originally written in 1726 by Jonathan Swift as an adult satire, bitter and biting, about politics, economy, science, and the fallen state of man. But the first part, about Lilliput, has always had a juvenile audience, attracted by the fascinating idea of adventures among very small people. Swifts' work was an outburst of imagination and fantasy in the early eighteenth century, when very little was written for children and such as did exist was dull and moralistic. Margaret Hodges has achieved a masterful retelling, respectful of the serious tone of the original in lightly touching upon some of the problems of morality and justice while providing delightful details of life in Lilliput. It emphasizes the adventures of Gulliver that are most appealing to children: the Lilliputians' descriptions of what Gulliver had in his pockets, for example, and how they managed to feed him, "man mountain" that he was. The illustrations [by Kimberly Bulcken Root] are exactly suited to the tale, with a rather tired and disheveled-looking Gulliver dealing as best he can with a topsy-turvy world.

Harry Ritchie

SOURCE: "All Things Weird and Wonderful," in *Times Educational Supplement,* No. 4145, December 8, 1995, p. 10.

The very mention of Gulliver and his travels, I have recently discovered, is likely to elicit the strangest reactions. One of my friends has been haunted by the book since childhood, when a pop-up illustration of Gulliver tied down by hundreds of Lilliputian ropes gave her a first frisson of sexual surrender. Another has fond memories of studying *Gulliver's Travels* for A-level two decades ago and persuading his teacher that, rather than produce essays analysing Swift's novel, he and his classmates could collaborate on a poster featuring drawings of furry Yahoos. It's that kind of book.

Few novels, in fact, have had such power to haunt, enchant and disturb. A gigantic Gulliver putting out the fire in the Lilliputian palace by pissing on it, a miniature Gulliver fending off wasps as large as partridges in Brobdingnag, an abashed Gulliver discovering that in the land of the Houyhnhnms humanity has been reduced to gibbering Yahoos. Rarely has a novel produced so many episodes and scenes that have entered the collective imagination. And rarely has a novel provoked such violently different reactions—so much so that *Gulliver's Travels* acts as a literary litmus test to the principles, attitudes and fears of its readers.

When the book was first published in 1726, the immediate reaction was one of universal delight. Swift's great friend Alexander Pope wrote to assure him that the book was read "from the cabinet council to the nursery". Ten thousand copies were sold within three weeks of publication, and soon pirate editions and translations into French and Dutch had also appeared. The combination of political satire, scatological wit, literary parodies and,

above all, the brilliantly simple fables in the storyline confirmed to Swift's contemporaries that he was, as Addison said, "the greatest genius of the age".

By the end of the 18th century, however, Swift and Gulliver were hated and reviled, due in no small part to the hostility of Dr Johnson who condemned the book as the sinister product of an author whose vile hatred of humanity drove him to terminal insanity. It was a fine double whammy, with this warped account of author and book providing evidence against each other. Walter Scott followed suit, judging *Gulliver's Travels* to be the "severe, unjust and degrading" vision of Swift's "gloomy misanthropy".

Scott was charitable by comparison with the Victorians who refused to stomach Swift's strong meat. Even Edmund Gosse found his customary benevolence tested when he took pity on a mind capable of conjuring up such a "sinister masterpiece". But it was Thackeray who really let rip. *Gulliver's Travels* was "Horrible, shameful, unmanly, blasphemous" and Swift "the most wretched being

' *Put the tip of it, with the utmost respect, to my Lip.*'

From Travels into Several Remote Nations of the World. By Lemuel Gulliver, First a Surgeon, and Then a Captain of Several Ships. *Written by Jonathan Swift. Illustrated by Charles E. Brock, 1894.*

in God's world" who "entered the nursery with the tread and gaiety of an ogre".

Why this level of vilification? Clearly, Swift had not displayed the proper "Victorian values". On the contrary—in the conflict between Lilliput and Blefuscu, for example, he had shown the humbug behind patriotism, he had lampooned glib notions of scientific progress with the creation of the ridiculous inhabitants of Laputa and Lagado, and then, of course, he had ended up reducing mankind to those vile Yahoos.

Just as, or even more, upsetting was the manner in which Swift revelled in his disgust at the human body. Where middle-class Victorians coped with the corporeal by hiding it behind locked doors and layers of clothing, Swift relished describing not only the horror with which Gulliver looked on the pock marks and sores of the great beauties of Brobdingnag but also the problems his hero faced in performing his massive ablutions in Lilliput.

The misreadings of critics such as Thackeray add a real poignancy to the scene in Glubbdubdrib, where Gulliver is entertained by the ghosts of great classical authors, accompanied by the shades of their commentators who are racked by shame and guilt, for they now appreciate how appallingly they misrepresented the work of their subjects.

But Swift and Gulliver have also found their champions, most fervently from political radicals—Hazlitt, Leigh Hunt and Cobbett were among their great admirers in the 19th century, and in our own Swift has been vividly appreciated by the likes of George Orwell and Michael Foot.

At first sight, this may seem odd, because Swift was a Tory and convinced reactionary. Nevertheless, he has been cherished by the literary Left because of his unerring ability to expose not just human folly in general but specifically the stupidities and corruption that accompany the follies of power. This leads Orwell partly to pardon Swift as a "Tory anarchist" who was propelled mainly by hatred of the Whigs, but he has to concede that he cannot sympathise with many of his preferences and prejudices, especially in their expression in Swift's Utopian vision of the Houyhnhnms—a species that has no use for science or indeed any form of curiosity, love, or hedonism. This dire Utopia encouraged Michael Foot to continue his rehabilitation of Swift by claiming that he was actually offering another satire here and describing his true ideal in the society of Brobdingnag—an interpretation that has the one disadvantage of being completely wrong.

The truth of the matter is that *Gulliver's Travels* continues to be an immensely problematic book. Some of the problems facing present-day readers are specific and minor. Much of the political satire which had Swift's contemporaries guffawing has little or no resonance now—whereas, say, the conflict between the Big Endians and the Little Endians (a civil war between factions who disagreed about how to open a boiled egg) has a timeless appeal.

Much of Swift's invective now seems fairly ham-fisted and often silly, not just when he attacks his own political foes. His satirical dismissal of intellectuals and scientists as a bunch of fools, whose discoveries and pursuit of abstract knowledge are all daft and useless, will only strike chords with the most Luddite of philistines. And then there is his eminently troubling indignation at humankind in general.

The least sympathetic part of the novel, to my mind, is Gulliver's encounter with the Houyhnhnms. Granted, in a century which has witnessed Hiroshima and the Holocaust, any portrayal of humanity as bestial carries real force. But those Yahoos just don't convince. Are they humans or not? And if human beings are so ghastly why do the Houyhnhnms have to behave anthropomorphically, sitting down on their flanks, pacing up and down as they have chats and so forth? And if those dull, passionless, smug, backward horses constitute some sort of ideal, then I am six inches tall.

Where contemporary readers enjoy a real advantage over Swift's Victorian enemies is in being able to enjoy many of his more revolting accounts of the body, especially those describing Gulliver's troubles in Bobdingnag. To readers accustomed to science documentaries and microscopic photographs which blow up to enormous size the parasites and bacteria inhabiting our bodies, Gulliver's stunned reaction to the all-too-noticeable defects of the Brobdingnagians will seem only realistic, even if Swift does dwell on this with uncomfortable insistence.

I feel it wise to end on that more positive note, for, as Hazlitt pointed out, the distinguishing feature of Swift's satire is his ability to "tear off the mask of imposture from the world; and nothing but imposture has a right to complain of it". In *Gulliver's Travels* Swift tore off that mask with such aplomb that, 250 years after his death, his inventions enjoy as vigorous a life as ever—the Lilliputians with their hilarious war with Blefuscu, the Brobdingnagian ladies of fashion oblivious to Gulliver's disgust, the intellectuals of Laputa with their heads so literally in the clouds that their tailor measures them for suits with a quadrant, ruler and compasses.

My own favourites are those academicians of Lagado who aim to extract sunlight from cucumbers, build houses from the top to the bottom, distinguish colours by their smell and regain food from excrement. Lest anyone think scientists could never be so stupid, Swift provides his best punch-line of all—every one of these experiments had actually been conducted by venerable members of the Royal Society. *Touché.*

Zena Sutherland

SOURCE: "The History of Children's Books: *Gulliver's Travels*," in *Children & Books*, ninth edition, Longman, 1997, p. 50.

[A] remarkable book emerged during the 18th century, a political satire not intended for children but read by them and known today as *Gulliver's Travels*. The author, Jonathan Swift (1667-1745), was born in Dublin and died there, Dean of the Cathedral. But between his birth and death, he spent considerable time in London and took an active part in the political life of the times. Recognized today as one of the greatest satirists in English literature, Swift wrote his book in Ireland to lampoon the follies of the English court, its parties, its politics, and its statesmen. Worried about the reception of the book, he published it anonymously in 1726 as *Travels into Several Remote Nations of the World,* in four parts, by Lemuel Gulliver. To Swift's surprise and relief, London society, the very society he was making fun of, was highly diverted. In these tall tales the humor sometimes overshadows the satire.

Children have always loved things in miniature, and they soon discovered the land of the Lilliputians. No one ever forgets Gulliver's waking to find six-inch people walking over him and Lilliputian ropes binding him. All the fascinating details are worked out to scale with logic and precision. Children are untroubled by any double meanings and like the fantasy for itself. The second journey, to the land of giants, Brobdingnag, is the next most popular, but is not so appealing as the omnipotent Gulliver in Lilliput. The remaining books most children never read.

If Gulliver's travels had not fascinated artists, the book might not have survived in children's reading as long as it has. An early edition illustrated by Charles E. Brock (1894) and later editions illustrated by Arthur Rackham and by Fritz Eichenberg would lure anyone into reading the story.

Additional coverage of Swift's life and career is contained in the following sources published by Gale Research: *Dictionary of Literary Biography,* Vol. 101; *DISCovering Authors; DISCovering Authors: British; Poetry Criticism; Something about the Author,* Vol. 19; and *World Literature Criticism.*

CUMULATIVE INDEXES

How to Use This Index

The main reference

> Baum, L(yman) Frank 1856–
> 1919 .... **15**

list all author entries in this and previous volumes of *Children's Literature Review:*

The cross-references

> See also CA 103; 108; DLB 22; JRDA
> MAICYA; MTCW; SATA 18; TCLC 7

list all author entries in the following Gale biographical and literary sources:

AAYA = Authors & Artists for Young Adults
AITN = Authors in the News
BLC = Black Literature Criticism
BW = Black Writers
CA = Contemporary Authors
CAAS = Contemporary Authors Autobiography Series
CABS = Contemporary Authors Bibliographical Series
CANR = Contemporary Authors New Revision Series
CAP = Contemporary Authors Permanent Series
CDALB = Concise Dictionary of American Literary Biography
CDBLB = Concise Dictionary of British Literary Biography
CLC = Contemporary Literary Criticism
CMLC = Classical and Medieval Literature Criticism
DAB = DISCovering Authors: British
DAC = DISCovering Authors: Canadian
DAM = DISCovering Authors: Modules
       DRAM: Dramatists Module; MST: Most-Studied Authors Module;
       MULT: Multicultural Authors Module; NOV: Novelists Module;
       POET: Poets Module; POP: Popular Fiction and Genre Authors Module
DC = Drama Criticism
DLB = Dictionary of Literary Biography
DLBD = Dictionary of Literary Biography Documentary Series
DLBY = Dictionary of Literary Biography Yearbook
HLC = Hispanic Literature Criticism
HW = Hispanic Writers
JRDA = Junior DISCovering Authors
LC = Literature Criticism from 1400 to 1800
MAICYA = Major Authors and Illustrators for Children and Young Adults
MTCW = Major 20th-Century Writers
NCLC = Nineteenth-Century Literature Criticism
NNAL = Native North American Literature
PC = Poetry Criticism
SAAS = Something about the Author Autobiography Series
SATA = Something about the Author
SSC = Short Story Criticism
TCLC = Twentieth-Century Literary Criticism
WLC = World Literature Criticism, 1500 to the Present
YABC = Yesterday's Authors of Books for Children

Author Index

Author Index

CUMULATIVE INDEX TO NATIONALITIES

CUMULATIVE INDEX TO TITLES

Title Index

Title Index

Title Index

Title Index

Title Index

Title Index

Title Index

Title Index

Title Index

Title Index

Title Index

ISBN 0-7876-2081-5

90000

9 780787 620813